HIROHITO AND THE

MAKING OF

MODERN JAPAN

HIROHITO AND THE MAKING OF MODERN JAPAN

HERBERT P. BIX

HarperCollins*Publishers*

HarperCollins books may be purchased for educational, business, or sales promo-
tional use. For information please write: Special Markets Department, Harper-
Collins Publishers Inc., 10 East 53rd Street, New York, NY 10022.

FIRST EDITION

Designed by Jackie McKee

Maps by Paul Pugliese

Library of Congress Cataloging-in-Publication Data

Bix, Herbert P.
   Hirohito and the making of modern Japan / Herbert P. Bix.
      p.   cm.
   Includes bibliographical references and index.
   ISBN 0-06-019314-X
   1. Hirohito, Emperor of Japan, 1901–89.   2. Emperors—Japan—Biography.
3. Japan—History—Shōwa period, 1926–1989. I. Title.
DS889.8.B59 2000
952.03'3'092—dc21
[B]   99-089427
00 01 02 03 04 ❖/HC 10 9 8 7 6 5

To Toshie, and my grandchildren—
Maia, Isamu, Lily, and others who may follow

CONTENTS

Illustrations follow page 244.

MAPS

Acknowledgments

My principal thanks go to my wife, Toshie, to whom this book is dedicated. Her hard work is reflected in the wealth of materials I was able to cover and in insights that found their way into the text.

Sam Hileman, an artist and former editor who lives in relative solitude in the Shenandoah Valley, in Millboro, Virginia, deserves special credit for brilliantly commenting in detail on the entire manuscript. He not only improved the flow in every single chapter but was a fertile source of ideas, a keen critic, and a good friend as well. I owe him a vast debt for enriching the book. Tim Duggan of HarperCollins was a splendid editor: incisive in his criticisms, patient, and supportive in every way. To him too I am greatly indebted. I particularly want to thank Susan Llewellyn of Harper-Collins for her wonderful copyediting of the entire text. My literary agent, Susan Rabiner, made it happen and gave her support throughout.

John Dower offered wise counsel; he also made valuable comments on early versions of two war chapters. More than a decade ago, while on a visit to Sheffield, England, another old friend, Nakamura Masanori, gave me a copy of his book on the postwar Japanese monarchy; around the same time Glenn Hook, who lives in Sheffield, sent me the emperor's "Monologue." These two works started me off. David Swain provided critical feedback during the initial stages of my research and writing. Martin Sherwin commented incisively on an early version of the manuscript, and Mark Selden, who has always been unstinting with his help over the years, commented on the last chapter. I am grateful to all of them, and to Feroz Ahmad, Brian Victoria, Ed Friedman, and Jon Halliday, for leaving their marks on the text. Noam Chomsky kindly made insightful suggestions for improving the countdown to war. Andrew Gordon helped by enabling me to return to Harvard University for a year of teaching

I extend thanks to Harvard-Yenching Library and Hitotsubashi University Library, where I did my research; to Elly Clay for reading an early draft of chapter 7; to Jonathan Dresner and Christine Kim for responding to numerous requests for materials from the Harvard libraries, and to Kikuchi Nobuteru for his computer skills and helpful participation in my course on the Shōwa monarchy.

A research fellowship from the U.S.–Japan Educational Commission (Fulbright Program) enabled me to launch this project at Hitotsubashi University in Tokyo in 1992. There I met Yoshida Yutaka and Watanabe Osamu, both of whom have written extensively and brilliantly on the metamorphosis of the modern monarchy. They discussed their views on Hirohito and shared with me their profound knowledge of the military, political, and constitutional history of modern Japan. Over the years they answered my queries and were always understanding and generous in their help. Awaya Kentarō, another old and valued friend, made available materials on the Tokyo trials and was a rich source of ideas and suggestions. Were it not for them, I am sure that this book would be less than it is, and that I would also have overlooked scores of important Japanese sources. Toward the end of the decade, I joined the faculty of the Graduate School of Social Sciences at Hitotsubashi, and in that most ideal environment completed the research and final rewriting of the manuscript.

Okabe Makio and Yamada Akira also deserve my deepest gratitude for sharing materials and discussing issues. Many other distinguished historians helped me make sense of Hirohito's life through their extensive writings, but Tanaka Nobumasa and Fujiwara Akira deserve special mention, as does Tanaka Hiromi, who made available the unpublished memoirs of Gen. Nara Takeji. To Akagawa Hiroaki I express thanks for his support and for supplying materials.

Over the ten years in which I pursued this project, my father-in-law, Shigeaki Watanabe, shared his recollections of early Shōwa. Mrs. Yoshida Ryōko also cooperated by sending a constant stream of Japanese-language materials.

Parts of chapter 13 derive from my essay "Japan's Delayed Surrender: A Reinterpretation," in *Diplomatic History* (1995); many passages in chapters 14 and 16 come from "Inventing the Symbol Monarchy in Japan," in the *Journal of Japanese Studies* (1995). I owe thanks to both journals for permission to use my material.

INTRODUCTION

By the late winter of 1946, pressure had mounted both at home and abroad for forty-five-year-old Emperor Hirohito to be indicted as a war criminal. If indicted, he would face trial for appointing General Tōjō as prime minister in 1941 and later declaring war on the United States and Great Britain. Questioning under oath as to when he had learned of the planned attack on Pearl Harbor and about his role in various imperial conferences and in the treatment of prisoners of war loomed ahead, as did disgrace, and punishment in some form if his innocence could not be established. Members of his own imperial family were calling for him to abdicate as a way of avoiding political responsibility and protecting the monarchy. His country's leading liberal intellectuals were publicly asking him to leave the throne in order to set a good moral example for the nation.

The American occupiers of his country, meanwhile, had just finished drafting their model for a new constitution that would preserve the monarchy but strip the monarch of all political powers. Parliamentary debate on the new constitution and his own emasculated status under it was about to begin.[1] Hoping to continue to use him for occupation purposes but recognizing that the burden of proof had fallen on him, Hirohito's American defenders needed to know how he felt about the lost war that had been fought in his name. They especially wanted him to address the glaring contradiction of why, if he had been strong enough to surrender his empire at the end of the war, he had not been equally strong enough to have prevented war in the first place, thereby saving millions of lives.

1

To stave off all these threats to his throne and to himself personally, Hirohito had to furnish an account exculpating his actions as the sovereign head of the Japanese state over the previous twenty years—one that would defend him against charges he might never have to face but could not be sure of escaping. And he had to do so secretly, for his self-defense necessarily entailed assigning responsibility for war and defeat to some of his most loyal subjects. If that had been revealed at the time, the already weakened spiritual ties that bound him and the Japanese nation would have shattered, and with them his usefulness to Gen. Douglas MacArthur.[2]

So at 10:30 on March 18, 1946, a chilly Sunday morning, Hirohito, though ill with a cold, summoned five of his most trusted aides to his office in the concrete bunker on the palace grounds, where he had lived during and since the Pacific War. They were to listen to his recollections of the extraordinary events of his reign. Upon entering the office, the aides found him propped up in a Western-style single bed that had just been moved into his study for the occasion. Seats had been placed for them at its foot. The emperor was wearing pajamas made of bright white silk, and his pillow and quilted blankets were also of finely woven soft white *habutae* silk. In the Shinto religion, of which he was the highest priest, such garments signified ritual purity, not penitence. The aides seated themselves and began to ask pre-scripted questions, suggested to them in part by General MacArthur's military secretary. They listened as Hirohito dictated his responses and Inada Shūichi took down the emperor's words. Later Inada wrote in his notebook: "People might ask why at such a moment we were hastily requested to listen to the emperor's account. Around that time, however, some people were questioning his responsibility in connection with the war crimes trials, and there was a need to record the emperor's candid feelings quickly."[3]

A summary of what the emperor said that morning, and at five other dictation sessions over the next three weeks, was later given by one of the emperor's aides to MacArthur's military secretary. Nothing came of the summary, however, perhaps because the top American officials at General Headquarters (GHQ) were already among the emperor's greatest protectors and mythologizers. In the original Japanese text of his "Monologue" the emperor sought to convey the impression that, except on two special occasions after 1928—a military rebellion in 1936 and the ending of the war in 1945—he had stood aloof from politics and refrained from direct intervention in decision making. The war with the United States and Great Britain, he implied, had been inevitable. Although he had personally opposed it until the very last minute, he had been unable to use his influence to prevent war—partly for fear of a domestic uprising but primarily for constitutional reasons. "As a constitutional monarch under a constitutional government, I could not avoid approving the decision of the Tōjō cabinet at the time of the opening of hostilities."[4]

Approximately ten days after completing his "Monologue," Hirohito had the same aide draw up another document, in English, summarizing key points of his defense but emphasizing that "Actually I was virtually a prisoner and powerless."[5] The longer "Monologue" remained unknown to the public until after Hirohito's death in 1989. The greatly abbreviated English version, depicting him as a helpless puppet of "the militarists," was not discovered and publicized in Japan until 1997. Both were apt symbols of the secrecy, myth, and gross misrepresentation that surrounded his entire life.

One of the most fascinating and complex political figures in twentieth-century Japanese history, Hirohito began his reign in late 1926, on the eve of renewed conflict in Japan's relations with China. It continued for sixty-two years of war, defeat, American occupation, and Cold War peace and prosperity. During the first twenty years he was at the center of his nation's political, military, and spiritual life in the broadest and deepest sense, exerting authority in ways that proved disastrous for his people and the those of the countries they invaded. Though the time span of his great Asian empire was brief, its potential was enormous. He had presided over its expansion and had led his nation in a war that cost (according to the official estimates published by governments after 1945) nearly 20 million Asian lives, more than 3.1 million Japanese lives, and more than sixty thousand Western Allied lives.[6]

Events had not turned out as he had anticipated and hoped. Yet when his turn came to provide explanations of the role he had played in those events, and to set the record straight, he and his aides were far from candid. They skillfully crafted a text designed to lead to the conclusion that he had always been a British-style constitutional monarch and a pacifist. Hirohito omitted mention of how he and his aides had helped the military to become an enormously powerful political force pushing for arms expansion. He ignored the many times he and his entourage had made use of the Meiji system of government by consensus to stifle a more democratic, less militarized political process. He intentionally fudged the details about his role as both a military leader and a head of state, blurred his motives, and obfuscated the timing of his actions and the logic that informed them. He was silent too about how he had encouraged the belligerency of his people by serving as an active ideological focus of a new emperor-centered nationalism that had grown up around him.

The aide who wrote the introduction to the "Monologue" claimed that the emperor had limited himself to describing briefly "the background causes and the immediate causes of the Greater East Asia War, its development, and how it came to an end." That too was untrue. Not included in Hirohito's explanation were the many ways he and his court entourage had destabilized the party cabinet system that had developed during the middle and late 1920s by insisting on selecting the next prime minister and forcing on him their own national-policy agenda. He omitted discussing how the war in China had begun, his direct leadership role in its expansion, and the conduct of Japanese forces on the ground and in the air. Hirohito also remained silent about the many experiences and circumstances that had most strongly affected his life, the values he placed on them, and the ideas that had shaped his actions and made him the person he was. In his single-minded dedication to preserving his position, no matter what the cost to others, he was one of the most disingenuous persons ever to occupy the modern throne.

This work attempts to study precisely those formative events and ideologies that underlay, deeply or near the surface, Hirohito as a monarch and a man. It focuses on the forces that shaped his thoughts and actions, as well as those of his close palace aides before, during, and long after the Asia-Pacific War (1931–45). It seeks to describe his actual role in policy making when he was at the center of events; and it is necessarily complex, for my concern embraces not only the modern, divinely legitimized monarchy that was constructed under Hirohito's grandfather, the emperor Meiji, and used to convert the Japanese people to militarism, war, and the values of subjecthood. It embraces also the reformed monarchy, which was artfully disconnected from the war and its official remembrance, and which has continued its existence down to the present day. It traces the impact of both the sacred and the secular monarchy on Hirohito, his interaction with the various organs of the state, and the monarchy's continuous transformation under him. Ultimately I am concerned with the whole of Hirohito's long life, for he illuminates, more than any other Japanese figure, the broader world of Japanese politics and government-military relations. His life has much to tell us about the changing political attitudes of the Japanese people over the past century.

This is not, however, an orthodox political biography. Hirohito was not a gregarious, outgoing person with a wide assortment of friends fond of writing candidly about him. He was a reticent person who spoke most eloquently sometimes by not speaking at all.

Socialized to public opacity, he was trained also to private wariness. He left behind no abundance of texts with his signature on them, revealing his thoughts and enabling us to capture his responses to the major events that he lived through. On ceremonial occasions, it is true, he wrote *waka* poems in the style of his grandfather Meiji, of which so far more than 860, most of them written after 1945, have been printed.[7] But he published no reminiscences and usually expressed his ideas or intentions only through others, who found it disrespectful and inappropriate for a Japanese subject to write critically about him.

He was also a lonely man. He is said to have kept a diary faithfully from the age of eleven. Probably he did. But that diary—held tightly by the Imperial Household Agency—is not and probably never will be freely accessible to researchers. The same agency is now compiling the chronicles of Hirohito's reign, but the work is proceeding "on the premise that it will not be made public . . . because it might constitute an infringement of the privacy of the people referred to, and those related to them."[8] Also off limits is Hirohito's correspondence with family members, the entire "Record of the Emperor's Conversations" (*Seidan haichōroku*) in its various versions, as well as a wealth of unpublished documents, such as diaries of people who served him, and that someday may illuminate Hirohito's whole existence. Neither has the U.S. government opened to the public all the secret records it holds on Hirohito, such as, for example, his conversations with Gen. Douglas MacArthur and the folder in the U.S. National Archives bearing his name.[9]

To pry open Hirohito's life and access his motives one must rely on his entourage of note takers and diarists, who worked closely with him, thereby came to know him well, and have actually published their notes and diaries. One must rely also on accounts by senior military officers and diplomats who recorded his words during the war years. Recently, due largely to the efforts of a new generation of Japanese scholars, the publication of hundreds of new documents, diaries, reminiscences, and scholarly studies pertaining to him during the war and postwar years, and the greatly changed valuation that the Japanese now place on the imperial institution, we in the West and in Japan have the chance finally to understand the intellectual, moral, and social forces that molded his life. Although far too many source gaps remain, these new materials justify retelling the story of Hirohito in the century of total war.

The work of Japanese scholars also enables us to appreciate how isolated Hirohito was from the Japanese people. Although he became the center of fanatical national worship and was greeted by some as a living deity whenever he traveled on visits to different cities, he was never "popular" in any lay sense of that term. He operated within a bureaucratic monarchy, and was considered at once an "organ" of the modern centralized state yet also an entity whose "will" transcended all law.[10] Above all, the new materials make it possible for us to appreciate how Hirohito embodied—as no other Japanese did—the contradictory logic of Japan's entire modern political development.

That development had begun in the time of Hirohito's grandfather, Emperor Mutsuhito, known posthumously as Meiji, "the Great." On becoming emperor in 1868, Meiji was made to serve as the polestar of the nation's modern transformation. Eventually the way his powers were built up and institutionalized during the late nineteenth century shaped the parameters of Japan's political development down through 1945. The imperial court was separated from the government and reorganized in accordance with models of European monarchy. A written constitution followed. Bestowed by Meiji in 1889 as his "gift" to the nation, the constitution asserted that the emperor was the successor in an unbroken, sacred blood lineage, based on male descendants, and that government was subordinated to monarchy on that basis.[11] It defined him as "sacred and inviolable," "head of the empire" (*genshu*), supreme commander (*daigensui*) of the armed forces, and superintendent of all the powers of sovereignty. He could convoke and dissolve the Imperial Diet; issue imperial ordinances in place of law; and appoint and dismiss ministers of state, civil officials, and military officers and determine their salaries. The underlying assumptions were that the emperor, as the source of law, transcended the constitution, whose purpose was not to place limits on his powers but the very opposite—to protect him and provide a mechanism enabling him to exercise authority unimpeded by limits. This system of government can be called a kind of constitutionally guided but by no means constitutional monarchy.[12]

Japan's colonial empire and new status as a great regional power in control of both continental and insular possessions was the second great legacy Meiji bequeathed to Hirohito. In 1894, nearly a decade after having decided to catch up with the advanced Western nations by joining them in the competition for Asian colonies, the oligarchic leaders of the nation declared war on China for the purpose of occupying and controlling Korea. China lost and the next year ceded Taiwan, along with the Liaotung Peninsula of southern Manchuria, and the Pescadores Islands. China agreed to pay a huge indemnity and later signed an unequal commercial treaty that allowed Japanese ships to navigate the Yangtze River and Japanese businessmen to operate factories in the inland and coastal treaty ports (such as Tientsin, Shanghai, and Canton).

Victorious war further enhanced Emperor Meiji's prestige. Mainly a protector of the interests of the nation's oligarchic rulers, at forty-three he became a national symbol and acquired the dual image of a monarch by divine right and a hands-on ruler making decisions in all affairs of state. In a people long habituated to an antimilitary outlook and to regarding samurai warriors with suspicion, fear, and disdain, the victory in 1895 evoked support for the new conscript military. It also stimulated xenophobic nationalism and implanted a sense of superiority to the Korean and Chinese peoples.

After Japan's defeat of China the international situation throughout East Asia became more complicated. Threats from Germany, Russia, and France forced Meiji and the oligarchs to return the Liaotung Peninsula to China. Immediately the Great Powers intensified their struggle for territorial and trade concessions at China's expense. Russia acquired leasehold rights in the Liaotung Peninsula, moved into Manchuria in 1898, and made its influence felt in Korea, thereby checking Japan.[13] That same year the United States fought the Spanish-American War, annexed Hawaii, and seized the Philippines, Wake, Guam, and Midway. In 1900, when the Western powers mounted an international expedition to put down the Boxer uprising in China, Japanese troops participated. The next year Japan joined the leading Western powers in signing the Boxer Protocol, which gave them indemnities and the right to station troops permanently in designated Chinese cities to protect their nationals and diplomats.

Three years later, starting in 1904, Japan launched a surprise attack on the Russian fleet at Port Arthur. The ensuing conflict cost an estimated 110,000 Japanese lives and ended with a brokered peace, no indemnities, riots in the capital, and the prospect that someday Russia would seek revenge. Emperor Meiji played no role in the fighting but nonetheless again added luster to his image. Japan gained the unexpired Russian leasehold rights to the Liaotung Peninsula, a seven-hundred-mile-long railway running through southern Manchuria, and the southern half of Karafuto (Sakhalin Island) in the Sea of Okhotsk, and these were praised as his epochal achievements.

Hirohito entered the world right at the dawn of this new era of imperial rivalry in Asia and the Pacific, and under him the drama of Japanese politics reached its disastrous conclusion in war and defeat. We can gain new perspective on Japanese politics by seeing how this man, who was so often out of step with his people, ignorant of their lives, never entirely sure of their real support, survived war and occupation, and how he maintained his place on the throne to continue the imperial tradition well into the second half of the century.

Hirohito and the Japanese nation formed a political unit based on sentiment and ideology, as well as shared memories of war. In looking at his life, we can see how he and his nation stood beside each other in a deeply symbiotic relationship, the manipulation and exploitation of which came chiefly from the emperor's side. Before, during, and immediately after the trauma of war and defeat, he presented himself to the people as a "traditional" exalted being, looking down on them while manifesting only their ideal features, never their shortcomings. They in turn were supposed to hold him in awe and trembling as a living deity and a model of the ideal father. They were to assist him in the construction of his authority, and to take responsibility for his exercise of power because he, in theory, could not. Never were the people to discuss where this model and organizing principle of their national life fell short of perfection. (Nevertheless, in every single period, some of them always did.)

Following Hirohito's enthronement in 1926, politics in Japan became enflamed over foreign and domestic policy issues. Political and military elites began to debate the meaning of the national polity, or *kokutai*. Centered on the imperial house, *kokutai* meant the best possible principles of Japanese state and society. As dissatisfaction with society deepened, the belief spread that reform could be achieved by utilizing the emperor's authority. In this context a new, spiritually driven, and powerful nationalism called the "imperial way," *kōdō*, arose and spread widely. The "imperial way" was a motivating political theology sprung from the idea of the emperor as the literally living embodiment of Japan past and present, a paradigm of moral excellence all should follow. The term denoted a kind of ideological warfare but also, on the other hand, an action plan. It was designed to make Japan free of all externally derived isms, such as Western democracy, liberalism, individualism, and communism. Free to be itself only, the nation would regain self-esteem and be able to wage a "holy" war of ideas against Western political doctrines. Although the roots of *kōdō* went back to the crisis of the mid–nineteenth century, its revival at the end of the 1920s, and its actual application in real-life Japanese diplomacy during the early 1930s, helped Japan break with its immediate past—and also greatly narrowed the nation's range of possible choices.

The "imperial way" became a formula for overcoming the Japanese people's keen sense of spiritual and economic subjugation by the West. It provided channels for thought and emotion in all areas of life, not just the military. It worked to make people insensitive to the hurts imposed on others by wanton aggressiveness and self-righteousness, just as its American counterpart—the rhetoric of "Manifest Destiny"—had done in certain periods of aroused American nationalism. Almost overnight the spirit of international conciliation disappeared from the deliberations about and conduct of Japan's foreign policy. In its place came expressions of the Shinto impulse to purify Asia from the polluting influences of Anglo-American political culture. Also embedded in the "imperial way" was the millenarian belief, shared by all Japanese Buddhist sects but preached with especial vehemence by the Nichiren sect, that the Japanese state, because of its unique monarchy, was a tremendous power for teaching morality and unifying the entire world. References to the sacred principle of the "imperial way," the "eight corners of the world" under the emperor's rule, and the "emperor's benevolent heart" became commonplace, and were linked to a willingness to use force against those who rejected his fatherly benevolence.

In this setting—a nation that interpreted itself as emperor centered and racially superior, with officials who recognized no morality higher than the state itself—Hirohito and his key advisers participated, directly and decisively, as an independent force in policy making. Acting energetically behind the scenes, Hirohito influenced the conduct of his first three prime ministers, hastened the collapse of political party cabinets, and sanctioned opposition to strengthening the peace machinery of the League of Nations. When resistance to his interventions provoked open defiance from the army, he and his advisers drew back and connived at military aggression.

From the very outset Hirohito was a dynamic emperor, but paradoxically also one who projected the defensive image of a passive monarch. While the rest of the world dissociated him from any meaningful personal role in the decision-making process and insisted on seeing him as an impotent figurehead lacking notable intellectual endowments, he was actually smarter and shrewder than most people gave him credit for, and more energetic too. In Hirohito's case there is as much to be learned from what he does not say and do as what he does. During the first twenty-two years of his reign, he exerted a high degree of influence and was seldom powerless to act whenever he chose to. When Hirohito did not exercise his discretion to influence policy or to alter some planned course of action, his decision had consequences.

From late 1937 onward Hirohito gradually became a real war leader, influencing the planning, strategy, and conduct of operations in China and participating in the appointment and promotion of the highest generals and admirals. From late 1940, when more efficient decision-making machinery was in place, he made important contributions during each stage of policy review, culminating in the opening of hostilities against the United States and Great Britain in December 1941. Concurrently he and his advisers acted as a weathervane of the moods and frustrations of Japan's ruling elites. To stay on top of the decision-making process and to respond to new international developments, he consciously broke with precedents set by his grandfather, Emperor Meiji, and changed direction in foreign policy. Slowly but surely he became caught up in the fever of territorial expansion and war.

After defeat in World War II, Hirohito's life entered a new

phase. His immediate priorities shifted to preserving his throne and avoiding indictment as a war criminal. In this he proved as adept at the give-and-take of politics with Americans as he had been in his dealings with his own generals and admirals. American-imposed reforms destroyed the triangular relationship between the relatively independent monarchy, the government (as represented by the cabinet), and the Japanese people. Deprived of sovereign status, Hirohito was forced to become a "symbol" of national unity. Even as an American-created "symbol monarch" under a new constitution, however, he continued to act as a restraint on democratic trends, and to lobby secretly for Japan's return to a balance of power system operating against the Soviet Union under strong American leadership.

By the time the occupation ended, in 1952, the monarchy had reverted to its premodern, relatively powerless, private form, stripped of all masculine military and law-giving roles and relocated, once again, on the periphery of national life. For the first time in his adult life, the reality of Hirohito's political role came together with the perception of him as a figurehead. The return to power of conservative elites who had earlier been purged from office, however, offered Hirohito hope while setting the stage for nearly a decade of largely unsuccessful political struggle to revive some of his lost powers. Thereafter the monarchy itself underwent further decline, but not the many moral and political problems generated by Hirohito's continuation on the throne and the failure of the Japanese people to question their support of him.

The history of the Shōwa monarchy and its justifying ideologies up to 1945 is inextricably bound up with the history of Japanese militarism and fascism; after that date it is connected to efforts by ruling elites to roll back occupation reforms, check Japanese pacifism, and regain the attributes of a great-power state. The first half of Hirohito's life, like that of his grandfather Meiji, illustrates the tendency of military power, in any polity, to expand in situations where democratic institutions are either absent or nonfunctioning, the voices of ordinary people are shut out of national political affairs, and the only institutional restraint on the growth of militarism is the supervisory power of a lax or indulgent chief executive. The lessons of the second half of his life, when he was deprived of deity and stripped of constitutional powers, are less obvious. Hirohito and his advisers were involved in the staging of the Tokyo war crimes trials, and later in the making of the military alliance with the United States. The way he and the monarchy operated during and after the occupation of Japan also reveals how the power of the throne helped tame the liberation of the Japanese people and deflate their sense of empowerment.

This book therefore challenges the orthodoxy, established long before the Asia-Pacific War and fostered afterward by the leaders of the Allied occupation, that Hirohito was merely a figurehead within a framework of autocratic imperial rule, and a puppet of the military. It also challenges the idea that the army was mainly responsible for Japan's aggression during the 1930s and early 1940s, and points out the long-neglected role of upper-echelon naval officers in lobbying against arms reduction in the 1920s, bombing undefended Chinese cities during the 1930s, and pushing for war in the Pacific at the start of the 1940s. It argues further that, starting in the mid-1920s, party cabinets and Hirohito himself professed commitment to the new international "peace code" (stated in the Covenant of the League of Nations and the Kellogg-Briand Pact of 1928) that criminalized aggressive war, but pursued a policy toward China that violated the spirit of Japan's voluntarily assumed treaty obligations embodying that code.

Even after the nation's capitulation in August 1945, Japan's ruling elites remained indifferent to the obligations imposed by international law on all sovereign states. Concerned about some of the wartime actions of the imperial state, and needing to protect the emperor, cabinet officers ordered the destruction of documents that would have aided in trying war criminals and reconstructing the Shōwa past. Later attempts by conservative politicians and intellectuals to portray the Tokyo war crimes trials as a judicial lynching by the victors, although derived partly from the limitations of the trials themselves, were also fueled by such prewar attitudes toward international law.

For more than twenty years Hirohito exercised, within a complex system of mutual constraints, real power and authority independent of governments and the bureaucracy. Well informed of the war and diplomatic situations, knowledgeable about political and military affairs, he participated in the making of national policy and issued the orders of the imperial headquarters to field commanders and admirals. He played an active role in shaping Japanese war strategy and guiding the overall conduct of military operations in China. In 1941 an alliance between Hirohito and his palace advisers on the one hand, and hard-line army-navy proponents of war against the United States and Britain on the other, made the Asia-Pacific War possible.

Two years into that war, long after Japan had lost the initiative and been forced onto the defensive, Hirohito and his imperial headquarters still imagined they could buy time to check American offensives and rebuild war power in order to fight and win a decisive battle somewhere in the Pacific. During the last year of the war, Hirohito continued to exercise a direct, sometimes controlling, influence on military operations and to project his mythic presence into Pacific battles. Only toward the end, during the first half of 1945, did he vacillate in his determination to fight the decisive battle on the homeland. It was his reluctance to break with the military proponents of fighting to the bitter finish that mainly delayed Japan's surrender.

Hirohito's relations with his military commanders were often strained. He frequently scolded them, hindered their unilateral actions, and monitored their implementation of military policy decisions. Yet throughout their drive for territorial expansion, he stood by his generals and admirals, forgiving acts of insubordination as long as the result was military success. His own modus operandi as supreme commander, and the influence he exerted on operations, remain among the least studied of the many factors that contributed to Japan's ultimate defeat, and are therefore the most in need of reexamination.

Hirohito was not only a political and military leader, he was also his nation's highest spiritual authority. He headed a religiously charged monarchy that in times of crisis allowed the Japanese state to define itself as a theocracy. In a wooden building in the southwest corner of the palace compound, he regularly performed complicated rituals that clearly implied his faith in his mystical descent from the gods, and the sacred nature of the Japanese state and homeland. The fusion in one individual of religious, political, and military leadership complicates the study of the emperor. It is further complicated by his standing from early manhood at the center of a changing group of advisers who exerted influence on others through him because they exerted influence on him—while always taking care never to step out ahead of him. The composition of that changing entourage and the ideas of its members must be taken into account in trying to understand Hirohito. Similarly one must be open to the possibility that at key moments of decision, his rivalry with his brothers may have had some degree of influence on Hirohito's behavior.

A major concern of this book is Hirohito's failure to publicly acknowledge his own moral, political, and legal accountability for the long war fought in his name and under his active direction, both as head of state and supreme commander. Hirohito did not abdicate when disaster came, for he believed himself to be a monarch by divine right, and the indispensable essence of the Japanese state. He lacked all consciousness of personal responsibility for what Japan had done abroad and never once admitted guilt for the war of aggression that over thirteen years and eleven months cost so many lives. Believing that his debt was to his imperial ancestors, he resolved to rebuild the empire to whose destruction he himself had contributed so much. American policy and the Cold War helped him to remain on the throne for forty-two more years—a symbol of national, ethnic continuity but also an object of recurring political debate. Eventually Hirohito became the prime symbol of his people's repression of their wartime past. For as long as they did not pursue his central role in the war, they did not have to question their own; therefore the issue of Hirohito's war responsibility transcends the years of war and defeat. It must be discussed within a context of changing Japanese perceptions of the lost war, and judgments as to how that war came about and about its true nature.

For the past half century, Japanese historians, journalists, and writers in different fields have tried to "work through" and establish the various meanings of their wartime and postwar pasts. Partly for want of adequate sources, critical inquiries into Hirohito's role in the war started only in the early 1970s, but they have continued ever since. Prodded by conscientious researchers, and reacting against assorted apologists, negators of atrocities, and deliberate obfuscators of the truth, many Japanese have continually reassessed their views of Hirohito, the war, the Tokyo trials, and other key events of the occupation period: often to rationalize them, but just as often to see them more objectively, to criticize and learn from them.

The emperor who emerges from this work was a fallible human being, susceptible to the same desires, drives, instincts, and faults common to all human beings, but with a prolonged educational experience such as probably no one in the entire world, except himself, was given. For much of his life he was at or near the center of power, the active agent of his and the ruling elites' interests. The knowledge he had of both the public stage and the hidden machinations of government no other individual has shared. When he equated the survival of his own imperial house with that of the nation, he was both proud and selfish, as well as mistaken. To think of him as the one individual whose very existence manifested the deepest political dilemmas of modern Japan would be quite accurate. Neither an arch conspirator nor a dictator, he was rather the leading participant in, and remains a key to understanding, the major political and military events of his nation in the twentieth century. I believe he was also a tense and troubled human being who deceived himself even more than others in struggling to perpetuate hierarchy and order at the expense of the democratic ideals enshrined in Japan's postwar constitution.

PART 1

THE PRINCE'S EDUCATION, 1901–1921

The Boy, the Family, and the Meiji Legacies

E mperor Meiji's first grandson was born on April 29, 1901, within the Aoyama Palace in Tokyo. The moment was one of national delight, and virtually the entire nation celebrated, especially the court. The spirits of the reigning emperor's ancestors were duly notified that the blessed event had come to pass, and that the baby seemed hale and vigorous. An heir had been born; the ancient dynasty would continue, "unbroken," for at least a few more generations. Scholars wise in the complexity of names and titles conferred. The infant, they announced, would be given the title "Prince Michi," connoting one who cultivates virtue, and given the name "Hirohito," taken from the terse Chinese aphorism that when a society is affluent, its people are content.[1]

The young but chronically ill Crown Prince Yoshihito, next in line to the throne, was twenty-one that spring. The bloomingly fit Princess Sadako was just sixteen. In time she would bear him three more sons: Yasuhito and Nobuhito in 1902 and 1905 respectively, and Takahito (Prince Mikasa) in 1915.[2] As for the baby's grandfather, Emperor Meiji, at forty-eight he had occupied the Chrysanthemum Throne for thirty-four years, and would continue to reign for eleven more.

According to custom, the children of Japanese royals were raised apart from their parents, under the care of an appropriate surrogate. Yoshihito had been taken while still a very small infant to be raised the time-honored way. Shortly after his birth in 1879, he contracted cerebral meningitis. Meiji insisted that he be treated according to traditional (Chinese herbal) rather than Western medical practice.[3] The baby failed to respond quickly and thereafter struggled through a hard, painful, often bedridden childhood. At different periods lasting several years he could seem more or less normal, but there were other times when he was hopelessly afflicted, and he was never robust. He became a royal dropout after managing somehow to graduate from the primary course of the Peers' School (Gakushūin) and to finish one year of middle school.[4]

Could the origin of the crown prince's problems have been in part genetic? Emperor Meiji had fathered fifteen children by five different women, and lost eleven of them. Yoshihito, the third son, was the only male to survive, and his mother was not the empress but one of Meiji's many concubines. Inevitably the court suspected that hundreds of years of imperial inbreeding had resulted in a genetic defect of some sort that might show itself in the generation that would be sired by Yoshihito.

Naturally enough Meiji and his advisers took extreme care in choosing the princess who would marry Yoshihito and bear his offspring. Their ultimate choice was Princess Kujō Sadako, a young girl from one of the highest-ranking court families. The Kujō were a branch of the ancient Fujiwara, a lineage that reached back to the late twelfth century, when its founding ancestor had become regent for the then-reigning emperor. Sadako had excellent evaluations at the girls' division of the Peers' School. Intelligent, articulate, petite, she was especially admired for her pleasant disposition and natural dignity. In all her attributes she was just the opposite of Yoshihito.[5]

The couple, who had met on several chaperoned occasions, were married in early 1900. As the years passed, Sadako grew in self-confidence and maturity, and the wisdom Meiji had shown in choosing her for his son was more and more praised.

Emperor Meiji, in consultation with Yoshihito and Sadako, had decided that his grandson Hirohito should be reared in the approved modern manner, by a military man. It seemed wise, therefore, that the parental surrogate be a married army or navy officer who could provide the child not only with a good family atmosphere but also a martial influence. His first choice, Gen. Ōyama Iwao, declined to undertake this heavy responsibility. They then turned to the elderly Count Kawamura Sumiyoshi, a retired vice admiral and ex–navy minister from the former Satsuma domain (a feudal fiefdom equivalent to a semisovereign state), and asked him to rear the child just as though he were his own grandson. Kawamura, a student of Confucian learning, could be further trusted because he was a distant relation by marriage of Yoshihito's mother.[6] On July 7, the seventieth day after his birth, Hirohito was removed from the court and placed in the care of the Kawamura family. At the time Kawamura allegedly resolved to raise the child to be unselfish, persevering in the face of difficulties, respectful of the views of others, and immune from fear.[7] With the exception of the last, these were characteristics that distinguished Hirohito throughout his life.

Hirohito was fourteen months old when his first brother—Yasuhito (Prince Chichibu)—joined him at the Kawamura mansion in Tokyo's hilly, sparsely populated Azabu Ward. The two infants remained with the Kawamuras for the next three and a half years, during which time three doctors, several wet nurses, and a large staff of servants carefully regulated every single aspect of their lives, from the Western-style food they ate to the specially ordered French clothing in which they were often dressed. Then in November 1904, at the height of the Russo-Japanese War, the sixty-nine-year-old Kawamura died. Hirohito, age three, and Chichibu, two, rejoined their parents—first at the imperial mansion in Numazu, Shizuoka prefecture, and later in the newly built Kōson Palace within the large (two-hundred-acre) wall-enclosed compound of the crown prince's Aoyama Palace. In 1905 Nobuhito (Prince Takamatsu) was born, and toward the end of that year joined his brothers at their Kōson Palace home. Their care was directed at first by Yoshihito's newly appointed grand chamberlain, Kido Takamasa; later their own special chamberlain was appointed.

During this earliest formative phase of Hirohito's life, one of the chief nurses attending him was twenty-two-year-old Adachi Taka, a graduate of the Tokyo Higher Teacher's School and later the wife of Hirohito's last wartime prime minister, Adm. Suzuki Kantarō. Taka could well have been called his substitute mother. Remembering this period later in her own life, Taka contrasted Hirohito's calm, deliberate, sedate nature and body movements as a baby with those of the more energetic, curious, and temperamental Chichibu.[8] The brothers were indeed very different emotionally, both as little boys and as adults. But young Hirohito was more assertive than she intimates, while the mature Shōwa emperor was the embodiment of energetic monarchism, and much more driven by emotions than nurse Taka ever foresaw.

Throughout the first decade of Hirohito's life, Crown Prince Yoshihito lived only a few minutes away, within the same walled compound as the Kōson Palace, and had almost daily physical contact with the boys. In his later years Chichibu talked often and freely about his father but not about the emperor Meiji. In Chichibu's uninhibited recollection Meiji's withholding of tenderness stifled any sense of devotion. "Never did I receive the warm, unqualified love that an ordinary grandfather gives to his grandchildren," he wrote. "So I never had any feeling of adoration for my grandfather. . . . Nor did I ever hear his voice."[9] Hirohito, for the most part, kept his memories of his father and his feelings toward him to himself, but he would always talk admiringly about his grandfather.[10] Perhaps he sensed from an early age that emulation of Meiji was expected of him, while emulation of his own father was not.

Emperor Meiji, according to nurse Taka, was extremely

reserved with his grandchildren and seldom saw them except on their birthdays.[11] These meetings usually lasted only two or three minutes and were more like imperial audiences than tender encounters between a grandfather and his grandsons. Meiji, in full military uniform, would stand at his desk and nod his head as the small boys bowed and then immediately exited.[12] If he ever showed them affection, it was by sending them toys. One has the impression, therefore, that Hirohito probably related more to the idealized emperor, "Meiji, the Great," than he did to the real grandfather whom, after all, he never really knew. Given the unusual emotional climate in which Hirohito was reared, ambivalence marked his relationship with his own father but less so with Meiji.

Hirohito was a docile child, fussed over and pampered by nurses and relatives during his kindergarten years. Like other children of his exalted class, he and his brothers grew up enacting in play the Russo-Japanese War.[13] As the emperor-to-be, Hirohito—little "Michinomiya"—had to be respected in play and could never be the recipient of anger or ill treatment. Even in make-believe war games, he always had to be the commander in chief, on the winning side. One day Prince Chichibu, according to his own memoir, quarreled with Hirohito over toys, and in anger whacked his older brother with an artillery piece. A horrified servant woman immediately grabbed Chichibu and dragged him off to the prayer room, where she made him apologize before pictures of the sun goddess, Amaterasu Ōmikami, and of their parents, the crown prince and princess. After admonishing the small prince, she made him swear to the deities never again to strike his brother. Chichibu, however, leaves the impression that he did so quite often.[14]

Between the ages of four and eight, Hirohito and his brothers were frequently taken by carriage to visit sites in the central part of the capital that were repositories of the nation's modern history. Occasionally the military leaders of the Russo-Japanese War and the Meiji oligarchs paid visits to them at the Kōson Palace. To familiarize Hirohito and his brothers with the world of militarism and war, they were taken to watch military parades and to see the museum where captured weapons from the Russo-Japanese War were displayed. They were also taken to the Yokosuka Naval Base, and in August 1906 Hirohito and Chichibu were both given a special tour of the warship *Katori*.[15]

When Hirohito was six years old, in 1907, Marquis Itō Hirobumi returned to Tokyo to report on the political situation in Korea, where, as a result of the Russo-Japanese War, Japan had gained the opportunity to establish a protectorate. Itō had been serving there since December 1905 as the first resident general. In September, Emperor Meiji bestowed upon him the highest hereditary title, "prince." Just at this time nurse Taka brought Hirohito and his brothers, dressed up in their sailor suits, to the palace to visit their grandfather. Unexpectedly they encountered Itō, Yamagata Aritomo, and five other oligarchs from the former feudal domains of Satsuma and Chōshū. The *genrō*, or "senior statesmen" as they were now called, had come to the palace to thank the emperor for their gifts. When Hirohito saw them in a waiting room, he stared at Itō's medals, causing Itō to approach and ask, "Are you the future crown prince?" Unafraid, Hirohito replied that he was. "And who are you?" Itō explained who he was and why he was there. To the great delight of all the elderly *genrō*, Hirohito questioned him in detail about his many medals as if he were much older than his age and used to having his questions answered.

I

In the year 1901 Tokyo's population was reaching nearly 1.5 million.[16] Though by no means wholly modern any more than the country itself, the city was bursting with energy. Emperor Meiji, for instance, lived not too distant from Hirohito's birthplace in a still new, sprawling palace consisting of three dozen wooden buildings, joined by a single corridor—which he never allowed to be wired for electricity.[17] His huge, stone-wall-enclosed Imperial Palace compound was encircled by a moat and spread over some 240 acres—a green island of emptiness and stillness amid the bustle that surrounded it. On one side were the Marunouchi and Kasumigaseki sections of Tokyo, where the nation's leading financial, business, and governmental institutions were just beginning to cluster. Between these future core business districts, which included the new Diet building and the office headquarters of the Mitsubishi Company, lay Japan's first Western-style park—Hibiya Park. To the east of the vast Imperial Palace grounds lay the head of Tokyo Bay, along which, on both sides, light and heavy industry were already concentrating.

Hirohito was brought up to believe that the entire history of modern Japan centered on his grandfather and the small group of talented officials who had assisted him. Virtually unknown beyond Kyoto when he had succeeded to the throne at age fifteen, by the time of his first grandson's birth, Meiji was revered all over Japan. In that interim not only had the monarchy evolved and gained political, economic, and military power, but the Japanese people themselves had acquired a new national identity as his "loyal subjects," or *shinmin*. The ideology of virtuous subjecthood implied a special type of conduct: absolute loyalty and service to the emperor, conceived ideally as the parent (both father and mother) of an extended family that included the whole nation as his "children." The entire family of subjects was expected to value hard work and competition, to honor the stories of the origins of the state, to subscribe to state Shinto, and to put service to the state and duty to the emperor ahead of private interests and pleasures. Hirohito was reared within this same imperial ideology, but viewed from the other side, as the one to whom all loyalty and service were owed.

An official cult of the emperor was also firmly in place at Hirohito's birth. Repressive laws governing speech and writing critical of the emperor had been enacted in 1893, 1898, and 1900. Restrictive publication and newspaper laws soon followed.[18] The mass media reported on the emperor and his family in a uniform way, using special terms of respect. Police regulations also governed the taking of his picture.

Of the many highly ambiguous legacies of the Meiji era, the constitutional system and the ideology of rule bequeathed by Meiji to Hirohito were by far the most important. Through the constitution Hirohito inherited political traditions of autocratic rule combined with an ethos of restraint in its exercise. Later, when he began to be educated to take over, he learned that no laws or imperial ordinances could be made unless the emperor gave his assent first.[19] Court and cabinet had been joined formally by the emperor himself—in whom the two worlds came together. But the structural division of court and government could easily lead to problems of communication. As Hirohito grew older he would experience this division, and be confronted constantly by the confusion that the architects of the constitutional order had institutionalized at the highest level.[20]

Although the constitution specified that the emperor was to share the exercise of legislative power with the Imperial Diet, Meiji and his advisers assumed that the Diet would reflect only the "imperial will," never its own. In case of a conflict between the emperor and the Diet, the emperor possessed a veto power by withholding his sanction. The constitutional order, codified by this great imperial "gift," was already undergoing change on the eve of Hirohito's birth. In 1900 Itō had founded a new political party, the Rikken Seiyūkai, or "Friends of Constitutional Government," to build parliamentary support for the oligarchic government and to help make the constitution work.

The Seiyūkai—representing mainly the preferences of large landlords and industrialists—came to dominate party politics in the Diet.[21] The *genrō* persuaded Emperor Meiji to acknowledge this new reality of party politics, even cabinets in which party men participated. Once again Itō played the key role in getting Meiji to abandon his opposition. He did so, however, only by promising that his new party would leave the appointment and dismissal of the prime minister and other ministers of state entirely to the discretion of the emperor.[22] By yielding to the emperor's autocratic prejudices, Itō denied the key parliamentary principle that cabinets should be organized by the head of the majority party in the elected lower house of the Diet.

In general Meiji was indeed an autocrat, and the constitution by no means changed his view on that. He continued to support the military in disputes within the cabinet. And the *genrō* continued to admonish him to restrain his exercise of despotic powers and to operate within the confines of a system of consensus. While the emperor could appoint and dismiss prime ministers and other high officials in a way he had been unable to before the constitution, Itō and the other *genrō* retained their exclusive power to nominate the prime minister.[23]

The emperor's chief advisers had also crafted and handed down to Hirohito, through Meiji, an ideology of rule grounded in the fusion, ever since antiquity, of religious awareness and state consciousness. "[A]ll religions are extremely weak and none furnishes a foundation of the state," Itō had asserted. The throne, therefore, had to serve as a substitute, and its occupant had to be the source of authority for all governments. Itō, in his famous *Commentaries on the Constitution* of 1889, had furnished the classic rhetoric for the theocratic emperor.

> "The Sacred Throne was established at the time when the heavens and the earth became separated." (*Kojiki*) The Emperor is Heaven descended, divine, and sacred. He is preeminent above all his subjects. He must be reverenced and is inviolable. He has indeed to pay due respect to the law, but the law has no power to hold him accountable to

it. . . . He shall not be made a topic of derogatory comment nor one of discussion.[24]

The imperial ideology in which religious myth figured so prominently was not ancient, however. Allegedly nonreligious "state Shinto" (as opposed to "sect Shinto") took shape during Meiji's reign directly from the belief that Japan was a holy realm protected by Shinto deities and ruled by an emperor who was descended from the sun goddess. The nationalization of core elements of Shinto entailed the establishment of the Grand Shrine of Ise Jingū as the major Shinto shrine in which the sun goddess was enshrined. Ise became the main symbol of Shinto as well as a center of national devotion and the apex of a hierarchy of lesser shrines in villages and towns throughout the country.

In 1890 Emperor Meiji issued, without the countersignature of any minister of state, the short Imperial Rescript on Education. "Know ye, Our subjects," it began, using the newly coined compound term *shinmin* to denote "loyal-officials-directly-subordinated-to-the-emperor, and people-who-obediently-comply-with-their-orders."[25] Then it went on to list the Confucian virtues, starting with filial piety, which were to inform human relationships, adding that "should emergency arise, offer yourselves courageously to the State; and thus guard and maintain the prosperity of Our Imperial Throne coeval with heaven and earth." The final line of the rescript asserted that emperors were the source of all morality.[26]

At the start of the Restoration both Confucianism and Buddhism had been considered foreign accretions to the national essence, and as such to be expunged. The education rescript, however, was part of a late-Meiji course reversal, using traditional Confucian, not Shinto, language to counter progressive, democratic thought and ideals and to drum in the new notion of "loyal subjects." The rescript molded generations of Japanese to be loyal servants to the emperor-state, in which governance was an essentially paternalistic exercise, carried out in a paternalistic manner, by officials who were supposed to know best what was good for the people. In addition the education rescript accustomed all Japanese to the notion that morality and culture were closely tied to, yet never transcended, the state.

Education and military affairs—two spheres of national life affecting all Japanese—had been placed under the emperor's direct extraconstitutional control, making him the sacred pedagogue with the power to proselytize, as well as the supreme generalissimo with the power to issue orders to the armed forces.[27] Without the emperor's support and assistance, no cabinet or prime minister could rule for long.

The strengthening of the monarchy, through the promulgation of the Meiji constitution and the Imperial Rescript on Education, changed the whole intellectual climate in Japan.[28] During Hirohito's childhood the institutions and ideology of the Meiji state underwent further development. State Shinto, and the notion of "the unity of rites and governance" through the emperor, gained a new lease on life through the establishment in 1900 of a Bureau of Shrines and Religion within the Home Ministry.[29] Soon each member of a household, whether Buddhist or Christian (then about 1 percent of the population), had to become a parishioner of a local shrine and have a connection with a tutelary deity. When the local shrines raised their status to the state level by choosing names from ancient myths or historical legends, all the gods of the shrine became connected genealogically to the ancestral goddess of the imperial house, Amaterasu Ōmikami. Feelings of veneration for Emperor Meiji deepened, and many people began to imagine that they themselves existed because of him.[30]

Hirohito turned seven in 1908, the year the government reaffirmed its foreign policy of expanding Japan's colonial position on the Asian continent within a framework of continued division of spoils with the European powers and the United States. That same year the Ministry of Education began to rewrite school textbooks to describe Japan as an organic, harmonious, moral, and patriarchial "family state" in which all Japanese were related to the emperor. Revision was needed because society was changing rapidly and interpretations of Meiji's "Imperial Rescript on Education," written in archaic language, needed to be unified. Now the education rescript acquired a meaning it had not had in the 1890s. Children continued to be taught the foundation myths: that they were the subjects of the emperor and had to obey him just as they obeyed their fathers and mothers. But for the first time the impersonal emperor-state itself was presented as the supreme entity that took priority over all other values. The relationship of the imperial house to the nation began to be described as that of a progenitor "head-family" to its various "branch" and "stem" families. When the text-book revision was completed in 1911, the premises of monarchical absolutism had been written into public education, and state power had, in theory, been grounded in the intimate sphere of the family.[31]

In the real world, of course, not all Japanese sided with the gov-ernment or identified strongly with the imperial house as the new textbooks assumed. Significantly the years 1910–11 witnessed the highly publicized High Treason Incident, in which a small group of radical socialists and anarchists were charged with lèse-majesté and executed for allegedly plotting to assassinate Emperor Meiji. One of them was a young priest of the Sōtō Zen sect, Uchiyama Gudō, who had written and widely circulated a scathing denunciation of the entire imperial system:

> The Big Bullock of the present government, the emperor, is not the
> son of the gods as your primary school teachers and others would have
> you believe. The ancestors of the present emperor came forth from a
> corner of Kyushu, killing and robbing people as they did. They then
> destroyed their fellow thieves. . . . When it is said that the [imperial
> dynasty] has continued for 2,500 years, it may seem as if [the present

emperor] is divine, but down through the ages the emperors have been tormented by foreign opponents and, domestically, treated as puppets by their own vassals. . . . Although this is well-known, university professors and their students, weaklings that they are, refuse to either say or write anything about it. Instead, they attempt to deceive both others and themselves, knowing all along the whole thing is a pack of lies.[32]

II

If Hirohito associated Japan's entire modern history with his grandfather and the loyal circle of advisers who assisted him, he perceived his own world largely in terms of the empire his grandfather bequeathed him. The two major wars fought in Meiji's name— against Ch'ing China in 1894–95 and czarist Russia in 1904–5— altered the conditions of Japanese national life and changed the international environment surrounding Japan.

The war with China deepened national integration and furthered the monarchy's transformation into a crisis-control mechanism for oligarchic, authoritarian rule. Concurrently it hastened a process of logrolling that advanced the power of political parties in the Diet, thereby imparting a measure of liberalization to the authoritarian state. Thereafter, as Japan's economic development proceeded apace, the elites in the military, the bureaucracy, the Diet, and big business found their interests frequently at odds, making domestic politics more and more fractious.

Ten years later came the Russo-Japanese War, followed by another period of growth in political party activity, as well as increased military spending to secure Japan's possessions on the Asian continent. By then the Army and Navy General Staff commands had been made directly subordinate to the emperor, and their bureaucracies had begun to elude cabinet control. To counter this danger Itō revised the Cabinet Regulations, restoring to the prime minister some of the power that had been lost in 1889.[33] Nevertheless, the relative independence of the military was never checked, and the cabinet never became the emperor's highest advisory organ. In March 1907, the navy minister appealed to the emperor to overturn Itō's work, and Meiji concurred.[34]

Six months later the army and navy ministers enacted General Military Ordinance Number 1, stipulating that "Regulations pertaining to the command of the army and navy which have been decided directly by the emperor are automatically military regulations (*gunrei*)." Emperor Meiji sanctioned the ordinance. With this, the army and navy acquired "the authority to enact, independently of the cabinet, a new form of law, called *gunrei*." Thus, while the prime minister's power of unification of the cabinet remained weak, the military—with Meiji's support—was able to advance the argument that the emperor's "right of supreme command" was an independent right, free of government control.[35]

During Hirohito's school years—the post–Russo-Japanese War period from 1907 to the eve of World War I—the military was allowed to arrogate power that it did not legally possess. Meiji sanctioned, as the new guiding principle of Japanese defense policy, the protection of "the rights and interests we planted in Manchuria and Korea at the cost of tens of thousands of lives and vast sums of money during the war of 1904–5."[36] New efforts were also made to infuse emperor ideology and *bushidō* (the way of the warrior) into the armed forces. Infantry manuals and training procedures were revised to emphasize the importance in warfare of human spirit, offensive-mindedness, small-arms fire, and hand-to-hand combat. Also incidentally, the rank and authority of the emperor's aides-de-camp were strengthened.[37]

In 1907 Japan's long struggle to subjugate the Korean people through control of their royal house entered a new phase. In September, Korean king Kojong dispatched three envoys to a peace conference at The Hague to plead that Korea's protectorate status had been forged without his official sanction. The Great Powers denied Kojong's envoys admission to the conference on the ground that, as a protectorate of Japan, Korea had no power in foreign policy. Following this embarrassing incident, Emperor Meiji sent Crown Prince Yoshihito to Korea to shore up relations with its royal family. Shortly after Yoshihito's return to Japan in late October, Meiji approved Itō's policy of forcing King Kojong to abdicate and removing his young heir, the "Crown Prince Imperial" Yi Un, to Tokyo—ostensibly to be educated but in reality to deter further anti-Japanese actions by Korean royals. On December 15, 1907, holding Itō's hand, ten-year-old Yi Un came to the Kōson Palace and was introduced to Hirohito, Chichibu, and Takamatsu. Over the next two years, while the oligarchs made their fateful decision to change Korea's status from protectorate to colony, Meiji acted as guardian to Yi Un, lavishing more attention and gifts on him than he ever had on his own grandsons. Itō made sure too to bring the Korean prince with him whenever he visited Hirohito and his brothers.

The last occasion Hirohito met Yi Un in Itō's presence was on September 14, 1909, soon after Itō had stepped down as resident governor of Korea and assumed the presidency of the privy council. Six weeks later, on October 26, a Korean nationalist assassinated Itō in Harbin, Manchuria, where he was on his way to discuss Russo-Japanese relations. As for the hostage Yi Un, Tokyo became his permanent home, and he was not allowed to visit Korea until his mother's death in 1911.[38]

During Hirohito's boyhood and afterward, Emperor Meiji was propagandized as the very touchstone of all virtue. Though Meiji's public persona was that of a progressive, "Westernizing" monarch, the fount and essence of all moral values, he was far from that. He was privately "anti-Western" in his inclinations, and politically reactionary. His personality was not very pleasant either. He tended toward dissoluteness and obesity, and spent an inordinate amount of time satisfying his prodigious appetites. Many of the maladies that afflicted him can be traced to his excesses in food and especially drink, which eventually ruined his health.[39]

During the years that Japan's elites hyped the suprahuman virtues of Meiji, justified the post–Russo-Japanese War status quo, and rewrote the textbooks to promote emperor worship, Hirohito was attending the elementary course at the Peers' School, which he entered in the spring of 1908, at the age of seven. Located in Yotsuya, Owari-chō, near the front gate of the old Akasaka Palace (about a twenty-minute walk from his Kōson Palace), the Peers' School had been established thirty years earlier, under the aegis of the Imperial Household Ministry, to educate all children of the imperial family (*kōzoku*) and the old court nobility. After the Peerage Act of 1884, the children of newly titled peers (*kâzoku*) could also attend, and the school expanded. The Meiji emperor had appointed General Nogi, a hero of the Russo-Japanese War, as the school's tenth president and charged him with educating his eldest grandson.

General Nogi favored a strict military-style education and was a firm believer in Confucianism, *bushidō*, and the precepts of Zen. He refused to pamper the little princes. On his instructions they were made to walk to school every morning, escorted by a medical attendant and two employees of the Imperial Household Ministry. As passersby looked on, they marched along in single file, with little Hirohito resolutely in the lead, Chichibu behind him, and Takamatsu in the rear. On rainy days they were allowed to ride in carriages; Hirohito rode alone while his brothers rode together and behind—the only exception being when one was sick.[40]

Because Hirohito was not a robust child, the teaching staff at the school focused, on Nogi's orders, on physical education and health as much as on deportment and academic achievement. At the same time they sought to implant the virtues and habits Nogi considered appropriate for a future sovereign: frugality, diligence, patience, manliness, and the ability to exercise strong self-control under difficult conditions. Devotion to duty and love of the military stood equally high in Nogi's vision of the ideal monarch. Under Nogi's tutelage Hirohito came to an early recognition of his physical weakness, and the need to overcome it by dint of hard work. From this experience as a child, he may also have come to feel that with the right education one could overcome all shortcomings.

Nogi was aware that the armed forces of modern Japan had been since their inception the armed forces of the emperor, and that they were supposed to be directly commanded by him.[41] Since the little prince would one day be in charge of the nation's military affairs, exercising the prerogative of supreme command in a way his grandfather had never been trained to do, the instructors at the Peers' School were told to "pay careful attention to guiding him in military matters."[42] In 1910 Meiji issued Imperial Household Regulation Number 17, requiring military training and service experience for the male members of the imperial family.[43] This law completed a process of compulsory militarization of the imperial family that had been going on for more than thirty years. For young Hirohito, however, military matters at this stage merely denoted training in horsemanship, which he began as early as the fourth or fifth year of elementary school, and the playing of war games (reenacting battles of the recent war) with his brothers and classmates.[44]

In formulating his spartan curriculum, Nogi must have borne in mind the failures experienced in trying to educate Hirohito's father. Crown Prince Yoshihito had had so many chief tutors and general supervisors of his education (including Itō Hirobumi and Gen. Ōyama Iwao) that no one could ever tell who was really in charge of educating him.[45] Nogi, however, benefited from an established system of ideological indoctrination and his own intense, overpowering character. When Nogi insisted that the boys salute and address him every morning as "Excellency," Hirohito and his brothers readily complied.[46]

Throughout his years at the Peers' School, Hirohito passed his winter school term and vacations in Numazu, Shizuoka prefecture, and his summers in Ikaho, Gumma prefecture, and in Hayama, Kanagawa prefecture. He had frequent contact with his brothers but was more often in the company of his specially selected classmates—thirteen boys, later reduced to nine. Already he received instruction in Shinto rituals from court nobles serving as "ritualists" within the Imperial Household Ministry. Hirohito would be the high priest of state Shinto—a religious as well as a political monarch.[47] Ancestor worship was also implanted early, before his character began to crystallize, by his performance of Shinto rituals. While he and his brothers lived in the Kōson Palace, every morning on rising, after splashing water and soap, and then toweling, they were taught to pray in a small, two-mat room by bowing in the direction of the Grand Shrine of Ise and the Imperial Palace.[48] As Hirohito grew older his visits to shrines and imperial mausoleums deepened his sense of the importance of his ancestors.[49] The religious identity that worked its way into his thought was one of the main results of his early childhood upbringing.

The central component of this identity was Hirohito's strong sense of moral obligation to imperial ancestors, who were the source of his being, his authority, his household fortune, and indeed whatever sustained both him and the nation. The creed of the ancestors bore on Hirohito, as the future head of the patriarchal imperial family. He was obliged to learn to perform solemn rites for them.[50] This relationship to tradition and the essence of his public obligation was summed up in the expression *kōso kōsō* ("the imperial founders of our house and our other imperial ancestors"). *Kōso* denoted his mythical forebears, starting with the sun goddess, Amaterasu Ōmikami, and continuing through Emperor Jimmu. *Kōsō* meant "our other imperial ancestors," or the line of historical emperors who had succeeded to the throne over time.[51] *Kōso kōsō* thus linked Hirohito directly to mythology and to the artificially constructed imperial tradition as a whole. It served as one source of his moral viewpoint and as the basis for his later assessments of the state. *Kōso kōsō*, his eternal public burden, determined the course to which his life was dedicated: preserving the throne so long as he was its occupant.

The rhetoric of "the imperial founders of our house and our other imperial ancestors" and "our imperial ancestors through a line of succession unbroken for ages eternal" [*bansei ikkei no kōsō*] had great historical depth. It can be traced back to such early politico-historical tracts of the imperial house as the *Shoku Nihongi* [Chronicle of Japan] of the early eighth century. It reappeared in Meiji's numerous imperial edicts, including his Rescript of 1889, establishing the Constitution of the Empire of Great Japan, the preamble to that constitution, the Imperial House Law of 1889, and the Imperial Rescript on Education of 1890. Hirohito's many imperial rescripts also contain the term *kōso kōsō*, as does the rescript in which he staked his family fortune in a declaration of war on Britain and the United States. Above all *kōso kōsō* expressed Hirohito's sense of himself as a ruler who had inherited the spiritual authority of his dead ancestors, and was more morally accountable to them than he was to his subjects, who after all were not the *source* of his authority but rather its objects.[52] Acknowledging responsibility to his imperial ancestors rather than to his "subjects" would always be a significant feature of Hirohito's character.

When Hirohito turned eleven in 1912, he became crown prince and was given the ranks of second lieutenant in the army and ensign in the navy.[53] That year the long reign of his illustrious grandfather finally ended, and the circumstances of his own life changed as well. Ever since Emperor Meiji had come of age politically, in the 1880s, he had been a power wielder, centralizing the organs of the state, protecting the oligarchs from their critics, and mediating disputes among them as they aged and became known as the *genrō*. His crowning achievement had been the glorification and sanctification of the empire that the hated oligarchs had actually created. In so doing, Meiji became the living symbol of Japan's nationalism and its empire, as well as the symbol of the legitimacy of imperial rule itself. His death at the age of sixty-one, on July 30, 1912, marked the loss of that dual symbol and precipitated questioning of the modus operandi of the throne.[54]

Hirohito's father, Crown Prince Yoshihito, made emperor at thirty-three, was unable to continue Meiji's legacy. Physically weak, indolent, and incapable of making political decisions, he was utterly lacking in knowledge of military matters, even though he was now the commander in chief. Less than one month after Yoshihito's accession to the throne, at the start of the new Taishō era (1912–26), the press reported the appointment of extra doctors to the court. In December 1912 Adm. Yamamoto Gonbei told *genrō* Matsukata Masayoshi that when it came to recommending a successor prime minister, Emperor Yoshihito "is not [of the same caliber] as the previous emperor. In my view it is loyal not to obey the [Taishō] emperor's word if we deem it to be disadvantageous to the state."[55]

Thus, without any institutional change having occurred, the accession in 1912 of Hirohito's father became an important turning point in the conduct of state affairs. The *genrō*, especially Yamagata, began to exert stronger control over the court, checking the will of the impetuous, always unpredictable new emperor. Imperial rescripts, which until recently had carried the force of law, and which the oligarchs had long relied on to curb recalcitrant Diets and ministers of state, suddenly became an object of fierce dispute and lost some of their authority.[56] A new interpretation of the constitution emerged: Professor Minobe's "organ theory," in which the state was viewed as supreme and even the monarch was subordinated to it as one of several "organs." Among Diet politicians a new movement arose to "protect the constitution" from the arbitrary rule of the "Satsuma-Chōshū cliques" that had dominated Japan under Meiji's protection. Because the franchise had doubled after the Russo-Japanese War, many politicians also began to press for passage of a universal male suffrage law.[57]

Historians mark the post–Russo–Japanese War period, culminating in the 1912 political change, as the start of Japan's "Taishō democracy" movement. By the use of this American-English term they mean a series of public campaigns, waged mainly by politicians, journalists, and intellectuals, to demand universal male suffrage, cabinet governments organized by the head of the leading political party, and politics conducted by parties in the Diet rather than by the older fief-based political cliques, which functioned apart from the Diet. After World War I, "Taishō democracy" also came to denote the transmission to Japan of American cultural and political products, lifestyles, and such ideologies as individualism.[58] The latter especially challenged the premise that the Meiji state rather than the individual had the capacity and was responsible for defining and enforcing the proper moral life.

III

The death of their grandfather was a major turning point in the lives of Hirohito and his young brothers. For Hirohito it marked the start of a new stage in his training. In order to prepare him to succeed to the position of supreme commander, he was assigned a new chamberlain and a military aide-de-camp, both supervised by a high-ranking official of the Imperial Household Ministry.[59] This man, former minister of education and longtime president of Tokyo Imperial University, Hamao Arata, was now known as the lord steward of the crown prince and was charged with overseeing Hirohito's education, and instructing him in the extraordinary complexities of court and social etiquette.

In addition the daily contact among the brothers declined, their educational paths separated, and their mentor paid them his last visit. On September 10, 1912, three days prior to Meiji's funeral, sixty-four-year-old General Nogi came to Hirohito's residence, already renamed the Crown Prince's Detached Palace. After informing Hirohito that he would "not be here when school starts," Nogi urged him to be vigilant and study hard. He then presented the prince with his two favorite history books, one by the seventeenth-century Confucian scholar and military strategist, Yamaga Sokō, the other by Miyake Kanran, a founder and leading representative of the early Mito school of nationalist learning.[60]

At the beginning of the Taishō period, on the day of Emperor Meiji's funeral, General Nogi and his wife closed the door to their second-floor living room and prepared to end their lives. He had removed his uniform and was clad in white undergarments; she wore black funeral attire. They bowed to portraits of Meiji and of their two sons, killed in the Russo-Japanese War. While the funeral bells tolled, they proceeded to commit ritual suicide. Mrs. Nogi acted first; he assisted, plunging a dagger into her neck, and then he disemboweled himself with a sword. The departed hero of the Russo-Japanese War left behind ten private notes and a single death poem. (The writing of *waka* death poems was another practice from Japanese antiquity that was revived in the nineteenth century.) In one note he apologized for his action to four family members, including his wife, and acknowledged having contemplated suicide ever since losing his regimental flag in the war of 1877; he also mentioned his aging and the loss of his sons. In another note, to a military doctor, he bequeathed his body to medical use.[61] Nogi also left notes for Capt. Ogasawara Naganari and Gen. Tanaka Giichi.[62]

Nogi's death poem, intended for public consumption, told the nation that he was following his lord into death—a practice known as *junshi* that even the Tokugawa shogunate had considered barbaric and outlawed "as antiquated in 1663."[63] Conservative intellectuals Nitobe Inazō and Miyake Setsurei, both given to decrying the collapse of traditional Japanese morality, interpreted Nogi's suicide as a signal act of samurai loyalty, pregnant with positive lessons for the nation, and for its armed forces. Nantenbō, Nogi's Zen master, was so enthralled by the majesty of his pupil's action that he sent a three-word congratulatory telegram to the funeral: "Banzai, banzai, banzai."[64] The *Asahi shinbun*, however, editorially criticized those who called for the establishment of a new morality by reviving *bushidō*, and asserted that Nogi's harmful action could teach the nation nothing.[65] Kiryū Yūyū, a writer for the *Shinano Mainichi shinbun*, went further, not only decrying Nogi's death as "thoughtless" and "meaningless" but warning presciently that "to comprehend death as loyalty" was a mistaken ethical idea that could only "end up encouraging great crimes in international relations."[66]

When informed of "Schoolmaster" Nogi's death by the chamberlain in charge of supervising his education, Hirohito alone of his three brothers was reportedly overcome with emotion: Tears welled up in his eyes, and he could hardly speak.[67] Doubtless he was too young really to understand the general's action, let alone the harmful effect that his anachronistic morality of *bushidō* might have had on the nation. But as Hirohito remarked late in life to an American reporter, Nogi had a lasting influence on him,[68] instilling precepts of frugality and stoic virtues of endurance and dignity to which Hirohito never failed to adhere. The brave Nogi was to Hirohito a giver of orders who meant what he said and was willing to lay down his life for his master. Hirohito not only identified with Nogi, he also derived from him the conviction that strong resolve could compensate to some extent for physical deficiencies. In Hirohito's imaginings, Nogi was to be emulated almost as much as his other hero, Meiji.

Hirohito still had two more years of primary school ahead of him. Then his education would be directed largely by two new figures in his life: Fleet Adm. Tōgō Heihachirō and naval Capt. Viscount Ogasawara Naganari, eldest son of the last lord of the tiny domain of Karatsu, and a prolific author of war stories and semifictionalized military histories. Later both men were to figure as major opponents of the first national defense policy embraced by Hirohito.

IV

Between the ages of thirteen and nineteen—in a decade when most Japanese students still received no military instruction in school, and normal "middle school" lasted for only five years—Hirohito and five of his classmates, specially selected from the Peers' School by Captain Ogasawara, were given a two-sided (military and liberal arts) education at the Tōgū-Ogakumonjo.[69]

The Ogakumonjo was a white-painted, Western-style, wooden school building that had been specially constructed for Hirohito within the precincts of the Takanawa Palace.[70] Nogi and Ogasawara had drawn up the plans for the school; the Meiji emperor had approved them shortly before his death. Fleet Admiral Tōgō presided over the Ogakumonjo as president, while Ogasawara recruited and supervised the entire teaching staff. The rationale behind Ogasawara's, the *genrō's*, and the court's choice of pedagogues was apparently quite simple: They all thought that the best way to educate a future monarch was to select the nation's most outstanding military officers and leading scholars from Tokyo Imperial University. Because Ogasawara chose (with only one exception) from the top of the academic hierarchy, his instructors were not agents of fanatic emperor worship, which may be one reason why Hirohito, in a later era of dictatorship and war, was usually uncomfortable with those who did hold such views.

The Ogakumonjo's strong suit was its military foundation. Besides training in horsemanship and military drills by junior army officers, Hirohito and his classmates studied map reading and did map exercises; military history; the principles of military leadership, tactics, and strategy; and chess.

Their regular military teachers included the president of the Peers' School, Gen. Ōsako Naoharu, an expert on the Russo-Japanese War; two navy rear admirals; and four active-duty lieutenant generals, most of whom had served as naval attachés abroad and taught at the Naval War College. Starting in 1919 the naval theorist Capt. Satō Tetsutarō delivered lectures to Hirohito on the American admiral Alfred Thayer Mahan's theories of sea power, which emphasized that control of the sea lanes of communication by large battleship fleets was the key to a successful expansionist foreign policy. Mahan had posited Japan's navy as a direct threat to future U.S. interests in the Pacific, though whether Satō noted this in lectures to Hirohito is not known.[71] Satō also lectured on Western and Japanese military history (including the Battle of the Sea of Japan, in which the combined fleet under Admiral Tōgō destroyed the Russian Baltic squadron).

Another naval officer who lectured at the Ogakumonjo was Hirohito's own uncle, Adm. Prince Fushimi Hiroyasu, an expert on German military theory. Prince Fushimi had spent his impressionable late teens studying in Imperial Germany, and had graduated from the Kiel Naval School in 1895. To Captain Ogasawara, supervising the Ogakumonjo, Prince Fushimi was a useful conduit to the imperial house, and thus a friend who should always be accommodated when the prince requested personal favors on behalf of his son's naval career. To Hirohito, Fushimi was merely the relative supervising the first stage of his naval training, which started in July 1916, and a familiar face since childhood.[72] What Fushimi taught and what, if anything, Hirohito learned from him is not known.

Hirohito's army lecturers were two generals who had recently commanded troops in China during World War I and Gens. Ugaki Kazushige and Nara Takeji. With the exception of Nara (who had come out of the Artillery Section of the Bureau of Military Affairs) they had previously served as superintendent of the War College. General Ugaki had graduated in the first class of the reformed (German-style) Military Academy (1890) and from the War College in 1900. In 1917 he participated in planning the Siberian Expedition to stop the spread of the Russian Revolution and establish a buffer state in eastern Siberia. When Ugaki began his lectures at the Ogakumonjo, in April 1919, he was fifty-one years old and just starting to rise in party politics under the patronage of Gen. Tanaka Giichi.[73]

Most important in influencing Hirohito on military issues was General Nara, an officer with a reputation for diplomatic skill. Nara, fifty-two, was appointed Hirohito's guide and adviser on military affairs on July 18, 1920, and stayed with him as chief military aide-de-camp until 1933. Nara had fought in the Russo-Japanese War, served in Germany, commanded the Japanese garrison at Tientsin, and worked in the Bureau of Military Affairs. He had also attended conferences of the League of Nations and in 1920 had chaired the committee to investigate the massacre, by Russian partisans, of more than six hundred Japanese civilian and military personnel at Nikolaevsk, on the Amur River.

Nara participated in the Ogakumonjo military lectures only during the prince's last term there, which began in September 1920. Acting on the request of *genrō* Yamagata Aritomo, he drafted a seven-point guideline for the prince's future education, stressing that Hirohito should place emphasis on military affairs and take a deep interest in actually commanding the army and navy. "To achieve this goal," wrote Nara, "he should practice commanding company-size units of the Imperial Guard. *Genrō* Field Marshal Yamagata, citing the situation at the time of Emperor Meiji's youth, laid particular emphasis on this point." Mastering horsemanship, cultivating the prince's interest in weapons, and giving him experience in firing them were some of Nara's other educational goals. In early October 1920 Nara had a trench dug inside the crown prince's compound so that Hirohito could practice firing machine guns. "I guided Lieutenant Katō and was able to carry out most of this plan," Nara wrote after World War II. "However, there was a view at court that the killing of living creatures would harm the moral sensibility of an emperor. Clearly the chamberlains did not like [the prince's] firing-line practice."[74]

The curriculum of the Ogakumonjo was modeled on the War

and Naval Colleges, where military instructors taught lessons drawn mainly from the Russo-Japanese War. One lesson for all officers, and for the future commander in chief in particular, was the primacy of tactics over strategy. Thus military decisions taken to fight and win battles were stressed. The study of war as "an element of statecraft"—that is, decisions concerning whether to go to war and about the mobilization and allocation of forces, taken to attain the ultimate goals of war—was slighted by comparison.[75] Hirohito's naval instructors impressed on him the notion that in war the purpose of a naval engagement was to win by hurling a large, powerful fleet into a single decisive battle such as the Battle of the Sea of Japan, considered the perfect model of a naval encounter. His army instructors taught him that infantry units were the core of the army. Hand-to-hand combat rather than firepower determined victory or defeat in battle. Artillery and cavalry (later tanks and aircraft) were to be developed and used mainly to support bayonet charges by the infantry.[76]

The daily routine of the school was highly regimented by Captain Ogasawara and Admiral Tōgō. From Monday to Friday and half a day on Saturday, the routine seldom changed. The five aristocratic boys who were his classmates were awakened by their servants at 6:00 A.M. and breakfasted together. When the crown prince, whose private quarters were on the second floor, above theirs, finished his morning preparations, he walked into a large, carpeted Western-style study (called the "class preparation room"), whereupon a bell rang, signaling the other boys to go upstairs and greet him. Filing into the study, where each boy had his assigned desk and attached bookcases, they lined up and bowed to the prince (who alone in all Japan wore the chrysanthemum crest on his cap). Then they all took seats for a short period of reading in preparation for class that lasted until around 7:45. At that point they excused themselves to Hirohito, returning to their separate rooms to put on their shoes and gather up their school equipment. Afterward they assem-

bled with their teachers at the entrance to the Ogakumonjo classroom to await the prince's arrival, just as they had done when Hirohito attended the Peers' School.

Usually there were four morning hours of classroom instruction, followed by recess for lunch. In the back of the room, seats
were set aside for guests who visited at different times. These were
usually Captain Ogasawara, Admiral Tōgō, various military aides,
members of the imperial family, and officials of the Imperial
Household Ministry.[77] The tension generated by this constant
monitoring of Hirohito's performance, which went on both inside
and outside the classroom, can easily be imagined. At noon the
prince took his classmates' bows and departed to eat alone or in the
presence of a military aide. While he usually ate a Western-style
meal, often topped off by a glass of milk, the other boys went off
together to their dining hall for a Japanese-style meal. Only on
occasional Saturdays were one or two members of the class allowed
to lunch with him.

In the afternoons there would be one hour of formal classroom
instruction, followed by physical exercises and military instruction.
Then the boys would have an activity such as riding, tennis,
Japanese fencing, or target practice with pistols. Although Hirohito
was clumsy and certainly did not excel in any sport (including *sumō*;
kendō; swimming, which he had practiced since kindergarten; and
golf, which he took up later in life), he persisted in athletics, fiercely
determined not to be outdone. Nagazumi Torahiko, his classmate
through thirteen years of primary and middle school, remembers
the seriousness and extreme diligence with which he pursued them
all. When the afternoon session ended, the boys lined up again and
bowed before Hirohito, whom they addressed, even at play, as *denka*
(prince), while he called them by their surnames. A short period of
free time was set aside for unsupervised play in the imperial garden
after school hours. In the evenings there was more study and private
visits to the prince by his military aides-de-camp, who taught him

how to read maps and played war-strategy games with him. As Hirohito grew older, his naval aide-de-camp had him read secret military plans and ask questions about them. By 9:30 P.M. the school day ended and all the boys retired to bed.

In the third term of their academic year—the winter months of January through March—staff and students moved to the imperial mansion in Numazu, where the climate was warmer. There classroom instruction was carried out in somewhat less formal surroundings. During the summer months of June through September, when his classmates returned to their families, Hirohito spent only a short period of time with his parents. His summers were mostly given to pursuing a busy schedule of tours of the main army camps, naval bases, and military arsenals in the country.[78] He also toured the military academies, paid regular visits to the General Staff Headquarters of the army and navy, acquired experience in seamanship during training cruises aboard frigates and cruisers, inspected artillery tests, and observed divisional and regimental maneuvers.[79]

Hirohito's teachers, seeking to prepare him for the different roles he was to play as an emperor in the Meiji mold, taught him the official interpretation of the nation's history, which combined elements of nationalism and racism in the myth of his descent from the gods. Although as crown prince he inhabited a moral sphere in which questions of personal accountability for the exercise of power and authority would not arise, he was indoctrinated in the same myths that were put forth in the nation's primary and military schools. The "imperial family" (kōzoku), at the apex of the national hierarchy of hereditary houses, and the titled peers (kazoku), directly below them, may not all have agreed that Crown Prince Hirohito was descended from the gods, but he understood the utility of that tenet. Eventually it became a working part of his identity.

Hirohito was born to be the leader of a highly militarized imperial family (kōzoku), whose adult male and female members played unique public roles in Japanese life. The kōzoku was a self-governing, homogeneous group composed of nine ranks of royalty, extending through cousins, of which there were many. The upper ranks consisted of the reigning empress, the emperor's eldest son, or crown prince, the dowager empress, the princes and princesses of the blood, and their children. Hirohito's brothers, called *jiki miya*, consituted a separate order within the *kōzoku*. Unaffected by seniority, they were expected to behave differently from other *kōzoku*. The emperor, as head of the eternal imperial house, *kōshitsu*, was not, technically speaking, a "member" of his imperial family but stood above it as a chieftain, closely supervising and unifying its members. The second and third sons of *kōzoku*, upon reaching adulthood, automatically became hereditary peers (*kazoku*) and most were granted the title of "count."[80] Enjoying ownership of land, stocks, bonds, multiple residences, servants, and generous stipends administered by the Imperial Household Ministry, some *kōzoku* traveled abroad and lived far freer lives than did most ordinary Japanese. Some also tended to express "liberal" views, though that certainly cannot be said of Hirohito's mother, his brothers Chichibu and Takamatsu, or of his uncles, Field Marshal Kan'in Kotohito and Fleet Admiral Fushimi, who were later used by the central command of the army and navy as levers for influencing the throne.

Adult male princes of the blood were eligible for direct appointment by the emperor to the House of Peers, an upper branch of the Imperial Diet that had equal authority with the lower house. Some of them also participated—together with the lord keeper of the privy seal, the president of the privy council, the prime minister, the justice minister, and the president of the Court of Cassation (the highest court of appeals)—in an Imperial Family Council, established under the Imperial Household Law.[81] The infrequently convened family council addressed questions pertaining solely to the imperial house. Since *kōzoku* were prevented by law from formally assisting the emperor as political advisers, their real influence lay in holding strategic positions of command within the armed forces and in their frequent access to the emperor.

An affluent, landed class that participated in state activities as military officers, the *kōzoku* may be compared to the Prussian "Junker" nobility, though without that class's narrow-mindedness and pietism, and with a much stronger bourgeois rather than professional military character. Having become militarized in the course of strengthening the imperial state, however, the male members of the imperial family, regardless of their wishes or their suitability for military life, received military instruction, starting at the Peers' School. On becoming professional officers, they were incorporated into the armed forces at the highest levels of command and given opportunities to pursue military studies abroad. Their importance as a service elite, diffusing within the armed forces the consciousness of being directly subordinate to the emperor, cannot be overestimated.[82]

Young Hirohito pursued his first four years of military training while World War I was being fought, and his last three during the Siberian Expedition. In the first stage, 1914 through early 1918, the European war should have dampened the glory of the Russo-Japanese War, in which military men still basked. Although Japan was allied with Britain and the United States against Germany—the model for its professional military class—the Japanese army failed to learn the lessons of the critical role played by modern weaponry in mass warfare. Officers of the seventeen divisions into which the standing army was then divided preferred the idealized tradition of *bushidō* as expressed in the classic text *hagakure*, which glorified death and loyalty unto death as the highest values.[83] Harsh training and frequent punishments, an emphasis on military spirit, and the fostering of regionalism (by keeping together in the same regimental units men who came from the same geographical area, so that they would fight for the honor of their local region) remained the army's chief characteristics. Indoctrination centered on cultivating *bushidō* and the "spirit of Japan" (*Yamato damashii*), which connoted racial superiority and a sense of invincibility.[84] Both elements were "indissolubly linked" to Japan's national polity, or *kokutai*, centered on the emperor and expressed in the Imperial Rescript to Soldiers and Sailors of 1882.[85] The severe punishments and bullying by superiors at all levels led to a steady erosion of army morale, and to an increasingly open resort to violence by officers to maintain discipline and manage troops.[86]

During Hirohito's last three years at the Ogakumonjo, 1918 to early 1921, the maintenance of discipline in the ranks became an urgent task. Concurrently the values of military men changed, as did the times. World War I brought in its wake the Bolshevik Revolution abroad and the "rice riots" at home, creating a situation that forced the army once again to examine its own character. The riots that erupted throughout Japan in the summer of 1918 led to the callout of more than 57,000 troops to suppress them. These protests were followed over the next three years by disturbances connected with labor and tenant disputes and with the campaign for universal male suffrage. The most violent strikes in Japanese history occurred in this period: at the Tokyo Artillery Arsenal (1919 and 1921), the Kamaishi iron mine (1919), the Ashio copper mine (April 1921), Yawata Steel (1920), and the Kawasaki-Mitsubishi Shipyards in Kobe in the summer of 1921. The Kobe strikes, involving more than 35,000 workers, led to the army being called out again—as always, in support of management. Before the turmoil in Kobe ended, more than 300 workers were wounded and some 250 arrested.[87] Thus the army returned to its original mission of maintaining domestic law and order, and its standing in ordinary Japanese life plummeted. For the second time since its creation—the first being in the 1870s and 1880s—the army became an object of open public criticism, especially reviled whenever troops were used to put down peasant protests and labor strikes.[88]

Because the military was a microcosm of society, as well as a major employer of factory workers in its arsenals and shipyards throughout the country, the changes that occurred in Japanese life during the six years between the outbreak of World War I in 1914 and the end of the war boom in 1920 also inaugurated a new phase in the military's relationship to the monarchy. The industrial sector was already outgrowing the agricultural sector in productivity. The sphere of imperial rule was contracting. The demeanor of Commander in Chief Emperor Taishō, his utter lack of charisma, and the genrō's gross manipulation of him were almost common knowledge in political circles. After 1918 Taishō was increasingly unable to attend the army and navy grand maneuvers, appear at the graduation exercises of the military schools, or perform any of his other annual ceremonial duties, including the convoking of the Diet. He faded from public view just when the ideological climate was most unsettled and the military was searching for ways to overcome its social isolation. These developments made it more difficult to persuade conscripts to obey orders just as though they came directly from the emperor.

Rather than counterpose itself dogmatically to the new trends in thought, the army followed the current mood, revising its education system and initially taking a tolerant attitude toward many aspects of the Taishō democracy movement.[89] Some army officers began studying the social causes of industrial and rural conflicts. Within a short time they started to question whether a kokutai based on the founding legends was an adequate spiritual source of their institutional identity. Articles soon appeared in the official journal of the army, Kaikōsha kiji, which implicitly downgraded the importance of the imperial house as a symbol of the unity between the military and society.[90]

V

By the time Hirohito graduated from the Ogakumonjo in 1921, what had begun as a crisis of oligarchic government in 1912, occasioned by the transition from Meiji to Taishō, had developed into something much more serious: a burgeoning crisis of legitimacy for the monarchy. While anticolonial movements in Korea and China buffeted the empire abroad, militant labor and tenant movements suddenly arose and began to spread, testifying to growing public dissatisfaction with the status quo at home. In this new post–World War I setting, with the Japanese people forcefully asserting their own views of the *kokutai* and questioning the unequal social order dominated by bureaucrats, the military, and capitalists, the late-Meiji image of a harmonious family-state became impossible to sustain.

Hirohito's middle-school tutors failed to register any of these changes. The calls for social reform; the decline in the army's consciousness of being the emperor's army, which had set in after 1918; the sudden acquisition by many groups of a more realistic concept of self-interest—these developments did not figure in his middle-school curriculum. The dissonance between what he was taught at home and in school about his family, the world, himself, and what was happening outside his classroom doors would increase over time.

To appreciate why Hirohito's educators felt as they did about his future role as commander in chief, two other features of the imperial military need to be considered. From the moment of their establishment, the idea existed that the modern armed forces of Japan were to be commanded by the emperor. The principle of supreme imperial command had been maintained in all the wars of the Restoration period; and long before the Meiji constitution had explicitly mandated the emperor to command the armed forces, the idea that he alone possessed the moral authority to do so existed in the ancient notion that the emperor was the medium through which the gods worked their will.[91]

Furthermore, the emperor's right of supreme command of the armed forces was considered to be an independent power, antedating the constitution and superior to his sovereign power in matters of state affairs. This was quite different from the clauses in the American Constitution of 1787, which designated that the president had authority as commander in chief, but only Congress had the "power" to declare war and make "rules" for the army and navy. The emperor possessed autocratic military power, and in exercising it did not constitutionally require any prior ministerial advice or consultation.[92]

Though the imperial armed forces at the time of their establishment (in the 1870s and 1880s) had the look of a modern military based on European models, they were far from modern in spirit and values.[93] The peasants who made up the bulk of its recruits remained unliberated from feudal social relations in agriculture, disposed to resist the authority of superior officers, and so deeply resentful of conscription that oldest sons were eventually exempted from military service. The solution that the autocratic founders of the armed forces devised was to introduce extremely harsh forms of punishment and discipline to control the situation, and to bring the emperor's moral authority right into the basic relationship between superiors and subordinates. Inferiors were taught "to regard the orders of their superiors as issuing directly from" the emperor. This meant that orders were infallible and obedience to them had to be absolute and unconditional.[94]

In addition to taking military order and discipline to excessive lengths, the Meiji government had invested the imperial forces with a vague dual mission. The army and navy were to defend against further expansion of the European powers; on the other hand the army had to engage in coercive law enforcement as an instrument of the central government. Certainly the initial motive behind its formation was to smash the defenders of feudalism, thereby furthering Japan's modernization. But whether the army existed primarily for the protection of the people from foreign aggression or for the protection of the government in the pursuit of its purposes was never clarified during Meiji's lifetime.[95]

Unfortunately Hirohito's instructors did not explain to him how his future exercise of this sovereign independent right of supreme command would someday eclipse his role as a "constitutional monarch." Nor did his teachers communicate to him how the sphere of the right of supreme command had expanded over time, producing rifts between the high command and the government, as well as dissension between the Army and Navy General Staffs and their respective ministries. In short, his education at this stage only allowed him to see the outer workings of the system, not its actual functioning. Only through experience, in the third decade of his life, would he learn the dynamics and pathology of the political structure—when the raw despotism of the monarchy reared its ugly head.

2

CULTIVATING AN EMPEROR

The care and attention that Hirohito's pedagogues lavished on the military side of his education were meant to teach him that the imperial house had a much deeper relationship with the military than it did with any other national institution.[1] There was, however, another side to Hirohito's training for the monarchy that had nothing to do with socialization for war but was intended to prepare him for involvement in governance, educational, and international affairs. This was "instruction for the emperor" (*teiōgaku*), imparted in a formal classroom setting by professional educators and specialists from Tokyo Imperial University and the Peers' School. The reasoning behind it was that the Meiji constitution had ascribed to the emperor enormous civil powers, as important as his military ones, and he had to be taught how to exercise them. If the Meiji constitution had created a true "constitutional monarchy" rather than something close to an autocracy, there would have been no need to place so much emphasis on educating the emperor, and he could have remained as badly educated as any of Britain's kings or queens had been.

Also mandating both civil and religious "instruction for the emperor" was the official ideology taught in the schools to counter democratic thought. The theocratic ideal of the unity of religious rites and political administration (*saisei itchi*), which had imparted religious significance to state actions throughout the Restoration era, required that the emperor be trained to perform rites. Equally important in the rationale for educating the emperor was the core notion, dating from the Restoration, that Japan's emperor should always be "a charismatic political leader who stands at the head of and promotes the process of civilization and enlightenment."[2] If the emperor was to continue leading the drive to modernize and Westernize, he had to be educated in a wide range of practical subjects as well as in modern political, social, and economic thought. Given this outlook, it is striking that until the age of seventeen, Hirohito was reared in total isolation from Japanese daily life and not even allowed free access to the newspapers.[3]

From May 4, 1914, when he first started, to late February 1921, when he graduated—two months short of his twentieth birthday, and a few weeks before the school permanently dissolved—Hirohito was instructed in any and all subjects considered useful at that time for the education of an emperor.[4] Math, physics, economics and jurisprudence, French (at that time still the language of diplomacy), Chinese and Japanese, calligraphy, ethics and history—all were part of *teiōgaku*: the making of an emperor. So too was natural history, which became one of Hirohito's favorite subjects.

Hirohito's military educators, with their stress on hygiene, physical fitness, and direct imperial command, represented a radical departure from two and a half centuries of Tokugawa practice in educating a Japanese monarch. Before the Meiji restoration, monarchs—with the notable exception of Meiji's own father—were educated in subjects that would not involve them in either the political or military affairs of the Tokugawa regime. They studied abstract Confucian philosophical texts, practiced reciting Shinto prayers, and steered clear of politics. Ritual and prayer, poetry and the arts preoccupied them.

Keenly aware of the complex system of state institutions that

Meiji had bequeathed the nation, Hirohito's educators, military and civilian alike, dispensed with this Tokugawa tradition, focusing instead on the monarch's need for secular education and knowledge of statecraft to make the system work. Thus they acted on the premise that even though the monarch had inherited the throne, he still had to be initiated into its rites and procedures and made technically fit to rule. For the imperial throne, situated at the very apogee of power in all its forms, had to function as an integrating and legitimating center, the keystone in the arch that held in place all the other institutions of the state: the cabinet, the separate bureaucratic ministries, the Diet, the privy council, the military, and the parties.

The men who were to "make" Hirohito into a suitable monarch for operating in this system of rule were mostly middle-of-the-road academics associated with Tokyo Imperial University and the Peers' School. They were a hybrid of the old unchanging Japan and the new, changing everywhere as it followed blindly the path of modernization. As pedagogues who worshiped the Meiji emperor, they constructed an orthodoxy of what the ideal monarch ought to be and do. They always tried to avoid forcing Hirohito to choose between the conflicting moral visions and norms contained in the Confucian model of the virtuous, peace-loving ruler and the Japanese *bushidō* model of the ideal warrior. Both norms would be attractive to Hirohito, and he would seek to act in ways that conformed to both.

In short Hirohito was the product of a hybrid education, and no serious portrait of him can neglect the tension that this produced. The late-Meiji invention of tradition, grounded in Restoration ideology, gave him his sense of identity and his basic orientation. Clashing with that tradition was modern scientific learning. The tension between these two worldviews lay at the heart of everything Hirohito did.

I

Hirohito became fascinated with nature in his tenderest years. While attending the Peers' School, under the guidance of a chamberlain who delighted in collecting seashells and insects, Hirohito opened his eyes to the natural world. In 1913, at age twelve, he had made his own insect specimen book, illustrating with butterflies and cicadas the symbiotic relationship between plants and insects.[5] It was an early step in the development of his capacity to assess objects critically and rationally.

From 1914 to 1919, when Hirohito was in middle school, Professor Hattori Hirotarō became his teacher of natural history and physics. Hattori remained his servant in scientific pursuits for more than thirty years, cultivating Hirohito's childhood fondness for insects and helping him to develop a keen, lifelong interest in marine biology and taxonomy.[6] Under Hattori's guidance Hirohito read Darwin's theory of evolution as interpreted by the popular writer Oka Asajirō, whose book *Shinkaron kōwa* (Lectures on evolution) was published in 1904. He may also have read a Japanese translation of Darwin's *Origin of Species*. Around 1927 he was given a small bust of Darwin, which thereafter adorned his study alongside busts of Abraham Lincoln and Napoleon Bonaparte.

In September 1925, during the fourth year of his regency, Hirohito had a small, well-equipped biological laboratory established within the Akasaka Palace. Three years later, during the second year of his reign, he built, within the Fukiage Gardens, the Imperial Biological Research Institute, consisting of a greenhouse and two large laboratories, each with specimen rooms and libraries. Hattori became associated with this laboratory and for the next four years lectured before the emperor once a week on basic science. Until 1944 Hattori and other aides also accompanied Hirohito to his personal marine research facilities in Hayama three or four times a year. There, using two rowboats and a larger, remodeled fishing vessel, they would dredge for sea specimens. Years later

Hattori edited *Sagamiwan sango erarui zufu* (Pictorial specimens of marine life in Sagami Bay), while Sanada Hiroo and Katō Shirō did the colored drawings, Baba Kikutarō wrote the accompanying explanations. Because the re-formed Imperial Household Agency held the copyright,[7] the book was ascribed to Hirohito. Nowhere in the book, however, did the emperor's name appear, which raised the question, How much of its research had actually been done by him?[8]

Hirohito himself was always very modest about his interest in biology. When *Sagamiwan sango* appeared, Hattori offered an assessment of his former pupil's scientific bent in a discussion that appeared in the *Sandē Mainichi* on October 2, 1949. Asked whether the emperor's studies should be viewed as genuine scientific research rather than the work of an amateur, Hattori replied:

> Recently Professor Satō Tadao [of Nagoya University] wrote in the Nagoya newspaper that it belonged to the category of an amateur's research. Indeed, depending on how one looks at the matter, I think that is true. He never published anything under his own name and ended up furnishing raw data to various specialists. Therefore, from one point of view he is, in the final analysis, probably a mere collector. But I don't think so. He did not just hand them material he had collected. Rather, he first thoroughly investigated that material himself, and on that point he is no amateur.[9]

Hattori's assessment makes sense. Specimen collection and the study of taxonomy without question fitted Hirohito's methodical nature. And certainly during his most active years, when surrounded by great disorder, by problems to which all solutions were hard and uncertain, science was a steadying, relaxing constant in his life. Taught by Hattori, the emperor became a naturalist and a patron of marine biology, pursuing as a hobby the collection of sea plants and animals, such as slugs, starfish, hydrozoa, and jellyfish.

As a would-be scientist and a serious student of the biological evolution of sea creatures over many thousands of years, Hirohito had to be aware of the vastly different time scale of the Japanese imperial house, which by arbitrary official determination went back only twenty-six centuries. It is doubtful, though, that awareness of this discrepancy led him to reject completely his early ingrained belief in the divinity of his own ancestral line. Hirohito always placed a premium on the values that were inculcated in his youth. And as he grew older, he learned to appreciate only too well the value of ideological illusions in strengthening obedience to official codes of behavior. For him the relationship between modern science and the account of the *kokutai*, or national polity, taught by his other teachers were reconcilable, not inherently conflictual.

The more general point, however, is that science cultivated the rational, scientific pole in Hirohito's outlook: his sense of himself as a disengaged thinker, open to arguments and counsel based on reason and evidence. But there was another side to Hirohito, associated with his sense of morals and vocation. This side worked to adjust his scientific bent and practice to the imperatives and constraints of divine emperorship. Here the ideas he received from Sugiura Shigetake, Shiratori Kurakichi, and Shimizu Tōru were far more influential, for they formed the context in which his rational, objective thinking was embedded.

II

Sugiura Shigetake was an ultranationalist Confucian educator who had received a Western education in England and returned home to become a founding member of the Society for Political Education, and contributor to its famous magazine *Nihonjin* (The Japanese), "whose express purpose was the 'preservation of the national essence.'"[10] Sugiura took part, with his friend Tōyama Mitsuru, in the conservative intellectual reaction against the Civilization and

Enlightenment movement that had dominated Japan in the first decade and a half after the Meiji restoration. Later he served as an official of the Ministry of Education, concerned with moral instruction. In 1892 Sugiura became the founder and principal (until his death in 1924) of the Japan Middle School. By the time Ogasawara recommended him as Hirohito's (and later Nagako's) ethics teacher, many of his former students already occupied distinguished positions in Japanese political and economic life.

Sugiura was fifty-nine years old, an ideologue and monarchist of the highest repute, when he lectured Hirohito on the principles that should guide his behavior. To Sugiura these were embodied in the three imperial regalia of sword, jewel, and bronze mirror, which the sun goddess, Amaterasu Ōmikami, allegedly bestowed on her grandson, Ninigi-no-mikoto, to use in pacifying the Japanese people. The regalia had mainly ethical significance, in that they denoted the three virtues every monarch should possess: courage, intelligence, and benevolence.

Hirohito did not openly dispute this teaching, but he came to view the regalia in his own way, mainly as symbols of his political and moral authority. As such, they required constant guarding and occasional display to insure the security of the throne. Moreover, Hirohito could not seek the ultimate source of his sovereignty in legitimacy of blood. As a descendant of the fourteenth-century northern court, his genealogical line had not been regarded—by either the nineteenth-century scholars of the "National Learning school" or the Meiji government—as the most legitimate line of succession.[11]

The other fundamental rules Hirohito was taught to respect were contained in the Charter Oath of Five Articles (1868) and the Imperial Rescript on Education (1890).[12] These documents had enhanced the Meiji emperor's power and authority, and Sugiura believed that the ideals in them (which all subjects were supposed to live up to) should also become Hirohito's standard for the future.

Sugiura's approach to Meiji's Charter Oath emphasized the wisdom in the document but played down its political contingency. Here too Hirohito went beyond Sugiura and, from his own reading in nineteenth-century Japanese history, learned to situate the document within its times. The staging (on April 6, 1868) of the "oath" rituals, in which Meiji swore to the sun goddess, mythical progenitor of the imperial family, and the Charter Oath of Five Articles, which guided reforms early in his reign, were expedient concessions to potentially obstructionist feudal lords and Kyoto court nobles. The latter might have challenged the power of the samurai coup (that is, Restoration) leaders. The performance of the oath rituals marked a first step in establishing the independent authority of the "imperial will." Hirohito would later insist that the Charter Oath was an ahistorical, timeless document—a "Magna Carta" of Japanese liberalism—but he spent his first two decades as emperor seeking to realize the "imperial will."

The Imperial Rescript on Education (including the special readings Sugiura gave to key words) also deeply impressed Hirohito. Sugiura's very first lecture on the education rescript focused on the term *kōso kōsō*, which appears in that document, in order to determine exactly how it should be interpreted.[13] "*Kōso kōsō*," he declared, "refers to the ancestors of His Majesty the Emperor and the Japanese nation. When our ancestors founded this nation it became coeval with heaven and earth and everlasting."[14] Sugiura went on to observe how successive emperors through the ages had always sought to carry on the "unfinished work of their imperial ancestors."[15] Because Sugiura believed in the moral superiority of the Japanese throne, his subsequent lectures on the education rescript could not avoid elevating the Japanese monarchy at the expense of other countries.

Thus Sugiura taught that in foreign countries the relationship between ruler and ruled was determined by power and limited to submission, whereas in Japan, "the emperor rules the people without power. Benevolence has been planted so deeply in the minds of the people that the sovereign/subject relationship has become indestructible. Therefore the people joyfully submit themselves to the emperor."[16] It is doubtful whether Hirohito ever accepted Sugiura's notion of rule "without power." But the idea of emperor-as-embodiment-of-benevolence was infinitely attractive to Hirohito, and the more he chose to act in his military capacity, the more attractive this alternative became for him. Sugiura was not only implanting a sense of morality in the future monarch, he was also fostering dissonance and frustration.

Summarizing Sugiura's twelve introductory lectures for Hirohito and his fellow students in their first year, and highlights of his later lectures, Nezu Masashi, the early biographer of Hirohito, noted:

These were titled the Imperial Regalia, the Rising Sun Flag, the Country, the Military, Shrines, Rice, Swords, Clocks, Water, Mount Fuji, Sumō, and Mirrors. Only in the second year of his ethics course did Sugiura have them read about abstract topics such as benevolence, fairness, rectification of wrongdoing, fidelity, justice, and uprightness, as well as concrete topics such as the imperial enthronement, Uesugi Kenshin [a late-sixteenth-century samurai warrior], the forty-seven masterless samurai of Akō [the classic tale of feudal vendetta], and Tokugawa Mitsukuni [an exemplar of imperial loyalty and Shinto nationalism]. In the third year he lectured on George Washington, Columbus, Malthus's theory of population, Peter the Great, and Rousseau, and in the fourth year he selected Kaiser Wilhelm II and Muhammad. There were only thirty foreign examples. The vast majority of his topics were from Confucian learning and the history of the Japanese emperors. Sugiura lectured four times on the Boshin Edict [of 1908], five times on the Imperial Rescript to Soldiers and

Sailors [of 1882], and eleven times on the Imperial Rescript on Education [of 1890]. But he gave just one lecture on the Meiji constitution—an indication of the relatively low value he placed on this.[17]

In his lectures Sugiura tended to undercut the scientific knowledge that Hirohito was discovering by celebrating Japanese nationalism and expansionism. He talked about the chrysanthemum flower—the crest of the imperial house—and concluded that "We call the European powers advanced civilized countries. . . . [However] just as we can say that the chrysanthemum is the most outstanding flower, so Japan is unsurpassed in both its national strength and its civilization." He also sought to convey a sense of rivalry between whole races, noting that "The European nations and the United States are of the same racial stock, the 'Aryan race'. . . . Our Japanese empire must be conscious of confronting the various Aryan races by our own power in the future."[18] Hirohito never warmed to Sugiura as an individual the way he did to Hattori. But he also never broke away from Sugiura's neo-Darwinian view of the international order. Nor did Hirohito ever abandon the notion, as implanted by Sugiura, that superior moral and spiritual qualities ultimately determined the outcome of conflict.

Of the foreign leaders whose lives, Sugiura felt, exhibited positive lessons for Hirohito, two were men with whom the Meiji emperor was often compared. During the first five years after Meiji's death, journalists and bureaucrats frequently ranked Meiji's achievements with those of the seventeenth-century Russian czar Peter the Great and Germany's Wilhelm II.[19] In his lecture on Peter, given in 1917, Sugiura explained that the twenty-five-year-old czar Peter went abroad to study foreign technology and returned to lay the foundations of the modern Russian empire. But his successors failed to build on the foundations Peter had laid, and so contributed to the upheaval in Russia.[20] When lecturing on Kaiser Wilhelm II of Germany, Sugiura treated the deeply flawed and racist kaiser as a great man who had failed for lack of competent advisers, and enthused over the good fortune of the Japanese emperor to be surrounded by many excellent advisers.[21]

The eighteenth-century French thinker Jean-Jacques Rousseau, on the other hand, he described as a rootless, self-indulgent character who could never keep a job and was worthy of no admiration at all. Rousseau's theories "have led to cursing against the state and government." Japan, he concluded, could avoid "the residual poison of European liberal thought" provided its leaders "show benevolence to the people, the people show loyalty to those above them, and everyone knows his place in the scheme of things."[22]

Hirohito never abandoned the rhetoric of benevolence, loyalty to superiors, and proper place. His attitude toward new foreign ideas, however, was more pragmatic than Sugiura's. For him any Western system of thought was acceptable if it could be used to further the achievement of national independence and power. The only absolute value, whether in a time of reaction or in one of liberal awakening, was the state, which he learned in his early twenties to equate with the throne.

"Love of Learning," "Posthumous Names," "Remonstrance," "Measure," "Piety," and "Sagacity" were other topics in Sugiura's syllabus. In these ethics lessons he mainly extolled past emperors as described in the eighth-century Japanese dynastic histories the *Kojiki* and the *Nihon Shoki*, written in Chinese. In a Sugiura lesson titled "Cherry Blossoms," Hirohito was told that the Japanese people were like the falling cherry blossoms: "When our imperial fatherland was in peril, our people rushed forward without regard for their lives."[23] And in "The Scientist" Hirohito was advised:

> In times of war the scientist fully prepares large artillery, airplanes, and warships, together with other modern implements. If they are used with a spirit of loyalty, courage, and justice, then, for the first time, we can say that war preparations are fully completed. With such

preparations we can proudly declare that we have no enemy in the
world. This is the meaning of Article 5 of the Charter Oath.[24]

In 1919, when the problem of racial conflict came to a head at
the Paris Peace Conference and the Japanese Foreign Ministry was
complaining of the racial discrimination suffered by Japanese subjects in various countries, Sugiura dwelled on the hostility that
existed between undifferentiated "Caucasians (so-called whites)"
and "Mongolians (so-called yellows)" as a whole, without regard to
their national identities. For him these were the only two (of "seven
common") racial groups "that have formed powerful states and possess advanced civilizations."[25] The history of the European advance
in Asia from the time of Vasco da Gama in the late fifteenth century
down to World War I, was shown as:

> an attempt by the white race to overpower the yellow race. Siam is
> nominally independent, but it obviously has no real power. Although
> China is a big country, due to many years of internal strife the Chinese
> lack the power to unite as a state, and are thus utterly incapable of
> competing with the forces of the white race. In the Far East the
> Japanese Empire alone has been able to deter the Western invasion in
> the East.
>
> In addition the Americans too have . . . adopted imperialism and
> are gradually extending their power into the Pacific. They have taken
> Hawaii and the Philippines and are trying to expand their commercial
> rights even in China and Manchuria.
>
> Viewed in this way world history is the history of rivalry and con-
> tention between the yellow and white races. . . . The whites shout
> about the yellow peril and we are angry about the white peril.[26]

To counter the rhetoric of racial strife, a rhetoric of racial harmony was suggested. "The ideal of humanity could be realized,"

Sugiura continued in his lecture on "Race," if the different races of the world cooperated with one another and advanced civilization. Unfortunately:

> the Europeans and Americans . . . are apt to look down on the yellow race with preconceived notions. I think it will be very difficult to abolish racial prejudice. Looking at our country, equality of the people has been our principle ever since the restoration of imperial rule. Yet even today there is a tendency to look down on the *eta* and *hinin* [despised hereditary status groups[27]] of former times. . . . Regardless of whether we can achieve our stand to abolish racial discrimination, it is most important to resolutely maintain our own principles. If we put benevolence and justice thoroughly into practice, then the Europeans and Americans cannot help but admire us. If we can do that, we will not have to be concerned about abolishing racial prejudice.[28]

Such ethics lessons may inadvertently have raised questions in Hirohito's mind about what exactly he was supposed to do as a benevolent monarch.

Sugiura's lectures elevated the ideal of the imperial house based on Confucianism and Japanese hegemonism; denounced foreign thinkers who talked about liberalism, individualism and socialism; and encouraged a conventional, social-Darwinian view of international relations in terms of conflict between the white race, led by Europeans and Americans, and the yellow race, led by Japan.[29] Essentially Sugiura taught that the emperor's authority derived from the teachings of his ancestors, going back in time to the sacred progenitor of the imperial line. This view connected with Japanese expansionism, as well as with the we-they distinction in "race relations" and the notion that Japan—and the Japanese spirit—was superior to the West and to Western things. It also assumed that for the emperor to lay burdens on his subjects was entirely natural because they existed to sacrifice themselves for him, not the other way around.

III

Another formative influence on young Hirohito's life was Shiratori Kurakichi, who brought him Japanese and Western history. Shiratori had studied in Germany. In 1909 he published articles in the journal *Tōyō jihō* (Oriental review) debunking the Confucian legends of the Chinese sages Yao, Shun, and Yu, thereby highlighting the irrationality of traditional Chinese culture.[30] His attitude toward China can be understood as compounded of an impatient "escape from Asia" way of thinking (associated with the noted Meiji educator Fukuzawa Yukichi) and attitudes of contempt toward others that welled up in his generation after the Sino-Japanese War. A liberal, positivist historian in the tradition of the nineteenth-century German Leopold von Ranke, and a recognized expert on Asian and Western history, Shiratori was fifty when he became a court official and took charge of general academic affairs and the teaching of history at the Ogakumonjo.[31]

To instruct the crown prince and his five classmates, Shiratori wrote five volumes of "national history," titled simply *Kokushi*. The first chapter of volume 1 of the *Kokushi*, or "General Introduction," addresses the racial origins of the Japanese and begins by stating the essence of his views on the national ideology:

> The imperial house unified our land and people and created the empire. Not only did it rule as the head of state, it also became integrated with the people and the head of their religion. Because of the ineffable feeling of intimacy between the throne and the people, the imperial house was able to create an extremely firm foundation for a state. However, just as the imperial house is a line of emperors unbro-

ken for ages eternal; the people too, from generation to generation, father to child, have propagated down to today. Not once has there been a change in the race. Therefore we, descendants of the people who assisted the founder at the time of her creation of the state, have carried out the will of our ancestors and become eternally loyal subjects. The successive imperial families have loved the loyal subjects of their progenitor and always trusted in the people's cooperation in carrying out their grand plans. This indeed is the essence of our *kokutai*. . . . There is no mistake . . . in saying that we have been a homogeneous race since antiquity.[32]

Shiratori's unusually clear statement of the national ideology starts with the exceptional nature of the Japanese "race" and ends with the theme of its homogeneity. In between it entrenches myth and the sacred at the point of origin. It stresses the unbroken line of imperial succession from the divine "foundress," implying that Japan has been under the continuous control of a descendant of the gods. The uniqueness of the polity lies also in the inexpressible connection between the imperial house and the people. Japanese subjects have been, and will continue to be, "eternally loyal," always serving successive emperors "in carrying out their grand plans."

Shiratori implanted in Hirohito's mind the very same ideas about the "national polity" that had been taught in the public school system ever since Emperor Meiji, in the early 1880s, had ordered that history instruction start with the meaning of the foundation myths.[33] By highlighting the notion of the divine origin of the imperial line, and linking it to the myth of the racial superiority and homogeneity of the Japanese, Shiratori impeded anything near an objective discussion of Japanese history. These two key elements of prewar emperor ideology became a critical part of Hirohito's intellectual inheritance.

Kokushi does not explicitly distinguish between myth and history. It narrates myths about the emperor's divinity in the spirit of the Imperial Rescript on Education—the document that placed the emperor at the center of the nation's spiritual life and guided the Japanese people in worshiping him as a god. In "Emperor Jimmu" Shiratori continues "the story" of the founding of the state as narrated in the *Nihon shoki*. Although the *Nihon shoki* projected an idealized, fictional "Jimmu" (the direct descendant of Amaterasu Ōmikami) rather than historical fact, Shiratori nowhere indicates the difference in his text.

> [Emperor Jimmu] . . . fought battles in many places, lost soldiers and imperial brothers, but never was beaten by disasters. Each time he met difficulty, he renewed his courage, became ever stronger . . . and suffered together with his own soldiers. With the divine protection of his imperial ancestors and the assistance of loyal subjects, he finally accomplished his great purpose. Thereupon he built a palace in the land of Kashiwara at the southeast foot of Unebi Mountain, where he stored the imperial regalia and was enthroned as emperor.[34]

Shiratori went on to observe that Jimmu had been able to accomplish his great project because of "the people's love and affection for the imperial house, their loyalty and courage, their perseverance in difficulties, and their mutual cooperation and assistance of the emperor." After his enthronement Jimmu rewarded those who had made contributions by appointing them as local governors, "thereby treating the people with boundless affection."[35]

Shiratori wrote his "national history" to harmonize with the modern "emperor system," of which he was a loyal servitor. He neither applied his critical skills to Japan's legendary beginnings nor insisted that the old stories related events that had never occurred and therefore constituted myth rather than fact. His textbook helped shape the religious imagination of the emperor every bit as much as Sugiura's ethics lectures did. We cannot know what Shiratori may have communicated verbally to Hirohito in discussions, but he certainly did not *write* a more nuanced interpretation of the manifest deity concept until much later.[36]

Every single chapter of all five volumes of *Kokushi*, from Emperor Jimmu onward, is (as historian Tokoro Isao noted) named after an emperor. In the course of his narrative, Shiratori describes how the sacred mirror and sword came to be enshrined at Ise and Atsuta, how the imperial household compelled local rulers to surrender their sacred objects—the mirrors, jewels, and swords that were once the symbols of their authority; and how these "regalia" became the symbol of legitimacy of the imperial household.[37]

Through his examination of the "sacred virtues" of the leading emperors in Japanese history, Shiratori (like Sugiura) came to believe and to teach that emperors were often a driving force in the modernization of the country. The idea of the emperor as a promoter of progress had its roots in the early Meiji period and was another of the key concepts of modern emperor ideology. It meant the monarch's active promotion of the nation's material and spiritual culture and not simply the notion, common to all monarchies, of *noblesse oblige*, or the monarch's concern for his people. It is precisely this "modernizing" side of imperial leadership that Shiratori emphasized.

Shiratori's historical survey put at Hirohito's disposal numerous examples of activist emperors who had combined power and authority in their own person. Although his lectures teemed with examples of ancient and medieval emperors who embodied moral goodness and benevolence, Shiratori concluded that some medieval emperors, for all their virtues, were unable to rectify long-standing political evils and so "the sufferings of the people steadily increased."[38] Even when regents for child, adult, and abdicated emperors took the initiative, the deadlock of politics and economics remained unresolved until Japan entered the Kamakura period (1193–1336), when the *bakufu* (military government) controlled the country. Having brought his narrative forward into the age of the

warriors, Shiratori set out to show how the Imperial House continued to play an important role in government long after it had delegated political and military affairs to the *bakufu*.

He also cast a positive light on the northern dynasty, which had
been neglected since the Meiji restoration, and from which Hirohito was descended. Only a few years earlier, in 1911, the old historical controversy over the question of imperial legitimacy during
the period of the northern and southern courts (1336–92) had been
resolved when the government of Prime Minister Katsura Tarō
"decided in favor of southern legitimacy and decreed that henceforth the [primary school history] texts should deal with the years
1336 through 1392 as 'The Period of the Yoshino [that is, southern]
court.'"[39] Thus, at a time when Japanese general education deliberately obfuscated the existence of a major dynastic schism in the
national history, fearing it might undermine popular belief in imperial sovereignty, Shiratori acknowledged the schism and treated the
northern line of emperors sympathetically.[40]

Finally Shiratori reviewed the foreign wars of the Meiji era,
explaining to Hirohito and his classmates how the modern empire
was won through a process of constantly seeking "peace in the Orient," taking into account the interests of other nations, and always
acting toward neighbors benevolently and justly. Shiratori acknowledged Chinese resistance to the colonization of Taiwan after the war
of 1894–95, but he was silent about the injustice involved in Korea's
loss of sovereignty, presenting what occurred as of benefit not only
to Koreans but to the "Orient" in general.

> Of all the countries in the world, only our empire was able to secure
> peace in the Orient. Because Korea was the original reason why our
> empire had to fight earlier with China and later with Russia, the
> empire tried to destroy the root of this problem forever. As soon as the
> war of 1904–5 [against Russia] began, we made Korea promise to lis-
> ten to our advice and concluded a type of treaty with it. When it came

to 1905, our empire made a new treaty in which it took control of Korea's diplomacy [that is, stripped it of its diplomatic rights], established a resident-general in Seoul, and had him manage Korean affairs.

After taking charge of Korea's diplomacy in order "to protect it" from threats by "other strong countries," Japan encountered obstruction from the Korean court, which "turned its back on this agreement in 1907." This led to a new treaty, by which the resident-general obtained the right to "supervise Korea's domestic politics" and "Korea became our protectorate."

Nevertheless, this system proved insufficient for improving the institutions of Korea and enhancing the peace and welfare of that nation. So, in 1910, we made a treaty with Korea and permanently annexed it. Thus the root of the problem in the Orient, which had troubled the empire for many years, was completely removed.[41]

Shiratori's interpretation of Japanese-Korean relations reflects the moral complacency and hypocrisy of Japanese popular attitudes toward Korea at the time of its annexation. He also implies that the imperial project itself was sensible and rational, for annexing Korea established peace in the region and meant progress for Koreans.

Having reached the end of the Meiji era, Shiratori concluded by describing in superlative detail Crown Prince Hirohito's grandfather, Emperor Meiji. From early childhood Meiji was active and courageous but also subdued, self-disciplined, frugal, benevolent, and wise, and always generous to his subjects. Meiji learned from the lectures of his entourage and listened attentively to those who brought him information. Moreover, "The emperor had a deep fondness for *waka* poetry and day and night recited verse. By writing his own poetry he naturally gained a benevolent heart [*ōmigokoro*]."[42]

Shiratori was successful in his main aims of furnishing Hirohito with examples of imperial benevolence, explaining the process of development of Japanese history, and stimulating his interest in history in general.[43] In later years Hirohito acquired more detailed knowledge of the Meiji era from reading *Meiji tennō-ki* [Chronicles of Emperor Meiji], which was edited and completed by officials of the Imperial Household Ministry in 1933 but kept hidden in the Imperial Household Ministry until the centennial year of the Meiji Restoration, 1968, when the first volumes began to be published. Even today scholars are not allowed to examine the primary materials on which it is based.[44]

Western history was also introduced to Hirohito by Professor Mizukuri Genpachi, whose *Seiyōshi kōwa* (Lectures on Western history) became one of his favorite textbooks.[45] Hirohito devoured all of Mizukuri's major works: *Napoleon jidaishi* (History of the age of Napoleon), *Furansu daikakumei shi* (History of the great French revolution) (1919, 1920) in two volumes, and *Sekai taisenshi* [History of the great world war) (1919), which appeared right after the Bolshevik Revolution and the collapse of monarchies all across Europe. These books presented revolution and war as the greatest threats to monarchy, and underscored the importance of a strong middle class as a bulwark against revolution.

Mizukuri's writings provided Hirohito with rational explanations for the fall of the Romanov dyanasty in Russia and the Hohenzollern dynasty of Prussia. They deepened his interest in history and European politics, and may have helped him to think in broader terms and to look for elements of general relevance in particular events. Shiratori's writings on the other hand, left him with a rich store of historical narratives to draw on when confronting policy decisions. Yet they were also intellectually constraining insofar as they followed the official line, transmitted the Japanese obsession with racial origins, and indoctrinated Hirohito to think in terms of emperors as developers of national power, prestige, and empire.

IV

Shimizu Tōru, a professor of law at Tokyo Imperial University, unlike Sugiura and Shiratori, was definitely not recognized in academic circles as an outstanding scholar. The choice of Shimizu as Hirohito's teacher of constitutional law may simply have reflected the opinion of Ogasawara and the *genrō* that the leading scholars of the constitution at that time—Hozumi Yatsuka, Uesugi Shinkichi, and Minobe Tatsukichi—were entirely too controversial to be instructing the crown prince. Shimizu belonged to no school and had spelled out his constitutional doctrine in a massive tome, published in 1904. In 1915 Shimizu became an Imperial Household Ministry official and took up his duties at the Ogakumonjo. There, and later at court, he instructed Hirohito on the two dominant accounts of the Meiji constitution that defined the parameters of constitutional government.[46] One, the direct imperial rule theory of Hozumi Yatsuka and Uesugi Shinkichi, affirmed imperial absolutism and taught that the emperor had responsibility for arranging the various organs of state and directly exercising his power to appoint and dismiss his officials. This was the view favored by many army officers (with the notable exception of General Ugaki), and by navy officers such as Fleet Admiral Tōgō and Captain Ogasawara. The other interpretation was the liberal "emperor organ theory" of Minobe, who sought to rein in the emperor's autocratic powers by making the cabinet his single highest advisory organ and curbing the power of extraconstitutional bodies to advise the emperor.

Shimizu, an eclectic, contradictory thinker outwardly eschewed both of these positions, though his writings were, overall, much closer to Hozumi's than Minobe's. Shimizu considered the main point at issue in constitutional interpretation to be the locus of sovereignty [*tōchiken*], which he situated in both the emperor and the state. For him the state represented "an indissoluble combination of the land, the people and sovereignty," while in a legal sense it "is a person and the subject of sovereignty."[47] He continued: "In our country sovereignty resides at one and the same time in the state and in the emperor. On this point state and emperor are assimilated to one another. They have become not two but one. In other words the emperor is the subject of sovereignty."[48]

This kind of argument meant that Shimizu was utterly unable to clarify the relationship between the monarch and the state. Constitutional scholar Uesugi, Hozumi's disciple in the law department of Tokyo Imperial University, argued that the emperor *is* the state and anything he does, no matter how arbitrary, is justified. Shimizu regarded the state as an independent moral personality [*jinkaku*] and claimed that the emperor always acts, by definition, in its interests. The two were never in conflict because the emperor was, at all times, thinking and acting in the interests of the state. For Shimizu the question of priority could never arise. On this point, Shimizu reinforced Sugiura's teaching that, historically, emperors have always acted in the interest of the state.

By expounding on the constitution from the perspective of the primacy of the *kokutai*, something Minobe felt it was unnecessary to do, Shimizu came to embrace the standard argument of prewar and early postwar conservative ideologues who wanted to prevent the *kokutai* from being destroyed by civil discord. Such people argued that in times of crisis, promoting to high office only those officials who believed most firmly in emperor ideology mattered far more than developing political institutions. As long as loyal, well-indoctrinated officials were in control, and they had strong personalities, they would always prevent the *kokutai* from being overthrown from within.

Shimizu never directly addressed the problem of the Diet and its powers, or the issue of extraconstitutional bodies like the privy council or the *genrō*. Essentially he was hostile to the principle of parliamentarism and against restricting the powers of any legal organ of the state that aided the emperor. Shimizu fostered in Hirohito the attitude that, for the emperor, *all* the organs of state were on the same level and had the same measure of authority. The emperor decided, on the basis of circumstances, which advisers to respect and gave his assent to them. But he did not always have to listen to their advice, whether it was unanimous or not.

Significantly, Shimizu failed to clarify the issue of the emperor's political nonaccountability for his actions. Although the Meiji constitution failed to make explicit the emperor's nonresponsibility, commentators generally agreed, from the outset of the constitution, that the operative word "inviolable" in Article 3 ("The emperor is sacred and inviolable") automatically approved that interpretation.[49] Thus, even if the emperor acted illegally according to domestic law and committed a crime, he could not be punished. He also could not be held accountable for the actions of the government if it acted illegally, even though he was the head of state. The only guarantee that the emperor would not violate the constitution was Article 55, which stipulated that ministers of state bore advisory responsibility for the advice they offered the monarch.

Yet this was not really a guarantee of nonaccountability, because cabinet ministers were excluded from giving advice on decisions involving matters of supreme command, the emperor did not have to accept the advice of his minister, and no procedures or institutions were ever developed for questioning the emperor on his constitutional responsibilities.[50] Shimizu tended to read into the term "inviolable" the idea of an emperor who possessed so much political and moral power that he stood above and beyond constitutional monarchy. In that respect too, Shimizu leaned toward the Hozumi-Uesugi line without actually endorsing it.

Shimizu portrayed the state as a human body with the emperor as its brain, noting that the "brain functions as the central force of the organization."[51] Hirohito liked this metaphor—the idea of being the brain for the state—and evoked it during the early 1930s when Minobe was under attack and had to resign his official positions. It was common in late-nineteenth-century German constitutional thought, particularly that of Georg Jellinek (1851–1911), a legal philosopher who exerted a strong influence on Japanese constitutional thinkers. Minobe himself had used it in 1912 when he said the emperor was like the head of a human body, except that he was thinking not of himself but the country. In the end it was precisely the vagueness and ambiguity of Shimizu's thought that most appealed to Hirohito, who, despite his later claim to the contrary, was inclined toward the same thing.

Finally, when memory of the emperor Meiji was still a vivid part of Japanese hagiography, Shimizu reinforced both Sugiura and Shiratori in idolizing Meiji as the perfect model of a monarch. Shimizu contributed to the Meiji myth by stressing that emperors could not act arbitrarily but had to reflect "public opinion" in their conduct of state affairs just as Meiji had done in his Charter Oath. All three teachers told fairy tales of Meiji's personal qualities, which had enabled him to achieve his great enterprise of transforming Japan into a major imperial power but were conspicuously lacking with Taishō. All three wanted Hirohito to retrieve the lost image of Meiji, which they had built up and romanticized in their different ways. And so they drove home the point that Japan needed a new Meiji, and that he would be the one to fulfill the role and match his grandfather's attainments.

Influenced by the ideas of Sugiura, Shiratori, and the hopelessly contradictory Shimizu, Hirohito strove to measure up to his symbolic grandfather whom he was so unlike in temperament, character, and interests. Hirohito also came to believe in the sacred nature of his own authority, as defined in the Meiji constitution. But the liberal "organ theory" created by Minobe and used by the party cabinets[52] of the 1920s he always regarded as a mere academic theory, good for debating in the universities but not something on which to base his own actions. Nor did he act in accordance with absolutist theological interpretations. In fact Hirohito was never a devotee of *any* theory of constitutional monarchy; the constitution did not provide standards for him in making important political decisions, for, like his grandfather, he believed he stood above all national law. The real constraints on his behavior, including Meiji's spiritual legacy, had nothing to do with the constitution, and even that he set aside when circumstances dictated.

V

The process of educating Hirohito never ended. Its ultimate goal was to enable him to understand and realistically evaluate viewpoints and options, embodied in policy documents presented to him by the government and the high command, while appearing to stand outside the process of political struggle and discord that had produced the documents. Another goal was to serve Japan—an invincible, sacred land—by making its system of checks, balances, and contending bureaucratic factions work to achieve unity and consensus. This function Hirohito would fulfill not through skill in dialectical questioning and theoretical argumentation, for Japan's leaders seem not to have set high store on the effectiveness of argument to clarify issues and resolve disputes. Rather he would do so by learning how to bring his detailed knowledge of civil and military affairs and his sacred authority to bear in reaching consensus. If he performed his role properly, his judgment and will would penetrate all the groups in the ruling system and generate unity. Here Hirohito's own modest physical endowments—his slightness, his squeaky voice, and his only average intelligence—were an educational asset; an anchor, tying him to reality, helping to counter the dangerous mythological hype. He was also a person who did not understand things intuitively but learned them soon enough, by necessity.

3

CONFRONTING THE REAL WORLD

When Crown Prince Hirohito celebrated his coming of age at eighteen, in the spring of 1919, the institution of the monarchy was in decline and being buffeted from many directions. The authority of the Diet and the prime minister was increasing; the political parties were becoming more powerful. Abroad, centuries-old monarchies had collapsed overnight: the Romanovs in Russia, the Hohenzollerns in Germany, the Hapsburgs in Austria-Hungary, and the Ottomans in Anatolia, the Balkans, and the Middle East. Never had hereditary monarchy appeared so unstable, or the international environment so hostile to it. At that moment Japan's delegates at the Paris Peace Conference were discovering the powerful trends toward international peace and democracy then sweeping across postwar Europe and the world.

The German kaiser, to whom Emperor Meiji had often been compared, had abdicated in early November 1918. A short time later, he escaped into uninvited exile in Holland. When the Versailles Peace Conference officially convened on January 18, 1919, the Allies immediately set up a Commission on Responsibility to consider indicting ex-Kaiser Wilhelm before a special international tribunal for infringing on "international morality" and violating the sanctity of treaties. As the work of the conference proceeded during 1919, the Japanese press reported the Allies' rejection of Japan's proposal on racial equality, and the dispute over Japan's wartime seizure of Shantung (now Shandong) Province. Of the threat to the inviolability of monarchs that was involved in putting a former sovereign on trial for war crimes the Japanese newspapers printed very little. Behind the scenes, however, the Foreign Ministry as well as the chief Japanese delegates, Makino Nobuaki and Chinda Sutemi, worried about how the trial of a head of state would affect Japanese beliefs at home regarding the sacred *kokutai*.[1]

This was the background against which Hirohito's coming-of-age ceremony and the last three years (1918–21) of his education at the Ogakumonjo must be set: abroad, the discrediting of the monarchical principle; at home, growing public indifference to the throne, increasingly open criticism of the social and political system, rising demands for reform of the state, and the dimming of the image of a monarch able to rule directly. The ruling elites had good reason to worry about the stability of the throne and the future of the young crown prince in these years.

A further source of concern was Hirohito's personality, a topic frequently overlooked in biographies that fail to set in context his multifaceted life. Hirohito's reticence, his voice, and the impression he conveyed of a lack of "martial spirit" were character traits that emerged again and again in his reign as emperor. So too did his highly impressionable nature, one of the earliest examples of which being a school essay Hirohito wrote in 1920, at the age of nineteen, which clearly aped the viewpoints of the elders surrounding him. The tour of Western Europe he made from March to September 1921 proved a maturing experience, and he returned from it resolved to assert himself in political affairs and to prepare himself to do so.

I

Early on the morning of May 7, 1919, one week after he turned eighteen, Hirohito departed the Akasaka Palace in a horse-drawn carriage, accompanied by a contingent of Imperial Guard cavalry. As his procession entered the Imperial Palace through the Nijūbashi (double bridge), crowds of well-wishers cheered. Changing into ceremonial garb, Hirohito purified himself and began to mark his coming of age by performing Shinto rituals in the palace's major shrines. When the ceremony ended, multiple-gun salutes were fired, and there were celebrations in the capital and in cities throughout the country.[2]

By this time Hirohito had completed a large portion of his middle-school studies and was in training to become the next monarch. The coming-of-age ceremony afforded the occasion for Sugiura, Shiratori, and other Ogakumonjo teachers to publish congratulatory newspaper messages, extolling his virtues. Ogasawara, the school principal, pointed out that:

> The crown prince is intelligent to begin with, and he has also worked hard at his studies. He has, therefore, mastered all of his courses, and when his teachers question him on various matters, he always gives excellent answers. We teachers are all deeply moved by his achievements. Moreover, from time to time, he recites orally, and here too we have been profoundly impressed by his superb ideas, lucidity, and strong voice. Because his . . . high school courses include military science, martial arts, and physical training, he has gained military knowledge at the same time as a sturdy martial spirit, while also strengthening his physique.[3]

Ogasawara's evaluation of Hirohito's intelligence, diligence, and mastery of his subjects accords with what has been written about him by virtually all who knew him intimately. It is his "moreover" and "also" that pose the problem. If Ogasawara seems to be going out of his way to convey that the prince was skilled in oral recitation and had a "sturdy martial spirit," it may have stemmed (as historian Tanaka Hiromi has pointed out) from his concern about criticism of the Ogakumonjo. In late March 1919, shortly before the coming-of-age ceremony, the *Jiji shinbun* had reported that as a consequence of the protected, closed society of the Ogakumonjo, the crown prince almost never spoke in public and lacked a martial spirit. Viscount Miura Gorō, a close confidant of the *genrō* Yamagata as well as of Prime Minister Hara Kei, had also called for reform of the school's rarified education policy.[4] Ogasawara, like Hirohito's other teachers, knew that the crown prince was shy and lacked interest and skill in making speeches. In fact, after this public assessment of the prince's progress, Nara Takeji, Hirohito's future military aide-de-camp, wrote in his diary about the prince's silence at the banquet held on May 8, 1919, as part of his coming-of-age celebration:

> The prince simply received the guests and then sat through the party without saying a word. Even when he was spoken to, he gave hardly any reply. During the intermission Viscount Miura Gorō, who has a reputation for boldness, vehemently attacked the lord steward of the crown prince, saying, "This is the result of your so overprotecting the crown prince that he knows nothing whatsoever of the real world." As a consequence, probably, an argument arose among the *genrō* Yamagata, Saionji, and others over the need to reform the crown prince's education and guidance.[5]

Nara then recorded a conversation with General Field Marshal Yamagata. Yamagata had been granted an audience with the crown prince, and now he recalled that when he had asked questions of Hirohito, he had received no answers at all. Neither had the prince asked any questions himself.

> [H]e seems just like a stone statue. This is very regrettable and must be due to the overprotective education Hamao is giving him. Hereafter we must encourage [the crown prince] to become more active and

free-spirited by affording him a more open education. This is why I
feel that it is also necessary for him to go abroad. . . . How unfortunate
that Hamao is procrastinating.[6]

Nara might also have noted that the late adolescent not only
failed to convey any "personality" in public, he also moved clumsily
and his voice was still high-pitched, neither of which was the case
with any of his brothers. But what should be said about Hirohito's
reticent mien? Was it the product of his inexperience and lack of
confidence, or was it part of an identity created for him by others, a
consciously cultivated product of his monarchical studies? And what
is to be made of his strange voice? Was it, too, an artful construction, or the result of slow-arriving hormones?

Like his brothers but much more so, Hirohito was a person of
strong emotions trained never to show them. He was also a lonely
person who had developed, as early as his middle-school years, the
habit of talking to himself when under stress.[7] The example of his
grandfather, who hardly ever spoke to him and whom he so desired
to emulate, probably served to increase his youthful reticence. In
addition Professor Shiratori had given him numerous examples of
imperial ancestors who fitted the Chinese Confucian (and popular
Buddhist) image of the taciturn monarch who said little but accomplished much, and whose silence was exemplary. Hirohito may have
come to think of taciturnity as a tactic, a way of shielding himself
from the intrusive gaze of his pedagogues.

His limited virtuosity in verbal expression, moreover, was in
keeping with Japanese cultural and aesthetic traditions. Unlike his
grandfather, a pure autocrat, Hirohito had a keen sense of being a
monarch *under* (in the narrow sense of being protected under or by)
the Meiji constitution. He had constitutional duties to perform, and
when performing them showed his face more as mask than as personality. The mask was a part of his psychological attire, which, like

physical vestments, he also donned in performing his religious, ceremonial duties. And one of his most important duties was to embody Japanese morality.

Paradoxically the mask of silence called attention to his inner self and was seen as praiseworthy. On the other hand, when he wore silence in the performance of his political and military duties, his mask sometimes caused problems. Those who reported to him directly then had to understand not only his words, which were often fewer than the situation called for, but his countenance, or how he seemed to be "moved." Expecting him to say little even when the matter was of the gravest personal importance to him, they learned to watch his facial expressions for the slightest indications of his inner thought and future behavior.[8] In a society that historically valued the wearing of masks and had turned them into the highest form of symbolic expression, the emperor's mask of silence resonated with meaning.

The same was true of his voice, in which many Japanese also came to "hear" their sense of national identity. Before Hirohito's accession to the regency in November 1921, the few among the elite who heard his voice regarded it as a cause of concern. Only as his tutors worked on it, as he became more experienced in government, and as the country plunged ever deeper into war, did people come to imagine it as suprahuman. Discussion of his voice would arise again at the time of Japan's surrender in August 1945, and later when he toured the nation during the occupation period.[9]

Apart from the matter of young Hirohito's inarticulateness, and the widely divergent ways in which Japanese apprehended his voice, the ruling elites after World War I had to wrestle with the problem of how to deal with his mentally disabled and physically sick father, and with the societal changes that were causing the monarchy's authority to diminish in a time of democratic ferment. In this additional context the question of the heir apparent's physical presence may have seemed exceedingly important. Naturally the *genrō* and their successors began to worry about Emperor Yoshihito's quiet, frail-looking son, who failed to convey with words any personality to a public accustomed to Meiji's impressive demeanor. It is also hardly surprising that with his glasses correcting his near sightedness, his slight frame, stooped shoulders, twitchy nervousness, and far-from-booming voice, the press eventually reflected the concerns of the top political leaders about his "sturdy martial spirit."[10] But Hirohito was intelligent and often strong willed. He practiced frugality and set a high value on military accomplishments and military preparedness in a modern, professional sense. The reality of his character, in other words, belied in many ways his unassuming physical appearance.

Hirohito also had behind him a childhood of training in self-control as well as a military education that had accustomed him to rigid routine. His grandfather had personally commanded the army and navy during occasional maneuvers staged against hypothetical foreign invaders and, quite unlike his own father, had been diligent in attending the graduation ceremonies of the army and navy schools.[11] But Meiji had not received a military education and knew virtually nothing about strategy and tactics. His training in military matters was designed to get him into the open air and reform his unhealthy lifestyle. Seeking to follow in the idealized footsteps of a fabricated Meiji, whom he had installed as his life's model, was one of Hirohito's dominant desires, though it never prevented him from freely altering Meiji's example whenever circumstances required. Hirohito, unlike his grandfather, was constantly accompanied by military aides-de-camp, who encouraged him to act in a military manner, and particularly after becoming emperor in December 1926, he was nearly always in uniform except during religious festivals (when he donned the ancient attire of a Shinto priest). This daily conditioning had a profound effect on his evolving personality.[12]

Equally important, Hirohito accepted, and felt no compulsion to question, the duly constituted order of authority into which he had been born. From an early age he acquired a sense of himself as a person who decided—and was destined to be required to decide—matters in the spheres of political power and military command. As he entered manhood and assumed the duties of emperor, however, his intellectual interests began to flow toward history, politics, and particularly natural science. These other values and aspirations did not prevent military matters from occupying the largest portion of his time.

The young man on the way to becoming Japan's "absolute" monarch and supreme military commander pursued a scientific hobby, but spent most of his time, and may even have had the most satisfactory personal relations, with military men who were not scientists. During his last two years at the Ogakumonjo, he seems to have befriended the vastly self-confident General Ugaki. Later, while participating with his ministers in ruling the state, he would add the mask of supreme commander in chief (*daigensui*) and begin to express himself more often. His words, uttered in a spirited manner, carried tremendous political influence. Hirohito usually gave wholehearted trust to bureaucratic types whom he appointed to high position. But he had little natural predilection for dogmatic saber rattlers and political reactionaries like the principal of his middle school, Captain (later retired Admiral) Ogasawara, the Imperial Navy's first public relations expert, and the school's principal, the renowned Fleet Admiral Tōgō.[13]

The problem therefore is: How should one understand the coexistence and specific content of the different, potentially conflicting, identities that Hirohito assumed as his life unfolded through so many distinct phases? How did he manage to control his emotional life so as to be able to survive the many different roles he took on and the demands made upon him, and at what cost to himself? Certainly his most deeply embedded, never effaced identity was that of an emperor by divine right. His education is the story of how he came to think of himself as a giver of orders, a participant, along with others, in the policy-making process, and the leader of a nation that was bringing modernity to Asia.

II

Inevitably Hirohito had acquired attitudes about political life that delighted his teachers.[14] One can gain a rough idea of his view of human affairs at this time from a recitation for Sugiura passed on to Imperial Household Minister Makino Nobuaki, who reproduced it in his diary. In "My Impressions Upon Reading the Imperial Rescript on the Establishment of Peace"—his short (two-page) composition written in January 1920, after the peace treaty between the Allied Powers and Germany had finally gone into effect, nineteen-year-old Hirohito looked ahead to the day when he would "bear the great responsibility of guiding political affairs" and cited the words of "my father, the emperor."[15] This essay reveals a young man concerned about "extremist thought" who wishes to uphold the virtues of military preparedness, yet also wants to realize "eternal peace." His first point is that:

> The realm of ideas is greatly confused; extremist thought is about to overwhelm the world; and an outcry is being made about the labor problem. Witnessing the tragic aftermath of the war, the peoples of the world long for peace and international conciliation among the nations. Thus we saw the establishment of the League of Nations and, earlier, the convening of a labor conference. . . . On this occasion, just as stated in the imperial rescript, our people must make strenuous efforts and always adopt flexible ways.

"Extremist thought" may be read here as a metaphor for ideas of democracy, antimilitarism, socialism, and communist revolution that had swept over Japan and the world following World War I. Having declared his concern about this phenomenon and referred to the "labor problem" as troublemaking, Hirohito continues his reading, sticking very close to the letter of the rescript:

> Concerning the League of Nations in particular, the imperial rescript states as follows: "We [*chin*; that is, Emperor Yoshihito] are truly delighted and, at the same time, also feel the grave burden of the state." I too offer my congratulations on the coming into being of the League of Nations. I shall obey the Covenant of the League and develop its spirit.

The enthusiasm with which Hirohito affirms the new world assembly should not be mistaken for an endorsement of either the Anglo-American worldview or the principles of the "new diplomacy" on which it was constructed. Rather his affirmation of the spirit of the League merely reflects his youthful idealism and optimism. At this stage, however, his idealism stands in stark contrast to the skepticism of the Hara government, which had wanted to delay acceptance of the League and had instructed the Japanese delegation at Versailles to keep quiet on European issues and concentrate on securing Japan's "rights and interests" in China.

Continuing with his resolutions, he declares in the very next line: "I must fulfill this important duty to establish permanent peace in the world. What should I do to carry out this duty?" His answer is that Japan, as a great colonial empire, must act in concert with other countries, on the basis of "universal principles," while eschewing luxury and extravagance at home. Then, linking "military preparations" and industrial-infrastructural development to "profitable diplomatic negotiations" and "keep[ing] up with the Great Powers," he hints at a premise of future action: "Without military preparedness profitable diplomatic negotiations will be difficult. Also, we cannot become a rich country unless we make industry and transportation flourish and increase the efficiency of workers. If we do not do this, we will be unable to keep up with the Great Powers."

Hirohito concluded his essay by stressing the ideal of total national unity in the face of foreign competition in order to fulfill "the nation's destiny."

"Confused realm of ideas," "extremist thought," "extravagance," "luxury," "military preparedness," "eternal peace," going along with the trend of the time, and achieving total unity as a prerequisite to realizing the national destiny—these were words and concepts that Japan's conservative ruling elites and military leaders used when describing the siutation at the end of World War I; so did young Hirohito. More broadly these terms belonged to an ideology conservatives paraded in order to deny growing social tensions in Japan. These tensions, the result of the widening gaps in wealth and power between different groups and classes, called for more than rhetorical surgery, however.

III

Japan's World War I prime ministers—Ōkuma Shigenobu (1914 –16) and Terauchi Masatake (1916–18)—had tried to govern within the fiction that the Taishō emperor both reigned and ruled. Postwar prime minister Hara Kei (1918–21) could not even pretend seriously that Yoshihito was more than a figurehead—a necessary formality but at most no more than that.[16] Hara and the aging *genrō* were deeply disturbed by the emerging trends: nationwide food riots in 1918, the deteriorating health of the emperor, and repeated lèse-majesté incidents involving criticism of the imperial house.

The lèse-majesté incidents of the postwar period were part of the larger Taishō-era challenge to veneration of the throne.[17] After Hirohito became regent in November 1921, however, people were also arrested and charged with lèse-majesté simply for saying,

"What a lot of people for just one youngster"; or "This is too much! His majesty the emperor is only a cocky young kid. Yet whenever he goes by, all traffic is stopped for several hours beforehand. Some fools even wait more than ten hours to see the procession pass."[18]

Reverence for the throne was being undermined not only by the public's growing awareness of the emperor's protracted illness, but by socioeconomic changes and the Taishō democracy movement, which cogently argued the case for a broader suffrage.[19] Yet the Hara government and the *genrō* would allow only a modest revision to benefit rural male elites. Rather than undertake a fundamental rationalization of political power to reflect societal changes, they vetoed demands for a universal male suffrage law, left the privileged hereditary peers and the privy council intact, and groped for ways to protect the throne and counter the Taishō democracy movement.

One of Hara's very first concerns was public criticism of the immense wealth of the imperial house. "If you make people think the wealth of the imperial house is the wealth of the nation," he told Imperial Household Minister Hatano Takanao, "then no matter how large the income is, no one will ever complain."[20] In a nation increasingly divided by class conflicts, Hara knew that the throne stood in danger of being drawn into controversy. More than a million people in farming and fishing villages, but most in towns and cities spreading through thirty-seven prefectures, plus Hokkaido, Tokyo, Osaka, and Kyoto, had just taken part in mass protests known as the "rice riots." Although the rioters had directed their anger against rising commodity prices, the underlying cause of the riots was the landlord system, which required tenants to deliver the largest portion of their crops as rent. Hara could not deny the "enormous income" of the imperial house, for the imperial house was indeed Japan's largest landowner, and care had to be taken to ensure that henceforth it not be involved in economic activities perceived as inflicting hardship.

The *genrō* Yamagata concurred. In October 1919 he too warned Hatano immediately to sell shares from the emperor's stock hold-

ings, and also to dispose of wetlands and dry fields from the imperial estates. The imperial house at that time enjoyed an annual
income of 6 to 8 million yen from its management of mountain
forests alone.[21] It owned palaces, mansions, schools, mausoleums,
and museums in Kyoto, Nara, and Tokyo, and received income
from its investments in corporate stocks and bonds, together with
an annual government allotment of 3 million yen. It also earned
profits from the purchase of stock in colonial banks and enterprises,
such as the Bank of Korea and (starting in 1925) the South
Manchurian Railway Company. That wealth, added to its income
from domestic mines and other sources, enabled the Imperial
Household Ministry to function as the guarantor and trustee of
some of Japan's largest capitalist enterprises—a "great creator of
credit and confidence for the development of Japanese capitalism as
a whole."[22] Due to its immense wealth, on a par with the largest
zaibatsu (great financial institutions or capital groups, with which
prewar and wartime Japanese corporations were affiliated), the
throne could relate to the nation in countless ways that had not been
possible in Meiji's time. If Hatano did not understand that fact,
Hara and Yamagata did. The time had come to use the imperial economic power to buy the nation's goodwill.

Against this background there occurred, during the second half
of 1920, prior to Hirohito's graduation from the Ogakumonjo, an
incident at court which showed how easily the monarchy could be
drawn into the political strife of the Taishō democracy era. It began
as a fuss within the upper stratum of the ruling class over the question of color blindness in the family of Hirohito's fiancée. Questions
about the crown prince's education, which had arisen around the
same time as his engagement, in June 1919, were also involved.
Hirohito's education, engagement, and European trip, which were
entwined from the outset, quickly fueled conflict over who would
ultimately control the political and economic power inherent in the
imperial institution.

To wit: In 1917, one year after Hirohito's formal investiture as crown prince, Captain Ogasawara had presented his mother, Empress Sadako (later Dowager Empress Teimei), with the names of three princesses he felt would be suitable partners in marriage for the crown prince. She chose Princess Nagako, the daughter of Prince Kuni Kuniyoshi, to be Hirohito's future wife. Then as now, the engagement of a crown prince was considered a major national event requiring much advanced preparation. Since Hirohito had already met Princess Nagako and liked her, and she had all the qualifications needed to become an empress, Hatano informed Prince Kuni by letter, in January 1918, of his daughter's selection as the crown prince's fiancée. The Kuni family thereupon hired Sugiura, Hirohito's ethics teacher, to begin giving her weekly lectures in ethics.

The imperial engagement ceremony was scheduled to be held at the end of 1920, but in June 1920 the most powerful of the remaining *genrō*, Field Marshal Yamagata, attempted to have the engagement canceled on the ground that color blindness existed in the Shimazu family, on Nagako's mother's side. On June 18 Yamagata forced Hatano to resign—ostensibly for not having thoroughly investigated the matter but also in order to expedite sending Hirohito on a foreign tour—and began to install his own Chōshū-faction followers, starting at the top with Gen. Nakamura Yūjirō, as the new minister of the imperial household. Supporting Yamagata was Prime Minister Hara. He too was troubled by the possibility that the Taishō emperor's chronic ill health and mental debility might have been caused by genetic defects in the imperial family, but he was also hoping to strengthen his influence in court affairs by cultivating good relations with Yamagata. Thinking of a healthy imperial family in the future, rather than the maintenance of the purity of the imperial bloodline for its own sake, Yamagata wrote to Prince Kuni asking him to "withdraw out of respect for the imperial house."[23]

Instead of submitting, Prince Kuni dug in his heels and secretly fought back, enlisting the support of Empress Sadako and Sugiura. It is doubtful if Hirohito, who had been involved in Nagako's selection, was aware of all that happened next. Sugiura tried to rally officials within the Imperial Household Ministry by maintaining that breaking an engagement would set a bad precedent for the imperial house and also scar the crown prince for the rest of his life. When his "ethical" arguments failed, Sugiura proceeded to mobilize the families of the nobility and titled peers on the Shimazu side of the Kuni family, hoping that once they became involved against Yamagata, they would exert their influence on high officials descended from the old retainer band of the Satsuma fiefdom.

Sugiura's attempt to manipulate the genealogically based marriage networks that linked the Satsuma clan failed to yield results. Yamagata and Hara continued to worry about the future of the imperial family, and their rational concerns could not be easily discounted. Makino Nobuaki, the second son of the great Restoration leader Ōkubo Toshimichi, had just returned to Japan from the Paris Peace Conference and was considered a leader of the Satsuma clique. After Sugiura's disciple Shirani Takeshi, an elite bureaucrat and head of Japan Steel, had visited Makino to discuss the problem, he reported to Sugiura that Makino "is having a hard time deciding."[24] Admiral Yamamoto of the Satsuma clique was also cool to Sugiura's importuning.

Despairing of being able to overcome the most powerful *genrō*, Sugiura decided to escalate his conflict with Yamagata by informing another former student, Kojima Kazuo, then a member of the House of Representatives and a leader of the Kokumintō Party, of Yamagata's attempt to break the crown prince's engagement. Kojima thereupon informed Kokumintō president Inukai Tsuyoshi, and soon Ōtake Kanichi of the Kenseikai Party also learned of the trouble. If the Kokumintō and Kenseikai Parties—the two leading enemies of Hara's Seiyūkai—had been willing to break the silence that surrounded the lives of imperial family members, they could have used this explosive issue against Hara at a time when the suffrage issue was before the forty-fourth session of the Imperial Diet, which had convened on December 27, 1920. Also, the media had learned of Sugiura's resignation of his position at the Ogakumonjo, officially for reasons of ill health, yet with only a few months to go before the crown prince's graduation. Apparently the more isolated, powerless, and desperate Sugiura felt in trying to change the situation, the more he alerted others, and the more politicized the issue became.

Finally Sugiura told his old friend Tōyama Mitsuru, the ultranationalist leader of the "old right," that Yamagata hated Prince Kuni and intended to aggrandize his own power at the court. In 1881 Tōyama, with Hiraoka Kōtarō, had formed the Dark Ocean Society (Genyōsha), a pressure group with allies in government, business, and the universities, which sought to make Japan the center of an Asian confederation to combat European imperialism.[25] Tōyama's comrades in the Amur River Society (Kokuryūkai, founded in 1901), as well as members of Uchida Ryōhei's Society of Masterless Samurai (Rōninkai), now began to harass Yamagata physically. Sometime in January 1921 two pan-Asianists of the "new right," the Orientalist scholar Ōkawa Shūmei and the China "expert" and Nichiren Buddhist thinker Kita Ikki, learned about Yamagata's attempt to annul the crown prince's engagement. Ōkawa had recently formed, with Professor Mitsukawa Kametarō of Takushoku University, a nationalist, anti-Marxist discussion group, the Yūzonsha (literally, the "pine trees and chrysanthemums"), which Kita later joined. From its ranks rumors spread of a plot to assassinate Yamagata.

In early February 1921, with the forty-fourth Diet still in session and the problem of the *kokutai* threatening to surface as a weapon in the hands of the opposition parties, Prime Minister Hara withdrew his support for Yamagata. Fearful of losing control of the situation and of being labeled a "national traitor," Yamagata, one of the most powerful figures in the Japanese political world, yielded to the forces centered in the civilian right wing. Imperial Household Minister Nakamura also submitted to Sugiura, as did another Yamagata backer, the high court official Hirata Tōsuke. Faced with all these losses, and sharing Hara's deep concern about the growing politicization of the crown prince's engagement (not to mention the activities of the Rōninkai and the threat to his own life), Yamagata gave up the struggle.

On the evening of February 10, 1921, officials of the Imperial Household Ministry and Home Ministry informed the Tokyo newspapers that the crown prince's engagement would go ahead as planned and that Nakamura and his vice minister, Ishihara Kenzō, had both resigned.[26] On February 12, the *Yomiuri shinbun* published a scathing editorial against Yamagata, for having precipitated "a certain grave incident at court." Ten days later Yamagata offered to resign as *genrō* and president of the privy council and to return his many medals and renounce his titles. He noted in his diary that "Today's Home Ministry and Metropolitan Police Board seem unable to control [the forces of the far right]. . . . I would like to borrow about fifty stalwarts from the army minister and wipe them all out."[27] Hara and the court declined to accept his resignation, but Yamagata had clearly fallen from power. The positions of *genrō* Matsukata and Saionji, who had sided with Yamagata in his opposition to the marriage, had also been slightly weakened. To help calm the situation at court, the *genrō* recommended that Makino step in and assume a prominent role in managing court affairs.

On February 15, 1921, the Hara cabinet had the Imperial Household Ministry formally announce that the crown prince would depart on a Western tour. The right wing (represented by Sugiura and Tōyama), having won on the issue of Hirohito's marriage, lost on the issue of his Western tour, which had arisen at the onset of the engagement dispute. Hara, the imperial princes, and all the *genrō* supported the tour, seeing it, in part, as a way of coping with the postwar enthusiasm for democratic reform; the ultranationalists opposed it as "a rash act of worshipping foreign thought."

The "grave incident at court" shows how easily problems involving the imperial house could engender heated partisan political controversy. From this seemingly minor episode in the history of the imperial house emerges the prototype of 1930s-style right-wing terrorism. On the issue of Hirohito's marriage, the forces of the right succeeded in frustrating the will of the *genrō* and the president of the strongest political party, creating a situation in which the legitimate leaders of the Meiji state were called national traitors.[28]

On another level this incident reveals the delicate competition between the current of Taishō democracy on one side and the imperial house and civilian right-wing groups on the other. It also illuminates the entire lineup of political actors in late Taishō politics. These were the Seiyūkai and its Diet opponents, the *genrō* and the younger members of the political class, Satsuma and Chōshū (or the fief-based political cliques), and the pro- and anti-Yamagata camps. Other protagonists were the Europeanists and pan-Asianists, advocates of continued Westernization and reform of the imperial throne; and advocates of the traditional concept of the *kokutai*, based on myths credulously accepted as fact. All made their appearance just as the *genrō* receded from the scene and new political alliances began to form.

Equally noteworthy was the Japanese public's unawareness of the dispute over the crown prince's marriage, while the civilian leaders of the right wing—for whom resorts to gangster methods were second nature—easily kept abreast of developments at court and exercised hidden influence there and also in the world of conservative party politics.[29] Tōyama, for example, was on close personal terms with many court officials well before and long after the incident. Kita (later executed for his minor role in the February 26, 1936, military uprising) used the incident to strengthen his relations with members of the imperial house, such as Prince Chichibu, to whom he presented a copy of his famous "Plan for the Fundamental Reorganization of Japan." Its opening chapter, on "The People's Emperor," called on the military to seize power in a coup d'état and reorganize the state. The emperor would provide legitimation and, in the process, move closer to the people. Starting in 1922 Kita began to exert political influence on Tōgō and Ogasawara Naganari just as they were beginning their new careers as lobbyists for an expanded navy.[30] (Ogasawara, who had converted to Nichiren Buddhism around the time of the Russo-Japanese War, was a particularly close friend of the demagogic Nichiren preacher Tanaka Chigaku.)

After the closing of the Ogakumonjo, Tōgō and Ogasawara— the ex–school president and the school's director—tightened their cooperative relationship. Tōgō, then seventy-five, was able to maintain his public activities only through his energetic spokesman, Ogasawara. And in 1921 Ogasawara went on the reserve list, after which the most effective way for him to maintain his relationship with those in power was to draw nearer to Tōgō, who as a fleet admiral remained on the active list, attending meetings of the Field Marshals and Fleet Admirals Conference, where he was privy to top naval secrets. Tōgō and Ogasawara—men with close ties to the religiously inspired ultranationalist right—soon became prominent advocates for construction of a fleet of submarines and a naval air force. Following the signing in Washington of the Five-Power Naval [Limitations] Treaty in February 1922, they, together with Adms. Katō Kanji and Suetsugu Nobumasa, formed the core of a naval pressure group hostile to the new international order and opposed to further arms cuts.[31]

Makino Nobuaki also came to the fore in Japanese politics during 1921. Makino had served in cabinets headed by Saionji and attended the Paris Peace Conference in 1919 as the de facto leader of the five-man Japanese delegation. He returned home deeply worried about the collapse of bourgeois monarchy in Europe and anxious to check the democratic current that had begun to sweep the world. After Imperial Household Minister Nakamura took responsibility for the dispute over the crown prince's marriage and resigned, Saionji, with the support of Matsukata, recommended Makino as the new imperial household minister.[32] On February 19, 1921, Makino assumed his duties, bringing with him as his vice minister Sekiya Teizaburō, a Home Ministry bureaucrat with firsthand knowledge of colonial and police affairs.

Makino's initially strong affinities with the future intellectual leaders of Japanese-style "fascism from above," such as Kita Ikki and Ōkawa Shumei, and his long-term ties with the moderate rightist Yasuoka Masahiro, clearly mark him as a transitional figure.[33] In March 1925 Makino became lord keeper of the privy seal—Hirohito's most important political assistant—a post he held until his resignation in 1935, at the age of seventy-five.[34] During most of that time he interacted with Hirohito mainly through his secretary, but actually saw Hirohito in audience only about once or twice a month.[35] Although British and American officials considered Makino to be the leader of the pro-Anglo-American faction at court and one of the most prominent court "moderates" and "liberals," his entire career belies such easy labeling.

Chinda Sutemi, a Christian educated in the United States, also entered the circle of high court officials in late 1920. He had served as ambassador to Austria, Germany, the United States, and England before joining Makino at the Versailles Peace Conference. His appointment as grand chamberlain to the crown prince and to Empress Sadako was part of the shake-up in the Imperial Household Ministry, which brought veteran diplomats and military men with firsthand experience of Western countries into the court.

The months of February and March 1921 marked a watershed in Hirohito's own existence. The phase dominated throughout by his earliest defining communities—court-centered society and figures from the Peers' School—ended with the formal dissolution of the Ogakumonjo on March 1, 1921. His basic spiritual and physical preparation for life was completed. A new group of palace officials, recently moved into high positions, was about to establish the court's independence from control by the government. In the process they would restructure his life and shape the monarchy as an independent political force between the government and the nation. Two days later Hirohito departed for Europe on a tour designed to further his education, push him into adulthood, and counter popular perception of the imperial house's decline.

IV

Crown Prince Hirohito graduated from the Ogakumonjo two months short of his twentieth birthday, just when the domestic political struggle outside the palace compound had entered a progressive phase. The government at the time was searching for ways to stave off the threat to the monarchy posed by the new thought that had entered Japan—ideas such as parliamentary democracy, antimilitarism, Marxism, and communism—since the end of World War I. For Prime Minister Hara the best way to proceed in the circumstances was to send the prince on an "inspection" tour of Western Europe, while seeing to it that he continued his formal education surrounded and influenced, as always, by men old enough to be his father or grandfather.

The professed reason for the prince's foreign trip was to pay his respects to the duke of Connaught (the brother of King George V) who had visited the Japanese court in June 1918, at the end of the Terauchi cabinet. But for Hara and the *genrō*—the tour's chief advocates—the real reasons were political and psychological and had everything to do with recovering the declining authority of the monarchy.[36] The imperial family, fearing for Hirohito's safety, initially opposed the idea of the tour, as did some Diet members, such as Ōtake Kanichi of the Kokumintō and Oshikawa Masayoshi of the Kenseikai, and leading civilian rightists such as Uchida Ryōhei and Tōyama Mitsuru. The right-wing patriots protested vehemently for weeks before Hirohito's departure, claiming that, in view of his father's illness, the trip would be seen as an unfilial action and have a harmful impact on the *kokutai*.

The ruling group—Saionji, Matsukata, Yamagata, and Hara—felt it a matter of "grave importance for the state" that the crown prince go on a "Western tour" before his imperial wedding. They had already written off Emperor Yoshihito because of his illness and his inability to speak in public. They wanted Hirohito to meet more people, to become accustomed to participating in political matters, and to begin learning how human affairs were managed.[37] In 1920, with the fiction of the Taishō emperor's direct rule increasingly apparent, they became more anxious than ever to bring the crown prince forward as a surrogate for his father. Their main opposition was from Hirohito's mother, Empress Sadako, who didn't want her first son to go abroad because of the physical dangers involved in such a trip. But Hara and the *genrō*, concerned about what they perceived as the serious inadequacies of the crown prince's education, felt the risk had to be taken. In late 1920 they finally persuaded her to allow the trip as "a matter of political necessity."[38] The journey to post-Versailles Europe had to go forward because, as the *genrō* Matsukata explained in a letter to her: "There may never be another time like this to inquire into the reasons for the popular movements and intellectual unrest that are occurring right before our eyes. This is a great chance for the crown prince to observe personally, at first hand, the rise and fall of the power of many states."[39]

Once Sadako's resistance was overcome, government and court officials could discuss more candidly among themselves the deeper reasons behind the trip. It was increasingly clear that Hirohito would soon become regent. He needed to investigate conditions in foreign countries in order to be able to deal with the new sentiments of the Japanese people.[40]

The great continental monarchies had collapsed and the war had unleashed worldwide movements for peace, democracy, disarmament, and independence. Operating in an antimonarchical world, as regent he would have to deal with the momentum for social reform that was steadily gathering force in Japan. He would also have to cope with the new tendency in Japan to disparage nationalism, militarism, and the state. Above all Hirohito represented the crucial "third generation" of Meiji's dynastic lineage, thus the one who had to be successful if the imperial house itself was to survive and prosper.[41] Precisely in relation to these external and internal pressures, coupled with fears for the future of the imperial house and its growing isolation, lay the necessity for Hirohito's Western tour.

Although initially conceived on a small scale, the tour developed into a formal state visit. At home it marked the start of a public relations campaign, centered on the crown prince, to counter popular perception of the imperial house's decline and the Taishō emperor's total physical and political incapacity. The entire campaign turned on building up Hirohito's image as "our" wise and great regent, representing "the nation's imperial house." Makino and the top officials of the Imperial Household Ministry made unprecedented efforts to tutor Hirohito on how he was to behave abroad and to mobilize the press corps to cover the trip.[42]

Five months prior to his departure for Europe, on October 28, 1920, Hara had told Imperial Household Minister Nakamura:

> Regarding the crown prince's habits, such as his frequent body movements, I want everyone in attendance close to him to correct this. I also observed that he is unfamiliar with Western table manners. I want someone to instruct him very carefully in this too. This matter is particularly important . . . [43]

In short, in order to ensure its success the tour was carefully choreographed down to the smallest details. And because of the precarious condition of the Taishō emperor's health, the tour could not be prolonged. The crown prince would have time to visit only five European countries: England, France, Belgium, Holland, and Italy, plus the Vatican. The Harding administration was planning to invite the prince, but the Hara government decided to omit the United States from his itinerary largely on the recommendation of the Japanese ambassador in Washington, Shidehara Kijūrō. In a secret telegram to the Foreign Ministry, Shidehara expressed fear that the prince might not be able to handle "the difference in national sentiment between Japan and the United States" and "the rough behavior of ordinary Americans," particularly newspaper reporters.[44] Shidehara also worried about the uncertain state of Japan–U.S. relations on the eve of an arms reduction conference. Should any incident occur during a royal visit, it could have extremely damaging effects on public opinion in both countries.[45] So Hirohito was denied the chance to visit the United States.

On March 3, 1921, Crown Prince Hirohito and his thirty-four-man entourage led by Prince Kan'in, Count Chinda Sutemi, and Lt. Gen. Nara Takeji, and accompanied by Prime Minister Hara, entrained at Tokyo Station for the port of Yokohama. There they boarded a boat that took them to the newly refitted warship *Katori*. After bidding them good-bye, Hara returned to join more than fifty thousand well-wishers standing on shore, and the *Katori* steamed out to sea, accompanied by a cruiser escort.[46]

Bound for Europe and his first encounter with the world outside Japan, Hirohito grew elated. During the next six months of travel, he followed a daily routine of study and physical activity and never eased up. He received his strongest impressions in France and especially England, the country originally scheduled as his main destination. The Western tour was the first major attempt by Japan's ruling elites of the Taishō era to manipulate Hirohito's image, and defenders of Hirohito often cite it as a source of his alleged commitment to "constitutional democracy."

Hirohito's outbound passage aboard the *Katori* took him through the Asian and European territories of the British Empire, starting from Hong Kong, where for fear of Korean assassins he went ashore only briefly. Accompanied by the British governor-general and guarded by the entire British police force on the island, they strolled through the city for about forty minutes, then had lunch aboard a British warship.[47] Next he sailed to the island of Singapore, already a vital center of commerce for all of colonial Southeast Asia. During his three-day stay in Singapore (March 18–21), he attended British receptions in his honor, visited a Japanese-managed rubber plantation and a museum, and circumnavigated the island.[48]

On March 22 the *Katori* departed for Ceylon (now Sri Lanka), second largest island in the Indian Ocean and a British colony that produced rubber and tea for the industrialized economies of the West. Six days later the warship arrived at the capital, Colombo. With neither Japanese nor expatriate Koreans living on the isolated island, the imperial party felt free of danger for the first time. After five days in Columbo, the *Katori* departed on April 1 for the warm waters of the Red Sea, their destination the Suez Canal, the famed "lifeline" of the British Empire. They reached the canal on April 15 and the next day began the hundred-mile journey through its locks with barren desert sands stretching away on each side.

After docking at Port Said, at the entrance to the canal, on April 17, they traveled to Cairo, the ancient capital of Egypt, then in its last year as a British protectorate. The next day, in Cairo, Field Marshal Viscount Allenby, the British high commissioner, acted as Hirohito's host and arranged for him to see the Pyramids and the Sphinx, and visit with the Khedive Fuad, soon to become the first king of formally independent Egypt. Leaving Cairo on April 20, the imperial party sailed into the Mediterranean, bound for the British colony of Malta, a military outpost guarding the route to Suez. On Malta, where the *Katori* anchored on April 25, they were welcomed by the British residents and guided to the graves of Japanese sailors killed during World War I. Another diplomatic welcome awaited them on April 30 in the British colony of Gibraltar, where they stayed for three days before departing on the last leg of their long sea journey.

Hirohito had just turned twenty years of age when the *Katori* finally arrived at Portsmouth, England, on May 7, and he was greeted by rows of flag-decorated British warships with their crews standing at attention. His subsequent itinerary called for him to stay twenty-four days in England, twenty-six days in France, five days each in Belgium and the Netherlands, and eight days in Italy. Except in Italy, where out of consideration for the king and the shortness of his visit he stayed on in the palace, the monarchies gave him the same formal treatment: three nights in the palace as the honored guest of the monarch, followed by stays in private hotels or private residences as the guest of the nation.

In England high military officials and diplomats formed a welcoming committee, headed by the Prince of Wales. Members of this select committee and other royalty always accompanied Hirohito on official visits and ceremonies. The high points of his visit to Britain included a three-night stay in Buckingham Palace, speeches at London's Guildhall and Mansion House, visits to numerous British military facilities (where he sometimes wore the uniform of a British army general), visits to both houses of Parliament, the British Museum, the prime minister's mansion at Chequers, the towns of Windsor and Oxford, the universities of Oxford, Cambridge and Edinburgh, a three-day stay at the castle of the duke of Atholl in Scotland, and a tour of Manchester and the Midlands industrial region.

The French leg of his tour (which began on May 31 and was divided into two periods of ten and sixteen days each) gave him considerably more freedom than he had been able to enjoy in monarchist Britain. On his first day in Paris, he visited stores and the Eiffel Tower, where he ordered Captain Yamamoto to purchase miniature Eiffel Towers as gifts for his fiancée, Princess Nagako, and for his brothers.[49] Later he toured the Louvre and visited the parliament, the Sorbonne, and the Invalides. He also spent much time while in republican France touring battlefields, military schools, and observing French army maneuvers in the company of Generals Foch and Joffre, and Marshal Pétain. He visited more war monuments and battlefields while in Belgium (June 10–15), as the guest of King Albert I. In the Netherlands (June 15–20), he toured Amsterdam, The Hague, and Rotterdam and was feted at numerous official ceremonies and banquets, including one hosted by Queen Wilhelmina, who later wrote his father a warm letter about the prince's visit. En route to Paris from The Hague, on June 20, his train stopped in eastern Belgium so that he could visit the city of Liège and tour yet another World War I battlefield. The second phase of his French visit took him to cities in eastern and southeastern France, where on July 8 he reboarded the *Katori* at Toulon and headed for Italy.

Hirohito arrived in Italy—a country with a large nobility but an insecure monarchy—on July 10, 1921, some fifteen months before Mussolini and the Fascists came to power. He spent eight days visiting Naples, Rome, and Pompeii, often in the company of his guide, King Victor Emmanuel III, soon to be a keen admirer of Mussolini. On July 15 and 16, while staying in Victor Emmanuel's palace, Hirohito removed his military medals and decorations and twice visited the independent Vatican, where he exchanged greetings with Benedict XV, the pope who had attempted unsuccessfully to mediate a settlement of World War I and later defended the kaiser from the threat of a war crimes trial. For the remainder of his Italian stay Hirohito attended the usual ceremonial functions, visited patriotic war monuments, and observed a sports tournament held under the auspices of the Italian military, then already under the influence of Mussolini's Fascist movement.

On the return voyage to Japan, which began on July 18, Hirohito did little sightseeing as the *Katori* retraced its course through the Suez Canal and the Indian Ocean to Singapore. Only when his ship anchored to take on coal at Cam Ranh Bay in French Indochina did he go ashore to walk in the tropical forests and later to ride in a motorcar along the newly constructed Highway Number 1, which ran parallel to the railroad linking Hanoi and Saigon. On August 25 the *Katori* finally departed Cam Ranh Bay for Tateyama, Chiba prefecture, arriving there on September 2. The next day it steamed into Yokohama Harbor, where Prime Minister Hara rode out in a boat to greet the prince personally aboard the *Katori*, while his cabinet and members of the imperial family waited at dockside.[50] Although it remained for Hirohito to make reports to his parents and to the spirits of his imperial ancestors, he had successfully completed the government's first public relations campaign to counter popular perception of the imperial house's decline.

Japanese press coverage of the Western tour was extensive and noteworthy. On Hirohito's departure from Japan, the *Tokyo Asahi shinbun* proclaimed grandly: "The crown prince's flag of the country of the rising sun bears down on the waves heading toward the West. Mark this glorious March 3 in history."[51] Thereafter the *Asahi* and other large dailies sensationalized "our crown prince's" triumphant tour of Europe, while the Home Ministry relaxed its restrictions on printing photographs of the imperial family. On June 4 the newspapers ran pictures of a smiling crown prince in military uniform. On June 24 the papers showed Hirohito in a frock coat with a high collar, holding a walking stick. Previously the press had been permitted to photograph him only in a motorcade on an official visit. While in Europe, however, he was shown walking on a street in civilian attire. When Hirohito visited the duke of Atholl in Scotland, where he was deeply impressed by the warm intimacy between the lord's family and his tenants, the Japanese press was allowed to report his official statement: "The duke's family live frugally and love their people deeply. If we have this type of politics, there will be no need to worry about the rise of extremist thought."[52] The press also reported his comment, on July 9, on touring the battlefield of Verdun, that those who still glorified war should "see this 'scene.'"[53]

Long after Hirohito's return, the press continued to show him in military uniform more often than in civilian dress, and to print assessments by Japanese journalists who had accompanied him to Europe.[54] In 1922 Nagura Bunichi, a writer for the *Asahi shinbun*, noted how Hirohito seldom spoke during the tour, never smoked, and drank only carbonated water (unlike his grandfather, who tippled heavily and often). Rather than dwell on the prince's reticence and sobriety, however, Nagura went on to express his pique at the failure of the English to overcome their outmoded stereotypes of Japanese:

> The interesting thing is that a paper like *The Times* showed understanding and printed an article welcoming the crown prince. Of course, the Japanese Embassy put up the money to propagandize [the visit], and so on the last day *The Times* printed a special Japan issue. Generally speaking the articles contained few errors, but even today they still think that all Japanese wear the topknot and dress in kimonos. . . . Worst of all was an article in *The Herald*, organ of the Labour Party, reprinted from the *Church Times*. I assumed that because it was the Labour Party they must have disliked Japanese militarism. The article said that the emperor of Japan is ill and the crown prince, being too busy with political affairs, was utterly unable to travel abroad. Therefore the visiting crown prince is a proxy for the real one, and the authorities, in order to prevent people from finding out, have confiscated all pictures of the crown prince that were displayed in stores in the city. When they go so far as to say things like that, we can no longer laugh. . . . On May 12 [he] visited the House of

Commons. . . . but had to sit in the commoners' gallery. At that moment Lady Astor was interpolating concerning the problem of housing improvement. . . . At the House of Lords he saw how the Lords passed a bill from the Commons. Here he sat next to the head of the Lords. No welcome was read out for him, and no one stood to greet him. I wonder what the Japanese Diet will do when the English crown prince visits Japan.[55]

Mitearai Tatsuo, a reporter for the *Hōchi shinbun*, produced an account of the tour that was more reflective of the Taishō democracy spirit. He began by contrasting his own ideal image of an intimate relationship between the emperor and the people with the actual relationship of constraint and rigidity that had developed since the death of the Meiji emperor. "The imperial family must feel the same way," he opined. "Judging from the style of living of Prince Higashikuni, studying in Paris, and Prince Kita Shirakawa, studying in Greece, the Imperial Household Ministry's way of thinking is just too rigid."[56]

For Mitearai the tour marked the crossing of the threshold of invisibility for the imperial house.

[I]ts biggest achievement was to have removed the veil between him and the people and to have swept aside the rigid thinking of the Imperial Household Ministry authorities. Everywhere our crown prince went, he had an opportunity to receive the stimulation for change, especially from the welcomes given him by high and low in England, and, I suppose above all, from witnessing the sophisticated social interaction of the crown prince of England [the future duke of Windsor] and the duke of York [the future King George VI].[57]

Hirohito's Western tour helped popularize the new image of a young, enthusiastic crown prince in touch with the times, keenly interested in British-style colonial management, and open to change. To those who looked at what was going on in the country as a call to reform, the message was clear: A vigorous successor to the throne was meeting Europe's leaders and immersing himself in world affairs. Someday he would use his will to move the country forward. In this way too the tour strengthened preconceptions of the monarchy's indispensability for political renewal.

Prime Minister Hara had expressed joy at the good press Hirohito had received in Europe, noting in his diary, on July 6, 1921: "This trip seems a really great success. There can be nothing more beneficial for the state and the imperial house."[58] When Hirohito returned home, Hara was anxious to learn from the entourage everything he could about the prince's progress.[59] Hirohito's teacher of French, navy captain Yamamoto Shinjirō, immediately reported to Hara all the grooming the prince had received while en route to Europe:

> You know the prince is extremely unaccustomed to foreign countries and to social intercourse with other people. Therefore we instructed him in his table manners and in his every movement and action. Concerning general principles, Prince Kan'in spoke with him on three occasions while the chief attendant informed him on other matters. The young attendants like Saionji [Hachirō] and Sawada [Renzō] spoke with him with particular frankness.[60]

When Hara later learned that the crown prince had invited two members of the imperial family to the palace and had gone out of his way to tell them to wear ordinary business suits instead of formal court dress, he expressed his pleasure:

> There are envious people who say that in England the relationship between the royal family and the people is such and such. I think this relationship is not a question of reason but arises totally from sentiment. Although the relationship between our imperial house and the

nation cannot be compared with that in England, it is a mistake to
hope for intimacy between the two only on the basis of reason. Surely
we must rely on feeling. From this point of view one must applaud the
success of the recent Western tour in producing harmony between
high and low.[61]

But the climate of opinion at home had not been unanimously
supportive of the tour, and when press photographs and a newsreel
showed the crown prince acknowledging the saluting of sightseeing
crowds, it rekindled the opposition of many extreme nationalists.[62]
Moreover, Hara's opinion notwithstanding, the ruling elites themselves were by no means satisfied with Hirohito's performance in
Europe, or with the new attitudes that that experience had evoked
in him. Chinda had been unenthusiastic about sending the crown
prince abroad but, at Hara's urging, had accompanied him to England where he looked after him. On September 6, 1921, four days
after Hirohito's return to Japan, Chinda described to Makino the
crown prince's behavior during his European tour: "It seems as
though the shortcomings in [the prince's] qualities of character are
insufficient calmness and a lack of intellectual curiosity."[63]

"Insufficient calmness" and "nervousness" are defects underscored by many who commented on the young prince in this period,
including his own mother, Empress Sadako. In an audience granted
to Makino on September 22, 1922, she made the revealing comment that her son was unable to attend the "annual food offering
ceremony" (*kannamesai*) because "he cannot sit on his knees."
Worse still, he had stopped taking his religious rituals seriously and
had recently become "extremely passionate about physical exercise.
She wants him to calm down and use his mind rather than go to
excess [in exercise]. His devotion to various physical exercises might
harm rather than help the nervousness, which is his weak point."[64]

But why Chinda could say that he lacked "intellectual curiosity"
is far from clear. On the basis of his school performance, the many

comments about his powers of recollection by those who knew him, and what has been written about his devotion to biological studies, just the opposite would seem to have been true. Chinda's comment, with its intimation that the prince was not overly bright, merely reflected the complications inherent in a tutorial relationship between a conscientious sixty-five-year-old diplomat and a twenty-year-old prince happily enjoying his newfound freedom.[65] Or it may just as easily have reflected an honest opinion of a senior official.

This suggests, however, that those closest to young Hirohito were at least uneasy about his ability to perform the enormous tasks about to be placed on his shoulders. They were agreed that he exhibited an average intelligence and an exceptionally good memory, though they never praised him for his boundless imagination or original thought. Mainly they were concerned about his health, and because he exhibited a level of personal insecurity ("nervousness") and social awkwardness that they found worrisome in a monarch but believed could be corrected with time and the assistance of his retinue.[66]

V

In England the primary mission of the crown prince had been to learn from King George V, who had skillfully survived the storm of political reform into which Britain and the rest of the world had been thrown as a result of World War I and the collapse of monarchies all across Europe.[67] George had "from the outset of his reign [in 1910] . . . sought to identify the monarchy with the needs and the pleasures of ordinary people, paying repeated visits to industrial centres, attending football matches, driving through the poorer districts of London, and visiting miners and workers in their homes."[68] Thereafter he helped check a trend toward pacifism at home and strove to raise morale in the British armed forces. According to George's official biographer, Harold Nicolson, he paid visits to the

Grand Fleet and various naval bases, inspected the armies in France, visited three hundred hospitals, conferred tens of thousands of decorations, and repeatedly toured the industrial areas. George was particularly keen to visit damaged areas "and talk to the injured in the wards. No previous monarch had entered into such close personal relations with so many of his subjects."[69]

Apart from contributing in important ways to Britain's war effort, George V had also furthered Britain's national interest and strengthened the cause of the British monarchy through his dealings with other royal families.[70] He had refused to grant asylum in Britain to his doomed cousin, Czar Nicholas II, during the Bolshevik Revolution; but in 1919, with the war over, he assiduously undermined Lloyd George's effort to place his cousin Kaiser Wilhelm II on trial in London as a war criminal.[71] When given an opportunity to shore up the authority of the Japanese imperial house, George decided to use Hirohito's visit to strengthen Britain's cooperation with Japan.[72]

George V had nearly reached the age of fifty-six when, on May 9, he came in person to Victoria Station to greet an excited twenty-year-old crown prince. He went out of his way to treat him as the monarch of a great power, and on May 29, near the end of Hirohito's stay in England, George brought Queen Mary and the highest officials of the land with him to Victoria Station to bid farewell to the prince. The king's welcoming strategy, riding with Hirohito to Buckingham Palace in an open carriage while crowds cheered along the route, later going out of his way to be seen with him, certainly impressed the prince and left him with friendly feelings toward the British. Indeed, all of Hirohito's experiences in England, including the academic degrees and royal accolades bestowed on him, strengthened his sense of national pride.

The whole spectacle of Hirohito's visit to England also impressed the first secretary of the Japanese Embassy in London, Yoshida Shigeru, as can be seen in this letter to his father-in-law, Makino:

> The current visit of the crown prince was greatly welcomed in this
> country. Needless to say, one could not have wished for a more cordial
> reception by the [British] imperial house. I am utterly overjoyed to see
> how popular he is among high and low alike. I think our crown prince
> received the natural adoration of everybody because he expresses him-
> self simply, straightforwardly, and honestly. Although such qualities
> are inborn, he is indeed very wise.[73]

Yoshida may have had few opportunities to meet and observe
the crown prince before he wrote to Makino. Yet one cannot doubt
for a moment his profoundly positive emotions on looking at Hirohito and seeing an image of "inborn" qualities that, by definition,
were associated with the national polity, centered on the Imperial
House. Even if what Yoshida was seeing was his own idealized image
of the throne in the persona of the crown prince, the image that
reached his eye was the same one seen by many Japanese elites. Precisely this eagerness and idealism of people like Yoshida to believe
that the crown prince symbolized a future Japan that was better than
the present one must be counted among the reasons for the success
of the Western tour.

Later in life Hirohito claimed that his European tour led him to
realize that he had been living like "a bird in a cage" and henceforth
needed to open himself to the real world.[74] He also implied that
King George V had taught him how the British monarch counseled,
encouraged, and, on occasion, warned his ministers regarding the
conduct of political and military affairs, and that he had come to
admire British-style constitutional monarchy. But the real image
George conveyed was that of an *activist* monarch who judged the
qualifications of candidates for prime minister and exercised his
considerable political power *behind the scenes* (always pretending, of
course, to be neutral and above the fray). If George's example
impressed the young crown prince, it encouraged him to retrieve
the imperial prerogatives his father had been unable to exercise.

Since George felt that the cabinet should reflect the monarch's political judgments on cabinet appointments, the expulsion of government ministers from office, or the altering of policies he disliked, that lesson too would have encouraged Hirohito (and his entourage) to regain the waning powers of the throne.

To the extent that George V strengthened Hirohito in the belief that an emperor should have his own political judgments independent of his ministers, George's "lessons" had nothing to do with "constitutional monarchy." They were also incompatible with the spirit of Taishō democracy, which at that time sought to reduce the emperor's political powers and turn him into a symbolic figurehead. If George really was Hirohito's role model, as was later claimed, then the lessons he learned from George could not have led him to become a true constitutional monarch.[75] Given the profound differences between the British and Japanese variants of constitutional monarchy, that is hardly surprising. In the pre–World War II Japanese imperial system, politics, religion, and military command were inseparably connected, the emperor had dictatorial authority and vast powers. In military affairs he did not require the advice of any minister of state, and he was expected to rule in order for the system to function properly. The British model was entirely different.

The most important instruction Hirohito and his entourage received from their observations of George V concerned public relations and the use of large-scale ceremonies and court rituals to popularize monarchy and strengthen nationalism.[76] George V had saved the Germanic British monarchy from destruction at the hands of the British people by abruptly Anglicizing it during World War I, when "people were calling for the abdication of the 'German King.'" By changing the surname of the royal house and family from Hanover to Windsor and inventing the "ancient" ceremonial monarchy, George V "made the Royal Family seem timeless and firmly rooted in the moral landscape, enabling them to shield so effectively the system of class privilege."[77] Hirohito and his staff were not as innovative as King George V, but they did take notice of George's fine sense of public relations in the new age of mass media, and of his skillful use of ritual as a strategy for perpetuating the political influence of the monarchy.

Apart from teaching him the real lessons of George V, the Western tour emboldened Hirohito to make a significant disclosure of character to unnamed members of his entourage. According to the unpublished memoirs of his military aide, Nara, shortly after Hirohito returned, he confessed to his disbelief in the divinity of his father and his imperial ancestors. In Nara's words it seemed as though:

> the very rational-minded prince does not believe that the ancestors of the imperial house are truly gods nor that the present emperor is a living deity [*arahitogami*]. I once heard that he divulged the thought that we ought to maintain the status quo, keeping the *kokutai* as it is; but he seems to think that it is too much to completely separate the emperor as a god from the nation. He thinks it would be best to maintain the imperial house [along British lines] and that the relationship between the state and the people should be that [in which] the monarch "reigns but does not rule."[78]

Nara completed his memoirs in late 1956, a decade after Hirohito's postwar disavowal of his divinity. Many defenders of the throne were still trying to whitewash the problem of Hirohito's unacknowledged war responsibility and obscure the fact that he had previously been regarded as an object of religious worship. If Nara was correctly reporting Hirohito's moment of candor, then Hirohito, at age twenty, made three noteworthy points:

He declared that he no longer believed his ancestors were living gods or that his own father was a living deity—something for which he could hardly be blamed. Second, and nevertheless, he affirmed the right of the state to impose on ordinary Japanese the belief that "the ancestors of the imperial house are truly gods and that the present emperor is a living deity." On the other hand, rather than defend what he now seemed to believe, or work to change the *kokutai*, which inhibited objective discussion of Japanese history, he felt he should accept the deceit that was expected of him and keep the *kokutai* just "as it is." His pragmatic, voluntary subordination of his own mind to the precepts of the imperial system forecast his (and his entourage's) active acceptance of the heightened cult of emperor worship that arose as a destroyer of careers in the mid- and late 1930s. The public actions of this prince would never be governed by his own private standards of goodness, morality, and integrity.

Third, by stating his preference for a British-style relationship between the throne and the nation, Hirohito inadvertently challenged an operative principle of the Japanese monarchy. In the process he revealed how unready he still was to play the role of emperor. For if the system of civil and military relations under the Meiji constitution was to function smoothly, with the imperial house as the one effective force for integrating state and nation, civil government and military affairs, then the emperor really had to exercise his enormous—indeed dictatorial—political and military authority. Moreover, prewar Japanese nationalism also demanded a real monarch who ruled, not a nominal one who merely reigned.

Keenly aware of these imperatives, and of the crown prince's impressionable nature and idealistic sentiments, Nara implied that Hirohito's confession of disbelief was not so serious as it might seem. The prince was merely reflecting the mood of those around him. He was not really uncomfortable in his unbelief. In fact, rather than expressing deeply held convictions, he was succumbing to thinking that had "flared up suddenly all over the world after the Great European War" and filled Japan. In this Hirohito was not alone, for, as Nara continued:

Even the *genrō*—Yamagata and Saionji in particular—were greatly tinged by the new thinking. This mood existed among a fairly large number of young officials in the Imperial Household Ministry and Saionji [Hachirō], Futara [Yoshinori], and Matsudaira [Yoshitami] apparently were in the vanguard. I can see the strong influence of these young Imperial Household officials who, after having been influenced by the *genrō* Saionji and others, passed their thoughts to the Crown Prince. . . . The right way to maintain the security and peace of the Imperial House is to have it gradually draw close to the nation while holding to the existing concept of the *kokutai*. I realize that most officials of the Imperial Household Ministry feel as I do. But . . . since the Imperial House of Japan is different from England, we must naturally refrain from saying such things as, "The monarch reigns but does not rule." As for the concept of the *kokutai*, I firmly believe nothing has changed from the way it was before. Therefore I shall always bear in mind the crown prince's predicament, and whenever there is an opportunity I will try to create an environment in which he can relax.[79]

Young Hirohito's "predicament"—his personal discomfort in early manhood with the attribution of divinity to him and his ancestors—clearly should not be exaggerated. At some level of mental awareness he had to believe in the myth of divinity in order to act as the chief priest of Shinto. After a brief period of doubt during the 1920s, he submitted to the party line, overcame his youthful idealism, and moderated his initial enthusiasm for court reform. Eventually, Hirohito learned to reconcile skepticism about his own personal divinity with belief in the *bansei ikkei* myth—the idea, enshrined in the Meiji constitution, that he embodied a timeless, genealogical line of sovereign emperors, descended through the male line, and "unbroken" from the age of the gods. The myth of the imperial regalia—the idea that his possession of the regalia legitimized his authority and preserved his family—presented an equally vexatious problem, and one that could be solved the same way. Hirohito's piety could be seen in the seriousness with which he later applied himself to performing Shinto rites at court and "reporting" important affairs of state to the gods. But the main modes in which it expressed itself were his dedication to the cults of imperial ancestor worship and Ise Shrine worship.

By the time Hirohito became emperor, he had grasped the utilitarian value of myths and clung to them as to other notions of statecraft. Whenever convenient he used such myths to rationalize his own behavior, to buttress the power of the imperial court vis-à-vis other elites in the ruling bloc, and to position himself outside political and secular responsibility. At the same time the more Hirohito lived the role of "sacred and direct" monarch, the more he came to rely on religious belief as a mechanism of power as well as a source of strength under trying conditions.

VI

On November 4, 1921, two months after Hirohito returned from Europe, a nineteen-year-old railway switchman, one Nakaoka Konichi, stabbed Prime Minister Hara to death. The assassin was alleged to have been the grandson of a Meiji-era loyalist from the former domain of Tosa. His motivations remain obscure but appear to have been connected mainly with Hara's assumption, a few weeks earlier, of the duties of navy minister while the incumbent, Adm. Katō Tomosaburō, was in Washington, Hara's defense of Yamagata, and his Seiyūkai cabinet's decision to send the crown prince to visit the European heads of state.[80] The public downfall of Yamagata, followed by Hara's assassination, demonstrated the enormous destructive power that could be generated whenever an issue involving the imperial house became a focal point of politics. With Hara gone and Makino (assisted by Sekiya and counseled from afar by Saionji) in control of palace affairs, the monarchy stood poised to enter a period of growing independence from the cabinet.

The next day, while the press was inadvertently invoking sympathy for the killer by focusing on his "indignation" at the "corruption of the times," Imperial House Minister Makino informed Empress Sadako of Hara's death. Anxiety swept over her as she tearfully told Makino that Hara was "such a rare person. I always wondered how he kept his balance and never failed to smile even when he had the weight of so many problems on his shoulders."[81] She sent an envoy to Hara's burial in Morioka, Iwate prefecture. But it was the plight of her husband, Emperor Yoshihito, straining just to rubber-stamp documents and unable to comprehend what was happening around him, that most unnerved her. It was his worsening condition, combined with the political crisis produced by Hara's death, that now hastened the establishment of a regency.

Concurrently the *genrō* Matsukata and Saionji decided that the rump Hara cabinet could not afford to resign just when it was preparing for an important international conference of the leading Pacific powers, scheduled to open later that month in Washington, D.C. Without bothering to consult Emperor Yoshihito, they asked Finance Minister Takahashi Korekiyo to assume the post of prime minister.

On November 25, 1921, Hirohito became regent for his father. As he assumed the duties of emperor, he already knew he was going to marry Nagako and be the monarch that Meiji had envisioned in the constitution. He may also have believed that it was his obligation to compensate for his father's inadequacies by doing all that was required to preserve the authority of the throne and defend the empire. These important aspirations depended on him gaining greater freedom of action, however. Given his youth, his peculiar upbringing, the respect he accorded the elders who constantly surrounded him, and the weight of court tradition, this would not be easy.

PART 2

THE POLITICS OF GOOD INTENTIONS, 1922–1930

THE REGENCY AND THE CRISIS OF TAISHŌ DEMOCRACY

When Hirohito became regent, in November 1921, the government had already begun promoting the image of an energetic, robust crown prince, capable of going on field maneuvers with the army, and splendidly suited to becoming the supreme commander of the imperial forces.[1] Through the mass media it continued to validate the image of the crown prince in constant motion, meeting with government officials and foreign dignitaries, convening the Diet, traveling to different parts of the homeland for military reviews and maneuvers, doing staff duty at army and navy headquarters, and touring the colonies. In 1922 Hirohito was indeed trying (with mixed success) to settle into the routine being laid out for him by his new entourage, while continuing to imagine that he could make the customs of the court comport more with what he had seen in Europe. But he was spending most of his time exercising, riding, and studying French.

Aware of how worried the *genrō* and government leaders were about his inexperience and what seemed to them excessively high spirits, the elderly Hirata Tōsuke (appointed lord keeper of the privy seal the previous year) and Imperial Household Minister Makino (who formally assumed that post on March 20, 1925) urged the prince to work harder. To carry out the duties of regent, they told him he had to continue his education, with particular emphasis on developing the proper imperial demeanor and gravity of expression, and to gain a better understanding of political, economic, and military affairs.

The initial Hirata-Makino study plan to develop Hirohito's interest in governmental affairs required his attendance at round-table conferences of the high palace officials. Afterward he was to submit to questions to see if he had grasped the issues discussed. This technique proved unworkable. Hirohito was simply not interested in what was being taught, and Hirota's health was failing. Too ill to devote himself to training the regent, Hirota increasingly absented himself. Toward the end of 1922 Makino stepped in to advise Hirohito on the written and unwritten rules of the monarchy, and on political affairs.

Meanwhile the mood at court began to change during 1922 as senior palace officials reacted to the breakdown of domestic cooperation and elite consensus. Disagreements among the ruling elites had surfaced during World War I about foreign and domestic policies, and had been papered over by the establishment of the Foreign Policy Research Council, which lasted from 1917 to early 1922. During that time the parties widened their electoral base and looked for ways to extend their influence to the colonies, up to now the special bailiwick of the army. Political leaders like Takahashi of the Seiyūkai believed, as Hara Kei had before him, that in order to flourish economically Japan had to adopt policies that appeased American interests. The major arms reduction obligations that the government had recently assumed under the Washington treaties were in line with Takahashi's views. But right-wing groups and some military leaders railed against the Washington treaties. Hirohito's chief aide-de-camp, Lieutenant General Nara, noted in his memoirs of this period: "We have been wearing civilian clothes such as swallow-tailed coats and morning clothes out of consideration for the regent ever since his European tour. Now, however, we have begun to consider the mood of the public. In early November 1922,

I conferred with Chinda and tried as much as possible to wear military uniforms, but did not say anything to the regent."[2]

I

Over the next few years a better system of instruction was put into effect, and Hirohito began listening to lectures, two to three hours a day, on any and all subjects that Makino, Kawai, Nara, and he himself considered useful. This in itself was highly unusual. Only since the Meiji period had the imperial court operated on the assumption that the reigning monarch, though born to his role in life, needed to be continually in training to rule. Just by means of daily study, organized and closely supervised by high officials of the Imperial Household Ministry, the monarch strengthened his skills, polished his virtues, and corrected his intellectual and physical shortcomings. Special court pedagogues, admirals, generals, diplomats returning from service abroad, and members of the titled peerage were employed for this purpose.

Makino believed, as did the "faculty" he put together, that ample historical precedent existed for officials serving at court to see themselves as part of an organization committed to "forming" the monarch through lifetime learning. In the imaginations of both Makino and Hirohito the classic figure who had ascended the throne as a helpless, uneducated teenager, and afterward mastered the art of ruling through the discipline of study, was Meiji, a man who disliked studying. Meiji furnished the specifications and was supposed to be proof of what miracles court advisers could perform by continuously cuing the monarch and by an exhortatory approach that responded to his psychological needs.

During the regency Hirohito learned how, throughout World War I, the lord keeper of the privy seal and the imperial household minister had worked with the *genrō* to restrain his father from interfering in political affairs. He came to see how important it was to prevent cabinets headed by political party leaders from gaining control of the court. He witnessed the practice of reducing the sphere of imperial assent to the smallest possible extent, so that neither his father the emperor nor he himself would need to express the "imperial will." He also saw how weak the political influence of palace officials was compared with the representatives of other advisory organs of the throne. Youthful, inexperienced Hirohito listened and learned while his entourage encouraged him to defend more explicitly his imperial prerogatives, which seemed threatened by the rise of party cabinets. As his desire grew to become a political actor and to retrieve the lost powers of the throne, so did the influence of Makino and the others who advised and assisted him while standing entirely outside the constitutional structure. They too believed that by exercising influence on Hirohito they could reestablish the monarchy on a stronger, independent basis.

At the start of the regency, three princes—Inoue Katsunoshin, the grand master of ceremonies, Kujō Michizane, the chief ritualist, and Saionji Hachirō, the *genrō*'s adopted son who served on the Board of Ceremonies—began training Hirohito in court rituals, a subject his mother was keenly intent that he master. Meanwhile Makino and other members of the entourage focused on setting up an ambitious program of imperial lectures so that Hirohito could continue his studies at a more advanced level.[3] Four Tokyo University professors were recruited to deliver "regular lectures." These were printed, and portions were given to Hirohito ahead of time, on a daily or weekly basis according to a fixed schedule.[4] Constitutional scholar Shimizu Tōru, historian Mikami Sanji, economist Yamazaki Kakujirō, and international law specialist Tachi Sakutarō delivered the lectures.[5] Because these four were teachers of the emperor but also expert consultants for Makino, Kawai, and other key members of the entourage, the influence of their ideas is immeasurable.

Little is known of the lectures on economics given by Yamazaki and others, including Inoue Junnosuke, president of the Bank of

Japan. In fact, it is doubtful that they or any other economists had a great impact on Hirohito. Court officials were generally both ignorant of economic policy and untrained to understand principles of finance. The trivial cost-saving measures Hirohito instituted in 1929 in response to the Shōwa financial panic left the impression that neither he nor his court team understood basic economics. It might well be that Hirohito's main interest in the economy derived from his concern for law and order, domestic tranquillity, and international stability.

Law professor Shimizu's influence on Hirohito is also difficult to assess but seems to have been much more important than Yamazaki's. Every Tuesday he would lecture on the Meiji constitution and on "administrative law," a topic that included discussion of contemporary political events. On Fridays he would expound on the Imperial Household Law (*kōshitsu tenpan*), which governed such matters as the ordinances (*kōshitsurei*) based on it, establishment of the regency, and the formal ceremonies of accession to the throne.[6] Shimizu always aimed to present proper conservative attitudes on questions of constitutional and civil law, though exactly what themes he emphasized and what positions he staked out in his lectures of the regency years is unclear.

More is known about Hirohito's history professor Mikami Sanji, who lectured before the regent on the political history of the Meiji period and was a prime creator of the stereotype of Meiji, "the Great." On January 14, 1924, for example, Mikami spoke of a famous incident from the prehistory of modern Japanese imperialism: the argument over whether to "conquer Korea," which had split the Meiji government in 1873. Meiji had listened dutifully to the instruction of the president of the Grand Council of State, Sanjō Sanetomi; afterward Meiji advised the self-designated leader of the proposed expedition to Korea, Saigō Takamori, not to proceed before a diplomatic mission to the Western nations, headed by Iwakura Tomomi, returned. In that way a costly foreign project was deferred until the country was better prepared to undertake it. Makino felt Mikami's lecture was a good reference for the young crown prince. "The . . . [Meiji] emperor," wrote Makino in his diary, "made a wise decision, and it resulted in good fortune for the nation in a difficult period when the Restoration reforms were being established. For the prince to hear such stories will have a great effect in nurturing his virtue."[7] Given Hirohito's reticence, however, neither Makino nor anyone else could be certain how he had reacted to what a lecturer said (or did not say) about a particular subject.

Mikami's lectures to Hirohito focused on Meiji's inexhaustible virtue and benevolence. He hammered home this theme over and over again as the Taishō emperor lay dying and the court prepared for Hirohito's accession. Vice Grand Chamberlain Kawai mentions that on November 19, 1926, Mikami spoke on how the Restoration leaders had encouraged Meiji always to do good and eschew evil. Makino's diary entry of that day notes that Hirohito seemed deeply moved, continuing:

> There were bold words of remonstrance concerning how one must really exert oneself to manifest generosity, love and esteem, prudence and dignity. . . . Professor Mikami culled examples from all over the world and amplified them. Such a lecture is very timely today. Therefore, in another room, I expressed my satisfaction to the professor and drew his attention to a few more points for his reference.[8]

Meiji's virtues continued to furnish lecture material throughout 1926 on his frugality, learning, and pedagogical intentions concerning his son. The painstaking efforts of Meiji's advisers to nurture his benevolence was never overlooked.[9] Mikami's last talk in 1926, delivered on December 3, stressed that: "The emperor should be generous and think of the people as his treasure; he should preserve his health . . . ; he should labor to heighten his

augustness and high virtues, yet also try to be gentle; he should care
well for his subjects."[10]

Mikami's lectures also affected the entourage and contributed to
its plan to establish in 1927 a national holiday to commemorate
Meiji and celebrate his "great virtue."[11] The impact of Mikami's
ideas on Hirohito was more complex. The weekly lectures on the
almost-mythical Meiji probably strengthened Hirohito's resolve to
live up to the ideal of an activist, dynamic monarch, manifesting the
qualities of benevolence Meiji was supposed to have possessed. On
the other hand, his "nervousness" and tension may have been exacerbated by the hyping of Meiji. An overelevated, unrealistic standard of behavior was set before him to emulate and attain. And
almost certainly this pressure caused him a great deal of anxiety.
Moreover, at the same time as he was being asked to be a gentle and
benevolent monarch, he was also being instructed in military science, economics, and international law and diplomacy, which
required a completely different, more disciplined, vigorous type of
behavior.

During these years Hirohito was taught about the morally dubious activities in which rulers, of necessity, normally engage. His
instructors imparted to him the doctrine that in making international policy decisions, states must eschew ethics and sometimes use
force to optimize their interests. The only question that really mattered, he learned, was: Is it in the national interest?

To focus Hirohito's attention on the pursuit of national advantage was the task of Professor Tachi, Japan's preeminent international lawyer. Tachi offered his answers to the question of what constituted the national interest in lectures on the history of diplomacy
and the precepts and prohibitions of international law. Before joining the faculty of Tokyo Imperial University, Tachi had studied in
Germany, France, and Britain between 1900 and 1904.[12] He was a
member of the Japanese delegations at the Paris Peace Conference
of 1919 and the Washington Conference of 1921–22.[13] His nation-

alist positions on questions of international law made him well regarded in both the Japanese Foreign Ministry and the army high command. It was hardly surprising that a private scholar who took his orders from the Foreign Ministry should have been chosen to teach international law at court.

Tachi came to lecture Hirohito after Japan (though not the United States) had signed on to the new Versailles-Washington framework of institutions based on principles of formal equality among sovereign nations, peaceful resolution of conflicts, and outlawing of aggressive war. Unlike Mikami, Tachi did not talk about virtue and benevolence. He avoided moral criteria in understanding international law, and shied away from restricting the rule of force by the rule of law. Tachi taught that war in general was always legal, never illegal; "established international law" existed to subserve the interests of states; the right of self-defense included war that expanded territory or protected the lives and the private property of nationals living in other states. This nineteenth-century view of international law had been generally accepted before Versailles and the Covenant of the League of Nations had declared new basic principles and established new (American-inspired) organizations to govern and resolve disputes among nations. Those new principles, however, failed to impress Tachi or the Japanese Foreign Ministry under any of its ministers, including the liberal Shidehara.

Tachi's nationalistic view of international law was the official Japanese view, in which Hirohito was instructed from the late 1920s through the early 1930s. As historian Shinohara Hatsue pointed out, those were precisely the years when U.S. Secretary of State Henry L. Stimson and many leading international law experts in the United States—such as Quincy Wright at the University of Chicago, James T. Shotwell at Columbia University, and Clyde Eagleton at New York University—were developing an opposing theory to criminalize aggressive war and abolish the principle that belligerents should be treated impartially.

As Hirohito built up his knowledge and gained experience of political and diplomatic affairs, he increasingly took the initiative in ordering "special lectures" on matters that he felt required the advice of outside experts.[14] Lectures on the political situation in Weimar Germany, Soviet Russia, China, Korea, and the League of Nations were intended to keep him abreast of main developments in foreign affairs and in the Japanese colonies. Senior military officers, the army and navy ministers, and various aides-de-camp delivered military science lectures to him, usually on a weekly basis, then augmented their instruction by having him partieipate in annual military field exercises and "grand maneuvers." These provided opportunities for him to meet and question the rising stars of his professional officer corps, and to signal to army and navy leaders how he might respond to their formal submission of requests.[15]

II

From the start of the regency, government and Imperial Household Ministry officials experimented with new ways of making the throne more responsive to Japanese society. In their efforts to recover lost authority, they relaxed the legal restrictions that before World War I had kept the press from photographing the monarch. In 1921 all the print and visual media of the period—newspapers, magazines, and film—were harnessed as the crown prince became de facto monarch. Photographic equipment soon was coming into Japan on a scale that rivaled the import of electric machinery and cotton textiles. An advertisement in the *Tokyo Nichi Nichi shinbun*, using a picture of the regent Hirohito and Princess Nagako together, was allowed to pass without question.[16] Books containing previously banned pictures of Hirohito's autograph and the imperial seal were published without incident.

Under Makino's direction the Imperial Household Ministry dispatched the crown prince on his first "experimental tours" to Kanagawa prefecture, and to the home island of Shikoku, in preparation for a later journey to the colony of Taiwan.[17] These tours did not draw on the precedent of Meiji's six imperial excursions, undertaken annually between 1872 and 1877, long before the establishment of the "emperor system."[18] Meiji's tours had carried the message that he was a living deity engaged in the project of national unification. Hirohito's first domestic tours, by contrast, carried no ideological message but were designed primarily to allow court officials to witness his performance and make suggestions for improvement. Secondarily, however, it was hoped that the tours would bring the imperial house closer to the people and, in that way, restrain the Taishō democracy mood that Hirohito's own father was inadvertently assisting simply by being passive, nonperforming, and often disoriented.

Makino wrote:

> The train departed at 9:45 A.M. for the grand army maneuvers. I accompanied [the prince regent]. We arrived at Shizuoka Station at 2:15 P.M. and went to the imperial mansion. . . . He viewed old documents and saw a display of fireworks in the evening.
>
> I shall be brief for we plan to write out our report on this trip later. . . . dealing with matters that must be reformed after adequate deliberation. . . . For example, [the regent's] posture . . . [and] his demeanor. . . . An appropriate demeanor should be adopted for the simple-hearted folk in Shikoku. Their expectations are naturally different from urbanites in places like Hokkaido or Tokyo. In this area, just to have the chance to worship the person of the emperor is a supreme honor. There is no need [for him] to nod in acknowledgment for *every* courtesy. The word I heard most often among the welcomers was *ogameta*: "I reverently beheld him." One should assess the public mind by just that one word.[19]

After the Shikoku trip, a more reassured Makino wrote (December 4, 1922), "We feel better now about him. Prudence and meditation will enhance his virtue. He seems more aware of his role and this gives us more confidence for the future."[20]

On April 12, 1923, Hirohito departed from the Yokosuka naval base aboard the warship *Kongō*, bound for Taiwan, a colony governed outside the Meiji constitution, where the Japanese population was a distinct minority and the climate, customs, and sentiments of the people were unlike those of Japan. His tour, another rite of passage, took him to the island nearly four years after the powerful Hara Kei cabinet had abolished the system of colonial government by the military and placed day-to-day decision making in the hands of a civilian governor-general.

This change had been carried out partly to placate anti-colonial movements in the Japanese colonies and partly to improve Japan's image by bringing it into apparent line with Western colonial practice in Asia. The military, however, had continued to rule in Taiwan just as in other Japanese colonies, though not so harshly as in Korea.

Hirohito's visit had two aims: first and foremost to remind the people at home that the moral source of all their worldly achievements was the imperial house, now represented by him; and second to reaffirm Japan's possession of Taiwan by putting his own seal on Meiji's colonial legacy. His imperial motorcade went first to "the place where the Japanese expeditionary force initially landed on Taiwan and Imperial Prince Kita Shirakawa, commander of the Imperial Guard Division, had died from malaria." In other words the regent began by demonstrating concern not for the colonized population but for his own imperial family, one of whom had died in the conquest, and whose spirit was enshrined in all but ten of the island's sixty-eight Shinto shrines.[21] In the 1930s Japan would compel Taiwanese (and Koreans) to worship at such shrines under the pretext of pursuing an assimilationist policy, but in this period it followed a less harsh program.

Apart from his visits to shrines, a number of military facilities, and a Japanese sugar refinery, Hirohito targeted the youth of the

colony by visiting thirteen Japanese-built schools. In another symbolic gesture of benevolence, he reduced the prison sentences of
535 political prisoners who had been arrested in 1915 for plotting
an armed uprising against Japanese rule.[22] But he had undertaken
the tour mainly to reinforce belief in the monarchy and to project an
image of exemplary moral perfection; and this aim he achieved simply by the dignified way in which he displayed himself and by the
press's extremely detailed coverage of his visit.

When he arrived at the governor-general's headquarters in
Taipei, for example, the *Tainichi shinbun* reported that a band played
"Kimigayo" (the Japanese national anthem) as his train entered the
station area. The stationmaster opened the train door and "onto the
platform stepped the bright, glorious, splendid figure of the prince."
Guided by numerous officials, and their accompanying military and
civil attendants, they all formed a line on the left side of the platform.
Hirohito "advanced and saluted the recipients of imperial accolades,
Japanese and Taiwanese alike. Then he drove off with his grand
chamberlain in a car emblazoned with a shining golden chrysanthemum
seal." Military police and civil police chiefs guarded him in front, while
the governor of the colony led the procession of cars that followed.[23]

The order in which the imperial entourage and the colonial
bureaucracy arranged themselves here vis-à-vis the crown prince
was characteristic of *all* public imperial functions and not specifically intended to reflect the special relationship of hierarchical
inequality between Japan and its colonies, which had been forced on
them without their consent.

In the May–June 1923 issue of *Taiwan jippō*, after Hirohito's
departure from Taiwan, Chief of General Affairs Kaku Sakatarō
affirmed the regent's importance as a model of morality and benevolence for the entire Japanese empire. "I believe," Kaku declared, that:

> our people's moral values are generated from the imperial house and
> that the crown prince's visit clearly shows this reality. We are most
> grateful that he has presented himself as the model of morality for the

common people. The prince is richly imbued with the value of filial piety toward his parents; he gets along well with his brothers. He is open but composed and does not display emotion. His majesty's philanthropy and humaneness extend even to animals. His modest, frugal way of life is a guide for all his subjects. His every word and action show the essence of morality. What especially moves me is that regardless of his subjects' class or office, wealth or poverty, he always smiles warmly on all.[24]

Hirohito's tour had helped Kaku to communicate the image of the imperial house as the source of the nation's morality and the emperor as the "model of morality for the common people." Kaku's emphasis on "filial piety" and the prince's amicable relations "with his brothers" was premised on the expectation that the Chinese population of Taiwan would respond enthusiastically if addressed in such terms of Confucian family relationships. But however one interprets the regent's performance, Kaku's language attempted to justify to the Chinese people a colonial order that had already become questionable as a result of rising demands for national self-determination and nationhood.

Hirohito sailed home from Taiwan as he had traveled there, departing Keelung on April 27, 1923, aboard the *Kongō*. Two days out to sea he celebrated his twenty-second birthday. Ahead of him lay his long-postponed marriage to Princess Nagako, continued academic study at court, and more tours and ceremonies as required by the new policy of bringing the imperial house closer to the people.

On his return to Tokyo, two events occurred that were to have an unforeseen impact on Hirohito's later life. One was the discovery in June 1923 of the newly formed, illegal Japanese Communist Party, the first group in Japan's modern history to call for the abolition of the monarchy; the other, which followed his first experience of a cabinet change, ranks among the worst natural disasters of the twentieth century.

On August 14, 1923, Prime Minister Katō died, and Admiral

Yamamoto Gonbei was appointed his successor. Two weeks later, on September 1, while Yamamoto was forming his cabinet, the great Kantō earthquake struck the Tokyo-Yokohama region. The quake and the fires that followed killed more than 91,000 people, left 13,000 missing, injured more than 104,000, and destroyed more than 680,000 homes in the Tokyo area alone.[25] While the fires raged and the aftershocks continued in both cities, Japanese vigilante groups, abetted by military and police officials, carried out murderous pogroms against Koreans and leftists rumored to have ignited fires, looted, and poisoned wells. More than six thousand Koreans were hunted down and killed throughout the Kantō region and in many other parts of the country.[26] Hirohito now gained his first experience as an active commander in chief issuing emergency imperial edicts. He placed Tokyo and its environs under martial law on September 3 and, after all danger from the earthquake had passed, toured sections of the devastated capital on horseback, in military uniform, accompanied by martial-law-commander General Fukuda. On October 10 he paid a similar visit to the Yokohama-Yokosuka area.[27]

After the Kantō earthquake incidents of lèse-majesté increased and culminated in the infamous Toranomon incident in Tokyo, causing a further postponement of Hirohito's marriage. On December 27, 1923, a young anarchist, Namba Daisuke, fired a small pistol at Hirohito's carriage as he was en route to the Diet to deliver his inaugural address. The bullet shattered the glass, cutting his chamberlain but leaving Hirohito untouched. Namba, the son of a Diet member, had employed a weapon commonly used for shooting birds. Had he not targeted the crown prince, he would have been charged with the lesser crime of attempting to inflict bodily injury.[28] Because he had intended to harm the future emperor, however, his action went beyond the parameters of lèse-majesté and sent a shock wave through the entire nation.

This incident quickly caused the highest officials of the land, from Prime Minister Yamamoto and his entire cabinet to the head of the national police, Yuasa Kurahei, to submit their resignations. Ordinary policemen in the area of the incident were dismissed en masse. Thereafter the strategy of displaying and guarding Hirohito in public was completely reevaluated.[29]

The day after this incident, December 28, at the start of the Forty-eighth Imperial Diet, the House of Peers held its first secret session in sixteen years.[30] Discussion focused on Namba's motivation, social background, and the need to tighten controls over thought. Diet member Nakagawa Yoshinaga observed: "Once people awaken socially [to defects in society] and [those defects] become unbearable, they will erupt, and it will be too late to do anything about it." He urged the "renovation of unjust institutions." Another peer, Tsuchiya Mitsukane, observing that Namba had been reading articles written by national university professors in magazines such as *Kaizō* [Reconstruction] and *Kaihō* [Liberation], urged the government to strengthen controls over dangerous thoughts.[31]

Namba was charged under the criminal code and speedily tried by the Great Court of Cassation. The chief judge in the case, Yokota Hideo, reportedly urged Namba to repent in the hope that his statement could later be used to bolster popular respect for the imperial house. Replying tartly, Namba asked whether the chief judge really believed in the emperor's divinity or merely professed such belief out of fear. When Yokota refused to answer, the would-be assassin reportedly declared, "I've proved the joy of living for the truth. Go ahead and hang me."[32] When his death sentence was read, on November 13, 1924, Namba shouted three *banzai*s: to the proletariat and Communist Party of Japan, to Russian socialism and the Soviet Republic, and to the Communist Internationale.[33] He was executed two days later, and on November 17, 1924, eleven months after his crime, secretly buried in an unmarked communal grave.[34]

Makino's diary entry on the day of the Toranomon incident registered the "tremendous change in popular thought" behind

Namba's assassination attempt. "Even concepts connected to the *kokutai* have undergone astonishing change among some people," Makino observed. "Of course they are still a very small minority, but I am more worried about the future now that a person has emerged and actually tried to act out his ideas. I fear that the people might lose their presence of mind by witnessing such a great act of lèse majesté."[35] Hirohito reacted more calmly to the shooting; later, when Nara informed him of Namba's execution, he is alleged to have said to Chinda Sutemi and Grand Chamberlain Irie Tamemori:

> I had thought that in Japan the relationship between his majesty and his subjects was, in principle, a monarch-subject relationship, but in sentiment a parent-child relationship. I have always devoted myself to the people on that understanding. But seeing this incident, I am especially saddened that the person who dared to commit this misdeed was one of His Majesty's loyal subjects. I want this thought of mine to be thoroughly understood.[36]

At age twenty-three Hirohito was emotionally detached and thought of the imperial system in ideological terms dunned into him since early childhood: The emperor is to the people as a father is to his children. Interestingly, military Aide-de-Camp Nara advised Hirohito not to make his sentiments public, for they would only provoke more dissent from socialists and communists. Whether Hirohito was persuaded to change his mind or (less likely) the entourage ignored his wishes is unclear; but no statement by the crown prince on the assassination attempt was ever issued.[37]

While the Toranomon incident was still being widely discussed, further acts of less unusual lèse majesté occurred as some ordinary people expressed their lack of appreciation for the prince regent's efforts to come into closer contact with them.[38] According to Hirohito's earliest biographer, Nezu Masashi, there were thirty-five such incidents during the six years between 1921 and 1927.[39] These episodes deepened concern among government officials about the spread of communism and other "dangerous thoughts."[40] They also exposed the fragility of Hirohito in the role of "crown prince for the age of the commoner."

Nevertheless the idea of popularizing both him and the imperial house remained alive during the early regency years. When the moment for Hirohito's wedding finally arrived at the beginning of 1924, he and his aides decided that a lavishly staged imperial wedding would be out of place in a physically devastated capital that was just beginning to reconstruct. Sensing that ordinary Japanese sought stability and continuity in a time of rapid economic and social changes, Hirohito tried to meet their expectations. An imperial wedding with a modest display of monarchical dignity and an emphasis on traditional court practice was sufficient for him, and would also serve to bring him closer to the people.

Crown Prince Hirohito and Princess Nagako celebrated their marriage in a series of short ceremonies on January 26, 1924. In an ancient tradition dating back to Heian times, the marriage was preceded by a carefully choreographed exchange of love poems. A court chamberlain in full dress coat and top hat delivered Hirohito's sealed poem (written on light pink paper, placed in a white willow box) to the Kuni family mansion, which had been specially decorated with red and white bunting. A few hours later a servant delivered a similar box to the Imperial Palace containing Nagako's reply.[41]

On the day of the wedding Princess Nagako rose at 3:00 A.M., went outside to a small garden shrine, and prayed to her family ancestors. After her bath and a light breakfast, she spent three hours having her hair arranged in the Heian manner and dressing in the heavy ceremonial robes of a lady of the court. At 9:00 A.M. she said farewell to her entire family and classmates and was driven off in a car sent from the imperial house.[42] Hirohito had arisen at 5:30, prayed to his ancestors, breakfasted, and put on the full-dress uniform of an army lieutenant colonel. They left for the Imperial Palace at about the same time in separate carriages, preceded and followed by mounted honor guards, and were cheered along the way by large crowds. Arriving at the palace, Hirohito donned the special saffron-yellow robes reserved for an imperial Shinto priest and performed religious rituals in the "Place of Awe," where they notified the gods of their marriage.

Thousands of people lined the heavily guarded route of their carriage procession after it had crossed over Nijūbashi (double bridge) and proceeded back to the Akasaka Palace. Hirohito and Nagako bowed to the crowds that cheered their arrival at the crown prince's residence, decorated with red-and-white bunting, then proceeded into the palace for further marriage rituals and a dinner that lasted late into the night.

Forty-seven military airplanes flew over the capital on their marriage day, dropping small parachutes with messages of congratulations. There was a 101-gun salute from the Army General Headquarters and a 21-gun salute from the battleship *Nagato*, anchored at the Yokosuka Naval Base. The *Osaka Mainichi* reported that the imperial house was using the occasion to bestow monetary awards on distinguished individuals, including about 258 Japanese settlers who had made contributions to society in each of the colonies. It also announced Emperor Yoshihito's pardon and commutation of sentences for criminals, his bountiful funding of social projects at home and abroad, and his grant of imperial property to Tokyo and Kyoto for public parks and museums.[43]

Thus the young couple, on Makino and Saionji's recommendation, used their wedding to obtain political support for the throne and to strengthen the groom's image as a benevolent prince. Imperial almsgiving on this and many other occasions was a way to recover the emperor's declining authority and to bring the imperial house closer to the people. Income from corporate stock dividends was now occupying an ever-larger part of imperial finances, and as the economic power of the throne increased, so too did Hirohito's bestowal of benevolence money and resources, along with other giftgiving connected to his enhanced diplomatic activities.[44] Though the giving of charity was a standard way for monarchs to diffuse their authority, what remains unclear, even today, is whether Hirohito's benevolence was paid for by his subjects' taxes or by his own imperial house assets.

Seven months after their wedding, when the nation had begun to recover from the great earthquake, Hirohito and Nagako departed the capital for a month-long retreat, a honeymoon of sorts, in the countryside. After two nights in Nikkō they journeyed to Inawashiro Lake in Fukushima prefecture, where they stayed at Prince Takamatsu's country villa. They played tennis, went fishing, climbed in the mountains, and enjoyed moonwatching.[45]

In December 1925 Hirohito became a father. He ordered Makino to arrange a series of court lectures for him and Nagako on child rearing and child psychology. Four years before, on becoming regent, Hirohito had put Makino on notice that someday he and Nagako intended to rear their children in the palace and not entrust them to servants.[46] His mother, Makino, and *genrō* Saionji had resisted, but by persisting Hirohito had gotten his way, making clear to Makino and others that he had no higher priority than his own "household." He now had the satisfaction of seeing Nagako breastfeed their own children, starting with daughter Teru no miya, and raise them until the age of three.[47] And because the wedding had been used as the occasion to reform the old system, whereby women of the inner court household lived in the palace instead of merely serving there during the day, Nagako was not surrounded by uneducated ladies-in-waiting who Hirohito feared might exert a harmful influence on her, not to mention leaking to outsiders any improper remark he might make.[48]

In this way Hirohito secured a sphere of private life free of constant surveillance. This achievement came about through his total ending of the practice of imperial concubinage and cutting back the number of ladies-in-waiting. These actions did not make him a court reformer, however, any more than his public performances during the regency made him a "child of Taishō democracy." Even in his young manhood Hirohito was a champion of nationalism and tradition against Taishō democracy. This was true also in his attitude toward the three wars Japan had fought since 1894. Though proud of the victories, he was open to the viewpoints of those in his entourage who had attended the Paris Peace Conference at the end of the Great War, and understood the dangers of renewing a naval race and expanding too vigorously in China.

III

The regency period saw Japan's foreign policy shift focus to reliance on multilateral treaties, the League of Nations, and the "peace code" embodied in the Covenant of the League.[49] To appreciate the boldness of this move away from an international order based on militarism, imperialist spheres of interest, and bilateral treaties, one need only recollect that during World War I Japan's leaders had secretly embraced "Asian Monroeism."[50] Led by the navy and supported by Prime Minister Ōkuma and his Anglophile foreign minister, Katō Kōmei, they had resolved to participate in the European war by expelling the German military from Tsingtao, one of China's most important ports, even before the British government requested that they do so.[51] At different times while World War I unfolded, Katō and the high command—acting in opposition to some of the *genrō*—had formulated secret and grandiose war aims that anticipated Japan's strategic expansion during the late 1930s: All of China was to become a Japanese protectorate, the Russian sphere of interest in northern Manchuria was to be pushed back, the resource-rich Dutch East Indies (present-day Indonesia) were to be wrested from Dutch colonial control, and the West was to be put on notice that Asia should be controlled by Asians (that is, Japanese).

Although Japan was allied with Britain, Japan's army strategists had hoped that the Western powers would be sufficiently weakened by their internecine strife as to be unable to oppose Japan's aims in postwar Asia. These war aims had to be set aside, however, when Germany was defeated and the United States, on which Japan depended for imports of capital, steel, and raw materials, put pressure on it to respect American and Allied rights and interests in China. But they offered a good foretaste of the future policies Japan would implement in the 1930s.

At the Washington Conference (November 12, 1921–February 6, 1922), Prime Minister Takahashi's Seiyūkai government had signed three treaties designed to establish a new basis for Japan's relations with the great European powers and the United States, which had emerged as the de facto world power. The Four-Power Treaty replaced the Anglo-Japanese Alliance that had been the backbone of Japanese diplomacy since the Russo-Japanese War; it also guaranteed the Pacific possessions of its signatories: Japan, Britain, the United States, and France. These powers plus Italy then pledged, in a Five-Power Naval Arms Limitation Treaty, to reduce their mainline battleships and aircraft carriers, while Japan agreed to limit its capital ships to 60 percent of the U.S. total, or a 10:6 ratio in naval power vis-à-vis the United States.[52]

The signatories to the Nine-Power Treaty vowed to respect the territorial integrity, sovereignty, and independence of China, and to abide by the "open door" and "equal opportunity" for all the powers in China to exploit China's natural resources and cheap Chinese labor. This had been the professed policy of the United States toward Asia ever since Secretary of State John Hay's "Open Door Notes" of 1899. Other resolutions called for convening a conference to restore China's tariff autonomy, and for the establishment of a commission to consider the question of extraterritoriality, on which rested the whole structure of unequal treaties with China.

During the 1920s young Hirohito, his entourage, and the Shidehara faction in the Foreign Ministry supported this American-led reorientation in international relations, with its emphasis on cooperation with the West in China, arms reduction, and the abrogation of Japan's previous military alliance with Britain. To be sure, they knew the postwar world order was far from just. The Great Powers had rejected Japan's modest request for a racial equality clause in the Covenant of the League; the United States had designed the Washington treaties to restrain Japan in China and roll back the advances it had made there during World War I. Still they supported the new order, just as they supported the League, in the hope they might thus be able to lessen the excessive arms spending that was driving the government to the verge of bankruptcy. In addition, although the United States had changed the rules of the game, organizations like the League of Nations and the International Labour Organisation (ILO) embodied the principle of the equality of nations which Japan itself had espoused in Paris in 1919. The new order did indeed recognize Japan as a great power (even though it did not recognize the principle of racial equality). This was reason enough for Hirohito and Makino to support the Washington Conference.[53]

In addition the new international order appeared to build on, but not change, the special international status of China under the "unequal treaty" system. It allowed for the possibility of China developing into an independent nationalist state, but ensured the hegemony of the "treaty" powers in Asia. For Japan, therefore, cooperation in this new Anglo-American order, however unjust and inequitable, at least promised stability, and was less a matter of siding with democracy than opposing the disorder associated with antimonarchist Russian Communism, and its spread in China.

Nevertheless, the schema of the white and yellow races locked in conflict and competition, which Hirohito had learned in middle school, had stayed with him. It was an intensely held belief that had also served as the premise of Japanese strategic thinking and war aims during World War I. The passage by the U.S. Congress of the blatantly racist Immigration Act of 1924 reinforced his awareness of racial conflict. Similarly Hirohito retained the knowledge he had received during the early 1920s from civilian court lecturers such as Shimizu Tōru, who rejected any urgent need for arms reduction. To counter the antimilitary mood arising from the Washington Conference, Shimizu had emphasized to Hirohito that "In a situation like the present, where the nations of the world vie with one another, every country must possess armaments to defend from danger."[54] This was the view of the entire entourage; it was Hirohito's view as well.

Hirohito's embrace of the idealistic Washington Conference goals of arms reduction and lasting peace also reflected the political influence on him of Makino, Chinda, and (to a much lesser extent) Saionji. They, together with the diplomat Shidehara, had directly participated in constructing the postwar framework and in tying the imperial court to conciliation with the West. Yet none of them ever gave his total, unqualified endorsement to the postwar "peace code," or to the notion that peace and international cooperation were ends in themselves. The imperial court's support of the Washington treaty system, in other words, rested on unstated assumptions regarding internationalism, and the economic advantages to be gained from diplomatic cooperation with Britain and the United States.

Essentially the entourage assumed that a cooperative, peaceful foreign policy would be compatible with defense of Japan's colonial interests, especially in Manchuria. They also believed Japan could go on developing the "rights and interests" it had extorted from China in "Manchuria-Mongolia" by earlier faits accompli, and that it could do so regardless of Chinese nationalism—a phenomenon for which none of the Washington treaty powers at the time had much regard or understanding. Another shared assumption was that China would not defect from the Washington Conference framework and repudiate the older system of unequal treaties that had been built up ever since the Opium Wars.

Last, Hirohito's entourage held two other largely unsupported beliefs: namely, that the leading Western powers would not prevent Japan from rising to dominance in Asia; and that Japan would be able to separate domestic affairs and foreign policy, cooperating with the West while pursuing narrowly nationalistic, repressive policies at home. Later, when some of these assumptions proved incorrect, Hirohito and his entourage withdrew their support of the Washington treaty framework, abandoned cooperation with other powers in China, and proceeded to sanction actions that directly violated the Nine-Power Treaty, not to mention the principles Japan had subscribed to in the Covenant of the League of Nations.

IV

During the regency years Hirohito and his entourage accepted without question the coalition nature of cabinet government, in which the military was privileged over other organs of state. Under this system army and navy ministers were appointed from the list of active-duty senior officers. Therefore every cabinet was necessarily "mixed"—a coalition of military and civilian officials. In the forty-two mixed cabinets that governed Japan between 1888 and 1945, "the military was guaranteed the right of being able to interfere legally in politics," while prime ministers could control the military only through the emperor or the military ministers.[55] Because of the regent's youth and inexperience, the military ministers and the chiefs of staff worked *within* the cabinet to avoid taking unresolved disputes to the sick and incompetent emperor or bothering the inexperienced regent. But there were a few important exceptions to this sheltering of the regent.

As early as 1923 Hirohito confronted changes in Japan's long-term defense plans arising out of the Washington Conference. The chiefs of the Army and Navy General Staffs, responding to the rise of Lenin's revolutionary regime in the Soviet Union, the abrogation of the Anglo-Japanese military alliance, and the naval arms reductions agreed to at Washington, revised their operational plans for the defense of the Japanese empire. They continued to define Russia as the number one enemy, just as they had been doing ever since the Russo-Japanese War. They showed an increased awareness of China by targeting it as the number three potential enemy, though they did not draft any plans for war against China. But now, for the first time in Japan's history, both chiefs of staff named the United States as the second main enemy after the Soviet Union.

Henceforth the army would prepare for a war on the Asian continent with a wartime force of forty divisions. The Imperial Navy would remain within the parameters of the Washington Naval Arms Reduction Treaty but organize and train for the defense of the homeland and the maintenance of sea lanes of communication with the Asian continent "north of the Taiwan Straits."[56] This meant targeting, primarily, the naval forces of the United States. The new challenge facing the navy, in the view of Prime Minister Adm. Katō Tomosaburō, was to avoid war with the United States at all costs, while building up auxiliary ships. A minority viewpoint, associated with Admirals Katō Kanji and Suetsugu Nobumasa, held that war could arise if Japan's conflict of interests with the United States in China turned into a major political problem, and Washington resorted to diplomatic and military pressure to make Japan submit. Hirohito, as regent, accepted the views of Admiral Katō Tomosaburō and the navy mainstream, who would be called, starting in the early 1930s, the "treaty faction." He approved this change in defense policy in early 1923, but only after securing detailed explanations from his chiefs of staff.

First, on February 17, 1923, he had the chiefs give formal reports to him at his Numazu mansion. The next day he asked for the views of his highest military advisory organ, the Board of Field Marshals and Fleet Admirals. On February 21 Field Marshal Oku Yasukata reported to Hirohito at Numazu, and on the twenty-fifth

Hirohito allowed Prime Minister Katō to view the revised defense policy draft. Finally, on February 28, Hirohito again summoned his two chiefs of staff to Numazu and gave them his approval of the draft. Thus, rather than blindly putting his seal to the revised national defense plan, he approved it "only after he had fully understood it."[57] This insistence on withholding his assent until he had been made fully informed was his standard operating procedure after he became emperor in his own right.

Following the adoption of the 1923 national defense plan, the army began to implement the first of the three personnel reductions that it was to carry out between 1922 and 1924. The navy stopped building capital ships and began scrapping old vessels in order to develop a modern fleet air force and a submarine force. And in 1923 the nonparty cabinet of Prime Minister Katō (who had led the Japanese delegation at the Washington Conference) began withdrawal of Japanese troops from China's Shantung Province. Two years later, in May 1925, Army Minister Ugaki (in the party cabinet of Katō Kōmei) deactivated four divisions and used the resulting savings to begin the modernization and reorganization of the army in order to prepare it for a future "total war." As a result, military spending by the army and navy as a percentage of total annual government expenditures decreased steadily throughout the decade.[58]

These reductions in personnel, armaments, and expenditures went forward amid deep regrets and angry recriminations in the officer corps. The feeling grew that Japan had fallen behind the other Great Powers economically, socially, and politically. Yet both services avoided fundamental institutional reform during the twenties. And because the army retrenched when it was under no foreign pressure to do so, General Ugaki became the object of bitter resentment among middle-echelon officers for yielding to the wishes of fiscally conservative politicians and industrialists.

Meanwhile the erosion of military discipline and morale that had resurfaced during the undeclared war in Siberia against the Bolsheviks (1918–22) continued throughout the 1920s. Unquestioning obedience to orders weakened while incidents of insubordination in the ranks proliferated.[59] The Report Concerning the Thought and Actions of Returning Troops, sent to the army minister in March 1919 by the commander of a garrison division, noted that "due to the rise in general knowledge and social education that enlisted men receive from newspapers and magazines, along with changes in popular thought," they could no longer be counted on "to be blind followers of the orders of their noncommissioned superiors."[60] Two years later, in 1921, Army Minister Tanaka Giichi warned his divisional commanders of the weakening discipline in the lower ranks, where "in recent years .. . . they have become bold and rebellious in their attitudes, and criminal acts have increased, especially cases where men form small groups and act violently."[61]

In response to these warnings the rules and regulations governing military life inside the barracks were revised to encourage discipline based on more rationalistic criteria, while military education began to stress "awareness education."[62] These changes lasted only a few years, however. In 1924 Army Minister Ugaki alerted divisional commanders to give the utmost attention to their soldiers' behavior in view of "the increase in criminal actions by low-ranking officers" and "the influence of [new] social thought."[63] Four years later, at the start of Hirohito's reign, when workers' and peasants' protest movements had intensified, senior officers again sounded the alarm about the number of soldiers coming into barracks with attitudes critical of the imperial system.

These circumstances forced Japan's military leaders to question whether the armed forces should continue to characterize themselves as the forces led by the emperor and his government, or turn to the nation and become the people's military. Army Ministers Tanaka and Ugaki—both supporters of fiscal restraint and cooperation with the political parties—argued the need to reemphasize the army's traditional "founding principles": namely, that all Japanese are soldiers; the emperor directly commands them; they do not interfere in politics or let politicians interfere in military matters; and their mission is to protect the state and spread the foundations of imperial rule. But the army in the early and mid-twenties was divided. Some officers argued over these principles; others said that the military, formed from the masses of the nation, was totally independent of the central government.[64]

Eventually Gen. Araki Sadao, a future army minister and a leading opponent of Ugaki's retrenchment policy, would settle the dispute by advocating the notion of the "emperor's army" (*kōgun*). For Araki the "emperor's army" was a force of workers and peasants for the defense of the nation under the emperor's guidance, rather than a "bourgeois force" for the defense of the ruling establishment.[65] But in the mid-twenties, the army had not yet begun to indoctrinate its troops to Araki's idea.[66]

Toward the end of his regency Hirohito became aware of the army's crisis of institutional identity and of mission. General Nara reported to him on the growth of factional fighting within the military, and General Ugaki lectured at court on the great importance that the army attached to the "independence" of the right of supreme command (*tōsuiken no dokuritsu*). The term *tōsuiken* carried both military and legal connotations and had always been used by military men broadly and vaguely.[67] Although the emperor's power to command the armed forces was already "independent" before the drafting of the Meiji constitution, the constitution never clearly recognized that "independence." It specified only that "[t]he emperor has the supreme command of the army and navy" (Article 11) and "determines the organization and peace standing of the army and navy" (Article 12). Moreover, the first sentence of Article 55, declaring that "[t]he respective ministers of state shall give their advice to the emperor and be responsible for it," left open a possible constitutional ground for "interference" by civilians in the *tōsuiken*.

During the regency the *tōsuiken* became, for the first time, an ideology of organizational self-assertion and a device for the military to keep civil officials and party politicians at bay. Military men still remembered that the Meiji emperor had originally empowered them. They took pride in the way he had exercised his direct command over them, and they credited Japan's victory in 1905 over numerically greater Russian forces to the superiority of their supreme command authority. But not until Yamagata's death in 1922, and the rise, starting in 1924, of governments headed by party cabinets, did they come to revere the very words "supreme command" and to react wrathfully against any politician or civil bureaucrat who interfered in the emperor's exercise thereof.

Forced to confront growing public criticism, declining respect for the imperial institution, and party cabinets that practiced strict fiscal austerity, the army especially bore down hard on the "independence" of the *tōsuiken*. This meant the denial of cabinet participation in matters of military command, and the denial also of the principle of "civilian control" over the armed forces—in effect, a military independent of all civilian authority.[68] The issue of civilian control first arose in October 1920 when Finance Minister Takahashi proposed in a letter to Prime Minister Hara that the Army and Navy General Staff Offices, among other institutions, should be abolished.[69] Thereafter the army began studying how best to defend itself against civilian control.[70] On November 5, 1925, Army Minister Ugaki used a special imperial lecture to influence Hirohito against civilian control.[71] Rather than alter militarism institutionally when popular sentiment might have supported such action, Hirohito, on his own, rejected the notion of civilian control of the military and embraced the theory of the supreme command's "independence" from cabinet interference.

This was definitely not an instance of Hirohito's following tradition, for in the mid-1920s the army and navy were making an entirely new departure by their unqualified emphasis on "independence." According to this new doctrine, not only were the army and navy directly subordinated to the emperor rather than the cabinet, but whatever affected their institutional interests was far more important than the fate of any particular government and its financial constraints, let alone any other organ of state. Military officers influenced by such thinking were bound to hold the civil government in contempt.[72] As political parties continued to gain power, that attitude of contempt made it easy for military officials to believe that party cabinets were to blame for all the social discontent generated by economic hard times, and for the problems Japan was confronting in China. Nevertheless, during the regency, senior military leaders were more interested in strengthening the imperial system and introducing military education into the public school system than in political reform of the state.

In 1925 Army Minister Ugaki secured Hirohito's assent to posting active-duty officers in the nation's middle schools and universities to provide military training. This move was unpopular with professional educators and soon led to clashes between civil and military officials. But in chief aide General Nara's view, it at least "had the good medicinal effect of quieting down the military."[73] It is tempting to imagine that Hirohito viewed the move as a way of igniting student passion to serve the country and himself, while spreading knowledge of how the military worked, but no documents reveal what he really thought about it.

The year 1925 was also noteworthy in terms of Hirohito's own increased military duties, his travels in connection with them, and his slow awakening to serious factional problems in the army. On August 10 he and Prince Takamatsu sailed from Hayama aboard the battleship *Nagato*, accompanied by four destroyers, to Ōdomari port in Karafuto (southern Sakhalin) for a one-day tour of the empire's northernmost colony. Some sixty thousand Japanese settlers greeted him as he came ashore. Traveling by motorcade, he inspected a wood-pulp factory and a school but spent most of his time viewing local flora.[74] When he returned to Tokyo, he went to see his parents in Nikkō. On October 11 he attended the last phase of the grand army maneuvers in the Tōhoku region, but after two weeks in the field "came down with a fever due to constipation" and had to return to Tokyo.[75] Shortly afterward he was promoted to army colonel and navy captain.

By this time Hirohito had become aware of opposition to Army Minister Ugaki within certain army circles. Perhaps Nara told him that the mood of displeasure and indiscipline among young and middle-echelon army officers was a reaction to the antimilitary mood of the times, but also to the ongoing defense cutbacks. He appears to have taken this information in stride. At twenty-four Hirohito lacked the experience to imagine where such unrest could lead and failed to see in it any portent of future trouble for himself. By his support for sending active duty officers into the classrooms, he inadvertently endorsed the egoistic assumption of military officers that they were ideally fitted to be the moral leaders of society. In the process, he sanctioned a major step forward in preparing the nation for the mobilization of all its resources in the event of war.[76]

V

In a time of political fluidity and challenge to established institutions from below, Hirohito accumulated military experience and observed how Makino worked to strengthen the independence of the court from party cabinet control. This was exactly what Makino and Saionji had wanted after Hara's death. Neither of them believed the regent was yet mature or knowledgeable enough to intervene in politics on the basis of his own judgment. Thus Hirohito witnessed but was not consulted on the five cabinet changes that occurred between 1921 and 1926. He also observed the activities of seven regular sessions of the Diet: the forty-fifth to the fifty-second. The first three prime ministers of his regency—Takahashi Korekiyo, Katō Tomosaburō, and Yamamoto Gonbei—had all been chosen by the *genrō*. But in July 1924 the *genrō* Matsukata Masayoshi died, leaving only Saionji Kinmochi to undertake the role of recommending the next prime minister. When the Yamamoto cabinet resigned to take responsibility for the Toranomon incident, Hirohito followed the advice of Prince Saionji (considered a great "constitutionalist") and ordered Kiyoura Keigo, president of the privy council and a sworn enemy of party cabinets, to form the next, non-party, government.

Kiyoura's "transcendental cabinet," based on leaders drawn from the imperially appointed House of Peers, ignored the wishes of the elected House of Representatives. Ultimately it galvanized the parties in the Diet into launching a movement to protect their political rights (termed the "second movement to protect the constitution").[77] Within five months the parties had succeeded in frustrating Kiyoura despite the support he had from the regent. In the general election of May 10, 1924, the "three-faction alliance to protect the constitution" won an overwhelming victory; and on June 7, 1924, Kiyoura resigned. Hirohito thereupon sent an emissary to Saionji, then convalescing in Kyoto, and the latter recommended Katō Kōmei, president of the Kenseikai, to succeed Kiyoura.[78] Kato immediately formed a three-party coalition cabinet, signaling a major triumph of the Taishō democracy movement. However, this victory of party unity over the forces of oligarchy and privilege lasted only until the summer of 1925, after which parliamentary conflict resumed, with the *kokutai* (thus the throne) emerging as a powerful weapon for the parties to use against one another.

Katō's tenure as prime minister spanned the Forty-ninth Imperial Diet, which began on June 28, 1924, to the start of the Fifty-second on December 26, 1926. During these months Hirohito and the court group supported General Ugaki's military reforms, the noninterventionist China policy associated with Foreign Minister Shidehara, and a highly repressive peace preservation bill. In Saionji's view the latter was needed to keep the Left from winning seats in the Diet. Thus a suitable "framework" would be maintained within which "normal constitutional government" could someday develop.[79] Saionji did not worry that the new security law, by emphasizing the sacred nature of the *kokutai* based on the imperial house, would enable political groups to begin using the concept of the unassailable *kokutai* as a political weapon against opponents.[80]

On March 7, 1925, the lower house of the Diet passed the Peace Preservation Law, aimed at making anarchist, communist, or republican ideology unthinkable. It was the first law to include the word *kokutai* since the era of the Council of State, which had ended in 1885.[81] The Diet debate brought out the problem of whether to confine the *kokutai* solely to the throne, the locus of sovereignty, or to tie it tightly to human relationships and the family system so that it might serve as a guide to wider action. The Katō cabinet and the leading political parties took the position that the *kokutai* should be confined only to the emperor's superintendence of the rights of sovereignty and *not* expanded to include the social order and the moral sphere.[82] Thus organizations that stood for reform of the state could be tolerated so long as they professed loyalty to the imperial house. Soon after the new security law went into effect, however, this situation began to change. By late 1926 the *kokutai* had become a destructive weapon in the conflicts of the political parties, just as it had shown signs of becoming during the battle over Hirohito's marriage.

The palace entourage quickly became alarmed at the growing friction among the conservative parties, and the tension between interest groups: elected ones in the Diet, and nonelected ones in the emperor's privy council and House of Peers. The breakdown of cooperation among the parties in the Diet began in the summer of 1925 and deepened during the last year of Hirohito's regency and the first months of his reign as emperor. Wakatsuki Reijirō (prime minister from January 30, 1926, to April 20, 1927) had to endure intense conflicts in the Diet that contributed to making the entire

political situation more unstable and tense than ever. While Hirohito kept fully abreast of these conflicts, he seems not to have
grasped the danger. Professor Mikami's lectures on Meiji's "benevolence" had made him totally committed to demonstrating his own
benevolence: aroused by the behavior of the parties in the Diet, and
influenced by Makino, he became so benevolently active behind the
scenes that the situation quickly worsened.

First, during the Fifty-first Diet, the Seiyūkai raised an issue of
corruption in the ruling party by charging two high Kenseikai officials with involvement in a brothel scandal, and calling on Wakatsuki to resign. Next, following the conclusion of the Fifty-first Diet,
on July 29, 1926, the Seiyūkai brought the *kokutai* issue forward by
circulating to Diet members a photograph showing a young
Japanese woman, Kaneko Fumiko, sitting in a police interrogation
room on the lap of her Korean husband, the political dissident Pak
Yol. The couple had been arrested in September 1923, detained for
nearly three years, and finally convicted for plotting the assassination of the crown prince. On April 5, 1926, eleven days after they
were sentenced to be executed, the Wakatsuki cabinet commuted
their punishments to life imprisonment in the name of the emperor.
Now an anonymously printed pamphlet accompanying the photograph accused Wakatsuki's Kenseikai cabinet and Justice Minister
Egi Tasuku of lacking a sense of the *kokutai* for having commuted
the couple's death sentence.

No mention, of course, was made of the crown prince, though it
was his action behind the scenes that had helped to bring about the
commutation. Hirohito had simply informed Chinda that he felt
the couple had not done anything to justify such harsh punishment.[83]
The rowdy criticism coming from the Diet chamber and the position of the Home Ministry on this affair were so at odds with his
commitment to the ideal of imperial benevolence and compassion
as to rouse him to action. The unintended consequence of Hirohito's personal need to demonstrate proper imperial behavior by

saving Pak Yol and Kaneko Fumiko, however, was to intensify Diet debate on the issue of the *kokutai*.

The politicians Ogawa Heikichi, Mori Tsutomu, and other leaders of the Seiyūkai and Seiyū Hontō parties supported the anti*kokutai* charges against Wakatsuki in the Diet.[84] At a general meeting of Diet members in September 1926, Seiyūkai president Tanaka declared that "This [Pak Yol photograph] problem . . . goes beyond the rights and wrongs of policy. It is against the essence of the *kokutai* concept."[85] In October at a regional meeting of Seiyūkai members, a party leader declared, "We have to say that it sets a bad precedent, destructive of the *kokutai*, for them [the Wakatsuki cabinet] not to discuss the importance of politics. Where the imperial house and the fundamental concept of the *kokutai* are concerned, we cannot go along with a government that deliberately slights this problem."[86]

Thus once the parties had defeated their oligarchic opponents, they could not refrain from using the throne as a political weapon. In Diet discussions on the Peace Preservation Law and on the Pak Yol affair, emotional issues connected with the legitimization of state power and of Japanese national identity figured prominently. In this situation Hirohito and his entourage found it impossible to avoid being drawn into the political conflict.

VI

Searching for some fundamental, enduring concept of identity and purpose to hold to in a Japan that was undergoing very rapid industrial and social change, Japanese in all walks of life debated the meaning of *kokutai* during the regency years. If the presence of the young regent, the rise of Taishō democracy, and the change in the basis and direction of Japanese foreign policy gave meaning to this period, so did the experience of national questioning and redefinition expressed in *kokutai* debates. Neither Hirohito nor Makino or

anyone else in the entourage knew what to make of the slow, continuous erosion of belief in established ideology. To deal with this
challenge, which was most visible on the Left, the court attempted
to strengthen both the orthodox version of *kokutai* ideology and
imperial authority, in preparation for Hirohito's accession to the
throne.

In the regency years *kokutai* discussions flourished among elite
and nonelite groups alike, signaling a remarkable loss of confidence
in the monarchy, a weakening of the ideological ties binding some
segments of the officer corps to the imperial house, and a gradual
unwinding of belief in orthodox *kokutai* thought itself. By the end of
the regency, the very word *kokutai* had become detached from its
dreamlike referents in mythology and was floating freely, ready to
be adapted to the needs of any person or group seeking to redress a
grievance, punish an opponent, aggrandize power, or adjust the
political horizons of the Japanese people.

This is to say that in Japan the 1920s was a time of intense
ideological and cultural conflict: While the government, the
regent, and his court entourage all clung uncritically to an official
version of *kokutai*, reform-minded people in different fields of
endeavor attempted to make Japan's national ideology compatible
with modern scientific thought, as well as with the trend toward
impersonal bureaucratic rule. The political world debated the *kokutai*, and so too did officers in the armed forces, priests in shrines and
temples, and professors in the universities. Invariably these discussions had to address the legitimacy of the emperor's rule and the sort
of moral value that he and the imperial system had, or ought to
have, in Japanese society.[87]

A small minority of liberals sought to reconcile the Imperial
House with the spirit and logic of Taishō democracy. In mainstream
kokutai debates of the period, they envisioned a political system
along the lines of a Western-style parliamentary democracy, and
wanted to preserve the imperial house by simply removing it com-

pletely from politics. Most reform-minded writers, however, aimed only at an updating of the "original story" by which the nation rationalized its political life. Standing against them were traditional conservatives, who sought the foundation of the *kokutai* solely in the imperial bloodline of succession and emphasized the direct personal rule of male emperors and their absolute political authority. Traditionalists were aggrieved by Japan's subordination to the West and wanted nothing to do with democracy. They held that the *kokutai* was immutable, and that those who tried to turn the emperor into a mere symbol were guilty of lèse majesté.

For the ruling elites discussion of the *kokutai* was invariably linked to the problem of controlling dangerous thought. A truly stable moral basis for Japanese politics required universal acceptance of the *kokutai*. But the more the *kokutai* was debated, questioned, and interpreted, the more difficult it became to maintain that common moral foundation. Seeking to resist the democratic current and build up the waning imperial authority, on November 10, 1923, the Kiyoura cabinet adopted a "cultural policy" based on the regent's Imperial Rescript on the Promotion of the National Spirit. Prime Minister Kiyoura thereupon formed, in February 1924, a Central Association of Cultural Bodies in response to Hirohito's call for the improvement of thought and "the awakening of the national spirit." Invited to the association's convocation meeting to discuss a national campaign against "dangerous thoughts" associated with the labor movement and the Left were representatives from Shinto, Christianity, and Buddhism, including the leaders of Nichiren.

The sect, founded in the thirteenth century, was then enjoying its golden age of influence and growth, and two of its leading proseltyzers—Honda Nisshō and Tanaka Chigaku—immediately seized on this "national spirit" campaign to draw up an appeal asking the court to issue a rescript conferring on Nichiren, the founder of their religion, the posthumous title of "Great Teacher Who Established the Truth," so that they could then use it for proseltyzing purposes.[88] After the court granted Nichiren the title, Imperial Household Minister Makino is alleged to have declared: "This decision was due to the emperor's benevolent awareness that the present ideological situation in Japan requires better guidance by sound thought, and especially, firm religious belief."[89]

In fact the imperial house, controlled by Makino and Hirohito, awarded the title because it considered the social situation bad enough to warrant the services of the most passionate enemies of Taishō democracy, the Nichiren believers. When Honda went to the Imperial Household Ministry to receive the award, he met Makino and told him that the Nichiren religion "is the banner of an army on the offensive in the 'ideological warfare' of the present day." Honda also expressed his patriotism and boasted about the Nichiren sect's antidemocratic, anticommunist nature.[90] That Buddhism (or the faith of Nichiren believers, many of whom were upper-echelon military officers and civilian right-wing ideologues) had to be called on to supplement emperor ideology indicates that the official creed was never able to exercise a controlling influence on all groups in Japanese society.[91]

Other forces deeply concerned in these years about guiding the people's thoughts and maintaining the *kokutai* were the military services, activist right-wing political organizations, and the new nationalist "study associations."[92] Baron Hiranuma Kiichirō's National Foundation Society (*Kokuhonsha*), established in 1924, and the Golden Pheasant Academy (*Kinkei Gakuin*), founded by Yasuoka Masahiro in 1927, later became influential in the bureaucratic reform movement of the 1930s. The Golden Pheasant Academy had direct links to the throne via Yasuoka's patron, Makino Nobuaki, who arranged to have Vice Imperial Household Minister Sekiya Teizaburō contribute to its educational and propaganda activities as his personal representative.[93]

Despite these government-supported campaigns to control discussion of the *kokutai*, unofficial attempts to widen the political horizons of the people by reinterpreting the *kokutai* continued. House of Peers and ex–Home Ministry bureaucrat Nagata Shūjirō wrote a book in 1921 defending the throne in terms of its symbolic and social utility.[94] He rejected the orthodox view of the *kokutai* based on mythology and offered the belief that the imperial house could win the hearts and minds of the people provided it became a "palliative force," standing outside politics.[95] Imperial Household Ministry editor and writer Watanabe Ikujirō published *Kōshitsu to shakai mondai* (The Imperial house and social problems) in 1925, a work that sought to encourage young workers and activists in the labor movement to rely on the imperial house to solve the nation's social ills.[96]

The mythological view of the *kokutai* came under attack even in military circles. In 1923 Lt. Hōriki Yūzō published a book on modern thought and military education in which he argued that "the danger to the state lies not in the intrusion of new thought but in the effort to stubbornly maintain the old state thought." The end result, he predicted, "will be to invite the misunderstanding that our *kokutai* no longer harmonizes with new ideas."[97] In 1924, when the Army Officer's Aid Society (*Kaikōsha*) solicited essays for its journal *Kaikōsha kiji* on the subject of educating soldiers as to "why the *kokutai* is so dignified and prestigious," the officer in charge of judging the essay papers, Maj. Gen. Okudaira Toshizō, complained that "young officers do not take this problem too seriously."[98]

Recent evidence suggests a slow, gradual decline, starting around the end of World War I, in the common reference point of the Japanese national identity: the myths that constituted "the fundamental principles of the founding of the country."[99] Many military officers blamed the growing lack of belief in the founding principles on the Taishō democracy movement, just as they blamed "democracy" for the decline of discipline in the ranks, and for the estrangement that had developed between the military and the people.

Studies on the "image of the emperor" in the armed forces during the interwar decades also suggest erosion in Hirohito's "approval rating" on the part of those who were supposed to have been most committed, by occupation, to dying for him.[100] The Imperial Army and Navy provided three years of schooling in cadet schools for a select number of young boys from about the age of fourteen or fifteen. Graduates of these schools usually went on to either the Military or Naval Academy.[101] In his study based on contemporary opinion surveys and post–World War II questionnaires given to thousands of former graduates of the service academies and cadet schools—most of whom served in staff positions in Tokyo during the Asia-Pacific War—Kawano Hitoshi determined that during the period from 1922 to 1931, awareness of "service to the emperor" as a motive for choosing a military career grew progressively weaker.[102] Kawano also found, in both services (but particularly among the naval elite), that over the entire survey period, from 1922 to 1945, a slow decline had occurred in respect for the emperor and in willingness to die for him.[103]

To counter such trends the government resorted to repression, lowering the threshold of tolerance for critical discussions of the *kokutai*. The lèse-majesté case of Inoue Tetsujirō, which arose in the last months of Hirohito's regency and was carefully monitored by Kawai and Makino, shows how the *kokutai*, the "legitimizing" concept of the Japanese state, could be used not only to divide Japanese from one another, but even to overturn power relationships in the sphere of civil society.

In October 1926 the Home Ministry had banned a book by Inoue (a member of the House of Peers) after Vice Grand Chamberlain Kawai Yahachi had read and discussed it with Privy Seal Makino, and after it had incurred the wrath of rightists.[104] Inoue, author of the official commentary on the Imperial Rescript on Education and a conservative critic of Christianity, had analyzed the relationship between the *kokutai* and national morality, seeking rational grounds for legitimizing the imperial institution. His 1925 study criticized "myths" pertaining to the three imperial regalia and the notion of the imperial line "being coeval with heaven and earth." He also attempted to demonstrate that the official theory, based only on the "myth" of the "unbroken line of imperial succession for ages eternal," was not acceptable for a modern nation.[105] According to Inoue the uniqueness of the *kokutai* lay in its "moralistic," "humane," and reformist nature. It was the latter that made "democracy" and "the liberation of the working class" part of the traditional spirit of the imperial house.[106] In staking out these positions, Inoue, after a long career as a political reactionary, was clearly aligning himself with the Taishō democracy current.

Inoue's book had passed the police censors and was being sold in Tokyo bookstores during September 1925. But after coming under attack the following month, it was recalled and banned.[107] A rightwing pamphlet attacking him (and sent to the Home Ministry and the Imperial Household Ministry) claimed that he had committed lèse majesté against the three imperial regalia, and called for an injunction against the sale and distribution of his book.[108] Those who initiated the censorship against Inoue, however, were his former colleagues at Daitō Bunka Gakuin, the college whose president he was. Angered by his firing of professors who opposed his school reforms, they went on strike, shut down the institution, and instigated the venerable "leader of patriots," Tōyama Mitsuru, and his rightist ideologues to compose an anti-Inoue pamphlet with the aim of bringing suit against him for expressing skepticism about Japan's ideology of control.[109] Ultimately both the Inoue lèse-majesté incident and the Seiyūkai's politicization of the Pak Yol affair were signs that the Taishō-era search for some new basis of legitimacy for the imperial state was drawing to an inconclusive end.

Hirohito's entourage monitored the Inoue incident but appears to have paid little attention to the various subcurrents of heterodox, fundamentalist thought (such as the Shinto-based religion known as Ōmotokyō) that ran beneath the main currents of debate and contributed to making Japanese nationalism "ultra." Unable to understand the moral viewpoint of people attracted to the messages of the millenarians, high court officials ignored them in their diaries, though they may have tracked them through police reports. Hirohito probably took no notice of them. If they have a place in his story it is only because they influenced politics in late Taishō and helped prepare the soil for relaunching the monarchy on more nationalistic lines at the start of the Shōwa era.

One particularly influential form of millenarian *kokutai* thought that flourished during the 1920s was expounded for urban, middle-class audiences by nationalist groups within Nichiren Buddhism. Tanaka Chigaku, the spiritual leader of one of these groups, was deeply hostile to Taishō democracy. Tanaka linked Nichiren to the expansion of the Japanese empire and made "clarification of the *kokutai*" his lifelong theme. A man whose fundamentalism was xenophobic but not radical, Tanaka worked to ingratiate himself with the imperial court and to make the Nichiren faith the state religion of Japan. In 1914 he renamed his main proseltyzing organization "Kokuchūkai" (Pillar of the state), wherein "pillar" denoted the *kokutai*, and began to lecture on its "clarification."[110] Like many other conservatives who took democracy as the enemy during the 1920s and 1930s, Tanaka added hatred of Jews to his agenda, and for the remainder of his life often referred to the "Protocols of the Elders of Zion," a czarist police tract that was the main doctrinal source of Japanese—as well as much European—anti-Semitism.[111] Through the activities of the Kokuchūkai, and his own lectures and voluminous writings preaching partnership with the imperial state in a grand project of global unification, Tanaka made an impact on popular sentiments in the Taishō era.

From the ranks of Kokuchūkai emerged military officers whom Hirohito promoted to important positions, such as Ishiwara Kanji, who had joined the organization in April 1920, after graduating from the War College, and occasionally lectured under its auspices.

Ishiwara went on to become a prophet of world war and the chief plotter of the 1931 Manchurian Incident. It was not only fear of the threat to Japan's interests in Manchuria, posed by Nationalist China and the Soviet Union, that drove Ishiwara to act but the millenarianism of Tanaka's Kokuchūkai. Honjo Shigeru, Ishiwara's colleague and commander of the Kwantung Army in Manchuria at the time, was also a Nichiren believer. Kita Ikki had no direct connection with Tanaka's Kokuchūkai, but his family belonged to the Nichiren sect, and his own spiritual development made him a Nichiren believer.[112]

The nationalistic Nichiren movement thus figures as an important catalyst in generating the phenomenon of Japanese ultranationalism. Not only did the sect influence many military men who participated in the politics of the interwar period, it also became part of the context in which the idea of Japan's national mission to unify the world was revived during the course of Hirohito's formal enthronement.

5

THE NEW MONARCHY AND
THE NEW NATIONALISM

Prince Hirohito's regency for his father ended with the Taishō emperor's death in Hayama at 1:25 A.M., December 25, 1926. Hirohito succeeded immediately to the throne. The imperial regalia were transferred to him, and at the age of twenty-five he became, by right of blood, tradition, myth, and history, but also by authority of the constitution, the so-called 124th emperor of Japan.[1] Thus, after a brief rite, Article 1 of the constitution, which stipulated that "[t]he empire of Japan shall be reigned over and governed by a line of emperors unbroken for ages eternal," was fulfilled. Simultaneously, he became commander-in-chief of the armed forces with the authority to issue orders that required no cabinet advice.

The privy council thereupon met and, in accordance with the custom inaugurated at the time of the Restoration, constituted the calendar by the reign of the new emperor. His imperial reign and future posthumous title would be "Shōwa," meaning literally "brightness" and "harmony" or "illustrious peace"—a name duly announced on December 28.

That same day the new emperor issued a series of imperial edicts: to soldiers and sailors; to Prince Kan'in, Prime Minister Wakatsuki and Prince Saionji, and to the nation at large, informing all that he had succeeded and asking for their continued loyalty to the throne. Through these rescripts Hirohito let the nation know that, in his eyes, the military still enjoyed a privileged status, and that the last *genrō*, Prince Saionji, would continue to control the selection of the next prime minister.[2] He promised that he would abide by the constitution, "cultivate inherited virtue and . . . maintain intact the glorious tradition set by our ancestors," starting with "Our imperial grandfather," whose "educational developments" and "military achievements" had "enhanced the grandeur of the empire."

I

Hirohito could now enter more fully into political life, intent on realizing his youthful idea of imperial rule. Firmly supporting but also guiding him was his defining community: seven polished, urbane gentlemen, all much older than himself, who exercised a continuous influence on him through their presence at court. I refer to these seven men, variously, as the "court group," "staff," or palace "entourage." The members of the court group who occupied official bureaucratic positions during the late 1920s were Lord Keeper of the Privy Seal Makino, Grand Chamberlain Chinda, Imperial Household Minister Ichiki, and Chief Military Aide-de-Camp General Nara, as well as three key secretaries who functioned as heads of staff.

On January 22, 1929, one week after Grand Chamberlain Chinda died, Makino brought in retired Admiral Suzuki Kantaro, a supporter of naval arms reductions, as his replacement. Suzuki served for seven years until his resignation in 1936. Meanwhile, Chief Military Aide Nara continued until his retirement in April 1933. Although Nara played the same role with respect to military matters that Makino played with respect to political affairs, he was less of a court man and had less political weight than Makino.[3]

The three chief secretaries were Kawai, Sekiya, and (for a short period) Okabe Nagakage. They helped to resolve disputes within the government, gather information for the emperor, and exert political influence on him. Kawai began his bureaucratic career as a secretary in the House of Peers. In the summer of 1926, he entered the Imperial Household Ministry as Makino's assistant, and the next year took on extra duties, becoming chief steward to the empress and chief secretary to the grand chamberlain. Kawai held all these posts concurrently until 1932, when he became director of the Office of Audits of Imperial Accounts. He was fastidious, hard-working, somber: a man with a keen sense of mission to serve the emperor, whom he held in awe. During this phase of his palace career, Kawai met Hirohito almost daily, maintained close contacts with the heads of the Home Ministry's political police, and kept Hirohito informed of national trends through police sources.

Sekiya started out as a Home Ministry bureaucrat and gained experience in the Japanese colonial empire. In 1921, after a short stint as governor of Shizuoka prefecture, he entered the Imperial Household Ministry as Makino's trusted information collector and messenger. He participated in Hirohito's Western tour and in the arrangements for his marriage in 1924. With his firsthand knowledge of colonial administration, Sekiya aided the court group when the Imperial Household Ministry began investing the profits from the emperor's vast landholdings in shares of stock in colonial enterprises. Like Kawai, Sekiya was methodical, efficient, and diligent— just the sort of bureaucrat Hirohito liked to have around him. He was also as dedicated as Makino was to keeping the court an independent force, free from control by party cabinets.

The wealthy nobleman Viscount Okabe Nagakage, the third member of the court group, played the role of liaison between court and government ministries. In February 1929 Okabe became chief secretary to Makino, concurrently holding the position of vice grand master of ceremonies. Of higher rank and social status than either Kawai or Sekiya, Okabe was both more relaxed in his personal attitude toward the emperor, and also more complacent in his assessment of political problems. He was also much less inclined to the radical right than either Makino or Sekiya.

Interacting with these palace officials, and a part of the court milieu even though situated outside the palace, were the special guardians of the throne. Foremost among them was the venerable last *genrō*, Saionji Kinmochi. Although Saionji's seasoned judgment and experience carried weight, and he sometimes gave important direction to Hirohito and the court group, historians have exaggerated his influence on the politics of the late 1920s and early 1930s. Born in 1849 of an ancient family of civil nobles (*kuge*) of the second rank, Saionji enjoyed a special relationship with the palace bureaucrats, who drew on his advice even though he was seldom in their company.[4] He was also the staunch defender of the economic interests of the Sumitomo *zaibatsu*, which was headed by his younger brother, Baron Sumitomo Kichizaemon.[5]

During the years Makino served as imperial household minister, Saionji executed by proxy the emperor's prerogative of recommending the successor to a prime minister. Thereafter, until May 1932, when Hirohito effectively deprived him of that control, Saionji still had influence on each succession of regime. He could also speak out on the appointment of members to the court group.[6] From 1927 onward, however, whenever the court group had completed its deliberations to select a new prime minister, they would send a messenger to the aged Saionji in Kyoto, Odawara, Yozu, or wherever else he happened to be residing. Saionji would sanction their decision, then resume his essentially nonpolitical life, far removed from the daily pressures of the court. Saionji listened well, advised carefully, but stirred himself to act personally only in extreme situations, such as assassinations and mutinies.[7] Whenever he did act, however, his efforts were disastrous for the causes of liberalism and party government in Japan.

Nevertheless, of the entire court group and those in its milieu, Saionji alone wanted to move to a multiparty system of politics in which the two main conservative groups—the Seiyūkai and Ken-seikai (later Minseitō), representing the interests of big landlords and big business—would control the Diet, support the orthodox view of the *kokutai*, and always remain totally dependent on the will of Emperor Hirohito rather than the confidence of the Diet.[8]

In 1929, when party cabinets were nearing the height of their power, a sharp division emerged between Saionji and the court group (including the emperor). Saionji shared with Makino a basic ignorance of the workings of modern political parties and an aversion to the principle of parliamentarism. But where Makino and the palace entourage believed that difficult political problems could be resolved only by the emperor's intervention, Saionji wanted the emperor to avoid political judgments.[9] Saionji also looked askance at Makino's radical rightist sympathies. Because Saionji stood outside the process of decision making at court during this and later periods, Makino and the other members of the entourage often had to persuade him to go along. Usually Saionji would swallow his doubts and assent to their decisions.

Finally three other special guardians of the throne and members of the court milieu by reason of aristocratic birth were Baron Harada Kumao, Prince Konoe Fumimaro, and Marquis Kido Kōichi, who enters the picture in 1930 and immediately begins playing an active role. They shared in common the belief, eschewed by Saionji, that the authority of the emperor should be used to solve political problems.

Harada spent two years as a special official of the Imperial Household Ministry before becoming, in 1924, the private secretary of Prime Minister Katō Kōmei. Upon resigning his government position in the summer of 1926, Harada joined the staff of the Sumitomo Company but immediately took leave to become Saionji's personal secretary, a position he held until Saionji's death in November 1940.[10] As Saionji's information collector, messenger, and "brain," Harada was the go-between and adjuster of views of

Saionji in Kyoto and Makino in Kamakura. He was, at the same time, a highly respected information gatherer and analyst of political trends for the three chief secretaries—Kawai, Sekiya, and Okabe—as well as for his close personal friends, Prince Konoe and Marquis Kido.

Konoe, born in 1891, was a true aristocrat as opposed to Harada and Kido, whose hereditary statuses were products of the Meiji restoration. In early Shōwa, Konoe was *the* rising star among young conservative and radical-right members of the House of Peers, a body he was soon to lead, first as vice president in 1931, then as president in 1933. His ideological vision of an Asian and Chinese economy dominated by Japan, and his view that Japan's mission was to save Asia from European encroachment, had wide appeal. Konoe was on the closest personal terms with the key members of every court group from the moment he made his debut on the political stage in 1921 until his death by suicide in December 1945.[11]

Konoe had been a member of the Japanese delegation at the Versailles Peace Conference. What he saw there and in travels through early postwar Europe and the United States confirmed his belief that Japan should support the spirit of the League of Nations and develop Asia in cooperation with the other Great Powers. But Versailles had also led him to reject what he called "the Anglo-American standard of pacifism." Complicating his thought, and making his belief in the international order crafted at Washington highly unstable, were very strong elements of racism and pan-Asianism. Basically Konoe believed that, by reasons of race, history, and geography, Japan was perfectly entitled to aggrandize Chinese territory to meet the needs of its own exploding surplus population.

At the start of Hirohito's reign, Konoe was a member of the leading faction in the House of Peers and president of the East Asia Common Culture Society (Tōa Dōbunkai), founded by his father. He chafed at the Washington treaty order that allowed the United States and Britain to shut out Japanese immigrants from their territories yet distrusted Japan's intentions on the Chinese continent. This particular feature of his thought separated him from Hirohito, who still accepted the limitations of the Washington system. Yet, in other respects, Konoe stood on common political ground with the palace "moderates." The latter may not have shared Konoe's dream of joining with China against the white races, but they were all virulently anticommunist in outlook and shared with Konoe the thought that it was only natural for China to sacrifice itself for the sake of Japan's social and industrial needs.[12] Last, Konoe (and the court group as a whole) worried about how to protect the essentially unstable monarchy in a postmonarchic world. The *kokutai* had to survive; his task was to help the emperor preserve it while using his authority to effect needed reform.

Kido Kōichi, born in 1889 and thus, like Konoe, a member of the third and least secure generation of the hereditary aristocracy, was impelled by fear that the impact of the Russian revolution and the tide of Taishō democracy would sweep away his privileged class. To counter such trends he had studied the writings of Russian socialists and nobles who had groped for ways to survive the Bolshevik challenge. He had also joined with fellow aristocrats Okabe Nagakage and Arima Yoriyasu to establish and manage a night school for educating workers; and he had pushed for reform of the Peers' School.[13] In the course of these activities Kido and other reform-minded peers formed the Jūichikai, a discussion group whose members aspired to take the lead in promoting political and social change. By the late 1920s, however, Kido's fears of left-wing revolution had ebbed, and his attention had turned to governmental reform.

Kido had state reform on his mind when he moved from the Ministry of Commerce and Industry to become Makino's chief secretary in late 1930. He quickly proved an indispensable adviser and information collector (through the Jūichikai) during the last two years of party cabinets, 1930–32. Working closely with Harada

Kumao, Kido rather than Makino took the initiative in restructuring the court's modus operandi after the rise of the military. Like Konoe he was essentially a 1930s-style "renovationist," never a traditionalist. In 1937, when Konoe formed his first cabinet, Kido left the court to serve as Konoe's education minister and adviser. In the last stage of Kido's political career, 1940–45, he returned to the palace and became Hirohito's most important political adviser, charged with the duty of helping to select the next prime minister. Kido worked tirelessly to forge a consensus between the court and the military, and was instrumental in effecting the court-military alliance that made possible Japan's declaration of war against the United States and Britain.[14]

From the beginning of the Shōwa era, Hirohito's small, highly cosmopolitan court group advised and assisted him entirely outside the constitution. It was an enclave of privilege and the nucleus of the Japanese power elite, composed of men from both the traditional ruling stratum and newly privileged and enriched groups from Meiji. Situated at the apex of the pyramid of class, power, and wealth in Japanese society, the court group represented the interests of all the ruling elites of imperial Japan, including the military. The court group cannot be understood, however, if it is set only in stark contrast to the military—as seen by Western observers at the time, and conventional academic historians since. Nor can it be understood if discussed apart from the imperial family, particularly Hirohito's younger brothers, who often interacted closely with those in the court milieu.

The different members of the court group collected, processed, and conveyed to Hirohito political data they had gathered from many quarters, including the British and American Embassies. The emperor had sole possession of their information plus vast amounts of political and military intelligence furnished by government and military officials who reported directly to him, orally or in writing. As head of the imperial family (kōzoku), Hirohito also received secret reports on the political activities of his brother, Prince Chichibu, from Chichibu's steward. Like a silent spider positioned at the center of a wide, multisided web, Hirohito spread his filaments into every organ of state and the army and navy, absorbing—and remembering—information provided by others.

His staff could spin the web and feed him their information precisely because the advisory organs of the imperial state—the cabinet, the Diet, the privy council, the Army and Navy General Staffs, and the bureaucracy—connected directly to the emperor yet were separate and independent of one another. In their own eyes ministers of state and chiefs of staff believed themselves to be directly subordinate to the emperor; in Hirohito's eyes, as Shimizu Tōru never tired of reminding him, they were all on the same level as far as their authority was concerned, regardless of their different constitutional status.

The membership of the court group changed over time, as did their political ideas, special characteristics, and operating strategy vis-à-vis the other forces in the Japanese political structure. Yet on political issues in all periods they were careful not to get ahead of the emperor. Usually, without cueing from his privy seal, Hirohito took the initiative in spurring his entourage to diffuse his intentions (the "imperial will") into the political process and, when necessary, to focus his will on any advisory organ or its representative. In short Hirohito "commanded" his court group, which had no power to act except because it was his conduit; and at his direction it acted by disseminating counsel and advice, which, as it was known to be on his behalf, exerted powerful influence on ministers and ministries.

From 1927 onward the court group struggled to place the monarchy within a new ideological framework and, at the same time, find a way to break through the constraints on the emperor's powers that had developed over the nearly fifteen years of the Taishō emperor's debility. To that end they perpetuated the convenient fiction of the emperor as a "constitutional monarch." In their own eyes, of course, "constitutional monarchy" was never a device for restricting the emperor's formidable powers, as it is in the West. It merely provided a protective facade behind which his powers could be freely exercised and even expanded as the situation required, while he remained nonaccountable.[15] The main objectives of the court group at the start of the new Shōwa era were to help Hirohito exercise real supervision; to act as an electoral college, helping him to choose a prime minister; and to ensure that his purposes were incorporated into decisions of the cabinets. In their reasoning the idea of "the normal course of constitutional politics" required that the will of the cabinet reflect the young emperor's will.

This convergence of wills was to be achieved through a process of constant informal reporting (*naisō*) by the prime minister, by other cabinet ministers, and by the military, coupled with questioning by the emperor (*gokamon*) before any cabinet decision could ever be formally presented to him. This process of maneuvering behind the scenes to obtain the emperor's consent was how Hirohito effected his purposes in policy making, and in the appointment and promotion of high-level military personnel. It was also how the court group always understood the meaning of the *kokutai*: For them the *kokutai* was a political system that allowed the emperor to use his power to rule, never merely to reign.[16]

However, in providing direct imperial rule in the age of mass suffrage, with the prime minister as the emperor's most important adviser, the court group had to be vigilant lest the throne be pulled down into partisan controversy. In the words of Privy Seal Makino, the cardinal rule whenever a political problem arose was that "the matter should never implicate or cause harm to the emperor" (*heika ni rui o oyobosazaru koto o daiichini*).[17] Thus the chief task of the court group from the beginning of Shōwa was to ensure that the party cabinets accepted both Hirohito's supervisory role and the need to shield him from either credit or blame for his actions in that role.

Essentially the court group reasoned that with a real ruler in the

Meiji mold now on the throne, the proper way to govern was for the prime minister to inform himself of the emperor's intention, through prior and full consultation with him on an informal basis (that is, *naisō*), and then to act to realize the emperor's wishes. In practice this meant that the court group had to develop situations and networks by which the emperor could influence, and implicitly give his sanction to, a solution, a problem, a policy, or a bill in the Diet before any of his constitutional advisers (his ministers) ever got around to presenting the matter to him in a formal report. That required keeping politics out of the public view. The more the emperor involved himself in civil and military decision making, the more deeply involved he and his closest aides became in deception, and the greater their stake in not ever admitting the truth.

Under the Shōwa emperor, therefore, the operating conditions for correct governance required extreme secrecy and constant simulation, dissimulation, indirection, and conniving on the part of high palace officials; unity, restraint, and profound humility on the part of ministers of state and heads of the emperor's advisory organs, some of whom were deeply antagonistic and suspicious toward one another; and the embrace by the emperor of the dual morality that princes and politicians have practiced from time immemorial. For this convoluted approach to work, the prime minister had to be willing to consult constantly with the emperor and heed his intentions, even when they might not coincide with his own—but as the living god was the emperor, and vice versa, that was more than appropriate.

II

The Fifty-second Imperial Diet, which had adjourned following Emperor Taishō's death, had reconvened on January 18, 1927. Hirohito and his entourage lost no time in trying to influence political trends and make the political world aware of his presence.

First, on January 19, 1927, the idea of a fourth national holiday was proposed in the House of Peers as if it had originated there rather than in the court. Two days earlier, however, Privy Seal Makino's secretary, Kawai, had visited Prince Konoe and suggested that both houses of the Diet consider designating a holiday to commemorate the great virtues of the Meiji emperor.[18] A short time later, the Diet approved a bill establishing November 3 as Meiji's holiday (*Meiji setsu*), and the sanctioning announcement was made by imperial ordinance on March 3.

The tenth anniversary of Meiji's death, July 30, 1922, had passed relatively unnoticed by the court and the public, except for visits by the regent to Kyoto and the Momoyama mausoleums.[19] Why now the new holiday? Because Hirohito's enthronement was in the offing, and his entourage needed every device it could muster to invest him with greater charisma and blot out Taishō's image. Hirohito could hardly be sent back in time to participate in great victories that had been won when he had been only four years of age. But Meiji could be transported, via the new holiday, and the appropriate fanfare, to a new generation and era, and Hirohito thereby made to shine brighter, if only by reflected radiance.

Due to the official mourning for Taishō, the first national celebration of Meiji's birthday could not begin until the following year. The honoring of Meiji therefore would occur during the enthronement and deification of his grandson, the noncharismatic Hirohito, whom the press was describing already as the new "incarnation of Emperor Meiji."[20] Before the year of mourning for Taishō had even ended, the public had grown accustomed to thinking of the preenthronement emperor as the new Meiji, and as the grandson who would perfect his imperial legacy.[21]

Later, intending to remind the young emperor of the toil rice cultivation required, and so identify him in the public mind with the plight of rice farmers in a period of agricultural depression, Kawai invented a new court ritual. He suggested that Hirohito cultivate rice within the palace precincts. Hirohito agreed and a field was prepared inside the Akasaka Palace grounds for this purpose. On June 14, 1927, Hirohito received rice plants from different regions of the country and staged his very first rice-planting ritual. Later, after his enthronement, he moved his residence to the palace, and seventy and eighty *tsubo* (280 and 320 square yards) of dry and wet field, respectively, were reclaimed for the purpose of ceremonial rice planting. A small mulberry grove beyond the wet fields was also prepared for Empress Nagako to engage in sericulture, thereby identifying her with Japan's most important export commodity, silk.[22]

The second series of political interventions by Hirohito and the court group concerned Prime Minister Wakatsuki's management of the Diet. In early 1927 leaders of the Seiyūkai and Seiyū Hontō renewed their attack on the Wakatsuki cabinet over the issues of the Osaka brothel scandal and the Pak Yol affair. Just before their formal motion of no confidence in the government came up for debate, however, Prime Minister Wakatsuki announced a three-day adjournment. He then met secretly with Tanaka of the Seiyūkai and Tokonami of the Seiyū Hontō and requested that political fighting stop out of consideration for the beginning of the new emperor's reign.

This compromise was brokered by the leaders of the main faction in the House of Peers. Behind it stood Lord Keeper of the Privy Seal Makino and Imperial Household Minister Ichiki Kitokurō,who deplored the possible dissolution of the Diet and the holding of elections right at the start of a new imperial reign. They wanted the parties to show restraint out of consideration for the new emperor. Makino and Ichiki had been instructing Wakatsuki on political matters ever since he became prime minister. They now told him to meet with the leaders of the opposition and resolve any further political strife in the Diet. The no-confidence motion should be withdrawn and the budget passed.[23] In this way they could postpone the first democratic election to be held under the recently enacted universal manhood suffrage law—an election that the parties expected to be very costly.

When the lower house reconvened after Wakatsuki's sudden adjournment, the court group prevailed. The main opposition parties withdrew their no-confidence bill, prompting a nonaffiliated member of the Diet to charge that the conference of the three party leaders had been an attempt to stifle free debate. Although political fighting in the Diet based on problems of the *kokutai* abated temporarily, the parties now understood that they could make more political capital at the expense of their opponents by "protecting the *kokutai*" than by "protecting the Meiji constitution."

Three months later, on April 17, 1927, the Wakatsuki cabinet collapsed: overthrown by its opponents in the privy council rather than in the Diet. Wakatsuki's fall was brought about by the opposition of Privy Councillors Itō Miyoji and Hiranuma Kiichirō to the moderate China policy of Foreign Minister Shidehara, who had refused to send Japanese troops to China after earlier Chinese provocations against Japanese living in the treaty port settlements. For Emperor Hirohito and the court group, Wakatsuki's resignation furnished another opportunity to play a determining role. Kawai, Chinda, Ichiki, and Makino conferred among themselves and then with Hirohito, and decided that Gen. Tanaka Giichi, president of the largest party in the Diet, should form the next cabinet. Having established a consensus among themselves, they notified *genrō* Saionji, who immediately agreed to their choice. Thereafter, until the assassination of Inukai Tsuyoshi, five years later, Japanese prime ministers were chosen not by the last *genrō* but by a system of consultations centering on the lord keeper of the privy seal, with Saionji ratifying the choice of Hirohito and the court group after the fact.

Tanaka formed his cabinet on April 20, 1927—the same day that Gen. Chiang Kai-shek established his Nationalist (Kuomintang) government in Nanking (now Nanjing) and renewed his Northern Expedition to unify China. Japanese foreign policy thenceforth took a decidedly more interventionist turn, as the intensification of the Chinese civil war increased the possibilities for dispatching troops to protect Japanese lives and property in China. The court group, having played the major role in the selection of General Tanaka as prime minister, now tried to impose its own political agenda and goals onto those of the new constitutional government.

Tanaka was the first prime minister to discover that a strong-willed emperor capable of playing a determining role in politics could make life absolutely miserable for the leader of a political party. Almost from the moment Tanaka became prime minister, Hirohito and the court group took a keen interest in his performance and soon found themselves at odds with most of his policies. They disapproved of the way the Seiyūkai Party had expanded its power through an aggressive policy of personnel appointments. With his Confucian and *bushidō* education, Hirohito wanted officials appointed solely on the basis of ability, not political criteria or affiliation.

On June 15, 1927, Hirohito summoned Makino to complain about Tanaka's personnel policies. Makino also felt that the political parties—the Seiyūkai in particular—were slighting the young emperor. He promised to speak to Tanaka about it. Disturbed that the parties were using the *kokutai* as a political tool, and ashamed of their behavior on the floor of the Diet, Makino believed that the emperor's interest in politics was "the greatest blessing for the state and the imperial house at a time of difficulty in national affairs." He saw nothing wrong in a politically active emperor, and credited that "achievement" to "our imperial entourage, which has contributed to cultivating his imperial virtues."[24]

Tanaka had difficulty understanding why Hirohito was displeased with his handling of personnel appointments. After all, by placing as many Seiyūkai Party members as possible in bureaucratic posts, he was merely following a traditional practice in "normal constitutional government," one that went back to Hara Kei. "We did not increase the number of officials we replaced in a short period of time as compared with what the practice was before," he reportedly told Hirohito in audience in the summer of 1927.[25] But Tanaka's remark merely irritated Hirohito, who again ordered that the prime minister be set straight.

III

Meanwhile the attention of Hirohito and the court group was focusing increasingly on his forthcoming enthronement. The declaration of national mourning for Taishō and the staging of the enthronement rituals for Hirohito were conducted in accordance with the Shinto principle of the unity of politics and religion, and a separate tradition of court law, which had priority over the constitution. The rites and rituals of this key moment did not derive from the constitution or from legislation by parliament. The role of the Imperial Diet in these activities was only to vote the funds needed.

The Shōwa enthronement rituals, festivities, and national unity banquets were planned and staged under recession conditions. Nevertheless, to finance these activities at different levels of government, the Fifty-fifth Imperial Diet unanimously passed a budget that, in U.S. dollar terms at that time, amounted to $7,360,000. In cost, scale, amount of advance preparation, numbers of participants, and numbers of policemen assigned to supervise them, these events outshone all previous enthronements.[26] But as the times were not considered "normal"—Hirohito had recently been the regent and Taishō had been largely hidden from the public—the oligarchic elites who decided these matters felt it necessary to skip over the vacuum of Taishō and link Hirohito directly to Meiji. This required rearticulating all the myths about the monarchy. After all, tradition and mythology helped to hold society together, despite its underlying conflicts.

Technology was also harnessed to the glorification of the monarchy. In 1928, when the enthronement year began, Japan had entered the age of mass advertising and mass consumer culture. For nearly three years, regular nationwide radio broadcasts had been affecting public opinion and values.[27]

Symbolically the enthronement was an exercise of power taking place at a time of renewed Japanese military activities on the Asian continent, and of increased reliance by the state on repression to prop up the fragile monarchy. Hence its total impact may best be understood when it is related to the rise of political reaction in Japan. Such reaction was evidenced by the Tanaka cabinet's repeated dispatch of troops to China's Shantung Province, and the increase, from 1928 onward, in the number of officials specializing in thought control.

After revision of the Peace Preservation Law, the government appointed in all prefectures "thought procurators" and "special higher police." The armed forces established their own "military thought police," and special Home Ministry police officials were assigned to work full-time on uncovering anti-*kokutai* "conspiracies" being plotted by communists and other radicals. As a result, from 1928 onward the imperial state assumed a sterner attitude toward its critics. First, communists and leaders of the sectarian Shinto organizations of Ōmotokyō and Tenrikyō, which refused to recognize Amaterasu Ōmikami as a superior deity, were subjected to increased police surveillance and repression; later the surveillance was extended to liberal intellectuals in journalism and the universities.[28] Thus the process of manufacturing a new emperor through ritual and propaganda went hand in hand with a major expansion and dispersion of the thought-control apparatus.

A Grand Ceremonies Commission, with Prince Kan'in as president and Prince Konoe as director, took charge of staging the Shōwa enthronement rituals. Serving on the commission were Chief Cabinet Secretary Hatoyama Ichirō, Imperial Household Ministry officials Sekiya and Kawai, various vice ministers, and the governor of Kyoto, where the ceremonies were to be held.[29] The

commission's task was to ensure that all the events and commemorative projects of the enthronement were carefully scripted so as to
reflect the themes of loyalty and service to the new emperor.[30] Its
main accomplishments, therefore, would be largely organizational
and ideological. Checking the process of monarchical demystifica-
tion and decline, keeping everything controlled that could be controlled, the commissioners reduced spontaneity to a minimum
while enhancing, so far as it could be enhanced, Hirohito's distinctively uncharismatic personality. They also instilled the feeling that
Japan was a "divine land" in which the monarch who became one
with the gods at the same time bonded with his subjects as their collective "parent."

Assisting the commission in this remaking of the monarchy
were the still new and relatively independent mass media, mainly
radio and newspapers, which rose to the occasion by instructing the
nation on the meaning of the unfamiliar rites and celebrations that
were planned. Japanese newspapers were expanding their circula-
tion and becoming national rather than local and regional. Their
reporters were anxious to ingratiate themselves with the central
bureaucracy. So, too, were radio announcers, who, in reporting on
the pageantry at Kyoto, were dependent on scripts prepared in
advance by the Imperial Household Ministry.[31]

For a whole year, press and radio reported the ceremonies and
rituals on a daily basis, day and night, throughout the home islands
and in the Japanese colonies, as Hirohito and his entourage skillfully implemented the real lessons they had learned from King
George V—lessons not about the constraints of constitutionalism
but the importance of state spectacle and ritual in enhancing the
monarch's dignity and authority.[32] When it was all over, the commission gave the print media unqualified praise for having acted as
the new holy scripture of the Japanese state.[33] Compliance with the
wishes of the state, abject submissiveness to the fashions of the
time—these were roles the modern Japanese press would continue

to play. Censoring itself whenever it was not censored by authority, the press never became a free voice of conscience for the Japanese nation.

The enthronement rituals and ceremonies, from their start in January to their climax in early December 1928, helped to manufacture a new imperial image for the young emperor. The rituals began with Hirohito's dispatch of emissaries to the mausoleums of his four predecessors, and that of Emperor Jimmu, notifying the imperial spirits of his forthcoming enthronement. At the same time the year-long schedule of ceremonial events at the three permanent shrines within the palace compound was made public. Next, on February 5, the emperor participated in rituals that chose by divination the fields where rice was to be grown to present to the sun goddess, Amaterasu Ōmikami. Through spring, summer, and fall the pace of events quickened. Using the press, radio, and public lectures, government officials and famous intellectuals instructed the nation in the revived themes of emperor ideology, which they often presented in explicit contrast to heterodox sentiments, such as communism and anarchism, that ran counter to official *kokutai* thought.[34]

The enthronement culminated during the months of November and December 1928. In November, in towns and cities in every prefecture and metropolitan district throughout the empire, hundreds of thousands of people took part in banquets and award ceremonies; millions of schoolchildren joined in flag parades and lantern festivals. Before the year ended the throne had dispensed millions of yen as an expression of imperial benevolence for the nation's poor, liberally awarded medals, granted titles, and bestowed posthumous decorations on historical figures from the thirteenth, fourteenth, and nineteenth centuries who were noted for loyalty to the throne.[35] Also in the name of the emperor, the government reduced the sentences of 32,968 criminals, including the assassin of Hara Kei; commuted the punishments of 26,684 prisoners in the colonies; and granted special amnesty to another 16,878 prisoners.[36]

Municipal and prefectural authorities, town and village governments initiated construction projects at all levels that gave unprecedented numbers of ordinary people the chance to participate actively in ushering in the new monarchical era.

For a typical example, in colonial Karafuto almost the entire population of more than 295,000 (including approximately two thousand Ainu and other aborigines) was mobilized to participate in the enthronement.[37] When the ceremonies ended, the Karafuto colonial government followed up by undertaking more than five hundred memorial projects, ranging from the construction of public parks and agricultural experimental farms to the building of "a youth hall, sacred storage places for safekeeping the emperor's picture, monuments for Japan's war dead, and government office buildings."[38]

Activities similar to those in Karafuto went on in a much more restrained manner in colonial Korea, where Governor-General Saitō Makoto had tolerated the growth of an indigenous Korean press as part of Japan's 1920s "cultural policy." The colonial government began the month with a luncheon banquet at the Kyongbok Palace on Meiji Day, November 3. Schoolchildren participated in flag-waving (Japanese, of course) and lantern processions. Accolades of the emperor were generously bestowed; more than eight hundred elderly men received gifts from the emperor; a banquet for designated collaborators was hosted at the Korean monarch's royal shrine; a contingent of dancers was enlisted from Seoul's Chinese community to perform in street processions. The newly established Keijō (Seoul) Broadcasting Company covered the November ceremonies and rituals of accession in the prescribed manner. So too did the colonial government's official Korean-language newspaper, which had more than twenty-two thousand subscribers or approximately 22 percent of the colony's three major dailies.[39]

The Korean public at large, however, was far more influenced by the colony's three other Korean newspapers, which countered the official coverage with strikingly nationalist articles. They denied space to the imperial pageantry and brazenly put down the imperial celebrations by running scores of articles that called attention to the increased police repression and preemptive arrests of Koreans. On November 9, eve of Hirohito's deification ceremony, *Tong'a ilbo* (Oriental daily) reminded its readers of Korea's own uniqueness by publishing an article on the foundation myth of Tan'gun, progenitor deity of the Korean race and so counterpart to Amaterasu Ōmikami. Also, to make sure its readers did not forget, the newspaper carried notices on "Han'gul Day," set aside to honor the invention of characters for writing the Korean language.

Thus the magnificent imperial pageantry and rituals of 1928 evoked sharply different nationalist responses, and in Korea revealed the deep tensions that beset the empire. But insofar as vast segments of the Japanese population played a role in these celebratory events and commemorative public projects, and the nation as a whole tuned in to radio descriptions of the rituals at their climax in November, as well as the military reviews of early December, these practices may have shored up waning ideological beliefs and made people more supportive of the state.

IV

The formal ceremonies (termed *sokui no rei*) of ascending to the throne, based on the myth of Amaterasu Ōmikami, began with an imperial procession from Tokyo to Kyoto on November 6, 1928, and reached a ritual climax in Kyoto four days later, when Hirohito took possession of all three sacred imperial regalia and reported his temporal accession to the spirits of his ancestors. In an afternoon ceremony on November 10 before an audience of about 2,700 civil and military officials and Diet members, Hirohito read aloud the following words to the people of Japan:

Domestically I sincerely wish to bring harmony to the people by kindheartedly guiding them to the good, thus promoting the further prosperity of the country. Externally I sincerely wish to maintain eternal world peace and advance goodwill among nations through diplomacy, thus contributing to the welfare of humanity. You, our subjects, join cooperatively with one another, put aside self-interest, and take on service to the public, thereby allowing me to nurture the great legacy of my divine ancestors and respond to the spirit of their benevolence.[40]

After completion of the *sokui no rei*, sacred dances were performed before the emperor's portable shrine. Two days later, on the night of November 14–15, a "great food-offering ceremony" (*daijōsai*) was held in Kyoto, followed by two consecutive days of banquets.[41]

The *daijōsai*, the most important and dramatic of the enthronement events, marked the emperor's deification and confirmed his "descent from the gods." The idea of the rulers' sacred divinity lay at the core of emperor ideology as it had in Meiji, and had proved itself to be necessary to the survival of emperor ideology into the middle of the twentieth century. Based on an imperial ordinance of 1909, the *daijōsai* ceremony departed from the ancient form of that religious rite by its heavy emphasis on the myth of the emperor's descent from heaven and by its connection with his postenthronement ritual visits to the Grand Shrine of Ise and to the mausoleums of Emperor Jimmu and four previous emperors of the late nineteenth and early twentieth centuries.[42]

The *daijōsai* started on the night of November 14 and lasted into the early morning hours of the fifteenth. First the official guests seated themselves inside special structures near the compound where the *daijōsai* was to be performed, while honor guards in ceremonial costume took up their places. Next the Shōwa emperor, wearing ritual garments of raw white silk and attended by court ladies and a chef, entered a specially constructed compound, containing three main wooden structures, wherein he reinacted symbolically the descent from the "plain of high heaven" in Shinto mythology. After purifying himself for the gods in the first chamber, he and his attendants passed through a hallway into two thatched huts in succession, called the *yukiden* and *sukiden*. Placed within these innermost chambers were rectangular matted beds—the *shinza* and *gyoza*—on which he performed secret rites. The *shinza* was believed to embody the spirit of the sun goddess, Amaterasu Ōmikami. By reclining on it in a fetal position, wrapped in a quilt, the emperor, according to Shinto theology, united with her spirit, thereby consummating his symbolic "marriage" to his progenitor deity. Afterward, sitting on the *gyoza* facing Amaterasu Ōmikami, he made the food offerings to her and other deities that completed the process of his becoming a living god or "manifest deity (*arahitogami*)."

So, staged behind a thick veil of secrecy in the dark of night, the rituals of the *daijōsai* climaxed in Hirohito's deification, giving him, it was claimed, an attribute that, as emperor, he had lacked until that moment.[43] Members of the imperial family and invited guests were unable to watch the ceremony. The press cautioned the general public, which had also been prevented from scrutinizing the "awe-inspiring mystery," to suspend rational judgment about the *shinza*.[44] On the other hand, the press did not suggest that judgment should be suspended about the amount of money being spent on the enthronement while the nation was in a depression, for that would have been an act of lèse-majesté. At least a few critical placards were made, saying, "Oppose the succession ceremonies! Celebrate the anniversary of the revolution!" There is also a line in a collection of "proletarian" *tanka* poems published in honor of May Day, 1929, that reads: "The big hoopla succession ceremonies are costing $7,360,000! They will break the backs of the poor!"[45]

On December 2, 1928, two weeks after acquiring his god-persona, Hirohito traveled to the Yoyogi Parade Ground in Tokyo to review the biggest display of army and air might in Japanese history. For hours he watched from an elevated stand as more than 35,000 troops, including 4,500 cavalry, marched past in a chilly drizzle.[46] Two days later he went on to Yokohama for a Grand Review of the Fleet. A total of thirty-nine submarines and 208 ships, including the giant aircraft carriers *Kaga* and *Akagi*, and about 45,000 crewmen took part in this final event, along with 25,000 members of the Imperial Reservists Association, and thousands of minor dignitaries from around the country. Hundreds of thousands of ordinary Japanese formed the crowd of spectators in Yokohama. Millions listened to running radio commentary of how the supreme commander reviewed his fleet while 130 naval aircraft flew over the harbor in slow, droning battle formation.

These two huge displays of military power marked the real completion of Hirohito's enthronement.[47] Both were broadcast from Tokyo and replayed throughout Japan by a special nationwide radio hookup, so that the people could hear the "boom of the imperial salute guns, the strains of the national anthem, the tread of the soldiers, the clatter of the cavalry, and the hum of airplane propellers."[48]

In his splendid history of the enthronement, Nakajima Michio noted that the grand military reviews were designed to show the people that their sovereign had now acquired all the attributes of his position and become a complete emperor. They emphasized that his abstract, symbolic identity as the nation's highest religious authority was, in practice, always combined with his concrete image as supreme military commander. Two images, two concepts—but one perception: one emperor performing two distinct but combined roles of equal gravity.

V

So began what became an official and accelerating emperor cult. It worked to enhance the personal image of a ruler who physically was not imposing, and whose demeanor was not godlike, though very controlled. It worked also to strengthen national unity and the subjective ties that bound individuals and groups to the nation through the emperor.[49] And if the dogma of the divine emperor required that limits be set on rational thought and debate about the monarchy, then let the limits be set by the policies of repressing "unhealthy thought" (that is, political dissent) and heightening martial spirit.

By late December 1928 the yearlong enthronement festivities had ended. The press less frequently reflected the nationalistic fever associated with them. The Kyoto Palace remained open to the public, though. Enthronement memorial books continued to be published. Officials continued to declare that the emperor and his subjects had been joined as one entity: "one mind united from top to bottom."

Newspapers continued to editorialize on the mission of "young Japan." The "thought police" pressed ahead with their work of arresting communists and other dissidents. And many Japanese, because of the enthronement, probably were more strongly than ever convinced of their innate moral superiority as a people and a race. Such thinking would soon have profound repercussions on the political events of the 1930s, tainting the mood of the country with the belief that Japanese culture was spiritually redemptive and a force for the regeneration of the world, while Western culture, on the contrary, was defiling and needed to be purged.[50]

This political reconstruction of Japanese identity, with renewed emphasis on race-people-nation rather than classes within a nation, must be carefully examined. The new racial consciousness was created in a context of worsening economic conditions and intensified rural class strife, with tenant organizations challenging the landlord regime, on which the imperial system in the countryside was partly based. Tenant disputes rose steadily from 1,866 in 1928 to 3,419 in 1931; industrial strikes also increased, reaching a prewar peak of 984 in 1931.[51] And just when social conflict was heating up, along came a clarifying, soothing, heaven-sent racism to infuse Japanese nationalism with a universalizing impulse.

As time passed Hirohito lessened his exposure to the Japanese people. During 1928 he made many tours and visits to the army and navy academies and their graduation ceremonies, the Diet, his private mansions, his relatives, and his ancestral mausoleums—all places where there was little chance of anyone approaching him with a dreaded direct appeal. His travels as supreme commander (*daigensui*) in connection with special military reviews and exercises continued at a rate of about four to six annually from 1928 to the start of World War II; but his longer, regional excursions (*chihō-junkō*) in his divine capacity as heavenly sovereign declined abruptly and then just stopped after a visit to Hokkaido in 1936.[52] The emperor's trips in connection with naval reviews and army grand maneuvers served to mobilize the nation and, at the same time, to highlight his divine and militaristic emperor images, not his secondary status as a "constitutional" monarch. Instead of creating intimacy with his subjects in their period of economic suffering, these pseudo-public appearances left him as remote from, and as uncomprehending of, their daily lives as ever.[53]

On those rare occasions in the first two decades of Shōwa rule when the consecrated emperor traveled on civil inspection tours, Home Ministry and prefectural officials regarded his visits as very serious events requiring the most careful advance preparation and allowing for zero human error. When an error occurred, the consequences could be unfortunate. On November 16, 1934, for example, a motorcycle policeman leading the imperial motorcade through Kiryū City, Gumma prefecture, was supposed to take a left turn at an intersection. Instead he led the procession straight on, slightly upsetting the itinerary of the tour. Seven days later the erring policeman committed suicide, the governor of Gumma and all the top officials involved in staging the tour were reprimanded, police officials in Gumma had their salaries docked for two months; and the home minister himself was questioned and severely criticized in the Imperial Diet.[54]

To protect and welcome the emperor, to ensure that the crowds who bowed before him remained silent and controlled, that nothing went amiss while he was in the prefecture, local officials formed special committees, and those serving on them, after praying to the gods for strength and guidance, rehearsed every minute detail of his approaching benevolent visit.[55] They mobilized all resources, laid out red carpets for Hirohito to walk on, swept and decorated the streets along which his motorcade would pass, disinfected (literally) and purified (ritually) the limousine in which he would ride, his railroad cars and the imperial locomotive, even the stations where he would stop. Sometimes the railroad tracks along his route were scoured and doused with disinfectants, especially where he was scheduled to alight.

The excessive, almost morbid need to make Hirohito's way spotless and germless, and his presence invisible (as all eyes had to be looking down, not at him), provides insight into the assumptions underlying Shinto beliefs. Threaded through the emperor's enthronement rituals, and his travels in connection with them, are many obsessive dualisms: clean against unclean, pure against impure, the self against the other. From these deep conceptual and emotional dichotomies would follow a natural, almost inevitable progression during the 1930s and early 1940s: We Japanese confront the world as a racially pure nation; therefore our wars are just and holy wars, and our victories create "new orders" in East Asia.[56]

To present Hirohito as deity incarnate, untouched by the evils of the political world, of his court, and of society—as pure, "sacred and inviolable"—required smoke, mirrors, and other magic—or, at the very least, concealment. Here the court group found additional

reason to hide from the public Hirohito's political actions during
the Wakatsuki and Tanaka cabinets. If they had been concerned to
cover up their own political interventions and those of the preenthronement regent, they dissembled even more in order to conceal
the numerous interventions of the postenthronement emperor.
Precisely this combination of secret political maneuvering and public deception, authoritarianism and lack of consciousness of personal responsibility became the hallmarks of the Shōwa emperor
and the men of "moderation" who served him at court.

The Shōwa enthronement rites, celebrations, and festivities of
1928 affected Japanese political culture at all levels but served
chiefly to reindoctrinate those in positions of public responsibility—especially government officials, schoolteachers, and policemen—in the sacred myths of Japan's origin. Taishō's incompetence
had abetted the rise of Taishō democracy; Hirohito's enthronement hastened its demise and revived the theocratic ideal of the
fusion of religion and politics. The rites and celebrations of Shōwa
thus contributed to closing Japanese society once again to the
absorption of new Western thought. Above all, his enthronement
pronounced that the emperor, ruling as well as reigning, had been
made into a living god.

Many dignitaries invited to the Kyoto ceremonies sounded this
theme of the emperor's divinity in a special issue of the popular
business magazine *Jitsugyō no Nihon* that appeared in November
1928. Tōyama Raita, president of the Great Japan Sugar Company
and member of the House of Peers, gave expression to it when he
wrote: "Witnessing this ceremony, I really felt that our emperor is
the descendant of the gods and that our nation always has a god"[57]
The court ritualist Hoshino Teruoki reiterated:

> [T]he enthronement showed that the emperor had assumed the reins
> of government with the benevolent heart of his ancestors. In so doing
> he has renewed the glory that he inherited from their virtuous spirits

and become the basis of the belief we have kept in our hearts and minds for thousands of years: namely, that our majesty is a deity [*kamisama*] and a living god [*ikigami*].[58]

No student of the enthronement can fail to be struck by the zeal with which this message of manifest divinity was proclaimed, and the significant numbers of ordinary Japanese who received it enthusiastically. As for Hirohito, neither then nor later did he ever publicly do anything, on his own initiative, to make people question that he was a "living god" or question the idea that Japan was a "divine country" because he and his people had united as one.[59]

In his analysis of Yokohama newspaper editorials devoted exclusively to the enthronement that appeared between January 1928 and January 1929, the historian Nakajima Michio identified three themes to which the enthronement gave heightened expression. First, the enthronement was seen as a great opportunity to indoctrinate the people in the national morality, thereby aiding the government's campaign to control dangerous thoughts.[60] To that end the editorialists urged the adoption of the "Oriental principles" of "the father's way and the mother's way" (*fudō bodō*), premised on the notion that the mother personified love while the father was the "main carrier of morality."[61] The view that men—or at least Japanese men—were morally superior to women was dear to monarchists of the period. But the supreme values in national morality were loyalty to the emperor and filial piety (*chūkō*). The emperor's awards of sake cups to elders over eighty, and the honoring by village and town authorities of persons over sixty years of age, reflected this way of thinking.[62]

Enthronement propaganda also stressed the compatibility of the *kokutai* with modern science. Considering that the mainstream position in earlier *kokutai* debates had underscored the estrangement of the *kokutai* from modern thought, this represented a remarkable reversal of argument. Now journalists asserted that "modern science" actually validated the *kokutai*. Scientific studies were daily demonstrating that "the spirit of respect for the gods, reverence toward ancestors, the unity of the monarch and the people, the unity of rites and governance, and the identity of loyalty and filial piety . . . constitute the most sublime human principles."[63]

A third editorial theme of 1928 was that the enthronement of the Shōwa emperor had inaugurated a new era in which youthful Japan was poised to become the hub of the entire world and to assume the mission of guiding all peoples.[64] An editorial in the *Yokohama Bōeki Shimpō* of December 1, 1928, titled "Young Japan and its Global Mission," claimed that loyalty and filial piety constituted a leadership principle for the entire world:

> Today's Japan should indeed not confine itself to its own small sphere. Neither should it remain in its position in the Orient or continue to occupy the place it holds in the world. This is an age in which Japan bears a global mission. It has become the center, the principal, and the commander and is advancing with the times to lead the entire world.[65]

Nakajima concluded his analysis of the Yokohama newspapers of 1928 by noting that "Japan had not yet entered the age of fascism yet the editorials were already preaching the theme of 'the eight corners of the world under one roof' (*hakkō ichiu*) without using that term."[66] The idea of the universal reign of peace in which each nation would take its proper place in the sun and recognize the leadership of Japan had lain dormant in the writings of Tokugawa-era scholars.[67] During the opening of Japan in the 1850s and 1860s, *hakkō ichiu* was revived and linked to the new conviction that Japan's emperor should always be "a charismatic political leader who stands at the head of, and promotes, the process of civilization and enlightenment."[68] The latter idea had influenced Meiji's image throughout his reign. Starting around 1928 Hirohito and his reign became associated with the rediscovery of *hakkō ichiu*, an expansionist belief that imparted new dynamism to Japanese nationalism.

Clearly the long enthronement process of the late 1920s built up and released enormous popular energy and enthusiasm.[69] Because the celebrations were set against a background of literary and artistic representations of an earlier military triumph—the Russo-Japanese War—the enthronement at its point of climax was experienced as a victorious foreign war. Undoubtedly it played a major role in enticing people to the side of the emperor and the state, and in mobilizing self-governing bodies, such as court-sponsored youth groups, the Imperial Reservists Association, neighborhood associations, and right-wing gangs. While that was going on, the Rising Sun flag was also diffused, and the Photography Department of the Imperial Household Ministry made preparations for "bestowing" on the nation's schools the most important symbol of the new nationalism—the sacred portrait of Emperor Hirohito and Empress Nagako, he in his new supreme generalissimo's uniform, with decorations on his chest; she beside him wearing a low-cut Western gown with a decorated sash.

Campaigns of national spiritual mobilization continued after 1928, pushing the nation's pride in Hirohito and in itself to new heights, and making belief in his sacredness the touchstone of political correctness. On December 1, 1928, the Tanaka cabinet issued a Statement Concerning the Guidance of Thought that advocated "promotion of education" and the "cultivation of the concept of the *kokutai*." Nine months later another cabinet launched a project dear to the court group since the start of Hirohito's regency: a national movement to give instruction and guidance to the nation on the danger of antiestablishment mass movements and on "improving economic life and nurturing national power." The propaganda campaign also sought to "clarify the *kokutai* and promote national spirit." With these multiple goals in mind, the Ministry of Education shortly afterward issued a directive to all schools and colleges throughout the country concerning the implementation of the new thought campaign.[70]

In this way the Shōwa monarchy became ideologically empowered through the indoctrination of the masses in the religion of Japanese spirit and deep veneration for—even worship of—the sacred ruler. It cannot be overlooked that these tendencies of Japanese nationalism emerged in the late 1920s, on the very eve of the great world economic slump, when Italian Fascism first registered itself internationally and the Nazi Party began its electoral surge in Germany. These themes and obsessions of Shōwa nationalism at first descended mainly "from above" into mainstream culture rather than rising from the common people. As they unfolded they subverted the Meiji constitutional structure while reconnecting with Shinto orthodoxy. The popular enthusiasm engendered by war and imperialist expansion during the fourth year of Hirohito's reign added new elements and motivations from below, which further transformed the constitutional order. When Hirohito began his reign, emperor ideology was definitely eroding and had become a psychological burden. Hirohito and the court group did their utmost, from the very start, to impart a new lease on life to all the irrational beliefs associated with the throne. They actively encouraged people to look to the emperor as the source of their morality—an omnipotent ruler conjoining political and military power with religious authority.

The political activities of Hirohito and the court group relaunched the monarchy in ways that gave a more militaristic configuration to Japanese nationalism. By embellishing the Meiji past, by celebrating the personality and "virtues" of the Meiji emperor, while simultaneously exalting the Shōwa emperor, they erected the springboard for the 1930s cult of emperor worship. Hirohito was its vehicle, and under him, with his active encouragement, the campaign soon took off and transformed Japanese politics, which were already becoming more pluralistic, divisive, and repressive.

Furthermore, during the very period in which political parties were rising to the apogee of their power, Hirohito's ritual enthronement and deification gave mystical intensity and strength to his double image as living diety (*arahitogami*) and supreme commander of the armed forces (*daigensui*). The powerful emotions released by these rites countered "democracy" and pacifism at home and antimilitary initiatives abroad. Only *after* Hirohito and his entourage had delivered all these blows to the Taishō democracy movement did military officers act out their dissatisfaction with party governments by resorting to aggression in Manchuria.

Whether early Shōwa nationalism, grounded in emperor ideology and imperial myths and rituals, can properly be seen as part of a worldwide "fascist" phenomenon remains contested among historians. Deification of the national racial community through its embodiment in a cult figure was a common element. Militarism, dictatorship, and the glorification of war, as well as youth, spirit, moral regeneration, and national mission, were certainly other common elements. And while Japan was always itself and sui generis, and Hirohito was no rabble-rousing, mesmerizing, crowd-dominating Führer or Duce, neither were Germany and Italy identical ideologically or organizationally. On balance, therefore, the ideological similarities among the leading revisionist fascist states during the 1930s, the similar psychological roles played by their cult leaders, as well as their historical trajectories of late development, all seem to be more important than their obvious differences.

6

A POLITICAL MONARCH EMERGES

Starting in 1927 stories of conflict with China over Manchuria returned to the front pages of Japanese newspapers, the Shōwa financial panic erupted, and both crises worsened with each passing year. Simultaneously criticism of the monarchy and of capitalism—referred to by opinion makers as the "thought problem"—spread even as the rituals of enthronement were unfolding around Hirohito, implanting in the Japanese a new image of him as a charismatic authority on a par with Meiji.

Equally disturbing to Hirohito, naval officers now presented him with conflicting views on how best to meet the navy's national defense requirements.[1] Adm. Katō Kanji, the leading opponent of the Washington Naval Treaty, began to pressure Hirohito to enlarge the geographic sphere of national defense. Kato argued that "the safety of the empire's homeland required confronting American naval forces deployed in the western Pacific" rather than in waters closer to home as specified in the 1923 policy.[2] Hirohito approved Katō's report, delivered to him on November 27, 1929, but clung to the arguments of Katō's opponents, the "treaty faction" admirals. They too wanted a big navy and believed in the doctrine of winning a war by fighting a decisive naval battle; but they insisted that the difference in national power between Japan and the United States ruled out, for the time being, anything but a passive defense of the empire.

At the start of his reign Hirohito avoided facing up to this continuing disagreement in national defense thinking within the navy. Although he maintained a very keen interest in the military side of his public life, he and his entourage preferred to concentrate on domestic affairs. There, they imagined, he would leave his mark in the march of emperors through the ages. Their initial, overriding goals, therefore, were to insert Hirohito's "will" into the conduct of government, to revive the power of the monarchy, and to strengthen his image as an authority figure equal to Meiji.

In affairs with the West the spirit of conciliation lingered, as attested by Japan's two main diplomatic projects of these years: the Kellogg-Briand Pact of August 1928, and the London Naval Treaty of April 1930. Yet signs of change, and of movement away from the pacifism and openness of the post–World War I era, were beginning to multiply. On February 20, 1928, representatives of left-wing parties, campaigning for progressive reform, opened a new front against the ruling elites by winning eight seats in the first national elections under the expanded suffrage law. Seventeen days later, on March 15, the government of Prime Minister Tanaka carried out mass arrests on a national scale of 1,568 Communist Party members and activists of the labor and peasant movements.[3] In April came the first expulsions of Marxist professors from the imperial universities in Kyoto, Tokyo, and Kyushu. On June 29 the Tanaka cabinet suspended normal constitutional processes and issued an emergency imperial edict revising the Peace Preservation Law of 1925 with respect to the crime of "altering the *kokutai*," now made punishable by death.[4]

For Communist Party members and intellectuals influenced by Marxist thought, the general election and the repression that followed in its wake became the occasion for redefining the new emperor as an oppressor, and for pointing to the social determinants of the throne. At the same time the imperial state was arresting Communists and their supporters, the new partisan slogan "overthrow the emperor system" spread in intellectual circles affected by Marxism. Meanwhile, abroad, on June 4, officers of the Kwantung Army guarding the South Manchurian Railway Zone murdered the local warlord, Chang Tso-lin. The next year, 1929, young Emperor Hirohito condoned the army's cover-up of this incident, thereby encouraging further acts of military defiance.

The groundwork for the future commission of war atrocities by the Japanese military was also being laid during this period. In 1928 the Tanaka government failed to endorse an international protocol banning chemical and biological warfare. The next year the privy council, responding to pressure from the military, failed to ratify the full Geneva Prisoner of War Convention, signed two years earlier. The privy councillors accepted the argument of the ministers of the army and navy, and of the foreign minister, that the clause concerning treatment of POWs was too lenient and could not possibly be implemented because the emperor's soldiers would never allow themselves to become prisoners of war.[5] This action in particular helped pave the way for later Japanese denials of the validity of international legal conventions for the treatment of prisoners of war and military wounded.[6]

In diaries and memoirs covering these crucial early years of his reign, Hirohito's close advisers—Makino, Kawai, Nara, and Okabe—painted a laudatory portrait of the young emperor. They admired Hirohito's unwillingness to be used by the parties—as if it was not in the nature of the imperial institution to be used—they praised him for his determination to take the supervisory role in politics that his father had been physically unable to perform, and they expressed satisfaction in their own tutoring skills for helping to bring this about. Only General Nara's account suggests that Hirohito was, at this stage, less than enthusiastic in asserting over his armed forces the control that was required of him by law.

The diaries of the entourage reveal Hirohito's abiding concern with political action. Discontent with merely looking on passively as history proceeded along its own path, he intervened in the decisions of the party cabinets and the privy council, arbitrated indirectly disputes among the leading political parties, and even forced the parties in the Diet to halt their debates to suit his convenience. Hirohito, influenced by Makino and the palace staff, soon did what Emperor Meiji had never done: scold, and effectively fire, a prime minister, Gen. Tanaka Giichi, president of the Seiyūkai—thereby nullifying Minobe's "organ" theory of the state, which the political parties were then drawing on to rationalize their actions.

Having rid themselves of Tanaka and his Seiyūkai government, Hirohito and his staff gave full backing to Hamaguchi Yūkō, president of the less diplomatically adventuristic Minseitō, installing him as Tanaka's successor in July 1929. In April 1930, months after Hamaguchi had formed his cabinet, Emperor Hirohito, with the full support of his entourage and Saionji as well, overrode the advice of his naval chief of staff and vice chief of staff, Admiral Katō and Vice Admiral Suetsugu, on the contentious matter of naval tonnage reduction. Although Washington and London had hinted they might form a naval alliance against Japan if it did not comply with the warship ratios worked out at the Washington Conference, Katō and his supporters on the Navy General Staff balked at the final compromise negotiated at London. They refused to accept "any limit on the navy's heavy cruiser tonnage of less than 70 percent of the individual cruiser strengths of the American and British fleets."[7] Katō's position, as he explained to protreaty Adm. Okada Keisuke, was that "[t]his problem concerns the fate of the navy, and therefore I want you to be aware that that is more important than the fate of the government."[8]

Strongly supportive of the navy's blatant intervention in politics during 1930, and sharing Katō's contempt for party government (and for what Katō called Japan's "Judaized society" or "the Jewish enemy in our hearts"), were General Araki and Admirals Ogasawara and Tōgō.[9] All four men maintained close ties to civilian ultranationalist ideologues and exerted influence on the Navy and Army Ministries, the Diet, the privy council and the palace (via Prince Fushimi). Their efforts accomplished nothing, however; for Hamaguchi stood firm against Katō, Suetsugu, and Tōgō and accepted the compromise cruiser tonnage ratios, as court officials had urged him to do. Thereupon the Seiyūkai joined with the military to publicly attack Hamaguchi and the court entourage, accusing them of having signed the treaty without the support of the Navy General Staff, thereby infringing on the *emperor's* "right of supreme command."

Determined to overthrow the Minseitō cabinet, and resentful of the palace entourage for having earlier forced Tanaka to resign, the Seiyūkai leaders accused Hamaguchi and the "evil advisers" around the throne—Makino, Suzuki, and Kawai—of relying on arms limitations treaties and on the "cooperation" of Britain and the United States to defend Japan's interests in China. By charging that Grand Chamberlain Suzuki had blocked the formal report to the emperor of the chief of the Navy General Staff, and that the government was pursuing a mistaken defense policy, the Seiyūkai politicians contributed to an atmosphere that fostered extremism.

Meanwhile literary, artistic, political, and international events were all coming together to create a new mood in Japan. Little had been written on the victorious Sino-Japanese and Russo-Japanese Wars during the entire Taishō period. In 1930, however, the military commemorated the twenty-fifth anniversary of the Russo-Japanese War, after having remembered it only five years earlier. In the interim, many emotional articles, books, picture books, and plays had appeared that gave national prominence to the Russo-Japanese War and to the admiral whose "divine action" (*kamiwaza*) had saved Japan in its confrontation with Russia.[10] These stories featured, as "paragons of the military man" and leading "war gods" (as opposed to mere heroes), Fleet Admiral Tōgō, who was still alive and active, and Comm. Hirose Takeo, who in 1904 had died attempting to seal the harbor in the second battle of Port Arthur.[11] In 1930, at the Kabuki Theater in Tokyo, *The Fall of Port Arthur*, in which General Nogi lost two sons, was enacted. When a Russian general in the play extended his sympathy to Nogi, Nogi replied, "'I could not have returned to Tokyo with my sons alive. As a father, I am pleased with the death of my two sons for the emperor.' At this the frenzied crowd cheered wildly."[12]

Thanks to these numerous literary conjurings of concrete memories, the long blackout on the wars of the late Meiji era ended. Children and young adults whose parents had fought in 1904–5 became better informed about the war that had won Japan a continental empire. Thus the decade that had begun as antimilitary ended with quite a different spirit: a massive reaffirmation of empire, the placing of hope in the myth of "war gods" like Admiral Tōgō and General Nogi, and the "virtues" of the young emperor.

Concurrently, in the foreground of national happenings, the Navy General Staff, the Seiyūkai Party leaders, and members of the privy council fomented public passion against the London Naval Treaty of 1930, which Japan signed with Britain and the United States on April 22. The treaty restricted the number of capital ships of each signatory and set limits for the first time on the number of cruisers and other auxiliary ships that each could build. The Japanese delegation had initially declared that it would maintain a 70 percent ratio vis-à-vis the United States on all auxiliary ships. In the end it compromised its differences with the Americans, accepted a 69 percent ratio plus parity in submarine tonnage, and agreed to renegotiate the treaty after six years.[13]

Two months after the ratification of the treaty in Tokyo, on November 14, while Hirohito was commanding special army maneuvers in Okayama prefecture, Sagoya Tomeo, a right-wing thug who belonged to the Aikokusha, an organization headed by the Seiyūkai politician Ogawa Heikichi, shot and mortally wounded Prime Minister Hamaguchi at Tokyo Station. On being informed of the shooting and of Hamaguchi's condition by Imperial Household Minister Ichiki, Hirohito's first concern was that "constitutional politics" not be interrupted.[14] His feelings about the vicious propaganda campaign that the naval lobby had stirred up against the treaty, and that apparently had led directly to the shooting, are unknown, as are the conclusions, if any, that he drew from Hamaguchi's death, which occurred in August of the following year, right on the eve of the Manchurian Incident.

The brief period of amity between the imperial court and a party cabinet was over, ended by the first political assassination of the 1930s. The stage was set for the last party cabinet in imperial Japan.[15] With the military honing a new entitlement—its "right of supreme command"—and the public lining up in its support, a new era was about to begin. The army and navy ministers continued to be sharply at odds with their general staffs over the issue of arms reduction. Discipline within the officer corps continued to loosen; the army as an institutional entity showed signs of spiraling out of control. The stoking up of emperor worship had lowered the whole level of national political debate, not to mention public morality.

Thus, by the imprudent and highly untraditional way in which Hirohito and his staff exercised power—firing Tanaka in 1929 and then throwing domestic consensus among the elites to the winds rather than risk a diplomatic setback in the London naval talks— they helped to ignite the anger of all who were dissatisfied with social conditions and with the economy of early Shōwa Japan. From their exalted position at the top of the polity, the court group never imagined they were contributing to the destruction of party government. Yet in pursuit of their own political agenda (sometimes ignored by Tanaka but executed forcefully by Hamaguchi) they introduced elements of instability that had not existed during the regency.[16] The more Hirohito made use of his authority, the more he widened rifts among the ruling elites.

I

While the grand enthronement ceremonies unfolded for the mass audiences at home and abroad, Hirohito, as part of his change of persona, prepared to move his private residence and office to the Meiji Palace, then being remodeled to suit his and his family's needs.[17] At the same time politics in Tokyo moved along—more and more a process of intrigue hidden by secrecy.

The Fifty-fifth Imperial Diet, meeting from April 23 to May 7, 1928, provided the occasion for the next clash between the court group and Tanaka. This time the issues were several: Tanaka's reorganization of his cabinet to bring in Kuhara Fusanosuke, a businessman and first-year member of the Diet, regarded by many as a dangerous right-wing extremist; his management of the Diet; and what the emperor regarded as his erroneous reporting of the proceedings inside the Diet. Hirohito had his own intelligence network. He knew that Tanaka's cabinet was deadlocked in its conflict with the opposition parties; its management of the Diet was certainly not proceeding smoothly. Hirohito complained several times to Makino that Tanaka's reports to him were inadequate and that his "imperial will" was being abused. In the end Kawai had to talk to Tanaka about the emperor's wishes.[18]

For Hirohito's aspirations to coexist with the constitutional order, the prime minister was expected to maintain absolute secrecy regarding the emperor's will. Tanaka refused to accept that. He kept trying to associate the emperor, the court entourage, and the *genrō* with his own Seiyūkai policies, until, finally, on May 14, 1928, one week after the Fifty-fifth Diet had ended and more than a year after Tanaka had become prime minister, Makino's chief secretary, Kawai, gave up on him and noted in his diary that the imperial court had become totally dissatisfied with Tanaka's performance:

> All of today's morning papers carried the gist of what the prime minister said when he visited Prince Saionji. If what they report is true,

then he lacks common sense in publicizing such things; his qualifications to handle constitutional politics must be doubted; and one must pity his thoughtlessness and immaturity. He is unable even to understand Prince Saionji's intentions. There is a very strong possibility, therefore, that he will disappoint the nation.[19]

Soon after Kawai wrote these words, Seiyūkai politician and Education Minister Mizuno Rentarō, leader of the campaign to keep Kuhara out of the Tanaka cabinet, submitted his letter of resignation to the emperor. The next day, to prevent the collapse of Tanaka's newly reorganized cabinet, Hirohito indirectly told Mizuno to remain in office. On May 23 Mizuno retracted his resignation, saying he would stay because of "the emperor's kind words." Mizuno's statement immediately precipitated a political uproar, for it was interpreted to mean that the emperor had taken sides, benefiting the Seiyūkai while undermining the Minseitō. The Minseitō reacted first by denouncing the Seiyūkai for exploiting the emperor's wishes in order to remain in power, then by establishing a Committee on the Problem of the Emperor's Message.[20] The committee resolved to wage a great national campaign to protect constitutional government and the *kokutai*. The Minseitō formulated its resolution in clear doublespeak: "We firmly aspire to overthrow the Tanaka cabinet in order to protect the *kokutai*, which has its core foundation in the imperial house."[21]

If, at this time, Hirohito had reflected on the Mizuno incident, he might have recognized the inherent contradiction in his very existence. In the process he might also have gained a better appreciation of the need to veil his interventions in absolute secrecy. But he was still young, relatively inexperienced, and not the least bit self-reflective. In due time he would gain some degree of insight into his predicament, and with that would come a worsening of his nervousness, for Hirohito's chronic psychological stress had its root in the institution of sacred monarchy itself, and the ingrained but never acknowledged friction between himself and the Japanese people.

With political debate over *kokutai* issues having rekindled, and the court group at odds with the Tanaka government over the whole range of its policies, there now occurred four events in quick succession that were to have lasting effects on both Sino-Japanese relations and Japanese politics during the next decade. Hirohito was at the center of each of them. These were the Tsinan Incident (May 1928), the assassination of Chang Tso-lin by staff officers of Japan's Kwantung Army (June 4, 1928), the signing of the Kellogg-Briand Pact (August 27, 1928), and the introduction into the public arena, during the second half of 1928, of the ideology of enthronement and deification.

II

On March 24, 1927, soldiers of China's Nationalist Revolutionary Army pillaged the Japanese Consulate in Nanking and assaulted the consul; they also attacked buildings housing the American and British Consulates. Later that same day British and American warships on the Yangtze River bombarded the city. The Japanese press immediately sensationalized the Nanking Incident, in which six Westerners died, Japanese rights were violated, and no Japanese troops had been dispatched. Against this background, in the middle of the official mourning for the Taishō emperor, Hirohito sanctioned Japan's first military interventions in China's civil war. Twice, in May and July, he gave his consent to the army's dispatch of troops to China's Shantung Province, ostensibly to protect Japanese residents from assaults by Kuomintang soldiers on their way north toward Peking. Less than a year later, on April 19, 1928, he consented to a third deployment: this time five thousand troops of the Sixth Division, under Gen. Fukuda Hikosuke, to the port of Tsing-tao, Shantung, a center of Japanese textile capital and once a Japanese protectorate. He did so after first asking Chief Military

Aide Nara whether the intervention would lead to another massacre of Japanese lives such as had occurred in the Russian city of Niko-laevsk (now Pugachev) in 1920. Nara said that it would not.

When General Fukuda arrived in Tsingtao, however, he decided on his own initiative immediately to proceed inland (by rail) to Tsinan. There, a few days later, the first of several clashes occurred between Japanese and Nationalist soldiers. Later, on May 8, Hirohito sanctioned without hesitation the dispatch of reinforce-ments to Tsinan to protect some two thousand Japanese civilians. Instead of making an issue of Fukuda's going beyond his authoriza-tion, the emperor silently directed his anger at Prime Minister Tanaka.[22] The Tsinan affair dragged on into early 1929, during which time seventeen thousand Japanese troops unleashed a reign of terror on the Chinese citizens of the city, wrecking chances for Sino-Japanese rapprochement. For Hirohito this incident was yet another example of Tanaka's inadequacy as a prime minister.

Less than a month after Hirohito had sanctioned a fourth deploy-ment of troops to Shantung Province, on June 4, 1928, senior staff officers of Japan's Kwantung Army, led by Col. Kōmoto Daisaku, assassinated the Chinese warlord and territorial sovereign, Chang Tso-lin, on whom Prime Minister Tanaka had based his Manchurian policy. This incident (and the prime minister's alleged mishandling of it) pulled Manchuria into the turmoil of Japanese and international politics. For the young emperor and his entourage, it provided the opportunity they had long been seeking to remove Tanaka and his entire Seiyūkai cabinet.

Leaders of the Minseitō were the first to discover that the real assassins were Kwantung Army officers rather than rogue elements of China's Southern Army, as the Kwantung spokesmen falsely alleged. By early September the court entourage too had heard that Japanese army officers had committed the crime and were blaming it on Chinese soldiers.[23] Prime Minister Tanaka was alone in slowly uncovering the truth because the top army leaders had wanted

Chang Tso-lin removed and were uninterested in pursuing the matter, let alone making a full disclosure of the facts. When, in October 1928, Tanaka finally learned the truth, he resolved to punish them and reestablish discipline in the army. His fellow cabinet ministers and the army, however, strongly opposed holding the assassins accountable. Led by Army Minister Shirakawa Yoshinori and Railway Minister Ogawa, who had the status of vice prime minister, the cabinet formed a coalition against Tanaka, claiming that disclosure would harm the imperial house, worsen Sino-Japanese relations, and undermine Japan's special rights in China. Additionally the cabinet did not want to be held accountable in the Diet for what had happened.

Isolated in his own cabinet but supported by Saionji, Tanaka went ahead anyway. His formal report to the emperor was made on December 24, 1928. He told the emperor that he intended to court-martial the criminals, purge the army, and reestablish discipline. The next day he said the same thing to Makino and Chinda in the mistaken belief that they would help him. However, when the cabinet learned of Tanaka's formal report, the ministers refused to support a court-martial and wanted the matter to be handled as an administrative affair of the army. On December 28 Shirakawa reported to the emperor that the army would investigate Chang Tso-lin's death but made no mention of a court-martial.[24]

When the Fifty-sixth Imperial Diet convened in early 1929, the opposition parties muted their attacks in questioning the government about the incident; they already knew or suspected the truth and did not desire full disclosure in any case. On this matter the Minseitō in particular wanted to accommodate the wishes of the army whose support it needed to form the next cabinet.[25] Meanwhile the emperor and his staff worried only about whether Tanaka would assume responsibility for what had occurred.

On January 17, 1929, the emperor pressed Shirakawa to investigate. Two days later the emperor asked Tanaka about his strategy for handling the Diet. On February 2 he again questioned Tanaka about the progress of the investigation; the prime minister hinted that his government would not take responsibility for the Chang Tso-lin incident.[26] One month later, on March 4, Makino told his secretary, Okabe, to inform Saionji that Tanaka no longer had the emperor's confidence and that the emperor intended to admonish him the next time he reported.[27] By this time Tanaka knew that the entire army had united against him and that he would have to yield and let the army off the hook. Thereupon the cabinet agreed to cover up the incident and have the army treat it as an internal administrative matter.

On March 27 Army Minister Shirakawa reported the cabinet's decision to the emperor. Colonel Kōmoto and Kwantung Army Commander Muraoka Chōtarō had committed the crime, explained Shirakawa, but to announce the truth and severely punish those responsible for the murder would be highly disadvantageous to Japan. At that point, if not earlier, Hirohito accepted the army's intention to lie to the public about the incident and to give merely administrative punishments to those involved.[28] Hirohito, Makino, and Admiral Suzuki thus sided with Shirakawa and those in the Tanaka cabinet who wanted to prevent the army's reputation from being blackened. In so doing they obviously, if unwittingly, abetted the forces plotting further aggression in China in order to maintain Japan's rights and interests there.[29]

Many years later, in his famous "Monologue," Hirohito claimed that "youthful indiscretion" had led him to speak to Prime Minister Tanaka in an angry tone and to request his resignation when Tanaka came and told him that he wanted to settle the Chang Tso-lin assassination "by hushing it up."[30] He conveniently failed to note that he too had wanted to hush up the murder. He also failed to note that he had carefully rehearsed with his staff what he would say to Tanaka, and that he really had no grounds for scolding the prime minister on the basis of his second, informal report of June 27, 1929. Hirohito directed attention to the scolding itself, and to the Tanaka cabinet's subsequent resignation. He thereby deflected attention from his constitutional responsibility as supreme commander in chief, for punishing a crime by two officers in what was essentially a military, not a civil affair.

After relating to his aides in his "Monologue" how he had secured Tanaka's resignation, Hirohito tried to explain why criticism was heaped on his entourage. In so doing, he revealed his keen sensitivity to charges of a "court conspiracy" that were circulated around that time and later helped to undercut the convenient fiction that the Imperial House always stood aloof from politics. Kuhara Fusanosuke, Minister of Communications in the reorganized Tanaka cabinet of May 1928, was to blame—for telling the truth—and Hirohito hated him for it. Instead of protecting the *kokutai*, Kuhara, one of Tanaka's "sympathizers":

> made up the phrase "bloc of the senior statesmen" and eventually spread the word that the cabinet fell because of a conspiracy by the senior statesmen and the imperial court. Thus believing in the truth of such . . . concocted phrases . . . resentment was created and left a disastrous legacy that lingered long into the future. This affair had a considerable influence on the incident of February 26, 1936. Thereafter I resolved to approve every report the cabinet laid before me even though I personally might hold an opposite opinion. . . . When I had told Tanaka, "Why don't you resign?" it was a warning, not a "veto." However, afterward I decided I would state my opinions but never exercise any "veto."[31]

After firing Tanaka, Hirohito tended to be more cautious in choosing when to intervene politically. But the degree of his restraint depended on the times and was therefore situationally (rather than constitutionally) determined. Moreover Hirohito seems never to have understood the deep resentment generated in

Seiyūkai circles by what he had done to Tanaka.[32] Nor did he grasp that the constant political attacks on the court by the military and the right wing, which marked his reign from 1929 onward, were one price he and his palace advisers had to pay for their active participation in politics and for reviving the fetish of imperial will as necessarily distinct from the will of the cabinet.[33] A real "constitutional monarch" would not have believed that constitutional monarchy required the monarch to approve every report of the cabinet. But Hirohito's sense of a constitutional monarch was "impoverished," devoid of any respect for the will of the nation as expressed through the lower house of the Diet.[34]

By repeatedly censuring and then finally firing his prime minister, General Tanaka, Emperor Hirohito had signaled to the political community that a cabinet led by the head of the Seiyūkai Party was not qualified to govern under his rule. He reacted quite differently, however, in the case of the Minseitō, the other main conservative party, on whose president, Hamaguchi, he bestowed the mantle of prime minister in July 1929.

Hamaguchi, having understood the lesson in Tanaka's failure, kept the young emperor fully informed before implementing policy measures. Moreover his personal values, as well as his policy goals of military and financial retrenchment, were entirely agreeable. The court group at this stage also approved of Hamaguchi's attempt to come to terms with Chinese nationalism by returning Shidehara to the post of foreign minister and signing a customs treaty with China.

Unfortunately, a few months after Hamaguchi formed his cabinet, the international financial system based on gold collapsed when, on October 14, 1929, the stock market crashed in the United States, the world's leading creditor nation and market for industrial goods. Soon the entire world economy fell into an unprecedented slump, with profound effects on the established international order. Emperor Hirohito's earlier decision to indulge the army in its insubordination, and to dismiss the only prime minister who had treated him as though he were a real constitutional monarch, had given young army officers in Manchuria a feeling that they could take matters into their own hands.

A small minority of them now proceeded to do so. During the year that elapsed between Chang Tso-lin's assassination in June 1928 and the Tanaka cabinet's resignation in early July 1929, Colonel Kōmoto resigned his post as senior staff officer. His successor on the staff of the Kwantung Army, Lieutenant Colonel Ishiwara, began the planning that would lead to the Manchurian Incident. Middle- and upper-echelon officers who advocated reform of the state for the purpose of waging "total war" strengthened their organizational unity and their ties with civilian right-wing groups; while elements of Tanaka's Seiyūkai (led by the dynamic Mori) joined forces with the military and the civilian right wing.

On December 29, 1928, Chang Tso-lin's son and successor, Chang Hsueh-liang, the warlord of the Three Eastern Provinces ("Manchuria"), united his territory with that of new Kuomintang government at Nanking. As China completed its nominal unification, the stage was being set in Japan for the coalescence of new forces of aggression and the neutralization of groups that supported policies of international cooperation and compromise in China. Neither the emperor nor his staff showed any understanding that the political attacks on the court by the military and the right wing, which marked his reign from 1929 onward, were the price they had to pay for infusing religion into politics and helping to create the fetish of imperial will in the first place.

III

On August 27, 1928, Japan became a signatory to the General Treaty for the Renunciation of War, known in the West as the Kellogg-Briand Pact (or the Pact of Paris) and in Japan as the

No-War Treaty. The pact's signers renounced war "as an instrument of national policy" and promised to settle all disputes by peaceful means. France and the United States had presented this treaty to Japan as another project in the spirit of international conciliation endorsed at the Washington Conference. The Tanaka cabinet accepted it and dispatched Privy Councillor Uchida Kōsai to Paris with instructions to use the occasion of the signing to inform the United States and other powers of Japan's special position in Manchuria. Uchida was not to arouse foreign suspicions of Japan's territorial ambitions, however, by indicating that Manchuria would be exempted from the obligations imposed by the treaty.[35]

How this treaty fared in Japan revealed much about the court group's attitude toward international law. By signing the Kellogg-Briand Pact, the Japanese government accepted that the concept of "aggressive war" was a recognized crime in international law.[36] In the first of the pact's two articles, the signatories pledged "in the names of their respective peoples that they condemn recourse to war for the solution of international controversies, and renounce it as an instrument of national policy in their relations with one another." In the second article they agreed to resolve "by pacific means . . . all disputes or conflicts of whatever nature or of whatever origin . . . which may arise among them."[37] When the Tanaka government submitted this short treaty for review by the Imperial Diet, the phrase "in the names of their respective peoples" immediately became an object of dispute.[38]

In the United States, where the postwar peace movement had spawned the idea of criminalizing war, the treaty enjoyed wide support from the intellectual community and the public.[39] Similar general acceptance might have been secured in Japan if the emperor had put his prestige behind it and made the outlawing of aggressive war his own personal project. That never happened. Instead the treaty immediately bumped against the unfolding crisis in Manchuria and a government-sponsored campaign to bind the people to the emperor, overcome the nation's increasing political fragmentation, and promote martial spirit after a decade of reviling the military.

More particularly the import of the treaty was obscured by contention over the twin issues of the emperor's sovereignty and his foreign policy prerogative. When the Imperial Diet convened in early 1929, the opposition Minseitō accused the Tanaka cabinet of infringing on the emperor's sovereign powers of state because "the High Contracting Parties" in Article 1 of the No-War Treaty called for outlawing war "in the names of their respective peoples" rather than in the emperor's name.[40] Although Minseitō and Seiyūkai politicians were at one in supporting the No-War Treaty, the former could not refrain from scoring points against the governing party by claiming that the wording in Article 1 of the treaty assumed the principle of popular rather than monarchical sovereignty and was therefore inconsistent with the *kokutai*.

The Diet debate on the treaty thus highlighted the ruling elites' unanimity in denying any popular agency in the making of foreign policy. At the same time it revealed the profound rhetorical shift then under way in the very process of political deliberation itself: from not dragging the throne into politics to "fighting night and day by implicating the imperial house" in political debate.[41]

In addition the No-War treaty fared poorly in Japan because Hirohito was personally advised on this issue by his teacher of diplomacy and international law, Tachi Sakutarō. At the time Tachi went on record deprecating the pact's intent and significance.[42] Hirohito certainly wanted Diet debate on his sovereign powers ended and the pact ratified, in keeping with the spirit of conciliation with the Western powers. On many occasions from March through early June 1929, he questioned Prime Minister Tanaka on how the treaty was faring in the Diet and in the privy council.[43] Yet Hirohito did not see the pact as a commitment to resolving by peaceful means all disputes that might arise with China over Japan's leasehold rights in Manchuria (due to expire during his reign). For him the Manchurian treaties and rights—contracts originally negotiated with the Ch'ing dynasty, later augmented by agreements secured by military faits accompli—were part of his grandfather's legacy. As such they were sacrosanct and deserving of protection even by the use of armed force.

On this score young Hirohito's view of the world was as unenlightened and rigid as Tachi's. Tachi's advice was that the pact would not inhibit Japan's resort to force to protect its interests in China, and that the moral element in it was of little consequence. Tachi focused, then and later, on defining self-defense broadly, seeking "loopholes" in the No-War pact to permit Japan to protect its interests and extraterritorial rights in Manchuria should a future need arise for armed intervention there. Tachi's position, moreover, was fully in tune with Japanese intellectual opinion at the time, which, unlike American opinion, responded skeptically to the No-War Pact.[44]

Specifically Tachi, like many other Japanese "realists," was dissatisfied with the way the liberal democracies—Britain and the United States—required all nations to adhere to the brand-new ethical code forbidding recourse to war as a means of resolving international conflicts. He saw this as an attempt by the Anglo-American powers to freeze the postwar international order to their own advantage.[45] Publicly, however, he did not reject either the peace ethic informing the new international law or the institutions that embodied that ethic, but rather sought to undermine both by developing loopholes and defining self-defense so broadly as to justify virtually any act of force as an instrument for resolving disputes.

While legalistic debate over the phraseology of the No-War Treaty raged during late 1928 and early 1929, Hirohito and the court group backed off. Instead of encouraging the new spirit of peace and antimilitarism to which the state (in Hirohito's name) was then committing itself by treaty, they decided to pump up his enthronement and thereby strengthen the trend toward chauvinistic nationalism. On the tenth anniversary of the signing of the European armistice ending World War I, the court group had a perfect opportunity to make the pacifism of the No-War Treaty the emperor's personal project, and to lead the Japanese nation to an understanding that wars of aggression had been made illegal. Before Hirohito got around to ratifying the treaty formally (June 27, 1929), however, his enthronement ceremonies had helped tilt Japan in the direction of a heightened nationalism that would prove difficult to retreat from.[46]

In Geneva, as the historian Ikō Toshiya has pointed out, Japan's delegates to the Council of the League of Nations did not seek ways to improve the Covenant and promote security. Instead, under Foreign Minister Shidehara's direction, they resisted bringing the Covenant into conformity with the new treaty banning aggressive war. Claiming that the peace machinery of the League could not work in the Far East, they repeatedly opposed mediation by third nations in disputes involving China. On every occasion between 1928 and 1931, the party cabinets sought to leave open the possibility of exercising force in China in the name of self-defense. If Hirohito, his court entourage, and the Foreign Ministry had not been so negative about strengthening the Covenant and preventing League intervention in Sino-Japanese disputes, and if new collective security agreements had been in place when the Manchurian Incident occurred, it might have been harder for the Kwantung Army to justify its arbitrary use of military force.[47]

IV

Despite having been informed by his chief aide, Nara, of the degeneration of discipline in the army and navy, the emperor continued to overlook problems of factional conflict, service rivalry, and growing fragmentation within both military branches. As the army's senior leaders grew lax in their exercise of control over the professional officer corps, officers of all ranks began to denounce their superiors and spread rumors to the public that the political parties were harming Japan's defense. Hirohito responded to this situation by avoiding battle. He shifted responsibility for dealing with the recalcitrant Navy General Staff onto the shoulders of Grand Chamberlain Suzuki, and onto General Nara responsibility for quelling insubordination and disobedience in the army. He also had Nara pressure Fleet Admiral Tōgō into agreeing to the ratification of the London Naval Treaty.[48]

In early 1930 Hamaguchi, strongly supported by Hirohito, clashed with the Navy General Staff over the signing of the London Naval Treaty. No sooner had that controversy ended than many navy leaders resigned their posts, and opponents of the treaty carried out a purge of officers who had supported it. The navy's political intervention influenced the army and undermined the position of Army Minister Ugaki, who continued to control the core personnel of the army.[49] The Seiyūkai immediately took advantage of the turbulent domestic situation to avenge itself on the Minseitō and the court entourage for the latters' previous interventions.

Ultimately the controversy over the London Naval Treaty did most to hurt the young emperor's image. Disaffected right-wing politicians joined military officers in viewing the signing of the treaty in September 1930 as the transgression of a moral boundary. By crossing it, they charged, the Minseitō had violated the honor of the state. Since they could not criticize the emperor, they blamed the court entourage for having monopolized his will and abetted the corruption of the parties. As early as 1929 Hiranuma Kiichirō, a leading ultranationalist in the judicial bureaucracy and an adviser to many right-wing groups, had privately criticized Hirohito for relying too much on Makino, and for repeatedly dispatching emissaries to Saionji, whether to learn the *genrō*'s wishes or to convey his own will.[50] In Hiranuma's extreme right-wing circles, the mistaken impression grew that the emperor's "will" was entirely in the hands of Saionji and the court entourage who guided his movements.

Critics of the palace and the parties railed against Western liberalism and democracy, which for a whole decade they had equated with Judaism and "Freemasonry." What they really wanted to smash was the restrictive Washington treaty system, which they had come to view as an Anglo-Saxon "iron ring" preventing Japan from expanding abroad. For them Japan had submitted once again to the United States and Britain, white powers that had earlier tried to curb its World War I Asian continental expansion. Drawing the inference that the West no longer acknowledged Japan as a first-rate power because of Anglo-American insistence that Japan adopt an inferior ratio in capital ships, opponents of the London Naval Treaty came to feel a keen sense of alienation from the Meiji constitutional order. The exaltation of the Shōwa emperor had charged the state itself with energy and vigor, while sanctifying the policies implemented in the emperor's name. The problem facing the disaffected military and some political leaders was how to reverse those policies. Casting politics based on the political parties as inordinately corrupt, and the court entourage as obstructive of the emperor's will, was their chosen procedure.

When Sagoya shot Prime Minister Hamaguchi on November 14, 1930, he was angered by Hamaguchi's role in expediting the London treaty and also wanted to see the birth of a Seiyūkai cabinet. That disaffected members of the Navy General Staff had also influenced him was rumored but never proved.[51]

At the time military spending was only slightly more than it had been at the start of the Shōwa era: nearly 29 percent of the annual budget, or 3.03 percent of GNP.[52] The Army and Navy General Staffs, however, were fiercely at odds with their service ministers over the issue of continued arms reduction and stagnating military allocations; the press had begun to build popular support for the military's "right of supreme command;" and the army as an institutional entity showed signs of marching out of control.

At the start of the new year, 1931, Justice Ministry bureaucrat and Privy Council Vice President Hiranuma, surveyed the scene in depression-stricken Japan. For nearly a decade Hiranuma had attacked Western liberalism, the values of the political parties, and Taishō democracy in general. Now he heralded the parting of the ways between the new nationalism and the internationalism that Japan had pursued since 1922.

> [T]oday the Great Powers openly emphasize the League of Nations while behind the scenes they steadily expand their military armaments. We cannot simply dismiss as the foolish talk of idiots those who predict the outbreak, after 1936, of a second world war. Our nation must be prepared to serve bravely in the event of an emergency. If other peoples [i. e., Europeans and Americans] obstruct world peace and the welfare of mankind, we must be prepared to display our nationalism in a grand way, based on the spirit of the founding of the state.[53]

Hiranuma went on to declare that if Japan was to pursue its ideals, it would have to build up its military power, which was hard to do:

> The depression in the business world is reaching its height. Unemployment is increasing daily. The family is breaking up. Starving people fill the streets. Do you think people are satisfied with this situation? This is the responsibility of statesmen who govern under the auspices of the emperor's will. To ignore this situation is to ignore the emperor's will. Therefore, at the start of this new year . . . to hide the reality and pretend that everything is peaceful would be the height of disloyalty. Because I firmly believe that one who respects the imperial house and loves the fatherland would not embellish the situation, I am clarifying here the essence of nationalism.[54]

V

By the summer of 1931 the political dispute beween the military and the Minseitō government of Wakatsuki Reijirō, Hamaguchi's successor, had become too threatening for the court officials to ignore. On June 13, 1931, Kawai recorded in his diary that

> the highest leaders of the army are conducting a united, organized campaign against arms reduction, saying that only the military may decide, as a matter of command, the size of the armed forces. The *genrō* [Prince Saionji] says that we should not slight the argument for dispatching troops in the event that a great disturbance erupts in Manchuria.[55]

Two weeks later Kido informed Privy Seal Makino that he had "heard from Harada Kumao [information gatherer for Saionji and Kido] about 'rather considerable plans for Manchuria that are being prepared by the military.'"[56] Then, in July, fighting erupted between Chinese and Korean farmers at Wamposhan, in the border area between Manchuria and Korea; the fighting led to anti-Chinese rioting and attacks on Chinese residents throughout the Korean Peninsula. The Japanese colonial authorities there failed to prevent the loss of 127 Chinese lives at the hands of Koreans, with the consequence that the mainland Chinese responded with a boycott of Japanese goods. To many Japanese suffering from the worldwide Great Depression, the boycott seemed a calculated plot by the Nationalist government in Nanking and the regime of Chang Hsueh-liang in Mukden to destroy Japan's strategic and economic interests in China.[57]

The crisis on the Asian continent worsened in August, when the Japanese army announced the disappearance in Manchuria of Capt. Nakamura Shintarō of the Kwantung Army staff. Japanese press accounts disclosed that Nakamura had been apprehended by Chinese soldiers and murdered near the border of northern

Manchuria.[58] Immediately the Seiyūkai charged that the Chinese were treating the Imperial Army with contempt. Played up by the parties and the press, the Wanpaoshan riots and the Nakamura incident heightened Japanese hostility against the Chinese. Behind that useful pretext the Kwantung Army increased pressure on the Mukden authorities.

As the confrontation between the Chinese and Japanese escalated, the political crisis within Japan deepened. Officers belonging to the thirty-fifth class of the Military Academy sent *genrō* Saionji a private manifesto "which affirmed that 'the Shōwa Restoration means the overthrow of political party government' and urged that captains and lieutenants all over the country become the 'standard bearers of the Shōwa Restoration.'"[59] The reference was to the current reign of the young Emperor Hirohito, but the message was that he should be a great reformer like his grandfather, or at least his era should be one of reform. For junior officers to issue such an admonition to the surviving *genrō* was an act of unprecedented audacity, reflecting the ongoing breakdown in military discipline and hierarchical order. It was also a hangover of the older practice of the young generation privately importuning the only member of the older generation to get to the emperor.

In early August, Army Minister Minami Jirō broke military precedent and disclosed to the press a speech he had given to a special meeting of regional and division commanders. In his speech General Minami denounced arms reduction proposals as "a sellout" and urged his fellow officers to protest military cutbacks.[60] Thereafter Army Chief of Staff Kanaya Hanzō and Gen. Suzuki Sōroku spoke out publicly against the curtailment of military spending in general.[61]

As these danger signs mounted, Hirohito and the court group finally began to consider how to cope with the politicized officer corps. On Hirohito's instruction Makino discussed with Saionji the problem of "maintaining military discipline," and the venerable elder statesman advised him to handle the situation by dealing directly with the military authorities rather than with Prime Minister Wakatsuki.[62] The Wakatsuki cabinet had been struggling unsuccessfully with the economic depression and alienating the military with its policies of financial retrenchment. To add insult to injury, Wakatsuki had chosen the summer of 1931 to compensate for revenue shortfalls by cutting the salaries of civil bureaucrats.[63]

Not until Japan was alive with rumors of imminent war in Manchuria, however, did Hirohito personally intervene. On September 10 and 11, he queried Navy Minister Abo Kiyokazu and Army Minister Minami respectively concerning the state of military discipline. Abo answered that he had just questioned the fleet commanders and had been told there was no problem in the navy.[64] Abo did not inform the emperor that the navy was very concerned about the army's activities in Manchuria, or that it would soon establish a "special organ" in Manchuria to spy on the Kwantung Army. Abo may also have been unaware that two months earlier—"in June or July"—senior officers of the Army General Staff had actually informed the heads of the Navy General Staff of their plan to seize Manchuria by force, and had asked for the navy's cooperation; the naval staff officers had failed to express any opposition to what the army was about to do.[65]

Minami was, however, in on the Kwantung Army's secret plans to bring Manchuria and Inner Mongolia under Japanese control by force, and he frankly admitted to the emperor that certain "young army officers have recently criticized our diplomacy as weak-kneed; the wording of their criticism was not precise and has led to their being misunderstood." He immediately added, however, that "we cannot permit such actions, and intend to suppress them fully. The army believes that diplomacy should be conducted as a national policy by Foreign Ministry officials and shall caution [our junior officers] about this."[66]

Hirohito responded that the army's political partisanship was interference with national policy, and he ordered Minami to tighten control. The army minister replied, duplicitously, "Ever since I heard such rumors, I have been carefully controlling matters." Hirohito then summoned Grand Chamberlain Suzuki and told him to inform Makino that "although the army minister reported to me that he has been controlling matters sufficiently so as to prevent [further acts of] military indiscipline, I urged him to be even more cautious."[67]

Minami explained the emperor's attitude to those senior officers in the Army Ministry and at General Staff Headquarters who were privy to the plot—timed to begin sometime in late September. They decided to move more cautiously. Their goal of wresting Manchuria from China by force did not change, but the emperor's stance led them to postpone action and not to defy the cabinet. Minami, newly chastened, thereupon circulated admonitory instructions within the army.

On September 15 Foreign Minister Shidehara received a top secret telegram from his consul general in Mukden, informing him that the Kwantung Army was about to launch a large-scale offensive action. Other reports over the next few days kept Shidehara fully informed of the Kwantung Army's plot. Nevertheless, throughout the early months of the Manchurian Incident, Shidehara functioned as the leading defender of the Kwantung Army to the Western world, claiming that victimized Japan was merely acting in self-defense, upholding the sanctity of treaties.[68]

Minami entrusted a letter to Gen. Tatekawa Yoshitsugu, chief of the General Staff's Intelligence Section, and told him to deliver it personally to the newly appointed Kwantung Army commander, General Honjō. Tatekawa, who had participated in Chang Tso-lin's assassination, was thought to have influence in Kwantung Army circles. Before leaving for Mukden with his message urging patience and postponement of action, Tatekawa disclosed to Col. Hashimoto Kingorō, planner of the abortive March coup, the decision of the army's senior leaders to postpone the planned hostilities. Immediately Hashimoto sent telegrams to Col. Itagaki Seishirō, the senior staff officer of the Kwantung Army at Mukden, one of which warned him to act quickly: "Plot discovered. Tatekawa coming; strike first to avoid implicating him. If Tatekawa arrives, take action before receiving his message."[69] Three days later, Lt. Colonel Ishiwara Kanji and Colonel Itagaki put their plans into effect.

Circumstantial evidence indicates that the senior editors of the Tokyo *Asahi* and Osaka *Mainichi* newspaper chains, Ogata Taketora and Takaishi Shingorō, were also party to this deception. For two months earlier, on the night of July 16, 1931, they had attended a meeting in Tokyo (probably at the residence of Baron Harada Kumao) where, in the company of Foreign Ministry officials, they had heard the Military Affairs Bureau Chief, Major-General Koiso Kuniaki, advocate the "independence of Manchuria" and say that if the army starts a war the Japanese people will support it.[70]

So on the eve of the Mukden fighting many influential persons in Tokyo either knew or strongly suspected that the Kwantung Army was about to start trouble. Hirohito and his top palace advisers—Makino, Suzuki, Sekiya, Kido, and Nara—also sensed the growing unrest in the military but misread the situation and were laggard in responding to it. Believing they had acted in ample time for the imperial admonition to work its dampening effect, they never imagined that the Kwantung Army would seize the initiative, completely overturn the Minseitō cabinet's policies, and undermine the emperor's authority. Hirohito and the court bureaucrats had deeply underestimated the factionalism and discontent that had been brewing for some time among the army, the foreign ministry, and the political parties. But they also failed to counter this danger because they naturally supported the army's mission in Manchuria, and had ever since 1905.[71]

PART 3

HIS MAJESTY'S WARS, 1931–1945

7

THE MANCHURIAN TRANSFORMATION

During the night of September 18, 1931, Kwantung Army offi-cers detonated an explosion near the Japanese-controlled South Manchurian Railway line at Liut'iaokou (north of Mukden) and blamed it on the soldiers of Chang Hsueh-liang and armed Chi-nese "bandits." Using an incident they themselves had staged as a pretext, and that had left the rail line itself undamaged, Staff Officer Col. Itagaki Seishirō ordered the Independent Garrison Force and the Twenty-ninth Infantry Regiment to attack the barracks of the Chinese Manchurian Army within the walled city of Mukden. Taken by surprise, the Chinese troops fled or laid down their arms. An hour later Itagaki's co-conspirator, Lt. Col. Ishiwara Kanji, sta-tioned in Ryojun [Port Arthur], conveyed the false report of what had happened to Kwantung Army Commander Honjō Shigeru. Honjō then issued attack orders that Ishiwara had carefully pre-pared long in advance. Over the next twenty-four hours Kwantung Army units advanced beyond the leased territory and seized control of the strategic towns along the railway. The army then prepared to move on the major population centers of southern Manchuria.[1]

The next day, September 19, the palace learned—through newspaper reports based on Kwantung Army explanations—of the clash in Manchuria. Responsibility, according to the army spokes-men, rested with the Chinese. Chief Aide-de-Camp Nara Takeji promptly informed the emperor, adding that he believed "this incident [would] not spread."[2] Nara may also have suggested, then or a few hours later, that Hirohito convene an imperial conference to take control of the situation—an idea that Makino and Saionji quickly negated on the ground that "the virtue of his majesty" would be "soiled" if the decisions of such a conference should prove impossible to implement.[3]

Once started, the Manchurian Incident set off a chain reaction of international and domestic crises that interacted and fundamentally altered the whole trajectory of Japanese state development. China immediately sought redress before the League of Nations; the Kwantung Army sought reinforcements. Gen. Hayashi Senjūrō, commanding in Korea, sought permission, through central army headquarters in Tokyo, to send units across the Yalu River into Manchuria. On September 19 the government was still helpless and ill-informed. Prime Minister Wakatsuki appealed to Harada Kumao, secretary to *genrō* Saionji, for assistance:

> I am not being kept informed by either the Foreign Ministry or the Army Ministry. . . . I have just warned them through Chief Cabinet Secretary Kawasaki. . . . The Chinese forces in Manchuria and Mongolia number more than two hundred thousand [*sic*] while we have only some ten thousand. I asked the army minister, "What are you going to do if, by chance, your challenge causes something you haven't anticipated—something that given you are so outnumbered you can't stop?" The army minister told me, "We'll send in troops from Korea . . . indeed, they may have already gone in." I rebuked him: "How can you allow dispatch of soldiers from Korea without government authorization?" He said, "Well, the fact is that during the Tanaka cabinet [1927–29] troops were dispatched without imperial sanction." I gathered he had not foreseen any problem at all. . . . Under these circumstances I am quite powerless to restrain the military. How can his majesty's military act without his sanction? What can I do? Maybe I

should not be talking to you like this, but can you do anything? . . . I
am in serious trouble.[4]

That evening members of the court group met at Harada's residence. In attendance were Kido (his diary is the available source);
Konoe; Okabe Nagakage, first section chief of the Foreign Ministry's Bureau of Political Affairs; and another titled peer.[5] All were
in their forties and tended to be critical of Saionji and Makino and
sympathetic to the military's attempt to resolve the Manchurian
problem by force. They agreed that the orders of the high command were not being fully obeyed, and that the emperor concurred
with the cabinet's initial desire to prevent the incident from getting
worse and doing more damage to Japan's public image. The problem, Kido reported, was twofold. The military was angry both at the
palace entourage for influencing the emperor's statements, and at
Saionji, whom it considered hostile. Hence "it would be better
hereafter for the emperor himself not to speak except when a situation is out of control;" and Saionji should be dissuaded from coming to Tokyo "unless the situation changes."[6]

In effect those meeting at Harada's mansion agreed that Hirohito should approve the military's actions, and that Saionji and the
senior palace officials should neither pursue the illegal infringement
of the emperor's powers of military command, nor do anything else
to provoke the military. Holding this attitude, the court group, over
the course of the entire Manchurian war, would never take a firm
stand against the army.[7]

On September 21 Wakatsuki convened his cabinet for six hours.
They decided not to authorize reinforcements from either the
homeland or Korea, and to treat the fighting in Manchuria as only
an "incident," thus avoiding a declaration of war.[8] The Kwantung
Army, meanwhile, had for three days been pressing army central
headquarters for permission to allow General Hayashi, commander

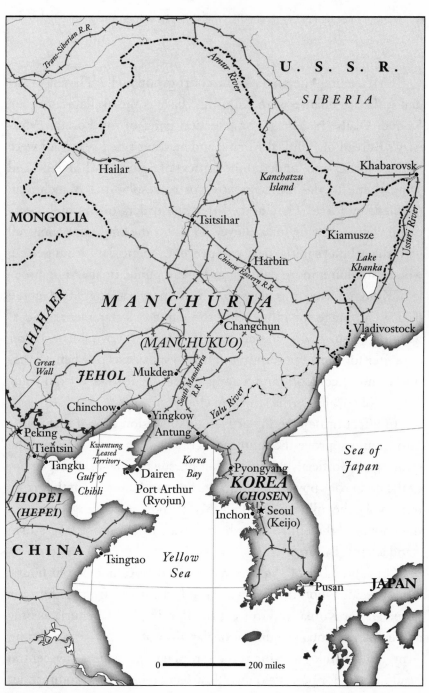

Manchuria, 1931–1933

of the Korean Army, to send reinforcements across the Yalu River into Manchuria. At 1:00 P.M. on September 21, while the cabinet was still meeting, Hayashi on his own authority ordered troops to cross the border. Shortly afterwards, Army Chief of Staff Kanaya reported to the emperor that despite orders to stand by on alert, the Mixed Brigade of the Japanese colonial army in Korea, in accordance with the principle that the field commanders have such discretion, "had crossed the border and advanced on Mukden."[9] Kanaya, of course, knew well that in this instance no such principle of operational autonomy could justify Hayashi's illegal action.

Thirty-year-old Hirohito now had an excellent opportunity to back the Wakatsuki cabinet, control the military, and stop the incident from getting worse. Politically the military was still weak. National opinion regarding Manchuria was divided. If he wanted to rule as a British-style "constitutional monarch" instead of an autocratic monarch saddled with a constitution, this was his chance.

Nara's diary entry for September 22 says what Hirohito did at this critical moment:

> In the afternoon, when I was summoned by the emperor, he asked me whether I had warned the chief of staff [Kanaya] not to broaden the action. I replied, "Yes, I did warn him, but even without my warning he understood very clearly both the cabinet's intention and your majesty's will, and he is already addressing each part of the problem in turn. Regrettably it is touch-and-go with the outlying army, and they often go their own way." . . . [Later] At 4:20 P.M. Chief of Staff Kanaya had an audience with the emperor and asked him to approve, post facto, the dispatch of the mixed brigade from the Korean Army. I heard the emperor say that although this time it couldn't be helped, [the army] had to be more careful in the future.[10]

Having now understood the need to reinforce the vastly outnumbered Kwantung Army's forward units, Hirohito accepted the situation as a fait accompli. He was not seriously opposed to seeing his army expand his empire. If that involved a brief usurpation of his authority, so be it—*so long as the operation was successful.*[11]

By October 1, 1931, two weeks into the incident, most Japanese had begun to rally behind the army. Hirohito knew that the incident had been staged. He knew who had planned it, who had ordered it, and who had carried it out. He was totally aware that several senior officers had violated the army's own penal law of 1908 by ordering troops into areas that lay outside their command jurisdiction. Nevertheless, as Chief Aide-de-Camp Nara's diary makes quite clear, Hirohito intended to order only the lightest of punishments for the army chief of staff and the Kwantung Army commander.[12]

A week later the emperor carried his silent endorsement of his officers further. Chinchou, a city in southern Liaoning Province, on the rail line between Peking (now Beijing) and Mukden, was "the last vestige of Chinese authority in Manchuria."[13] The air attack on it that Hirohito sanctioned was one of the first on a city since the end of World War I. As described by Nara in his diary entry of October 9:

> Before Vice Chief of the General Staff Ninomiya [Harushige] departed from the Imperial Palace, I told him that His Majesty wanted to know whether an expansion of the incident would become unavoidable if Chang Hsueh-liang should reorganize his army in the vicinity of Chinchow. If such an expansion should become necessary, his majesty would probably consent. [General Ninomiya] said he would speak with the chief of staff and in a short while would report to the throne.[14]

Buoyed by these encouraging words from General Nara, Ninomiya immediately ordered briefing materials drafted on the need to bomb Chinchou. The Operations Section of the General

Staff Office thereupon explicitly noted that the emperor regarded the bombing as "only natural in view of conditions at this time."[15] If Nara's October 9 diary entry is taken at face value, then Hirohito had changed his mind overnight. Earlier he had expressed disapproval to Nara of General Honjō's public denunciation of the Chang Hsueh-liang regime, and on October 8 he had told Nara that "the outlying military and the Foreign Ministry are at odds—the army wants to create an independent Manchuria-Mongolia regime and negotiate with it, while the diplomats consider that undesirable. I believe the army on this point is wrong. With my thinking in mind, warn army headquarters."[16]

A special meeting of the Council of the League had been called at Geneva to consider China's complaint. Opinion there had quickly hardened against Japan. On October 27 Nara's diary records imperial uneasiness:

> After lunch I visited with the privy seal for a while. [He] said the emperor had told him that he [the emperor] intended to have the chief military aide-de-camp question the army and navy ministers on their resolve and preparations if we are subjected to an economic embargo or are faced with military hostilities with the Great Powers.[17]

By early November the attitude of the Foreign Ministry and the court had changed. On the sixth Foreign Minister Shidehara reported to the emperor that the ministry had decided to abandon negotiating with only the Nationalist government of Chiang Kai-shek. Support should be given to Gen. Hsi Hsia and a puppet regime established based on the Chinese landlord class in *southern* Manchuria.[18] Settlement of the Manchuria and (Inner) Mongolia problem might then be negotiated directly with the notables of that regime rather than with Chang Hsueh-liang or Nanking. Shidehara afterward sought and received support for this plan from Makino and Saionji, as well as Ugaki, the new governor-general of Korea.[19]

This policy shift came when army headquarters in Tokyo was trying to restrain the colonial army from invading *northern* Manchuria, risking a clash with Soviet forces. On November 5 Hirohito made a partial, special delegation of his authority to Chief of the General Staff Kanaya, allowing him to decide on "small matters" concerning troop operations and tactics. During the next three weeks, while the Kwantung Army moved by rail through northern Manchuria, Kanaya used that special authority on five separate occasions to check actions by the field army.[20]

Meanwhile, at the urging of U.S. Secretary of State Stimson, the League council had invoked the Kellogg-Briand Pact against both China and Japan. Over the objection of the Japanese delegate, the council then passed a moral resolution setting a time limit of November 16 for Japan to withdraw its troops from the occupied areas.[21] Foreign criticism of the aggression mounted, and the Japanese public, led on by the press, radio, entertainment industry, and the Imperial Military Reservists Association, rallied to the Kwantung Army and denounced both China and the West. When Uchida Kōsai, president of the South Manchurian Railway Company, came to Tokyo to promote the establishment of a new Chinese regime in Manchuria in accordance with the ideas of the Kwantung Army, crowds greeted him enthusiastically.

Faced with the Kwantung Army's deep distrust of party government and its inflexible determination to bring both northern Manchuria and Inner Mongolia under Japanese control, the senior generals in Tokyo yielded to the wishes of their subordinates and withdrew their support for a southern Manchuria regime. While the emperor was participating in grand maneuvers at Kumamoto, the Kwantung Army penetrated the population centers in north Manchuria. Then, suddenly, after a week of offensive operations, the main force entrained for the south and moved toward Chinchou, far from the railway zone, where about 115,000 Chinese troops were based.[22]

Emperor Hirohito now acted decisively through Chief of Staff Kanaya and Army Minister Minami, stopping the field army from launching a ground attack on Chinchou, though only for a short period of time. Nevertheless, when the high command in Tokyo endorsed the Kwantung Army's idea of establishing "independent" Chinese regimes in all three provinces of Manchuria so that Japanese forces could be positioned in the north to block any future Soviet invasion, neither the emperor nor the court group raised objections. On November 23, Shidehara sent a mendacious message to the Associated Press of New York, placing responsibility not only for starting the incident but also for the occupation of Tsitsihar and Harbin in north Manchuria squarely on the Chinese. "Japanese troops were not in the railway zone as ornaments," he declared. "When the Chinese attacked, they could not but perform the duty for which they were there—namely, to repel the attack and prevent its repetition."[23]

With the Chinchou affair weathered for the time being, the attention of the court group shifted to a political crisis at home. In March 1931, and again in October, radical officers on the General Staff, members of Col. Hashimoto Kingorō's secret Cherry Blossom Society, had decided to simplify their problems by overthrowing the government.[24] Hashimoto's March plans were discovered; the conspirators were arrested. When Baron Harada learned of the March incident, he concluded that the Manchurian crisis was "the opening act of an army coup d'état," which "has made some military officers firmly believe that because they succeeded in Manchuria, they will succeed at home."[25] When the army tried to cover up the October plot, Nara, Suzuki, and Chief of Staff Kanaya reported the incident to the emperor. On November 2 Nara gave Hirohito a more comprehensive written report.[26] But neither Hirohito nor any of his senior generals demanded punishment for the conspirators, who as a consequence were treated leniently: they were let out of detention and their crimes quickly forgotten.

The October conspiracy and Hirohito's weak response to it undermined the Wakatsuki cabinet's effort to control the army. As for the court group, they were now persuaded that nothing in Manchuria could be so important as preventing a domestic crisis that could bring down the monarchy and the entire Meiji political system. More particularly the October affair initiated open factional conflict between two groups of Army Staff College graduates. One, the Imperial Way faction, or Kōdō-ha, comprised Gens. Araki Sadao, Mazaki Jinzaburō, and Obata Toshishirō and the "young officers" who supported them. Contemporaries labeled their opponents—a much more amorphous grouping—the Control faction, or Tōsei-ha, and included within it Gens. Nagata Tetsuzan, Hayashi Senjurō, Tōjō Hideki, and others of high rank, plus their young-officer supporters. Both groups aimed to establish "military dictatorship" *under* the emperor and promote aggression abroad. The Kōdō-ha would use a coup d'état to achieve that aim. The Tōsei-ha, though not averse to assassination and intimidation, leaned more toward legal reform of the government.

In terms of strategic doctrine the Kōdō-ha considered the Soviet Union to be Japan's main enemy. They emphasized military and national "spirit" over material force, a principle that had become army doctrine after the Russo-Japanese War. The Tōsei-ha, on the other hand, gave priority to military modernization and the establishment of a "national defense state," a term borrowed from Nazi Germany. Tōsei-ha officers were aware that modern war had become a confrontation between whole societies requiring calculations of total national power. War against both the United States and the Soviet Union would require the technological upgrading of the army and navy, the modernization of industry, and the spiritual mobilization of the entire Japanese nation.[27]

As the Manchurian Incident unfolded, the conflict between these two loose groupings, which differed mainly over means, not ends, intensified and became a permanent feature of Japanese politics throughout the 1930s.

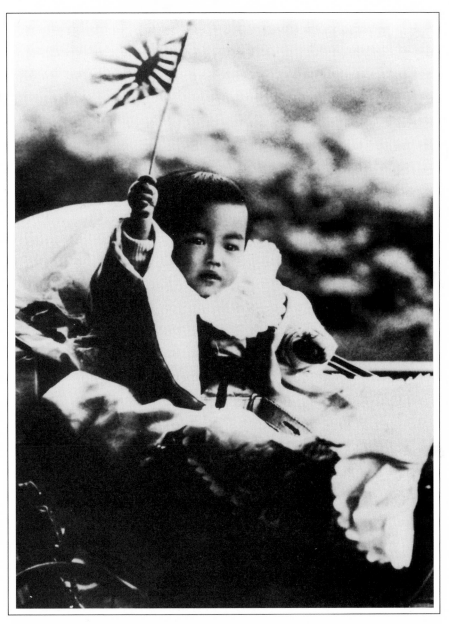

1902: Born into an age of rampant imperialism, one-year-old Hirohito clutches the military flag of the Rising Sun. (*K.K. Kyodo News*)

Resplendent in his supreme commander's uniform, Emperor Meiji posed for portraits that were frequently retouched to enhance his dignity, then widely diffused and handled in accordance with specially invented rites. Meiji was the lodestar of Japan's transformation from a late-feudal to a modern nation-state. (*Mainichi shinbunsha*)

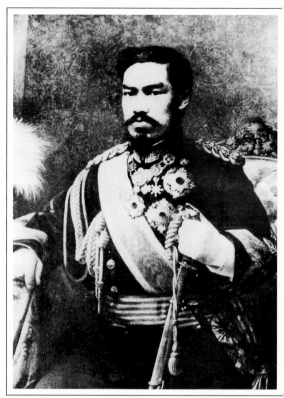

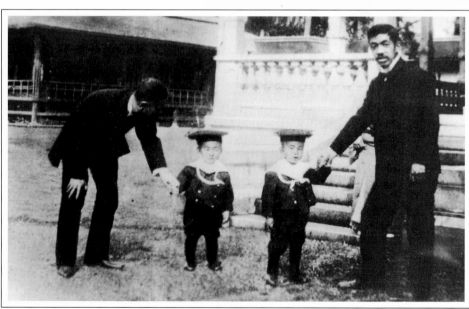

1905: Crown Prince Yoshihito, the future Taishō emperor, suffered from chronic ill health throughout most of his life. At the time of the Russo-Japanese War, he poses (*standing, right*) at his Aoyama Palace holding Hirohito's hand; an unidentified person holds the hand of his second son, Chichibu. (*K.K. Kyodo News*)

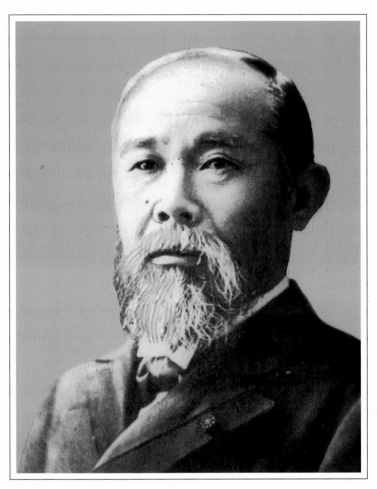

Itō Hirobumi, the chief architect of Japan's modern bureaucratized monarchy, established a Western-style hereditary peerage. Ito designed a constitution that defined the emperor as a theocratic monarch with near absolute political and military powers. (*Mainichi shinbunsha*)

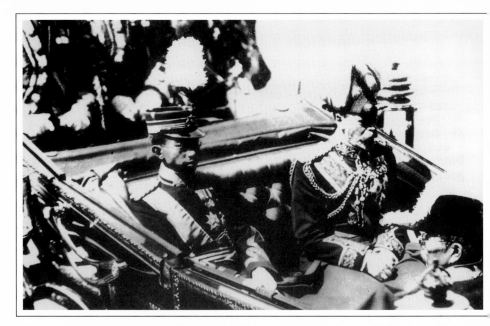

May 9, 1921: Crown Prince Hirohito with Britain's King George V. The real "lessons" George taught Hirohito had nothing to do with constitutional monarchy. The king exercised political judgments behind the scenes, used ceremonies to strengthen Britain's wartime nationalism, and in various other ways perpetuated the influence of the monarchy in a postmonarchical age. (*Mainichi shinbunsha*)

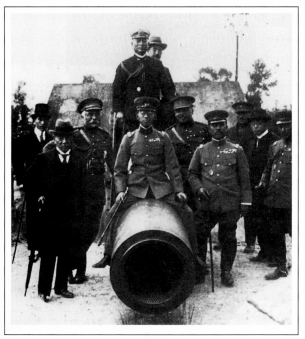

June 1921: Crown Prince Hirohito sits astride a cannon in Dunkirk, France. On his left is diplomat Chinda Sutemi, on his right Prince Gen. Field Marshal Kan'in and chief military aide Lt Gen. Nara Takeji. Standing atop the cannon, behind Hirohito is Vice Adm. Takeshita Isamu. Visiting the major battlefields of World War I in the company of his former military instructors deepened Hirohito's knowledge of Western military history. (*Mainichi shinbunsha*)

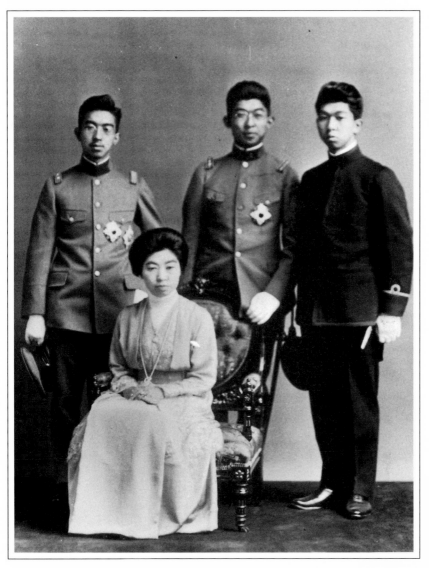

Proud Empress Teimei with her three grown sons: Prince Regent Hirohito, Prince Chichibu, and Prince Takamatsu. This photograph probably dates from the early 1920s, when public respect for the throne was on the decline and Hirohito was studying at court and listening to lectures in preparation for his future role as sovereign. (*Mainichi shinbunsha*)

November 10, 1928: Emperor Hirohito was formally enthroned, wearing traditional full court dress: a glossed-silk costume, dyed brownish yellow and printed with distinctive designs used only for emperors. The vertical pendant of his ceremonial cap also distinguishes him; the wooden tablet in his hand, a symbol of authority, may have been inscribed with thoughts he wished to remember . (*Mainichi shinbunsha*)

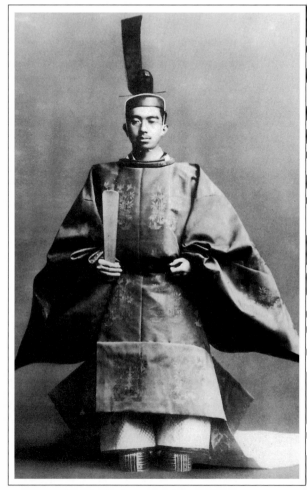

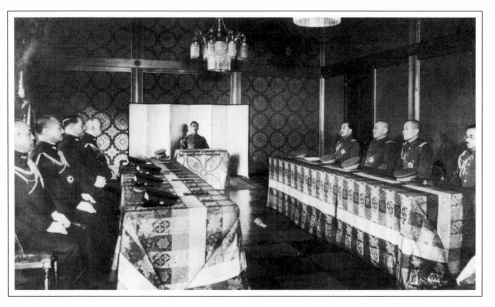

January 1938: Hirohito's political power grew in tandem with the military's rising voice in policy making. Presiding at his first Imperial Headquarters Conference, without uttering a word, he backed a stronger military policy toward China than the Army General Staff proposed and supported those pushing for continuation of the war. (*Mainichi shinbunsha*)

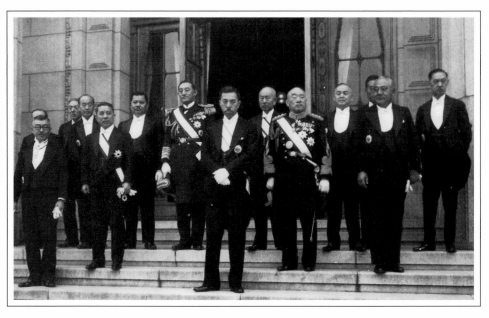

March 1938: The first Konoe cabinet led Japan into a protracted war of attrition with China. Prime Minister Konoe in the center, flanked on the left by Navy Minister Yonai and on the right by Army Minister Sugiyama Gen. Kido Kōichi, Konoe's friend, is in the last row, far left. (*K.K. Kyodo News*)

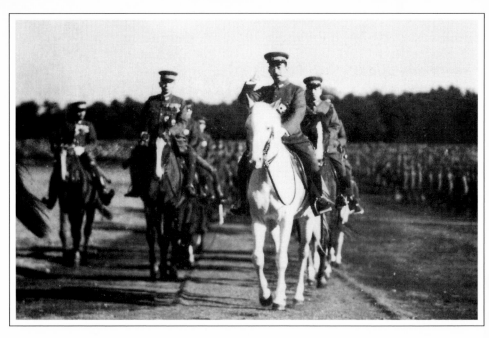

1938: As Japan began full-scale national mobilization for war in China in 1938, Hirohito confronted the problem of managing conflicts among the nation's ruling elites. Here he participates in an army review at Tokyo's Yoyogi Drill Ground. (*Mainichi shinbunsha*)

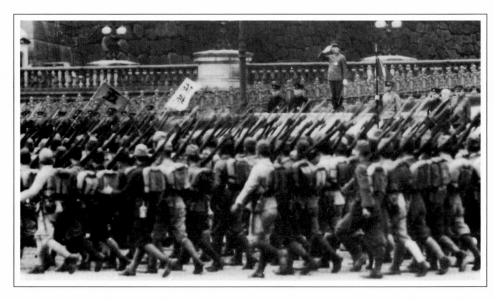

May 22, 1939: Hirohito saluting as more than 22,000 young students in military uniform march past him. That day, as part of the national campaign to promote "spiritual mobilization" for the China war, he issued an imperial rescript calling on all youth to play a leading role in developing the nation's fighting spirit while also fulfilling their occupational duties. (*K.K. Kyodo News*)

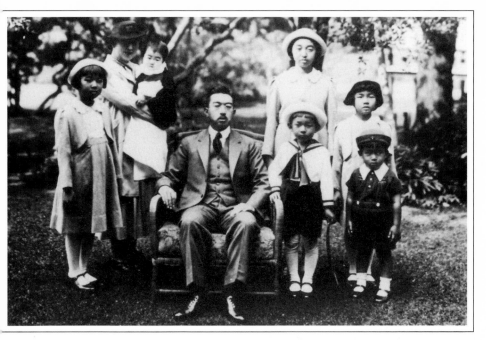

October 1939: Hirohito, a devoted family man, with Empress Nagako and their six children. In a garden of the Meiji Palace, the empress holds Princess Suga. To her left is Princess Taka and to her right fourteen-year-old Princess Teru. Five-year-old Prince Akihito (the present emperor) stands closest to his father; while Prince Yoshi and Princess Yori stand beside Akihito. (*K.K. Kyodo News*)

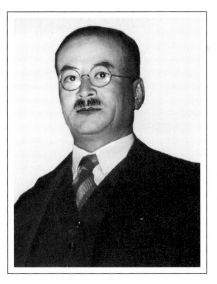

Kido Kōichi, a "revisionist" bureaucrat and member of the third generation of hereditary aristocrats, served at court for six years before becoming the last lord keeper of the privy seal in 1940. Kido was a great fixer and maker of alliances between the throne and hard-line expansionists in the military. (*Mainichi shinbunsha*)

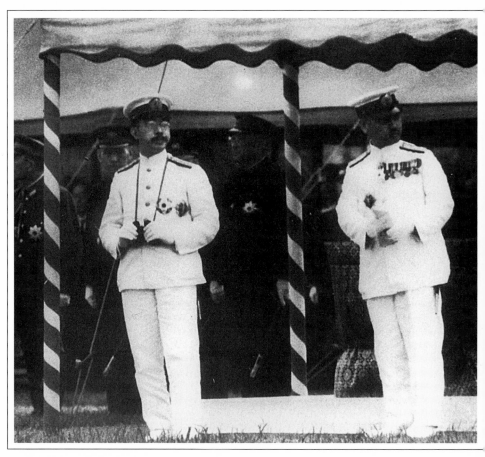

1942: Hirohito inspecting naval air exercises at the Kasumigaura air base, Ibaragi prefecture. With the Battle of Guadalcanal raging, he worried about how to strengthen air power in the Southwest Pacific. (*Mainichi shinbunsha*)

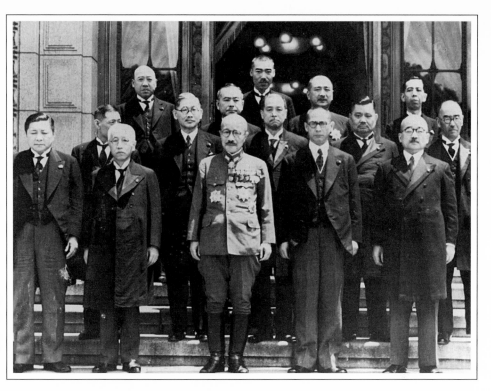

October 1941: Prime Minister General Tōjō Hideki with his cabinet of "wise men." No previous prime minister exceeded Tōjō in his passion to carry out Hirohito's slightest wish. In the third row (*rear, far right*) is the face of Kishi Nobusuke, a war criminal suspect who became a postwar prime minister. (*K.K. Kyodo News*)

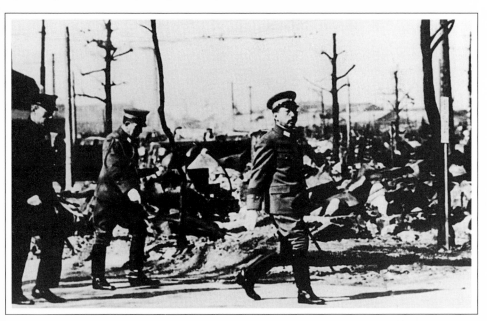

March 1945: Having resolved many weeks earlier to continue the war to the bitter end, Hirohito rushes past fire-bombed ruins in the capital—evidence of the American incendiary raids, designed to destroy civilian morale. (*K.K. Kyodo News*)

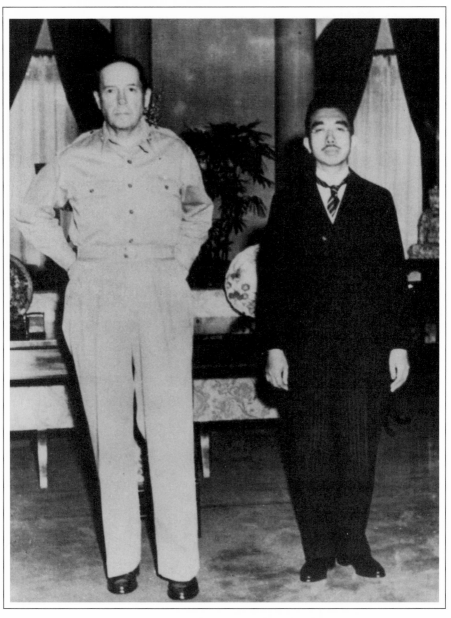

September 27, 1945: This famous photograph of General MacArthur and Emperor Hirohito at the American Embassy marked the beginning of a useful partnership. Printed in the Japanese press soon afterward, the photo played on the thin line that separated American informality from an act of disrespect to the throne. (*K.K. Kyodo News*)

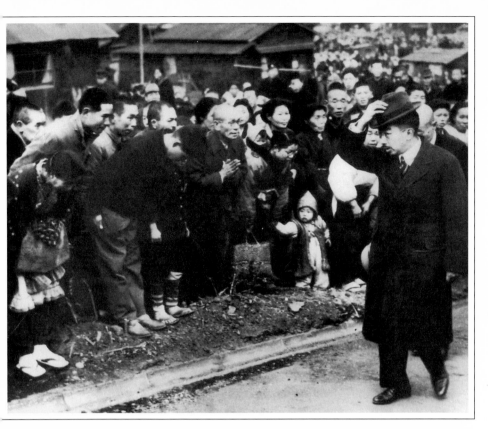

February 1946: The new "human emperor" inspecting war-damaged areas in Kanagawa prefecture, at the beginning of his national tours. Undertaken at the suggestion of occupation officials, Hirohito's carefully choreographed tours helped "democratize" and transform the monarchy. Newsreels of him "at one with his people" were shown in the United States, where they also generated helpful publicity for MacArthur. (*Mainichi shinbunsha*)

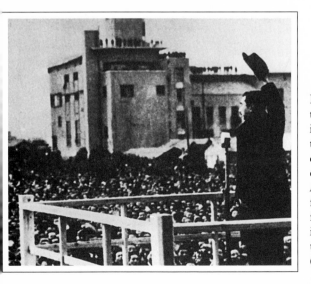

December 1947: Hirohito on tour in Hiroshima. Totally ignorant of his role in delaying the surrender, most Japanese continued to welcome him emotionally wherever he went. Allied criticism of the lavishly funded, highly political tours finally led GHQ to cancel them in 1948, the year the Tokyo trials entered their final stage. (*K.K. Kyodo News*)

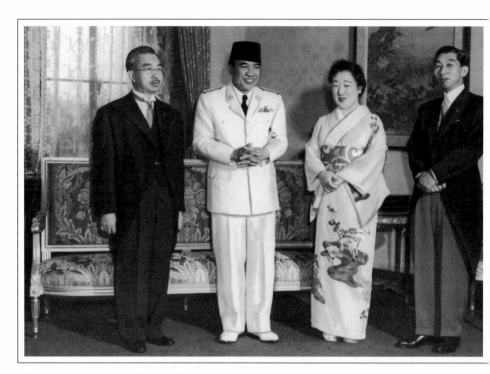

June 1959: As part of Japan's U.S.–supported effort to promote itself as a model of rapid economic growth, Hirohito greeted many Asian heads of state in the late 1950's. Here, accompanied by Empress Nagako and Prince Takamatsu, he receives President Sukarno, the dictator of Indonesia who had come to power in August 1945 by cooperating with Japan's wartime occupation regime. (*Mainichi shinbunsha*)

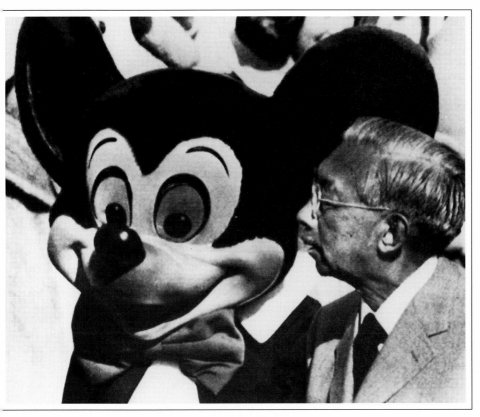

October 1975: The long-standing perception of Hirohito as a politically impotent, innocuous figurehead was confirmed for many Americans when the elderly emperor made a walkabout with Mickey Mouse at Disneyland, California. Here he also signed the visitor's book
and acquired a Mickey Mouse wristwatch. (*AP/Wide World Photos*)

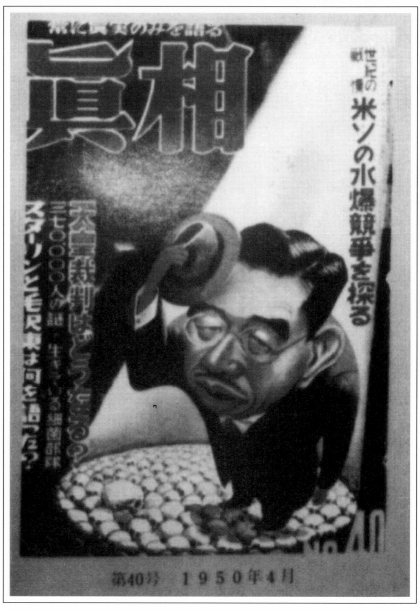

Shinso 40 (Apr. 1, 1950): Even as the political mood in Japan shifted to the right, the satirical magazine put hat-doffing Hirohito, standing on a ground of human skulls, in the limelight. Although American policy prevented the International Military Tribunal for the Far East from indicting the emperor as a war criminal, a small but significant minority of Japanese understood the enormity of his wartime role and were never so forgiving.(*San Ichi Shobo K.K.*)

I

It is fair to say that through 1931 Hirohito had less ruled than presided over his people, and that his performance had been dilatory, inconsistent, and self-contradictory. He had asserted his authority at petty moments; at more serious ones, he had caved in to insubordinate army officers. More aware of Japan's economic dependency on the West than the staff officers who had engineered the Manchurian Incident, he had worried about diplomatic isolation and economic sanctions, but never once said, publicly or privately, that the Manchurian action of the army had been wrong. Instead, with excessive tolerance, he ratified each expansion of the action while pampering and refusing to punish senior officers who had committed criminal acts of insubordination. For young officers throughout the army and navy, the message went out that the emperor's main concern was success; obedience to the central command in Tokyo was secondary. Signaling to the plotters and advocates of a "Shōwa restoration" that his priorities were not always those of his advisers, Hirohito made further acts of military insubordination more likely—a consequence he certainly did not intend.

Prime Minister Wakatsuki resigned on December 11, 1931. He had failed to control the army, to contain the Depression, and, most vitally, to maintain the backing of the court group. The Manchurian Incident now entered a second stage. The court officials conferred and decided that the more chauvinistic Seiyūkai, then a minority party in both the Diet and the prefectural assemblies, should form the next cabinet. Inukai Tsuyoshi, president of the Seiyūkai, had sided with the opponents of the London Naval Treaty in 1930 and later had affirmed the legitimacy of the Manchurian Incident. He had also publicly rejected the League of Nations' recommendations on Manchuria and declared (in a phrase that recurs throughout the whole history of twentieth-century Japanese diplomacy) that Japan should "escape from the diplomacy of apology" and develop a "new, more autonomous road."[28]

Aware of Inukai's indulgence of the military regarding

Manchuria, the court group instructed Saionji to discuss with him the terms of his appointment, which were to include avoidance of any radical changes in either foreign or domestic economic policy. This Saionji did, late on the afternoon of December 12, after having conferred with Makino, Suzuki, Ichiki, and the emperor. Four days later Inukai secured Hirohito's permission for a cabinet composed of discordant factions, with Mori Tsutomu as chief secretary, Lieutenant General Araki as army minister, and the more liberal Takahashi as finance minister.[29]

On becoming prime minister Inukai immediately ended Japan's two-year adherence to the gold-standard exchange system on which the free flow of commodities and loan capital had been based during much of the 1920s. With this action Japan joined Britain and other powers that had begun to pursue divergent—and defensive—economic recovery policies that undermined international trust. Next Inukai requested the emperor's permission to dispatch two battalions to Tientsin and a brigade to Manchuria, where since early December Kwantung Army troops had been massing for a ground assault on Chinchou. On December 23, as Hirohito was instructing Inukai, then serving as his foreign minister, "to adopt a policy of not attacking Chinchou" and "to maintain international trust," the Kwantung Army moved on the city.[30] The United States, Britain, and France warned Japan that its actions contravened the Nine-Power Treaty. On December 27 Nara noted that the emperor had again cautioned Inukai about "the impact that the Chinchou incident is having on international affairs."[31] Nevertheless the Kwantung Army proceeded to occupy Chinchou, worsening the strain in Japanese-American relations.

Once the Rising Sun Flag flew over occupied Chinchou, however, Hirohito put aside his misgivings. On January 4, 1932, he took the occasion of the fiftieth anniversary of Meiji's Imperial Rescript to Soldiers and Sailors to issue his own rescript calling on all military men to meditate on its meaning—in effect, a very mild admonition. Four days later, perhaps on the recommendation of Prince Kan'in, he issued an imperial rescript that praised the insubordinate Kwantung Army for having fought courageously in "self-defense" against Chinese "bandits" and for having "strengthened the authority of the emperor's army [kōgun]." Widely disseminated nationwide through the radio and the newspapers, the rescript quieted dissent and nudged people toward war.[32] Needless to say it did nothing to support Inukai's efforts to restore discipline in the army.

Moreover, over the next few years Hirohito granted awards and promotions to approximately three thousand military and civil officials for meritorious service in connection with the Manchurian war and the Shanghai Incident, both of which were tremendously popular at home, and the opposite abroad. Kwantung Army Commander Honjō, Army Minister Araki, and Navy Minister Ōsumi Mineo were awarded the title of baron.[33] Hirohito's public support of the army's campaign in Manchuria fits right in with his failure to punish them even when they disobeyed orders.

Between late January and March 1932, the Japan-China conflict spread to Shanghai, and condemnation of Japan continued to grow in the West. When a puppet Manchukuo government under Pu Yi, the last Ch'ing Dynasty emperor (from 1908 to 1912), was established, Inukai deliberately withheld recognition from the new state. Heading a divided party cabinet, he governed with the help of the privy council and relied on emergency imperial edicts and emergency financial measures that flouted the Diet's budgetary authority.[34] Even after his Seiyūkai Party had won overwhelmingly in the February general election, Inukai still faced intense opposition in his efforts to maintain the status quo at home as the court had instructed him to do. Right-wing extremists and terrorists repeatedly assailed him verbally, while the leading reformer in his own party, Mori, sought to break up the party system itself and ally with the military to create a new, more authoritarian political order.

Early in Inukai's tenure the army underscored its ties to the imperial bloodline by promoting Prince Kan'in, the senior member of the (extended) imperial family, to chief of the Army General Staff, thereby also eliminating from the high command General Kanaya, a key member of the Ugaki faction. The navy responded by bringing to the fore, as Chief of the Navy General Staff, Prince Fushimi, who had recently led a purge of supporters of the London Naval Treaty. The advancement of these two hard-liners signified a decline in the authority of the service ministers. The rival services could now use their respective princely "authority figures" to influence the emperor and to control their forces on the Asian continent.[35]

During the five-month life of the Inukai cabinet, Hirohito became a publicly active, voluntary participant in the incident, which he had definitely not been at its start. His main priorities at the beginning of 1932 were to maintain the throne's independence from the political parties but not from the suddenly popular military, while mobilizing public support for the Manchurian operation. He also wanted to ensure continuity of both government policy and top personnel. Consequently, when a Korean nationalist tried to assassinate him as he was returning in his horse-drawn carriage from a military review (the Sakuradamon incident of January 8), the emperor insisted that the cabinet stay on rather than resign en masse, as would have been customary.[36] At that time Inukai had held power for less than a month. So Hirohito downplayed the seriousness of the incident and avoided any direct, public expression of his private feelings about terrorism, as Kido advised. An indirect, further downplay was provided by press reports that he had bestowed "an imperial gift of three and a half kilograms of carrots" to two horses injured in the bomb-throwing attack.[37]

Meanwhile the Japanese takeover of Manchuria and Inner Mongolia continued without meeting military opposition from either China or the Soviet Union. On December 31, 1931, the Soviet government, deeply disturbed by Japanese aggression in the vicinity of the Soviet Far East, where the border with northern

Manchuria was ill defined, offered Japan a nonaggression pact. Hirohito's reaction to the Soviet offer (or if he even knew of it) is not known, but the Inukai cabinet simply ignored it. Formal Japanese rejection came a year later in December of 1932. Nevertheless Stalin kept the offer of a pact open until late 1933, by which time he judged the Japanese threat to have subsided temporarily.[38]

On February 16, 1932, the Kwantung Army command convened a meeting in Mukden of leading Chinese collaborators to establish a Northeast Administrative Committee. The next day that committee declared the independence of the new state of Manchuria.[39] On March 1 Manchukuo was formally proclaimed. The Kwantung command, confident that the Inukai cabinet would implement the army's policies, pressed Tokyo to recognize the new state immediately. Eleven days later the Inukai cabinet did endorse separating Manchuria and Inner Mongolia from China and setting up an "independent" state; on the all-important question of legal recognition of the new entity, however, Inukai delayed.

On this matter Inukai was at odds with the military; his chief secretary, Mori; and those in the Foreign Ministry who were prepared to put the obligation to Manchukuo above all other international duties and alignments. And while Inukai struggled to contain the radical faction in the army, he was not happy with Japan's worsening relationship with the United States, on which it depended for markets, technology, capital, and raw materials.

The administration of U.S. President Herbert Hoover hardened its view of Japan right after Inukai approved the army's occupation of Chinchou. Secretary of State Stimson then took a fateful step that determined American policy toward Japan for the remainder of the 1930s. On January 7, 1932, he ratcheted up the pressure by sending formal notes to Japan and China declaring that the U.S. government could not recognize the legality of any political change in Manchuria if it was made by force from Japan.

II

The effectiveness of Stimson's nonrecognition principle depended entirely on whether the Hoover administration was willing and able to force Japan to give up Manchuria. When, three weeks later, the Sino-Japanese conflict spread to Shanghai, where the Chinese had organized a highly successful boycott of Japanese goods, and Britain and the United States had important commercial interests, Washington could do little more than protest faintly. Even when Stimson implied, in a public letter to the chairman of the Senate Foreign Relations Committee on February 23, 1932, that the United States might start rebuilding its fleet if Japan continued to violate the open-door principles in China, Tokyo ignored the threat.[40] As the emperor and the Inukai cabinet well knew, with the Great Depression worsening, neither Washington nor London was prepared to do anything very serious about Manchuria.

Tensions in Shanghai had begun after Japanese residents took umbrage at a Chinese newspaper article, on January 9, decrying the failure of the assassination attempt on the Shōwa emperor. Nine days later army Maj. Tanaka Ryūkichi, hoping to divert foreign attention from the army's operations in northern Manchuria, instigated an attack by a Chinese mob on a group of Japanese Nichiren priests.[41] The Imperial Navy found this incident a tempting chance to demonstrate its prowess to the army. The Shanghai fleet was quickly reinforced and on January 28, 1932, marines under Rear Adm. Shiozawa Kōichi went ashore and that night challenged China's Nineteenth Route Army—a 33,500-man force stationed in the vicinity of the International Settlement, which ran along the waterfront. In the ensuing battle the Chinese gave the Japanese marines a good thrashing.[42] Unable to retrieve the situation despite reinforcements from the fleet, the navy had to call on the army for help. Inukai secured the emperor's permission to order troops to Shanghai. But the Chinese army still held firm and again inflicted heavy losses. The high command in Tokyo then organized a full-fledged Shanghai Expeditionary

Force under General Shirakawa and reinforced it with two full divisions.[43] Intense fighting ensued; the Chinese finally fell back, and Japan was able to announce a face-saving cease-fire, followed by an armistice, negotiated with British participation on May 5, 1932, which also ended the Chinese boycott.

The Shanghai Incident should have awakened Hirohito to the recklessness and aggressiveness of his senior admirals—the very officers he and the court group regarded as sophisticated, cosmopolitan men of the world. Driven by service rivalry, they had deliberately sought a confrontation with Chinese forces in the heartland of China, knowing that problems with the United States and Britain were sure to result. Equally important, this incident was an unlearned lesson for both military services. Neither army nor navy drew any new conclusions from the heavy losses they incurred in this first large battle with a modern Chinese army. They continued as before—utterly contemptuous of the Chinese military and people, whom they saw as a rabble of ignorant, hungry peasants, lacking racial or national consciousness, that could easily be vanquished by one really hard blow.[44] Hirohito himself may have held that view privately. But the emperor was more aware than his commanders of Japan's vulnerability to economic blockade. Going out of his way, he told Shirakawa to settle the Shanghai fighting quickly and return to Japan.[45] At Shanghai, Hirohito acted decisively to control events; in rural Manchuria, on the other hand, he was pleased to watch passively as his empire expanded.

At Shanghai, both during and after the fighting, Japanese officers and enlisted men alike exemplified the pathological effects of the post–1905 battlefield doctrine of never surrendering. Captured by the Chinese in February 1932, Capt. Kuga Noboru was returned to Japan in a prisoner exchange; he committed suicide to atone for his capture.[46] Praised for his martial spirit by Army Minister Araki, Kuga was later enshrined at Yasukuni. From this time on, officers who survived capture were often openly pressured to commit suicide. A plethora of books, movies, and stage dramas glorified the "human bombs" and "human bullets" who gave their lives on the Shanghai front. These tales heightened the popularity of the army at home, while also reinforcing its mystique abroad.[47]

Disagreements within the Inukai cabinet worsened after the first engagement at Shanghai. In trying to limit troop deployments and operations at Shanghai, Inukai could rely on backing only from the emperor—who was unwilling to discipline his uniformed officers despite the disruption of normal political life they were causing. While fighting raged at Shanghai, war fever in Japan deepened; public criticism of Seiyūkai cabinet policies mounted. Not surprisingly "direct action" suddenly went too far—and became terrorism. Two prominent business leaders—Inoue Junnosuke, former finance minister in the Wakatsuki cabinet, and Baron Dan Takuma, director of the Mitsui *zaibatsu*—were assassinated on February 9 and March 5, respectively. Their killers were civilian members of a secret band the press labeled the "Blood Pledge Corps." While these murders were under investigation, Inukai pressed the army and navy not to expand operations in the Shanghai area. He also sought Prince Kan'in's support for dismissing about thirty officers to restore discipline. Such was the situation when another clap of terrorist thunder ended Inukai's own life and precipitated the start of a fundamental transformation in Japanese politics.

On May 15, 1932, young naval officers murdered Inukai in his office, and two other groups of would-be (army, navy, and civilian) assassins threw bombs at the headquarters of the Seiyūkai Party, the Bank of Japan, the Metropolitan Police Office, and, most significantly, the official residence of Lord Keeper of the Privy Seal Makino. Demanding abrogation of the London Naval Treaty, they "distributed leaflets calling for the purification of the court entourage."[48]

In the ensuing political confusion, the emperor and his advisers decided to abandon the experiment in party cabinets that had begun in the Taishō era. Guided by Kido and Makino, Hirohito placed his support behind a fully bureaucratic system of policy making, and cabinet politics that no longer depended on the two main conservative parties in the Diet. Diet party activities continued, but the court group's fling with constitutional government by means of party cabinets working in tandem with elected representatives was abandoned. Moreover, navy and army leaders now abjured coups to seize political power, turning their attention to restoring discipline in their respective services. Precisely this interruption in the high command's effort to extend its political power gave the court group a chance to rally and settle on a leader of a countercoup cabinet.[49]

The day after Inukai was assassinated, the rump Inukai cabinet resigned, and the court group began deliberations to choose the next prime minister. As before, they called Saionji in from the periphery of events so that he could be seen as the emperor's proxy in presenting the imperial decision. Formerly the decision itself would have been made by the *genrō*, but no longer. On May 19 Grand Chamberlain Suzuki gave Saionji a paper (drawn up by the emperor, Makino, and Kido) containing Hirohito's "wishes" regarding choice of the next prime minister.[50]

Hirohito's first "wish," that the "prime minister should be a man of strong personality and character," reflected the thought of Makino and his intellectual adviser, Confucian scholar Yasuoka Masahiro [Masaatsu]. Yasuoka had recently formed the State Restoration Society (Kokuikai) to develop an ideological rationalization for moving "new bureaucrats" to positions of political power.[51] Loyal officials who believed in emperor ideology were, in his view, more important than institutions in carrying out the interests of the Imperial House. Only loyalists could prevent the *kokutai* from being overturned by internal movements and factions. The way to protect the throne was to nurture powerful personalities who were totally dedicated to the emperor. On this score Hirohito was at one with the "new bureaucrats" of the 1930s.

Hirohito's second point—that "Reform of the evils of present-day politics and the restoration of military discipline depend mainly on the prime minister's character"—expressed his concern that *public* responsibility for this most important task rest on the chosen prime minister. His other wishes reflected his displeasure with the revolving-door between the two main conservative parties in power, and the policy changes that invariably resulted. Hirohito blamed party-based cabinets rather than insubordinate officers for the erosion of his own authority as commander in chief. More distrustful of representative parties than of military insurgents, he would strengthen the power of the throne by weakening the power—indeed the very principle—of party government.

Presumably the aged Admiral Saitō at the head of a cabinet of "national unity," rather than Seiyūkai president Suzuki Kisaburō, would bring in trustworthy officials of stern character. These would be the "new bureaucrats" who, freed from loyalties to partisan political groups, and sharing the emperor's values and goals, would serve the nation by serving Hirohito. So emperor and bureaucracy had meshed in the time of Meiji. That cooperation must now be returned, and new autocratic officials appointed to join Hirohito in containing the forces agitating for radical reform.[52]

Naturally enough, therefore, Hirohito ruled out the choice of "any person holding fascistic ideas," a prohibition directed implicitly (as Masuda Tomoko has suggested) at the newly appointed vice president of the privy council, Hiranuma. Head of the Kokuhonsha, an antidemocratic, right-wing pressure group that nevertheless was within the political mainstream, Hiranuma advocated that the constitution be changed. He wanted to form his own cabinet, and was backed in this by Mori.[53] Civilian right-wingers had earlier campaigned for Hiranuma to be taken into the court bureaucracy, and he had many supporters in the privy council, the military, and civilian right-wing organizations. Hirohito and his entourage, not to mention old *genrō* Saionji, had ample reason to oppose Hiranuma.[54]

Yet to most Japanese in 1932 the term "fascism" was vague and mysterious, and referred mainly to Italy. Hirohito's disavowal of "fascism," therefore, may have sprung (as Masuda also conjectured) from his belief that anyone who criticized his entourage and wanted to change the Meiji constitution was politically unfit.[55] Hirohito needed to feel at ease with his prime minister. If that person was absolutely loyal and obedient, it did not matter if he held fascist ideas, for so long as an exponent of fascism opposed change by coup d'état, the emperor could regard him complacently. Two years later, for example, Hirohito registered no objection to the army's key concept of a "national defense state," even though the term was of Nazi German provenance and implied a state organized along lines entirely different from that of Meiji.[56]

"Protecting the Meiji constitution," another imperial wish, probably implied that Hirohito understood the extraordinary usefulness of the 1889 constitution—a document that neither guided the exercise of power nor protected the limited freedoms and rights of Japanese subjects. Why should he allow the constitution to be changed? It already could legally produce, "constitutionally," virtually any type of political rule that he and the power elites desired.[57]

Hirohito's final desire, to have diplomacy based "on international peace," was not an affirmation of the Washington treaty system, but referred to the new, post-Manchukuo status quo that had arisen from aggression. Although the "empire" had just gobbled up new territory, Japan remained economically dependent on its main critics and rivals, the Anglo-American powers. In this circumstance Hirohito naturally wanted to avoid new frictions with Britain and the United States. Therefore the consolidation of Manchukuo should be energetically "peaceful."

Ten days following Inukai's assassination, Hirohito bestowed the premiership on elderly Admiral Saitō. The cabinet of "national unity" that Saitō now formed included Uchida as foreign minister; Takahashi as finance minister; the leader of the new reform bureaucrats, Gotō Fumio, as minister of agriculture; General Araki as army minister, and Admiral Okada Keisuke as navy minister. This cabinet would weather four Diet sessions and numerous changes in cabinet posts over a period of more than two years, before finally falling in July 1934 in a corruption scandal involving the Teijin Rayon Company. During that time Saitō would preside over the construction of Manchukuo, Japan's withdrawal from the League of Nations, and a partial reorganization of the machinery of government.

Saitō at once began preparations to recognize Manchukuo. Violation of treaties would be required, and established relations with the United States would have to be risked. The League, international law, and the West now came under intensified attack by Japanese politicians, journalists, military officers, and intellectuals. The League's resolutions on the Sino-Japanese dispute were likened to the Tripartite Intervention of 1895, which had forced the Meiji government to give up the Liaotung Peninsula.[58] Army Minister Araki denounced the League for endorsing Stimson's nonrecognition doctrine and for judging Japan's actions to be contrary to the Kellogg-Briand Pact and the League Covenant. General Araki also elaborated on the theme of Asia oppressed by the white West.

Outwardly Japan would proclaim the existence of an independent state; in practice it would exercise suzerainty over a colony.[59] On August 25 Foreign Minister Uchida informed the Sixty-third Imperial Diet that:

> [t]he measures we have adopted toward China, especially since the start of the incident of [last] September 18, have been most just and appropriate. I view the formation of Manchukuo as the autonomous will of the people who live there—yet also as a result of the separatist movement in China. Recognition of the new state in no way conflicts with the Nine-Power Treaty.[60]

And in respect to Manchukuo: "this government has unanimously resolved not to compromise one step, even if the country is turned into a scorched earth."[61]

Reinforcing Uchida, Mori opined that "the new Manchukuo is a declaration to the world that our diplomacy has become autonomous and independent. . . . This action is akin to a declaration of diplomatic war."[62] Such ideological bombast and bravado clearly proclaimed the extraordinary notion that Japanese policy was unconcerned, in the short run at least, with national security and economic well-being.[63]

On September 15, 1932, the Saitō cabinet formally recognized Manchukuo and signed the Japan-Manchukuo Protocol agreement. Japan assumed responsibility for Manchukuo's defense and was granted, in a secret annex, permission to do there what it wanted.[64]

The League of Nations Lytton Commission, established to investigate the conflict, submitted its report on the Manchurian Incident to the assembly on October 2, but the latter delayed considering it in order to give the Japanese government still more time to get its house in order.

III

No issue caused Hirohito more anxiety than the prospect of the Kwantung Army opening military operations in the Peking-Tientsin area as a result of its offensive in Jehol Province. Prior to the offensive the army high command in Tokyo had tried to regain control by replacing many Kwantung Army senior officers and unifying the bureaucratic agencies in Manchuria. Senior Gen. Mutō Nobuyoshi was given triple appointment as commander of the Kwantung Army, chief plenipotentiary of Manchukuo, and governor of Kwantung—positions that had formerly been divided among three ministries.[65] At the same time the size of the Kwantung Army was increased.

In November 1932 Hirohito learned that the Kwantung Army considered Jehol Province (an important source of revenue from opium) to be part of Manchukuo, and planned to invade the province in the spring.[66] By December 23, however, advanced units of the Kwantung Army had already reached Shanhaikuan, the eastern terminus of the Great Wall and the entrance to Jehol Province. There they clashed briefly with the forces of Chiang Hsueh-liang. A more serious clash occurred a week later, on January 1, 1933, and the Japanese occupied the entire town. Hirohito, aware that this latest army advance could complicate relations with the League, tried to warn the army (through Nara) not to allow the incident to expand; two days later he suggested to Makino that the problem be addressed by convening an imperial conference.[67] But the entourage was divided; no imperial conference was called.

On January 14, 1933, when Chief of the General Staff Prince Kan'in asked the emperor to sanction more troops in Manchuria, Hirohito warned him about Jehol Province.[68] According to Makino (verified by Kido), Hirohito told Kan'in, "We have been very lucky so far in Manchuria. It would be regrettable if we should make a mistake now. So go carefully in Jehol."[69] In other words the emperor instructed Kan'in not to let the operation overreach. What worried him was not territorial expansion per se, but failure, and fear of where accountability for failure might ultimately come to rest.

A few weeks later Hirohito went out of his way to honor Lt. Gen. Tamon Jirō and Gen. Yoda Shirō, former commanders of, respectively, the Second Division and the Thirty-eighth Mixed Brigade of the Korean Army, which had taken part at the beginning of the incident. The generals had just landed at Ushina port in Hiroshima prefecture. Hirohito sent an attaché to deliver a personal message to them. Later he invited Tamon and Yoda to a palace banquet, where they and other ranking officers received gifts bearing the imperial crest.[70] Such gifts were, of course, standard palace procedure at imperial fetes, but in this instance indicated that the commander in chief approved and was proud of what his senior officers had accomplished. With lightning speed and very few Japanese casualties, they had expanded the Meiji colonial inheritance for which he was responsible.

On the other hand, grateful though he was, Hirohito still had reason for concern. Military expansion beyond China's Three Eastern Provinces carried dual risks, major war with China and opposition from the Great Powers, particularly the Soviet Union. Already Moscow was rapidly building up its Far Eastern Army, flying in air units from European Russia, and beginning to form a Pacific Fleet.[71] When the time for Hirohito to sanction the Jehol campaign arrived on February 4, 1933, Prince Kan'in asked permission to redeploy Kwantung Army units into Jehol. Not bothering to check with the Saitō cabinet on the invasion, Hirohito gave his conditional consent. Expansion to consolidate Japan's acquisition of Manchukuo was acceptable—but not an attack on North China proper. So he would approve the Kwantung Army's Jehol operation, he told Kan'in, "provided that 'they not advance beyond the Great Wall of China.'"

Four days later, on the eighth, Prime Minister Saitō informed the emperor that his cabinet opposed "the invasion of Jehol because of our relationship with the League of Nations." Realizing, but not openly admitting, that he had acted too hastily, Hirohito tried to stop the invasion. Nara should tell Prince Kan'in that he (the emperor) had decided to withdraw his previous approval; Nara demurred, pointing out that the chief of the Army General Staff was scheduled for an audience in two days, and it would be better for His Majesty to tell him directly at that time. Hirohito agreed. On February 10, Prince Kan'in came to court, and Hirohito conveyed the Saitō cabinet's disapproval and asked that the Jehol operation be cancelled.[72]

Contemporary accounts indicate that Hirohito was in quite a bad mood the following day, February 11. Joseph C. Grew, the newly appointed American ambassador, saw him at a court luncheon that day and noted: "The Emperor seemed very nervous and twitched more than usual."[73] In the afternoon Saitō went to Hirohito saying that Japan might be expelled from the League if it carried out the invasion of Jehol. He (Saitō) had tried to stop it "but the military strongly insisted that they have already received the imperial sanction."[74] Saitō departed; Hirohito summoned Nara and said, "somewhat excitedly," that he intended to stop the operation by using a supreme commander's direct order. Nara tells us in his unpublished memoirs that he recommended further reflection: "If Jehol was dangerous for national policy, there was no reason the cabinet could not stop it. . . . Cancellation should be ordered only by the cabinet. Any attempt to use a direct imperial command was apt to precipitate a major disturbance and cause a great political upheaval."[75]

Later that night Hirohito sent a chamberlain to seek out Nara's views again. Nara knew perfectly well that the cabinet could control the military only by going through the emperor. Nevertheless he replied in writing that "[i]t is improper for anyone other than the cabinet to stop the operation."[76] Hirohito acquiesced. The Saitō cabinet subsequently approved the Jehol operation; on February 12, Hirohito sanctioned Jehol for a second time on the condition that they "never cross the Great Wall during the course of the invasion, and if they do not listen to this, I shall order a cancellation."[77] These were the words of a highly frustrated commander in chief, not one who acquiesced unconditionally in the conduct of his high command.

The Japanese invasion of Jehol—an area "approximately the size of Virginia, Maryland, and West Virginia combined"—commenced on February 23, 1933, one day before the assembly of the League adopted the Lytton Report, rejecting any change in the status of Manchuria.[78] Encountering little effective Chinese resistance, the twenty-thousand-strong Japanese force completed its operation in about one week.

The emperor had tried very seriously to delay, cancel, guide, and limit the invasion according to his judgment of the international situation. His chief aide-de-camp, General Nara, had worked actively to block him. Managing to dissuade the emperor from employing the imperial power of supreme command was Nara's last major achievement. Shortly afterward Prince Kan'in nominated Honjō, former commander of the Kwantung Army, as Nara's replacement. First expressing mild dissatisfaction with that choice, Hirohito then sanctioned it when asked to do so by Grand Chamberlain Admiral Suzuki and Prince Kan'in.[79] Later the emperor would take Honjō's measure and learn how totally untrustworthy he really was. At this time, however, Hirohito was not strongly opposed to a general whom, after all, he had feted as a national war hero just a few months earlier.

IV

As the year 1933 opened, the Japanese delegation at Geneva found itself totally isolated. In Tokyo there was angry debate over the refusal by the League to believe the official Japanese version of events. When Foreign Minister Uchida alerted the emperor to the imminence of Japan's withdrawal, Hirohito queried him only about its effect on Japan's guardianship of the former German possessions in Micronesia.[80] One month later, on February 20, the Saitō cabinet formally—but secretly—decided to quit the world organization. On the twenty-fourth the League, by 42 votes to 1 (Japan), adopted a report denying recognition to Manchukuo and mildly criticizing Japanese aggression; no one was surprised. The English-speaking head of the Japanese delegation, Matsuoka Yōsuke, thereupon faithfully followed the cabinet's withdrawal scenario and walked out.[81] On March 27, the Japanese government formally notified the League that it had withdrawn.[82]

Hirohito marked the occasion with an imperial rescript to the nation. Drafted by the chief of the Foreign Ministry's Asia Bureau, Tani Masayuki, in consultation with the emperor and Makino, the rescript contained a pitifully feeble admonition that "Organs of military command and political organs should try not to infringe on their respective spheres."[83] Its real burden, however, was its assertion that a difference of opinion over the Manchuria problem had forced the government to withdraw from the world organization.[84] Nevertheless, that withdrawal did not go against "the fundamental spirit of the League" and Japan would continue to work "for the welfare of mankind." Depicting an obviously negative action as inherently positive and benevolent, the imperial rescript achieved a rhetorical mish-mash that obfuscated everything. This was an early instance of a practice that soon became standard procedure—the papering over of unresolved internal disputes by combining opposing actions and assertions in a bland—and blind—show of consensus when no one really agreed on anything.

Interestingly, too, the same day that the cabinet voted on the League, Makino had noted in his diary:

> I do not applaud our quitting the League. The people act as if by withdrawing we have achieved something great, or they believe our achievement is withdrawal itself. And the media rush about . . . [trying to realize] that goal. All of this shows the shallowness of thought in the Japanese public. As time passes, they will surely come to realize how superficial they have been.[85]

Perhaps Makino could have expanded on the role of the media in generating support for the Manchurian war, but he was not wrong about the uncritical popular response to anti-League propaganda.[86] Many people were easily persuaded to move right, left, or about-face. But what about himself and the emperor? Belief in a policy of expansion, disagreement over how to use imperial authority to control the army, and fear of domestic unrest all lay behind the court's appeasement of military expansion. Makino, particularly susceptible to such fear, had abruptly abandoned his support for Japanese-Anglo-American-cooperation when he was confronted by the advocates of a Monroe Doctrine for Asia. Rather than clash with the military, he abjured his long-held belief in the Versailles-Washington treaty system. He supported Hirohito's decision to quit the League, which he himself had helped establish. Hirohito and Makino, standing at the top of the polity, became, in a sense, the earliest apostates in a decade of apostasy.[87]

No documentation has been presented to show that Hirohito or his palace advisers ever sought to avoid a break with the League by proposing alternatives to the army's continental policy. Influenced perhaps by the euphoric public response to the army's deeds of valor, Hirohito decided to gamble. With little or no questioning of where the resulting diplomatic isolation might lead, he sanctioned the cabinet's decision. Maintaining a good standing with his recalcitrant army was more important to him at that moment than international goodwill. Hirohito failed to see that international isolation would not heal the internal, structural rift between the cabinet and the army, which only widened the more he exercised his direct authority as supreme generalissimo.

Prime Minister Saitō was equally shortsighted. In reporting on the League to a secret session of the House of Peers (February 21), Saitō, like the emperor, expressed concern only over small, immediate possible consequences of withdrawal, such as whether the League and the United States would allow Japan to continue controlling the mandated islands in the South Pacific.[88] One would have expected Hirohito to question Saitō on the long-term consequences of withdrawal. So far no evidence indicates that he did.

The new direction in foreign policy encouraged changes in how the Japanese understood themselves and the outside world. The old ruling elites had failed to give hope and encouragement to the people during the worst phase of the depression. The nation had responded by supporting the military, which at least seemed aware of their suffering and frustrations, and to want to help. Once the nation succumbed to anti-Chinese, anti-Western xenophobia and embraced the Manchurian Incident, the only chance of checking the military lay with the court group. If Hirohito and his entourage had stood firm, the shift toward Asian Monroeism—the rhetorical assertion of a Japanese right to safeguard Asia from the West— might have been reversed. But the court group and those in its milieu also tended to see international affairs in antagonistic racial terms, disagreed among themselves as to which line to follow, and were opportunistically inclined to begin with. Ultimately they cooperated with the army.

A policy of military and economic expansion on the Asian continent in defiance of the Great Powers was made easier by developments abroad. The Saitō cabinet appeared on the scene when the industrialized West had come to be characterized by very different systems of national organization and values. In Germany, Hitler and his Nazi Party—the most revolutionary, nihilistic, racist movement ever to arise in Europe—were goose-stepping toward power in January 1933. Their open intention was to destroy the Versailles system and build up Germany's armaments in preparation for war.

In Britain the Conservatives had a keen sense of rivalry with Japan over control of the China market. At the Imperial Economic Conference in Ottawa in 1932, the Tories had gone over to protectionism and had resolved to form a British imperial sterling bloc, hedged in by preferential tariffs for members of the empire.

In the isolationist United States, Franklin D. Roosevelt, starting his first term as president, took a different approach to the economic crisis. He upheld free trade and offered reciprocal trade agreements to as many nations as possible to lower tariff duties. Above all he sought to give people hope by reforming some of the nation's worst social ills and launching it in a new direction. But his New Deal recovery measures left intact the Jim Crow system of domestic racism in the south, while tending to reduce trade outlets for Japan in the Western Hemisphere and in the Philippines.[89]

As for the Soviet Union, its centrally planned economy had come to symbolize heavy industrialization without democracy. In 1932 the Soviet regime was returning to the international scene after having completed its first five-year plan. It was also starting to build up production of military aircraft and tanks and reequip its "Special Red Banner Far Eastern Army"—largely in reaction to Japanese expansion on the continent.[90] It could be cogently argued that Soviet Russia, with its enormous military potential, was a barrier to Japanese strategic ambitions, and that communism was an ideological threat.

Japanese supporters of continental expansion could point to other frictions with the United States and Britain. Although Britain and the United States disagreed on how to cope with the depression and had difficulty coordinating their policies with respect to Japan, British and American politicians could justly be depicted as hypocritical practioners of formal democracy at home and defenders of the imperialist status quo abroad—and Japanese journalists were happy to provide such depictions. Conversely, Japanese proexpansionists could soon suggest that the rise of National Socialism in Germany augured well for Japan. Germany had followed Japan out of the League, and was the potential enemy of Britain, the United States, and Russia. Moreover, in 1933, Nazi Germany was also in a state of emergency and like Japan aiming for a racial and cultural renaissance.

Thus ideas advanced by Japan's leaders to justify their actions in Manchuria gained reinforcement from the breakdown of global capitalism, emergent monetary and trade blocs, and contending domestic systems of politics and ideology. In a lecture delivered at court before Hirohito and his entourage on January 28, 1932, former army minister General Minami emphasized national security, raw materials, and the need for territory to explain the army's creation of an independent Manchurian state. "Japan-Manchuria joint management," he told the emperor, would enable Japan to "withstand an economic blockade from abroad" and "[continue] indefinitely as a great power."[91] The acquisition of Manchuria in its entirety would also solve the Japanese "population problem" by providing space for Japan's rapidly increasing people, whose numbers by the end of the decade were expected to reach seventy million.

Following up, Matsuoka (a former corporate officer of the South Manchurian Railway Company) delivered a court lecture on February 8, 1932, entitled "Japan-Manchuria Relations and the Diplomatic History of Manchuria." When questioned by Hirohito, Matsuoka somewhat vaguely stressed the difficulty of sustaining amicable relations among nations so closely related racially as Japan and China. "This is a principle in biology," he informed his marine biologist monarch.[92]

Konoe, a frequent participant in court group discussions, cast the problems besetting Sino-Japanese relations in terms of conflict between the white and yellow races and asserted the spiritual superiority of the Japanese over their pale opponents. For Konoe the Manchurian Incident was a bolt of illuminating lightning that had "pierced the dark cloud of economic blocs encroaching around Japan." "Even if the incident had not occurred and taken the form it did," argued Konoe, "sooner or later an attempt would necessarily have had to be made to dispel the cloud and open a path for the destiny of Japan." In "Sekai no genjō o kaizō seyo" (Reform the world's status quo), an essay he published in February 1933, Konoe sounded a Malthusian warning on the causal relationship between population pressure and war:

> Unequal distribution of land and natural resources cause war. We cannot achieve real peace until we change the presently irrational international state of affairs. In order to do that, we must . . . recognize two great principles. The first is freedom of economic exchange—that is to say, abolition of tariff barriers and the emancipation of raw materials. The other is freedom of immigration. Few possibilities exist for

implementing these principles in the near future, however. . . . As a result of our one million annual population increase, our national economic life is extremely burdened. We cannot wait for a rationalizing adjustment of the world system. Therefore we have chosen to advance into Manchuria and Mongolia as our only means of survival.[93]

For Konoe natural necessity, natural inevitability, and self-preservation justified Japan's right of conquest in Asia. He sneered at Westerners who dared

. . . to judge Japan's actions in Manchuria and Mongolia in the name of world peace. They brandish the Covenant of the League of Nations and, holding high the No-War Treaty as their shield, censure us! Some of them even go so far as to call us public enemies of peace or of humanity! Yet it is they, not we, who block world peace. They are not qualified to judge us.[94]

For Japanese who felt that the home islands and colonial Korea needed a territorial "buffer" against Soviet Communism and Chinese anti-imperialism, the idea of an "independent" Manchurian state was highly appealing. Defenders of Manchukuo also argued the great economic advantages of its vast resources. Manchukuo in time would become a life-space, providing land, homes, and food for a Japanese rural population, while its coal, iron, and agricultural resources would enable Japan's economy to accelerate and grow, and in the process prepare for any future protracted war with the United States.[95]

The idea of turning imperial Japan into a self-sufficient economic "empire" that could face down its Western colonial rivals in Asia militarily was, at one level, a rerun of the "Asian Monroeism" pursued by the Terauchi cabinet during World War I.[96] Autarchy acquired widespread public appeal, however, only when the Western powers were seen as wantonly bullying Japan. Self-sufficiency also had special appeal to Japanese capitalists at a time when they were seeking to reduce their dependence on foreign resources and technology, and shifting their domestic investments from light industries to heavy and chemical industries.

Of the many exaggerated, self-serving representations of the international situation proferred by Japanese opinion leaders during the incident, none was more effective in winning support for the army than the depiction of Manchuria-Mongolia as Japan's economic, strategic, and moral "lifeline," "our only means of survival." The lifeline metaphor, first coined by Matsuoka, stirred widespread feelings of patriotism. Gripped by a false account of their army's behavior in Manchuria, many Japanese seemed willing to confront even the greatest of the Great Powers in order to preserve their nation or uphold its honor. If recognition of Manchukuo and withdrawal from the League led to rejection of international law itself on the ground that international law was a Western construct, designed to freeze the international order at a point in time advantageous to the Anglo-Americans, then so be it. Japan would create its own hierarchical international framework grounded in norms that emanated from the emperor, who was morality incarnate and more real than the abstract Law Anglo-Americans cherished.

Konoe best captured this Japanese sense of aggrieved nationalism. Years earlier, in his famous essay of December 1918, "Reject the Anglo-American Standard of Pacifism" (*Ei-Bei hon'i no hei-washugi o haisu*), he had argued that the white race, by discriminating against the yellow, and advanced states such as Britain and the United States, by monopolizing colonies, had violated international norms of "justice and humanity." Japan, "an undeveloped country of the Yellow Race," should not advocate a "servile type of status quo," but a "standard of pacifism" which put Japan at the center of the world and ordered events from a Japanese perspective.

This Manichaean view of the age as a confrontation between

have and have-not nations, and antagonistic racial groupings, now predisposed Konoe to support the incident, and to advocate dismantling both the Versailles-Washington system and the various international treaties supporting it.[97] In a speech given in November 1935, Konoe denounced the League of Nations, the Kellogg-Briand Pact, the Nine-Power Treaty, and the London Naval Treaty, saying: "Italian officials preach with great boldness and frankness why Italy must expand. German politicians openly proclaim in the Nazi program why Germany requires new territory. Only Japan lacks this frankness."[98] Konoe found the reason for this deficiency in "Anglo-American standards . . . diffused throughout our Japanese thought," thereby strengthening "the institutions devoted to preservation of the status quo."

Although often criticized by *genrō* Saionji for these hard-line views, Konoe was trusted by Hirohito. It cannot be proved that Konoe influenced the emperor's decision to permit Japan to leave the League. But Hirohito had long been exposed to the view that the Great Powers were motivated by racial rivalry and hoped to keep Japan from rising to the rank of the the dominant power in Asia. Moreover, we know that Konoe's ideas did affect the court officials closest to the emperor, as well as the different elites with whom they had to deal in their role as consensus builders.

Ultimately, however, short-term political considerations caused Hirohito to align with the military. Hirohito recognized and drew confidence from the fact that most states had accepted Japan's faits accomplis. So far no Western power had recognized Manchukuo; but neither, so far, had any made Japan suffer economic punishment for that conquest. The most important need, in Hirohito's view, was to stabilize the domestic political situation, which had been shaken by assassinations of prime ministers, attacks on his entourage, and aborted coup attempts. That priority required him to avoid a confrontation with the commanders of the Kwantung Army, which was needed to defend Manchukuo.[99]

*   *   *

Of Hirohito's private life during the Manchurian Incident there are virtually no published materials, apart from a two-page document in Kawai's diary, and a few anecdotes by fiction writer Koyama Itoko, who claims to have met the emperor unofficially, and been shown court documents.[100]

By 1932, Hirohito and Nagako had been married for eight years. She had borne four girls, of whom three had survived, and was pregnant with a fifth child. That summer, when the situation in Manchuria forced them to remain in the capital instead of traveling to their vacation retreat in Hayama, they spent many hours of the day in each other's company, and maintianed carefully regulated work days. He awoke, as a rule, at seven-thirty, she a little earlier. They dressed without the aid of servants and usually breakfasted on milk and food prepared by two "court ladies" (that is, maids). When they finished, one of the maids rang a bell to let the chamberlain on duty know that he could enter and greet them. Their day started with baths, followed by outdoor exercise taken separately. For the pregnant Nagako, exercise consisted of tending flowerbeds or a round of golf accompanied by a nurse. Toward noon Hirohito returned from his office to lunch with her, then left for work until about four o'clock, when he again joined her for tea. They took dinner together around six-thirty and snacked again around nine before retiring to their bedroom, usually at ten. When Nagako was not tending her garden, she spent part of each weekday rolling bandages for the troops in Manchuria.

The summer and fall of 1932 were a particularly stressful period in their lives. He was struggling to cope with the Manchurian crisis; she worried over her inability to produce a male heir to the throne. Having been socialized to live strictly regimented lives of public service, they had recently submitted to pressure from Privy Seal Makino, Secretary Kawai, and Grand Chamberlain Suzuki and agreed to let their first child, six-year-old Princess Teru, move out of the palace to live in a separate building within the imperial compound. Neither of them were happy about the move, but they did not seek to defy the court tradition that seemed to mandate it.

In this atmosphere, sometime in late 1932, Empress Nagako miscarried. Afterward pressure mounted for Hirohito to fulfill his monarchical duty by taking a concubine. The elderly Count Tanaka Mitsuaki, a former president of the Peers' School and Imperial household minister, who had served both Meiji and Taishō, searched in Tokyo and Kyoto for a proper mate. Ten princesses were selected, of whom three made the final cut, and one (allegedly the prettiest) was rumored to have visited the palace and played cards with Hirohito (in the presence of Nagako). The monogamous Hirohito supposedly took no further notice of her. In early 1933 Nagako became pregnant again and on December 23, 1933, she gave birth to Prince Akihito. The personal crisis was over.

V

After the invasion of Jehol and Japan's withdrawal from the League of Nations, the Kwantung Army widened its sphere of occupation: In early April 1933, the army entered Hopei Province, south of the Great Wall, in the vicinity of Peking. Hirohito intervened, the offensive was halted, and the army withdrew to Shanhaikuan. But on May 7, the army again crossed into North China. This time Hirohito sanctioned the action post facto, but made sure Honjō knew he was infuriated. Honjō noted in his diary entry of May 10: "The emperor does not intend to obstruct the operation, but neither can he permit decisions made independent of the supreme command." Of course, the emperor did permit it because he had no alternative.[101]

That same month a spokesman for the Kwantung Army command announced that Jehol had been annexed to Manchukuo. Though not stated publicly, the annexation also included outer districts of Hopei and Chahaer Provinces, which lay within China proper. The decision for this annexation had not been made in advance by the cabinet; neither was it based upon "treaty rights." On the last day of May, Nationalist emissaries signed the humiliating Tangku Truce Agreement, granting de facto recognition to Greater Manchukuo and establishing a demilitarized zone south of the Great Wall in eastern Hobei. The Manchurian Incident was now closed, at least temporarily, as an issue of Western concern.

Having stabilized by truce a profound political and military instability, the contending forces drew apart. Chinese guerrillas kept up their warfare in Manchukuo. For the next four years the "buffer" zone between Manchukuo and North China proved to be less a zone of peace than a Kwantung Army staging base for unremitting political, military, and economic pressure on all five provinces of North China within the Great Wall.[102] But the mere presence of the zone, combined with Soviet willingness to sell Japan the Chinese Eastern Railway, and Britain's efforts to improve relations, allowed the emperor to believe that international tensions would soon ease.

As for Chiang Kai-shek, having opted to appease Japan for the short term in order to buy time to build up his forces and develop economic power, the generalissimo could now concentrate on fighting the Chinese Communists. But so long as a Japanese army controlled Manchuria, and stood poised to sweep Kuomintang influence from North China, Sino-Japanese relations could never return to normal. Neither Chiang nor the Chinese public had the least intention of letting Japan get away with its aggression.[103]

In Japan the contending forces and groups also turned inward. The Imperial Way generals and their supporters remained in positions of power; the army and navy remained at odds. As twenty-eight-year-old Prince Takamatsu, serving aboard the battleship *Takao*, confided to his diary on June 11, 1933, the army was enveloped in a "fascist mood," which the politicians needed to understand. The truce agreement pleased the emperor, but it was not enough. "We must somehow restore harmony, end bullying by the military, and restrain the selfishness of the *zaibatsu*."[104] A few weeks later Takamatsu noted that "90 percent of the national income now accrues to about 10 percent of the people." On July 21 his worries shifted to the "unappreciated effort" of naval power, not only in "bombarding Shanhaikwan and the Shanghai Incident," but in enabling "the army to act and diplomacy to work" throughout the crisis. Over the next few months the prince noted growing signs of radicalism in the navy and in society at large. As 1933 drew to a close, the birth of Prince Akihito to Empress Nagako evoked in him both joy and relief that the burden of imperial succession had finally been removed from his shoulders. The news that the imperial line would be perpetuated brought widespread relief to the nation as well, though only momentarily.

Toward the end of 1933, national policy remained in flux, with Manchukuo undigested and enthusiasm for the war beginning to subside, which was not what military leaders, bureaucrats, and journalists wanted. Fearing that the new penchant for militarism and war was about to reverse itself, army propagandists took action. The movie departments of the large newspapers had already been competing to produce "visual newspapers," or newsreels, of the incident.[105] Now the Osaka *Mainichi* newspaper company saw a chance to promote business and boost profits by making a new type of patriotic film that would show the nation what needed to be done in the period ahead.[106] As producer Mizuno Yoshiyuki explained, "communism and totalitarianism were contending with one another. Terrorism was everywhere. So we thought we could use the great power of film to make the nation understand the ideological confusion and the international situation."[107] The result was *Japan in the National Emergency*, a widely acclaimed documentary, produced in August with the assistance of the Army Ministry and shown throughout the country during late 1933.

Japan in the National Emergency is important today primarily for the light that its landscape of patriotic images and scenes, culled from the years 1931 to early 1933, shed on emperor ideology. In this film the armed forces used Hirohito's spiritual authority to endow the empire—and themselves—with a moral mission to expand. By processing a wide variety of visual images of national unity, the film reinterpreted the logic of Japanese ultranationalism for the early 1930s.

Army Minister Araki narrated half of the film's twelve segments, and at different moments in his presentation showed large maps of Asia and the Pacific, and a picture of Geneva. Araki equated military power and morality, using myth as his frame of reference for understanding the meaning of the incident. His two main rhetorical devices were the "great mission" bestowed on the "divine land" by the gods, and the hostile efforts of the Chinese and the Western powers to isolate Japan and prevent the "Yamato race" from realizing its sacred destiny, "secur[ing] peace in the Orient." Later in the film Araki defined Japan's role more concretely, seeing it as both strategic and cultural. The task was "to create an ideal land in East Asia," which meant constructing Manchukuo and there realizing a harmony of the races. In effect Araki presented imperial aggrandizement as an idealistic effort to realize an antiracist utopia in Manchukuo.

To Araki the internal threat confronting Japan was as serious as the external one. "Having uncritically accepted [Western] culture in everything," he declared, "we now find we have lost our hold on the autonomous ideals of the Japanese race." As he spoke the screen flashed to scenes of Western cultural influences that increasingly appealed to the Japanese in the early 1930s—modern couples dancing in Ginza dance halls, strolling hand in hand along busy, darkened Tokyo streets—juxtaposed against shots of imperial troops battling in the freezing cold and stifling heat of Manchuria, schoolgirls writing letters of encouragement to soldiers under the direction of their teachers, worshipers at Shinto shrines, and so forth. Araki denounced dancing, golfing, American movies, women wearing cosmetics and smoking in public, communists—everyone who had succumbed to Western decadence and Western values of individualism, hedonism, and materialism. The alternative to such defilement was traditional consciousness, exemplified in village life, Shinto shrine worship, and military service. The urgent need was to abandon the pursuit of pleasure and accept personal sacrifice and pain in order to accomplish the great national mission.

Throughout the film Araki sought to distill the significance of the recently concluded incident. It was a "providential blessing" that had unleashed the tremendous energy of the Japanese people. But it was also a "warning to us from heaven" to return to the great principles of the "imperial way" that had governed Japan since its founding. Highlighting Araki's words, the screen linked the age of the gods to the present: Takachiho-no-mine, the place where the male and female deities Izanagi and Izanami had descended from heaven, a depiction of Emperor Jimmu's enthronement, Ise Shrine, Kashihara Shrine, Atsuta Shrine, Meiji Shrine, the Imperial Palace at Nijūbashi, and Hirohito's enthronement in 1928.

In the last few segments Araki defined national defense and explained how "spiritual mobilization" could enable Japan to break "the encirclement offensive of the entire world, centered on the League" and symbolized by an "iron ring" surrounding Japan. As he spoke, the film audience heard "Kimigayo" and saw the Shōwa emperor reviewing troops, mechanized units passing in parade, and warships steaming in review and firing a salute. Araki:

> . . . the imperial forces exist as moral entities. They defend not only Japan's territorial needs [literally "expansibility in space"], but also the enterprising spirit of the state and its everlasting nature, which is coeval with heaven and earth. Consequently, when discussing national defense, I cannot agree with those who define Japan narrowly in a

geographic sense and in terms of coping [with other coun-
tries]. . . . Our armed forces are, simultaneously, the armed forces of
the emperor and a national force. They are, therefore, . . . a great
embodiment of our national virtue. Since we are implementing the
imperial way, manifested in the three imperial regalia, the carrying out
of the emperor's way is the spirit of the founding of the military. The
spirit of the Japanese military manifests the sacred spirit of his majesty
who commands the Japanese military. I believe our spirit expresses the
emperor's heart, which is why the imperial forces move only at the
emperor's command.[108]

Having asserted that the armed forces incarnated "national
virtue," and manifested the "sacred spirit" of Hirohito by expanding abroad, Araki guided his audience to the main thrust of his
entire argument: namely, that Japan must prepare for total spiritual
mobilization. "Ninety million people must become one and join the
emperor in spreading the imperial virtue. For this we must unite
and advance until the very last minute [of the battle]. In this way, we
will secure the glory of final victory." A montage of quick shots
shows patriotic businessmen donating aircraft to the army, women
receiving military training, motorcycles on the road, the nation
industrializing, factory chimneys belching smoke, people walking
briskly. Two segments later the camera cuts to the "three human
bullets" (*bakudan sanyūshi*) departing for the Shanghai battlefront,
where they blow up an enemy encampment. A chart shows the elements that produced their bravery, and finally the film shows their
gravesites.[109]

As the film moves to a close, the camera evokes a sense of Japan
triumphing over adversity. Climbers persevere through storm and
snow to reach the summit of a mountain. General Mutō travels to
Manchukuo and meets Emperor Pu Yi. A black cloud rises over a
map of the distant city of Geneva and moves swiftly eastward to sur-
round Japan. Cheering Tokyo crowds welcome home from Geneva

diplomat Matsuoka, who bows deeply toward the Imperial Palace while another map shows Japan spreading open the iron ring. To round out the film, the departed Emperor Meiji returns through three of his war poems, connoting the need for spiritual mobilization and reminding the audience that nothing great is ever accomplished without tremendous exertion and sacrifice.[110]

The army's second consciousness-raising endeavor was the book entitled *Hijōji kokumin zenshū* (Essays on the time of emergency confronting the nation), published in March 1934.[111] This work, part of a seven-volume collection, was designed to present the ideas of military and diplomatic experts on all aspects of the "emergency." The fifteen army contributors—representing many of the core officer group—sought to raise public consciousness about the nature of modern warfare and the dangers confronting Japan. What they mainly conveyed, however, were the lessons that the army had drawn and had failed to draw from World War I.

The preface, by the new army minister, General Hayashi, revealed that the army was still in the grip of the simplistic victory ideology of the Russo-Japanese War. For Hayashi, future war would be an extension of Japan's previous wars though on a much grander scale, requiring total national mobilization. Vice Chief of the Army General Staff Ueda Kenkichi explained that preparing the nation for war meant building up armaments, "uniting politics, the economy, finance, and all other institutions," and perfecting war leadership.[112] Other writers equated the development of national power with the mere technical "fulfillment of war preparations."[113] None grasped that industrialized warfare at midcentury required a high rate of productivity, mass production, and a vibrant economy unblighted by backwardness in science and technology or by agricultural stagnation. The army leaders' analyses, however, clearly pointed to a coming great bureaucratic reorganization of Japanese society.

General Tōjō asserted: "The modern war of national defense

extends over a great many areas." It requires constructing "a state that can monolithically control" warfare in all of its forms: military, economic, ideological, and strategic. Filled with anti-Western resentment, Tōjō dwelt on how the victorious democracies of World War I had waged ideological warfare against Japan. Hereafter Japan must stand erect and "spread [its own] moral principles to the world," for "the cultural and ideological warfare of the 'imperial way' is about to begin."[114] Other contributors to *Hijōji kokumin zenshū* tended "to reduce national mobilization for waging total war to a problem of acquiring resources" for self-sufficiency.[115] Built into the thinking of these military leaders were visions of territorial conquest on the Asian continent and the possibility of war with Britain and the United States.

There is no doubt that Emperor Hirohito, indoctrinated in post–Russo-Japanese War tactics and strategy, believed that superior arms rather than superior productivity determined victory. Unlike his generals, however, he was reluctant to break with the British and Americans, and felt little need to press a rapid, radical overhaul of the machinery of government or an immediate militarization of the entire economy. To do so could endanger the stability of the imperial house. This difference in thinking concerned both the direction and the pace of change. To secure greater freedom of action for building a total war economy, the radicals in the armed forces would therefore have to confront the throne and its protectors directly.

RESTORATION AND REPRESSION

When Japan recognized Manchukuo and withdrew from the League of Nations, most Japanese felt that something fundamental had changed. Youthful, ancient Japan had fought another war of "self-defense," and in the process scored an armed victory over Chinese warlordism and a spiritual one over "Western moral decadence." By its own efforts, the nation had opened a new road to modernity and put forth a claim to becoming greater and more respected in the world than it had been.

For General Araki and other politically active officers of the army, the rhetoric of "crisis," "Shōwa restoration," "Anglo-Saxon encirclement," and so on was simply a mobilizing device too effective to let go. They prolonged the euphoria of victory and took advantage of it by continuing the Imperial Way theme, using it to strengthen army influence in politics and to reshape the emperor's image. The pleasant view of an indestructible and virtuous Japan confronting morally inferior, devilish foreign states spread widely. So too did notions of "national defense state," "empire," and "holy mission" to spread the "emperor's benevolence." These ideas led people to invest the military's expansion abroad with notions of goodness. They also strengthened their desire to overcome the West in every field of endeavor and, in that way too, structured a new, more exclusionary sense of collective identity.

Under Meiji, Japan had superficially "escaped from Asia"

(*datsu'A*), assimilating certain concepts, as well as the technology, and in certain ways even the identity of the leading Western societies. The practical consequence was a kind of hopeful, shallow, often resentful sense of solidarity with the white Western communities in Asia, including the adoption of their racist attitudes and epithets toward Chinese and other Asian peoples. Now, however, Japan was on the rise, independently striving, building, renewing its role as the—rightful—leader in Asia. Therefore many ideologues now discovered that Western political thought was essentially exploitative, hegemonistic, and aggressive—in short, a contagious plague that for a time had infected insular Japan and caused it to threaten the interests of fellow Asians. Henceforth Japan should act not so much in "self defense," as to spread the Shōwa emperor's virtues by establishing a morally superior society in Manchukuo, where the "five races" would live in hierarchical "harmony" in accordance with the "principle of the 'kingly way.'"

Japan's Manchukuo-vindicating new national image, as well as some characteristics of its worship of the state, resembled aspects of German Nazism and Italian Fascism. (The latter developed partly out of an Italian search for a counterpart to Japan's national political religion of emperor worship.)[1] With the arrest in 1933 of eighteen thousand dissidents, and the forced recantation of many left-wing leaders, the communist movement in Japan was all too easily suppressed.[2] Between 1934 and 1936, what remained of Taishō democracy and the institutions of constitutional liberalism were similarly enfeebled by intimidation and assassination. Although racial intolerance and bigotry never became a state policy as in Nazified, anti-Semitic Germany, racial discrimination against other Asians was habitual for many twentieth-century Japanese, having begun around the time of the Sino-Japanese War of 1894–95, with the start of Japanese colonialism. The Anti-Comintern Pact made with Germany and Italy in November 1936 brought in Nazi ideologues who gained many Japanese supporters and injected Nazi-style anti-

Semitic arguments into mainstream public discussion—where defamation of Jews was already widespread. Thereafter all Japanese governments shamelessly manipulated the popular image of the Jews, not so much to persecute them as to strengthen domestic ideological conformity.[3]

Ethnological studies of the rural areas from which the army recruited most of its troops during the 1930s suggest, however, that despite the best efforts of the Ministry of Education, many country people were relatively unaffected by official propaganda. To them emperor ideology was neither so meaningful nor so valid as their own nativism. Family and village considerations still took precedence over state considerations. Indeed, down to the start of the China war in mid–1937, many villagers displayed only the shallowest acceptance of the emperor's authority.[4] Knowing this, the army always acted on the premise that soldiers were rooted, above all, to their families and villages. The army's Field Service Code (*senjinkun*), issued on January 8, 1941, emphasized that "[t]hose who fear shame are strong. Remember always the good reputation of your family and the opinion of people of your birthplace." And: "Do not shame yourself by being taken prisoner alive; die so as not to leave behind a soiled name."[5]

Significant exceptions to rural ignorance of the emperor's authority were persons in posts of responsibility in local society. Village officials, schoolteachers, policemen, Buddhist and Shinto priests—the foot soldiers of Japanese nationalism—invoked the authority of the emperor and the power of the state to strengthen their local authority. Their loyalty to and veneration of the emperor often seemed spontaneous and deeply felt. But most villagers did not occupy positions of public responsibility and probably were not devout believers in the emperor. Their patriotism was of a different order.

In 1935, for example, anthropologists John and Ella (Lury Wiswell) Embree interviewed farmers in the remote agricultural village of Suye Mura on Kyushu Island. When Ella Wiswell's book, *The Women of Suye Mura,* appeared many years later, it described a world of hard-drinking, outspoken farm-women, who laughed at the emperor's pretensions. Wiswell recorded a conversation with a literate woman of the village:

> Having stopped by for a chat, I asked her, "You worship the Emperor like a god (*kamisama*) don't you?" indicating the hanging scroll portraying the Imperial couple in the *tokonoma* [ceremonial alcove in the main room]. "Yes, when we make a ceremonial offering to the gods, we make it to the emperor too. When we pray in front of the gods, it is also in front of the emperor, and to him we offer flowers," she said. "Why?" I asked. "Well, I suppose it is because he is head (*taishō*) of the country," she replied. Then she described the figures in the scroll. "There on the left is Jimmu-tennō", the very first . . . and on the right is his wife. Then come Taishō-tennō and the Empress. Below them is the palace, then the three princes, Chichibu, Mikasa, and Takamatsu-sama. Below, there behind the flowers (she had a tall vase in front of the scroll) are the present Emperor and Empress. They are all great people. . . ." "And who is above them all?" I asked. "That is Amaterasu-Ōmikami. . . . She is the number-one goddess." "So, but why are they all in the picture together? What is the relationship between Amaterasu and the present Emperor?" "I don't know, but they are both there most probably because she is the greatest *kamisama* and he is the head of the country, the greatest person in Japan." "Then the Emperor is not a *kamisama*?" "No, he is just worshiped like a god . . . , but he is not a real god. He is human, a very great man." . . . "If the policeman were to hear us, he would tie me up and throw me in prison. But he can't hear, can he?" I said I thought we were safe. I left her on the balcony, dusting and drying her lacquerware. So much for Emperor worship.[6]

Even allowing for Wiswell's leading questions, this interview, which occurred at the height of the "*kokutai* clarification movement," suggests that the effort to prepare the populace for war had not penetrated deeply or widely. Life in the countryside was not yet geared to the political objectives of the army and navy. Nonideological irreverence for the throne and ignorance of, or disbelief in, the foundation myths were realities behind the effort to pump up state Shintoism, and they were hard to overcome.

By the eve of all-out war with China, Japanese public schools, under orders from the Ministry of Education, were inculcating Shinto mythology as if it were historical fact; emperor ideology had become fused with anti-Western sentiment; and a conceptual ground had been prepared for the transformation of Hirohito into a benevolent pan-Asian monarch defending not only Japan but all of Asia from Western encroachment. Emperor Meiji's image as a Western-style monarch defending Japan (alone) from Western imperialism was thereby enhanced—and stood on its head. From this time one can see a deepening conflict in official ideology between an emphasis on the absolute uniqueness of divine Japan, and the pan-Asian ideal that stressed a fundamental identity shared by the Japanese and their fellow Asians.

I

In the spring and summer of 1933 Hirohito faced discipline problems in his military and attacks on his court entourage from within the military, from the Seiyūkai, the privy council, and civilian right-wing organizations. Hirohito's military critics faulted him privately for "obstructing the army."[7] They called him an incompetent "mediocrity" who was manipulated by his advisers. Others complained, privately, that he gave less importance to affairs of state than to his recreations—marine biology, tennis, golf, and even mah-jongg.[8] Young staff officers in Manchuria were irritated by his alleged dislike of war.[9] Members of the imperial family were also critical. His brother Prince Chichibu and Princes Higashikuni and Kaya frequently reported that younger officers were unhappy with Hirohito's expressions of dependency on his entourage.

The year before, in 1932, Prince Chichibu, next in line to the throne and the brother with whom Hirohito was least intimate, had repeatedly counseled him to implement "direct imperial rule"— even if that meant suspending the constitution. At that time the emperor told Nara of his intention to transfer Captain Chichibu out of the Third Infantry Regiment because he had "become very radicalized" there.[10] The regiment, commanded by Gen. Yamashita Tomoyuki [Hōbun], was home to many populist young officers, including Nonaka Shirō, who, two and a half years, later would help plan and carry out the mutiny of February 1936. Acting as head of the imperial family, Hirohito had Chichibu reassigned to Army General Staff Headquarters in Tokyo, then to a regional command in distant Hirosaki, Aomori prefecture.

In April 1933 Hirohito had tried to curb the young officers' movement by pressing Nara to have the inspector general of military education, Hayashi Senjurō, an opponent of Army Minister Araki, take appropriate "educational measures" against extremism in the army.[11] It was yet another example of rule by three-cushion indirection. Araki, however, was not easily deterred from his support of the young officers. He proceeded to undermine the emperor by calling for pardons for the army cadets, naval lieutenants, and ensigns who (together with one civilian) had been indicted for the unsuccessful coup on May 15, and the murder of Prime Minister Inukai.[12]

Through the summer newspapers and radio covered the separate army and navy trials of the indicted. As support mounted for these "true believers in the *kokutai*," military reservists throughout Japan and the colonies gathered more than seventy-five thousand signatures on a petition calling for a reduction of their sentences.[13] On September 11, 1933, a navy court-martial sentenced Koga Kiyoshi and three other naval perpetrators to death, but later reduced their sentences to fifteen years' imprisonment. An army court-martial handed down even lighter sentences (four years' detention) to eleven young army officers who had taken part in the coup. The lone civilian conspirator, tried in a civilian court without the benefit of a huge and popular bureaucratic organization behind him, received imprisonment for life. At this time the Japanese judicial process invariably gave perpetrators of mutiny and assassination lenient treatment if they claimed to have acted purely out of patriotism. Ordinary civilian criminals, tried under civilian jurisdiction, rarely got off so lightly.

Two weeks after the navy court-martial, Prince Takamatsu, who had served aboard ship with some of the criminals, wrote in his diary that their "act of violence" had been:

> . . . purely motivated. . . . As military men they wanted to end the corruption of the political parties, the selfishness of the *zaibatsu*, the paralysis of the farming villages, the decadence of social morals, and the attitude of the nation's statesmen. . . . But social problems were not their immediate objective. Rather their primary aim was to convert dissatisfaction and distrust toward the leaders of the navy into perfect order. Many [navy] people regard social reform as secondary. . . . Since such a thing has happened once, there is a possibility that naval personnel might generate a second May 15 incident. . . . [R]ight now we must restore discipline and order in the navy.[14]

Restoring discipline and order in the military became the primary concern of Hirohito and his palace advisers after the formation of the Okada cabinet in July 1934. On the surface the problem appeared two sided: Abroad, the Kwantung Army and the small China Garrison Force in the Peking-Tientsin region had begun plotting to establish Japanese influence in North China, and it was unclear in Tokyo whether they would succeed. Meanwhile radical army officers impatient for reform were fomenting civil discord and extremism at home as a way of gaining power for themselves. The need to impose strong central control became clear during 1935, but both the palace and the Okada cabinet were slow to respond. Officers implementing national policy in the field often disagreed with General Staff officers in Tokyo who participated in drafting policy, while policy planners on the General Staffs feuded with their counterparts in the Army and Navy Ministries and in the Foreign Ministry. The emperor's task was to stand above this dissension and, without becoming directly involved, foster unity. In 1935 he was still groping for a way to achieve this.

More particularly, small incidents of anti-Japanese resistance in the demilitarized zone separating Manchukuo from northern China led the field generals to demand that Chiang Kai-shek withdraw his forces from the Peking-Tientsin area. Chiang yielded, and in June 1935, the Chinese side approved the demands of the Japanese army by signing the Ho Ying-ch'in–Umezu Yoshijirō Agreement. Five months later an Autonomous Committee for Defense Against Communism in Eastern Hepei Province was established in the demilitarized zone under Kwantung Army supervision. Intelligence agencies in the army soon followed up this diplomatic "success" by inaugurating a second pro-Japanese puppet regime, the Kisatsu Political Affairs Committee in Tungchow, under Yin Ju-keng, a Chinese graduate of Waseda University in Tokyo, whose wife was Japanese.

Hirohito's reaction to this arbitrary conduct of diplomacy by military field commanders was to propose to eighty-eight-year-old Makino that an imperial conference conduct a full-scale reexamination of policies toward China. According to Makino's diary entry of June 15, the emperor said, "Even if you question the *genrō* [Saionji] concerning the North China problem, he is far from Tokyo and far from the [government] authorities. I doubt he can provide us with good ideas. It will be effective to have an imperial conference depending on the circumstances [at the time of defining fundamental policy]."[15] Yet because of deep divisions among the political elites, not to mention the opposition and chronically poor judgment of Saionji and Makino, no such conference was convened.

II

The premeditated efforts of the Kwantung Army and the China Garrison Force to separate North China further hardened Chinese opposition. Japan's "Monroe Doctrine" for Asia became an immediate source of conflict with the United States and Britain.[16] While this was occurring, domestic debate on the *kokutai* rekindled, gradually resulting in popular distrust of the nation's ruling elites. For nearly a decade the court group had initiated efforts to "clarify" the national polity—that is, counter antimonarchist thought and impart rationality to the tangle of statements and intellectual arguments pertaining to the nature of the state. The leaders of the army, frustrated by the slowness of political reform, now launched their own campaign to promote an ideal of Japanese nationhood within the concept of the *kokutai* and the myth of the emperors' divine ancestry.

The campaign began in the House of Peers on February 18, 1935, with an attack on Minobe's "organ theory" of the emperor's position as the "traitorous thought of an academic rebel." The speaker was Baron Kikuchi Takeo, a retired general and member of the Imperial Reservists Association as well as the Kokuhonsha—a radical rightist organization that was part of the mainstream of Japanese politics. Kikuchi demanded that the Okada government ban Professor Minobe's books. A week later Minobe spoke in his own defense, while outside the Diet right-wing groups associated with the Imperial Way officers demonstrated against him.

In early March, reserve Maj. Gen. Etō Genkurō charged in the House of Representatives that at least two of Minobe's books— *Kenpō satsuyō* [Compendium of the constitution] and *Tsuiho kenpō seigi* [Additional commentaries on the constitution]—fell within the purview of the crime of lèse-majesté. Shortly afterward, on March 4, Prime Minister Okada yielded to the hysteria by declaring in the Diet that "No one supports the emperor organ theory."[17]

The following month, after the Diet went into recess, Okada and his cabinet ministers asked Minobe to resign his imperial appointments and initiated administrative measures against his writings. The entire government bureaucracy was instructed not to refer to the emperor as an "organ" of state. Officials of the Education Ministry directed prefectural governors and heads of institutions of higher learning to participate in clarifying the meaning of the august *kokutai*, following up by initiating investigations of books, articles, and lectures by law professors in the nation's universities. Bureaucratic ministries and offices throughout the nation soon began holding seminars on the meaning of the *kokutai* and the national spirit. To deliver the lectures and teach the new courses, they enlisted specialists in Japanese racial thought, academic opponents of liberalism, and advocates of Nazi theories of law.[18]

In effect, in order to counter the unauthorized, radical movement denouncing Minobe's constitutional interpretation, Okada generated a government-sponsored, national *kokutai* clarification campaign, which also declaimed against Minobe's teachings and banned some of his books and articles. It was this official campaign that Hirohito supported. To control the radicals within the armed forces and resist the *kokutai* indoctrination movement from below, which aimed at overthrowing Okada, he lent his authority to a government campaign that fostered unbridled fanaticism.

On April 6, 1935, Superintendent of Military Education General Mazaki, a member of Hiranuma's Kokuhonsha and a dispenser of secret army funds to right-wing newspapers, had issued an instruction to the army on "clarifying the *kokutai*." In it Mazaki reminded one and all that Japan was a holy land ruled over by sacred emperors who were living deities.[19] At that point right-wing civilian groups allied with the army formed a League to Destroy the Emperor-Organ Theory and "accomplish the clarification of the *kokutai*." Member journalist Ioki Ryūzō and law professor Nakatani Takeo espoused totalitarian ideas of remaking Japan in the image of Germany. The league's immediate goals, however, were to remove Ichiki Kitokurō from the presidency of the emperor's privy council and to eliminate the influence of Makino and Saionji. The opposition Seiyūkai, hoping to overthrow the Okada cabinet, began cooperating with the League.[20]

Nationwide antigovernment agitation on the *kokutai* issue continued throughout the spring, summer, and autumn of 1935. Senior officers of the army and navy, the army-dominated Imperial Reservists Association (with branches in all the prefectures), and an alliance of many small and some large right-wing groups, led the agitation, while religious sects that outwardly had subjugated themselves to the state, such as "Imperial Way Ōmotokyō," also joined the campaign. In August, when public procurators dropped the lèse-majesté charges against Minobe because his intent had not been criminal, the antigovernment movement against his theory rekindled. Thereafter the demand grew that there be no dissent from the truth that Japan was a "peerless nation" led by a divine, precious, august ruler, and also that there be no public criticism of military budgets.

Behind these attacks lay the ideological desire to discredit not a particular interpretation of the Meiji constitution but all constitutional interpretations, whether Minobe's or his opponents', that differentiated the emperor from the state. The leaders of the "League to Destroy the Emperor Organ Theory" were fighting to abolish the advisory powers of ministers of state, and to return to a more flexible process of governance in which the voice of the military could be freely translated into national policy. At their head stood the Imperial Way generals Mazaki and Araki, Vice President of the Privy Council Hiranuma, certain Seiyūkai politicians, and right-

wing agitators outside the goverment, such as Ioki. Their underlying demand was for very radical reform, captured in Ioki's slogan of
a "Shōwa restoration," and it made the campaign against Minobe a
threat to the Okada cabinet and, indirectly, to Hirohito. When the
army and navy ministers mounted the rostrum at a convention of
the Imperial Reservists, meeting in Tokyo in late August 1935, and
publicly expressed solidarity with this radical anti-Minobe movement, the Okada cabinet realized that a crisis was at hand and it had
to act.

To control the agitation, Okada was forced to issue a second
statement clarifying the *kokutai*.[21] Based on a draft prepared by the
Army Ministry and revised by civil officials after discussions with
the vice ministers of the army and navy, this statement declared: "In
our country ninety million subjects believe absolutely that the
emperor exercises the sovereign powers of the state. On this point
no one in government holds the slightest difference of opinion.
Consequently the emperor organ theory, which is incompatible
with this belief, must be eliminated."[22] In effect Okada twice officially proscribed Minobe's constitutional theory as an alien doctrine. After his second statement was issued, senior army leaders
withdrew their support from further attempts to overthrow his cabinet. By this time the Ministry of Education had initiated the development of a new system of ethics based on Confucian social values,
Buddhist metaphysics, and Shinto national chauvinism. A united
front of the leading right-wing organizations formed, dedicated to
saying "Out!" to American and European thought, and "In!" to the
reformation of Japan's institutions on the basis of Imperial Way
principles.

Doctrinally, one of Minobe's main crimes in the eyes of militarists and political opportunists was his (correct) assertion that the
emperor's right of supreme command was not a responsibility of
ministers of state. Its "sphere of application," therefore, had to be
carefully circumscribed by the Diet if Japan was not to have "dual

government," with laws and ordinances deriving from separate sources. In extreme cases, he warned, military power could "control the government and there would be no end to the damage caused by militarism."[23]

Minobe did not stop with only admonishing the military for interfering in national affairs. He also interpreted Article 3 of the Meiji constitution ("The emperor is sacred and inviolable") to mean simply that the emperor was not by law required to suffer judgment for his actions in affairs of state. If the emperor could freely conduct politics of his own volition, "then he could not hope to be nonaccountable, and the unavoidable result would be to harm the dignity of the imperial house." In other words Minobe assumed that in Japan the constitution imposed limits on the power of the monarch even though he alone was personally nonaccountable. Not wanting the emperor to be an "absolute" ruler saddled with political accountability, Minobe took a stand against the notion of direct imperial rule and the dictatorship that the army leaders were then advocating. Minobe further argued that imperial rescripts issued in matters of state were not "sacred and inviolable" but could be criticized by the Diet and the nation. Only those that pertained to moral issues and were unsigned by ministers of state were immune to criticism.[24]

Many of the army's leaders, wanting to have things entirely their own way, opposed Minobe by resurrecting a constitutional theory of divine right that sharply counterposed "sacred" and "inviolable." They found the explanation of Article 3 that they were seeking in the writings of Uesugi:

> [Our] emperor is the direct descendant of the gods and rules the state as a living god. He originally dwelt with the gods and was inherently different from his subjects. . . . That being so, it is obvious indeed that Article 3 of our constitution has a nature completely different from the same article in the constitutions of other countries.[25]

Uesugi's interpretation triumphed because it neither assumed Western-style constitutional monarchy nor infringed on the army's independence of command authority. Moreover, his view, which highlighted the emperor's absolutist position, was much closer to the truth of the 1889 constitution than Minobe's, which sought to justify the transition from rule by the Satsuma-Chōshū oligarchy to rule by party cabinets.

However, many extreme rightist believers in "*kokutai* clarification" were really seeking to abolish the practice of constitutional interpretation per se. While Minobe was suffering for not succumbing to the lunacy of this *kokutai* debate, and campaigns against him and Okada (considered to be too moderate because he too was unwilling to implement radical reform) were spreading, demagogic attacks on the court entourage also increased. Earlier, anonymous allegations of improper behavior by high court officials had forced the resignations of Imperial Household Minister Ichiki and his secretary, Sekiya. Kawai had also resigned his post and assumed the job of chief of the Imperial Household Accounts Office. Kido, the most politically competent member of the palace entourage, had stayed on as Makino's secretary and in August 1933 had assumed the additional post of president of the Board of Peerage and Heraldry, with jurisdiction over the imperial family. Now the two "*kokutai* clarification" movements, one from above and the other from below, precipitated a further reshuffling. Makino resigned at the end of 1935; a few months later Hiranuma obtained his wish of succeeding to the presidency of the privy council in place of Ichiki.[26] Ultranationalists, however, were not contented with this shakeup of the palace entourage and weakening of the Okada cabinet. Until the army's voice in national affairs was further strengthened, and the use-value of the emperor pushed to its peak, they refused to allow the situation to stabilize.

When Chief Aide-de-Camp Honjō informed Hirohito of the spreading attacks on the Okada cabinet and the Diet debates on constitutional theories, the emperor—then thirty-four—made no attempt to intervene and end the crazy furor in which he personally was never mentioned. Privately he told Honjō that "the monarchical sovereignty argument" was "better." But in a country like Japan, "the emperor and the state are, generally speaking, the same. So it doesn't matter which [theory] prevails." Decades of effort to define a system of parliamentary governance under the Meiji constitution were at stake in this "debate," yet Hirohito was indifferent to its implications. On the other hand, Honjō also alleges in his diary that Hirohito told him: "[I]n dealing with international matters such as labor treaties and debt problems, the organ theory is convenient."[27]

These inconsistent statements reveal Hirohito's attitude: protect members of the entourage, such as Ichiki Kitokurō, but avoid commitment to specific constitutional interpretations of his role in governance. After the war, when discussing the attack on Minobe's rationalist interpretation of the Meiji Constitution, Hirohito observed that:

> Under the Saitō [sic; Okada] cabinet [in 1935], the emperor organ theory became a topic of public discussion. I once told my chief military aide-de-camp, Honjō, to tell Mazaki Jinzaburō that I liken the state to a human body in which the emperor is the brain. If we use the words "bodily organ," instead of "organ" in a social sense, then my relationship to the *kokutai* is not in the least affected. . . . In addition there was the question of the "living god." I am not sure whether it was Honjō or Usami [Okiie] who held that I am a living god. I told him it disturbs me to be called that because I have the same bodily structure as an ordinary human being.[28]

In fact the state was not for Hirohito an entity with an independent life of its own, capable of meeting the needs of ruled and rulers alike. It had to have an emperor who functioned as its "brain." In this respect Hirohito always stood midway between the modern, rationalist theory of the state propounded by Minobe and the absolutist theory of Uesugi, which, under army pressure, became the official orthodoxy from 1935 onward. Hirohito also found the myth of the living god to be helpful for amplifying his voice in the policy-making process and for strengthening loyalty to himself in the military. Moreover, banning Minobe's theory was a way of checking any further attempt to revise the Meiji constitution by reinterpretation. So he allowed Minobe—who had denied the absoluteness of the imperial will and taught that the Diet could freely criticize laws and ordinances sanctioned by the emperor—to be purged from public life.[29] And the Japanese people were encouraged to behave as if they thought the emperor was a living deity.

Yet Hirohito was by no means personally comfortable with a movement that sought to deprive him of his freedom. He realized, too, that the participation of commoners in antigovernment debates on the clarification of the *kokutai* could undermine faith in the nation's privileged elites and diminish his own charismatic authority. Nevertheless he did nothing to stop the chattering cult that surrounded the throne from reaching new levels of fanaticism. If Hirohito ever thought his military rightists were thinking and acting wrongly, he never let them know it. What his sardonic exchanges with Honjō mainly showed was his eclecticism, his irritation with the army's attacks on his entourage, and his belief that the constitutional order contrived under his grandfather was compatible with any form of authoritarian government. He had been educated to play an active role in political and military decision making; he intended to do so, and he knew that many of the people denouncing Minobe's theory wanted to deny him precisely that.

Honjō, a stubbornly persistent fanatic, repeatedly pressed the emperor to change his thinking regarding his deification. "Because we in the military worship your majesty as a living god," Honjō opined on March 28, 1935, "it is extremely difficult in military education and command to treat your majesty as only a human—which is what the organ theory [of Minobe] requires." Hirohito tried to enlighten Honjō somewhat the next day. Addressing the text of the constitution, he pointed out that "[a]rticle 4 says that the emperor is the 'head of state.' That says precisely what the organ theory says. If you wish to reform the organ theory, you must inevitably reform the constitution."[30]

Hirohito's view of the constitution had been shaped by Shimizu Tōru, who opposed the "emperor organ theory" yet also found fault with Uesugi. Like Shimizu, Hirohito straddled these two main interpretations. That he refrained from coming out in defense of Minobe, thereby allowing Uesugi's absolutist theory to triumph, was only to be expected. Essentially Hirohito stood for protecting and strengthening the imperial house, drastically reducing the importance of elected professional politicians in making policy, and allowing limited reforms only as needed to meet crises. Because he equated himself with the state, and hence the state of the state, as it were, he tended to view all who opposed the established order as standing in opposition to him, and a threat to his sovereignty.

On this last point he was not wrong. Many advocates of direct imperial rule rejected the very notion of a state based on law and sought a dictatorship unrestrained by any constitutional interpretation. Hirohito was never prepared to go that far. The irony is that, in sacrificing Minobe, he and the Okada cabinet sanctioned a war against heresy that not only wiped out academic freedom but also abetted the very military radicalism they sought to control.

III

In late 1934, several Imperial Way officers at the Army Cadet School were arrested on suspicion of plotting a coup. No punishments were imposed in this incident, but the following year two of the same group—Isobe Asaichi and Muranaka Takeji—were again arrested, for having distributed a document charging that officers of the Control faction, such as Maj. Gen. Nagata Tetsuzan, had once authored plans for coups d'état against the government. This time the highest echelons of the army reacted. The accusations by Isobe and Muranaka were condemned as disloyalty, and both officers lost their commissions. Other officers of the Imperial Way targeted for retaliation a stalwart of the Control faction, Military Affairs Bureau Chief Nagata Tetsuzan, who was rumored to be planning a major purge to rid the army of factionalism.

In August 1935—six months into the populist movement to denounce Minobe's interpretation of the constitution—Lt. Col. Aizawa Saburō of the Imperial Way entered Nagata's office and used his samurai sword to slash him to death. At that point the struggle within the military over reform of the state and the demand for increased military spending, which lay in the background of the movement to denounce Minobe, took a more dangerous turn.

The anti-Okada forces in the army, still using the slogans "*kokutai* clarification" and "denounce the organ theory," now stepped up their attacks on the emperor's entourage and the hereditary peers. Senior Imperial Way generals arranged to give Aizawa a public court-martial under the jurisdiction of the First Division, a hotbed of Imperial Way officers based in Tokyo. When Aizawa's show trial opened on January 12, 1936, his lawyers quickly turned it into an emotional indictment of the Okada cabinet, the court entourage, and the constitutional theory of Professor Minobe. They not only won popular support in many parts of the country but even in such unlikely places as the palace, where Hirohito's own mother, Dowager Empress Teimei Kōgō, now a woman of strongly rightist views, became an Aizawa sympathizer.[31] Before the trial could run its course, however, it was disrupted by a military mutiny in the capital. Army Minister Hayashi's earlier dismissal of Imperial Way General Mazaki as superintendent of military education, and the issuing of orders for the transfer of the entire First Division to

Manchuria, had triggered the largest army uprising in modern Japanese history.[32]

Around five o'clock on the morning of February 26, 1936, the word storm over the *kokutai*, which had raged throughout 1935, burst into rebellion. Twenty-two junior-rank army officers, commanding more than fourteen hundred fully armed soldiers and noncommissioned officers from three regiments of the First Division, plus an infantry unit of the Imperial Guards, mutinied in the center of snow-covered Tokyo. They seized the Army Ministry and the Metropolitan Police Headquarters and proceeded to attack the official and private residences of senior statesmen and cabinet ministers. The rebels—1,027 were recruits who had just entered the army in January—assassinated Lord Keeper of the Privy Seal Saitō Makoto, Finance Minister Takahashi, and the new Inspector General of Military Education, Gen. Watanabe Jōtarō, a known supporter of Minobe's constitutional theory. They also killed five policemen and wounded Grand Chamberlain Suzuki, among others. While the assassinations were in progress, other mutineers raided the newspaper offices of the *Asahi shinbun* and *Tokyo nichi nichi shinbun*. Shouting, "Traitors!" at the journalists, they overturned type trays and fired their weapons into the air.[33]

Yet within the first few hours the insurrection began to go awry. The rebel officers killed Prime Minister Okada's secretary, but Okada and Privy Seal Makino escaped; they failed to secure the Sakashita Gate to the palace, so allowing the palace to continue communicating with the outside; and they made no preparations to deal with the navy. In Yokosuka, naval base commander Rear Adm. Yonai Mitsumasa and his chief of staff, Inoue Shigeyoshi, ordered marines to guard the Navy Ministry building and gathered warships in Tokyo Bay in preparation for suppressing the rebels.[34] On the morning of February 28, after fruitless negotiations through sympathetic officers in central army headquarters, the martial-law commander in the occupied area transmitted an imperial order to disperse. Most of the troops returned to barracks, one officer committed suicide, the remaining leaders surrendered, and the uprising collapsed without further bloodshed.[35] Martial law in Tokyo, however, continued for nearly five months.

The rebel officers had originally planned to have the army minister, General Kawashima, who was associated with the Imperial Way faction, report their intentions to the emperor, who would then issue a decree declaring a "Shōwa restoration." Despite their radical aim—overthrowing of the political order—the mutineers (like other military and civilian extremists of the 1930s) assumed the legitimacy and intended to operate within the framework of the imperial system and the *kokutai*.[36] They saw the emperor as the puppet of his advisers and, in effect, devoid of a will of his own. Once the lord keeper of the privy seal and the grand chamberlain were out of the way, they believed, the emperor could be counted on to bestow the mantle of prime minister on General Mazaki, the hero whom they trusted to strengthen the military and resolve the China problem.

At the beginning of the insurrection they had a chance of success. The Tokyo military police commander, Gen. Kashii Kōhei, was an Imperial Way sympathizer; the emperor's chief aide, General Honjō, was the father-in-law of rebel officer Capt. Yamaguchi Ichitarō; and supporters of the mutineers could be found at military bases throughout the country.

According to the historian Hata Ikuhiko, the rebels contacted General Honjō both by phone and written message prior to the attack on the Okada cabinet. Honjō, the first of the entourage to learn of the mutiny, could have warned the intended targets of their danger if he had been so inclined. He did not. By the time Honjō came to court at 6:00 A.M. on the twenty-sixth, however, Chief Secretary Kido, Imperial Household Minister Yuasa Kurahei, and Vice Grand Chamberlain Hirohata Tadakata already knew that Saitō had been murdered and Suzuki seriously wounded. So too did the emperor. At 5:40 A.M. the chamberlain on night duty, Kanroji Osanaga, had awakened Hirohito and informed him that his old ministers and advisers had just been attacked and an uprising was underway.

From the moment Hirohito learned what had happened, he resolved to suppress the coup, angered at the killing of his ministers but also fearing that the rebels might enlist his brother, Prince Chichibu, in forcing him to abdicate. He put on his army uniform, received Honjō in audience, and ordered him to "[e]nd it immediately and turn this misfortune into a blessing."[37] Honjō departed, and Hirohito embraced a strategy devised by Kido and presented by Imperial Household Minister Yuasa. Kido had taken swift action earlier that morning when Honjō arrived at court, demanding that the chief-aide-de-camp immediately determine how the Imperial Guard Division would respond in the event the mutineers marched on the Palace.[38] Kido's plan was to prevent the formation of a new, provisional cabinet until the mutiny had been completely crushed. At 9:30 A.M., Army Minister Kawashima, who in January had met with Isobe, one of the main energizers of the rebel officers, came to court and performed the role that the rebels had scripted for him: He urged the emperor to form a cabinet that would "clarify the *kokutai*, stabilize national life, and fulfill national defense." Taken aback at his army minister's obtuseness, Hirohito scolded Kawashima and ordered him to give priority to suppressing the mutiny.[39] Hirohito also vented his anger that morning on Chief of the Navy General Staff Prince Fushimi, a supporter of the Fleet faction, who came to the palace to learn the emperor's intentions on forming a new cabinet and was told, in effect, to get lost.[40]

Later that day Kawashima met with the Supreme Military Council, an informal group of high-ranking army officers, most of whom were sympathetic to the rebels. Among those in attendance and controlling the meeting were the Imperial Way generals Araki,

Mazaki, and Yamashita and their supporters, including Prince Higashikuni Naruhiko and Lt. Gen. Prince Asaka Yasuhiko. The council decided to try persuasion on the rebel officers before conveying the emperor's order to them, which was precisely the opposite of what Hirohito had demanded. According to the historian Otabe Yūji, "the army minister's instruction" was issued from the palace to the rebel officers at 10:50 A.M., five hours and fifty minutes after the start of their mutiny. It declared that "(1) Your reason for rebelling has reached the emperor; (2) We recognize your true action was based on your sincere desire to manifest the *kokutai*. . . . (5) Other than this, everything depends on the emperor's benevolence."[41] This "instruction," expressing informal upper-echelon approval of the uprising and intimating to the rebels that the emperor might show leniency, was conveyed to the ringleaders by Tokyo martial law commander General Kashii.

On the evening of the first day of the uprising, when the ministers of the Okada cabinet came to court to submit their resignations, Hirohito again refused to permit it, telling them to stay on without their prime minister until the mutiny ended.[42]

Early on the morning of the second day, February 27, Hirohito declared "administrative martial law" on the basis of Article 8 of the Imperial Constitution, pertaining to emergency imperial ordinances. Formally he was invoking his sovereign governmental power to handle the crisis.[43] In reality he was backing his orders to suppress the rebellion in his capacity as commander in chief by freeing himself from any obligation to obtain the consent of any cabinet ministers for his actions.

Hirohito displayed unusual energy in working to crush the rebellion. At short intervals throughout the second day and into the early morning hours of the twenty-eighth, the third day, Hirohito sent chamberlains scurrying down the long corridors of the Meiji Palace to summon Honjō for repeated audiences. Each time he demanded to learn whether the rebels were being suppressed.

When he did not like Honjō's replies, he threatened to lead the Imperial Guard Division himself. But (as Hata notes) Honjō was equally stubborn in his defense of the rebel's actions: Indeed, Honjō's own diary account of this period shows him a virtual traitor to the emperor.[44]

During the uprising Hirohito met Prince Chichibu, who had just returned from his post in distant Hirosaki and with whom his relations were not always amicable. After their meeting Chichibu is alleged to have distanced himself from the rebels and ended his relations with the young officers and the Imperial Way generals.[45] Nevertheless, rumors of the prince's sympathy for them never ended, and two years later Prince Saionji twice revealed (to his secretary, Harada) his fear that sibling rivalry in the imperial family could someday lead to murder.[46] Also on the second day two senior naval officers distinguished themselves by their show of loyalty to the emperor: Rear Admiral Yonai and his chief of staff, Inoue.

By the morning of the fourth day of the uprising, February 29, the emperor had firmly maintained his authority, the troops were returning to their barracks, and most of the ringleaders were in custody. Court-martialed in April, secretly and without benefit of defense lawyers, seventeen of them were executed in July by firing squad. Shortly afterward, around the time of the Buddhist *obon* festival for the spirits of the dead, Hirohito is alleged to have ordered one of his military aides (who happened to have been on night duty at the Palace when the mutiny occurred) to secure seventeen *obon* lanterns. The aide later hung them somewhere in the palace. Hirohito said no more about the lanterns, which had to be kept secret because he could not be perceived as condoning mutiny. Perhaps this action made him feel more at ease with himself. Even after having sanctioned death sentences in order to extinguish threats to his entourage, he could still feel that he was living his belief in compassionate concern for his subjects.[47]

When the military investigated the February uprising, it discovered that the rebels' sense of crisis had been magnified by the general election held on February 20, in which voters had expressed antimilitary sentiments by supporting left-wing candidates. Further, despite the rural roots and populist rhetoric of the ringleaders, most had not become revolutionaries because of the agricultural depression, and their ultimate goals had little to do with agrarian reforms, as many contemporaries imagined. The aim of the insurgent leaders was to further the good of the *kokutai*, as they understood it, by accelerating Japan's rearmament. The military portion of the national budget had increased steadily since the start of the Manchurian Incident, going from 3.47 percent of GNP in 1931 to 5.63 percent in 1936. During that period the navy had steadily increased its tonnage; both services had begun to develop air forces; but the army had not expanded significantly and still totaled about 233,365 officers and men organized in seventeen divisions.[48] The insurgent officers blamed the political system, not economic conditions, for limiting military budgets in a time of national emergency.[49]

Interestingly, in their concept of total war the thinking of the ringleaders and their senior commanders in the Army Ministry and the Army General Staff was strikingly similar: Both wanted state control of industrial decision making and production in order to fully mobilize the nation's resources. Beyond their common ignorance of what "total" war really required, the rebel leaders were as disunited in their thinking as they had been in their actions throughout the uprising. Only the idea of a "Shōwa restoration" to reform the management of the state seems to have been widely shared. Notions of what such a "restoration" would mean in practice varied from individual to individual.[50] For Isobe, perhaps the most deranged of the ringleaders, it denoted "[s]tate consolidation of the economy together with completing the Meiji restoration and developing it into a world restoration."[51]

The February mutiny confirmed Hirohito's belief in the constitution's importance for securing his powers of military command. So rigidly did he heed that lesson that when General Ishiwara Kanji later drafted a plan to establish a separate, independent army air force, Hirohito would not even consider it for fear that an air force, not provided for in the constitution, might elude his control.[52] Ultimately the entire experience strengthened his sense of the enormous power he had when performing as a military commander. He seems to have resolved never to appear indecisive when confronted with decisions to act; and he began to move closer to the Control faction of the army, and to feel justified in sanctioning large military spending increases. Yet he never overcame the memory of this incident, and tended to infer from it that the throne was more insecure than it really was.

After World War II, when Hirohito was particularly concerned to play down his role as supreme commander, he offered a deliberately distorted account of the February mutiny:

> I issued an order at that time for the rebel force to be suppressed. This brings to mind Machida Chūji, the finance minister. He was very worried about the rebellion's adverse effect on the money market and warned me that a panic could occur unless I took firm measures. Therefore I issued a strong command to have [the uprising] put down.
>
> As a rule, because a suppression order also involves martial law, military circles, who cannot issue such an order on their own, need the mutual consent of the government. However, at the time, Okada's whereabouts were unknown. As the attitude of the Army Ministry seemed too lenient, I issued a strict order.
>
> Following my bitter experiences with the Tanaka cabinet, I had decided always to wait for the opinions of my advisers before making any decision, and not to go against their counsel. Only twice, on this occasion and at the time of the ending of the war, did I positively implement my own ideas.
>
> Ishiwara Kanji of the Army General Staff Office also asked me,

through military aide Chōjiri [Kazumoto], to issue a suppression order. I don't know what sort of a person Ishiwara is, but on this occasion he was correct, even though he had been the instigator of the Manchurian Incident.

Further, my chief military aide, Honjō, brought me the plan drafted by Yamashita Hōbun, in which Yamashita asked me to please send an examiner because the three leaders of the rebel army were likely to commit suicide. However, I thought that sending an examiner would imply that they had acted according to their moral convictions and were deserving of respect. . . .

So I rejected Honjō's proposal, and [instead] issued the order to suppress them. I received no report that generals in charge of military affairs had gone and urged the rebels to surrender.[53]

When Hirohito ordered the immediate suppression of the rebels on the morning of February 26, he was angry at them for having murdered his closest advisers, and at his senior army officers for procrastinating in putting them down. On the second day Minister of Commerce and Industry Machida assumed the additional post of finance minister, and fear of economic panic and confusion became a reason, though not the main one, for the emperor's action. Thereafter Hirohito felt that every hour of delay harmed Japan's international image.[54]

Repeatedly since the Manchurian Incident, the emperor had clashed with the military over infringements of his authority but never over fundamental policy. Occasionally, in step with the army's rise to power, he had impressed his own political views on policy making, just as he had done earlier under the Hamaguchi cabinet.[55] The February 26 mutiny taught him and Yuasa—his privy seal from March 1936 to June 1940, and the very first lord keeper of the privy seal to come to court daily—the importance of exercising the emperor's right of supreme command to the full whenever circumstances required. Even with Honjō acting against him, Hirohito had received support and gotten his way by taking a firm stance. His decisiveness abruptly ended the period in which alienated "young officers" had tried to use him as a principle of reform to undermine a power structure they could not successfully manipulate. Hirohito, however, had learned precisely how to manipulate that establishment in most situations and circumstances.

The decision-making process had built into it secrecy, indirection, lack of clear lines of communication, vagueness in the drafting of policy statements, and manipulation of information networks— in short, confusion, misunderstanding, and perpetual intrigue to negotiate elite consensus. That was the way things worked in Tokyo. It was how the emperor worked. Now, once again, he had reminded all the close-knit elites that *he* was *the reason* the system worked.

IV

On May 4, 1936, in his rescript at the opening ceremony of the Sixty-ninth Imperial Diet, while Tokyo still lay silenced under martial law, Hirohito had finally closed the curtain on the February mutiny. For a short time he considered sending the military and the nation a strong message of censure of the army, but after much thought and procrastination over a three-month period, he settled for one terse, utterly innocuous sentence: "We regret the recent incident that occurred in Tokyo."[56] Many in his audience of Diet members and military officials responded with startled "awe," and privately some were disappointed. Once again, at a crucial moment, Hirohito declined an opportunity to rein in his military publicly through his constitutional role. Nevertheless, owing to his actions behind the scene, the drifting and yawing in domestic policy that had characterized Japan since the Manchurian Incident now ended, and over the next fourteen months, the emperor and most of his advisers concurred with the demands of the army and navy for accelerated military buildup and state-directed industrial development.

The Hirota Kōki cabinet, formed immediately after the February 26 mutiny, following Privy Seal Yuasa's recommendation, is remembered for having furthered military influence in politics while allowing interservice rivalries and jealousies to affect national goals. In May 1936 Hirota, on the advice of his army and navy ministers, revived the practice of appointing military ministers only from the roster of high-ranking officers on active duty. He professed to believe the measure would prevent officers associated with the discredited Imperial Way faction from someday regaining power.[57] By narrowing the field of candidates and increasing the power of the army vis-à-vis the prime minister, Hirota's action paved the way for army leaders to use this weapon to overthrow the cabinet of Admiral Yonai in July 1940.[58]

In policy toward China, Hirota spurned cooperation based on equality and supported the army's plans to separate the five provinces of North China, with a population estimated at more than eighty million, from the Nanking government. Hirota had been foreign minister when the Japanese commander of the China Garrison Force, based in the port city of Tientsin, and the chief of the Mukden Special Agency had signed local agreements with Chinese Nationalist minister of war, Gen. Ho Ying-ch'in, by which Chiang Kai-shek withdrew both his political organs and his Central Army from North China. Like the emperor, Hirota had thereafter done nothing to counter statements by the commander of the China Garrison Force and other generals publicly suggesting that the coal- and iron-rich northern provinces be split away from the rest of China and, in effect, incorporated into the Japanese continental holding.[59]

Also like the emperor, Hirota shared an assumption that many Japanese officers considered self-evident: China was neither a nation nor a people but merely a territorial designation, and Japan was entitled to rearrange that territory and take whatever parts it wished. Emperor Hirohito, on April 17, 1936, sanctioned the army's request for a threefold increase in the size of its small China Garrison Force from 1,771 to 5,774 troops.[60] He also approved the establishment of a new military base at Fengtai, a rail junction in the southwest suburb of Peking, not far from the historic Marco Polo Bridge. Strong Chinese protests ensued, but the expanded garrison went ahead with the construction of its Fengtai barracks. Japanese troops were soon conducting training exercises with live ammunition, in close proximity to Chinese military facilities, setting the stage for repeated clashes with Chinese troops.[61]

Hirohito should have known that Japan needed time, capital, and more industry—in short, needed years of at least relative peace, if it was going to profit from its new territories on the continent and the industrial development already in place. And the Army General Staff also ought to have appreciated the dangerous animosity and distrust Japan had stirred up within China's educated public of workers, students, and intellectuals, and especially among such Manchurian exiles as Chang Hsueh-liang and his officer corps, who identified strongly with the northeastern provinces and were determined to go on resisting Japan.

Hirohito and his strategists were more concerned with protecting their overlong (and exposed) northern lines of supply and communication from possible Soviet interruption than with the "united front" that Chiang Kai-shek and his archrival Mao Tse-tung were forming throughout the first half of 1937. Japanese contingency planning under the Hirota cabinet focussed on defense against the Soviet Union. A major war with China was neither expected, desired, nor prepared for. Japanese relations with Moscow deteriorated as the Kwantung Army reinforced and expanded its activities in Inner Mongolia, and strengthened its positions along the northern border with Outer Mongolia.

The Hirota cabinet responded favorably to Nazi Germany's

policies of rapid rearmament on a gigantic scale, anti-Sovietism, economic autarchy, and racial and religious bigotry and intolerance. The signing of the Anti-Comintern Pact with Germany in November 1936 was preceded by the growth of military ties between the Imperial Army and Navy and the German military command, and came on the heels of a series of foreign policy coups by Hitler that destroyed the post–World War I settlement in Europe.[62] A secret protocol to the pact committed the signatories not to assist Moscow in the event of war between one of them and the Soviet Union.[63] A year later Italy joined the pact. Having aligned internationally with the rising Nazi and Fascist dictatorships, imperial Japan could now be expected to act together with them in the future.[64] For the democratically elected governments of Britain, France, and the United States, the Anti-Comintern Pact united the looming crises in Europe and Asia.

Hirota adopted his most important foreign policy measures in mid–1936, in four- and five-member ministerial conferences that departed from the practice of full cabinet meetings envisioned under the Meiji constitution. The "Criteria for National Policy," and the "Foreign Policy of the Empire," both decided on August 7, 1936, set forth a grandiose, provocative and unrealistic array of projects and goals, which, if they came to be concurrently attempted, would quite exceed Japan's national power. Manchukuo was to be built up; the resources of North China were to be secured for the empire through puppet regimes; preparations would be made for future war with the Soviet Union; control of the western Pacific and Southeast Asia was to be brought about, which would require new naval construction in competition with the United States, as well as the building of air bases and radio stations on Taiwan, the Marianas, and the Carolines (in the Central Pacific)—and, at the same time, there would be an increase in military and naval manpower and logistical support structures.[65]

The "Criteria for National Policy" registered the tendency of

Japan's bureaucratic elites to line up their respective positions, side by side, in vague official texts that could be interpreted to suit the convenience of their drafters.[66] This was to be the pattern of decision making for all later stages of the crisis of Japanese diplomacy. That this tendency made its appearance on the eve of war with China was significant, for it meant that the prime minister, foreign minister, army and navy ministers, and the two chiefs of staff had abandoned the task of thrashing out their disagreements in reasoned argument. Rather than struggle to reach genuine consensus, they adopted a simpler, easier procedure. They enscribed their respective positions in "national policy" documents that postponed reckoning over the resources needed to accomplish their goals, and also left unclear whether force or diplomacy, or both, would be employed.

The drafters of the national policy equated their first criterion—to "eliminate the hegemonistic policies of the Great Powers in East Asia"—with "manifest[ing] the spirit of the imperial way" in foreign policy. Henceforth foreign policy would become more expansionist and radical, for the "imperial way" implied, internationally, that the emperor's "benevolence" be extended until Japanese overlordship was established throughout Asia. The second yardstick of sound foreign policy required Japan "to become the stabilizing force in East Asia in both name and reality" by building up armaments. The third and fourth "criteria of national policy"—and the core of the document—were "to secure our footing on the East Asian continent, and to advance and develop in the Southern Oceans by combining diplomacy and national defense."[67]

The reference to the "East Asian continent" met the wish of the army to advance north with a view to countering the Soviet Union; the "Southern Oceans," an elastic geographical term, denoted the navy's goal of moving southward and preparing to achieve supremacy over the United States and Britain in the vast western Pacific. Neither service was happy with the goal of the other; neither trusted the other. By posting their plans side by side, thereby avoiding a clear decision as to which one should prevail, they prevented the pluralistic system of advising the emperor from breaking down.

Japan was now only a year away from all-out war in China, but the inability of its constitutionally mandated imperial advisers and the chiefs of staff to agree on a unified national policy was more than ever an endemic feature of the political process. And complicating these disagreements and splits between "the government" and "the military," under both Hirota and his successors, was continuing discord between the Army General Staff in Tokyo and officers in the field charged with implementing policy.

Once Japan entered a serious war emergency, with the prestige of the throne exalted far beyond the limits of ordinary times, this multitiered structure of bureaucratic conflicts created increasing room for Hirohito to maximize his influence in policy making. Constantly becoming more experienced in playing his designated political and military roles, Hirohito would watch as his advisers developed their policies, note their disagreements, and finally insist that they compose their differences and unify their military and political strategies. As it was impossible for them to do so, the pressure he exerted complicated the already confused decision-making process. His "unity" card would become Hirohito's special wedge for driving home *his* views, ensuring that those of "middle stratum" officers did not prevail in national policy making, and that the process itself remained primarily "top-down" in nature.

And the more Hirohito pressed "unity" upon the representatives of his chronically divided "government" and "high command," the more they papered over their differences in policy texts that virtually impelled expansion abroad and, soon, war without end. It was not just the Japanese military provoking aggression in China during the middle and late 1930s; the religiously charged monarchy was also driving aggression, while offering a shield from public criticism to those who acted in its name.

On August 25, 1936, the Hirota government announced that slightly more than 69 percent of the government's total 1937 budget (or nearly 33 billion yen) would be allocated to the military. This amounted to almost a threefold increase in the 1936 military budget of approximately 10 billion yen, or 47.7 percent of government spending.[68] To pay for all this, taxes would be raised and inflation tolerated, armaments manufacturers and the great *zaibatsu* enriched, and the patriotism of ordinary wage earners fanned up while their wages were held down.

These policies of the Hirota cabinet reflected and to some degree were impelled by backlash within the navy over the army's unilateral actions at home and abroad. On March 27, 1936, the Third Fleet commander, Adm. Oikawa Koshirō, had offered to the navy minister and the chief of the Navy General Staff his "Views on National Policy Centering on China." Writing from his flagship, *Izumo* in Shanghai Harbor, Oikawa pointed out that the Kwantung Army was rushing "political machinations" to "separate the five provinces of North China from the authority of the Nanking government and so form a buffer zone between Manchukuo and China."[69]

After urging the navy not to permit the Kwantung Army to act unilaterally in so grave a matter, Oikawa recommended a policy of expanding southward into Southeast Asia and the southwest Pacific, while also moving north. Although this should be done peacefully, Japan had to prepare and be ready someday to free itself of tariff and other obstacles to economic growth "by using military force." Therefore, even if war against the Soviet Union should be decided on and "preparation for a war on land" made the immediate national goal, the navy still should prepare for war at sea.[70] Oikawa also stressed the need to exercise care and prudence so as not to provoke the Great Powers and induce them "to unite against us."[71]

The reply to Admiral Oikawa by the navy vice minister and the vice chief of the Navy General Staff was later formally adopted as the Hirota cabinet's "Criteria for National Policy" and "General Principles of National Policy," approved in August.[72] The latter document spoke of making Japan the "stabilizing force in East Asia" while it expanded southward.[73] At this time, however, the navy's senior commanders clearly recognized the irrationality of separate army and navy advances, fearing that this would exceed Japan's national strength and "ultimately lead to war with more than two countries." They recommended a policy of "gradual and peaceful expansion" in both the north and the south.[74]

This was indeed the rational strand in the otherwise wildly ambitious strategy pursued by the cabinets of Hirota and his successor, General Hayashi. That influential groups in the navy, army, Foreign Ministry, and imperial court were still capable of lucid evaluations of Japan's problems during 1936 and the first half of 1937 is undeniable. Nevertheless, these same leaders were already beginning to be carried by the momentum of their choices. Sooner or later their policy goals—military expansion on the continent, naval control of the western Pacific and Southeast Asian sea lanes, and equalization of relations with the Great Powers—would provoke military clashes with China—and even more serious clashes with the United States and Britain.

Significantly, in the fall of 1936, after several incidents involving attacks on Japanese nationals living in central and south China, the navy began to study ways to improve its policing capabilities in south China. The air power theories of the Italian Maj. Gen. Giulio Douhet were then in vogue among navalists, and the resulting contingency plan included a punitive air campaign against the civilian population of China's major cities as well as preparations for conducting a coastal blockade should one ever be needed.[75]

Hirota's tenure as prime minister ended on January 23, 1937. He was followed on February 2 by General Hayashi, whose cabinet lasted only four months. Prince Konoe then organized his first cabinet on June 4. He was a descendant of the famous Fujiwara family of court nobles, whose women had for centuries regularly intermarried with imperial princes and during the Heian period (794–1185) had ruled Japan. Personal cleverness, charisma, and high lineage, as well as good connections with the navy and willingness to cultivate the army and the civilian right wing all combined to propel him to the top.

V

Following the February 26, 1936, uprising, under the prime ministerships of Hirota and Hayashi, the emperor and his entourage became more supportive of reinforcing his theoretically unassailable power from below. In this context the Ministry of Education accelerated efforts to further the nation's spiritual mobilization for a possible protracted war, and on May 31, 1937, published and distributed for school use an estimated three hundred thousand copies of *Kokutai no hongi* (The Fundamentals of the national polity). Eventually more than two million copies were sold nationwide.

Kokutai no hongi was a discourse on the *kokutai*, and on the emperor's ideological and spiritual role as the exemplar of national benevolence and morality. A transitional ideological tract, it did not completely reject Western thought and institutions, but went beyond merely emphasizing Japanese cultural distinctiveness. Extolling the "bright," "pure," and selfless "heart" of the Japanese, and counterposing the *kokutai* to modern Western individualism and "abstract totalitarianisms," it stressed the absolute superiority of the Japanese people and state over all other nations. "We loyal subjects differ completely in our nature from so called citizens of

Western nations. . . . We always seek in the emperor the source of our lives and activities."[76]

Kokutai no hongi also emphasized the centrality of the family-state, home, and ancestors, and reminded readers that the "divine winds" (*kamikaze*), which had twice saved Japan from Mongol invasions in the late thirteenth century, proved indisputably Japan's divinity and indestructibility. Above all the pamphlet implanted the image of the emperor as a military ruler and "a living god who rules our country in accordance with the benevolent wishes of his imperial founder and his other imperial ancestors."[77] All Japanese subjects had the duty to give Hirohito their absolute obedience. In practice that meant "to live for the great glory and dignity of the emperor, abandoning one's small ego, and thus expressing our true life as a people."[78] Here, in essence, was that peculiar amalgamation of Shinto, Buddhist, neo-Confusian, and Western monarchist ideals, known as *kōdō*—"the imperial way," that powered Japanese aggression, and was used by army leaders to browbeat critics and by right-wing thugs to justify their terrorist actions. For Hirohito the chief merit of the pamphlet was the possibility it offered of producing a stronger spirit of devotion to his person, thereby enhancing his influence over the military.

The myth of Japan as a tightly unified, monolithic state and society, which *Kokutai no hongi* perpetuated, was reaffirmed four years later in July 1941 in yet another hysterical Shinto-Buddhist tract published and distributed by the Ministry of Education. By this time Hirohito had become the symbol of Japan's "escape" from the West, and had begun the process that would lead to the momentous decision to declare war against the United States and Britain. He needed more than ever the strongest possible political influence over the entire nation. The country had taken on the identity of a fascist state and had even adopted the haunting rhetoric of fascism; its people labored under the burdens of food rationing and a total war economy; policies were in place designed to increase war production by lowering living standards; in the emperor's name all open dissent had been squashed.

Against this background *Shimmin no michi* (The Way of the subject) called for overthrowing "the old order based on the dominance of individualism, liberalism, and dialectical materialism," and building a new order in East Asia based on the principle of allowing "all nations to seek their proper places."[79] The pamphlet demanded that "a structure of . . . unanimity" be established in all realms of national life so that Japan could perfect its total war state and establish "a world community based on moral principles." With every subject involved in serving the emperor, it called upon all Japanese to purge egotism from their souls and practice daily a relation to the state in which nothing is "our own," and "even in our private lives we always remember to unite with the emperor and serve the state."[80]

HOLY WAR

Early on the morning of July 8, 1937, an ominous unplanned incident occurred some twenty miles south of Peking, when Japanese army units barracked at Fengtai clashed with Chinese garrison forces at the Marco Polo Bridge (in Chinese, Lukouchiao). Army headquarters in Tokyo was notified immediately and ordered that the problem—stemming from a brief exchange of rifle fire the night before—be resolved on the spot. The fighting in the vicinity of the bridge, located on the railway line from Peking to the interior city of Hankow, went on for three straight days. By the eleventh, negotiations by the local commanders resulted in the signing of an armistice. Thereafter, for about three weeks, the military leaders succeeded in making their armistice hold.

Now the serious consequences of a split in China policy within the military required the emperor, vacationing in Hayama, to return to Tokyo. One group, based partly in the Military Affairs Section of the Army Ministry and partly in the Operations Section of the Army General Staff, saw the incident at the Marco Polo Bridge as an opportunity. Manchukuo had never received lawful recognition by China; the terms of the armistice that had ended the Manchurian Incident were not being observed; the demilitarized zone separating the provinces of North China from Manchukuo was often violated; and there were other irritating issues. If the fighting near Peking was taken as a provocatory pretext, all outstanding problems with

China could be settled by one powerful military strike—for the Chinese would never be a formidable military match. Therefore troops should immediately be moved to the Peking area to "protect Japanese lives and property." The officers who held this hawkish position enjoyed the support of Kwantung Army staff officers and some civilian officials of the South Manchurian Railway Company (a major repository of imperial household investments) who hoped to extend the company's lines from Manchukuo into North China, and so wanted to see the incident expand.[1]

The other, more senior group, confined to the Army General Staff and centered on Major General Ishiwara, head of the First Department, and his Second Section chief, Kawabe Toshirō, feared becoming so embroiled in China that resources would be diverted from the buildup to defend against the Soviet Union. When, on July 9, the Konoe cabinet met in emergency session and decided temporarily to postpone sending more troops to North China, the views of this second group—the nonexpansionists who called for local settlement of the incident—momentarily prevailed. The expansionists, however, were already at work behind the scenes, placing homeland divisions on alert and drafting orders to send reinforcements, and when the Konoe cabinet met again on the eleventh, it reversed its decision of the ninth and decided to send thousands of troops to North China from the Kwantung Army, the Korean Army, and the homeland.

Meanwhile Hirohito reacted to the events in North China by first considering the possible threat from the Soviet Union. One week earlier, on June 30, Japan's recently mutinous First Division had been building fortifications on Kanchazu Island in the Amur River. At that point along the ambiguously demarcated border between northern Manchukuo and the Soviet Union, Russian troops came onto the island, a firefight ensued, and the Japanese destroyed two Soviet gunboats. The Russians, showing restraint, brought up more troops and artillery but did not immediately respond otherwise.[2] Tokyo and Moscow exchanged charges, and a test of resolution seemed imminent. Would the Russians now attack along the Manchukuo border? The emperor summoned his chief of staff, Prince Kan'in, before meeting, in succession, with Prime Minister Konoe, the new army minister, Sugiyama, and the chief of the Navy General Staff.

> "What will you do if the Soviets attack us from the rear?" he asked the prince. Kan'in answered, "I believe the army will rise to the occasion." The emperor repeated his question: "That's no more than army dogma. What will you actually do in the unlikely event that Soviet [forces] attack?" The prince said only, "We will have no choice." His Majesty seemed very dissatisfied.[3]

Hirohito wanted to know exactly what the contingency plans were, and Kan'in was evasive. Nevertheless, despite his disappointment with Prince Kan'in's report, the emperor approved the decision of the Konoe cabinet to move troops to North China, and put his seal on the order for their dispatch.

Aware of the armistice yet anxious to resolve all of its outstanding problems with China in one stroke, the Konoe cabinet had decided to enlarge the incident, and the emperor had tacitly agreed from the very start. The sequence of decisions following the Marco Polo Bridge flare-up was thus quite unlike the pattern at the time of the Manchurian Incident, when field officers had perpetrated illegal faits accompli and the emperor had explicitly sanctioned their actions after the fact. On this occasion the Konoe cabinet was taking the initiative in tandem with the army expansionists, and Hirohito was supporting that decision from the outset in opposition to the nonexpansionists on the Army General Staff. On the other hand, in one respect the first episode of what would become the China war was similar to the far more premeditated Manchurian Incident. The shooting in the vicinity of the Chinese barracks at

Fengtai near Marco Polo Bridge on July 8 had been arbitrarily ordered by a Japanese regimental commander without orders from the center, in order to rectify a perceived "insult to the Japanese army." Though this action did not really begin the war, Hirohito would later refer to it in blaming the army for expanding a skirmish, already calming, into the long and bitter China conflict.[4]

Three years into the war the emperor looked back and expanded on his thoughts and actions that day in early July when he had pondered what to do in North China. The number one priority had to be preparation to fight the Soviet Union. Therefore he believed he had no choice in China except to compromise and delay; and so he had talked with Prince Kan'in and the Minister of the Army Sugiyama Gen about the Kanchazu Island matter. They told him, in effect, that so far as the army was concerned there was no need to worry: "Even if war with China came, . . . it could be finished up within two or three months," which seemed reasonable to Hirohito. So he left the matter open for a short time, decided to talk with Prime Minister Konoe, convene an imperial conference, and work through to a decision. If his military opposed it, then that was that. He spoke with the service ministers and the chiefs of staff. They did not convince him either way, but "they were agreed with each other on the time factor, and that made a big difference; so all right, we'll go ahead." The war with China was launched. Then it soon became clear that Japanese forces in China were not large enough. "Transfer troops from the border between Manchukuo and the Soviet Union," he said. But his military chiefs told him, "No, that can't be done."[5] Hirohito was silent as to his own shortsightedness in the making of this decision.

The press report issued to the Japanese nation by the Konoe cabinet, also on July 11, 1937, stated that troops were being ordered to North China because "the Chinese side" had deliberately perpetrated an armed attack against Japan. "As our empire's constant concern is to maintain peace in East Asia, however, we have not abandoned hope that peaceful negotiations may yet ensure nonexpansion of the conflict."[6] Japan's domestic press emphasized the Konoe cabinet's hope to contain the fighting to the Peking-Tientsin area and left unchallenged the claim that the Chinese were wholly at fault. The emperor, who by now had acquired considerable experience in dealing with his divided and deeply flawed military apparatus, probably knew otherwise. But the incident had happened; it was ongoing; and it needed to be ended quickly.

Meanwhile, as preparations went forward for a general offensive in response to recurring small-scale clashes with Chinese troops, Hirohito's concern about Soviet intervention lessened, and he took satisfaction in the fact that the cabinet—which included Hirota as foreign minister, Sugiyama as army minister, Yonai as navy minister, and Kaya Okinori as finance minister[7]—had gone on record as opposed to expanding the incident beyond the Peking-Tientsin area.

Two weeks later, as the reinforcements from the Kwantung Army and the Korean Army were joined by the three divisions from the homeland, several minor clashes with the Chinese occurred, at Langfan, near Tientsin, on July 25 and at the Kuang'an Gate near the center of Peking the next day. Hirohito now pressed for a decisive, war-ending battle, and on July 27 sanctioned an imperial order directing the commander of the China Garrison Force to "chastise the Chinese army in the Peking-Tientsin area" and "bring stability to the main strategic places in that region."[8]

The broad Japanese offensive followed strictly orders sanctioned by the emperor and issued from Tokyo, and after only two days of fighting led to the occupation of Peking and Tientsin, in both of which cities the British and French maintained small treaty-port settlements.[9] By changing the mission of the China Garrison Force from protecting Japanese residents to occupying Chinese territory, Hirohito had abetted the escalation of the incident, leading to a new state of affairs in North China.

On July 29–30 there occurred a fresh incident which offered timely justification for Japan's renewed policy of aggression, undertaken in the name of "chastising Chinese violence." Tungchow, a small walled city east of Peking, was under the control of the collaborator Yin Ju-keng and his (Japanese-trained) Chinese security forces. On July 29–30, the latter rose up and attacked the Japanese civilian community, left undefended by the departure for nearby Peking and Tientsin of the main Japanese garrison. The uprising triggered a mood of blind fury against the Japanese occupiers. Assisted by students and workers, the Chinese troops slaughtered eighteen Japanese soldiers, nine intelligence officers, and 223 of the city's 385 Japanese and Korean residents, including many women and children.

In Japan the Tungchow massacre generated a mood of anger and belligerence. The press reported a "second Nikolaevsk," but failed to put the Chinese atrocity in perspective by mentioning that the Japanese invasion of the north was coming from the demilitarized zone, where Japanese and Koreans manufactured heroin and opium for smuggling into the provinces of North China.[10] Kido greeted the news with deep anger, as did, presumably, most policy makers. Prince Takamatsu discussed Tungchow with the emperor on August 2 and cautioned him to remember that the views of the nonexpansionists in the army did not represent the entire army. Takamatsu may also have told his brother that, as he observed in his diary, "[t]he mood in the army today is that we're really going to smash China so that it will be ten years before they can stand up straight again."[11]

In view of such incidents it can hardly be said that the Japanese government was being dragged into war by its own forces. Rather it is more accurate to say that Konoe, backed by one group in the army, had resolved to exploit a small incident for the larger aim of punishing the Chinese army and securing control of the Peking-Tientsin area. In this, Konoe enjoyed the active support of Hirohito, who had cut short his vacation to return to the palace and was being carefully briefed on developments. As the historian Fujiwara Akira noted, "it was the [Konoe] government itself that had resolved on war, dispatched an army, and expanded the conflict," and Hirohito had fully supported it.[12]

At this point Chiang Kai-shek decided to abandon the north and by shifting the war to the lower Yangtze River region, starting at Shanghai, possibly involve the foreign powers in defense of their citizens living in China's largest and most international city. Japan had close to twenty-five thousand residents there, the Europeans about sixty thousand, and the Americans approximately four thousand. Nearly all of them lived in the foreign-ruled International Settlement area.[13] The Battle of Shanghai began August 13; the next day Chinese air force planes joined in by attacking Japanese troops and naval airplanes on the ground and bombing the Third Fleet's flagship *Izumo*. Almost immediately the Navy Ministry under Admiral Yonai became the main advocate of war expansion, including the occupation of Nanking.[14] This second series of moves, by Chiang Kai-shek on one side and the Imperial Navy on the other, turned the "North China Incident" into the China war.

At Shanghai, Chiang's best-trained and -equipped troops plus assorted "auxiliaries," eventually totaling approximately 110,000 to 150,000 troops, took on some twelve thousand Japanese sailors and marines, who were quickly reinforced.[15] Gen. Matsui Iwane was made Hirohito's field commander on August 15, and five days later a Shanghai Expeditionary Force (consisting mainly of poorly disciplined reservists in their late twenties and early thirties) was dispatched. The Twelfth Infantry Regiment and the Tenth Brigade Headquarters of the Eleventh Infantry Division were placed on alert at Dairen in case they were needed at Shanghai.[16]

Concomitantly twenty naval planes based in Nagasaki made a four-hour transoceanic flight to bomb, for the first time, the Chinese capital of Nanking.[17] These aircraft were the "96-type long-range bombers," that had recently been developed under the guidance of Adm. Yamamoto Isoroku for use in a future air war against the United States; Yamamoto was anxious to test them.[18] On the seventeenth the Konoe cabinet, foreseeing quick victory, formally decided to abandon its nonexpansion policy and wage war for the singularly vague purpose of "chastising" China's armed forces. "The empire, having reached the limit of its patience," read the announcement, "has been forced to take resolute measures. Henceforth it will punish the outrages of the Chinese army, and thus spur the Nanking government to self-reflect."[19] Behind this decision, of course, lay the emperor's judgment and approval, just exercised in pushing troop reinforcements and strategic bombing—or it would never have come to pass. Equally important was his and the cabinet's arrogant disdain for the Chinese people and their capacity for resistance.

On August 18 Hirohito summoned his army and navy chiefs for a pointed recommendation. The war, he told them, "is gradually spreading; our situation in Shanghai is critical; Tsingtao is also at risk. If under these circumstances we try to deploy troops everywhere, the war will merely drag on and on. Wouldn't it be better to concentrate a large force at the most critical point and deliver one overwhelming blow?"[20] Peace, he went on, "based on our attitude of fairness," could be achieved only through such a staggering victory. "Do you," he asked them, "have in hand plans for such action? In other words, do we have any way worked out"—and here the emperor became victim of his own naive rhetoric—"to force the Chinese to reflect on their actions?"[21]

Three days after their audience with the emperor, the chiefs of staff delivered their written reports. A major air campaign could destroy China's air force, military facilities, vital industries, and political centers. But air attacks alone would probably not suffice to make the Chinese army and people "lose the will to fight." Japan should also occupy certain strategic points in North China, engage the Nationalist military forces directly, occupy Shanghai, and establish a naval blockade of the China coast.[22] To this policy, advocated most strongly by the navy at a time when many in the army and the government sought to avoid an all-out war, Hirohito gave his sanction, expressing concern only about the dispatch of troops to Tsingtao and the occupation of the air bases near Shanghai.[23] At this point too, he accepted the position of his admirals not reluctantly but actively, pressing his generals to move with decisiveness.

Hirohito's order of August 31 for the "Dispatch of the North China Area Army" bristled: "[D]estroy the enemy's will to fight" and "wipe out resistance in the central part of Hepei Province," with a view to ending the war quickly. But deleted from this imperial order, in accordance with his wishes, was the deployment of troops to Tsingtao.[24] Over the course of the next two weeks Hirohito sanctioned six troop mobilizations in preparation for reinforcing the Shanghai area, where the fighting had bogged down. On September 7 the emperor sanctioned the deployment of three divisions and the Taiwan Garrison Force to the Shanghai front; at the same time, because of his concern with the Soviet Union, he ordered other units sent to Manchuria to stand guard. Strongly disapproving of the troop buildup but unable to stop it, First Department Head Major General Ishiwara resigned and was appointed vice chief of staff of the Kwantung Army.[25]

At the beginning of the war in China, the question had arisen of defining Japan's war aims. On September 4, 1937, Army Minister Sugiyama issued a directive to his commanders stating: "Our present situation is completely different from any the empire has experienced before. We must bear in mind that this war has become total war."[26] On the same day Hirohito informed the Imperial Diet that while he was constantly preoccupied with "securing peace in Asia through cooperating with China, . . . China . . . does not really understand our empire's true intention. To our deep regret they have constantly caused difficulties and problems that have finally resulted in the present incident. Our troops, displaying loyalty and bravery, are suffering hardships solely to make China self-reflect and to quickly establish peace in East Asia."[27]

Japan needed to wage war without declaring war. Dependent on imports of American oil, iron and steel, cotton, and copper, Japan's leaders feared that if it became a formal belligerent, the United States would deny it these strategic materials. By fighting an "incident" rather than a war, Japan could enable American industrial and raw-material exporters to circumvent the U.S. Neutrality Act of 1935 and the even more stringent one of May 1937—a profitable arrangement that American business, in the grip of renewed depression, was eager to continue.

Other reasons Japan preferred not to define clearly its war aims as it had done in three previous foreign wars were more spiritual. There existed, after all, an official theology with a great number of theologians—university professors, Zen and Nichiren Buddhist priests, and government bureaucrats—to expound it: The emperor was a living god, the descendant of Amaterasu Ōmikami; Japan was the incarnation of morality and justice; by definition its wars were just and it could never commit aggression. Hence its effort to establish the "imperial way" (kōdō) in China and bring people there under the emperor's benevolent occupation by means of "compassionate killing"— killing off the few troublemakers so that the many might live—was a blessing upon the occupied people, and by no means colonial expansion. Those who resisted, naturally, had to be brought to their senses. But formally there was no "war," only an "incident."[28]

Consequently, from early on in the war the Japanese government regularly referred to the "China Incident" as its "sacred struggle" or "holy war" (seisen). And the longer the struggle dragged on, the more its ideologues insisted on using this term—"holy war"— which expressed the national mission of unifying the world under the emperor's benevolent rule (*hakkō ichi'u*), so that his and Amaterasu Ōmikami's august virtue could shine throughout the universe.

I

By early November the fighting in China had made clear to Prime Minister Konoe, the emperor, and the Army and Navy General Staffs that a more rational, more efficient high-command structure was needed to control the forces in the field and implement national policy. A Cabinet Planning Board had already been created in October. Now, on the twenty-seventh, Hirohito, on the recommendation of Konoe, ordered an "Imperial Headquarters" (*daihon'ei*) established within the palace as a purely military instrument through which he could exercise his constitutional role as supreme commander, and the army and navy could act more in concert. Thereafter, for a few hours in the morning a few days a week, the two chiefs of staff, the army and navy ministers, the chiefs of the operations sections, and Hirohito's chief aide-de-camp conducted business in the palace. With a staff of just over two hundred, the Imperial Headquarters was, initially, more a haphazard collection of officers rather than an effective organization for prosecuting war and coordinating politics and strategy, as Konoe had originally envisioned.

At the same time, also at the urging of Konoe, who wanted to bring the army and navy chiefs and vice chiefs of staff into closer consultation with the government, an intergovernmental liaison body was organized on November 19, 1937: the Imperial Headquarters–Government Liaison Conference.[29] Intended to help in integrating the decisions and needs of the two military branches with the resources and policies of the rest of the government, the liaison conference too at its outset was a temporary, seldom-convened conference for exchanging information.

Final decisions of the liaison conference were formally disclosed through special meetings, which Hirohito attended in person. These imperial conferences (*gozen kaigi*) were also neither established by government regulations nor related to the constitutional process. Because the emperor convened them and sanctioned their decisions, however, contemporaries regarded them as legitimate even though only a few ministers of state, such as the prime minister and finance minister, actually participated in them.[30] Imperial conferences were convened at least eight times between January 11, 1938, and December 1, 1941.[31] Those attending imperial conferences, in addition to the emperor, were the chiefs and vice chiefs of the two general staffs, the army and navy ministers, the prime minister, finance minister, foreign minister, president of the privy council, and president of the Planning Board. Army and navy Military Affairs Bureau chiefs and cabinet secretaries were not allowed to attend imperial conferences. Except in two critical instances, both in 1941, the newspapers informed the public of the meetings immediately after they occurred. Press reports were terse, noted who attended, what they wore, and always stressed the unanimity of the decision makers.[32]

At the imperial conferences Hirohito presided over and approved decisions impacting not only the destiny of Japan but of China and other countries affected by Japanese policy. Since these conferences were usually convened after the liaison conferences, at which all the interested parties had reached decisions in which the emperor shared, he already knew the contents of the matters to be "decided." Essentially the imperial conference was designed to allow him to perform as if he were a pure constitutional monarch, sanctioning matters only in accordance with his advisers' advice but not bearing responsibility for his action. At these meetings, civilian ministers wore morning clothes and military officers full-dress uniforms. The theatrical element of these affairs should not obscure their great importance, however. Nor were all imperial conferences the same, and the emperor's lips were not sealed at all of them.

The imperial conference was *the* device for legally transforming the "will of the emperor" into the "will of the state." And because everyone who participated in its deliberations could claim to have acted by, with, and under the unique authority of the emperor, while he could claim to have acted in accordance with the advice of his ministers of state, the imperial conference diffused lines of responsibility.[33] In that sense it was the perfect crown to the Japanese practice of irresponsibility, for it sustained four separate fictions: (*a*) that the cabinet had real power; (*b*) that the cabinet was the emperor's most important advisory organ; and (*c*) that the cabinet and the military high command had reached a compromise agreement on the matter at hand, providing the emperor with a policy that he (*d*) was merely sanctioning as a passive monarch. Reality was quite different: a powerless cabinet, an emasculated constitution, and a dynamic emperor participating in the planning of aggression and guiding the process, by a variety of interventions that were often indirect but in every instance determining.[34]

The senior members of the Imperial Headquarters all counseled Hirohito, but the chiefs of staff alone transmitted his orders to the various field and fleet commanders.[35] Through the Imperial Headquarters, Hirohito exercised final command over both armed services, including the field armies that were directly under his orders: the Kwantung Army and the area armies in China.[36] Through the liaison conference he and the high command attempted to coordinate policy with the civil government.[37] But that coordination and unity of war leadership proved impossible for Hirohito to achieve, for the Imperial Headquarters reproduced the rivalry of the military services, while the liaison conference was based on—and ultimately sabotaged by—the principle of separate and independent imperial advisory authority by ministers of state.[38]

Furthermore the cabinet (as a whole) could not exercise control over its military members because of its weak powers of integration and the unique position within it of the army and navy ministers, who enjoyed independent authority to advise the emperor. At the insistence of the navy, which feared both army control of the Imperial Headquarters and any weakening of its own independent "right of supreme command," the prime minister and civil officials were excluded from the Imperial Headquarters. Although Hirohito sanctioned this arrangement, it reduced efficiency and hampered communication and coordination with the civil organs of state throughout the war.

Having established the Imperial Headquarters, Hirohito found it somewhat easier to perform as an active supreme commander in chief, something his grandfather Meiji had never been. In communicating his highest orders, called Imperial Headquarters Army Orders (*tairikumei*) and Imperial Headquarters Navy Orders (*daikairei*), directly to the theater commanders, area army commanders, often division commanders, and fleet admirals, Hirohito's army and navy chiefs of staff acted as "transmitters." Although it was physically impossible for him to scrutinize all the orders of the Imperial Headquarters, these orders in the highest category—his supreme commands—were carefully examined by Hirohito before being returned to the chiefs of staff for transmission.

The same was true of the more important orders and directives that the chiefs of staff issued based on the *tairikumei* and *daikairei*. Drafts originated in the operations sections of the army and navy, were revised by department heads and bureau chiefs, moved up the chain of command to the vice chiefs of staff and chiefs of staff, and finally were presented to the emperor for his approval before being sent out.[39] Thus, not only as the force that animated Japan's entire war system, but as the individual with free agency who carefully examined and sanctioned the policies, strategies, and orders for waging wars of aggression, Hirohito's responsibility was enormous.

Hirohito interacted with his Imperial Headquarters through probing questions, admonitions, and careful repetition of his instructions and questions to his chiefs of staff and war ministers. Over time he also learned how to use his position to put constant psychological pressure on them. Usually he operated temperately, more in the courteous manner of George C. Marshall, one might say, than in that of George S. Patton. His "questions," however, were tantamount to orders and could not be ignored. Sometimes he met objections to the changes he wished to see implemented in ongoing military operations, but so long as he persisted, he prevailed—even if that meant his chiefs of staff had to override the wishes of important department heads and operations sections chiefs who desired different policies. The chiefs of staff, in short, were responsible to an energetic, activist emperor, and could never wage the China war just as they liked.[40] The same was true of the army and navy ministers, who were also subjected to Hirohito's interrogations and sometimes made to feel his anger.

Moreover, at key moments for which documentary evidence is available, Hirohito not only involved himself, sometimes on a daily basis, in shaping strategy and deciding the planning, timing, and so on of military campaigns, but also intervened in ongoing field operations to make changes that would not have occurred without his intervention. He also monitored, and even occasionally commented on, orders issued by area commanders to their subordinate units, though the extent to which he did this cannot be determined.[41]

Informal briefings (*naisō*) from the cabinet, which Hirohito had received ever since the start of his reign, were augmented from late 1937 onward by the Imperial Headquarters, which regularly supported Hirohito in his supreme commander role. To some extent the informal briefings were question-and-answer sessions—questions from his majesty (*gokamon*), answers from his briefers. The usual participants were the chiefs of staff and certain cabinet ministers. From time to time there were more formal sessions. At these the emperor silently received written or oral reports (*jōsō*) from his ministers or senior military staff. During the *naisō* briefings, exchanges of information and ideas could lead to discussions of policy, strategy, even tactical matters, and to decisions arrived at by Japanese-style "consensus"—with the result that cabinet decisions were predetermined "finished products" that mirrored Hirohito's thinking and therefore rarely had to be revised.[42]

II

In late October the positional warfare in and around Shanghai showed signs of drawing to an end. On November 9 the Chinese army began a partial withdrawal. Some three square miles of the city and large parts of its environs had been devastated by artillery shelling and by air and naval bombardment. Nearly a quarter million Chinese had been killed, including many women and children who had fought on the front lines. Japan had suffered 9,115 dead and 31,257 wounded.[43] Chinese defenses crumbled around mid-November, after the Shanghai Expeditionary Force's Sixteenth Division, commanded by Lt. Gen. Nakajima Kesago, came ashore unopposed at Paimaoko on the banks of the Yangtze River, threatening to link up with the Tenth Army, under Lt. Gen. Yanagawa Heisuke, which had landed a week earlier on the northern coast of Hangchow Bay.[44] The demoralized and disorganized soldiers of Chiang Kai-shek, exposed to constant bombing and strafing from Japanese navy planes and to shelling from Japanese gunboats, retreated pell-mell through villages and towns along the Yangtze toward Nanking, some 180 miles away.

Columns of Japanese troops, heavily reinforced but badly in need of rest and resupply, pushed west in hot pursuit. The original mission of the Shanghai Expeditionary Force had been to conduct only a limited war in the Shanghai area and to avoid problems with the British and the Americans. These restrictions were now ignored as field commanders began to exercise their own discretionary power in defiance of the high command in Tokyo. Entering for the first time into direct contact with ordinary Chinese civilians, the troops (who had been killing prisoners of war throughout the Shanghai fighting) were now ordered to disregard the distinction between combatants and noncombatants. As stated in the attack order of the Second Battalion of the Sixth Infantry Regiment, issued on November 11, "All the law-abiding people have retreated within the walls. Treat everyone found outside the walls as anti-Japanese and destroy them. . . . Since it is convenient in conducting sweep operations to burn down houses, prepare materials."[45]

Burning and plundering villages and towns as they proceeded inland along main roads and along the rail trunk line toward Nanking, the different units of the Japanese army drove ahead of them a vast exodus of Chinese troops and civilian refugees. On December 1 Hirohito's newly established Imperial Headquarters ordered the Tenth Army and the Shanghai Expeditionary Force to close in on the capital from different directions. The following day Prince Asaka took command of the Shanghai Expeditionary Force and General Matsui, then in poor health, was promoted to command the Central China Area Army, which comprised his own Shanghai force and the Tenth Army. On December 8 troops under Asaka's command began the assault on the Chinese defenses. The walled city of Nanking, with a population estimated at four to five hundred thousand, fell on December 13, after a defense of only five days.

There were no orders to "rape" Nanking. Nor did Imperial Headquarters ever order the total extermination of the enemy as the ultimate goal of the Nanking encirclement campaign. Standing orders to take no prisoners did exist, however. And once Nanking fell, Japanese soldiers began to execute, en masse, military prisoners of war and unarmed deserters who had surrendered. They also went on an unprecedented and unplanned rampage of arson, pillage, murder, and rape. The resulting slaughter continued in the city and its six adjacent rural villages for three months, and far exceeded earlier atrocities committed during the Battle of Shanghai and along the escape routes to Nanking. General Nakajima's Sixteenth Division, in just its first day in the capital, killed approximately 32,300 Chinese prisoners of war and fleeing soldiers. Another Japanese estimate reduces that total somewhat, to 24,000.[46]

When Generals Matsui and Asaka insisted on staging a triumphal victory parade on horseback down the broad main thoroughfare of Nanking on December 17, Asaka's chief of staff, Inuma Mamoru, ordered the Sixteenth and Ninth Divisions to intensify their mopping-up operations within the occupied city and its surrounding villages so that no harm would befall the imperial prince. On the night of December 16 and into the morning hours of the seventeenth, with the battle already won and the Chinese remnant troops, mostly unarmed and out of uniform, trying desperately to flee, Japanese soldiers rounded up and executed more than seventeen thousand men and boys just within the Nanking city walls.[47] Meanwhile the Ninth Division stepped up its murderous operation in Nanking's outlying administrative districts.

At 2 P.M. on December 17, General Matsui, accompanied by Admiral Hasegawa, concluded the victory ceremony by bowing to the east and raising the Sun Flag from the front of the former Kuomintang Government office building. "Banzai for His Majesty the Supreme Commander!" shouted Matsui three times. More than twenty thousand assembled combat troops—one-third the total number occupying the city—echoed in unison.[48]

The total number of Chinese atrocity-victims—both within the walled city and its rural districts—remains hotly disputed. The best Japanese estimates put the figure at "no fewer than two hundred thousand," while acknowledging that the true number may never be known. The postwar Tokyo War Crimes Tribunal accepted an estimate of "over 200,000" civilians and prisoners of war "murdered in Nanking and its vicinity during the first six weeks."[49] The war crimes trial held at Nanking accepted a figure of "over 300,000," and later uncorroborated estimates made in China increased that figure to 340,000 victims.[50] In December 1937 the first Western news accounts of the Nanking massacres, based on limited access to the city, gave estimates of from ten thousand to more than twenty thousand killings in the first few days.[51] Of the specific battlefield conditions that led Japanese soldiers to commit these horrendous crimes, the ones most frequently cited by Japanese historians are the breakdown of discipline, racial chauvinism, desire for revenge, and "extreme psychological frustration."

Also in dispute is the number of rape victims. Foreign observers at the time estimated that approximately one thousand women and girls of all ages were sexually assaulted and raped, daily, throughout the early stages of the occupation, when the imperial army had completely isolated Nanking from the rest of China. Raping continued into late March, by which time order in the ranks had been restored. "Comfort stations," where women from throughout the Japanese empire were forced to serve as prostitutes, were beginning to proliferate; and the army had established a new "National Restoration Government" for the central China area to match the one installed some three months earlier at Peking. Yet widespread violence against Chinese civilians continued. Between the start of the China war in August 1937 and the end of 1939, as many as 420 Japanese soldiers would be convicted by military courts for the rape and murder of Chinese women. Yet no Japanese soldier was ever executed for such crimes.[52]

Hundreds of Japanese reporters and newsreel cameramen accompanied the army in China at this time, and a relatively small number from the United States and Europe. Only the latter conveyed to the world what was really happening. The censored Japanese press, prohibited from quoting foreign news sources critical of Japan, did not discuss massacres, war atrocities, terrorized civilians, or rapes, but merely reported many prisoners captured at Nanking and large numbers of Chinese dead left unburied.[53] Nevertheless the story of two Japanese second lieutenants competing to cut down with their swords a hundred Chinese soldiers had appeared several times in the *Tokyo Nichi Nichi shinbun* prior to the capture of Nanking, so that a context for grasping the violence on the battlefields in China existed.[54] Yet only very discerning Japanese readers and those with access to foreign newspapers, such as the Christian scholar Yanaihara Tadao, made the connections and became aware that killers in uniform had committed crimes that did not accord with Japan's idealized self-image.[55]

Members of the imperial family, including Hirohito's fifty-year-old granduncle Prince Asaka, who had commanded the attack on Nanking under Matsui's supervision and was the ranking officer in the city at the height of the atrocities; forty-nine-year-old General Prince Higashikuni, chief of the army air force and an uncle of Empress Nagako; and seventy-one-year-old uncle Prince Kan'in, chief of the Army General Staff, all knew of the massacres and the near-total collapse of discipline.[56] So too, of course, did Army Minister Sugiyama. Many middle- and upper-echelon officers of the Imperial Headquarters knew. Reserve Maj. Gen. Etō, a member of the Lower House of the Diet, knew.[57] The Foreign Ministry certainly knew. Its East Asian Bureau chief, Ishigari Itarō, confided to his diary that "A letter arrived from Shanghai reporting in detail on the atrocities of our army in Nanking. It describes an horrendous situation of pillage and rape. My god, is this how our imperial army behaves?"[58] The diplomat and old China hand Shigemitsu Mamoru wrote soon after the war of how, at the time, he had "made great efforts to develop a good policy toward China in order to compensate for crimes [committed] when occupying Nanking."[59]

It seems unlikely that the Konoe government knew of the rape and pillage at Nanking but the well-briefed Hirohito did not. Hirohito was at the top of the chain of command, and whatever the shortcomings of the command system at that very early stage, he could not easily be kept ignorant of high- or middle-level decisions.

He closely followed every Japanese military move, read diplomatic telegrams, read the newspapers daily, and often questioned his aides about what he found in them. As the commander in chief who had sanctioned the capture and occupation of Nanking, and as the spiritual leader of the nation—the individual who gave legitimacy to the "chastisement" of China—he bore a minimal moral as well as constitutional duty to project—even if not publicly—some concern for the breakdown of discipline. He never seems to have done so.

Growing foreign diplomatic complaints about the behavior of his troops in the Shanghai-Nanking war zones may also have come to Hirohito's attention. Certainly they came to the attention of the high command and the Foreign Ministry, not to mention several members of the Diet. U.S. ambassador Grew twice formally protested the Japanese army's pillaging of American property and desecration of American flags in Nanking to Foreign Minister Hirota, who then raised the issue at a cabinet meeting in mid-January 1938.[60]

Diplomat Hidaka Shinrokurō, who visited Nanking right after its fall, also reported in detail to Hirota, and may even have briefed the emperor on the atrocities in late January, though the evidence for this is conjectural.[61] Hidaka spoke fluent English. He personally knew the Nazi German John Rabe, one of the organizers of the Nanking International Safety Zone, established by Westerners near the city's center to provide a sanctuary for refugees. *Manchester Guardian* reporter Harold J. Timperley, author of *Japanese Terror in China* (1938), the first book on the Nanking massacre, was his personal friend. He also discussed Nanking events with *New York Times* correspondent Hallett Abend. Hidaka even transmitted to the Foreign Ministry some of the complaints of members of the International Committee for the Nanking Safety Zone, including those written by Rabe and Nanking University professor Lewis Smythe. If either Hidaka or Foreign Minister Hirota had briefed Hirohito on the atrocities committed by the army, he would have been very well informed indeed.

Assuming, however, that Hirohito was not officially informed by them or anyone else in a formal position of authority of the true scale of the mass executions his soldiers were carrying out, under divisional, regimental, and even staff orders, in violation of international law, he still had secondary intelligence of the breakdown of army discipline from non-chain-of-command sources, such as the domestic and foreign press, or perhaps from his brothers, who might have passed on to him orally rumors of what was going on in occupied Nanking.[62] Since he did have such secondary intelligence, he could secretly have ordered an investigation. Yet no documentary trace exists of an imperial order to investigate. Instead there remains Hirohito's silence about the criminal behavior of the imperial forces whose movements he was following closely up to the very moment they took the city. There also remains the equally undeniable fact that throughout the prelude to the incident and during the entire period of the murders and rapes, rather than do anything *publicly* to show his displeasure, anger, or remorse, he energetically spurred his generals and admirals on to greater victories in the national project to induce Chinese "self-reflection."

On November 20, more than three weeks before the fall of Nanking and the day his new Imperial Headquarters was established, Hirohito had bestowed an imperial rescript on the commander of the China Area Fleet, Adm. Hasegawa Kiyoshi. He applauded the officers and men of the fleet for cooperating with the army, controlling China's coasts, and interdicting its lines of marine transportation. At the same time he had warned, "We still have a long way to go before we achieve our goal. Increasingly strive to accomplish more victories."[63]

Four days later, while attending his first Imperial Headquarters conference, Hirohito had given after-the-fact sanction to the momentous decision of General Matsui's Central China Area Army to attack and occupy the capital of China. During that meeting the head of the Operations Department of the Army General Staff explained to him that both the transportation corps and the artillery units of the army in central China were still lagging far behind the foremost units on the front lines, and that while the army regrouped, "the air forces of the army and navy will ... bomb Nanking and its strategic areas."[64] Thus Hirohito was quite aware of and approved the plans to bomb and strafe Nanking and its environs. He ratified (post facto) the removal of all restrictions on the army's perimeter of operations; he did nothing to hold back the army and navy during their headlong rush toward Nanking without prior authorization from Tokyo. On December 1—many days after aerial bombardment and sea and ground attacks on Nanking had begun—Hirohito gave the formal order for General Matsui to attack: "The commander of the Central China Area Army, acting jointly with the navy, will capture and occupy the enemy capital of Nanking (Imperial Headquarters Army Order Number 8)."

Hirohito had been eager to fight a decisive battle in "the enemy capital" because at that time, like most of his high command, he had subscribed to the view that one big blow would bring Chiang Kai-shek to his knees and end the fighting. Consequently, despite the diplomatic harm Matsui's and Asaka's actions were causing, the emperor publicly praised them. On December 14, the day after Nanking fell, he conferred an imperial message on his chiefs of staff expressing his pleasure at the news of the city's capture and occupation.[65] When General Matsui returned to Tokyo to be released from temporary active duty in February 1938, Hirohito granted him an imperial rescript for his great military accomplishments.[66] Prince Asaka had to wait until April 1940 to receive his honor, the Order of the Golden Eagle.[67] In such ways did Hirohito exercise his authority indirectly to condone the criminality of his troops. Although he may have been privately dismayed by what had happened at Nanking, he took no notice of it publicly, and did nothing to make up for it by taking an interest in and changing Japanese policy on the treatment of prisoners of war.

Both army and navy officers and men perpetrated the Nanking atrocities. Their start coincided with the shelling by the Japanese army of Chinese refugee vessels and the British gunboats *Lady Bird* and *Bee*. At the same time two Japanese navy planes deliberately bombed the U.S. gunboat *Panay*, at anchor on the Yangtze River some twenty-seven miles upstream from Nanking, with diplomats and American and European journalists and photographers aboard.[68] To add insult to injury, after the *Panay*'s crew and passengers had abandoned the burning ship, Japanese soldiers in motorboats boarded it and fired on the last lifeboat making its way to shore. Accounts of these incidents, in which three Americans later died and three others were seriously wounded, reached the West just when the British and American press began reporting the sensational news of the Nanking massacres.[69] The two events impressed American public opinion with the aggressiveness, cruelty, and sheer audacity of the Japanese military, which had attacked warships of the two powers that had been most critical of Japan's actions in China. They also gave new resonance to the image of Japan as a direct threat to American security.

Although Konoe and the Imperial Navy immediately apologized and paid more than $2.2 million in reparations for what they claimed was the "mistaken" sinking of the *Panay*, Hirohito once again took no personal action to counter the damage, though he could easily have sent telegrams expressing regret to President Roosevelt and King George VI.[70] Clearly, neither he nor the Konoe cabinet grasped the full extent of the military and diplomatic blunder Japan had just committed.

The massacres and the sinking of the USS *Panay* were neither quickly forgotten, nor forgiven—either in China or in the United States. News of Nanking's "rape" spread and was turned by many Chinese into a symbolic event: the prism through which, long afterward, they saw their entire war with Japan. In the depression-racked

United States, press reports of the massacres and the sinking of the *Panay* received rare front-page attention.[71] The Asian news momentarily raised international tensions, stimulating a wave of anti-Japanese, pro-Chinese sentiment that never entirely abated. Since the late nineteenth century, Americans had tended to view China not only as a market to be exploited but also as a proper field for the projection of their idealism and essential goodness in foreign relations. President Roosevelt's refusal to impose sanctions against the vulnerable Japanese economy came under criticism from a new movement to boycott the sale of imported Japanese goods. American voices advocating naval expansion also grew louder. Roosevelt, then in his third term but still unable to dominate foreign policy, sent Capt. Royal E. Ingersoll, the head of the Bureau of Naval Operations, to London for naval talks concerning possible cooperation with Britain to resist Japanese aggression in Asia and the Pacific.[72]

The *Panay* incident also brought Hirohito, briefly, to the attention of Americans. On December 14 the *Chicago Daily News* carried a banner headline warning BREAK WITH JAPAN WEIGHED unless the "Emperor of Japan" replied swiftly to "President Roosevelt's demand for apologies, compensation and guarantees against repetition of attacks on Americans in China." Beneath the caption "U.S. Demands Put to Mikado," was a picture of a small, bespectacled Hirohito, in military uniform, sitting astride his huge white horse.[73] The *Daily News* implied an emperor who possessed real political power, and thus should be held accountable for the sinking of an American warship. Journalistic realism such as this, however, was extremely rare.

The *New York Times* and the *Washington Post* tended either to treat Japan as a monolithic political entity or to focus solely on "Japanese war lords," "militarists," and "military extremists." The *Los Angeles Times* editorialized, on December 14, that Roosevelt's note to the emperor on the *Panay*

> wished to call attention to the fact that the Japanese armed forces are
> under the control of the Emperor alone, and not . . . bound to obey
> the Japanese government as represented by the Cabinet. . . . Whether
> the Japanese high command actually obeys the Emperor or controls
> him is of course another question. But there is a duality in the Japanese
> set-up which makes the Japanese government difficult to deal with.[74]

The *Los Angeles Times* thus left open the question of the emperor's real power.

Judging from these big urban dailies, Hirohito was largely irrelevant in the Japanese policy-making process. With few exceptions he existed (if he existed at all) in American minds mainly as a powerless "figurehead." And the steady worsening of relations with Japan after 1937 did little to undermine this stereotype. The dominant American image of the Japanese emperor down to Pearl Harbor was that of a monarch who, without ruling, reigned—without participating in political decision making was sustained by political decisions, and without influencing the thinking of his advisers was at all times and in all ways obedient to their counsels. These assumptions were both wrong and stubborn. Reinforced by earlier American exposure to the false image of the Meiji emperor, they persisted long after Pearl Harbor. Under the sway of the static "figurehead" image, American perceptions of Hirohito and the Japanese policy-making process leading to the Pacific War were never rooted in reality.[75]

III

The undeclared China war would last eight years, set the stage for the triumph of Communism in China, and end only after having given seed to Japanese involvement in World War II, and Japan's ultimate defeat. During these years the emperor was presented with several opportunities to consider a cease-fire or an early peace. The first and best came during the attack on Nanking, when Chiang's Nationalist Army was in complete disarray. Chiang had hoped to end the fighting by enticing intervention by friendly nations that had signed international treaties with China. Those major powers were not inclined to offer China positive support so long as a war crisis loomed in Europe, however, and isolationism was on the rise in the United States.

At the Nine-Power Treaty Conference in Brussels in November 1937, proposed by Britain and the United States and boycotted by Japan, the Nationalist representatives even failed to persuade the participants to declare Japan an aggressor.[76] When the Brussels Conference ended without enacting sanctions against Japan, the Konoe government and the Imperial Headquarters had immediately expanded the combat zone, disregarding the harm to the lives and property of the other treaty powers that could result from an offensive against Nanking. In late November, desperately hoping to slow down the Japanese advance by diplomacy now that arms were failing to defend Nanking, Chiang finally accepted a previous offer of German mediation. The Army General Staff in Tokyo was also willing. Thereupon Oscar Trautmann, the German ambassador to China, attempted to resuscitate Japan-China peace negotiations, but was unsuccessful.[77]

One day after the fall of Nanking, on December 14, Konoe signaled in a press conference a change in his government's attitude toward peace negotiations:

> Before we take joy in the news of the fall of Nanking, we cannot help but be saddened by the fact that 500 million people, sharing the same race and the same culture, are hopelessly deluded. The Nationalist government went to the edge both diplomatically and by its actions with its anti-Japanese movement. They failed, however, to assume responsibility for the consequences of their actions, abandoned their capital, and split their government. Now, when they are collapsing

into separate military cliques, it has become clear to us that they show
no sign of reflection. Accordingly we are forced to rethink our
course.[78]

Konoe and his cabinet now offered harsh terms. China must
formally recognize Manchukuo, cooperate with it and Japan in
fighting Communism, permit the indefinite stationing of Japanese
troops, and pay war reparations to Japan.[79] The no-escalation faction within the Army General Staff still hoped for an early reduction of army expenditures in China, and therefore wanted the
Trautmann peace mediation, begun in November, to continue.[80]
They pointed out realistically that Japan's refusal to recognize the
Nationalist regime would "drive [Chiang] into concentrating everything against Japan. . . . Inevitably, this will make the Soviets, the
British, and the Americans more active. . . . The Empire will be
forced to expend enormous national strength and resources for a
long time to come."[81]

On January 9, 1938, the newly established Imperial Headquarters–Government Liaison Conference decided on a policy for
handling the China Incident. After sending on the document—entitled "Fundamental Policy for Dealing with the China Incident"—
for rubber-stamping by the cabinet in order to ensure its formal
legality, Konoe reported it to Hirohito. The next day he asked the
emperor to convene an imperial conference but not to speak out at
it, for "We just want to formally decide the matter in your majesty's
presence."[82] Hirohito and Konoe were concerned not only with
blocking the views of the antiexpansionists on the Army General
Staff, they also wanted to prevent undue German influence in
Japanese affairs. On January 11, some thirty minutes before the
imperial conference finally met in the palace, its members convened
a special meeting to answer questions about the policy document
that Hiranuma Kiichirō, president of the privy council, insisted on
asking.

After the ministers of state had satisfied Hiranuma's concerns, the conference convened at 2 P.M. in the emperor's "august presence" and heard Foreign Minister Hirota argue that the Trautmann mediation had no hope of succeeding and therefore "we must strengthen our resolve to fight through to the end with China."[83] Prince Kan'in, speaking for the Army General Staff, expressed "a mild reservation about the prudence of a policy that regarded the Nationalist government as a totally defeated regime," but went along with the consensus of the meeting.[84] The imperial conference then adopted a document specifying that if the Nationalist government refused to accept peace entirely on the terms proffered, Japan would withdraw recognition and confer it upon a different, more pliant regime.[85] Presiding, in full-dress army uniform, at his first imperial conference since the one twenty-five years earlier, when his father had sanctioned Japan's participation in World War I, Hirohito gave his approval.[86] By sitting through the approximately seventy-minute-long meeting without uttering one word, he had appeared to maintain imperial neutrality in the matter, though in fact he was firmly backing a stronger military policy toward China than the Army General Staff proposed.

When the Chinese delayed in replying to Tokyo's harsh conditions, the Konoe cabinet abruptly broke off negotiations. On January 16, 1938, Konoe issued the promised statement that Japan would thereafter no longer recognize the Nationalist government.[87] A supplementary public announcement by Konoe two days later made clear that his real purpose in withdrawing recognition was to "eradicate" Chiang's government—an objective that Navy Minister Yonai in particular strongly endorsed.[88] Significantly, at both the liaison conference and the imperial conference that followed it, the emperor failed to support his Army General Staff on the crucial matter of continuing peace negotiations. Instead he tended to back the harder navy line.

The army opponents of an all-out "war of annihilation" in

China still tried to get their views heard. On the eve of Konoe's famous nonrecognition statement, Prince Kan'in tried unsuccessfully to make a report directly to the emperor before Prime Minister Konoe presented his formal report. By the time Hirohito finally heard Kan'in, at 9:30 P.M. on January 15, however, his mind was firmly set on continuing the war rather than negotiating. "We will be leaving an anti-Japanese Chinese force in the south, so what will our army do about that?" he asked the prince. Hirohito's other questions concerned whether it would be wiser to prop up the [client] regimes in North China indirectly, by using "advisers so as not to draw attention," what plans the army had made to counter "guerrilla tactics," and what plans had been prepared to counter "a Chinese reply."[89] Hirohito's questions mainly involved operations, but his last query could be interpreted as an indirect and dry criticism of the nonexpansionists on the General Staff for raising a matter that had already been decided at the liaison conference.[90] Thus the nonexpansionists were once again checked. Sharing the same stance on the China war as Konoe and the hard-line expansionists in the Navy Ministry, Hirohito would push for a quick resolution of the incident.

The Konoe cabinet now inaugurated a second intense stage of the China war, which lasted through December 1938. By that time Japanese combat casualties since the start of fighting at the Marco Polo Bridge had reached 62,000 killed and 6,667 wounded; deaths from illness in both China and Manchuria totaled 12,605. Over the course of the next two years, Japanese combat casualties decreased sharply but still remained high. From 30,081 killed and 15,760 wounded in 1939, they declined by almost half to 15,827 killed and 8,000 wounded in 1940.[91] Deaths from illness remained relatively stable, averaging over 11,500 per year. In other words, by the end of 1938 the China war had attained a plateau in respect to its cost in combat casualties, with the annual rate near 24,000. That the number of dead was, on average, about twice the number of wounded seems rather shocking, but precisely what conclusions can be drawn from that upside-down ratio is not clear. Equally important, Japan had lost all hope of being able to control the China war militarily or politically.

During 1938 the major cities and railways of northern, central, and southern China came under occupation by the Japanese army, while the vast hinterland of villages and mountainous areas in between served as bases for Chinese guerrillas. Everywhere during the first four years of the China war, the Japanese area armies slighted Communist troops controlled by Mao Tse-tung, regarding them as mere "bandits," and directed virtually all their main blows against the "Nationalist" forces of Chiang Kai-shek. The same was true of the army air force, which carried out five long-range bombing campaigns in the interior of northern and central China during this period. They bombed military facilities in the Communist base-area of Yenan on only two occasions in October 1939. The main target of air attack was always Chungking. Not until August 1941, did the army commit large numbers of its bombers to attacking Yenan.[92] Meanwhile, with the capture of Wuhan and Canton in October 1938, the Japanese ground offensive reached its apogee, and thereafter Japan shifted to the strategic defensive.[93]

Confronted with a deadlocked war and no prospect of victory in sight, Japan's leaders pressed on as if unable—more than unwilling—to change their ultimate goals. Against a backdrop of full national mobilization, tighter press censorship, and ever higher levels of military spending, they initiated numerous peace maneuvers. These turned on exploiting conflicts between the Chinese Nationalists and their domestic enemies. Prime Minister Konoe's famous declaration of a "New Order in East Asia" in November 1938 was the most significant of these initiatives. Konoe expressed his hope of achieving peace in China through Chiang Kai-shek's enemy—and leader of his own faction within the Kuomintang—Wang Ching-wei. This particular effort to supplement military action with political maneuvers eventually culminated in the establishment of the Wang regime in Nanking at the end of March 1940, and the signing of a Japan-China Basic Treaty in November 1940. Yet never really trusting Wang or believing in his ability to end the war, the Konoe government delayed recognizing his regime, and later forced him to cede to Japan, by treaty, a vast array of military, economic, and political privileges that turned his government into a puppet regime lacking any legitimacy in the eyes of most Chinese.

But whether focused on a direct settlement with Chiang Kai-shek in Chungking, or on the installation of a new sham government in Nanking, Japan's efforts at ending the war aimed ultimately at expanding, consolidating, and legitimizing its war gains. Never did its "peace feelers" manifest any intention to set a deadline for withdrawal of Japanese troops from North China, let alone relinquish control over the puppet state of Manchukuo.

The Japanese summer offensive against Wuhan was scheduled to begin in July 1938, and the Army General Staff was worried about the posture of the Soviet Union. On July 11, 1938, the commander of the Nineteenth Division precipitated a major clash with the Soviets over possession of a hill on the border of Manchukuo. Known as the Chang Ku-feng Incident, the result for Japan was a complete and costly defeat. At the time diarist Harada Kumao noted Hirohito's scolding of Army Minister Itagaki: "Hereafter not a single soldier is to be moved without my permission."[94] In other words he told his army minister that he would be in charge here, then took no disciplinary action at all against the officer who had provoked the incident. Shortly afterward, when it was clear that Soviet forces were not going to counterattack across the border, he gave the go-ahead for the planned offensive in China to begin.[95] It was yet another example of his selectivity in using his authority to intervene.

Once again Japan expected to crush the Chinese quickly. Enjoying overwhelming ground, naval, and air superiority, the Japanese offensive of late 1938 triumphed in virtually every encounter. But Chinese resistance was also stiffening, forcing Japanese troops to rely increasingly on chemical weapons. (Here too there were Western precedents: most notably, Germany's first use of poison gas in World War I and Fascist Italy's use of gas in Ethiopia in 1935.) By November, Japanese troops had occupied the "three Wuhan cities" of Wuchang, Hankou, and Hanyang on the Yangtze River in central China, and Canton in the far south; they controlled the main railways throughout the country and had established controlling enclaves in all of China's richest, most developed coastal provinces.[96] Chiang Kai-shek, proclaiming that the war must continue, retreated with his entire government farther into the interior to the walled, mountain city of Chungking, beyond Japan's power to pursue him.[97]

For Japan, Wuhan was indeed the high point of the war, the extreme limit of its offensive capability at that time. As news of its victories came back, the nation celebrated as it had when the press first reported (prematurely) the news of Nanking's fall: Sirens sounded, newspapers published extras, and the emperor, as he had done during the Manchurian Incident, donned full uniform and appeared astride his white horse.

Konoe soon issued his second statement on the war, on November 3, 1938. Maintaining that Japan intended to construct a "New Order in East Asia," he also declared that it would not veto participation by the Nationalist Chinese government. Eight weeks later, on December 22, Konoe made an important third pronouncement, which set forth the "three Konoe principles," thereafter considered to be Japan's official war aims. First, China must formally recognize Manchukuo and establish relations of "neighborly friendship." This principle implied that China cease all anti-Japan activities. Second, China would be required to join Japan in defending against Communism; this implied that Japan had a right to maintain armies within China. Third, there must be broad economic cooperation between the two governments, including acceptance of Japan's right to develop and exploit the natural resources of North China and Inner Mongolia.[98]

On these three principles, Japan hoped to establish its "New Order in East Asia." Konoe's statement was intended to drive a wedge between the factions in the Nationalist government—former premier Wang Ching-wei on the one hand and Chiang Kai-shek on the other. The eventual outcome would be a new collaborationist government to rule from Japanese-occupied Nanking over Japanese-controlled provinces.[99]

IV

On January 4, 1939, Konoe resigned, unable to end the fighting in China or to bring about a consensus within his divided cabinet on a military alliance with Nazi Germany. His departure opened the way for three successors—former privy council president Hiranuma, Gen. Abe Nobuyuki, and Admiral Yonai—to carry the "holy war" forward. An accommodation with Wang Ching-wei to establish a rival regime in Nanking was in the offing. But Japan had not crushed Chiang Kai-shek. On the contrary, it had aroused a deep spirit of national resistance wherever its often wantonly brutal troops had advanced. Unable to maintain control of the vast rural countryside, forced to stretch its fronts and their lines of supply and communications to the limit, the Japanese armies in China soon found themselves hopelessly frustrated, both militarily and politically. At that point World War II started in Europe, and Japan's ruling groups began to imagine that the rising power of Germany offered them a way out of their dilemma.

Following his resigned prime minister's recommendation, the emperor at the start of 1939 appointed Hiranuma as Konoe's successor. Hiranuma was a strong supporter of the army and a person whom Hirohito had once considered an outright fascist. Since the army mutiny of 1936, however, he had distanced himself somewhat from the radical right by dissolving the Kokuhonsha—at Prince Saionji's insistence—and cultivating ties with members of the court entourage. Now, under coaching from Finance Minister Ikeda Seihin and the court group, he redefined himself further, promising not to make enemies of Britain and the United States by entering hastily into a military alliance with Nazi Germany. His partial turnaround on the German alliance was enough to put him in Hirohito's good graces.[100]

For the next nine months Hiranuma grappled not only with military and diplomatic problems arising from the deadlocked war in China but also with the problem of the Soviet Union. In May the Kwantung Army clashed with Soviet and Mongolian forces near Nomonhan village, on the border between northwestern Manchukuo and Outer Mongolia (the Mongolian People's Republic). The fighting quickly developed into a full-scale border war, involving large numbers of tanks, artillery, and aircraft. Although the Kwantung Army brought biological warfare weapons to the front, no conclusive evidence shows that they actually used germ warfare against Mongolian and Soviet forces, as later charged.[101] Fighting at Nomonhan continued until September 15, when Soviet foreign minister Vyacheslav Molotov and Japanese ambassador Tōgō Shigenori signed a truce agreement in Moscow.

Japanese casualties—excluding their Manchukuoan auxiliaries—totaled more than 18,925 dead, wounded, or missing—virtually an entire division.[102] The officers responsible for provoking the disastrous Nomonhan incident—the commander of the Kwantung Army, Gen. Ueda Kenkichi, and his two senior staff officers, Maj. Tsuji Masanobu and Lt. Col. Hattori Takushirō—were merely reassigned. No rethinking of army plans and methods took place. The emperor again refrained from punishing anyone, and in 1941 he even allowed Tsuji and Hattori to be promoted and to serve in important positions on the Army General Staff, just as he had earlier allowed the perpetrators of the Manchurian Incident to be posted to central headquarters in Tokyo, and promoted.[103]

Moreover, it appeared that the officers involved had acted legitimately on the basis of a document—the "Outline for Dealing With Disputes Along the Manchuria-Soviet Border"—that Hirohito had sanctioned shortly before the incident erupted. As the troops were following orders he had approved, he certainly did not want to punish them; and the army high command also saw no need to give more attention to a reckless action that had ended so miserably.[104]

That summer of 1939 the Hiranuma cabinet confronted yet another serious diplomatic problem arising from the stalemated war in China. For several months the North China Area Army had been unhappy over London's decision to stabilize China's national currency. Alleging the presence of Chinese terrorists operating from within the British concession in the occupied city of Tientsin, the army began puting pressure on the enclave. Japanese troops encircled the entire concession with an electrified wire fence and started searching foreigners for their possession of banned Nationalist currency. In mid-June they escalated their harassment to a full blockade and started strip-searching British citizens, male and female alike. Concurrently, at home, the army and right-wing groups unleashed an anti-British propaganda campaign.[105] To the delight of army leaders, Hiranuma's home minister and close consultant, Kido, refused to rein in the campaign even though it had incurred Hirohito's displeasure.[106]

As Japan's relations with Britain worsened throughout the spring and summer of 1939, the pending problem arose of whether to strengthen ties with Germany, an idea the emperor opposed. When pro-Nazi ambassadors Gen. Ōshima Hiroshi in Berlin and Shiratori Toshio in Rome refused to convey the Foreign Ministry directive carefully circumscribing the terms under which Japan would join a new Axis pact, Hiranuma merely fretted. When he informed the emperor of their actions, Hirohito too grew excited but chose not to order their recall.[107]

Then, on July 26, 1939, the United States, having repeatedly protested Japanese actions in China, notified the Hiranuma government that it intended not to renew the U.S.–Japan Treaty of Commerce and Navigation, scheduled to lapse in January 1940. Up to that point the Roosevelt administration had pursued a policy of gentle appeasement of Japan, but its basic Asian policy had always been to maintain the imperialist status quo embodied in the Washington treaty system. Thus it had consistently refused to recognize any changes Japan had brought about by force in China. Roosevelt had also propped up China's national currency by making regular silver purchases—a policy that would eventually lead him to join the British in providing foreign exchange so that Chiang Kai-shek could stabilize his currency, counter the proliferation of Japanese military currencies in occupied areas, and go on fighting.[108] Now, however, anticipating that war would soon break out in Europe, the United States put Japan on notice that serious economic sanctions could follow further acts of aggression. Thereafter, if Japan's leaders were to continue the war in China, they would have to take more seriously the reactions of the United States, on which they depended for vital imports needed to wage war.

"It could be a great blow to scrap metal and oil," Hirohito complained to his chief aide-de-camp, Hata Shunroku, on August 5, shortly after the American move:

> Even if we can purchase [oil and scrap] for the next six months, we will immediately have difficulties thereafter. Unless we reduce the size of our army and navy by one-third, we won't make it. . . . They [his military and naval leaders] should have prepared for something like this a long time ago. It's unacceptable for them to be making a commotion about it now.[109]

But of course Hirohito did not enjoin his chiefs of staff to end the China war, or to reduce the size of anything; he simply got angry at them for not having anticipated the American reaction.

A few weeks later, on August 23, 1939, while the Japan-Soviet truce to end the fighting on the Mongolia-Manchukuo border was being negotiated in Moscow, Germany signed a nonaggression pact with its ideological enemy, the Soviet Union—which contravened the 1936 Japan-German Anti-Comintern Pact. After a fruitless three-year quest for "collective security" with the West against German territorial expansion in Europe, Stalin had declared Soviet neutrality and, in a secret protocol attached to the pact, made a deal with Hitler to take over the Baltic states and eventually partition Poland.[110] Stunned by this diplomatic reversal, and unsure how to interpret the enormous strengthening of both German *and* Soviet power that Hitler's alliance with Stalin portended, the Hiranuma cabinet resigned on the morning of August 28.

A very angry Hirohito used the occasion of this cabinet change to inform Chief Aide-de-Camp Hata that he intended to appoint someone he could trust as the next army minister, certainly not Isogai Rensuke or Tada Hayao (generals whose names had appeared in the press), and that Hata "should convey that to the army minister [Itagaki Seishirō]."[111] For many months Hirohito's displeasure with Itagaki's reporting had been building, and he had told him to his face that he lacked ability. Now, on the twenty-eighth, Hirohito appointed General Abe prime minister, telling him (according to Konoe, who told Kido) to chose either his chief aide, Hata, or Gen. Umezu Yoshijirō as army minister, and to try to "cooperate" with the United States and Britain. However, "the most important matter" was "preservation of internal order." "[B]e very careful in chosing your Home and Justice Ministers," he warned.[112] This seems to have been an authentic expression of Hirohito's distrust of the Japanese people; it may also have echoed, rather less clearly, his uneasiness with the German-Soviet rapprochement: nothing good could come of such an unnatural coupling, so be on guard against further Soviet and German maneuvering. On the afternoon of the next day, Hirohito formally appointed Hata Shunroku, the military professional he liked and trusted, as Army Minister.[113] Retired admiral Nomura Kichisaburō, a man who promised to reestablish good relations with the United States, came in as Abe's new foreign minister.

Meanwhile Hitler had already revealed to his generals, in May, his strategy for attacking and destroying the armies of the Allies and seizing control of the European continent. With Germany at the height of its power relative to Britain, France, and Poland, Hitler now decided to put one part of his overall plan into effect. On September 1, 1939, the first day of the Abe cabinet, German armies invaded Poland, starting a new European war. Two days later Britain and France intervened, declaring war on Germany, and on September 8, President Roosevelt, Hitler's most implacable enemy, proclaimed a state of limited national emergency.

Soon the United States, despite its declaration of neutrality, was shipping Britain and France growing supplies of war matériel. In October, Roosevelt ordered a large part of the American fleet, home-ported in Southern California, to Hawaii to relieve pressure on the British, French, and Dutch colonies and Pacific Ocean defenses. Positioning the fleet at Pearl Harbor, he hoped, might serve to deter revisionist Japan from overturning the status quo in Southeast Asia. These momentous events, all occurring during the early months of Abe's tenure, raised fears in Tokyo that the United States, despite its strong isolationist sentiment, would eventually enter the war on the side of Britain and France. Unable to respond to the new international situation, the Abe cabinet collapsed on January 14, 1940.

Immediately another frantic effort to choose a successor began. Privy Seal Yuasa queried the senior statesmen, even the venerable Saionji, but attended above all to the wishes of the emperor. At Hirohito's insistence Reserve Admiral Yonai, a man in whom he reposed great trust, formed the next cabinet, and Hata was asked by Hirohito to stay on and assist Yonai as the army minister.[114] To assuage criticism in the army at the selection of a naval officer, Hirohito also sanctioned at this time Gen. Tōjō's elevation to the post of vice army minister.[115]

From the very start of his reign, Hirohito had played an active role in high-level personnel appointments. At such times he had imposed conditions, telling the prime minister–designate he must do such and such, or appoint certain persons to this or that ministry so they could control one or another particular section chief.[116] Indeed, he and his advisers had destabilized the system of party government by insisting on determining who would be the next prime minister. Now, as the China war dragged on and the pace of European diplomacy quickened, his involvement in such matters increased. His interventions were made at his own choosing, and intentionally concealed from the public. When new calls arose from the army high command for a military alliance with Germany that would make Japan part of an anti–Anglo-American bloc, Hirohito continued to resist. The government, he insisted, should focus on bringing the China war to a swift conclusion and not ally Japan closer with Germany except to counter the Soviet Union.

Three months into Yonai's tenure as prime minister, starting in April, Germany invaded Western Europe, completing the drastic realignment in international relations that it had begun eight months earlier with its conquest of Poland. One after another Europe's remaining independent nations fell: Norway, Denmark, Luxembourg, Belgium, the Netherlands, and finally, with little military resistance, France, from which the British army was extricated at the last moment. Overnight the geopolitical perspectives in Tokyo changed. For three long years Japan's leaders had been locked in a war of their own making in China, with no military or political victory in sight. The Nazi victories in Europe had created unprecedented opportunities for Japan to take over the Asian colonies of Britain, France, and the Netherlands. The expectation grew apace of making gains and compensating for weaknesses by riding on the coattails of the rising power of Germany, which now controlled most of the resources of Europe up to the Soviet frontier and was preparing to invade Britain. When Yonai failed to act on the long-pending issue of a German alliance, the army brought down his cabinet, and Hirohito did nothing to prevent it.

Throughout this chaotic series of international crises under three prime ministers—Hiranuma, Abe, and Yonai—Hirohito was content to watch as both the China war and the policy of southern advance unfolded. Not once did he make a personal effort to extricate Japan from its deadlocked war in China. And because Japan's policy toward China remained unchanged, relations with the United States also failed to improve. Believing the policy of southern advance to be strategically desirable, Hirohito worried mainly over what stance the British and the Americans would adopt if the navy continued to move south.

By the summer of 1940, two new elements had entered the picture, increasing the pressure on him to align more closely with the advocates of a new German alliance. One was the conquest of Western Europe by the German military juggernaut, which left Britain apparently isolated, on the verge of invasion; the other was the realignment of Soviet foreign policy under the aegis of Stalin's pact with Hitler. The Soviet move seemed to have imparted new strength to the Axis alliance while also raising the specter of renewed Russian military aid to Chiang Kai-shek.[117] In this situation of rapid military conquest and intense diplomatic maneuver, Hirohito vacillated, uncertain whether to stand firm against the army on a tripartite pact directed against the U.S. and Britain, or to change sides and sanction what the army wanted. Ultimately his decision would have less to do with shared ideological goals with the Nazis than with preserving the unity of Japan.

STALEMATE AND ESCALATION

J apan's ruling elites had embarked on a war in China for which Hirohito and the authority of the throne were absolutely essential. Officially the armed forces were chastising the troops of Chiang Kai-shek and spreading the virtues of the emperor, not creating chaos and cruelty. Hirohito's symbolic role was to obfuscate the relationship between the government's principles of peace and its policies of violence. He personally made the whole military endeavor seem both ethical and rational. Outwardly he was the model of morality for Japanese society, the embodiment of its aristocratic and national values, a symbol of its professedly benevolent intentions. The role he played as supreme commander, shaping the fighting strategy and the conduct of the war from behind the scenes, was deliberately camouflaged. Yet the experience he gained in playing that role during the first four years of struggle against the Nationalists altered his attitude toward war in general and eventually made him more willing to risk Japan's security for larger purposes.

Hirohito did not regard China as a "modern" state and probably never believed Japan's aggression there to be wrong. He supported the policy of withholding a declaration of war against China and ratified and personally endorsed the decision to remove the constraints of international law on the treatment of Chinese prisoners of war as stated by the army vice chief of staff in a directive on August 5, 1937: "In the present situation, in order to wage total war in China, the empire will neither apply, nor act in accordance with, all the concrete articles of the Treaty Concerning the Laws and Customs of Land Warfare and Other Treaties Concerning the Laws and Regulations of Belligerency."[1] The same notification advised staff officers in China to stop using the term "prisoner of war." Throughout the war in China the Japanese military captured tens of thousands of Chinese soldiers annually. Yet, at the war's end, when Japanese authorities claimed to have had in their possession scores of thousands of Western prisoners, they acknowledged having only fifty-six Chinese prisoners of war.

Hirohito had studied international law under Tachi Sakutarō; he knew that Japan had signed (but not ratified) the 1929 Geneva Convention on the Treatment of Prisoners of War. He had also read the clause calling for respect for international law in the imperial war rescripts of his grandfather and father. Yet he never had orders issued to his armed forces that would have prevented the mass murder or mistreatment of Chinese prisoners. That act of omission reflected a widespread tendency among many Japanese bureaucrats, intellectuals, and right-wingers during the 1930s to regard international law itself as a purely Western fabrication. For them the rule of international law was something that, ever since the end of World War I, the British and the Americans had wanted to develop and spread because it served their interests, not Japan's.

For many Americans, Europeans, and Asians, the aspect of Japan's war of aggression that more than anything created the stereotype of the heartless, cruel Japanese—a stereotype that has never entirely been forgotten or forgiven—were the atrocities and the mistreatment of prisoners of war.[2] Behind the atrocities lay precisely the military's refusal to apply international law to China; for that void Hirohito shared responsibility. He alone was free to act in this area, needed to act, but did not act. If he had intervened and insisted on establishing rules and regulations, or even an organization for handling war prisoners, the result could well have been different.

Hirohito bore more direct responsibility for the use of poison gas, a weapon that caused the death of many Chinese and Mongolian combatants and also noncombatants. Before the China Incident had turned into a full-scale war, he had sanctioned the dispatch to China of chemical warfare personnel and equipment. Article 171 of the Versailles Peace Treaty, and other international agreements signed by Japan after World War I, banned the use of poison gas— including tear gas. Yet the army had no problem violating the ban in the case of a technologically inferior enemy. Neither, apparently, did Hirohito. His first directive authorizing use of chemical weapons was dated July 28, 1937, and transmitted by Chief of the Army General Staff Prince Kan'in. It stated that in mopping up the Peking-Tientsin area, "[Y]ou may use tear gas at suitable times."[3] A second imperial order, dated September 11, 1937, and again transmitted through Prince Kan'in, authorized the deployment to Shanghai of certain special chemical warfare units. These orders authorized the beginning, at first experimental and on a very small scale, of what would become, by the spring and summer of 1938, extensive use of poison gas in the main battle theaters in China and Mongolia.[4]

Gas was the one weapon over which Hirohito, the Imperial Headquarters, and the high command retained close, effective control throughout the entire China war. Front-line units were never free to use this highly effective weapon at their own discretion; even area army headquarters lacked the power to authorize that use. Gas could be employed only after explicit authorization had been requested and received from Imperial Headquarters–Army Department, usually in the form of "directives" issued by the chief of staff after having first obtained the emperor's permission.[5]

In the Wuhan offensive, from August to late October 1938, Imperial Headquarters authorized the use of poison gas on 375 separate occasions. In the concurrent offensive against Canton in the far south of China, it authorized the Twenty-First Division commander to use both tear gas and poison gas.[6] In March 1939 Imperial Headquarters granted Gen. Okamura Yasuji permission to use more than fifteen thousand canisters of gas in the largest chemical attack of the war. Okamura justified his request by saying that the gas canisters were needed to restore the reputation of the troops and to give them "the feeling of victory."[7] On April 11 the emperor approved Directive Number 11, issued by his army chief of staff, authorizing further use of poison gas by the North China Area Army and its Garrison Force in Inner Mongolia.[8]

By May, when the major transport center of Hsuchou fell, the Japanese army was using chemical weapons whenever they could be effective in turning the tide in closely fought battles.[9] "Imperial Headquarters Army Order Number 301," sealed by Hirohito on May 15, 1939, authorized the carrying out of field studies of chemical warfare along the Manchukuo-Soviet border.[10] What the content of those studies was remains unclear. In July 1940 Hirohito approved Prince Kan'in's request to authorize the use of poison gas by the commander of the Southern China Area Army. A year later, however, in July 1941, when the army moved into the southern part of French Indochina, Army Chief of Staff Sugiyama issued a directive explicitly prohibiting the use of gas. Presumably Hirohito and the high command were concerned that gas not be used against Western nations that could retaliate in kind.[11] Their well grounded fear of American possession (and forward stockpiling) of chemical weapons continued to deter them from using such weapons down to the end of World War II.

Hirohito also sanctioned during 1940 the first experimental use of bacteriological weapons in China.[12] It is true that no extant documents directly link him to bacteriological warfare. But as a methodical man of scientific bent, and a person who questioned what he did not clearly understand and refused to put his seal to orders without first examining them, he was probably aware of the meaning of the

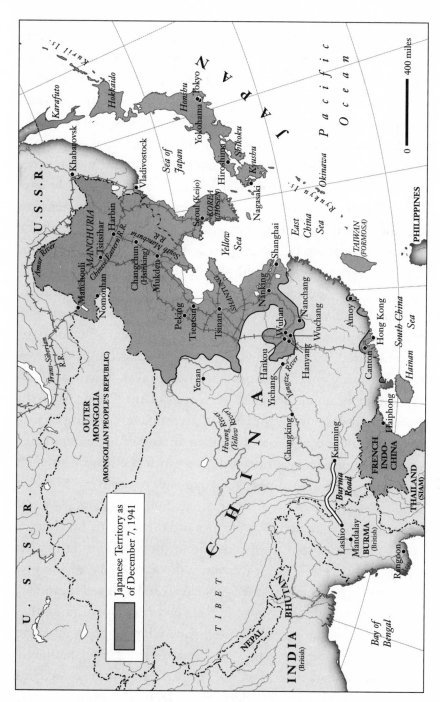

The Far East, 1930–1941

orders he approved. Detailed "directives" of the Imperial Headquarters that the army chief of staff issued to the Kwantung Army
command in charge of biological warfare, Unit 731, were as a rule
shown to the emperor; and the Army Orders of the Imperial Headquarters–Army, on which such directives were based, were always
read by him. Biological weapons continued to be used by Japan in
China until 1942, but the full consequences of this Japanese reliance
on both chemical and biological warfare would come only after
World War II: first, in the Truman administration's investment in a
large biological and chemical warfare program, based partly on
transferred Japanese BC discoveries and technology; second, in the
massive American use of chemical weapons in Vietnam.[13]

Though no documents directly tie him to it, another feature of
the brutal China war for which Hirohito should be charged with
individual responsibility was the strategic bombing of Chungking
and other cities, carried out independently of any ground offensives,
and using many types of antipersonnel explosives. Starting in May
1938 and continuing until the beginning of the Pacific War, the
Japanese naval air force initiated indiscriminate bombing against
China's wartime capital of Chungking and other large cities. The
bombing campaign was uncoordinated with the army's strategic
bombing of Chinese cities. First studied by military historian
Maeda Toshio, the navy's air attacks on Chungking anticipated the
German and Italian bombing of cities and the strategic bombing of
Japan's own cities that the United States initiated during the last
stage of the Pacific War. At the outset the navy deployed seventy-
two bombers (each with a seven-man crew) and dropped incendiary
as well as conventional bombs. In their first two days of raids, they
reportedly killed more than five thousand Chinese noncombatants
and caused enormous damage.[14] Two months later, in retaliation for
this indiscriminate bombing, the United States embargoed the
export of airplane parts, in effect imposing its first economic sanction against Japan.[15]

Apart from the strategic bombing of China's cities, Hirohito also knew of and approved the "annihilation" campaigns in China. These military operations caused death and suffering on a scale incomparably greater than the totally unplanned orgy of killing in Nanking, which later came to symbolize the war and whose numbers have probably been inflated over time. At the end of 1938 the North China Area Army inaugurated the first of many self-designated campaigns of annihilation against guerrilla bases in Hepei Province. These operations targeted for destruction "enemies pretending to be local people" and "all males between the ages of fifteen and sixty whom we suspect to be enemies."[16] They continued off and on for the next four years, gradually becoming larger in scale, more organized, systematic, and widespread.[17] Eventually the Chinese Communist Party labeled them the "three alls policy": that is, "burn all, kill all, steal all," or, in Japanese, *sankō sakusen*. Hirohito was apprised of the nature of the *sankō sakusen* and on December 2, 1938, signed off on the first one.

The pacification of the five occupied provinces of North China—Heipei, Shantung, Shensi, Shanhsi, and Chahaer—had by then become the main goal of the North China Area Army. During 1939 and early 1940, the area army had tended to overlook the organizing activities of the Chinese Communists and to target for destruction Nationalist military forces, though it did launch some small-scale operations against Communist base areas in Inner Mongolia as early as the summer and winter of 1939. As the Communist-controlled base areas in remote mountain regions expanded, during 1939–40, to include control over scores of millions of people, the area army finally took note, but before it could act, the situation changed dramatically. In August 1940 guerrillas of China's Eighth Route Army launched two surprise offensives—known as the "Hundred Regiments" campaign—against Japanese railways, bridges, coal mines, blockade houses, and communications facilities throughout North China. The most extensive physical damage and the heaviest loss of Japanese lives occurred in Heipei and eastern Shantung Province.[18]

In response to these destructive guerrilla attacks, Maj. Gen. Tanaka Ryūkichi of the North China Area Army, developed in late 1940 one of the first plans for attacking and so totally destroying the Communist guerrilla bases that "the enemy could never use them again." The first Japanese campaign of "total annihilation" was directed against Communist bases in Shanhsi Province.[19] Full-scale, highly organized extermination operations by the area army did not begin to be implemented, however, until July 1941, when General Okamura took command. Okamura's guidelines for subordinate commanders called for targeting mainly Communist forces, encircling and caging them by constructing interdiction and containment trenches. To that end North China was divided into pacified, semipacified, and unpacified areas. The latter were to be made unhabitable and cut off from the semipacified areas by the building of trenches. Hirohito gave his approval to this policy in Imperial Headquarters Army Order Number 575 of December 3, 1941, which ordered the theater army to "strengthen the containment of the enemy and destroy his will to continue fighting."[20]

Thereafter "annihilation campaigns" continued to involve burning down villages, confiscating grain, and forcibly uprooting peasants from their homes and mobilizing them to construct "collective hamlets." The Japanese strategy also centered on the digging of vast trench lines, many twenty feet wide and thirteen and a half feet deep, and the building of thousands of miles of containment walls and moats, watchtowers, roads, and telephone lines. Japanese police and collaborating Chinese constabulary mobilized millions of Chinese peasants to do this work for periods of up to two months at a time.[21] But except for killing Chinese, directly and indirectly, the enormous effort that went into these campaigns, which were always sanctioned by Hirohito, was for naught. Chinese guerrillas were invariably able to return to the no-man's land and control it after the Japanese had departed.

There are no Japanese statistics on the number of Chinese military casualties resulting from the *sankō* operations. But according to the recent rough estimate of historian Himeta Mitsuyoshi, "more than 2.7 million" Chinese noncombatants were killed in the course of those battles.[22] Although detailed empirical analysis of this aspect of the China war, by Japanese scholars, is now under way, it has been clear for some time that the well-planned *sankō* campaigns were incomparably more destructive and of far longer duration than either the army's chemical and biological warfare or the "rape of Nanking." Yet in the United States the latter, though extremely important and deserving of attention, figures as the centerpiece in the moral condemnation of Japanese wartime conduct, and is even compared—thoughtlessly, without regard to purpose, context, or ultimate aim—with the German genocide of European Jewry.

I

During the summer of 1940, Hirohito's judgment on how to direct the Japanese military to end the war in China was shaped by his perception of how the international situation was developing in Europe, and how Britain and the United States would react to any new Japanese military moves.

On July 22, 1940, Konoe formed his second cabinet, with Matsuoka Yōsuke as foreign minister and General Tōjō as army minister. Five days later Konoe convened the long-suspended Imperial Headquarters–Government Liaison Conference. In a mere ninety minutes the conference decided on a new national policy designed to exploit changes in the structure and dynamics of the international system brought about by Germany's victories in Europe.[23]

The vagueness of the July 27 "national policy" document,

adopted at this meeting, was seen in its emphasis on shifting focus to the "Southern area" if the war in China could not be concluded quickly, then deciding issues by exploiting foreign and domestic situations. Afterward Konoe and the chiefs of staff formally reported the document (entitled "Outline for Dealing with Changes in the International Situation") to the emperor. The July 27 outline also called for a military move into French Indochina to establish bases there, and the acquisition, by diplomatic means, of the raw materials of the Dutch East Indies. If Japan had to use armed force to realize these aims, it would seek to fight only Britain; at the same time it would prepare for war with the United States.[24] Hirohito approved this general prescription for renewed aggression knowing that whenever concrete policies based on it were formulated, they would be reported to him and his sanction sought on each occasion.

The army's interest in a military alliance with Nazi Germany had developed slowly until 1938, when, in response to German suggestions, a positive campaign for an alliance was initiated. Throughout 1939 and early 1940, Hirohito rejected the army's idea not so much because he thought there was anything fundamentally wrong in Hitler's racist, radically anti-Semitic regime, or the German quest for continental control, but because he wanted an alliance to be directed solely against the Soviet Union. Admirals on the navy high command also opposed the idea, but for a different reason: They believed a military pact with Germany would force Britain and the United States to increase their aid to Chiang Kai-shek and thus postpone resolution of the China Incident. The European war, and the frenzied international response to Germany's blitzkrieg offensive of spring-summer 1940, changed everything. An almost palpable bandwagoning mood arose. Hirohito's brother Prince Chichibu repeatedly importuned him to end his opposition to a German alliance. Then suddenly the navy high command, whose lead Hirohito often followed, abandoned its former skepticism and began to favor a military alliance with Hitler that would move Japan more firmly into the anti-Anglo-American camp.

The key moment in the navy's reversal came during the ninth month of the European war—June 1940—after the French government had fled Paris, Italy had entered the war, and the Germans had conquered France and taken control of the resources of most of Europe up to the Soviet borders. Several factors figured in the navy's conversion. Adm. Takagi Sōkichi, a navy leader with close ties to the palace, pointed out in an internal policy document that the navy hoped that so long as Germany was allied with the Soviet Union, if Japan became a military ally of Germany, the enthusiasm of Japan's generals for war against the Soviet Union would be at least dampened.[25] Both navy and army leaders also believed that Hitler would soon crush Britain, and that by "entering into a tripartite pact . . . Japan would be responding to Hitler's strategy and [so] joining in the new international order."[26] A third factor leading the navy to favor alliance was that the pact's negotiators had deleted from the treaty any automatic war-participation clause, thereby guaranteeing Japan would not be drawn against its will into Germany's war with Britain.

Furthermore the navy leaders projected not only an early end to the German-British war but the possibility that the Soviet Union might formally join the Axis, creating a four-power system. This possibility—not out of the question in the late summer of 1940—reflected an accurate assessment of the role of ideology in Stalin's USSR. More substantively the navy leaders believed that Germany could help Japan end its diplomatic isolation and confront the American diplomatic offensive from a position of greater strength. Finally, by agreeing to the treaty with Germany, the navy leaders hoped to eliminate a major part of their long-standing rivalry with the army. They might then be able to restrain the army's domination of the domestic political scene. With the navy lining up in support of the pact, and Germany triumphant in Europe, it remained only to persuade the emperor. A change in his chief political adviser helped to accomplish that.

On June 1, 1940, the emperor exercised his own discretion in choosing a new lord keeper of the privy seal. Ignoring *genrō* Saionji's qualms about Kido's right-wing bent, expressed through the former's refusal to recommend a candidate, Hirohito decided to heed Konoe and Yuasa's positive recommendations and appoint Kido, the revisionist bureaucrat and class-conscious leader of the hereditary aristocracy, to succeed the ailing Yuasa as his most important political adviser.[27] The youngest man ever to hold the post, Kido was nearly fifty-one; Hirohito was thirty-nine. More than a year earlier, Kido had reportedly told Harada that the emperor was "a scientist" by nature, and "very liberal and pacifistic at the same time."

Thus for Kido, who was trusted by the military and entirely willing to ally with Germany, the problem in advising the emperor would be to get him to change his thinking slightly so that no gap developed between him and some undefined "right wing." Or, in Kido's own words: "As with Emperor Kōmei in his last years, when his entourage had completely converted to the side of the *bakufu*, something quite like that might come about. We must adopt a more understanding attitude toward the army and lead while pretending that we are being led."[28]

Since 1930 Kido had served at court, where his responsibilities and influence had increased together with the military's rise to power. Having aided in the birth of the Saitō Makoto cabinet in 1932—the first step in the court's entrusting of politics to the military—Kido had drawn steadily closer to both the reform bureaucrats in different government ministries and the Control faction of the army, centered on Generals Tōjō and Mutō Akira. While serving in the Hiranuma cabinet, he had found nothing at all objectionable in a military alliance with Nazi Germany. Kido had also grown frustrated with the conduct of the incumbent privy seal, Yuasa, whom he criticized for sticking to the law on everything and not being as "advanced" as "the right wing."[29] By the time of his own appointment as privy seal, Kido knew how displeased the army had become with Prime Minister Yonai for stalling the negotiations with Germany. Last, Kido understood the sense of urgency in army and navy circles about seizing control of the British, French, and Dutch colonies in Southeast Asia.[30]

After becoming privy seal, Kido settled into a routine of closer daily contact with Hirohito than any previous political adviser. His task was to learn the emperor's intentions while alerting him to problems that lay ahead as the nation girded itself for even greater military efforts. Kido's family background, and their long prior association from 1930 to 1938, helped to cement their relationship. So too did Hirohito's belief in the rightness of the China war and in a peaceful "southward advance." Kido now began to move the emperor closer to those leaders in the army and navy who refused to abandon the China war and imagined they could extricate themselves from their predicament by taking advantage of the European war, in which Germany looked to be the likely winner.

At an imperial briefing on June 19, 1940, Hirohito asked Chief of Staff Prince Kan'in and Army Minister Hata: "At a time when peace will soon come in the European situation, will there be a deployment of troops to the Netherlands Indies and French Indochina?" This question revealed not only that Hirohito expected an early German victory but that he had also begun to consider the possibility of deploying troops in both Indochina and the Dutch East Indies, now that the French and Dutch had been conquered by the Germans, even if the less opportunistic side of his personality recoiled at the idea of doing so.[31]

When the problem of French Indochina arose again the next day in a conversation with Kido, the emperor revealed both his keen concern with appearances and his genuine vacillation over what to do about the undefended European colonies. Conscious of the ideological ideals that he, defender of the nation's moral integrity, was expected to uphold, he remarked that, historically, "there were actions such as those taken by Frederick and Napoleon." But "our country does not want to act in such Machiavellian ways. Shouldn't we always try to bear in mind the true spirit of *hakkō ichi'u* [benevolent rule], which has been our policy since the age of the gods."[32] Avowing "benevolent rule" and disavowing Machiavellianism, while simultaneously sanctioning the use of poison gas against the Chinese—these contradictory acts reveal Hirohito's divided nature. Here he was telling Kido, indirectly, I am the kind of person who favors action on the basis of ideals but when tactical needs and opportunities arise—well, it can't be helped. Needless to say, Hirohito's action fit a pattern of exterminating people while enveloping oneself in moral, humanitarian rhetoric that was just as much Western as Japanese.

On July 10, when Army Minister Hata and Chief of Staff Kan'in went to Hayama to report to Hirohito on military preparations, the emperor remarked that if the latest "Paulownia peace maneuver" in China should fail, then "we will have to employ the mediation of a third country. . . . In the final analysis, it will have to be Germany. But if we trust them and are not careful, they might come up with unreasonable demands later on. You must act on this matter after preparing thoroughly."[33] Begun in Hong Kong in late December 1939 by one of the army's many intelligence bureaus in China, the peace overture was targeted at T. V. Sung (Chiang Kai-shek's minister of finance) and Sung Mei-ling (Chiang's wife). When Hirohito made this remark he no longer took seriously the secret peace negotiations with Chungking, which had been discontinued and restarted. They were floundering over the stationing of Japanese troops in China, the recognition of Manchukuo, the arrangement of a truce, and the status of the client Wang Ching-wei regime in Nanking.[34] On the other hand he was not at all certain that Japan could use Germany to do its bidding in China without having to pay some unacceptable price.

The next day Kido, also in Hayama, recorded the emperor's concern that the United States could easily cut off oil supplies to Japan. Forecasting that "Britain will probably reject our request for closing down the route for supplies to reach Chiang Kai-shek," and that "we shall then be forced to occupy Hong Kong and might, ultimately, have to declare war," the emperor observed that: "Should that happen, I am sure America will use the method of an embargo, don't you agree?" Kido reassured him by saying that the nation must "be fully resolved to resist," to proceed cautiously, and "not [to] be dragged into events precipitated by the overseas agencies."[35]

Six days after this exchange Kido presided over a meeting at the palace with President of the Privy Council Hara Yoshimichi and five former prime ministers: Wakatsuki, Hirota, Okada, Hayashi, and Konoe. In record time (only thirty minutes) they nominated Konoe—the charismatic prince who in 1937 had enlarged the China war, then quit when the going got rough—to succeed Admiral Yonai as prime minister.[36] The emperor sanctioned their candidate, and on July 17, 1940, issued the order for Konoe to form a cabinet. Thus Konoe was able to return to office because five former prime ministers agreed to his nomination, his friend Kido pushed his candidacy, and Hirohito continued to trust him.

For army minister Konoe chose the tough, fifty-five-year-old General Tōjō, the leading representative of the army's hard-line, expansionist faction, a man bent on realizing the ethnocentric ideal of "direct imperial rule." For foreign minister he chose the voluble, high-strung Matsuoka Yōsuke, who was not afraid of either the emperor or the military, and with whom he shared many beliefs about the international order. Matsuoka promised to restrain the military abroad.

Given the absurdly contradictory mission of improving relations with the United States, strengthening cooperation with Germany, and eliminating Britain's economic and political interests in East Asia, Matsuoka tried to gain the attention of the American public. On July 21, one day before he took office, he gave an impromptu, off-the-record interview to an American correspondent, who immediately filed it with the Sunday *New York Herald Tribune*. In remarks largely ignored by journalists and editors in the United States (but not the State Department), Matsuoka had declared that:

> In the battle between democracy and totalitarianism the latter adversary will without question win and will control the world. The era of democracy is finished and the democratic system bankrupt. There is not room in the world for two different systems or for two different economies. . . . Fascism will develop in Japan through the people's will. It will come out of love for the Emperor.[37]

Matsuoka's preaching to Americans of the demise of democracy expressed his penchant for drawing attention to himself; his "love for the emperor" revealed the protean role that emperor ideology played throughout the history of the modern monarchy. Not only did the emperor serve to justify ideologies of militarism and war, he had also become, by this time, the ideology for Japanese fascism. Defenders and opponents of established political authority justified their projects in the emperor's name precisely because there had always coexisted within the official theory both a purely utilitarian view of the monarch as a "jewel" to be manipulated in order to furnish legitimacy, and an idealistic view of him that broke sharply with tradition and nurtured the fantasy of true, direct imperial rule.[38] Where Tōjō rejected a utilitarian approach to the throne and wanted the emperor to continue playing his highly active role behind the scenes, the emperor-loving Matsuoka straddled both views.

II

Shortly after the second Konoe cabinet started, on July 26, 1940, the ministers met and resolved to conclude the China Incident based on the principle of constructing a "New Order in Greater East Asia," and to complete war preparations as a "national defense state." The next day, hoping to impart authority to this consensus over national policies which his new cabinet ministers had just agreed to, Konoe convened a meeting of the liaison conference—the first since its suspension as a war leadership organ in September 1938, two and a half years earlier.[39] The July 27 liaison conference adopted a vaguely worded document—"Main Principles for Dealing with the Situation Accompanying Changes in the World Situation"—which formally affirmed the course of advancing to the south and tying up with the Axis powers, but left unclarified whether armed force would be used in the southern advance.

Specifically Japan would incorporate the Dutch East Indies, British Malaya, and other resource-rich areas of Southeast Asia into its "New Order" and, at the same time, strengthen its ties with the Axis states. After having been briefed on these deliberations, the emperor sanctioned the final decision as the policy of Konoe, whom he trusted, rather than of Matsuoka, whom he personally disliked. These moves placed Japan in strategic collision with the United States, at a time when it had become, for the first time in its history, a net importer of raw materials, and American strategists in and outside of government worried about who would control colonial Southeast Asia—a region they were beginning to see as essential for American national security.[40] Less than two months later, in accordance with these "national policy" decisions, Japan began its long-prepared-for "Southern advance" in September by sending troops into the northern part of French Indochina and concluding the Tripartite Alliance with Germany and Italy.[41]

Looking closer at Japan's decision to station troops in northern Indochina, one sees that Hirohito was briefed beforehand by Army

Minister Tōjō and the army and navy chiefs of staff, among others, about their plans for securing bases there. He agreed to authorize their plans because he thought that acquiring bases and stationing troops in French Indochina would contribute to toppling the Chungking regime and ending the China war. But he also sanctioned the entry of the army into northern Indochina because he believed in the value of the advance-southward policy, decided at the liaison conference, even though that policy carried the risk of war with Britain and, inevitably, the United States—powers that had their advanced military bases in the Philippines, Singapore, and Hong Kong. Naturally he wanted to carry it off without provoking the United States to retaliate. Influenced by Foreign Minister Matsuoka, he probably thought that could be done given Roosevelt's preoccupation with the European situation and his relative restraint in dealing with Japan so far.[42]

On July 29—many weeks after France and the Netherlands had been defeated, the huge German offensive in the West had achieved its mainland objectives, and Britain stood in danger of invasion—Hirohito summoned his chiefs and vice chiefs of staff to the palace. When they arrived he made the unusual gesture of offering seats to the elderly Princes Kan'in and Fushimi before proceeding to question Fushimi about prospects for war with the United States. Fushimi replied that victory would be difficult in a protracted war and therefore, "[u]nless we complete our domestic preparations, particularly the preparation of our material resources, I do not think we should lightly start war even if there is a good opportunity to do so."[43]

Also participating in this briefing was the Army Vice Chief of Staff Sawada Shigeru. According to Sawada's account, the emperor's questions spanned a broad range of issues. Hirohito asked if they were "planning to occupy points in India, Australia, and New Zealand." He wanted assurance as to how the army would handle the Chinese division that had concentrated along the border with

French Indochina and appeared ready to enter the colony if the Japanese did. Mainly Hirohito wanted to know about the United States, the Soviet Union, and Germany. Could Japan, he asked, "obtain a victory in a naval battle with the United States as we once did in the Battle of the Japan Sea? . . . I heard that the United States will ban exports of oil and scrap iron [to Japan]. We can probably obtain oil from other sources, but don't you think we will have a problem with scrap iron?"[44]

Turning to the Soviet Union and Germany, Hirohito asked:

If a Japan-Soviet nonaggression treaty is made and we advance to the south, the navy will become the main actor. Has the army given thought to reducing the size of its forces in that case? . . . How do you assess the future national power of Germany? . . . Both Germany and the Soviet Union are untrustworthy countries. Don't you think there will be a problem if one of them betrays us and takes advantage of our exhaustion fighting the United States?[45]

As his interrogation of his chiefs drew to a close, Hirohito observed:

[I]t seems as though you people are thinking of implementing this plan by force because there is a good opportunity at this moment for resolving the southern problem even though some dangers are involved. . . . What does a good opportunity mean? [To this question Sawada replied: "For example, if a German landing in England commences."] In that case wouldn't the United States move to aid Britain? . . . Well, I've heard enough. I take it, in short, that you people are trying to resolve the southern problem by availing yourselves of today's good opportunities.[46]

Hirohito's questions indicated his belief in the likelihood of continued Anglo-American cooperation but also his uncertainty as to what, at that juncture, constituted "a good opportunity." For Sawada and the army general staff it had to be Britain's defeat and military occupation; for Hirohito the good opportunity was some sort of readjustment of relations with the United States. On the other hand, Hirohito knew how deeply divided his army, navy, and the Konoe cabinet were about fundamental strategy for implementing the decisions of the liaison conference. He was troubled by the disunity, strife, and vying for leadership among the different bureaucratic organs and overseas military units wishing to carry out the advance south. Moreover, Kido claims that the emperor told him the next day, July 30, that:

> Prime Minister Konoe . . . seems to want to shift the nation's dissatisfaction caused by the lack of success of the China Incident toward the south. If there is a good chance, the Army wants to go south, leaving the China Incident as it is. The Navy seems to think that unless the China Incident is resolved first, they are not going to deploy military force in the south.[47]

Kido's account of what the emperor told him errs seriously in claiming that the admirals would not "deploy military force in the south" unless the war in China was resolved. Indeed, the war planners on the Navy General Staff had already begun to develop plans to secure Indochina predicated on fighting a war with the U.S. and Britain should it ever become necessary. The navy worried not about the stalemate in China but only about provoking war with the United States.[48]

Contrary to the hopes of the emperor and the bureaucratic groups responsible for the decision to advance militarily into Southeast Asia, the Roosevelt administration immediately interpreted Japan's move as a direct challenge. American policy planners, both in and out of government, believed that this area, Southeast Asia and the Indonesian archipelago—unlike China—had to remain open primarily for its beleaguered European allies, but also, in the longer run and more important, for commercial and financial control by the United States. Japan could not have ventured on a riskier course.[49]

The Konoe cabinet's professed reason for the entry of the army and navy into northern Indochina was to complete the encirclement of China—if possible through diplomatic agreement with French officials in Hanoi or with the pro-Nazi regime in Vichy France, but if necessary by the use of force. The real reason was to prepare bases and concentrate troops and ships for eventually striking farther south at the surrounding countries rich in oil, rubber, tin, and the resources needed for self-sufficiency in the age of total war. Hirohito's role in this expansion of aggression was to remain above the conflicts among his military elites and the Foreign Ministry, led by Matsuoka, while helping them to achieve consensus so that the policy-making process did not break down.

Kido's important diary entry of September 14, 1940, registers Hirohito's concern with the disunity between the high command and Matsuoka, but also his belief that it was best to go ahead and implement the advance, for "if we procrastinate, the machinations of Britain and the United States will become increasingly intense and there is a possibility of them joining up with French Indochina or with China."[50] Shortly afterward the emperor issued Imperial Headquarters Army Order Number 458, ordering the area army to begin the entry into French Indochina. Once again he had dealt with a situation of elite conflict at home by sanctioning new aggression abroad.

No war was declared, but Japan had now expanded its war in China by definitely stepping into World War II. The Roosevelt administration, which had in place a "moral embargo" on aircraft shipments to Japan, responded, symbolically, by embargoing scrap iron and aviation gasoline. Henceforth Roosevelt would seek to counter Japan by applying economic sanctions incrementally, by aiding China just enough to keep Japan bogged down, by negotiating with Japan on an informal basis, and—most important—by rapidly rearming and preparing the U.S. army and navy for war against the Axis.

III

Japan's leaders took their second fateful step toward a larger war when the liaison conference and the Konoe cabinet reached full consensus on a military alliance with Nazi Germany and Fascist Italy. To insure the legitimacy of their decision, an imperial conference—Hirohito's third—convened on September 19 and shortly afterward he sanctioned the treaty. When Kido saw him on September 24, Hirohito remarked that he wanted "to worship in person at the *kashikodokoro* [Place of Awe]" in the palace, and ask for the protection of the gods since "in this case we are not simply celebrating as at the time of the Japan-British treaty; we are going to face a serious crisis depending on how the situation develops."[51] Later the treaty was forwarded to the Privy Council which completed its purely formalistic deliberations in just one day.

On September 27, 1940, Japanese representatives in Berlin signed the Tripartite Pact with the dictatorships of Germany and Italy. The affiliation of fascist Rumania and Hungary followed. By the terms of the pact, Japan recognized the leadership of Germany and Italy in "the new order in Europe" while they recognized Japan's dominance in "Greater East Asia." The three powers pledged "to assist one another with all political, economic, and military means" if "attacked by a power at present not involved in the European War or in the Sino-Japanese conflict."[52] This last article was intended to check Britain and keep the United States out of the war.

The deliberations leading to this key event had gone on for three years. Hirohito had had ample opportunities to ponder its implications, including the near certainty that it would deprive Japan of diplomatic flexibility and end forever its chance for cooperation with the United States and Britain. Although he did not trust Nazi Germany, his opposition had never been to a military alliance with the Nazis that countered Soviet pressure on Manchukuo, but only to one that took Britain, France, and the United States as the main enemies.[53]

Thus, when Konoe was hinting he would resign, at the very end of 1938 and the beginning of 1939, Hirohito reportedly said to his new Chief Aide-de-Camp Hata: "If [the army] doesn't want Prime Minister Konoe to resign that much, instead of persuading him to remain, go along with the decision of the Five Ministers Conference, made earlier, to strengthen the defense against Communism, and . . . make this anti-Communist alliance just against the Soviet Union. Go tell this to the General Staff."[54] Hirohito was then clearly not against the Tripartite Pact itself; he was only opposed to including Britain and France among its targets.

A year and a half later, at the very moment President Roosevelt had increased his support for the hard-pressed British by making his Lend-Lease destroyers-for-bases deal, Hirohito, despite misgivings, abandoned his opposition and assented to the treaty. It was an opportunistic and dangerous move, certain to deepen Japan's difficulties with the Anglo-Americans once Germany renewed its conquests in Europe. More than that, it was a very self-conscious break with the Meiji legacy of Anglo-American friendship in foreign policy, and Hirohito knew it, which is another reason he vacillated so long before making it.

In the lead-up to his personal conversion to the military's line on foreign policy, Hirohito likened himself to his grandfather Meiji on the eve of the Russo-Japanese War, when Itō Hirobumi had pledged Meiji his loyalty unto death if Japan should lose the war. "When matters have come this far, Konoe should really share the joy and suffering with me," he told Kido on September 15, echoing

Itō's pledge to Meiji.[55] Later Konoe told Harada: "When I went to the Palace the next day [September 16], the emperor said that, 'Under the present circumstances this military agreement with Germany can't be helped. If there is no other way to handle America, then it can't be helped.'" Konoe added that the emperor also asked him, "What will happen if Japan should be defeated? Will you, prime minister, bear the burden with me?"[56]

Hirohito passively assented to the treaty, then rationalized his action as personal submission to an inexorable historical process. The conflicts of the different bureaucratic forces, he implied, had driven him into sanctioning the most fundamental shift in the monarchy's stance on foreign relations since his grandfather sanctioned Japan's alliance with Britain in 1902. Yet at the time Hirohito was fully aware that his flip-flop on the Tripartite Pact was a major turning point that carried the possibility of war with the United States.[57] Later, he blamed it mainly on Matsuoka, but also faulted his brothers—Chichibu and Takamatsu—and never reflected on his own mistaken judgement in sanctioning the Pact.[58]

Around this time a subtle shift occurred in the internal ranking of the imperial family. Hirohito's most outspoken critic and next in line to the throne, Prince Chichibu, had become seriously ill with tuberculosis. Chichibu's retirement from an active public life meant that Prince Takamatsu stood to become regent in an emergency. Henceforth he would be reading more official documents and gratuitously proffering advice that Hirohito usually did not consider helpful.[59] Rather than line up firmly with Hirohito in Japan's foreign policy crisis, Takamatsu drew closer to Chichibu. The brothers approved of the Tripartite Pact as the best hope in the circumstances, and continued to find Hirohito's performance lacking.

As for Kido, he later insisted that he and the emperor "had to adopt a balance-of-power policy in order to avoid becoming isolated and, at the same time, not be drawn into [the European war].

There was no way to negotiate with the United States without having the power of the alliance in the background. The explanations of Konoe and Matsuoka persuaded us. We didn't like it but couldn't help signing it."[60] Kido, unlike the emperor, held the army mainly responsible for the Tripartite Pact but never admitted the navy's decisive role.

On September 27, 1940, Hirohito issued an imperial rescript to the nation in which, contrary to his usual practice, he apparently chose to let stand the wording that had been prepared for him by others. The rescript declared:

> The great principle of the eight corners of the world under one roof [*hakkō ichi'u*] is the teaching of Our imperial ancestors. We think about it day and night. Today, however, the world is deeply troubled everywhere and disorder seems endless. As the disasters that humankind may suffer are immeasurable, We sincerely hope to bring about a cessation of hostilities and a restoration of peace, and have therefore ordered the government to ally with Germany and Italy, nations which share the same intentions as ourselves. . . . [61]

Soon after the release of the rescript, the Tripartite Pact was signed, and on October 4, Prime Minister Konoe issued a belligerent statement at a press conference in Kyoto declaring that, "If the United States does not understand the positions of Japan, Germany, and Italy, and regards our pact as a provocative action directed against it, and if it constantly adopts a confrontational attitude, then the three countries will fight resolutely."[62] Few Japanese leaders at the time understood the tremendous ideological significance of the Tripartite Pact for the United States, or how the Roosevelt administration would now use it to deepen anti-Japanese feeling. Meanwhile the emperor, accompanied by Kido, observed special grand naval maneuvers off Yokohama. A week later, still uncertain about his break with Britain, he reported in prayers to the gods that he had made an alliance with Germany and Italy, and asked for their protection.[63]

The following month the entire nation celebrated the 2,600th anniversary of the founding of the state by the mythical Emperor Jimmu. Preparations for this *kigensetsu* had been underway since 1935. One day before the start of the official commemorative events, on November 9, a government regulation established an "Office of Shinto Deities" within the Home Ministry to further the "spiritual mobilization" of the nation in preparation for total war. Started by the first Konoe cabinet at the beginning of the China war, the campaign sought the participation of youth about to be sent to war, exhorting them to "respect the Shinto deities," "serve the state," and rush forward to victory in the war against China.

For this event government agencies launched fifteen thousand new projects and festivities of various kinds, costing 1.63 billion yen.[64] At the peak of the celebrations, on November 10 and 11, an estimated five million people attended banquets. Food prepared as military field rations, in remembrance of the troops on the front lines, was consumed by celebrants in the palace plaza. Amid these reminders of the war, and of the new direction in foreign policy, the Tokyo *Asahi shinbun* on November 10 ran a column entitled "Questions and Answers About the New Order," which emphasized the important role that youth would play in the new world order.[65] On the eleventh, pictures of Emperor Hirohito and Empress Nagako spread across the pages of the leading newspapers. His imperial rescript of that date reminded readers of "the violent upheavals in today's world" and enjoined them "to promote at home and abroad the grand principle of the Way of the Gods, thus contributing to the welfare of humankind."[66] Any doubts that Hirohito had allowed himself to become not only the symbol and legitimizer of the "New Order," but also the mouthpiece for its rhetoric were put to rest. At 11:25 A.M. some fifty thousand representatives from all over Japan and the world, including members of the Hitlerjugend, shouted in unison, "Banzai!"; warships anchored in Tokyo Bay fired salutes; and radio coverage of the joyous event continued throughout the day.

Britain's response to the Axis military alliance was to reopen the Burma Road, which earlier it had agreed to close, and to look for ways "to cause inconvenience to the Japanese without ceasing to be polite."[67] President Roosevelt's response was to make another small loan to Chiang Kai-shek, and give assurances of further American support to keep China in the war. In November, Roosevelt assented to Adm. Harold Stark's "Dog" plan for the recasting of America's defense strategy on the premise that Germany was the main enemy. Henceforth the United States would follow a defeat-Germany-first strategy, focusing on the European front and aid to Britain. If war should come in the Pacific, the United States would initially wage a defensive campaign but not turn its full weight against Japan until after Germany's downfall.[68] In China, Chiang Kai-shek resolved to continue fighting Japan alone, without benefit of full-scale Anglo-American aid, but confident that war in the Pacific was only a matter of time.

PROLOGUE TO PEARL HARBOR

Following the outbreak of the German-Soviet war in the summer of 1941, the Japanese army and navy chiefs of staff, together with the emperor's other main advisers, began to spend more and more of their workdays at court.[1] Hirohito's command prerogatives were changing quickly, and he was about to become a commander in chief in every sense of the word. The liaison conference, which had been formed in November 1937 and suspended two months later until July 1940, was revived, convened with greater frequency, and gradually strengthened. The president of the Planning Board and the home minister became permanent constituent members of the liaison conference, and in the course of a year, it developed into the most important regularly convened body for deciding national policies and guidelines for policies.

The liaison conference also moved its deliberations from the prime minister's official mansion to the palace.[2] It eclipsed the cabinet, usurped its decision-making function, and became, in effect, a forum for debates and arguments that had to be resolved, ultimately, by the emperor himself. Between September 27, 1940, and November 1941, there were scores of liaison conference meetings. Many more followed thereafter until early August 1944, when the liaison conference was replaced by the Supreme War Leadership Council.[3]

Final decisions of the liaison conference continued to be formally disclosed through imperial conferences, which now began to convene more frequently. The Imperial Headquarters was also reorganized, and new agencies or sections added until 1945 to deal with such matters as intelligence, transportation, science and technology, occupied areas, and so forth. By May 1945 the headquarters staff, some working within the palace compound but the overwhelming majority outside, had grown to more than 1,792.[4]

Certain key features of the high command structure, and Hirohito's way of working within it, remained unchanged, however. The independent bureaucratic interests of the emperor's military and civil advisory organs continued to shape policy. Guidelines for the conduct of the war continued to be drafted far down the military chain of command and moved upward through a process of negotiation and consensus building. And the ever-wary Hirohito continued to search out contradictions and discrepancies in whatever was reported to him. Thus, whenever the army and navy chiefs of staff or top cabinet ministers made formal reports that were in conflict, and sometimes when they were quite consistent or nearly identical, if Hirohito was not convinced by the argument put forward, he would reject them.

As the danger of war with the United States and Britain drew nearer, and as senior general staff officers (like the often-chastised General Sugiyama) acquired a better understanding of Hirohito's character and the breadth of his military knowledge, the middle-echelon officers who prepared his briefing and background materials learned how their immediate superiors could avoid his scoldings and inconvenient questions. One cannot dismiss altogether the possibility that at least some materials intended for the emperor's study in ratifying (or rejecting) command decisions may have been shaped if not distorted by interservice maneuverings.[5] Complex systems of decision making often invite manipulation, if only as a means to prioritize and simplify.

On the other hand Hirohito understood very well how the policy deliberation process worked. He knew the names and careers of the most important bureau, department, and section chiefs of the Army, Navy, and Foreign Ministries, and their tendencies. His chief aide-de-camp's office in the palace was connected by a hot-line telephone to the offices of the Army and Navy Operations Sections and their First Departments so that his aides could immediately convey imperial questions or raise queries of their own.[6] Hirohito knew who headed the First Department of the Imperial Headquarters–Army, charged with the development of operations plans and troop deployments; and who within the First Department was in charge of the Twentieth Group (grand strategic planning) and the Second Section (operations). More important, he was familiar with the step-by-step bureaucratic procedures that led directly to the drafting of the "national policy" documents deliberated at the liaison conferences and studied by him.

From 1941 onward, the high-command machinery steadily became more elaborate. The emperor widened and deepened his access to include just about all military intelligence. Detailed question-and-answer materials were compiled by staff officers in the Operations Sections, and war situation reports reached him on a weekly, daily, and sometimes twice-daily basis. Monthly and annual state-of-the-war evaluations were also compiled for the emperor's perusal; and, as historian Yamada Akira documented, Hirohito routinely received drafts of developing war plans and full explanations of operations, accompanied by detailed maps, informing him why an operation should be mounted and the units that would be carrying it out.

Battle reports and situation reports were delivered to the palace daily and, after the Pacific war started, shown to the emperor at any time of the day or night. These included itemization of combat losses and their causes, places where Japanese troops were doing well or not so well, and even such details as where cargo ships had been sunk and what matériel had been lost with them. Sometimes "even telegrams coming into the Imperial Headquarters from the front lines" were shown to Hirohito by his three army and five navy aides-de-camp, serving around the clock on rotating shifts.[7] Among the many duties of these aides was the regular updating of Hirohito's operations maps.[8] In addition, throughout the Pacific war the chief of the Navy General Staff sent the emperor formal written reports, titled "Explanatory Materials for the Emperor Concerning the War Situation." These, added to his other sources of information, kept the emperor extraordinarily well informed. But a flaw in this intelligence system was that the army and navy prepared and presented their secret information to him separately, so that only the emperor himself ever knew the entire picture, especially in respect to losses.[9]

When the "facts" reported from the front lines were inaccurate, Hirohito's "information" was misinformation. Still, Yamada observes, the emperor's briefers "believed in what they reported." Certainly their intentions were not to deceive him but to present accurate figures on the losses in personnel and armaments sustained by Japanese forces, as well as the damage inflicted by them. The materials he received were timely, detailed, and of high quality—as indeed they had to be, for the emperor was not only directing the grand strategic unfolding of the war, but pressing for solutions to the inevitable mishaps and miscalculations of his staff and field commands.[10]

In addition, to check on the accuracy of the reports he was receiving, Hirohito would often send his army and navy aides, as well as his own brothers, on inspection tours to various fronts to gather information outside routine channels. According to Ogata Kenichi, Hirohito's army aide-de-camp from March 1942 to November 1945, the emperor "sent his aides as close to the front lines as possible and chose the seasons when the troops were suffering most. When they returned, the emperor received them as though he valued their reports more than anything else." When questioning his ministers of state and the chiefs of the general staffs,

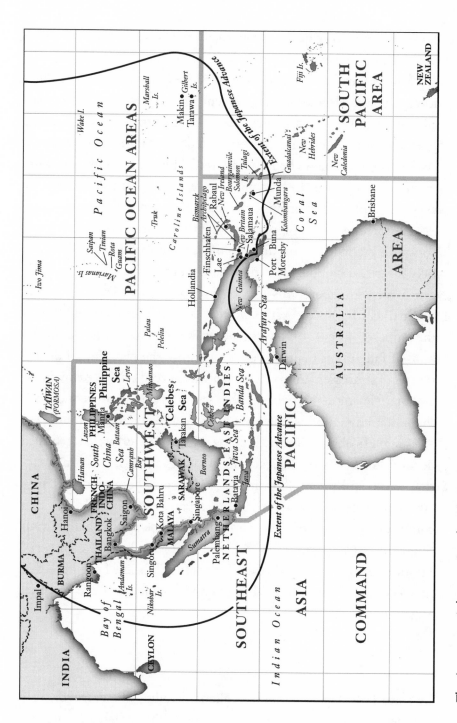

The Japanese Advance South, 1942

Hirohito frequently quoted from these reports.[11] In this way too, he kept his imperial eye constantly on his commanders.

Finally Hirohito continued his practice of viewing domestic and foreign newsreels and movies, screened for him at the palace, usually two or three times a week. He continued to read the censored Japanese press daily, and often pointedly questioned his military leaders about the news he found there.[12] Thus he not only knew the truth about the war, he was also aware of the slanted versions or even outright "brainwashing" the Japanese people were receiving.

As early as the eve of Pearl Harbor, this enormous, time-consuming effort by the high command to be sure Hirohito was fully informed had begun to detract from the efficiency of key officers involved in operations and strategic planning. Because the First Department head, for example, spent so much of his time keeping the emperor abreast of developments, he often could not immerse himself fully in his main duties, which were the planning of operations and strategies. Imoto Tokuma, who served on the Army General Staff during 1941, believed that this unintended consequence of the monarchy's modus operandi became a factor in Japan's defeat. Keeping Hirohito informed was a Herculean effort that forced department heads to delegate their top-level work down to "section chiefs and their subordinates," who soon became drawn into "the war leadership activities of the department heads. When that confusion occurred, officers who might still be able to handle routine administrative affairs were quite unable to meet the Imperial Headquarters operational planning responsibilities. I see here that they caused a wide dark void to open in command at the Imperial Headquarters."[13]

I

By early 1941 Japanese policy makers including the emperor were mesmerized by the connection between the stalemated war in

China and the course of events in Europe. German-Soviet relations particularly held their attention. Bound together by their nonaggression pact of August 1939, both powers were apparently positioning themselves for a further partition of Europe. But hidden complications in their relationship had developed. Hitler was secretly preparing to attack his new ally. Stalin, aware that Hitler was concentrating troops along the western border of the Soviet Union but not yet able to see an invasion imminent, mulled over the frighteningly swift triumph of the German war machine in the West, the German military campaign in the Balkans, and the overall deterioration of Russo-German relations. He felt an urgent need to secure Russia's Far Eastern borders, and also to block any further development, at Soviet expense, of the German-Japan axis.[14] And he found that he could avoid the nightmare of a two-front conflict by responding to the Konoe cabinet's renewed initiative for a treaty. Intent on deflecting Japan's attention away from the Soviet Far East and toward the sphere of Anglo-American interests—Southeast Asia and the South Pacific—Stalin would agree to a neutrality pact in exchange for Japan's pledge to relinquish to the Soviets its coal and oil concessions in North Sakhalin.

On April 7 Matsuoka Yōsuke arrived in Moscow from Berlin.[15] Several days of hard bargaining ensued, during which he resigned himself to the impossibility of securing a nonaggression pact, then accepted Stalin's conditions and settled for what the Soviets would offer. A newly released document in the Russian Foreign Ministry archives discloses that during his meeting with Stalin at the Kremlin on April 12, Matsuoka proposed that problems in Japan-Soviet relations be resolved "from a wider point of view." "[S]hould you wish access to the warm Indian Ocean through India," said Matsuoka, "I think that should be permitted. And if the Soviet Union should prefer the port of Karachi for itself, Japan can close its eyes. When Special Envoy Heinrich Stahmer (Gestapo agent and later German ambassador to Tokyo) visited Japan, I told him that, in the event the Soviet Union comes toward the warm ocean through Iran, the Germans should treat the matter exactly as Japan does." Reverting to his pet themes—"sav[ing] Asia from the control of the Anglo-Saxons" and "washing the influence of British and American capitalism out of Asia"—Matsuoka tried to have Stalin promise to end Soviet aid to Chiang Kai-shek.[16] Stalin replied that the Soviet Union could "tolerate cooperation between Japan, Germany, and Italy on the large issues," but that "at this time I want to talk only about the neutrality treaty with Japan, for on this issue there is no doubt that the time is ripe."[17]

The next day, April 13, Matsuoka and envoy extraordinary Gen. Tatekawa Yoshitsugu signed with Molotov, in Stalin's presence, a five-year neutrality treaty.[18] Under its terms the two nations "pledged to maintain peaceful, friendly relations" and to respect their mutual territories. In the event of military activity by a third state against one or both of them, the other party would "maintain neutrality throughout the entire period of the conflict." The treaty was to go into effect from the day of its ratification and remain binding for five years. In addition the Russians pledged, in a separate declaration, to respect the inviolability of Manchukuo while the Japanese recognized Russia's interest in the "Mongolian People's Republic." If neither Moscow nor Tokyo gave notice of abrogation by the end of the fourth year, the treaty would automatically be extended for another five years. Hirohito ratified the treaty on April 25, and the following day, the official Russian newspaper, *Pravda*, announced that the neutrality pact with Japan had gone into effect.[19]

Approximately nine weeks later, on June 5, the Japanese ambassador in Berlin, Gen. Ōshima Hiroshi, reported to the emperor and the high command that Hitler was about to invade the Soviet Union.[20] The Army General Staff's "Twentieth Group" immediately responded by drafting a plan for opening war against the Soviet Union while simultaneously advancing south into French

Indochina. The Army Ministry's Military Affairs Bureau just as immediately set to work on its own, different plan, which featured postponing the attack on the Soviet Union "until the time ripens." As these disagreements intensified between the Army General Staff and the Army Ministry over how to assess the new factor of a German-Soviet war, a new document—"Outline of the Empire's National Policies in View of the Changing Situation"—began to take shape.[21]

Then, on June 22, the situation changed as anticipated. Hitler turned on Stalin and, unconsciously following the footsteps of Napoleon Bonaparte after his standoff with Britain, invaded the Soviet Union.

On the following morning, June 23, a meeting of the top leaders of the Navy Ministry and Naval General Staff, attended also by Section Chiefs and Bureau Heads, firmed up the navy's position: Go for military bases and airfields in the southern part of French Indochina even if that move entailed "risking war with Britain and the United States." For, as explained a few days later by a key participant, liaison officer Lt. Col. Fujii Shigeru of the Navy Ministry's Military Affairs Bureau, a Japan–U.S. war was probably inevitable, but just might be avoided by taking "an extremely hard line" toward the United States and Britain, throwing fear into them, and persisting in that tough attitude whenever they appeared threatening. He likened this approach to "walking on a tightrope."[22] Today we would use "brinksmanship."

To all those who wanted to strike northward and destroy Soviet power throughout the eastern Siberian region as far as Lake Baikal, the German-Soviet war offered an obvious temptation. The participants in the liaison conferences and imperial conferences that led to Japan's declaration of war against the United States and Britain, were also influenced by the American tightening of economic sanctions against Japan after it had moved into southern Indochina, and by President Roosevelt's commitment to the defense of Britain, China, and the Soviet Union. Since the British blockade of Germany's ports necessitated a tightening of economic sanctions against Germany's ally Japan, British policy also contributed in a minor way to the worsening of Japan's relations with the Anglo-American powers, and thus to a further narrowing of the possibilities for diplomatic conciliation in Asia during late 1941.

Of all the background factors that influenced policy decisions during 1941, the deadlocked China war, then in its fourth year, was the most significant. Here, however, the conventional image of a Japan whose military "had its hands full" or was "tied down" in China is somewhat misleading. The war was indeed bogging down Japan's large continental army. Yet precisely because Japan was fighting in China, its army and navy had been able to expand the industries, stockpile the weapons, and secure the enormous funds needed to confront the United States and Britain during the fall and early winter of 1941. After four years and five months of war in China, the army had expanded from seventeen divisions totaling 250,000 men in July 1937 to fifty-one divisions and 2.1 million men by December 8, 1941.[23]

By conducting military operations in China with minimal logistic support, engaging in mass looting and plunder, establishing client "puppet" regimes rather than direct military administration of occupied areas, all the while diverting, annually, large percentages of emergency military appropriations to build up basic war power, the army and navy arrived at a position where they felt they could risk a Pacific war. In this sense, China removed the restraints on Japanese military spending. It figured not simply as the justification for Japan's rising military budgets but as their very source. Without war in China neither the army nor the navy, even if they had wanted to, would have been able to take the gamble of advancing south by military force in late 1941.[24]

II

On July 2, 1941, ten days after the German invasion of the Soviet Union, Konoe summoned an imperial conference to deal with matters debated but not resolved between June 5 and 23 within the Army and Navy Ministries and general staffs, and then aired at the June 30 and July 1 liaison conferences. The consensus of the conferences was that moving troops and planes into the southern part of French Indochina would not provoke the United States into coming out against Japan, but even if it did, vital national goals mandated taking the risk.

The document adopted at the imperial conference and immediately approved by the emperor—entitled "Outline of the Empire's National Policies in View of the Changing Situation"— opened the preparatory steps for new wars against the Soviet Union, Britain, and the United States. For the first time a policy statement used the expression "war with Britain and the United States." Specifically the July 2 document called for establishing the "Greater East Asia Coprosperity Sphere," expediting the settlement of the China war, and advancing "south . . . in order to establish a solid basis for the nation's preservation and security [literally, 'self-existence and self-defense']." It further stipulated:

> Depending on [appropriate] changes in the situation, we will settle the northern question [that is, attack the Soviet Union] as well. . . . In order to achieve the above objectives, preparations for war with Great Britain and the United States will be made . . . [and] our empire will not be deterred by the possibility of being involved in a war with Great Britain and the United States.

From start to finish the document was conditioned by circumstances and burdened by contingencies.

If the German-Soviet war should develop to the advantage of our empire, [then] we will, by resorting to armed force, settle the northern question and assure the security of our northern borders. . . . But *if* the United States should enter the [European] war, [then] our empire will act in accordance with the Tripartite Pact. However, we will decide *independently* as to the time and method of resorting to force [emphasis added].[25]

Where French Indochina was concerned, the policy outline projected movement of the army into the Cam Ranh Bay and Saigon areas to secure bases for further operations.[26] It also marked out for confiscation ("at the appropriate time") the remaining Western treaty enclaves in China, and specified the completing of preparations for the destruction of Anglo-American military power in Asia. On the other hand it neither approved Japanese intervention in the German-Soviet war (as sought by foreign minister Matsuoka and Privy Council President Hara Yoshimichi) nor ruled out the possibility of such intervention. In fact the July 2 imperial conference authorized secret preparations for a future attack against the Soviet Union, designated "Kwantung Army Special Grand Maneuvers." This decision led to a succession of secret troop mobilizations at home, and to the massing, during July and the first week of August, of approximately seven to eight hundred thousand Japanese troops in northern Manchukuo. Their mission was to be ready by early September for a war with the Soviet Union, which, however, would be started only if the Germans succeeded in quickly destroying Soviet resistance in the West.[27]

Hirohito sanctioned this hard-line policy reluctantly but sanctioned it nevertheless.[28] He ratified the idea of "not be[ing] deterred by the possibility of being involved in a war with Great Britain and the United States"; and his approval of the stationing of Japanese troops in southern Indochina very quickly provoked American and British military reaction. Later he caused one part of the new national policy to be reversed. All concerned were thereby reminded that decisions of an imperial conference were not immutable but could be changed by the emperor if he wanted to do so.

On July 30 Hirohito made a major operational intervention by suggesting to General Sugiyama that the buildup in Manchukuo stop as it was probably preventing the Soviet Far Eastern Army from redeploying to fight in the West.[29] No thought was given to aiding his ally Hitler. At this time the emperor did not desire a full-scale war with either the Soviet Union or the United States; but if war had to be, he was more inclined to risk it southward into the Anglo-American sphere of interest than fight the Russians; and if the Soviet Far Eastern Army departed westbound, in relative terms Japan's war-power in the North would immediately improve. The threat of Soviet attack to take advantage of Japanese operations in China and the South would become negligible. Ultimately, of course, the U.S. oil embargo would make a northward invasion impossible for the short term. For that reason also, the movement West of the Soviet Far Eastern forces would be gratifying. So, though for a short period of time in early July the "peace-loving" emperor had contemplated a military invasion of the Soviet Union even though he had ratified the Neutrality Pact with Russia a mere three months earlier, he changed his mind, gave an operational command, and as a result the liaison conference on August 9 cancelled for that year the "planned" invasion of the Soviet Union.[30] Hirohito's intervention thus prevented Japan from going to war with the Soviet Union as the army high command wanted. An initial imperial decision did not control the final one at this point in time.

In the interim between the July 2 imperial conference and the next one on September 6, several important changes occurred in Japan's ruling setup, and in the situation facing its policy-makers. The conflict intensified between Prime Minister Konoe and foreign minister Matsuoka, who had become the most vocal advocate of the go-north strategy. When Matsuoka forced a confrontation over how to handle negotiations with the U.S., Konoe, supported by the army and navy ministers, quickly reshuffled his cabinet in order to drop Matsuoka and bring in Admiral Toyoda Teijirō, a less mercurial figure. The formation of the third Konoe cabinet, however, provoked fear among middle echelon officers of the army and navy that Konoe would soon abandon both the Axis and the plan to advance into southern Indochina. As a result, the army and navy ministers—Tōjō and Oikawa—made increased preparations for war against the United States and Britain a condition for their entering the cabinet.[31] And, most important, Hirohito came to believe that war with the United States and Britain had to be risked, though he still hoped to avoid war if at all possible.

Meanwhile, the army and navy, acting in accordance with the complex, ambiguous national policy in effect after July 2, and in step with hasty diplomatic arrangements, accelerated the pace of their expansion into Southeast Asia. Negotiations with Vichy France set up the July 28 peaceful occupation of the southern part of French Indochina in preparation for seizing the resources of the Dutch East Indies and British Malaya. The incursion involved more than 40,000 Japanese troops but later grew to more than 185,000.[32] As the advance developed, it provoked President Roosevelt and his advisers into unleashing powerful economic sanctions against Japan along with a merely token military response.

On July 26, Roosevelt ordered defenses in the Philippines—America's main Pacific possession—strengthened, promising to send, as soon as possible, 272 B-17 long-range heavy bombers and 130 new P-40 fighter planes to protect them. He also appointed the retired Army Chief of Staff, General Douglas MacArthur, commander-in-chief of all U.S. military forces in the Far East. Five years earlier, in preparation for the Philippines to become a self-governing commonwealth, Roosevelt had sent MacArthur to Manila as the head of a military mission charged with the impossible task of arranging the islands' future defense against a Japanese attack. Now, in effect, the president moved America's own outer defense perimeter five thousand miles to the west, to an archipelago that, even though it lay on the side of Japan's southern advance, had been relegated to secondary strategic importance by the defeat-Germany-first-principle; and he placed in charge of the Pacific army a charismatic general, famous for his grandiose rhetoric and penchant for charting independent courses.[33]

That same day, July 26, Roosevelt also signed an executive order freezing Japanese assets in the United States, thereby bringing "all financial and import and export transactions in which Japanese interests are involved under the control of the Government."[34] American officials in the State and Treasury Departments, as well as the Office of Production Management (charged with preventing raw material shortages and coordinating America's own defense production) immediately proceeded to interpret the freeze order in such a way as to impose, by August 1, a total embargo on oil and gasoline exports to Japan.

The American economic sanctions threw near panic into the Konoe government and had the effect of further dividing opinion within the navy as well as between the navy and the army. Shocked, like everyone else, by this rapid escalation of Anglo-American economic pressure, Hirohito looked on as his navy and army leaders struggled to reach a consensus on how to respond to the crisis. He had been informed that Naval Chief of Staff Admiral Nagano had suggested war with the United States at the liaison conference of July 21, five days *before* the United States froze Japanese assets and followed with the oil embargo. If war with the United States began immediately, Nagano had declared prior to the oil embargo, Japan would "have a chance of achieving victory" because of the difference in their war preparations. As time passed, however, that "probability" would decrease and the situation would thereafter "become disadvantageous to the Empire." Moreover, he added, "if we occupy the Philippines, it will be easier for our navy to carry on the war. We can [then] manage the defense of the South Pacific fairly well."[35]

Hirohito, knowing the navy's preparations were by no means sufficiently advanced to fight the United States, which was the main reason opinion within the navy was so divided, was irritated by Nagano's words at the liaison conference. Neither had he been pleased with the admiral's recent formal reports to him. He summoned the naval chief of staff on July 30—the same day that he blocked war with the Soviet Union—and expressed his dissatisfaction. According to the *Sugiyama memo*, Hirohito bluntly told him, "Prince Fushimi said that he would avoid war with Britain and the United States. Have you changed that?" Nagano replied, "I have not changed the principle but if we are going to fight, then the sooner we do so the better because our supplies are gradually dwindling anyway."[36] According to the diary of Vice Navy Minister Sawamoto Yorio, the emperor also asked Nagano, "Do you have any plans for fighting a protracted war?" When Nagano replied that there was no way to be sure of victory in a long war, and also expressed his belief that the Tripartite Pact was harming the adjustment of relations with the United States, Hirohito, unwilling to blame himself for this state of affairs, merely listened.[37]

The political crisis produced at the start of the third Konoe cabinet, and intensified by the crisis in Japan–U.S. relations, had revived navy fears that the army, acting unilaterally, might start a war with the Soviet Union. In fact, from late July onward, arguments rekindled within the Army for just that, and for giving primacy to the Tripartite Pact with Germany over the Neutrality Treaty with the Soviet Union. On July 30, however, as noted earlier, the emperor had told Sugiyama to stop the Kwantung Special Exercises, and shortly afterward, on August 9, the Army General Staff shelved its plans for invading the Soviet Union during 1941, though without formally notifying the navy of its decision until late August. But key army planners stuck to the view that the German-Soviet war would be short and end in a decisive German victory. In this situation there developed in the army high command by the beginning of September, an attitude of "let's finish off down south before beginning operations up north in the spring [of 1942]." Thus, only a month after the American oil embargo, the army came around to wanting a quickly won war against the United States, so that within a year it could turn around and "do the north."[38] All these divisions and disagreements were thrashed out in liaison conference meetings before being informally reported to the emperor on September 5.

The American economic sanctions, meanwhile, were having their effect on Prime Minister Konoe. Britain had already placed economic restrictions on Japan as an ally of Germany; in late July it followed the American lead and froze Japanese assets. Japan's negotiations with the government of the Netherlands Indies for oil purchases had also collapsed; on July 28 the Dutch authorities also froze Japanese assets. Japan was now forced to draw down its reserves of oil and other stockpiled strategic materials.

In the spring of 1941 Konoe had hoped to negotiate a friendlier U.S. attitude toward Japan. The secret, unofficial "conversations" between Adm. Nomura Kichisaburō and U.S. Secretary of State Cordell Hull, at which Japan had asked the American government to cease supporting Chiang Kai-shek and to furnish strategic materials, continued for several months but got nowhere. Now, because of the Japanese move into southern French Indochina, the talks faced a complete breakdown, and Konoe's hopes were collapsing.[39] In despair, and believing that the man he had earlier appointed as ambassador to the United States was incompetent, Konoe resolved to meet Roosevelt directly and break the deadlock.

At 11:40 A.M. on August 4, Konoe spoke with the emperor for about forty minutes and probably received endorsement of the idea of a summit meeting. This was because Hirohito had by no means decided on war at this time, and whenever he felt unready to make up his mind, he often liked a substitute reason for postponement.

Later that evening Konoe met the army and navy ministers and informed them that a summit of heads of state might serve to reopen the talks.[40] Since neither the navy nor the army wanted to take responsibility at that moment for opposing Konoe, especially believing that he had the emperor's backing, they agreed to his idea.[41] Afterward Konoe instructed Nomura to propose to President Roosevelt that a meeting between himself and Roosevelt be held (at Honolulu or at sea in the mid-Pacific) to head off the looming war. Since Hull was cool to the idea of a summit, and the president was then aboard ship, en route to his historic meeting with Prime Minister Winston Churchill off of Argentia, Newfoundland, which would result in the Atlantic Charter, Nomura was unable to convey the message until August 17.

No Roosevelt-Konoe meeting ever took place. On October 2, the U.S. government indirectly rejected the summit proposal on the ground that Tokyo's negotiating position had yet to be clarified. To this day some Japanese conservatives and right-wing apologists for the "War of Greater East Asia" continue to see this rejection as proof that Roosevelt sought to "provoke Japan into a war."[42] But Konoe was only prepared to say that Japan would withdraw its troops from French Indochina *after* the China Incident had been resolved. On all the key issues that had crystallized after the oil embargo—the problem of how to resolve the China war, the withdrawal of Japanese troops from China, Japan's alliance with the Axis, and its southern advance—his negotiating draft was silent. Konoe had approved of Japan's aggression in China and the privileges it had secured there by force and had incorporated into the basic treaty with the Wang Ching-wei regime in Nanking; he intended to ask the United States to advise Chiang Kai-shek to stop resisting Japan. If a summit meeting had taken place, Konoe's set of stale positions, already proven inadequate, could never have led to a modus vivendi, and might even have hastened the coming of war.[43] Or, one may speculate, perhaps Konoe was calculating on deceiving

Roosevelt—the master dissimulator—by leaving issues vague.

Japan's leaders could either capitulate to the pressure of the anti-Axis coalition led by the United States and Britain—or continue the course they had set. As the shock of the American sanctions spread, disagreements emerged within the court group and among the senior statesmen (*jūshin*) over how to respond to the crisis. The "mainstream" of the Court group, centered on the emperor and Kido, tended to place their trust in the hard-line senior leaders of the army and navy, and to take a more positive attitude toward war with the United States and Britain. Konoe, Okada, and those around them constituted an "antimainstream" group. They had turned away from their prior infatuation with Nazi Germany, they were supportive of the army's Imperial Way faction, they did not accept the premise that further delay in the southern advance would mean certain defeat, and they wanted to continue the talks with the United States as long as possible. These differences within the court group were fermenting in September but would not emerge clearly until after Konoe stepped down in mid-October.

III

Meanwhile the rapidly rising tension in relations with Washington following the oil embargo had clarified the choices facing Japan's leaders. The Takagi Sōkichi papers offer a glimpse how the Konoe government, the navy, and the palace framed the risks of war during early autumn 1941. They could capitulate under economic pressure, which would give them a breather, or they could take some other course to end, neutralize, or escape the pressure. War, if they chose to wage it, had to supply the resources needed to make the empire invincible. During a dinner on August 4 with Hosokawa Morisada, Konoe's private secretary, Admiral Takagi was asked by Hosokawa if it was true that "war *must* be waged against the United States [emphasis added]." Takagi, replying, in effect contrasted the

U.S. with Japan in several respects: the Americans had more domestic raw materials, their navy was undergoing "strategic development," and they were strengthening their Pacific defenses. Admiral Takagi also mentioned "relations of mutual assistance among Britain, the United States, and the Netherlands." The United States was growing stronger vis-à-vis Japan, he stressed. "As time passes and this situation continues, our empire will either be totally defeated or forced to fight a hopeless war. Therefore we should pursue war and diplomacy together. If there is no prospect of securing our final line of national survival by diplomatic negotiations, we must be resolved to fight."[44]

Admiral Takagi's auditor knew exactly what he meant by "final line of national survival"—that strategic configuration of naval and army outlying island bases, garrisons, airfields, fortifications, colonies, which could provide protection of the sources of the raw materials Japan did not possess internally, and protect also the sea lanes for transportation of those essential materials. The "line" also involved home island defenses, and on the continent certain coastal areas stretching southward, from which enemy aircraft could attack the sea lanes linking the resource-rich colonies of Southeast Asia to Japan.

On August 8 Admiral Takagi had another conversation with a palace representative—Matsudaira Yasumasa, Kido's chief secretary, which once again reflected views about Japan's options that would emerge during the next imperial conference:

> *Matsudaira*: The other day I got the impression from the briefing that the chief of the Naval General Staff [Adm. Nagano Osami] gave to the emperor that it is now too late to avoid war with the United States even though it will be a most bloody war.
>
> *Takagi*: Absolutely not. I don't know what [Nagano] said, but I can't imagine him reporting that. In my view, if Japan lets the time pass while under pressure from lack of materials [the oil embargo], we will

be giving up without a fight. If we make our attack now, the war is militarily calculable and not hopeless. But if we vacillate, the situation will become increasingly disadvantageous for us.

Matsudaira: Prince Takamatsu said the same thing.[45]

Locked in a desperate struggle with Britain, the United States, and the Dutch regime in Batavia, all of whom were concerting to develop barriers to further Japanese expansion, the Konoe cabinet publicly complained of an "ABCD encirclement." The prowar Takagi blamed Japan's predicament on the oil embargo and the deadlocked Japan–U.S. negotiations. So too did the emperor, who understood technical, qualified arguments, supported by statistical data, and liked clear-cut, detailed analysis by competent specialists. Hirohito sided with Takagi and the navy, and showed no understanding that Japan owed its quandary to the bankruptcy of the Konoe cabinet's policies of relentless aggression against China and now Southeast Asia. Nevertheless, he wanted, in Kido's words, "to have more assurance of victory before he was willing to [take] the nation into war."[46]

Following Hirohito's ratification of the drive into Southeast Asia, the liaison conference, which now had fully usurped the cabinet's decision-making function, met on more than a dozen occasions. After each meeting Hirohito received briefings on the progress of the crisis from the prime minister and his chiefs of staff.

His brother Prince Takamatsu, serving on the Navy General Staff, also added his private views on the situation. In late August he warned the emperor that "October is crucial for our oil reserves." Hirohito answered (according to Takamatsu), "we will have nothing to bargain with when the time comes to make peace if we don't leave the fleet intact." The prince retorted, "I told him his idea was useless, taking the example of the German fleet at the time of the Great War in Europe. Or maybe I said that oil from northern Karafuto is not enough."[47]

Throughout the month of August, Hirohito became very familiar with the navy's argument that an early opening of hostilities was desirable because the American oil embargo would gradually sap Japan's military power. Soon he too came to believe that a decision to initiate a new war should ultimately be based on tactical and technical grounds offered by military specialists and supported by map drills conducted by the navy.[48] Those grounds included the size of the Imperial Army and Navy, the quality of their armaments, their considerable combat experience and readiness, their esprit de corps, their anticipated relative rates of consumption and resupply of war matériel, and their forward deployment in China and Southeast Asia.

Significantly absent from the calculations of Hirohito and the high command was any assessment of the enormous nonmaterial political power that Roosevelt also had in reserve and was rapidly mobilizing for possible war against the Axis. With the newly expanded American draft army in the process of completing its largest-ever "war games," the American public was gradually becoming supportive of the government and more martial in its own sense of national identity.

In Tokyo the navy's leaders were making the case for an early opening of hostilities while also pushing for continuation of diplomatic talks in order to persuade the United States to change its stance. At this stage, however, the navy's arguments were not being turned into national policies, for the main players in the drama—the ministers and vice ministers of the army and navy, the chiefs and vice chiefs of the two general staffs, Foreign Minister Toyoda, and Prime Minister Konoe—could not reach consensus. Unwilling to withdraw from China or to defect from the Axis, which most of them believed would emerge victorious over Britain and the Soviet Union, the decision makers kept incorporating changes in the international situation as the key element in their scenarios for war or diplomacy, but never once carefully examined the full range of policy choices open to them. Even Prime Minister Konoe, the main advocate of continued negotiations with the United States, was saying, "[W]e must be very cautious about procrastinating [diplomatically] or we may end up being forced to fight at the same time we are sliding into 'gradual decline.'"[49]

So the decision makers plowed ahead as if they were wearing large blinders and compelled to follow the furrow they were creating. On September 3 the liaison conference met and adopted a short document stating first, "The empire, for its existence and self-defense, shall complete war preparations by about the latter part of October with the resolve not to hesitate to go to war with the United States (Britain, and The Netherlands)." The second item read, "In tandem with this [decision], the empire shall endeavor to achieve its demands vis-à-vis the United States and Britain through diplomatic means." The third item indicated the degree to which Japan would "not hesitate to go to war" and was designed to meet the army and navy's need for time to prepare. It stated, "In the event there is no prospect for achieving our demands by about early October, we shall immediately decide to initiate war with the United States (Britain, and The Netherlands)."[50]

The time element had now been moved into the policy-decision-making process. If the emperor approved these time-lines, the government would continue its negotiations with the United States while also continuing to prepare for war; and if its diplomatic wishes were not granted "by about early October," there would be another imperial conference to make the final, fateful go-or-don't-go choice for war.

At 5 P.M. on September 5, Prime Minister Konoe came to the palace to brief the emperor on this newest "national policy" document of the liaison conference, which the cabinet had rubber-stamped late the previous day.[51] Forty-four-year-old Hirohito already knew the approximate burden of the document and could hardly have been taken aback by its arrival, or by the request for an imperial conference. The high command had kept him informed in detail about the steadily worsening crisis and the military plans for dealing with it. According to Kido's diary, he knew he would soon be called upon to make "a truly grave decision if the United States does not simply and straightforwardly accept our proposal."[52]

Now the moment had arrived for him to focus on the most important decision of his entire life. He was going to be asked to break Japan free of its own deadlocked foreign policy by resorting to a war strategy against a vastly superior adversary and continental giant, the United States, which Japan could not possibly defeat militarily.

A Japan–U.S. war was not predetermined. Hirohito did not have to hurry to accept the high command's introduction of a time limit on diplomacy with the United States; nor did he have to agree to subordinate diplomacy to war preparations. With the German invasion of Russia in its sixth week and far from producing a decisive victory, and with Britain and its empire still in the war, a man with his well-trained skepticism might have reasonably anticipated that Germany would not easily triumph over either of its enemies. Recently returned ambassador to Britain, Shigemitsu Mamoru, a strong supporter of the new order movement, had told him exactly that in both a private audience and a court lecture. Japan could maintain its great power status and exert influence in postwar politics if it stayed out of the European war. All he needed to do was call for "a reexamination of current policy."[53]

Hirohito clearly had options at this moment. He could have slowed the momentum to a new war by choosing to concentrate on the one already in progress. He could have thown into China Japan's huge army along the Manchuria-Soviet border area. He could have opted to profit commercially from the war in Europe by staying out of it, for the time being, as London and Washington were warning. This would have meant halting the southward advance and withdrawing troops from colonially partitioned Southeast Asia, thereby losing the chance to seize the Dutch East Indies.

Some of the navy's top officers had deep misgivings about going into Indochina, and all of them would have acceded to such a decision had the emperor made it.

An untitled document in the Takagi Sōkichi papers describes the briefing of the emperor on the night of September 5. When this account is collated with other contemporary evidence, an interpretation can be made of what actually transpired on the eve of Hirohito's formal ratification of the decision to initiate war under certain conditions. Unlike the postwar diaries of Kido and Konoe, or the Sugiyama "notes,"[54] this Takagi version contains not only the emperor's angry scolding of Sugiyama but also, at the end, his all-important exchange with Konoe: the only person in the room with a constitutional responsibility for advising him.

> *Emperor*: In the event we must finally open hostilities, will our operations have a probability of victory?
>
> *Sugiyama*: Yes, they will.
>
> *Emperor*: At the time of the China Incident, the army told me that we could achieve peace immediately after dealing them one blow with three divisions. Sugiyama, you were army minister at that time. . . .
>
> *Sugiyama*: China is a vast area with many ways in and many ways out, and we met unexpectedly big difficulties. . . . [ellipses in original]
>
> *Emperor*: Didn't I caution you each time about those matters? Sugiyama, are you lying to me?
>
> *Nagano*: If Your Majesty will grant me permission, I would like to make a statement.
>
> *Emperor*: Go ahead.
>
> *Nagano*: There is no 100 percent probability of victory for the troops stationed there. . . . Sun Tzu says that in war between states of similar strength, it is very difficult to calculate victory. Assume, however, there is a sick person and we leave him alone; he will definitely die. But if the doctor's diagnosis offers a seventy percent chance of survival, provided the patient is operated on, then don't you think one must try

surgery? And if, after the surgery, the patient dies, one must say that was meant to be. This indeed is the situation we face today. . . . If we waste time, let the days pass, and are forced to fight after it it is too late to fight, then we won't be able to do a thing about it.

Emperor: All right, I understand. [He answered in a better mood.]

Konoe: Shall I make changes in tomorrow's agenda? How would you like me to go about it?

Emperor: There is no need to change anything.[55]

Konoe, unconvinced by Nagano's logic, gave the emperor one last chance to revise the outline. Hirohito, persuaded by Nagano's and Sugiyama's hardline arguments, ignored it.

When Admiral Nagano recalled this meeting in a roundtable with his former wartime colleagues soon after the surrender, he remembered the emperor's "unusually bad mood" that evening and also suggested that Hirohito had not been pressured to approve the outline of the "national policies." Nagano, moreover, said that it had been he rather than Konoe who had asked, "Should I reverse the order of Articles 1 and 2?" The emperor had answered, "Let the order in the draft stand just as it is written."[56] Whether Konoe, who opposed war with the United States, or Nagano, who favored it, asked that question is unimportant. The point is that the emperor was reminded, not even subtly, that this was a chance to stop, or slow, or lengthen the countdown to all-out, unbounded war. Instead of using his opportunity in any way that would have displeased the pro-war forces in the military, Hirohito accepted their "rapid decline" arguments and ruled to set time conditions—ruled, that is, in favor of opening hostilities once certain conditions were met. The momentum toward war would continue to build.

The emperor was also far from pleased with the policy plan. At the September 5 briefing, he showed his irritation with Sugiyama and the army high command as a whole, and revealed differences in strategic thinking between him and his chiefs of staff. As would become clearer over the next four days, Hirohito was warning them that the global situation was still fraught with possibilities; for him to formally resolve on war at this stage would be premature.[57]

At 9:40 A.M. the next day, September 6, twenty minutes before the start of the imperial conference, Hirohito summoned Kido and told him that he was going to raise some questions at the meeting, whereupon Kido replied that "Privy Council President Hara should be the person to raise the important points of your majesty's concern." Therefore it would be "best for your majesty, to give your warning at the very end," saying something to the effect that everyone "should cooperate fully to bring about success in the diplomatic negotiations."[58]

The main topics at the conference that day were the preparations for war and when to finalize a decision to open hostilities. During the conference Sugiyama had in his possession, and may even have introduced, prepared question-and-answer materials for the emperor. These materials made two things clear: that the United States could not be defeated, and that it was therefore impossible to predict when a war with the United States would end. However, if Japan achieved a great victory in the southern operations, Britain would be defeated and knocked out of the war,

> producing a great transformation in American public opinion. Therefore a favorable conclusion to the war is not necessarily beyond hope. In any case we will have to occupy strategic areas in the south and establish strategic superiority. Concurrently we must develop the rich resources of the southern area and utilize the economic power of the East Asian continent in order to establish a durable, self-sufficient economic position. Moreover, we shall work together with Germany and Italy to break up the unity of the United States and Britain. An unbeatable situation would see us link up Europe and Asia, guiding the situation to our advantage. In this way we might see a hope of coming out of the war [at least even with the United States].[59]

Upon conclusion of the formal presentations, Hirohito gave the "Outline for Carrying Out the National Policies of the Empire" his sanction—with misgivings, without an optimistic prospect of victory, or even any notion of the course that a protracted war might take. All the participants now had to complete preparations for war with the United States, Britain, and the Netherlands by the last ten days of October, and they had to make the decision to start the war if there was no longer hope of achieving their demands through the Washington negotiations by an unspecific deadline in early October.

Hirohito at this stage was still taking his time. To drive home his wariness on the question of war or peace, and to make his high command cooperate in giving diplomacy more time to work, he spoke out (as prearranged with Kido) just before the September 6 meeting concluded.[60] "What do you two chiefs of staff think?" he asked. "Neither of you has said a word." Then, taking a piece of paper from his pocket, he read aloud a famous *tanka* by Emperor Meiji: "Across the four seas all are brothers./In such a world why do the waves rage, the winds roar?"[61] When he had finished, the chiefs of staff stated their intention to give priority to diplomacy, and the conference adjourned in a tense mood.

Meiji had written his poem at the beginning of the Russo-Japanese War to express his worries about the possible outcome. The next year, fortunately, he had been able to compose poems celebrating victory. Thus Meiji's poem had its roots in his anxiety about the chances for victory.[62] When Hirohito read aloud the poem to his two rarely fully cooperative chiefs of staff, the question "Why do the waves rage, the winds roar?" sent a strong, clear message. As the conference ended, the chiefs of staff—having been made aware of the emperor's apprehension over their readiness for the possible outcome of the two-track policy they were embarking on—promised to give diplomacy more priority, and over the next few days the chiefs of staff would strive to assuage Hirohito's doubts about their disunity, insufficient war preparations, and acting in haste.

On September 9 Army Chief of Staff Sugiyama gave Hirohito a detailed report on the planned southern advance operation. The emperor once again wanted reassurance about the Soviets, asking what he would do "if pressure comes from the north?" Sugiyama answered:

Once we have begun the southern operation, we cannot pay attention to anything else—we have to keep pushing forward until we achieve our objectives. Your majesty, we need your understanding. If something happens in the north, we will transfer troops up from China, but we must not stop the southern operation halfway.

Emperor: Well, then, I'm relieved. But don't you think it will be very hard to transfer troops from China?

Sugiyama: Yes. Because our strength in China will be weakened, we will have to contract our battle fronts and also do other things. These matters are considered in the annual operations plan just coming up. Under any circumstances, you don't have to worry about China.[63]

The next day Sugiyama briefed the emperor again and was again questioned, this time regarding the mobilization for the southern advance operation:

Emperor: You may go ahead and mobilize. But if the Konoe-Roosevelt talks go well, you'll stop, won't you?

Chief of the General Staff: Indeed, your majesty, we will.

Emperor: I will ask you one more time: Is there *any* possibility that the north [that is, the Soviet Union] may move against us while we are engaged in the south [emphasis added]?

Chief of the General Staff: I cannot say that will absolutely not occur. However, it is inconceivable that large forces will be able to attack us because of the season.[64]

In just three days a war with the United States, at which the emperor had balked on September 6, had become a matter of lesser importance than a two-front war.

A few days later the man designated to lead the attack on the United States, Adm. Yamamoto Isoroku, commander of the Combined Fleet, paid a visit to Prime Minister Konoe, who was becoming increasingly despondent. According to the "record" of their conversation (made more than a month later), Yamamoto tried to reassure Konoe: "I don't know about the army," he told him, "but as you try to adjust diplomatic relations [with the United States], you don't have to worry about the navy. The coming war will be protracted and dirty, and I don't intend to sit idle on the flagship neglecting my duty." The admiral intended to do everything he could to force an early, decisive, showdown battle in which he would commit his entire fleet, making especially important use of air and submarine forces. If he won that battle, a long war of attrition might be avoided—if not also won. In this top-level pep talk for the depressed prime minister, they both seem still to have believed that the hoped-for meeting at sea between Prince Konoe and President Roosevelt might come to pass. Konoe wanted a diplomatic breakthrough but feared that even if he did meet with Roosevelt, nothing would issue from their talk and war would begin. Admiral Yamamoto suggested using deception. "[I]f the talks at sea should break down, don't assume a defiant attitude. Depart leaving everything vague. And the fleet will take action while you are en route home."[65]

But Prince Konoe was now thinking of departing the cabinet he headed, not a summit with an American president who did not want to help the empire, but strangle it. On September 26, with the deadline set on September 6 fast approaching, he complained to Privy Seal Kido that he was getting out if the military insisted on mid-October for making the decision to open hostilities.[66]

Hirohito's early-October deadline for "adjusting" relations with the United States passed with no progress in the negotiations. On October 13 he told Kido: "In the present situation there seems to be little hope for the Japan–U.S. negotiations. If hostilities erupt this time, I think I may have to issue a declaration of war."[67] The next day Konoe held his last cabinet meeting. Army Minister Tōjō did most of the talking:

> For the past six months, ever since April, the foreign minister has made painstaking efforts to adjust relations [with the United States.] Although I respect him for that, we remain deadlocked. . . . Our decision was "to start the war . . . if by early October we cannot thoroughly achieve our demands through negotiations." Today is the fourteenth. . . . We are mobilizing hundreds of thousands of soldiers. Others are being moved from China and Manchuria, and we have requisitioned two million tons of ships, causing difficulties for many people. As I speak they are en route to their destinations. I would not mind stopping them, and indeed *would* have to stop them, if there was a way for a diplomatic breakthrough. . . . The heart of the matter is the [imposition on us of] withdrawal [from Indochina and China]. . . . If we yield to America's demands, it will destroy the fruits of the China Incident. Manchukuo will be endangered and our control of Korea undermined.[68]

Two days later, on October 16, Konoe resigned—a victim of the time element in the national policy document he himself had helped to craft. After the Manchurian Incident, Konoe had been vociferously anti-Anglo-American and pro-German. On January 21, 1941, he had declared firmly before a secret session of the Diet that "Germany will win."[69] Now he was just as sure that Germany would lose, and also sure that the senior officers of both services could not promise a Japanese victory. Konoe's policy of seeking to end the international pressure on Japan by negotiating in Washington had alienated pro-Axis forces in the government and military.

Rightly convinced that the emperor and Kido supported the arguments for war put forward by Tōjō, Sugiyama, and Nagano, and that the emperor no longer trusted him, Konoe prepared to withdraw from the scene.

One of Konoe's last official actions as prime minister was to join with Tōjō in recommending Prince Higashikuni to succeed him. Many believed that Higashikuni would be able to control both the army and navy and secure the highest degree of national unity. Hirohito, however, refused: As he had before, he did not want to expose in any unnecessary way the future of the imperial house. He himself later acknowledged, "I dismissed the army's choice and allowed Tōjō to form a cabinet," because, of course, Tōjō was the person he wanted, and he believed now especially that his personal preference should settle the issue.[70] Konoe's letter of resignation pointed out that on four separate occasions he had sought to withdraw troops in order to preserve peace with the United States, while Tōjō had opposed both the action and its purpose. With the China Incident unresolved, he, as a "loyal subject" of the emperor, could not take on the responsibility of entering into a huge new war whose outcome could not be foreseen. Hirohito accepted Konoe's resignation and threw his support to the army minister. He thereby also accepted Tōjō's reasoning: Army morale had to be maintained; troop withdrawal would not solve the problem of relations with China; and yielding to the United States would only serve to make the United States higher-handed than ever.[71]

A conference of senior statesmen convened at the palace to decide who should succeed. Kido, supported by army generals Hayashi and Abe, pushed Tōjō; Admiral Okada objected. Kido explained that Tōjō, abandoning the time limit for the war decision, would reexamine the whole problem of relations with the United States. He did not say that Tōjō would be explicitly charged with making avoidance of war the reason for that reexamination of national policy, for the emperor had never ordered avoidance; nor did Kido say that Tōjō's reexamination would review Japan's options prior to the imperial conference decision of September 6.

Thus General Tōjō, the army's strongest advocate of war and the main opponent of troop withdrawal from China, received consensus and was recommended. Later that day Hirohito unhesitatingly elevated Tōjō to become his, and the nation's, new prime minister. "[A]bsolutely . . . dumbfounded" was how Tōjō described his feelings to his secretary on being selected.[72] "Nothing ventured, nothing gained," was Hirohito's comment to Kido ten days afterward.[73] The emperor and Kido and those close to them now believed that war was unavoidable. On the day of Tōjō's appointment, Prince Takamatsu confided to his diary: "We have finally committed to war and now must do all we can to launch it powerfully. But we've clumsily telegraphed our intentions. We needn't have signaled what we're going to do; having [the entire Konoe cabinet] resign was too much. As matters stand now we can merely keep silent and without the least effort war will begin."[74] So too thought many in the Roosevelt adminstration. And Konoe out, Tōjō in, seemed a confirmation.

Konoe's chief cabinet secretary, Tomita Kenji, later recorded Konoe's reminiscences of the circumstances surrounding his resignation, in which he implied that Hirohito was clearly at fault.

> Of course his majesty is a pacifist, and there is no doubt that he wished to avoid war. When I told him, as prime minister, that to initiate war is a mistake, he agreed. But the next day he would tell me, "You were worried about it yesterday; but you don't have to worry so much." Thus, gradually, he began to lean toward war. And the next time I met him, he leaned even more toward war. In short, I felt the emperor was telling me: My prime minister does not understand military matters; I know much more. In short, the emperor had absorbed the views of the army and navy high commands. Consequently, as a prime minister who lacked authority over the high command, I had no way of making

any further effort because the emperor, who was the last resort, was this way.[75]

The emperor would one day, down the long bloody road of World War II, praise Tōjō for serving him loyally while saying of Konoe, who had tried to prevent war with the United States, that he lacked "firm beliefs and courage."[76] To add to the irony, it was Konoe, not the emperor, who was arrested after the war as a probable war criminal.

IV

The cabinet that General Tōjō formed on October 17 was committed to keeping the emperor fully informed on all important questions while they were under study. Kaya Okinori came in as finance minister and Tōgō Shigenori as foreign minister. Over the next two weeks both these men grew extremely pessimistic about the chances of success in a war with the United States, yet neither was willing to make any one-sided diplomatic concessions to secure American agreement. Nor did they, even once, openly threaten to resign and bring down the cabinet if they could not follow their convictions when it really counted.

At a marathon seventeen-hour meeting of the liaison conference on November 1, called to decide on a revised "Outline for Carrying Out the National Policies of the Empire," Tōgō tried to prolong the discussions in Washington beyond the time desired by the navy and army so as to avoid a war decision. Eventually he yielded to military pressure and the arguments of Prime Minister Tōjō, who insisted that "when hardship comes, the people will gird up their loins. At the time of the Russo-Japanese War, we took our stand with no prospect of victory, and that was the situation for one year from the Battle of the Yalu River. Yet we won."[77]

Tōgō responded, "Is there no way we can manage a decisive

battle in a short period of time?"[78] But after the liaison conference adjourned, Tōgō concurred with the army and navy on a cutoff date for negotiations with the United States, followed by the use of diplomatic trickery. Thereafter he repeatedly rejected Ambassador Nomura's requests to offer the Americans meaningful concessions.

On November 2 Tōjō and the military chiefs, Admiral Nagano and General Sugiyama, briefed the emperor on the previously decided national policies. Tōjō reported that his reexamination of eleven points, including the raw materials situation, begun on October 23, had been in vain; precious time had been lost.[79] The emperor seemed satisfied. No doubt he felt that he had gone an extra mile. He now had his excuse for ratifying the decision to initiate war. The stipulated next step was at hand, but he needed one more detail settled. "What," he asked Tōjō, "are you going to do to provide justification [for the war]?" Intent on shielding his public image, so different from the leader his military and cabinets knew, and even more concerned with total public support for the forthcoming conflict, Hirohito ordered the loyal Tōjō to devise the most plausible war rationale possible. Tōjō answered, "The matter is presently being examined. I shall soon report on it."[80]

That same day Hirohito ventured a surprise proposal to Tōjō. Develop an action plan for ending the war, he told him, so that the last act could be controlled and foreseen. Make contact with the "Roman pope" in the Vatican![81] Tōjō acted quickly, demonstrating his trustworthiness. However, his plan to move from war to peace, duly adopted at the liaison conference on November 15, was no more than a scenario for seizing opportunities for concluding a war not yet begun (and projected as likely to conclude no better than a draw) once Japan and Germany had already triumphed.[82] Still, it pleased Hirohito.

On November 8 Hirohito had received detailed information about the Pearl Harbor attack plan. On the fifteenth he was shown the full war plan, in all its details.[83] The single most important feature of this final, perfected plan was its hypothesis that an "impregnable" military system to defend economic self-sufficiency, needed for waging a protracted war, would be established following the completion of the first stage of the oceanic offensive in the South Pacific. Apart from that, no long-term, concrete plan for guiding the war in its protracted stage existed. The army and navy had different strategic concepts—and goals—for the offensive stage. Just as situational thinking had pervaded the policy-making process leading to the war decision, so now unknown future conditions and circumstances would determine the war strategy. Nor did the plan specify where and when to end the initial offensive. Despite this glaring flaw, Supreme Commander Hirohito confirmed it. The stage was set for Japan's fatal delay later in shifting to defense in the Pacific.

Worth noting are the following lines in the explanation of the full plan: "This surprise attack operation, comparable to the Battle of Okehazama, is extremely bold. Of course its success will largely depend on the luck of the battle. However, so long as the enemy fleet is anchored there on the day of the attack, it is possible to sink two or three battleships and aircraft carriers."[84]

Statistical evidence presented by the chiefs of staff, and by the president of the Planning Board, Gen. Suzuki Teiichi, coupled with enticing illustrative comparisons from Japanese military history, probably helped convince Hirohito that a protracted war was not only possible to fight but could be concluded satisfactorily even without any real plan for doing so.

The emperor had discussions with his high commanders on November 3. Toward noon on the fourth, he told Kido that two problems still bothered him about the operation:

> Suppose we invade Thailand, won't we need to provide a clear justification for that? How is the research on this matter going? And in the event that [enemy] airplane and submarine interdiction [on our lines

of supply and transport] occurs from bases in Australia, do we have countermeasures so we can be sure of uninterrupted acquisition of oil and supplies?[85]

That was indeed a serious question and indicated Hirohito's keen sensitivity to the strategic weakness in Japan's position in the South Pacific. If control of the sea-lanes could be weakened by Anglo-American air and submarine attacks, Japan's strategy for a long war would prove flawed. The emperor's questions also demonstrated his ingrained habit of sniffing through procedural and tactical details and sometimes losing sight of the big issue—a dangerous habit for a supreme commander.

That afternoon Hirohito broke precedent by attending for the first time a full meeting of the Conference of Military Councillors. For three and a half hours he sat silently listening to questions put to his chiefs of staff and Prime Minister Tōjō by Princes Higashikuni and Asaka, Gens. Terauchi Juichi, Yamada Otozō, and Doihara Kenji, and Adms. Oikawa Koshirō and Yoshida Zengo. Hirohito's purpose in being present at the discussions was to imbue the forthcoming national policy document with the greatest possible authority prior to his sanctioning it. In the evening Lt. Col. Tanemura Sataka entered in the secret war log of the Twentieth Group that "the emperor [okami] seemed extremely pleased. Now the decision of the state is further strengthened and the result will be fine."[86]

On another early November occasion, Hirohito once again went over the war plans with his two chiefs of staff:

Emperor: I understand you're going to do Hong Kong after Malaya starts. Well, what about the foreign concessions in China?

Sugiyama: We are studying the confiscation of concessions by right of belligerency.

Emperor: You are going to attend to the concessions after Hong Kong? Right?

Sugiyama: Indeed, Your Majesty. If we don't, our surprise attack in Malaya will fail.

Emperor: Then when will you take over the foreign concessions?

Sugiyama: It is mixed up with diplomacy, so I shall have to report to you later. But we are going to make sure that we don't [seize] the concessions beforehand.

Emperor: You say the landings will be difficult due to the monsoon. Can we land even in December? . . . Now, next, when does the navy plan to open hostilities?

Nagano: We are planning for December 8.

Emperor: That's a Monday [Japan time; Sunday in Hawaii].

Nagano: This day is better because [everyone] will be tired from the weekend.[87]

Clearly, in the early days of November Hirohito's mind had become fixed on war. He no longer agonized over the deadlocked negotiations with the United States. At his daily informal briefings by the chiefs of staff, he had approved the contents of the national policy document that was to be presented at the next imperial conference; approval had also come from the Conference of Military Councillors. All these decisions were made before the cabinet had ever met to deliberate them, though the issues were a matter of life or death.[88]

On November 5, at the imperial conference that was not reported in the press, Hirohito made the actual (though next to last) decision for war by sanctioning both the completion of "preparations for operations" and a deadline for terminating the Washington diplomatic negotiations, at midnight December 1.[89] The negotiations were to go forward on the basis of two proposals, A and B, to be offered in succession.

A, favored by the army, was communicated to the United States on November 7. It sought a full settlement of differences based on a revised version of ideas that had been presented during earlier stages of the Japan–U.S. talks, including the question of stationing troops in China, the principle of nondiscriminatory trade in China, and the interpretation of the Tripartite Pact. This time the army indicated its willingness to confine its forces to fixed areas in North China and Mongolia for a fixed period of time, and not automatically to act in accordance with the Tripartite Pact. On the principle of nondiscrimination in commerce, Tōgō insisted on attaching the condition that it was acceptable as long as it was applied not only to China but worldwide—that is, to Western possessions as well.

Proposal B, transmitted on November 20, omitted mention of China and simply sought a modus vivendi. It promised that Japan would not advance by armed force any further than French Indochina and would withdraw to the northern part of that colony after peace was reached in the war with China. In return the United States was asked to restore relations prior to the freezing of Japanese assets, furnish Japan with a million tons of aviation fuel, and assist it in procuring raw materials from the Dutch East Indies.[90] Each proposal comprised a package; each had a deadline of midnight, November 30. Since the decision to proceed with final war preparations had been made, and only a few weeks allowed for a settlement of issues, the result was a foregone conclusion.

Kido wrote on the fifth:

> Our policy toward the United States, Britain, and the Netherlands was decided upon at the imperial conference that convened in the emperor's presence at 10:30 A.M. and continued until 3:10 P.M. At 3:40 P.M. Prime Minister Tōjō came to my office and we discussed the matter of the organization of the Southern Area Army, the dispatch of Mr. Kurusu [special envoy] to the United States, and so forth.[91]

Simultaneously Admiral Nagano, navy chief of staff, went over the war plan in detail with the emperor. "Imperial Navy Operations Plan for War Against the United States, Britain, and the Netherlands" had been drafted by the general staff of the Combined Fleet aboard the battleship *Nagato*, then forwarded directly to the Navy General Staff before going up the chain of command.[92] No ministers of state attended this audience, at which Hirohito gave the final go-ahead to attack Pearl Harbor.

According to Sugiyama's notes, the emperor (who already knew the approximate time, places, and methods of attack at all points) was worried about maintaining secrecy. Hirohito wanted to know when the assault groups could be set in motion. The precise dates would be settled shortly, said Nagano. Secrecy was essential, so they had to be especially careful to avoid too-early forward deployment. Even with great care, in an operation involving so many units, one could not be sure how long it could all be kept hidden. Hirohito, worried as always about the Soviet Union, cautioned Nagano to be especially careful in the north so as not to provoke the Russians.

They next turned to China, where Japan, after four years and nearly five months of fighting, had built up huge forces and was potentially capable of destroying Chiang's armies. Sugiyama told his supreme commander: "Since it is unsuitable at this time to withdraw troops from Yi-ch'ang [a main river port near the entrance to the Yangtze gorges, and a natural jumping-off point for an army intending to move into Szechwan Province and attack Chungking], we are thinking of using home units to reinforce our assault force. We are going over that now." Hirohito, however, was of a different opinion. "We should probably withdraw the troops from Yi-ch'ang."[93]

The last remark seems somewhat cryptic, but no matter what the emperor was really thinking, he wanted Yi-ch'ang, which since 1940 had been the staging area for the Japanese Eleventh Army in the Wuhan area to launch an assault against Chungking, to be downgraded to secondary importance, at least for a time. He thus left open the possibility of returning to Yi-ch'ang once the primary operation had been successfully completed. The underlying strategic problem, of course, was that Hirohito and his high command were taking the nation into a completely new war while more than half the Japanese army was, and had to remain, tied down on the continent.

V

After November 5 all Japanese "negotiations"—whether still aimed at securing oil from the United States and the Dutch East Indies or at stopping the United States and Britain from interfering with Japan's activities in China or taking any other action that could threaten Japan's fleet operation in Southeast Asia—were partly sincere, partly fraudulent. For months these negotiations had been of utmost gravity and importance to Japan's leaders, including Hirohito, who had very detailed knowledge of them and had hoped to see them succeed. Though Hirohito did invest hope in proposal B, at the same time he felt it wouldn't work and that it was therefore better to string Washington along until the exact moment when he and the high command were ready for the showdown. To Roosevelt and his strategists the negotiations were expressions of Japanese weakness. To have agreed to anything proposed by Tokyo would have been seen, all across the United States, as an act of "appeasement." More important, they were under strong pressure from Britain and China not to compromise with Tokyo. By not taking seriously the Japanese military threat, the Roosevelt administration did not take seriously either the alternative to such a threat, which was a temporary settlement of differences that left the Japanese with a guaranteed minimum amount of oil and thus an incentive to go on talking at a moment when the anti-Axis coalition was at its weakest.

Hull had been reading decrypted Japanese diplomatic messages (intercepted and decoded by the system code-named MAGIC). He, like Roosevelt, was aware of the new Tōjō cabinet's military timetable for war and of Japanese troop movements toward Southeast Asia. On November 26, contrary to the advice of Ambassador Grew in Tokyo, Hull handed Ambassador Nomura and his special assistant, Kurusu Saburō, a "draft mutual declaration of policy" and a ten-point written outline of principles for a comprehensive agreement rather than a temporary truce or tactical delay. The two-part document was headed "strictly confidential, tentative and without commitment." The second part, entitled "Outline of Proposed Basis for Agreement Between the United States and Japan," omitted any reference to the earlier Japanese proposal for a temporary truce. It called for Japan to "withdraw all military, naval, air and police forces from China and Indochina" but left "China" undefined in all six places in the text where the word appeared. It also omitted any mention of Manchuria, for Hull had discarded Stimson's earlier nonrecognition doctrine from the start of the talks. Equally important, Hull stated no deadline for troop withdrawal. On the other hand the draft document made quite clear that the United States would not support any government in China other than Chiang Kai-shek's Nationalist government.

When this "Hull note"—a postwar Japanese term—arrived in Tokyo on the twenty-seventh, Tōjō misrepresented the American action by telling the liaison conference that Washington had issued an "ultimatum to Japan." Tōgō knew, of course, that Hull's statement was not really an ultimatum, for it was clearly marked "tentative" and lacked a time limit for acceptance or rejection. But Tōgō kept silent. Afterward some members of the privy council also pointed out that Hull's memorandum could not be considered as America's final word because of its heading—an observation that apparently made no impression on Tōgō. Soon he too consented to the opening of hostilities, just as in early November he had consented to the army's demand that the United States desist from supporting Chiang Kai-shek.

Perhaps Tōgō perceived in the spirit of Hull's memorandum a

tone of colonialist arrogance in the American position. Like everyone else in the room, he may have felt relief that the hard-line
American position, grounded in abstract principles, had absolved
them of moral responsibility for what they were about to do. Now
they could claim that the United States government had "forced"
them to opt for war in self-defense: We didn't do it of our own volition; the "Hull note" triggered the war, and hereafter we shall use
this American document to prove it.[94]

Through every stage of the Hull-Nomura secret talks, under
three foreign ministers—Matsuoka, Toyoda, and Tōgō—the Army,
Navy, and Foreign Ministries had practiced policy making by suspension, with nobody backing down and differences left unresolved
but papered over. All three ministries blocked and checked one
another, while the army especially never made meaningful concessions or acted in ways that might have begun to build trust by suggesting a new pattern of behavior.[95] All three foreign ministers clung
to an already existing agreement—the "Basic Treaty" with the client
Wang Ching-wei regime, which guaranteed the stationing of
Japanese troops in China. More important, they stuck to their system of policy making, which, because of bureaucratic conflicts and
divisions, never consolidated and, in late 1941, could only make for
continuous movement in the single direction of war.

Ultimately it was always more advantageous for each of the
forces in this process, including the emperor and Kido, to move to
expand war rather than risk paralysis and complete breakdown of
their system of rule. This was especially true of Hirohito, who, at
different times in the decade after the Manchurian Incident, had
expressed fears that not taking some warlike action—like not pump-
ing up the *kokutai* or not suppressing dissent—would jeopardize the
imperial system of government and eventually damage the imperial
institution itself. For Hirohito domestic conflicts were more dangerous than the escalation of war, for they carried the risk of eroding the monarchy. In the Japanese wartime system of decision mak-

ing, the major players worked toward consensus by subordinating the nation's interests to their own bureaucratic, institutional interests, all the while mouthing the false rhetoric of harmony and consensus. Whenever they failed to reach agreement, they glossed over their differences in vague policy documents that placated all sides and allowed the exigencies of the situation, the preparation for war, and their own special interests to determine their final course of action.

As the time approached for his final decision for war, Hirohito requested a last round of discussions with government leaders and senior statesmen. On November 27 a large Japanese task force, with six aircraft carriers, set off from Tankan (Hitokappu) Bay in the southern Kurile Islands headed toward Hawaii, and the liaison conference decided on the "Sequence of Administrative Procedures to be Taken Regarding the Declaration of War."[96] On November 29 the leaders assembled at the palace, and he listened to their comments. Prime Minister Tōjō and members of his cabinet spoke first. Next, the senior statesmen—Wakatsuki, Hirota, Konoe, Hiranuma, Okada, Yonai, Hayashi, and Abe—gave their opinions. Hirota, Hayashi, and Abe pushed for war. The majority argued that it was better to maintain the status quo and endure American pressure, but nobody expressed flat-out opposition to beginning hostilities.[97]

On November 30 Prince Takamatsu went to the palace and attempted to stop his brother from taking the empire into a new war. The navy had its hands full, he cautioned. Its leaders were not certain of ultimate victory and wanted to avoid war with the United States if at all possible. Although their encounter lasted only five minutes, Takamatsu would never forget his futile last-minute attempt to have a voice in the policy-making process. Afterward a puzzled Hirohito asked Kido, "What's going on?" Kido replied, "The decision this time [the next day] will be enormously important. Once you grant the imperial sanction, there can be no going back. If you have even the slightest doubt, make absolutely sure until you are convinced."[98] After next checking with Tōjō, Hirohito called in his top naval leaders, Nagano and Shimada, for yet another joint review. Both men reassured him that the war operation would be successful. Whether Hirohito also questioned them about the navy's confidence after the first two years of war—Takamatsu's concern—we have no way of knowing.

The last step in the countdown phase to war took place on the afternoon of December 1. Nineteen somber leaders, including the entire cabinet, assembled; the emperor entered, took his customary raised seat at the dais end of the room in front of a gold screen; and the meeting began.

An hour later, after everyone at the two long facing tables, at either side of and at right angles to the emperor, had completed his presentation, Privy Council President Hara questioned the cabinet and the military high command, presumably on the emperor's behalf. Hara's very first comment misrepresented Hull's statement by claiming that "the United States . . . has demanded that we withdraw troops from *all of China* [emphasis added]," when, in fact, Hull had used only the word "China." "I would like to know," said Hara, "whether Manchukuo is included in the term 'China'? Did our two ambassadors confirm this point?"[99]

Tōgō replied that the two ambassadors had not clarified the American meaning of "China" in their meeting with Hull on the 26th.

> However . . . the American proposal [early in the negotiations on] April 16 stated that they would recognize the state of Manchukuo, so Manchukuo would not be part of China. . . . On the other hand . . . there has been a change in their position . . . they look upon Chungking as the one and only legitimate regime, and . . . they want to destroy the Nanking regime, [so] they may retract what they have said previously.[100]

Tōgō's answer was astonishingly evasive and illogical. Throughout the Japan–U.S. negotiations, the Manchurian problem had been a low priority for Hull; never once had he raised the issue of troop withdrawal from Manchuria. Nor had Nomura included Manchuria in his talks with Hull when discussing "China." Both men always separated Manchuria from the rest of China. Moreover, as historian Sudō Shinji recently pointed out, if Hull had wanted to change the status quo in Manchuria, "he would have brought the Manchurian problem forward on its own in the course of negotiations."[101] Tōgō knew this but chose to emphasize that the secretary of state was demanding withdrawal from Manchuria because the United States had refused to recognize the Nanking government— a position that Roosevelt and Hull had never altered. After Tōgō's irrelevant reply, no one at the conference pursued the issue of Manchukuo because they all shared the same misperception that the United States was attempting to change the status quo in that area as well as China proper.

Hara concluded his brief questions to the high commanders by setting the war decision in a broad historical context leading from the war of 1894–95 to the Manchurian Incident of 1931. In Hara's opinion war was preferable to accepting Hull's proposal because:

> If we were to give in [to the United States], then we would not only give up the fruits of the Sino-Japanese War and the Russo-Japanese War, but also abandon the results of the Manchurian Incident. There is no way we could endure this. . . . [I]t is clear that the existence of our empire is threatened, that the great achievements of the emperor Meiji would all come to naught, and that there is nothing else we can do.[102]

Hara finished speaking, the emperor remained silent, whereupon Tōjō spoke: "Once His Majesty decides to commence hostilities, we will all strive to meet our obligations to him, bring the government and the military ever closer together, resolve that the nation united will go on to victory, make an all-out effort to achieve our war aims, and set his majesty's mind at ease. I now adjourn the meeting."[103]

At the end of these "minutes" Sugiyama noted that "[t]he emperor nodded in agreement to each explanation that was made and displayed not the slightest anxiety. He seemed to be in a good mood. We were filled with awe."[104]

Meanwhile, in another part of the palace, General Sugiyama met with the emperor and briefed him on the plans for the December 8 attacks.[105]

Between December 2 and December 8, or "X Day," while the Japanese people remained completely unaware, Emperor Hirohito met repeatedly with his chiefs of staff, questioned his aides about the country's air defenses, reviewed the organization of the fleet, examined war plans and maps, and received reports on the status of all the units moving into position on the various invasion fronts.

VI

In virtually everything he had done since becoming emperor, Hirohito had departed from the precedent set by his grandfather, the Meiji emperor. The drafting of his war rescript, starting in late October, was no exception.

Previous war rescripts had contained cautionary phrases such as "insofar as it is not contrary to international law" and "within the sphere of international law." Hirohito's contained no such limitations since it had to mesh with the operations plans for two simultaneous surprise attacks: an air assault on the American fleet and naval facilities at Pearl Harbor in Hawaii, and a ground landing at Kota Bharu in British Malaya.

From Kota Bharu, Japanese troops were to strike southward down the Malayan west coast, largely avoiding the rain forests and

mountains, to seize Singapore—at the tip of the Malayan Peninsula—linchpin of the British Empire in Southeast Asia and gateway
to the resources of the Netherlands East Indies. Japanese forces
headed for Singapore needed to violate Thailand's neutrality at Singora (Songkhla), a strategic port north of Kota Bharu on the Gulf
of Siam, in the Kra Isthmus area of southern Thailand. The entire
southern operation was thus premised on the violation of international law with respect to two major powers—the United States and
Britain—and a minor but diplomatically active third power, Thailand. Fully aware of these operational imperatives, and uncertain if
Thailand would enter the war on Japan's side rather than Britain's,
the emperor and Foreign Minister Tōgō removed from the draft
rescript the clause on respect for international law.[106]

Also omitted was any reference to the "Greater East Asia
Coprosperity Sphere" as an official war aim. The "Essentials for
Implementing Administration in the Occupied Southern Area," a
document prepared by the Foreign Ministry and adopted at the liaison conference of November 20 (that is, prior to the "Hull note"
and the final imperial decision for war), stated that if Japan were to
advocate "the liberation of the peoples of East Asia" from white
supremacy and colonial rule, its war aims would "become altruistic
and have little persuasive force on the nation . . . the world might
regard it as a racial struggle. However, it might be all right to advocate this unofficially."[107]

The emperor's active role in composing and fussily checking the
war rescript at all stages was in keeping with his character. Foreign
Ministry officials, assisted by cabinet secretary Inada Shūichi, journalist Tokutomi Sohō, and court official Yoshida Masuzō, a scholar
of the Chinese classics, did the actual drafting.[108] Officers in the Military Affairs Bureaus of both branches, as well as civilian bureaucrats
in the prime minister's office, participated in polishing it. The
emperor and Kido then read through the various drafts. The analysis by the historian Okabe Makio of three surviving versions—one

unnumbered, another numbered 4, and a third numbered 6—suggests that the rescript may have gone through as many as ten or eleven different versions.[109] Kido, Tōjō, Tōgō, and the emperor played active roles throughout this process; and at Hirohito's insistence several significant changes were inserted into the text.

The desire for peace had been a consistent element in the public personas of his father and grandfather, and had also been embodied in important instructional texts of his youth. Hirohito now carefully reiterated the peace theme in his only declaration of war. Thus, before the words "Our empire has been brought to cross swords with America and Britain," he ordered the insertion of formulaic expressions stating that the emperor did not want war ("It has been truly unavoidable and far from our wishes that . . . "). Such phrases underscored his supposed desire for peace—in the sense of global peace among the world's great regional spheres rather than among particular nations.

Second, the last line of the war rescript originally contained the phrase "Advocate the principles of the Imperial Way throughout the world [*kōdō no taigi o chūgai ni senyōsen koto o kisu*]." To the emperor it was unobjectionable for the Field Service Code (*senjinkun*) of the Imperial Army to use the amuletic term "Imperial Way" (*kōdō*); virtually every act of Japanese territorial aggrandizement since 1931 had been done under that name. But he did not want ideas of imperial expansion in his war rescript, crafted for everyone in Japan and the world to see.[110] On his instruction, therefore, Kido had this line changed to "preserve the glory of our empire" [*teikoku no kōei o hozen semu koto o kisu*]. Needless to say, none of these changes detracted from the overall message that Japan, "for its existence and self-defense," was setting out to eliminate the hand of Anglo-American imperialism in Asia.

The last step was the countersigning of the war rescript by the ministers of state so as to maintain the fiction that Emperor Hirohito, a genuine and truly constitutional monarch, sanctioned great policy changes only in accordance with the advice of his cabinet ministers. Thus was the finishing touch applied to the Japanese system of irresponsibility designed under Meiji.

Before dawn on December 8, Tokyo time, the Imperial Navy and Army launched nearly coordinated surprise attacks at Singora and Kota Bharu. More than an hour later, they struck at the well-defended American naval base at Pearl Harbor, and several hours later at Clark Air Base in central Luzon, thus hitting the main supports of the rising American empire in Asia. President Roosevelt now had the war he did not want, with the country he regarded as a secondary threat to American security.

The diaries of Privy Seal Kido and Hirohito's naval aide, Jō, allow us to follow the emperor hour by hour on that first day of the "War of Greater East Asia." According to Jō, "[T]he forces heading for Malaya started landing at Singora at 1:30 A.M. and completed the landing at 4:30 A.M. At 2:30 A.M. the foreign minister [Tōgō] presented the emperor with a message from President Roosevelt," which (according to the recollection of a chamberlain) seemed to annoy him.[111] And Jō continued:

> 4 A.M. (Japan time): Japan issued a final ultimatum to the United States. 3:30 A.M.: the Hawaiian surprise attack was successful. 5:30 A.M.: Singapore bombed. Great results. Air attacks on Davao, Guam, Wake. 7:10 A.M.: All the above was reported to the emperor. The American gunboat *Wake* was captured on the Shanghai front. The British gunboat *Petrel* was sunk. From 7:15 to 7:30 the chief of the Navy General Staff reported on the war situation. At 7:30 the prime minister informally reported to the emperor on the imperial rescript declaring war. (Cabinet meeting from 7 A.M.). At 7:35 the chief of the Army General Staff reported on the war situation. At 10:45 the emperor attended an emergency meeting of the privy council. At 11:00 A.M. the imperial rescript declaring war was promulgated. [At

11:40 A.M. Hirohito conferred with Kido for about twenty minutes.] At 2:00 P.M. the emperor summoned the army and navy ministers and bestowed an imperial rescript on them. The army minister, representing both services, replied to the emperor. [At 3:05 P.M. the emperor had a second meeting with Kido, lasting for about twenty minutes.] At 4:30 P.M. the chiefs of staff formally reported on the draft of the Tripartite (Germany-Italy-Japan) Military Pact. At 8:30 P.M. the chief of the Navy General Staff reported on the achievements of the Hawaii air attack. . . . Throughout the day the emperor wore his naval uniform and seemed to be in a splendid mood.[112]

THE ORDEAL OF SUPREME COMMAND

Confronted with military strangulation by oil embargoes and the choice of admitting defeat in China, thereby abandoning a large part of his continental empire and probably destabilizing the monarchy he had inherited, Hirohito opted for his third alternative: war against the United States and Britain. Like most of his top commanders he believed that Germany would triumph over Britain as it already had over all of Europe. If certain strategic schedules were quickly achieved, Japan would be able to counter superior American productive capacity and force at least a standoff with the United States.[1] Having made his choice, Hirohito dedicated himself totally to presiding over and guiding the war to victory at all costs. It was a most demanding and absolutely vital role.

Yet Hirohito was rarely adequate when exceptionally strong personal leadership was needed to coordinate and control the decentralized power structure and mediate conflicts between the general staffs and their ministries. Too inhibited and slow in producing ideas, he was never able to surmount rivalries between the military services and thereby maintain their unity of purpose and effort. This proved costly. What Hirohito did was provide his chiefs of staff with continuous oversight based on his strong sense of responsibility for the empire and, ultimately, the interests of the imperial house. He also reinforced their belief in the inherent superiority of offense over defense. Optimistic by nature, he approached

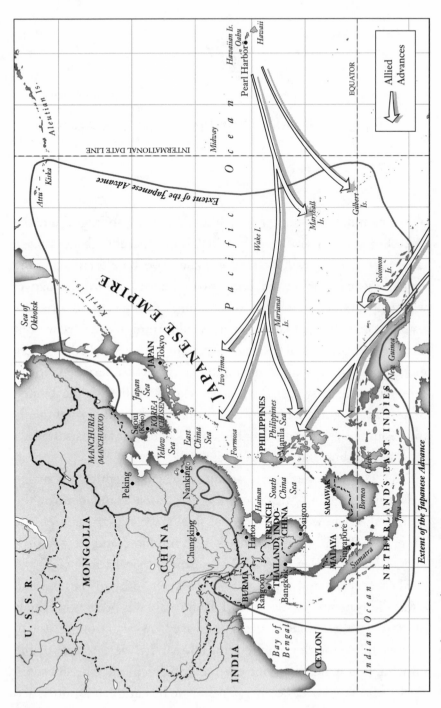

War in the Pacific, 1941–1945

difficult military situations with the attitude that the troops could succeed if only they tried harder. On the other hand, before approving campaign plans he was habitually cautious. He not only looked for what could go wrong and expected that it quite likely would, but actually *predicted* it would unless the high command took some action that he recommended. Hard-won experience had made him a deeply suspicious leader who did not have full confidence in the way his army high command conducted operations. He was pointed, sometimes extremely harsh, in criticizing command errors and rebuking overconfidence.

Although Hirohito never visited the war theaters as did other commanders in chief, he exercised a decisive and controlling influence on theater operations, both in planning and execution, whenever he chose to do so. As during the first four years of the China war, he went on issuing the highest military orders of the Imperial Headquarters, and sometimes audited the conferences that led to the decisions transmitted in his name. He continued to receive in audience generals and admirals returning on duty from the Pacific and China battlefronts. He publicly encouraged and praised front-line units (and, later, home-front organizations). He continued sending messages and messengers to the fronts, and bestowing rescripts (which carried far more honor and prestige than did presidential citations for American commanders) on meritorious officers. He carefully edited his rescripts to be sure exactly what words were used. He visited bases, battleships, and various army and navy headquarters. He inspected military schools, granted audiences to industrial leaders to encourage production, took a keen interest in weapons development, and everywhere drove home the message of sacrifice for the state.

But Hirohito's greatest strength during the war years may have been his ability to transform his natural reticence and inhibitions into a quality of leadership. His charisma resided in his whole imperial being, as distinct from his rather ordinary human qualities—in the myth of his ancient lineage and the traditions and obligations of emperorship over the centuries, down into the modern period of pure invention and manipulation by image makers. In many ways it was his stubborn persistence and determination not to fail as a monarch that helped him to survive the war.

The architects of the Meiji constitution of 1889 could not have foreseen an emperor with Hirohito's rigid character yet capacity for tolerating institutional change. Nor could his teachers at the Ogakumonjo have anticipated the great Asia-Pacific war that he would initiate, guide, and—after prolonged vacillation—end. Nevertheless, by empowering the emperor militarily as supreme commander, ultimately and solely responsible for declaring and waging war and making peace, Itō and his colleagues decades earlier had burdened the yet unborn Shōwa emperor with enormous responsibilities from which he could have no escape so long as he ruled.

There were also religious duties—the very essence of his inherited position—which some of his predecessors had found so onerous that they abdicated rather than be bothered with them. Hirohito clung to his religious obligations even in wartime. He also continued to perform ceremonies such as the annual *utakai-hajime* poetry party, at which he and his officials judged *waka* submitted by his subjects.

Since he had staked the destiny of the nation and the protection of his throne on war, it was more than ever necessary to invoke the favor of the Shinto deities. Thus, from the diary of Privy Seal Kido Kōichi three days after the attack on Pearl Harbor:

> December 11, 1942: Today the emperor travels to Ise Shrine to worship in person [rather than by proxy]. . . .
> December 12: . . . Departed Kyoto Palace at 6:45 A.M. . . . arrived at Yamada Station at 10:00. The emperor prayed first at the outer shrine. After taking his lunch . . . he proceeded to the inner shrine, where he worshiped. . . . It is unprecedented for an emperor to worship in per-

son during wartime. I am moved to awe before his great benevolence and feel profoundly honored as a loyal subject to be able to serve in this grand ceremony.[2]

From the diary of Lt. Comm. Jō Eiichirō, naval aide-de-camp to the emperor:

February 11, 1942: National Foundation Day. . . . Night duty. From 9:45 to 10:20 P.M. the emperor worshiped in the palace. I understand that in his Imperial Declaration to the Gods he reported on conditions at the battlefronts.[3]

December 12, 1942: 1:20 P.M. Emperor prayed at the Inner Shrine [Kōtai Jingū]. He gave thanks to the gods for victories on various battlefronts and asked for their protection in the future as he leads the nation in this time of extreme national emergency.[4]

January 28, 1943: The *outakai* began. I attended in the Hōōnoma [room] and was deeply moved by the poems of the emperor and empress.[5]

June 30, 1943: Today the emperor, at court, performed the *yoori no gi* purification ritual. I understand that he told Chief Aide-de-Camp [Hasunuma] that he had purified the stagnant war situation.[6]

Although Hirohito's position required him to perform Shinto rituals and annual court ceremonies, he voluntarily embraced fixed routines and traditional practices because rigid order suited his temperament and furnished outlets for his frustrations. Always, however, the chief demands on his time came from his role as supreme commander.

I

World War II in the Pacific was officially termed by the Tōjō government the "War of Greater East Asia" (*Dai Tō'A sensō*). It lasted for three years and nine months. The main theaters of battle were the South and Southwest Pacific, where the Imperial Navy and its naval air force had never anticipated decisive battles. Instead the navy had assumed, and Hirohito had believed, that the Combined Fleet would go fleet to fleet, ship to ship against the American enemy only in the Central Pacific. What developed was an unplanned, unprepared-for, and escalating war of attrition in the south. The army and navy made piecemeal responses to unexpected attack, reinforced slowly and inadequately, suffered more and more defeats, lost more and more aircraft and trained pilots, troop and supply transports, fighting ships, and whole ground units.

There, in the southern ocean, during the first twenty-six months of the war, the naval air force lost 26,006 warplanes—nearly a third of its total power—and thousands of experienced pilots.[7] Many hundreds of thousands of tons of fighting ships went down. The loss of merchant and naval transport was especially crippling. When, toward the end of 1943, American forces under Adm. Chester Nimitz, commanding Pacific Ocean Areas, finally began their full-scale counter offensives in the Central Pacific, Japan was desperately trying to contract its defense perimeter and rebuild the naval air and sea power that had been destroyed in the brutal and barbaric South Pacific campaigns.

From the outset Hirohito shared his admirals' mistaken strategic assumptions, and he also held his generals' misperception of the primary enemy. The Army General Staff focused on the Soviet Union; kept most of Japan's ground forces in Korea, Manchuria, and China; and neither researched nor prepared for combat on the remote jungle islands of the Pacific even after that area had become the main theater. Hirohito too was fixated on the Soviet Union, though not to the same extent as the army, and not for so long.[8] Moreover, he grasped the shortcomings of the army's approach before the high command did, and thereafter worked to redirect it.

During the first two months of the war, from December 8,

1941, through late January 1942, Japan's offensive against the weak, unprepared colonial armies in Southeast Asia unfolded almost exactly on schedule, and in accordance with the pre–Pearl Harbor war guidance plan, on which Hirohito based his initial interrogations. During this period the Imperial Army and Navy scored continuous victories. After destroying or crippling a large part of the American fleet at Pearl Harbor and sinking the British battleship *Prince of Wales* and the battle cruiser *Repulse* on December 9 off Singapore, Japanese pilots inaugurated the conquest of the Philippines by wiping out most of MacArthur's just-reinforced air force on the ground. Guam, Wake Island, and Hong Kong fell in succession. Joint navy-army task forces seized the Celebes and the Dutch oil fields in Borneo on December 16, and landed troops and planes in the northern, southern, and eastern parts of the Philippines during late December. On January 3 they occupied Manila, which MacArthur had declared an open city, ostensibly to protect its civilian population but also because his forces were too weak to defend it.

The Japanese blitzkrieg attack gave the Allies no time to recover. Capturing already-built British and American airstrips in Southeast Asia and the Philippines, the naval air force advanced step by step, providing air cover for the sea and ground advance. Pushing farther into the Southwest Pacific with the aim of capturing Java in the Dutch Indies, a task force seized the Australian naval and air base at Rabaul in New Britain on January 22–23. Most of the operational goals in the South Pacific that had been set prior to Pearl Harbor had now been achieved. Key strategic resource areas of the south were in Japanese hands; the war's first stage as initially calculated had ended.[9]

Sustained by the momentum of its success, determined to keep the enemy in retreat, and lacking any carefully thought-out plan for ending the war, Imperial Headquarters did not, at that point, stop its "drive to the south" and shift to a more flexible strategy. Instead, on January 29, it ordered the Combined Fleet to capture the strategic points of Lae, Salamaua, and Port Moresby in the British (eastern) part of the island of New Guinea, thereby implementing the first step of a plan to isolate and ultimately attack Australia.[10] On February 7, the emperor placed his seal on *Daikairei* Number 14, ordering the Combined Fleet to attack the island of Timor in southeastern Indonesia.[11] Hirohito was now as intoxicated by victory as his senior commanders. The joint navy-army task force captured the Portuguese and Dutch territories on Timor on February 20, Batavia on Java on March 5, and shortly afterward occupied Bougainville, the largest island in the Solomons chain, threatening American and British supply lanes to Australia.

On March 7 the liaison conference formalized the rapidly expanding Pacific offensive in a new policy document, whose first article declared: "In order to force Britain to submit and the United States to lose its will to fight, we shall continue expanding from the areas we have already gained," and while "working long-term to establish an impregnable strategic position, we shall actively seize whatever opportunities for attack may occur."[12] The next day Lae and Salamaua in New Guinea were occupied. By April 1942 the Japanese had captured strategic points in the remote Andaman and Nicobar Islands, territory belonging to British India and running from the Malacca Straits all the way to the mouth of the Indian Ocean, thereby forcing the small British fleet in the Indian Ocean to remove to the coast of East Africa.

Meanwhile, in Southeast Asia, Japanese army troops had earlier captured British Singapore on February 15. They had massed in Thailand and from there pushed into the British territory of Burma, capturing Rangoon (Burma's main port) on March 8, Lashio (the starting point of the Burma Road) on April 28, and Mandalay on May 1. In the South Pacific, at the start of May, the army and navy moved into the southern Solomons (Guadalcanal and Tulagi), and around July 21 they took Buna, on the extreme eastern end of New

Guinea, having earlier occupied Hollandia. Finally, on June 7, they pushed their vast Pacific defense perimeter north toward Alaska by placing garrisons on Kiska and Attu in the Aleutians.

While operations in the South Pacific were unfolding victoriously, the ground advance in the Philippines, despite initial, very quick successes, had soon slowed. American and Filipino troops withdrew to prepared positions in the Bataan Peninsula and the island fortress of Corregidor in Manila Bay; and there they remained. Right around this time Hirohito made his first major intervention in an ongoing Pacific front operation. Worried about the stalled offensive on Luzon, he pressed Army Chief of Staff Sugiyama twice, on January 13 and 21, to increase troop strength and launch a quick knockout of Bataan. Sugiyama, though prone to underestimate his enemy's powers of resistance, in this instance correctly observed that the Americans holed up on Bataan constituted no threat whatsoever to Japan's operations far to the south.[13] But no chief of staff could ignore the emperor's repeated "request." On January 22, despite shortages of food, munitions, and manpower, the Japanese renewed their attacks on the Bataan Peninsula, while the high command set about finding adequate reinforcements should they be necessary.

In the battles that followed, the besieged American and Philippine forces—numbering approximately eighty thousand—inflicted heavy losses on the Japanese. On February 9 and 26 Hirohito again pressed Sugiyama about the operation on Bataan. Finally, on April 9, weeks after General MacArthur had escaped by PT boat and B-17 bomber to Melbourne, Australia, the holdouts in Bataan surrendered. Those on Corregidor capitulated a month later.[14] The prolonged American-Filipino defense of Bataan-Corregidor had set the stage for the Battles of the Coral Sea and Midway that followed by allowing American intelligence analysts to intercept, decode, and analyze Japanese radio transmissions.

It is impossible to say whether Hirohito was notified of the

Imperial Army's gratuitous mistreatment of some 78,000 American and Filipino prisoners of war in the infamous "death march" out of Bataan. He was confronted by a prisoner-of-war issue soon after Bataan fell, however. Sixteen U.S. B-25 bombers, launched "no return" (with just enough fuel to land on friendly Chinese airfields) from the carrier *Hornet*, bombed Tokyo, Yokohama, and Nagoya. This event occurred on April 27, nine days after the fall of Bataan. Eight of the fliers, commanded by Col. James Doolittle, were later captured when their planes went down over Japanese-occupied territory in Kiangsi Province, China. Sentenced under the "military regulations" of the theater commander to be executed "because of their act against humanity," the Americans were soon transported to Tokyo, where their cases were referred to the Army Ministry.[15]

Tōjō initially opposed death sentences for the American prisoners, fearing (rightly) American retaliation against Japanese living in the United States. Sugiyama and the entire Army General Staff, however, insisted on executing all eight so as to teach Americans (whose bombing had killed about fifty civilians) an object lesson and thereby decrease the likelihood of further air attacks. The executions would be authorized by an *ex post facto* military regulation specially drafted by the Army Ministry.[16] Hirohito, however, chose to intervene and commute the punishments of five. Why he allowed the others to die in violation of international law cannot be answered; at the end of the war the Japanese destroyed all records and documents pertaining to prisoners of war. Perhaps Hirohito wished to demonstrate his "benevolence," but not an excess of that quality. Or perhaps, having sanctioned by this time so many violations of international laws, he was simply untroubled by breaching yet another one.

In addition to prodding the Bataan offensive and intervening in the case of the "Doolittle fliers," the emperor kept closely in touch with operations in Burma and China, still believing these would be the main battle fronts. On at least three occasions during 1942—

February 9, March 19, and May 29—Hirohito pressed Sugiyama to examine the possibilities for an eventual attack on Chungking.[17] "Can't you figure some way somehow to put an end to the China Incident?" he asked Sugiyama during an audience on May 29. At his urging Sugiyama set in motion the drafting of plans for a major offensive with fifteen divisions to wipe out Chiang's main forces in Szechuan Province and capture Chungking (Operation Gogō).[18]

While these plans were being considered, the navy sustained two successive defeats, and the Pacific suddenly emerged as the critical front in the war, though more than a year would pass before Imperial Headquarters recognized it as such. On May 7–8, as new victories in the Philippines were being reported to the emperor, the Battle of the Coral Sea was fought, giving Japan a tactical victory (in terms of American ship losses) but a strategic defeat in that the Imperial Navy lost a large aircraft carrier and 104 skilled pilots, and had to postpone its planned attack by sea on the Allied stronghold of Port Moresby in New Guinea.[19]

One month later, on June 5–6, the navy suffered another setback, losing four large aircraft carriers, one heavy cruiser, and approximately three thousand men, including 121 skilled pilots, in battles near Midway Island in the Central Pacific.[20] American morale soared; in Tokyo the profound significance of the defeat was overlooked. On June 10 the navy conveyed to the liaison conference an incomplete picture of the results of the battle, on the ground that the real extent of damage was a military secret not to be entrusted to all members.[21] Only the emperor was accurately informed of the carrier and pilot losses, and he chose not to inform the army immediately. Army planners, inaccurately briefed on the real significance of the Coral Sea and Midway defeats, continued for a short time to believe that the Combined Fleet was healthy and secure. Did Hirohito himself fail to grasp the import of the twin defeats? Kido, who discussed the naval battle of Midway with Hirohito on June 8, wrote that day:

I had presumed the news of the terrible losses sustained by the naval
air force would have caused him untold anxiety, yet when I saw him he
was as calm as usual and his countenance showed not the least change.
He said he told the navy chief of staff that the loss was regrettable but
to take care that the navy not lose its fighting spirit. He ordered him
to ensure that future operations continue bold and aggressive. When
I witness the courage and wisdom of the emperor, I am very thankful
that our imperial country Japan is blessed with such a sovereign.[22]

The navy conducted no post-mortem analysis on the influence
its Midway losses might have on future operations.[23] But later Hirohito and the high command cancelled plans to seize Fiji and Samoa
and to begin establishing control of the Indian Ocean. Midway did
not cause them to end the South Pacific offensive. The Combined
Fleet, however, was forced to conduct its operations around the
central and southern Solomons without adequate air cover.

II

A naval officer who assisted Hirohito through many difficult
moments of the war was Lt. Comm. Jō Eiichirō. A skilled pilot who,
late in 1937, had helped plan and direct the first air offensive against
China's cities from the aircraft carrier *Kaga*, he was also an amateur
scientist with an interest in meteorology. On returning to Japan, he
served on the Navy General Staff and taught at the Navy and Army
War Colleges. He then went back to China as vice commander of
the Thirteenth Naval Air Force, charged with bombing operations
deep within China. After a year in China, Jō was assigned to the
palace. His duties there required him to make daily war situation
reports and convey top-secret navy materials and orders to the
emperor. He also transmitted the replies of the navy chief of staff
and navy minister to the emperor's questions and assisted the
emperor as envoy and information collector.

Jō was descended from the Kyushu warrior Kikuchi Takefusa,

and his samurai background embodied one of the fundamental vindicating events in the history of Japanese national defense. Kikuchi (according to commentator Nomura Minoru) had participated in saving Japan from the Mongol fleet in the thirteenth century, when fortuitous "divine winds" (*kamikaze*) arose to destroy the would-be invaders.[24] This background surely figured in Jō's later determination to save Japan from the American fleet by drawing up the first detailed plan for a "kamikaze" Special Attack Corps in June 1943.[25] Jō's idea of recruiting and training young pilots willing to smash their *Zero* fighters, armed with 550-pound bombs, into the decks of American ships was later adopted and put into practice in the Philippines by his friend, Vice Adm. Ōnishi Takijirō.

Hirohito clearly liked Jō, for they shared interests in science and the environment.[26] During his tour of duty at the palace, Jō kept a detailed diary that again and again provides a very human view of Hirohito. For example, he suggests that Hirohito had an insatiable appetite for Japanese and German newsreels. (Even after Japan had lost air and sea control in the Pacific, Japanese cameramen at the fronts often managed to supply fresh footage.)[27] Jō describes Hirohito relaxing, celebrating, and performing various public duties. On February 18, 1942, the emperor conducted the first celebration of Pacific war victories by appearing for ten minutes on his white horse on Nijūbashi, the famous bridge leading into the palace, where he waved to crowds assembled on the Imperial Plaza. On the evening of February 20, he spent nearly two hours relaxing in the aide-de-camp's duty office.[28]

Watching movies, playing cards and chess with his military aides, or lecturing to them on his entomological collections were Hirohito's regular evening activities throughout the war. For example, on May 20, 1942, Jō wrote that in the evening:

> when the emperor joined us in our duty office, the subject changed
> from insects in general to special ladybugs called *tamamushi zushi*. He
> had a chamberlain bring his illustrated book of insects from his study

and began explaining them to us. Later, after dinner, he summoned a chamberlain to bring his box containing three rare ladybugs that he had collected in the palace (one of them was black.) He let Mitsui and me study them. I am deeply touched.[29]

These were the days of champagne victories, and in the daytime Hirohito often went horseback riding, worked in his laboratory, or attended palace lectures whenever his official duties permitted. On February 24, Jō noted that the emperor viewed a newsreel; the next day he "enjoyed [cross-country] skiing in the inner garden" of the palace.[30]

On February 26 and 28, the naval vice chief of staff briefed Hirohito on the war situation and the role of the "special submarine attack force." The vice chief also showed him "pictures related to the special attack force as well as writings [by the suicide volunteers] prior to their departure. After examining these photographs and writings, the emperor seemed very pleased."[31] The notion of "body smashing" (*taiatari*), or riding a device intended solely to crash into and destroy an enemy, was already well developed by this time, though it was still two years away from being applied to warplanes.

On March 9, 1942, while the army and navy were advancing in the islands of the Central and South Pacific, Privy Seal Kido noted in his diary that the emperor:

> was in a more pleasant mood than usual and smilingly said to me, "We are winning too quickly." The enemy at Bandung on the Java front, he continued, had announced surrender on the seventh, and we are about to force total collapse in the entire Dutch Indies. The enemy forces at Surabaya have also surrendered. Rangoon on the Burma front has fallen. The emperor was obviously delighted. I could only express congratulations.[32]

Two days later Hirohito's naval aide Jō departed Yokosuka on a six-week inspection tour of the Central and South Pacific theaters.

Jō's itinerary was a testament to the thinking of Japan's military leaders, who in their March "Assessment of the World Situation" (and again in July and November) estimated that the earliest the Americans would be able to launch their main counteroffensive would be the second half of 1943;[33] ergo, it was safe for Japan to continue its offensive below the equator. The enemy would not think it worth paying the price to reestablish the status quo over such vast distances.

Jō traveled first to Saipan in the Marianas Islands, then to Truk in the Carolines, and from there to Rabaul on New Britain Island in the Bismarck Archipelago, where the navy was establishing a major base that could be used to support advances further to the southwest. From there, he went to Kwajalein atoll in the Marshall Islands, then to Wake, Guam, Palau (now Belau), Peleliu, and the new Japanese seaplane base at Davao, on Mindanao in the southern part of the Philippine Archipelago. He continued his tour by visiting the Dutch East Indies. His return trip took him to Subic Bay and Manila in the Philippines, and finally home by plane to Yokohama (stopping en route at Saipan) on April 23. During his long journey Jō sketched pictures of tropical flowers and collected seashells and American films for the emperor's viewing, including Walt Disney cartoon films found on Guam.[34] Jō's diary conveys no sense of how radically overextended Japan's lines of transportation and communication had become. Indeed, he seemed completely unaware of the enormous and insoluble logistical problem that maintenance of such a far-flung system of bases implied for a nation whose war power was so inferior to that of its enemies.

III

While Imperial Headquarters was still reeling from Midway, Nazi Germany came to the rescue in the form of the Wehrmacht's summer offensive against Russian armies in the Soviet Union and General Rommel's successes against the British in North Africa. As if in compensation for the shock of Midway, Hirohito and the officers of the high command seem once again to have invested Germany with much greater military and industrial power than it actually possessed.[35] On June 26, 1942, Hirohito asked Kido: "Not only has the German army captured Tobruk in North Africa, it is continuing its advance into Egypt and has occupied Salûm and Sidi Barrani. Should we send the Führer a special imperial message congratulating him on his victories?"[36] Kido dissuaded him because the Führer had never congratulated the emperor. Nevertheless, Hirohito and the high command had concluded it might be possible to contribute to an eventual German offensive coming from the Middle East by launching an attack on Ceylon (now Sri Lanka), in the Indian Ocean.

On July 11 Hirohito sanctioned Nagano's request to abandon the operation to capture strategic points in Fiji and Samoa, which Imperial Headquarters had decided—and he had approved—on May 18. During his briefing of the emperor, Nagano suggested a campaign to destroy enemy ships and communications in the Indian Ocean. Such an operation would "cut communications between the United States and Australia, prevent Australia from being used as a U.S. base to launch attacks against Japan . . . and make our defenses impregnable."[37]

Meanwhile, five thousand sea miles from Tokyo, at Combined Fleet headquarters in Rabaul, plans were going forward to send construction troops and laborers to build an airstrip and naval facilities on Guadalcanal. As that work was nearing completion, on August 6 (two months after Midway) Sugiyama came to the palace to brief the emperor on the progress of the New Guinea campaign. The emperor used the occasion to make a disconcerting query: "I am not so sure the navy air [force] can count on effective enough army support in the landing operations in New Guinea. Don't we need to send in the army air too?"[38] It was just the sort of question that Hirohito, who knew the navy's total losses in skilled pilots, would ask. Sugiyama replied that the army was not considering doing so. He might have added (though he apparently did not) that Imperial Headquarters Army Department was actually withdrawing army air force groups from the south (mainly Rabaul) in order to begin the offensive against Chungking, which the emperor had urged in May. Sending army fighter pilots to the distant New Guinea and Solomons area was certainly not something the army cared to do.

The very next day, August 7, American forces under Admiral Nimitz and General MacArthur, the commander in charge of the Southwest Pacific Area, began their first, limited offensive thrusts against exposed Japanese positions in the south. Nineteen thousand U.S. Marines, divided into two groups, landed on the hot, wet, disease-ridden islands of Tulagi and neighboring Guadalcanal—ten degrees below the equator in the southern part of the Solomon chain. Two days later a nighttime naval battle took place off Savo Island, near Guadalcanal. Japanese shells and torpedoes sank four American heavy cruisers. The ensuing land and naval battles of Guadalcanal would continue for six full months, irrevocably crippling the Japanese navy air force and marking the first true turning point in the Pacific war.

From the outset the Imperial Navy's landing operation on Guadalcanal had been poorly planned, and the emperor had worried about it. Would the services be able to overcome their jealousies and cooperate in consolidating their newly won positions in the Solomons and in eastern New Guinea, where preparations were underway for launching a ground attack on Port Moresby?[39] When American naval, air, and ground forces attacked Guadalcanal, the high command in Tokyo was stunned. The chiefs of staff and the operations officers had assumed, correctly, that the major Anglo-American counteroffensive would not start until 1943. They were utterly unable to conceive that, in the interim, their enemy could execute with incredible speed the same sort of leap across the Pacific that they themselves had pulled off seven months earlier at Pearl Harbor.[40]

Army Chief of Staff Sugiyama agreed to the navy's request for an immediate deployment of troops to Guadalcanal to prevent an American buildup, but not perceiving the seriousness of the situation, he threw in only one small unit from Guam.[41] Most of this Ichiki Detachment (approximately fifteen hundred troops), was destroyed three days after landing on the island. In early September the army threw in a second small unit—the Kawaguchi Brigade (approximately three thousand soldiers)—from Palau, which attacked American positions on the night of September 13 and was also largely decimated. Later, early in October, the Seventeenth Army in the South Pacific decided to land its Second Division— some twenty thousand elite infantry troops—on Guadalcanal. Joining the starving survivors of earlier units, they soon launched two more suicidal attacks on American positions in the jungle; once again the outcome was failure. Thereafter the army landed more reinforcements, including parts of the Thirty-eighth Division.

Hirohito's reaction to the various land, naval, and air battles associated with Japan's loss of Guadalcanal is telling. When informed of the American landing, he immediately recognized the potential danger—"I wonder if this is not the start of the American-British counteroffensive?"[42]—but felt that Japan had to maintain its winning momentum while steadily building up its reserves of vital oil, rubber, and other resources. Despite his doubts about becoming locked in to a particular island battle, he continually encouraged his commanders in the Solomons to stay on the offensive and strike hard with all the weapons and men they could muster. Sugiyama had told the emperor on September 15, after the Ichiki Detachment had been effectively destroyed, that "I am sure it [Guadalcanal] can be held." Hirohito sought to hold him and Nagano to their word by disclosing his doubts about whether the army and navy really had the will to do the job. His pressure on them strengthened their resolve to retake and secure the island, and thus contributed to the very thing he feared most: getting trapped in a war of attrition.

For Hirohito and Prime Minister Tōjō the first month of the Battle of Guadalcanal was also a time of political crisis. For months the army had been planning to establish a new Greater East Asia Ministry that would have jurisdiction over all Japanese-occupied territory in the southeast and China, with the exception of Taiwan, Korea, and Sakhalin. Foreign Minister Tōgō disagreed with the plan and refused to compromise on ceding further political authority to the army. Moreover, Tōgō had learned about the navy's defeat at Midway and the battles on Guadalcanal, and may have secretly wanted to shake up the cabinet for failing to increase war power sufficiently.[43] When, on August 29, 1942, Tōjō's secretary informed Tōgō about the army's plan to establish the Greater East Asia Ministry at the next cabinet meeting, Tōgō was firmly negative. Thereupon Tōjō went to the palace and explained the situation to the emperor. Hirohito immediately decided to block any effort by Tōgō to topple the cabinet. As far as Tōjō was concerned, that settled the matter.

Armed with Hirohito's strong support, Tōjō brought the issue to a head during the September 1 cabinet meeting, at which time Tōgō threatened to resign. During the recess of the meeting, while Tōgō returned to the Foreign Ministry, Hirohito sent Navy Minister Shimada Shigetarō to act as a mediator. Tōgō now proposed a compromise plan, but Tōjō high-handedly refused to consider it, whereupon Tōgō quit and Hirohito immediately accepted his resignation. The next day he allowed Tōjō (temporarily) to assume the portfolio of foreign minister. Determined not to let the cabinet fall while Americans were taking the offensive in the Solomons, Hirohito stood solidly behind Tōjō. Under Hirohito's strong auspices, Tōjō was on the way to consolidating his "dictatorship."[44]

Throughout the fall of 1942, while Hirohito was discussing with the high command, and privately with Kido, the chain of battles in the Solomons, the toll in Japanese fighter planes, warships, transports, and casualties mounted steadily. Though the troops on Guadalcanal were dying of untreated tropical sickness, fever, and starvation, Hirohito kept demanding greater efforts from them. Only toward the very end of 1942 did he finally abandon hope of eliminating the American presence on Guadalcanal. His tenacity and offensive spirit influenced the high command and perhaps inspired the sick, malnourished defenders in the Solomons, who fought bravely to the very end. At the same time, and more important, his unyielding determination to hold Guadalcanal, combined with the navy's rigid notion of victory through a decisive sea battle, contributed to Japan's long delay in shifting to a defensive posture in the Pacific.

Hirohito intervened a second time on the Guadalcanal front after the Imperial Army launched another unsuccessful offensive there on October 23–24. This was followed a few days later by a second major sea battle in which the Imperial Navy engaged the American fleet, sinking the aircraft carrier *Hornet* and a destroyer.[45] According to the diary of Vice Admiral and Chief of Staff of the Combined Fleet Ugaki Matome, on October 29 Hirohito issued an imperial rescript addressed to Combined Fleet Commander Yamamoto Isoroku. The rescript stated: "We are deeply pleased that this time in the South Pacific the Combined Fleet has inflicted great damage on the enemy fleet." Hirohito added an extra line: "However, we believe the war situation is critical. Officers and men, exert yourselves to even greater efforts."[46]

Ugaki went on to write that a separate radio message came to him later that evening saying that after the emperor had handed Nagano the rescript intended for Admiral Yamamoto, his majesty had cautioned him: "What I want to tell you now concerns the latter part of my rescript. Guadalcanal is the focal point of the war and an important base for the navy. So don't rest on small achievements. Move quickly and recapture it."[47] When the emperor's rescript and verbal warning to Nagano were radioed to the Combined Fleet Headquarters on Rabaul, Ugaki immediately replied, "We are dismayed by the concern our failures on Guadalcanal have caused the emperor. Only the quickest possible achievement of our goals can excuse us before his majesty."[48] The navy was not only unable to improve on its "small achievements," but within two weeks it lost the battleships *Hiei* and *Kirishima* to a radar-equipped American battle group in the third great engagement in the Solomons.

Throughout the bitterly fought ground and sea battles for Guadalcanal, the emperor put constant psychological pressure on his naval commanders to recapture the island, and on three different occasions—September 15, November 5, and November 11—he pressed the army high command to throw in more troops and planes to assist the hard-pressed navy.[49] At first Sugiyama was reluctant— partly because army pilots were inexperienced in transoceanic combat but also because he planned to reinforce the North China Area Army and employ it, supported by the army air force, in a major offensive to reach Chungking.[50] However, the emperor's persistence forced his senior generals to relent. After his second request for army air force participation on the Solomons front, Sugiyama reported to him the next day that the army had decided to deploy its air power to New Guinea and Rabaul. This change in an ongoing operation had been opposed by both upper- and middle-echelon officers. Hirohito, nevertheless, forced the change.[51]

When Sugiyama reported on September 15 that "not much can be expected from the landing" of a second detachment of troops on Guadalcanal, the emperor not only pressed him to order the army air force into the battle but jumped far ahead by asking when it might be possible to occupy Rabi, the easternmost corner of New Guinea. Even while worried about Guadalcanal, Hirohito was already projecting a fresh offensive in New Guinea.[52]

In conveying his feelings to the fighting forces throughout the fall of 1942, Hirohito pointedly praised the navy for its successes in the sea battles of the Southwest Pacific, thereby making it extremely difficult for the navy to call a halt to the Guadalcanal campaign. Hirohito kept the same pressure on the army, telling the troops in one rescript, "try to live up to my trust in you," implying that the troops were not yet meeting his expectations.[53] Nevertheless, by November 1942, it had become clear to the emperor and Tōjō that the recapture of Guadalcanal was impossible, and that its abandonment would not necessarily unravel the whole Solomons front. Indeed, it might facilitate operations at other strategic points.

Hirohito's worries about the Solomons campaigns and the war situation in Europe, which was also worsening for the Axis, caused the army, around this time, to cancel its preparations for Operation Gogō. Yet at Eighth Area Army headquarters in Rabaul, where distrust of the navy was strong, most senior staff officers were too full of pride to admit openly the need to withdraw from Guadalcanal, let alone reorganize the entire army so that it might profit from its defeats.

The continuing drain on men and matériel, which led to the decision to withdraw from Guadalcanal, opened a new phase of sharp discord between the services over the allocation of ships and scarce raw materials. Japan's losses in naval warships were roughly equivalent to those sustained by the Americans. However, in just two months of fighting around Guadalcanal—October and November 1942—the Imperial Navy lost fifty-nine merchant ships, amounting to 324,000 tons, as compared to thirteen to fifteen, or 61,000 tons, lost monthly between the start of the war on December 8, 1941, and the end of September 1942. Most of the sunken vessels were transports loaded with troops, weapons, and supplies. As a result, conflict arose between the Army Ministry and the General Staff over whether to use as troopships and weapons carriers those transports that had been specially designated to move raw materials from Southeast Asia.[54]

Apart from its losses in naval and merchant ships, the Japanese navy lost 892 planes and 1,882 pilots during the six-month-long Guadalcanal battles from August 1942 to the final withdrawal in early February 1943. Yamada notes that this was "two and a half times the number of planes and fifteen times the number of pilots lost at Midway."[55]

Despairing over these enormous losses in a battle of attrition he had wanted to avoid but had actually helped to bring about, Hiro- hito made a special two-day trip to worship at Ise Shrine on Decem- ber 12, 1942.[56] On December 28 he told his chief aide, General Hasunuma, that he remained dissatisfied with the plans of the chiefs of staff, who had just made a formal report summarizing the war sit- uation for 1942. They had promised to submit their plans for with- drawal from Guadalcanal, complained the emperor, but "[w]hat I want to know is how they propose to force the enemy to submit. The situation is very grave indeed. I believe we should now convene an imperial conference in my presence, and it makes no difference whether we hold it at the end of this year or the start of next. I am ready to participate at any time."[57]

The Imperial Headquarters Conference was held on December 31, 1942. The chiefs of staff reported they would cancel the attempt to recapture Guadalcanal, and the withdrawal of troops would begin at the end of January. Hirohito sanctioned that decision but insisted, "It is unacceptable to just give up on capturing Guadal- canal. We must launch an offensive elsewhere." Sugiyama promised to "take the offensive in the New Guinea area and restore the morale of the troops."[58] By placing their hopes on a new offensive in New Guinea, Hirohito and the General Staff delayed once again Japan's strategic shift to the defensive in the Pacific.[59]

On New Year's Day 1943 the new head of the First Department, Maj. Gen. Ayabe Tachiki, flew to Rabaul to transmit the emperor's Guadalcanal withdrawal order.[60] At Hirohito's insistence the high command now planned to secure strategic points in the Solomons north of New Georgia and Santa Isabel, and north of the Stanley

Mountains, which run like a spine down the length of New Guinea. The focus of battle would shift to New Guinea. The navy would defend New Georgia, Santa Isabel, and some other small islands in the central Solomons; the army was to defend in the northern Solomons area, including the islands of Buka, Bougainville, and Shortland.[61] Tōjō, in his combined role as army minister and prime minister, had had to apply enormous pressure on the high command to bring about this change. Accepting, if not satisfied by, his commanders' promises, Hirohito now authorized withdrawal of the Japanese survivors from Guadalcanal (more than eleven thousand mostly broken men from a force that at its peak had numbered approximately thirty thousand). He thereafter closely attended the progress of the difficult evacuation, which the navy completed on February 7, 1943.[62]

IV

The United States had ended the overstretched Japanese offensive in the Pacific by taking Guadalcanal. The war was now entering the phase of protraction and defense. Imperial Headquarters nevertheless still delayed any major contraction of its Pacific defense lines. American, Australian, and New Zealand forces confronted reinforced Japanese troops in jungle fighting at Lae, Salamaua, and Finschhafen in New Guinea, pushing the Japanese back on the defensive before they had time to consolidate their gains. Hirohito and his chiefs of staff studied their maps and decided to strengthen their remaining strategic positions in New Guinea and the Solomons. The Army General Staff in Tokyo was aware of the treacherous terrain and climate the troops had to operate in, as well as their deficiencies in transport, air power, provisions, artillery, and ammunition. So too, in a distant, more abstract way, was Hirohito. Yet on January 26, 1943, he opposed any retreat from the Munda airfield on New Georgia (some 180 miles from Guadalcanal) since that would mark a movement back from the line of defense agreed to only three weeks earlier. Admiral Nagano, chief of the Navy General Staff, reaffirmed the navy's intention to hold at Munda, though he had earlier hinted to the emperor that Munda, under American naval bombardment since early January 1943, could well be abandoned.[63]

A few weeks later, in mid-February, Hirohito put pressure on Nagano for air attacks and a naval bombardment of Guadalcanal from bases on Munda and Koronbangara. "There is no sign of any attacks. Why aren't you carrying them out?" he asked.[64] Imperial Headquarters soon drafted concrete plans for prolonged defense in the central and northern Solomons. American forces landed on New Georgia in early June, and an estimated ten thousand Japanese defenders, heeding their emperor, managed to hold out for nearly three months.[65] Thereafter Bougainville remained the last major island in Japanese hands.

As the situation along Japan's entire defense perimeter in the central and northern Solomons deteriorated steadily, the emperor continued to demand that the navy fight decisive battles, regain the initiative, and provide supplies to the various island garrisons so that they would not be left totally isolated. During a briefing on March 3, at which he was informed that the navy's attempt to reinforce at Lae had failed, he remarked, "Then why didn't you change plans immediately and land at Madan? This is a failure, but it can teach us a good lesson and become a source of future success. Do this for me so I can have peace of mind for awhile."[66] "Do this for me" had become the signature message of the fighting generalissimo.

The failure of the navy to fully commit in the sea battles of Guadalcanal, and especially the heavy air losses throughout the Solomons, troubled Hirohito. On March 30, 1943, Kido noted in his diary a morning audience in which "[t]he emperor talked to me for an unusually long time about the prospects for the war, the future, and other matters."[67] What they discussed were the navy's losses since the defeat at Midway, and the emperor's fear that if such losses continued, the navy would lose control of the sea-lanes, making it impossible to sustain the far-flung outer defense perimeter.[68]

Gradually, the emperor's changed attitude toward the navy became clear. The easy victories were months ago, the current picture one loss and defeat after another. When the 2,500-man garrison on Attu Island in the Aleutians was destroyed on May 29, he dressed down Sugiyama and Nagano, telling them at their separate briefings on the Aleutian front that they should have foreseen what was coming—instead, "after the enemy landed on May 12" they took "a week to devise countermeasures." Lack of foresight, derived from misjudgement and overconfidence, irritated the emperor. "They're making excuses about how heavy the fog was," he told General Hasunuma, but:

> [F]og should have been anticipated. They should have known better to start with. I wonder if the army and navy have been holding frank discussions on this matter. Maybe this [defeat] is the result of one service making energetic demands and the other guaranteeing them irresponsibly. What they agree to between them they absolutely must implement. No matter how good an agreement between the army and navy may be, if it isn't carried out, that's worse than no promise at all. (The emperor has been complaining about this ever since Guadalcanal.)[69]

And again Hirohito fumed for a decisive naval victory:

> The way we're waging war now raises the enemy's morale just as on Guadalcanal. We're making neutral and third countries feel very uneasy; we're causing China to puff [its chest] up; and we are undermining all the countries of the Greater East Asia Coprosperity Sphere. Isn't there some way, some place, where we can win a real victory over the Americans?[70]

To appreciate the significance of Hirohito's disillusionment with his navy, it should be remembered that from early in the 1930s, he had positioned himself as a relative centrist within the Japanese political milieu. The "liberals" and "moderates" whom he had favored—Prime Ministers (and retired admirals) Saitō Makoto and Okada Keisuke and later Yonai Mitsumasa and Suzuki Kantarō—were, in fact, hard-line imperialists. By endorsing them, he had placed himself firmly in support of territorial aggrandizement and aggression in China. Later the leaders of the navy became more passionate than their army counterparts about expanding the fighting in China. Their changed posture influenced his attitude. Now, in the latter half of 1943, though the navy was still quite powerful despite its heavy losses, the army was in the process of taking over the main defensive role along the Pacific perimeter, and Hirohito's confidence in his admirals had waned.

As the withdrawal through the Solomons proceeded, Hirohito gave that operation close attention but also followed far-off events in Europe and North Africa, where German and Italian forces had also been thrown on the defensive. His first premonition that Germany might lose came when the Allies landed in Sicily on July 10, 1943, and then, several weeks later, on the Italian mainland. Mussolini became the first Axis leader to fall, and be carted off to jail. On September 8 the Italian king, Victor Emmanuel III, and the government of Gen. Pietro Badoglio fled from Rome to the south and surrendered unconditionally to the Allies. German armed forces moved into Rome. Overnight the Axis became bipartite, and the Italian armed forces were transformed from allies to the enemy—in theory at least.

Hirohito had, of course, visited Italy at the age of twenty. But more than twenty years had passed since that European tour, and his initial reaction to Italy's surrender was mostly concern about the Rumanian oil fields which fueled Germany's war economy. Would they now come under Allied air attack from bases in southern Italy?

Hirohito's uneasiness about Hitler's Rumanian oil was probably also a geographically displaced concern about Japan's own newly won oil resources in the Dutch Indies.[71]

As the Japanese Pacific defense perimeter slowly contracted, space was traded for time; but traded also were lost warships, transports, and decimated air squadrons with their irreplaceable veteran pilots. This trade-off could not be sustained much longer. In August 1943 the American advance through the Solomons accelerated, bypassing many islands and leaving their garrisons stranded and helpless. On the fifth, Hirohito was informed by General Sugiyama that everything in the Solomons and Bismarck Sea area was in peril. The emperor, always looking for opportunities to attack, attack, attack, responded: "Isn't there someplace where we can strike the United States? . . . When and where on earth are you [people] ever going to put up a good fight? And when are you ever going to fight a decisive battle?" Sugiyama apologized for the way the situation had turned out. Hirohito responded angrily, "Well, this time, after suffering all these defeats, why don't you study how *not* to let the Americans keep saying 'We won! We won!'[emphasis added]"[72]

Hirohito no longer hid his dissatisfaction with Admiral Nagano either. On August 24 he berated the navy chief of staff for the navy's cowardly performance in the sea battle off Bela Bela Island: "[Admiral,] the other day when the army dispatched a large unit, I heard that four of your destroyers guarding the troopships fled."[73] Hirohito's complaints were becoming increasingly specific and acerbic, as in this exchange with General Sugiyama on September 11:

> *Emperor*: I understand you're committing most of the seventeenth Division to Rabaul. Just how do you intend to keep them supplied? I'm not going to tolerate another, "Our men fought bravely, then died of starvation." I agree with the Meiji emperor, who held that when gentlemen are fighting a war, they must support one another. What

sort of agreement have you worked out with the navy? Just what do you people have in mind?

Sugiyama: First supplies, second secure enough shipping to move those supplies. Rabaul is vital to the navy and they have asked us to hold it somehow. If we lose Rabaul, we will lose all mobility [in that area]. They tell us they will make every effort to find supplies and transports. I thought we can somehow manage it because they have this intention, and so we reached agreement.

Emperor: You say you're sending troops to Rabaul. When and what will you be sending to western New Guinea? Unless you move something there, the military preparation is going to be weak.

Sugiyama: We'll send in backup units and work them hard. Build airfields and roads, then afterward deploy combat units.

Emperor: Are you going to send [troops] to Truk?

Sugiyama: Yes, the lead units of the Fifty-second Division.

Emperor: The enemy side has considerable power to counterattack. How are our defenses at Andaman, Nicobar, and Sumatra?

Sugiyama: Well, at Andaman and Nicobar we're still in the planning process, and we need to move as quickly as we can there. At Palenbang [in Sumatra] we have also taken [preliminary] measures to handle our defenses.[74]

Hirohito and Prime Minister General Tōjō had reviewed the entire war thus far and were now thinking of pulling the army out of Rabaul altogether, a move the navy high command strongly opposed for fear it would shut down the entire support setup in the South Pacific. But the emperor and Tōjō were determined to get Japan back on track strategically. They had reexamined their guidance of the war and agreed on the need to contract all Pacific fronts while at the same time launching a new offensive in the eastern part of New Guinea. The new "absolute defense line" would be established well behind the line of contact with the enemy; there, at strategically selected points in rear areas, the army and navy and their air forces would reorganize, rebuild, concentrate, and prepare to defend aggressively with immediate counterattacks.

On September 15 Nagano and Sugiyama made formal written reports to Hirohito that set forth a conflict between their interpretations of the "absolute defense perimeter" concept. While taking note of the need to strengthen defensive positions in the "rear" around the Caroline Islands, Nagano emphasized that the navy had to go on seeking opportunities in certain areas of the Pacific where the war situation had become "somewhat disadvantageous"—that is, near disasters. Those certain areas for a great naval victory happened to lie some twelve hundred miles outside the "absolute defense line." The navy, in short, still intended to fight the decisive battle in the Marshall and Gilbert Islands areas. Its concept of the rear line simply meant a foothold where war power would be accumulated, and from which the navy would launch attacks far forward at the line of contact.[75] General Sugiyama, on the other hand, stressed an energetic defense of "the presently occupied areas" to gain time in building stronger rear-area defenses—that is, the "absolute line" where supplies and troops would make ready for quick-reaction counterattacks or offensive thrusts—as the emperor had ordered.[76]

How Hirohito adjudicated this army-navy high command discrepancy is unclear. There is no record that he intervened forcefully to unify the services in their application of the "absolute defense perimeter" concept. It seems more likely that Hirohito tacitly approved the navy's continued offensive-mindedness, while not rejecting the army's insistence on contraction of the front lines. Two-track positions were entirely in keeping with his character. Over the next two weeks the liaison conference met on numerous occasions to discuss the shift toward the defense. Finally, on September 30, 1943, a conference of the Imperial Headquarters was convened in Hirohito's presence.

While the emperor sat silently listening, Privy Council President Hara put questions on his behalf to Tōjō, Sugiyama, Nagano, the president of the Planning Bureau, and the minister of commerce and industry. Hara's questions revealed that although the government had planned "to produce 40,000 aircraft" during 1944, the present annual output was, as Tōjō nonchalantly admitted, only "17,000 to 18,000 planes." When Hara asked Nagano if he was "confident of securing the absolute defense perimeter" with 40,000 aircraft, the navy chief of staff "stiffened the mood of the conference" by replying, "I cannot assure the future of the war situation." Tōjō came to his rescue, saying, "As the imperial rescript stated, this war is essentially for our self defense and very self existence. So whether Germany wins or is beaten, we have to fight on to the end regardless of how the war situation may develop hereafter. Nothing has changed in our resolve to fight until we achieve our aims."[77]

A curious exchange followed that showed how, though the huge disparity in national industrial power between Japan and the United States was already painfully manifest at the fronts, the high command had set aside rational calculations and had begun to rely on spiritualism:

> *Sugiyama*: We need 55,000 aircraft to meet operational requirements. But we cannot meet those demands even if we risk all of our national resources. So, we shall try to achieve our goal by compensating for deficiencies through the use of mobile task forces [*kidōryoku*].
> *Hara*: We are not gods. Therefore we cannot avoid mistakes. But now I am relieved. Both of you [high commanders] seem to be on solid ground.[78]

At the conclusion of the conference, both chiefs of staff agreed, at least on paper, to prevent further depletion of men and matériel by establishing the "absolute defense perimeter," and to rebuild, regroup, and redeploy to meet the coming Allied general offensive.[79]

The policy document adopted that day stated:

> ... we shall establish a strategic posture to cope with the American-
> British offensive, making mid–1944 our approximate target for full
> readiness. Whenever the occasion presents, we shall capture and
> destroy the enemy's offensive forces. To carry out the Empire's war,
> the strategic area in the Pacific and Indian Oceans that must abso-
> lutely be secured is a perimeter that includes the Kurile Islands, Oga-
> sawara, the inner South Pacific (the central and western parts), the
> western part of New Guinea, the Sunda Strait, and Burma.[80]

Within this "perimeter" lay the Japanese home islands, the
Kuriles, the Bonin (Ogasawara) Islands, Iwo Jima, the Marianas, the
Philippines, the Netherlands East Indies, and Andaman and Nicobar Islands in the Indian Ocean. Beyond it lay Rabaul, the central
Solomons, the eastern part of New Guinea, the Marshall Islands,
and Makin and Tarawa in the Gilbert Islands.[81] More than 140,000
troops of the Eighth Area Army, mostly on Rabaul, as well as the
troops in eastern New Guinea, would no longer be supported but be
left to fend for themselves.

During the last three months of 1943 and the first half of 1944,
Imperial Headquarters repeatedly drew down units on the continent in order to establish and hold the "absolute defense line."
Entire divisions and parts of divisions from China, the Kwantung
Army, and the Korean Army were rushed to the Central Pacific to
defend strategic bases and airfields on remote and ultimately
doomed islands. But American offensives always developed at a pace
that outstripped the ability of the Imperial Army and Navy to consolidate and respond effectively. Unable to read Allied radio messages (as the British and Americans could read theirs), the high
command was never sure where to concentrate to meet Allied
thrusts.

Despite the mounting losses Hirohito remained as undismayed, rigidly self-disciplined, and aggressive as ever. When naval aide Jō reported to him on September 21, 1943, that "enemy transports have concentrated in the northeastern part of New Guinea and our defenses are on full alert," Hirohito (aware from briefing materials that the Americans were headed for Finschhaven) replied, "Being ready to defend isn't enough. We have to do the attacking."[82]

By November 1, 1943, Bougainville was the last major Solomon island in Japanese hands, and its airfields were under American attack.[83] When, eight days later, Nagano reported good results in the second air battle off Bougainville, the emperor, according to the diary of naval aide Jō, "seemed satisfied and joined toasts with his aides-de-camp in their duty office."[84] An earlier report to the throne from Nagano concerning the first air battle off of Bougainville, on November 5, 1943, had greatly exaggerated the results, claiming that the American aircraft carriers "Independence" and "Bunker Hill" had been sunk when, in fact, only one torpedo boat was destroyed. Although no attempt had been made to deceive the emperor—Nagano and the Imperial Headquarters itself had believed the first front-line data—the incident pointed to the increasing difficulty Hirohito faced in obtaining accurate war reports from the Solomons.[85]

In late December, following its loss of control of the Vitiaz and Dampier Straits—the body of water between the island of New Britain and the north coast of New Guinea—the Japanese navy withdrew from the Solomons. The overall outlook for the army's position in New Guinea dimmed further when American and Australian forces under Gen. Robert Eichelberger, MacArthur's newly appointed field commander, captured Buna on January 2, 1944, and then continued to advance slowly, over several months, on the west along the New Guinea coast, and on the east through the central and northern Solomons. Approximately 50,000 Japanese troops of the Second Army in western New Guinea, and another 55,000 of the Eighteenth Army in the eastern part of the large tropical island, were isolated or bypassed, and went down to defeat, though not before killing or wounding some 11,300 Americans.[86] Meanwhile Rabaul had been encircled, and more than 130,000 troops had been left isolated there and on other islands in the Solomons.

American carrier task forces and marine assault troops had also moved into the Central Pacific and in bitter frontal attacks destroyed the Japanese garrisons on Tarawa and Makin in the Gilbert Islands. On February 18, 1944, American planes destroyed the main naval anchorage of the Combined Fleet on Truk Island, forcing the navy to evacuate it, leaving behind many of its tankers and eroding its future ability to maneuver. The dream of fighting one great decisive battle in the Central Pacific was finally over. Imperial Headquarters could do little but watch as the defense line on which they had placed their hopes was driven back to the Marianas. Two entirely separate drives were unfolding against them—one through the Southwest Pacific, the other through the Central Pacific—and there was not much they could do to stop either from accelerating.

In this situation Tōjō secured Hirohito's consent to a drastic shake-up of the command structure. On February 21, 1944, he took the unprecedented action of forcing army Chief of Staff General Sugiyama to resign so that he (Tōjō) could assume that position while also serving as army minister and prime minister. At the same time Navy Minister Adm. Shimada Shigetarō pressured Chief of Staff Admiral Nagano to resign so he himself could assume that post. Although the majority on both general staffs were opposed, Tōjō once again had the emperor's strong prior backing. When Sugiyama conveyed his worries about the changes directly to the emperor, Hirohito simply told him to cooperate.[87] That ended dissent. When he felt the need, Hirohito was willing to set aside one of the most hallowed Meiji-era military traditions—the division of power between military command and administration.

Behind Tōjō's effort to unify the operational and administrative structures of the services (and, indirectly, government affairs and military command) lay the Allied advance creeping ever nearer to the Japanese home islands, and growing distrust within ruling circles of the high command's handling of the war. The military peril was intensifying disputes over strategy—were the Marianas even defensible?—and over the allocation of scarce materials for the production of airplanes and ships. These disputes within the high command tended to delay production. Another supreme commander, less inhibited and worried about his own image, might have intervened forcefully and adjudicated these matters, but there is no indication that Hirohito did more than entrust their handling to his favorite prime minister, Tōjō. And as Tōjō briefed him on every slightest move he took or even contemplated taking, Tōjō could do no wrong in his eyes. In the end Tōjō's tinkering with the leadership structure and his assumption of three posts merely added to his enemies and hastened his ouster.[88]

Wartime diplomacy, which at this time chiefly meant relations with Nanking and the manipulation of Nanking's ties with Chungking, also engaged the emperor's attention, as did military operations on the Burma front. Starting in late 1943 and continuing into early 1944, Hirohito and Tōjō personally encouraged a new approach to China that they hoped would enable the armed forces to reduce their presence in China and thereby better sustain the attrition in the Pacific.[89] This changed policy had been discussed at liaison conference meetings for over a year but its implementation had been delayed because of widespread resistance on the part of the ruling elites to surrendering Japanese "rights and interests" in China.[90]

Finally, on January 9, 1944, the Tōjō government and the Wang Ching-wei regime in Nanking issued a joint statement announcing to the world that Japan would abolish its treaty-port settlements and extraterritorial privileges in China. Under this new policy the army was ordered to treat as a sovereign equal the client regime of

"National China," which had just declared war on the United States and Britain, and to withdraw from overseeing Chinese administration in occupied areas. To facilitate the acknowledgment of Nanking's autonomy and the partial restoration of its sovereignty, Hirohito sent his youngest brother, Prince Mikasa, to Nanking as a member of the China Expeditionary Army's headquarters staff.[91] Mikasa's mission was to engage in discussions with staff officers and promote understanding of the new China policy. While pursuing this and other peace maneuvers in China, the Tōjō government also prepared to implement Operation Ichigō to destroy American air bases in China, from which B-29s were operating. The "Ichigō" offensive unfolded successfully from April to October 1944.

Hirohito did not personally embrace the principle of national self-determination, a major issue of wartime diplomacy for the Allied powers. Nor did he ever call for a reexamination of Japan's relationship with colonial Korea and Taiwan. Like Foreign Minister Tōgō and his successor, Shigemitsu Mamoru, Hirohito thought in terms of the notion of "place," meaning each racial entity in its proper place within the Japanese-led, multitiered "coprosperity sphere," with the special privileges of Japan guaranteed by treaty. As the war worsened, however, he bowed to the exigencies of the situation and once again showed political initiative. Hirohito began discussing with Tōjō how to take advantage of the opportunities created by the "Ichigō" offensive. They decided to alter their policy toward Yenan, in effect granting tacit recognition to Mao Tse-tung's Communist regime in Yenan in order to use the communists against Chungking—while by the same action also appeasing the Soviet Union.[92]

Southeast Asia attracted the emperor's attention as well. On January 7, 1944, he sanctioned an offensive from Burma into Assam Province, India. The aim was to preempt an Allied drive to recover Burma and possibly bring about an uprising of Indian nationalists against British rule. Although no documents indicate that Hirohito himself actively promoted this particular offensive, it was just the sort of operation he had pushed for all through the war—aggressive and short-sighted. The Imphal campaign, justified partly to defend Burma and partly to restore troop morale, began on March 8 and bogged down in early April. Tōjō and Sugiyama, who had been dubious about the operation from the start, dispatched observers to the scene and kept the emperor abreast of the deteriorating situation.[93] Finally, on July 5, Hirohito accepted Tōjō's recommendation and ordered the disastrous Impal campaign halted. By then, approximately 72,000 Japanese troops had been killed or wounded.[94]

V

Despite the cumulative impact of one major defeat after another, the determination of Hirohito and the high command remained undaunted. When a huge American armada closed on Saipan in mid-June to begin the conquest of the main Japanese bases in the Marianas, the Combined Fleet threw in a restored strike force of nine carriers and more than 460 aircraft to oppose the landings.[95] The ensuing naval, air, and land battles of the Marianas, fought between June and August 1944, were the decisive battles of the war for the Japanese navy and its air force. Three Japanese aircraft carriers were sunk and 395 planes shot down, without inflicting any serious damage on the American invasion force.[96] After desperate fighting, in which Japanese ground commanders once again failed to prepare adequate defenses in depth, Saipan, Guam, and Tinian fell and quickly became forward U.S. bases for long-range B-29 ("Superfortress") bombers. The capture of Saipan on July 7, 1944, was a particularly heavy blow for the high command. Resistance was bitter, and when it ended, after three weeks, Japan had lost virtually the entire garrison of 23,811 as well as ten thousand noncombatants.[97] It had also lost control of the air and the seas everywhere in the Pacific.

Saipan and the remaining Japanese bases in the Marianas were now in enemy hands. In Europe the Allies had landed in Normandy and were fighting eastward and northward, while the Soviets were driving into Poland. Staff planners in Imperial Headquarters now had to anticipate that Germany would soon be defeated, and that enormous American military resources would presently be moving from Europe to the Pacific. The Philippines, Taiwan, Okinawa, and the Bonin Islands would be invaded. More important, the homeland itself was almost certain to become a battlefield, for Tokyo—1,272 miles away from Saipan—had at last come within range of B-29s.

Hirohito's reaction to this dismal state of affairs is of paramount importance in assessing the role he played in the war. Confronted with certain defeat, he dug in his heels and refused to accept it. "Rise to the challenge; make a tremendous effort; achieve a splendid victory like at the time of the Japan Sea naval battle [in the Russo-Japanese War]," he told Vice Chief of Staff Admiral Shimada in audience on June 17.[98] The next day he warned Tōjō: "If we ever lose Saipan, repeated air attacks on Tokyo will follow. No matter what it takes, we have to hold there."[99] Informed by his chiefs of staff on two successive days that the situation on Saipan had become hopeless, Hirohito ignored their advice and ordered Shimada to recapture it, whereupon the First Department of the Navy General Staff immediately poured all its energies into the problem. Working night and day, with a sense of "utter desperation," staff officers finally completed a draft plan on June 21.[100] Three days later, however, on June 24, after headquarters of the Combined Fleet had weighed in with its opposition, Tōjō and Shimada formally reported that the recapture plan must be cancelled; Saipan was gone for good.[101]

Still refusing to accept the loss of Saipan, Hirohito ordered his Chief Aide General Hasunuma to convene, in his presence, the Board of Field Marshals and Fleet Admirals so that he could consult them. The latter—two elderly princes, plus Nagano, Sugiyama,

Hasunuma, the chiefs of the general staff, and the heads of the operations departments—met in the palace on June 25. After they had presented their unified view that the previous reports of the chiefs of staff were appropriate, the recapture of Saipan was impossible, Hirohito told them to put that in writing and left the room.

In the ensuing discussion Tōjō announced to the conference that the army had designed "balloon bombs," and was planning to send thirty thousand aloft against the enemy in the autumn.[102] There is a strong possibility that Hirohito had received an informal briefing on the balloon-bomb weapon program sometime between December 1943 and January 1944, and thereafter had taken a keen interest in its progress.[103] At this bleak moment in the war, when Imperial Headquarters was about to turn to planning for future ground battles on the home islands, Hirohito may have drawn comfort from learning, in the report of the board, that army and navy preparations were well under way to retaliate for the anticipated B-29 bombing raids.

Reliance on such special reprisal weapons as wind-carried balloon bombs was an indication of Hirohito's growing anxiety. The loss of the Marianas had inaugurated not only a new stage in the war, but also a new political crisis in Tokyo, in which he himself was once again targeted for criticism by members of his own imperial family. Around this time in the diary of Hirohito's brother, Prince Takamatsu, there appear comments such as: The emperor doesn't realize the gravity of the situation; he cleaves rigidly to bureaucratic hierarchy and is liable to dismiss anyone who steps beyond his jurisdiction; he "flares up frequently."[104] Criticism from the member of the family who had long faulted Hirohito's performance as emperor was nothing new, of course. More important were criticisms arising within ruling circles, and directed against Tōjō, whose accumulation of power Hirohito alone had made possible.

Between the defeats in the Solomons early in 1943 and the fall of Saipan in July 1944, a small group of court officials and senior statesmen led by Konoe and aided by a navy group centered around Admiral Okada, had been working covertly to force Tōjō out of office. Knowing that Tōjō's power flowed from the supporting and far greater power of the emperor, these men never doubted that Hirohito could dismiss his prime minister whenever he decided to. Indeed, they regarded the emperor as the main obstacle in their path to peace.[105]

Personally disappointed with the state of the war, Hirohito finally decided to withdraw his support of Tōjō, opening the way for Tōjō's enemies to precipitate the collapse of the entire Tōjō cabinet on July 18, 1944.

Two days after Tōjō had resigned, Hirohito himself bestowed on his favorite general an unusually warm imperial rescript praising him for his "meritorious services and hard work" and telling him that, "Hereafter we expect you to live up to our trust and make even greater contributions to military affairs."[106] Although the rescript was not published, Tōjō's enemies within the government and in court circles knew of it and were put on notice as to the emperor's feelings toward the man many Japanese at that time feared as a virtual dictator.

Kido, the quintessential backstage man, who once was as great an admirer of Tōjō as the emperor, had played the key role in Tōjō's downfall. Yet during the tenure of Tōjō's successor, Gen. Koiso Kuniaki, Kido continued to support the prowar factions of the army and navy, as did the emperor. Tōjō's dismissal, in other words, did not reflect an intention on the part of either the emperor or Kido to end the war.

The emperor's view of the war became less sanguine after Tōjō's downfall. Nevertheless, knowing full well that B-29s would soon be bombing Tokyo, both he and Kido remained unwilling to even consider an early peace effort. The same was true of many senior statesmen who participated in "peace maneuvers" around Prince Konoe.[107]

Politically, however, Hirohito's dismissal of Tōjō signaled a profound shift. In the autumn of 1941, at the time of the decision to broaden the war by attacking Pearl Harbor, the emperor's chief political adviser, Kido, had been instrumental in forming a loose alliance between the court group and some senior statesmen on the one hand, and the prowar forces composed of the military elites, "renovationist bureaucrats," and top leaders of the business world on the other.[108] U.S. ambassador Grew had never even imagined such a grouping. As for Konoe, he had stepped down from office prior to Tōjō's appointment, becoming an opponent of war with the United States and Britain (though not, of course, publicly so).[109] Now, almost three years later, Tōjō's resignation brought Konoe and the men around him, representing the most powerful interests in all the key areas of Japanese life, back to the political stage. Not enchanted by the mystique of the throne, possessed of a realistic insight into Japan's military predicament, and able to influence members of the court group and the imperial family, Konoe was ready to take the initiative in trying to break out of the hopeless war by exerting influence on members of the court group and the imperial family.

VI

Tōjō's successor, Prime Minister Koiso, was a virtual unknown whose cabinet lasted for eight critical months. During that time, between July 22, 1944 and April 5, 1945, the war grew increasingly desperate, and the Japanese people were forced to make more and more sacrifices. On July 24, 1944, the emperor sanctioned plans for showdown battles in the Philippines, Taiwan, the Southwest [Nansei] Islands, the Ryukyus, and the Japanese home islands with the exception of Hokkaido and the Kuriles. Two days later, he told Koiso to stay in the capital as long as possible and let the war determine whether the Imperial Headquarters should be moved to the continent. As for himself, he intended "to remain in this divine land and fight to the death."[110]

Shortly afterward, on August 4, the Koiso cabinet decided to arm virtually the entire nation and have all subjects begin military training (with bamboo spears) in workplaces and schools throughout the country. Hirohito formally confirmed the new preparations for defense against the forthcoming enemy offensives at his imperial conference two weeks later. Emphasis was to be placed on air defense, fighting the enemy "in the interior" rather than "at the water's edge," and the rapid development of "sure victory weapons," which meant the large-scale production of "body-smashing" or "special attack" weapons, designed to "exchange" the life of the crew or the pilot for a specific military achievement.[111]

On August 5, 1944, the liaison conference changed its name to Supreme War Leadership Council and began new diplomatic initiatives aimed at making the Nationalist government in Chungking acknowledge Japan's "sincerity;" the council also mapped its first vague overtures to the Soviet Union. The latter plan, made by the Foreign Ministry, ostensibly sought Soviet help in bringing about reconciliation between the Chinese Communists and Chiang Kai-shek's Nationalists. Japan could then conclude peace with the new regime in China and be in a better position to wage the "War of Greater East Asia." In return Japan would endeavor to promote restoration of relations—that is, peace—between its Nazi ally, the German Third Reich, and the Soviet Union.[112] And why? So that Japan's crumbling hegemony in East Asia might be stabilized. This first Soviet-centered peace plan amounted to little and ended in nothing.

Awareness of the emperor's resolve to fight on was widespread in government circles, particularly after his rescript of September 7, 1944, on the occasion of convening the Eighty-fifth Imperial Diet. After noting that the enemy's offensive was intensifying and the overall war situation had "grown more critical," Hirohito had declared, "Today our imperial state is indeed challenged to reach powerfully for a decisive victory. You who are the leaders of our people must now renew your tenacity and, uniting in your resolve, smash our enemies' evil purposes, thereby furthering forever our imperial destiny."[113]

That Hirohito still had hope of victory could be seen in his and the Imperial Headquarters' performance during the Battle of Leyte, in the southern Philippines. The American reconquest of its former colony, by troops under General MacArthur's command, started in October with the air, naval, and land battles of Leyte and the Philippine Sea. Continuing into November, these battles virtually destroyed what was left of the Combined Fleet and took the lives of about eighty thousand Japanese defenders.[114] The decision of Imperial Headquarters, on October 18, to fight the decisive battle on Leyte made an effective defense of Luzon impossible. After the war, Hirohito himself admitted: "Contrary to the views of the Army and Navy General Staffs, I agreed to the showdown battle of Leyte thinking that if we attacked at Leyte and America flinched, then we would probably be able to find room to negotiate."[115] His statement reflects what actually happened: Hirohito and his chiefs of staff forced the field commander, Gen. Yamashita Hōbun, to engage the American invasion force where Yamashita had not wanted to fight and had not prepared defenses. It was one more example of the destructive influence Hirohito often wielded in operational matters.

Fighting on Leyte continued into late December 1944, and involved kamikaze suicide attacks that were initially highly effective as the planes came in from behind the cover of mountains. Finally Imperial Headquarters decided to write off the island as lost. The costly defense forced delays in preparations for fighting more important battles elsewhere, including the homeland. The development of "balloon bomb" reprisal weapons, which Hirohito on September 25 had placed under the control of Army Chief of Staff Umezu and ordered completed by the end of October, remained on schedule, however.[116] In response to the Leyte defeat, the first release of thousands of balloon bombs against the U.S. mainland occurred on or around Emperor Meiji's day of remembrance, November 3; by March 1945, about 9,300 had been released.[117] Very few reached the North American continent; those that did caused little damage.

Housewives and old people—everyone all over Japan practicing war with bamboo spears; wind-carried balloons with a small incendiary device hanging below; surely the military significance of these measures was more symbolic than practical. Kamikaze attacks on Allied warships and troop transports were an entirely different threat, however, a real and dangerous one.[118] They were a kind of weapon Americans, Australians, and Britons simply could not understand, and for that reason found all the more disturbing. Hirohito, however, clearly understood the rhetoric of sacrifice, and he may have hoped that the kamikaze tactic would prove militarily effective. On New Year's Day 1945, while the Japanese capital was under air attack, the emperor and empress inspected the special last-meal rations being provided to the departing members of the suicide units. Thereafter Hirohito continued to show gratitude for these "special attack forces" whose operations he had followed in the newspapers and watched on film since the summer of 1944, when he saw the first newsreel on the kamikaze ("The Divine Wind Special Attack Force Flies Off").[119]

Sometime after January 9, 1945, when the United States began retaking Luzon, and the self-destruction of kamikaze pilots and "human torpedoes" increased, the emperor's military aide Yoshihashi Kaizō was delivering a briefing on the battles near Lingayen Gulf in the Philippines. He had just mentioned the suicide attack of one of the "special pilots" when:

> suddenly the emperor stood up and made a deep, silent bow. I was
> pointing at the map and his majesty's hair touched my head, causing

me to feel as though an electric current had run through my body. On a later occasion, I informed the emperor about a corporal who had made a suicide attack on a B–29 in the sky over Nagoya, and the emperor did the same thing: rose and bowed deeply. Both times only the emperor and I were in the room.[120]

Enthralled like the rest of the nation by the rhetoric of sacrifice, the emperor began the most fateful year of his life by honoring the "Yamato spirit" in its supreme manifestation.

During the first half of 1945, American forces recaptured most of Luzon, though the fighting in the Philippines continued until virtually the end of the war. They also invaded Iwo Jima and Okinawa. Everywhere they encountered desperate and increasingly effective ground resistance and more and more kamikaze attacks, which, however, became gradually less deadly as American countermeasures were developed. On tropical Iwo Jima in the Bonin Islands, where, after three days of fierce naval bombardment, two marine divisions landed on February 19, outnumbered Japanese defenders for the first time did not try to stop the invaders at the beaches or resort to mass charges. Instead, they pursued a "dug-in" defense from caves and bunkers. When the battle there entered its final stage, the emperor said, on March 7, "I am fully satisfied that naval units have taken charge of defense and are cooperating very well with the army. Even after the enemy landed, they fought ferociously against much greater forces and contributed to the entire operation."[121]

American journalism made Iwo Jima symbolic of U.S. superiority in everything from technology, firepower, and tactics to raw courage. The image, partly falsified, of U.S. Marines triumphantly raising the flag atop Mount Suribachi glorified the bravery of Marines in single-minded pursuit of victory. In his bombproof command center in Tokyo, Hirohito too viewed Iwo Jima in terms of the courage of his forces there and their willingness to fight to the death. He had ordered all garrisons on islands forming the outer moat of defense to buy time during which the home islands could prepare for the final battle. Their mission was to make the enemy bleed as much as possible. General Kuribayashi, the Iwo Jima commander, had done exactly that. Virtually the entire Japanese garrison of twenty thousand men had fought to the death but the Americans had also died, nearly seven thousand of them, with more than nineteen thousand wounded.[122] Thus Hirohito took comfort in the proportionately greater losses that his doomed defenders had inflicted on the invading marines. As Guadalcanal had been, Iwo Jima had become a test of character. And Hirohito had abetted the killing by his bullheaded refusal to accept and deal with Japan's defeat.

In the defense of Okinawa, another island he had defined as an expendable moat area, the emperor intervened early and often for he believed—as he told Chief of Staff Umezu—"If this battle turns out badly, the army and navy will lose the trust of the nation. We have to think about the impact it could have on the future war situation." He seemed unable to comprehend just what was happening: "Why doesn't the field army go on the offensive? If there are insufficient troops, why don't you do a counterlanding?"[123] "Is it because we failed to sink enemy transports that we've let the enemy get ashore? Isn't there any way to defend Okinawa from the landing enemy forces?"[124] So spoke Supreme Commander Hirohito on the second day of the American invasion. And later that same day he told Prime Minister Koiso: "Nothing is going the way it was supposed to."[125]

On the third day Hirohito pressed Umezu to order the Thirty-second Army on Okinawa, under Lt. Gen. Ushijima Mitsuru, to either go on the offensive or launch a counter-landing.[126] Ushijima, having learned from the mistakes of his predecessors in the Central Pacific, was following a strategy of tactically retreating, digging in, and fighting a war of attrition from well-concealed bunkers. After Hirohito's intervention the Tenth Area Army, which was the upper echelon of command over the Thirty-second, ordered Ushijima to "launch an offensive against the northern and central airfields."[127] Ushijima could only comply, radioing back to Imperial Headquarters, "All of our troops will attempt to rush forward and wipe out the ugly enemy." The charge was made—but the "ugly enemy" survived it. Hirohito also urged the navy to counterattack in support of the defenders on Okinawa with every possible resource.[128]

While the Battle of Okinawa intensified, Hirohito cautioned Umezu about the army's plans to contract its defense lines in China and redeploy troops northward to defend Manchuria and Korea, but more particularly the home islands. On April 14, he warned Umezu: "Be cautious . . . of the enemy's propaganda. Destroying railroad lines and villages in enemy areas at this time might have a bad effect on the minds of the people." But his principal concern was that "we not hurt ourselves" by pulling out and allowing Americans to develop new air bases there.[129]

As late as May 5 the emperor was still hoping for a victory on Okinawa and radioing the Thirty-second Army, via radio messages, that "We really want this attack to succeed."[130] The battle for Okinawa had begun on April 1. It lasted until mid-June and cost an estimated 94,000 to 120,000 Japanese combatants and 150,000 to 170,000 noncombatants, including more than seven hundred Okinawans whom the Japanese army forced to commit collective suicide. American combat losses were approximately 12,500 killed and more than 33,000 wounded; among these casualties were more than 7,000 sailors, reflecting the toll taken by kamikaze attacks. The war was lost, and had been for more than a year, but defeated Japan stubbornly fought on.

At this critical pass Hirohito's personality and his approach to life and his office served him badly. He could see many things sooner than his chiefs of staff could, but was always prone to rigid procedures rather than flexible solutions. All his life he had been excessively earnest, preoccupied with detail. Now, confronting endless defeats, he carried his earnestness, his inflexibility, and his absorption with detail to extremes. The final, most destructive stage of the war was about to begin, with Hirohito, the helmsman, spurning rational judgments and refusing to see, let alone forestall, the catastrophe.

13

DELAYED SURRENDER

In February 1945, just before Iwo Jima was assaulted by U.S. Marines and less than six weeks before Okinawa was invaded, Hirohito consulted his seven senior statesmen concerning the war. They were the six former prime ministers—Hiranuma, Hirota, Wakatsuki, Okada, Konoe, and Tōjō—and former lord keeper of the privy seal Makino. The meetings, though interrupted by air raids, revealed an overwhelming consensus to go on with the struggle.

In Europe, Germany and its Nazi regime were heading toward defeat. Just how soon the Third Reich would collapse was not yet clear, but that its demise was fast approaching seemed certain. As for Japan's situation, it was equally grim. The army in Burma had been destroyed. The armies in China proper had fared better. Their "Ichigō" offensive of 1944 had opened a land corridor along the main trunk railway from Peking in the north to Wuhan, and from there to Canton in the southernmost province of Kwangtung.[1] But in all the occupied provinces the tide had turned against Japanese forces. They were stretched thin and fighting a costly guerrilla war that in 1944 alone had absorbed 64 percent of Japan's emergency military expenditures.[2]

Now, in 1945, the armies in China anticipated, and therefore had to prepare for, both a Soviet invasion from the north and an American landing in the Shanghai area. Neither in China nor Manchuria could the continental armies be drawn down further to supply veteran troops for the defense of the home islands.[3] Nor could the navy, which had suffered crippling losses, do much to transport them anywhere.[4]

On the other hand the kamikaze tactics that had been evolving since before Leyte were a potentially powerful resource. The high command was also strengthening army air power, stockpiling weapons, and organizing twenty-nine new divisions, fifty-one infantry regiments, and many artillery and tank regiments in preparation for defending the homeland. During 1945, 43 percent of the army would be stationed in Japan, Korea, and Taiwan. Given these factors, and the emperor's wildly optimistic belief that they could affect the outcome, this did not seem to him and Kido an auspicious moment to think of negotiating peace.[5]

The enemy must first be made to see "the disadvantages of continuing the war," Wakatsuki advised. Makino declared that "the ultimate priority is to develop an advantageous war situation." Okada said Japan should wait for "a moment favorable for us," then make peace. Hiranuma and Hirota advised the emperor to fight on until the end.[6]

Prince Konoe alone of the senior statesmen did not concur.[7] Distinctly unawed by the haze of emotion and reverence that surrounded the emperor, he had tried for more than eighteen months to convey a complex message of dire threat to the emperor if the war continued.[8] Many months earlier he had told the emperor's brother Prince Takamatsu that the army was plagued by "a cancer" in the form of the Control faction, but "Kido and others" did not see matters the same way he [Konoe] did, while "his majesty is relatively unconcerned with ideological questions." For the past four years, he went on, the emperor had been told and still believed that "the extremists are the Imperial Way faction." The real danger to the *kokutai*, however, came from the Control faction. Konoe added that, should the war worsen, they would try to change the *kokutai*. Whether the threat was from communists within the country—by which he meant mainly the left-wing radicals within the Control faction—or from the "Anglo-American enemy," Konoe surmised that both enemies would want to retain the emperor while communizing the country.[9]

Now, in his written report to the emperor, presented on February 14 with Kido in the room listening, Konoe elaborated on this conspiracy theory.[10] The Soviet Union, he declared, saw Japan as its biggest threat in East Asia; it had linked up with the Chinese Communists, the largest and strongest Communist party in Asia and was cooperating with the United States and Britain to expel Japan from China. It would enter the war when it saw the chance. Defeat, he told the emperor, was inevitable if the war continued, but more to be feared than defeat was the destruction of the *kokutai*. For the war was also eroding the domestic status quo, releasing forces that threatened Japan and its imperial house from within as much as from without. The danger lay in the emperor and Kido's trust in the generals of the Control faction who were unintentionally advancing the communization of Japan. Sue quickly for peace, Konoe pleaded, before a Communist revolution occurred that would make preservation of the *kokutai* impossible.[11]

Hirohito, sympathetic to Konoe's fears about the army, conceded that something had to be done. But he was taken aback by Konoe's view of Moscow's intentions, for he shared the wishful thinking of his high command that the Soviet Union would need Japan in its looming confrontation with the Anglo-Americans, and would not want to destroy Japanese power in East Asia. Thus he firmly rejected Konoe's recommendation that he act immediately and directly to end the war.[12] Hirohito agreed rather with his senior statesmen: To end the war would be "very difficult unless we make one more military gain." Konoe allegedly replied, "Is that possible? It must happen soon. If we have to wait much longer, . . . [a mere battle victory] will mean nothing."[13]

Nevertheless Hirohito stuck to his position. That same day he reportedly said, "If we hold out long enough in this war, we may be able to win, but what worries me is whether the nation will be able to endure it until then."[14] In a sense this was what Konoe was concerned about, too. In another sense, however, the emperor was invoking the age-old tradition of the power of Japanese spirit over material odds: My people are capable of superhuman efforts and sacrifice. Therefore, though we have lost our sources of oil and are suffering bombing every day, we still may triumph. The outlook for a negotiated peace could be improved if Japan fought and won one last, decisive battle.

Nor did Hirohito budge after his intelligence forecasters warned him, at a meeting of the Supreme War Leadership Council on February 15, that the Soviet Union intended "to secure a voice in the future of East Asia" and was therefore likely to abrogate its Neutrality Pact with Japan by spring, joining the war whenever thereafter it judged Japan's power to have weakened sufficiently.[15] The next day Foreign Minister Shigemitsu reiterated that warning. The Nazi Germans had entered their last stage, he declared in a private audience, and the "Three-Power [Yalta] Conference" had clarified the "unity of Britain, the United States, and the Soviet Union." Shigemitsu warned Hirohito not to count on the Neutrality Treaty; and just as Konoe had done, he too stressed the internal danger from Communism. But Hirohito refused to see the absurdity of his assumptions about the Soviet Union. At the end of the hour-long audience, he ignored Yalta and asked Shigemitsu a question about the "mood in the German Embassy."[16] And Hirohito's mind remained unchanged ten days later when Tōjō conceded, during his formal interview at the palace on February 26, that there was a "fifty-fifty" chance that the Soviet Union would turn against Japan.

The chances that the Japanese people could hold out long enough looked slimmer and slimmer as the spring of 1945 passed. On March 9–10, the U.S. Pacific Air Force launched 334 B–29s in the first night incendiary air raid over densely populated Tokyo, turning about 40 percent of the capital into ash and burning to death an estimated eighty to one hundred thousand people. So hot was the firestorm that water boiled in canals, glass melted, and heat from the updrafts destroyed some of the bombers.[17] Nine days later, on the eighteenth, the emperor, accompanied by his doctor and a chamberlain, inspected the capital by car. Aide Yoshihashi, who rode behind them in a separate vehicle, later commented that the victims were

> digging through the rubble with empty expressions on their faces that became reproachful as the imperial motorcade went by. Although we did not make the usual prior announcement, I felt that they should have known that his was a "blessed visitation" (gyōkō) just the same, for after all, three to four automobiles bearing the chrysanthemum crest were passing. Were they resentful of the emperor because they had lost their relatives, their houses and belongings? Or were they in a state of utter exhaustion and bewilderment (kyodatsu jōtai)? I sympathized with how his majesty must have felt upon approaching these unfortunate victims.[18]

Yoshihashi's observation of "exhaustion and bewilderment" on the part of the people is worth noting. By March factory production had started to fall; absenteeism was on the rise; so too were instances of lèse majesté—always of keen concern for the Imperial Household Ministry. Over the next five months, members of the militarized imperial family as well as the senior statesmen would speak of a crisis of the kokutai. The threat from within that Konoe had warned of seemed more and more palpable. Yet until the very end, most Japanese people, whether living in the country or large urban areas, remained steadfast in their resolve to obey their leaders and to work and sacrifice for the victory that they were constantly told was coming.

Two days after Hirohito's inspection of bomb damage in the

capital, no less a person than retired foreign minister Shidehara Kijūrō, once the very symbol of cooperation with Britain and the United States, gave expression to a feeling that was widely held by Japan's ruling elites at this time: namely, Japan had to be patient and resist surrender no matter what. Shidehara had earlier advised Foreign Minister Shigemitsu that the people would gradually get used to being bombed daily. In time their unity and resolve would grow stronger, and this would allow the diplomats "room to devise plans for saving the country in this time of unprecedented crisis."[19]

Now, on March 20, 1945, Shidehara wrote to his close friend Ōdaira Komatsuchi, the former vice president of the South Manchurian Railway Company, that, "[i]f we continue to fight back bravely, even if hundreds of thousands of noncombatants are killed, injured, or starved, even if millions of buildings are destroyed or burned," there would be room to produce a more advantageous international situation for Japan. With the country facing imminent absolute defeat, Shidehara still saw advantages in turning all of Japan into a battlefield, for then the enemy's lines of supply would become longer, making it more difficult for them to continue the war and giving diplomats room to maneuver.[20] This was the mindset of the moderate Shidehara; it was probably shared by Hirohito.

One day before American troops landed on Okinawa, while rumors were circulating in high court circles of an imminent cabinet change, Konoe allegedly remarked to his secretary, Hosokawa, that soon "the army will increasingly brandish the notion of fighting to the death. But Kido['s] . . . mind is completely set on [Chief of the General Staff] Anami. Considering our *kokutai*, unless the emperor assents to it, we can do nothing. When I think of the madmen leading the present situation, I can't help but feel weary of life."[21]

Konoe at that moment may well have included Hirohito among the "madmen."

On April 5, three days after Hirohito ordered an end to peace maneuvers in China through an ex-Kuomintang official (one Miao

Ping [Myō Hin], whom Koiso strongly supported), and five days into the Battle of Okinawa, the emperor and Prime Minister Koiso parted ways.[22] Blaming Koiso for Japan's succession of military defeats from Leyte to Iwo Jima, Hirohito brought down his cabinet. Hirohito now chose his former grand chamberlain and trusted adviser, seventy-eight-year-old retired Adm. Suzuki Kantarō, to lead a new government. At that time neither the emperor nor Suzuki was considering any policy change that might lead to ending the war. It was only *after* the Battle of Okinawa had been fought and horribly lost, leaving huge sections of more than sixty Japanese cities leveled by American incendiary air attacks, that Hirohito indicated his desire for peace and started looking for ways to end the war.

In Kido's diary the first clear indication that the emperor would be asked to think seriously of an early peace appears on June 8, 1945, when Kido prepared his own "Draft Plan for Controlling the Crisis Situation." It was a pivotal moment. This was after the Imperial Palace had been inadvertently bombed, all hope of saving Okinawa had been lost, and on the day that the Supreme War Leadership Council adopted the "Basic Policy for the Future Direction of the War."[23] Fighting in Europe had ended. Japan was now completely alone. Kido's "plan," a nebulous one, called for seeking the Soviet Union's assistance as a go-between so that Japan could obtain more leverage in negotiating with its enemies. By drafting it Kido indicated that he had ended his long honeymoon with the military hard-liners. By accepting it Hirohito indicated that he was at last ready for an early peace.

With the empire collapsing around him, Hirohito entered a period of high tension and emotional depression. In mid-June, shortly after hearing from Kido about the status of the underground bunker in the mountains of Matsushiro, Nagano prefecture, that had been constructed for transferring him and the Imperial Headquarters, he became sick and was forced to cancel his scheduled activities.[24] Only with great effort did he fulfill a promise to visit his mother on the afternoon of June 15. On June 22 Hirohito himself finally informed the Supreme War Leadership Council directly of his desire to commence diplomatic maneuvers to end the war. According to Kido's summary, the emperor told the assembled war leaders that the decision at the imperial conference on June 8 "concerned the leadership of the war." Now he wanted them "quickly to complete concrete studies concerning the conclusion of the war, without being confined to the former [decision], and bring it to a realization." He also added that they were not to lose the chance for peace by being overly cautious.[25] But neither Hirohito nor anyone else in the room was thinking of immediate capitulation. They were thinking only of an early peace and committing themselves just to that.

In early July, after Soviet ambassador Jacob Malik had broken off his inconclusive talks in Japan with former prime minister Hirota, Hirohito for the first time, showed a keen interest in expediting direct negotiations with the Soviet Union by dispatching a special envoy to Moscow. But neither the emperor nor the Suzuki government ever devised a concrete plan on the basis of which the Soviets could mediate an end to hostilities, assuming the Soviets were ever interested in doing so, which they were not. In the Japanese approach to war termination, negotiation with the Soviets to guarantee the emperor's political position and the future of the monarchy was always accorded more importance than the search for peace to end the killing and suffering.[26]

From April 8, 1945, until its capitulation, the Suzuki government's chief war policy was "Ketsugō," a further refinement of the "Shōsangō" (Victory Number 3) plan for the defense of the homeland.[27] Its defining characteristic was heavy reliance on suicide tactics, and the manufacture of weapons solely for the purpose of suicide missions using massive numbers of kamikaze "special attack" planes, human torpedoes shot from submarines, dynamite-filled "crash boats" powered by truck engines, human rocket bombs carried by aircraft, and suicide charges by specially trained ground units. While preparations for Operation Ketsu went forward, on June 9 a special session of the Imperial Diet passed a Wartime Emergency Measures Law and five other measures designed to mobilize the entire nation for that last battle.

The same day the emperor (who had not yet begun working to end the war) issued another imperial rescript in connection with his convocation of the Diet, ordering the nation to "smash the inordinate ambitions of the enemy nations" and "achieve the goals of the war." Concurrently the controlled press waged a daily die-for-the-emperor campaign, a campaign to promote gratitude for imperial benevolence, and, from about mid-July onward, a campaign to "protect the *kokutai*."[28]

Americans countered with their own propaganda designed to break Japan's will to fight. B-29s dropped scores of millions of leaflets, written in Japanese, announcing in advance the next scheduled target for B-29 attack or urging surrender while utilizing the emperor to attack the militarists. Leaflets bearing the letterhead of the chrysanthemum crest attacked the "military cliques" for "forcing the entire nation to commit suicide" and called on "everybody" to "exercise their constitutional right to make direct appeals [for peace] to the Emperor. Even the powerful military cliques cannot stop the mighty march for peace of the Emperor and the people."[29] Seven million leaflets alone revealed the terms of the "joint declaration" issued by the governments of the United States, Great Britain, and China.[30] "Today we come not to bomb you," they said. "We are dropping this leaflet in order to let you know the reply by the government of the United States to your government's request for conditions of surrender. . . . It all depends on your government whether the war will stop immediately. You will understand how to quit the war if you read these two official notifications."[31]

Pressed by imperial edicts to continue their preparations for the final homeland battle and to think only of victory, now assaulted from the air by the American psychological warfare campaign in addition to bombing, the Japanese people complied as best they could. During late July and August, when the nation's prefectural governors, police chiefs, and officers of the "special higher police" submitted to the Home Ministry reports on the rapidly deteriorating spirit of the nation, there was not a single reference in their nearly two thousand pages of reports to any popular inclination to accept the terms of the Potsdam Declaration.[32] Even immediately after the American dropping of the atomic bombs on Hiroshima and Nagasaki on August 6 and 9, and the Soviet declaration of war on the eighth, people generally clung to the hope of a final victory, and thus to the belief that their "divine land" was indestructible. Mobilized in the service of death, the collective memory of the "divine winds" (*kamikaze*) that would save Japan helped to maintain the will to fight on.[33]

American intelligence analysts, meanwhile, watched all these main island preparations. They saw how the Japanese had fought and died on Okinawa—thousands almost daily for eighty-two days—and how the whole nation had become enveloped in the imagery of national salvation through mass suicide. When political leaders in Washington said that the Japanese were likely to fight to the death rather than surrender, they were not exaggerating what the Japanese government and its mass media were saying.

I

Mindful of the mistakes that had been made in dealing with imperial Germany at the end of World War I, but concerned above all to maintain a high degree of patriotic fervor and international cooperation in the fight against the Axis, President Roosevelt and Prime Minister Churchill had relied on abstract war slogans and, after the first full year of war, the goal of "unconditional surrender." Their policy of no negotiated termination of the war aimed at smashing the fascist states and then putting new, nonfascist political entities in place. The objective was military occupation *and* postwar political and social reform—always the two together. The philosophies of fascism and militarism were to be uprooted totally, and the conquered nations democratized, reborn as peace-loving capitalistic societies.

Roosevelt had stated, at Casablanca in January 1943, that the Allies would punish the leaders of the fascist regimes but not destroy their peoples. But until they had won total victory over the Axis, he and Churchill steadfastly resisted pressures to clarify the meaning of their simplifying formula. Needing Soviet military power, yet keenly aware of Stalin's distrust of them for not yet opening a second front in Europe to relieve the hard-pressed Red Army, Roosevelt and Churchill had ample reason for displaying an uncompromising attitude toward the enemy states.[34] Their determination to make this the last total war, plus the imperatives of holding the antifascist alliance together, strengthened their resolve to eschew any formal contractual offers if made by the leaders of the aggressor nations, and to retain a free hand to occupy and reform those nations after destroying their military power and toppling their governments.

Roosevelt also projected his Wilsonian idealism into "unconditional surrender" and saw it as a means of realizing a liberal international order. The unconditional surrender formula, which sought to achieve reforms in the postsurrender period, stated the basic precondition for building a new world order after fascism had been vanquished.[35] In the case of Japan, it essentially assured the Allies the supreme authority to exercise powers in the Japanese homeland "beyond those given a military occupant by international law."[36]

After the German army signed unconditional surrender documents with the Allied forces on May 7 and 8, 1945, and the Third Reich, in the words of the American journalist William L. Shirer, "simply ceased to exist," Japan alone remained in the war.[37] At that point, with the Battle of Okinawa still raging, newly installed President Truman declared on May 8 that Japan's surrender would not mean the "extermination or enslavement of the Japanese people."[38] His remark suggested that future occupation measures would not be enforced in a vindictive spirit. But because it left the unconditional surrender principle unaltered, the former ambassador to Japan and leader of the "Japan faction" within the State Department, Joseph Grew, pressed the president to make public a clear definition of the term so as to persuade the Japanese to surrender.

Grew, a conservative Republican, saw Emperor Hirohito as the man who held the key to Japan's surrender. He was the "queen bee in a hive . . . surrounded by the attentions of the hive."[39] At various times before and during the war, he described the emperor as a "puppet" of the militarists, a constitutionalist, and a pacifist. Grew had enormous confidence in the influence on policy of those whom he termed the "moderates" around the Japanese throne. In the spring of 1945, with the final collapse of the Japanese empire approaching, Grew, who had always moved in high court circles and knew nothing about the Japanese body politic, was willing to allow these individuals "to determine for themselves the nature of their future political structure."[40]

In his memoirs, published in 1952, long after President Harry S. Truman and Secretary of State James F. Byrnes had rejected his efforts to include in the Potsdam draft declaration a clause guaranteeing the position of the imperial house, Grew wrote:

> The main point at issue historically is whether, if immediately following the terrific devastation of Tokyo by our B-29s in May, 1945, "the President had made a public categorical statement that surrender would not mean the elimination of the present dynasty if the Japanese people desired its retention, the surrender of Japan could have been hastened. . . . From statements made by a number of the moderate

former Japanese leaders to responsible Americans after the American occupation, it is quite clear that the civilian advisers to the Emperor were working toward surrender long before the Potsdam Proclamation, even indeed before my talk with the President on May 28, for they knew then that Japan was a defeated nation. The stumbling block that they had to overcome was the complete dominance of the Japanese Army over the Government. . . . The Emperor needed all the support he could get, and . . . if such a categorical statement [by Truman] about the dynasty had been issued in May, 1945, the surrender-minded elements in the Government might well have been afforded . . . a valid reason and the necessary strength to come to an early clear-cut decision. . . . Prime Minister Suzuki [Kantarō] . . . was surrender-minded even before May 1945, if only it were made clear that surrender would not involve the downfall of the dynasty.[41]

Immediately Grew met fierce opposition from his colleagues in the State Department—the "China crowd"—who argued that to keep the emperor and guarantee the future existence of the monarchy was to compromise on the very essence of Japanese fascism.[42] They—Dean Acheson, poet and future Librarian of Congress Archibald MacLeish, and James Byrnes—were aware of Grew's earlier misjudgments of Japan's political situation and his tendency to be protective of the emperor and Japan's conservative "moderates." They certainly did not want to treat Japan and its emperor, whom they saw as central to the Japanese philosophy of militarism and war, more leniently than Germany and by so doing leave an undesirable impression, at home and abroad, of appeasement. These bureaucratic disagreements reflected a lack of clarity at the highest levels in Washington as to what the American war aims were. More important, they highlighted the interrelationship, during the spring and summer of 1945, between wartime goals and postwar policies.

The Potsdam Declaration was issued on July 26, 1945, in the form of an ultimatum aimed at hastening Japan's surrender.[43] At

Potsdam, Truman had yielded to Churchill's advice and clarified the terms for implementing the unconditional surrender principle. To save Japan's leaders from their own folly, the president agreed to issue the "terms of unconditional surrender" *before* Japan surrendered, and to soften the fourth term of the declaration by permitting "Japanese military forces, after being completely disarmed . . . to return to their homes."[44]

The Japanese government read the declaration and was informed that if it fulfilled certain unilateral obligations ("our terms"), which the victorious powers would impose *after* the Japanese government had proclaimed "the unconditional surrender of all Japanese armed forces" and furnished "proper and adequate assurance of their good faith in such action," Japan would *then* be allowed to retain its peace industries and resume participation in world trade on the basis of the principle of equal access to raw materials. "The alternative for Japan," the declaration concluded, "is prompt and utter destruction." It gave no warning about the atomic bomb. Article 12 stated, "The occupying forces of the Allies shall be withdrawn from Japan as soon as these objectives have been accomplished and there has been established in accordance with the freely expressed will of the Japanese people a peacefully inclined and responsible government." Deleted from this article, however, was the phrase that Grew insisted on having: "this may include a constitutional monarchy under the present dynasty." Consequently the status of the emperor was not guaranteed, and the policy of unconditional surrender remained intact.

The Japanese government received the declaration on July 27 and showed no intention of accepting it. On the contrary, the Suzuki cabinet first ordered the press to publish the Dōmei News Service's edited version and to minimize the significance of the declaration by not commenting on it.[45] Next, on July 28, at the urging of Army Minister Anami Korechika, Chief of the Naval General Staff Toyoda Soemu, and others, Prime Minister Suzuki made

Japan's rejection explicit by formally declaring, at an afternoon press conference, that the Potsdam Declaration was no more than a "rehash" (*yakinaoshi*) of the Cairo Declaration, and that he intended to "ignore" it (*mokusatsu*). Underlying Suzuki's statement was Hirohito's resolve to continue the war, and his unrealistic expectations about negotiating through the Soviet Union. If Hirohito, who read the newspapers daily, had been displeased or even concerned about the impression of intransigence that Suzuki and his cabinet were conveying to the world, Kido probably would have mentioned it in his detailed diary of his conversations with the emperor. He didn't. Kido knew that Hirohito was still waiting for the Soviet reply to Japanese peace maneuvers, unable to make up his mind whether to surrender or continue fighting for more favorable terms.

Also on July 28, when the allegedly moderate senior statesman Navy Minister Yonai, was asked by his secretary, Rear Admiral Takagi, why the prime minister had been allowed to make such an absurd statement, Yonai replied: "If one is first to issue a statement, he is always at a disadvantage. Churchill has fallen, America is beginning to be isolated. The government therefore will ignore it. There is no need to rush."[46]

"No need to rush" directly contravened Article 5 of the Potsdam Declaration ("We shall brook no delay") and was a position that further supported the contemporary Western idea that, as of July 28, the Japanese, following the leadership of their emperor, had neither reversed their decision nor loosened their will to fight to the finish, while making vague overtures for peace on a separate track.[47] Suzuki's intention was not misunderstood.

The Americans now accelerated their preparations for the use of atomic bombs and for an invasion of southern Kyushu—termed Operation Olympic—scheduled to begin on November 1. At 8:15 A.M. on August 6 a single B-29 destroyed much of the undefended city of Hiroshima, immediately killing an estimated 100,000 to 140,000 thousand people and taking the lives (over the next five years) of perhaps another 100,000.[48] At the center of the explosion a "light appeared 3,000 times brighter than the sun," and a fireball formed, emitting thermal radiation that "instantly scorched humans, trees, houses. As the air heated and rushed upward, cold air flowed in to ignite a firestorm. . . . [Hours later] a whirlwind whipped the flames to their peak until more than eight square miles were virtually in cinders. Black, muddy rain, full of radioactive fallout, began to drop."[49]

Two days later, citing as a pretext Japan's rejection of the Potsdam Declaration, the Soviet Union declared war on Japan.[50] On August 9 the United States dropped the second atomic bomb on Nagasaki, immediately killing approximately 35,000 to 40,000 people and injuring more than 60,000.[51] That same day, in a nationwide radio report on the Potsdam Conference, President Truman gave full expression to the vengeful mood of most Americans:

> Having found the bomb we have used it. We have used it against those who attacked us without warning at Pearl Harbor, against those who have starved and beaten and executed American prisoners of war, against those who have abandoned all pretense of obeying international laws of warfare. We have used it in order to shorten the agony of war, in order to save the lives of thousands and thousands of young Americans.[52]

Meanwhile in Tokyo, during the crucial interval between the Potsdam Declaration and the August 6 atomic bombing of Hiroshima, Hirohito himself said and did nothing about accepting the Potsdam terms. Twice, however, on July 25 and 31, he had made clear to Kido that the imperial regalia had to be defended at all costs.[53] The three sacred objects—consisting of a mirror, curved jewel, and sword—symbolized the legitimacy of his rule through the northern court, and were integral to his sense of being the occupant of the throne by divine right. He wanted to protect them by having them brought to the palace. Fixated on his symbols of office when the big issue was whether to accept immediate capitulation, Hirohito was unprepared to seize the moment and end the war on his own.

Prime Minister Suzuki, after his initial rejection of the Potsdam ultimatum, also saw no need to do anything further. His Cabinet Advisory Council, composed of the president of Asano Cement, the founder of the Nissan consortium, the vice president of the Bank of Japan, and other representatives of the nation's leading business interests who had profited greatly from the war, met on the morning of August 3. They recommended acceptance of the Potsdam terms on the ground that the United States would allow Japan to retain its nonmilitary industries and participate in world trade. Suzuki replied to them at a cabinet meeting that afternoon. According to Minister of Agriculture and Commerce Ishiguro Tadaatsu, Suzuki's friend and defender, Suzuki told the head of the Cabinet Intelligence Bureau and advisory council member Shimomura Kainan:

> For the enemy to say something like that means circumstances have
> arisen that force them also to end the war. That is why they are talk-
> ing about unconditional surrender. Precisely at a time like this, if we
> hold firm, then they will yield before we do. Just because they broad-
> cast their declaration, it is not necessary to stop fighting. You advisers
> may ask me to reconsider, but I don't think there is any need to stop
> [the war].[54]

So for ten days, while Hirohito kept himself relatively secluded, the Potsdam Declaration was "ignored." The bombs were dropped, and Soviet forces invaded along a wide front from northern Manchuria to Korea. Then Foreign Minister Tōgō Shigenori, not a dove by any stretch of the imagination, persuaded the emperor that the declaration in itself really signified *conditional* surrender, not unconditional, though he probably had his own doubts about that interpretation. With that sticking point out of the way, Hirohito, strongly assisted by Kido, took the gamble and authorized Tōgō to notify the world that Japan would accept the Allied terms with only one condition, "that the said declaration does not comprise any demand which prejudices the prerogatives of His Majesty as a Sovereign Ruler." The next day, August 11, Secretary of State Byrnes replied to this first surrender communication by alluding to the subordination of the emperor's authority to the supreme commander of the Allied Powers, thereby leaving intact the vitally important principle of unconditional surrender. However, since Byrnes did not clearly answer the Japanese on the emperor's future status, his reply could also be seen as hinting that the emperor's position might be maintained after surrender.

At that point another dispute erupted among the leaders in Tokyo over the meaning of the Byrnes reply, forcing Hirohito to rule once again, on August 14, in favor of acceptance. Afterward he went before a microphone and recorded his capitulation announcement, which was broadcast to the Japanese nation at noon on August 15. By then victor and vanquished had entered into a noncontractual relationship based on the unconditional surrender principle, and the main concern of the moderates had already shifted to divorcing him from both his actual conduct of the war and the unrealistic thinking and failed policies that had brought Japan to defeat.

Why did Japan's top leaders delay so long before finally telling their people that they had "bow[ed] to the inevitable" and surrendered without negotiation? If Grew and the critics of unconditional surrender had had their way in May, June, or even July and had cut a deal on the issue of guaranteeing the dynasty, would Japan's leaders then have surrendered immediately? Or was there not more to this issue than meets the eye?

II

The conventional treatment of Emperor Hirohito's role in ending the war presents Japan's request for Soviet mediation—the Hirōta Kōti–Jacob Malik talks—and the secret messages that Foreign Minister Tōgō sent to Ambassador Satō Naotake in Moscow, as serious attempts to surrender. Yet the participants in these peace overtures, which went on through June, July, and early August, perceived them as a tactic that would merely delay the inevitable capitulation. Only Hirohito, anguishing over the prospect of losing sovereignty, and the army high command had inflated expectations about the Soviets.

After the war, the emperor advanced a short and misleading explanation of these Soviet negotiations:

> We chose the Soviet Union to mediate peace for two reasons: All other countries had little power. Therefore, even if we had asked those countries to mediate, we feared they would be pressured by the British and Americans, and we would have to surrender unconditionally. By comparison the Soviet Union had both the power and the obligation that came from having concluded a neutrality treaty.
>
> Because we did not think the Soviet Union was a trustworthy country, it was first necessary to sound them out. Consequently, we decided to go ahead with the Hirota-Malik talks, in which we said that if they allowed us to import oil, we would not mind giving them both southern Karafuto and Manchuria.[55]

Hirohito failed to mention how limited Japan's territorial concessions to the Soviets were for staying out of the war compared to what the Allies were offering Stalin for coming into it.[56] Neither did he mention earlier efforts, under Foreign Minister Shigemitsu, to promote peace between the Soviets and the Nazis.[57] Japan's Soviet policy had aimed at maintaining "tranquillity" in relations with

Moscow, promoting a Nazi-Soviet peace, and setting the Allies against one another. That policy had begun to change during 1943, and by late 1944—after he had learned that Stalin had labeled Japan an "aggressor state"[58]—Hirohito had approved a vague proposal for sending a special envoy to Moscow. By the time the Suzuki government decided to ask for Soviet good offices in ending the war, Soviet policy had shifted from maintaining neutrality to awaiting the right moment to attack Japan. But Hirohito paid no attention to the recent history of Japan-Soviet relations. He misread the evidence because it conflicted with his goal of negotiating an end to the war that would guarantee an authoritarian imperial system with himself and the empowered throne at the center.

Continuing with his postwar explanation of Japan's overtures to Moscow, the emperor added: "However, even when it came to the beginning of July [1945], there was no answer from the Soviet Union. For our part, we had to decide this matter prior to the Potsdam Conference. . . . For that reason, I consulted Suzuki and decided to cancel the Hirota-Malik talks and negotiate directly with the Soviets."[59]

Leaving aside the fact that Ambassador Malik, not the emperor, effectively ended the talks, Hirohito in early July did indeed become more concerned about negotiating an end to the war that would preserve the imperial prerogatives. Around July 12 he and Kido began pushing to open secret direct negotiations with the Soviets by sending Prince Konoe to Moscow as the emperor's special envoy. A few days earlier, however, in a July 9 report to the throne, former foreign minister Arita Hachirō had pointed out that, "There is almost no chance of our bringing Chungking, Yenan, and the Soviets to our side, or of using them to improve our position. . . . [I]f we try to do this, we will merely be wasting precious time in a situation where every minute counts." Judge the big picture coolly and rationally, pleaded Arita in his audience with the emperor, for "merely to call for absolute victory will produce nothing." In order to make "the divine land . . . imperishable," we must "bear the unbearable."[60]

More important, since June 8 Ambassador Satō in Moscow had been telling Tōgō it was unimaginable that the Soviets would ever help Japan.[61] On July 13 Satō warned Tōgō that although "we are overawed that the dispatch of a special envoy is the imperial wish," it would not mean anything at all to the Soviets, and would only cause trouble for the imperial house, "if the Japanese government's proposal brought by him is limited to an enumeration of previous concepts, lacking in concreteness."[62]

On July 20—one day after Satō had notified Tokyo that the Soviets had indeed refused to accept the special envoy "on the grounds that the mission is not specific" (just as he had been saying they would all along), the ambassador sent his most emotional telegram yet to Tōgō, summing up his feelings about the whole situation. Satō (like Arita on July 9 and Prince Konoe since February) urged immediate surrender because the state was on the verge of being destroyed. "[T]his matter of protecting the national polity [*kokutai*]," Satō emphasized, could be considered as "one of a domestic nature and therefore excluded from the terms of a peace treaty."[63] In other words there was no need for Japan to insist on securing a foreign guarantee of its monarchy: The *kokutai*, meaning for him the emperor's prerogatives, could be saved without delaying surrender, and restored later when Japan once again became independent.

Nevertheless, at Hirohito's insistence, Tōgō persisted, telling Satō that Japan could not reveal its peace plan in advance and that he should concentrate on learning Soviet intentions and getting them to accept Prince Konoe as the emperor's special peace envoy. On August 2 Tōgō sent another message to Satō telling him that the emperor, the prime minister, and the military leaders were "placing their hopes on this one matter. Although you may have your own opinion, understand this situation and somehow stimulate the Soviet side to accept our special envoy."[64] After receiving Tōgō's message, Satō cabled the Foreign Ministry again urging acceptance of the Potsdam Declaration.[65]

Neither Satō nor retired foreign ministers Shigemitsu Mamoru or Arita Hachirō believed that the war could be ended through the good offices of the Soviet Union. Foreign Minister Tōgō himself doubted it. But in compliance with the wishes of the emperor, who wanted his imperial prerogatives to be guaranteed internationally, Tōgō kept trying and would not agree to direct negotiations with the Allied governments even when the president of the Cabinet Intelligence Bureau, Shimomura Kainan, visited his residence on August 4 and pleaded: "It is not enough to deal only with the Soviet Union. There is no hope if we continue like this. Somehow, by backdoor channels, we must negotiate with the United States, Britain, and China."[66]

Tōgō sent his last message to Satō, still asking him to discover the attitude of the Soviet side, on August 7. But by then Stalin knew about the atomic bombing of Hiroshima. When American ambassador Averell Harriman met him in the Kremlin on the evening of August 8, Stalin said that "he thought the Japanese were at present looking for a pretext to replace the present government with one which would be qualified to undertake a surrender. The bomb might give them this pretext."[67] Caught off guard by the news of the American destruction of an entire Japanese city, Stalin had decided to enter the war formally the next day, a week earlier than previously scheduled, and a week earlier than President Truman had anticipated.[68] By dropping the atomic bomb on Hiroshima, Truman inadvertently deepened the Soviet dictator's suspicion of the United States, thereby contributing to the onset of the Cold War.

As the Japanese Foreign Ministry's messages to Moscow were intercepted and decoded by U. S. intelligence and read, at least in part, by Truman, it has been argued that the president could—and

should—have backed away at least somewhat from the unconditional surrender formula. But those messages clearly were always
too tentative and vague to be taken for serious attempts at negotiating an end to the war.[69]

Even the letter that the Foreign Ministry had already prepared
for Konoe's projected (but never realized) secret mission as the
emperor's special envoy is reported to have aimed mainly at obtaining
a Soviet guarantee of the future of the throne and its current occupant.[70] Preservation of the *kokutai* was the vital goal, the single condition for peace. Furthermore, the "emperor's letter" implied that the
war had been generated spontaneously, like a natural disaster, and
that in so far as the United States and Britain insisted on unconditional surrender, they, not Japan, were the obstacle to peace.

Unable to decide to end the war unless the future of the throne
and the all-important prerogatives of its occupant were absolutely
guaranteed, the Suzuki cabinet and the Supreme War Leadership
Council never framed a peace maneuver from the viewpoint of saving the Japanese people from further destruction. They waited,
instead, until their foreign enemies had created a situation that gave
them a face-saving excuse to surrender in order to prevent the *kokutai* from being destroyed by antimilitary, antiwar pressure originating from the Japanese people themselves. The bomb, followed by
the Soviet declaration of war, gave them the excuses they needed.
This is why (as Tanaka Nobumasa pointed out) Yonai Mitsumasa
could say to Adm. Takagi Sōkichi, on August 12, that

> I think the term is perhaps inappropriate, but the atomic bombs and
> the Soviet entry into the war are, in a sense, gifts from the gods [*tenyū*,
> also "heaven-sent blessings"]. This way we don't have to say that we
> quit the war because of domestic circumstances. I've long been advo-
> cating control of our crisis, but neither from fear of an enemy attack
> nor because of the atomic bombs and the Soviet entry into the war.
> The main reason is my anxiety over the domestic situation. So, it is

rather fortunate that we can now control matters without revealing the domestic situation.[71]

Similar reasons of political expediency also account for Konoe's calling the Soviet participation in the war "a godsend for controlling the army," and why Kido regarded both the atomic bombs and the Soviet entry as "useful" "elements for making things go smoothly."[72] An incipient power struggle was going on, making it immaterial to the persons involved whether one hundred thousand or two hundred thousand people died, so long as their desired outcome was gained: an end to the war that would leave the monarchy intact, available to control the forces of discontent that defeat would inevitably unleash. In the final scene of the war drama, as in earlier scenes, the Japanese "moderates" found it easier to bow to outside pressure than to act positively on their own to end the war.

Yet another example of ruling elite thinking about surrender terms was the "Essentials of Peace Negotiations" (*wahei kōshō no yōryō*), a document drafted by Konoe and his adviser, retired Lt. Gen. Sakai Kōji, after Konoe had reluctantly accepted his mission to Moscow.[73] The "Essentials," which appear never to have circulated, stipulated the preservation of the emperor system (including most of the imperial prerogatives) as the absolute minimum condition for peace. The document defined the "original" or "essential homeland" as including the southern half of the Kurile Islands but showed a willingness to concede to the enemy all overseas territories, including Okinawa and the American-occupied Bonin Islands, as well as the southern half of Sakhalin. The "Essentials" also accepted complete disarmament for an unspecified period of time, thereby compromising on the matter of demobilizing and disarming the armed forces.

More significant, an "explanation" attached to the "Essentials" noted that "the main aim is to secure the imperial line and maintain the political role of the emperor. In the worst case scenario, however, transfer of the throne to a successor might be unavoidable. If this should happen it must take a spontaneous form." Konoe and Sakai were also prepared to "return to politics predicated on *minpon seiji*" or "the people-under-the-emperor." They used this Taishō-era term to mean "democracy" at a time when the Japanese people viewed democracy as the culture of the enemy. Significantly, even Konoe did not dare to seek the emperor's approval of his attached "Explanation."[74]

In maneuvering for a "peace with honor" that would protect the throne, Konoe and Sakai also revealed their willingness to send some of their fellow countrymen into forced labor in lieu of material reparations if cutting a deal required it. Thus the "Essentials" declared that "We shall demobilize the military overseas in the places they are stationed, and endeavor to repatriate them. If that is impossible, we shall consent to leaving some of them where they are for awhile." Their explanation of this item noted: "We consent to offer some labor as reparations." Clearly the idea of interning Japanese POWs at forced labor for the Soviet economy (later implemented by the Russians in Siberian work camps) was not exclusively a Soviet notion but actually originated with men in the emperor's entourage.[75]

III

The twin psychological shocks of the first atomic bomb and the Soviet entry into the war, coupled with Kido's and the emperor's concern over growing popular criticism of the throne and its occupant, and their almost paranoiac fear that, sooner or later, the people would react violently against their leaders if they allowed the war to go on much longer—these factors finally caused Hirohito to accept, in principle, the terms of the Potsdam Declaration.[76]

At the first meeting of the six constituent members of the Supreme War Leadership Council, from 10:30 A.M. to 1:00 P.M. on

August 9, Army Minister Anami Korechika, Chiefs of Staff Umezu Yoshijirō representing the army and Yonai representing the navy, and Tōgō representing the Foreign Ministry were supposed to have discussed acceptance of the Potsdam Declaration. Instead they debated whether to try to surrender with conditions: one condition, preservation of the *kokutai*, or four?

After Suzuki had addressed the gathering about the atomic bombing of Hiroshima and the Soviet attack, Yonai, according to the account of Navy Chief of Staff Toyoda, was the first to speak and to frame the issue in terms of four conditions. "Let's start to talk," he began. "Do we accept the Potsdam Declaration with no conditions . . . ? If not, and we want to insist on attaching hopes and conditions, we may go about it this way. First, preservation of the *kokutai*, and then for the rest, the main items in the Potsdam Declaration: treatment of war criminals, method of disarmament, and the matter of sending in an army of occupation."[77] Thus the participants extracted what they considered to be the unclear points of the Potsdam Declaration and made them the basis for their discussions.

The army insisted on four conditions.[78] These were, first, preservation of the *kokutai*, considered by all as something distinct from the Potsdam Declaration. The other conditions were, second, assumption by the Imperial Headquarters of responsibility for disarmament and demobilization; third, no occupation; and finally, delegation to the Japanese government of the punishment of war criminals.[79] The army equated the *kokutai* with the emperor's right of supreme command. Its self-serving desire to have autonomous war crimes trials was predicated on the belief that the Allies would use such trials to indict the military on political grounds. Hence the army leaders wanted to preempt the work of any international tribunal by conducting their own trials—exactly as the uninvaded and unrepentant Germans had done after World War I.[80]

Supporting the military's views at cabinet meetings during the day were three civilian members of the Suzuki cabinet: Justice Minister Matsuzaka Hiromasa, Home Minister Yasui Tōji, and Minister of Health Okada Tadahiko.[81] At the imperial conference that night (it lasted into the early morning hours of the tenth), Foreign Minister Tōgō held that the sole surrender condition to be insisted on was preservation of the *kokutai*. And throughout the discussion "preservation of the *kokutai*" meant for Tōgō preservation only of the Imperial House or dynasty, not the continuation of Hirohito's reign.

This was not what it meant for the others. Hiranuma, also a supporter of one condition, had a very different interpretation of the *kokutai*, one in which the "emperor's sovereign right to rule the state [did] not derive from national law." Accordingly Hiranuma insisted that "Even if the entire nation is sacrificed to the war, we must preserve both the *kokutai* and the security of the imperial house."[82] Stated differently, there was no completely unified understanding of what the *kokutai* meant; the debate on one condition versus four was really about the future form of the Japanese state and concealed the competition for future political power that was already under way.

It is doubtful whether the emperor and Kido initially sided with Tōgō and opposed the four conditions of the senior military leaders. The more likely inference is that both men still sympathized with the diehards, military and civilian alike, who preferred to continue the suicidal war rather than surrender immediately and unconditionally. This may be why, on August 9, Konoe had Hosokawa Morisada go to Navy General Headquarters and urge the emperor's brother Prince Takamatsu to press Hirohito (via Kido) to accept the Potsdam terms, and why, later that afternoon, Konoe also enlisted the help of diplomat Shigemitsu Mamoru in persuading Kido to change his stand on four conditions. At the urging of Takamatsu and Shigemitsu, Kido did indeed shift to Tōgō's position.[83]

Credit for ending the war must also be given to the younger generation of bureaucrats who assisted the court leaders: Kido's secretary, Matsudaira Yasumasa; Suzuki's secretary, Sakomizu Hisatsune; Tōgō's and Shigemitsu's secretary, Kase Toshikazu; and the assistant to Navy Minister Yonai, Rear Admiral Takagi. Not only were these men instrumental in pressing the emperor's top aides to accept the Potsdam terms, they also played a major role behind the scenes, after the surrender, in shielding the emperor from the consequences of defeat.[84] The desire to protect the emperor would thereafter limit and distort how the entire process of surrender was depicted. Matsudaira even managed to get the false official version of the emperor's role in the war inserted into *The Reports of General MacArthur*.[85]

The manufacture of historical memory of the end of the war began in Tokyo at the imperial conference held in the early morning hours of August 9–10. There the emperor, who had belatedly joined the "peace camp" in June by calling for an early though not yet an immediate surrender, and had thereafter vacillated, formally accepted the Potsdam Declaration, in a speech to his ministers scripted for him by Kido. Shortly before the conference opened, Suzuki asked for and received special permission from the emperor to have Hiranuma, representative of ultraconservative opinion, attend.[86] Sakomizu, who knew beforehand that the forty-four-year-old emperor was going to give a speech that night, came to the midnight meeting prepared to document it. He wrote up the emperor's words in smooth, businesslike language.

Many months later the emperor himself recounted what was most relevant to understanding the motivation for his "sacred decision" (*seidan*) at the Supreme War Leadership Council meeting on the night of August 9–10. Past 2:00 A.M., with the meeting deadlocked over whether to accept the Potsdam Declaration, Suzuki:

> expressed his wish that I should decide between the two opinions. . . .
> Although everybody agreed to attach the condition of preserving the
> *kokutai*, three—Anami, Toyoda, and Umezu—insisted on adding

three further conditions: not to carry out an occupation with the aim of securing specific surrender terms, and to leave disarmament and the punishment of war criminals to us. They also insisted that negotiation on these matters was still possible at the present stage of the war. But four people—Suzuki, Hiranuma, Yonai, and Tōgō—argued against them, saying there was no room to negotiate.

I thought by then that it was impossible to continue the war. I had been informed by the chief of the Army General Staff that the defenses of Cape Inubō and the Kujūkuri coastal plain [in Chiba prefecture] were still not ready. Also, according to the army minister, the matériel needed to complete arming the divisions that would fight the final battle in the Kantō region could not be delivered until September. How could the capital be defended under such conditions? How was a battle even possible? I saw no way.

I told them that I supported the Foreign Ministry's proposal. Hiranuma's revision of the Foreign Ministry's original draft, concerning the phrase "the position of the emperor in the national law," was accepted, but later on that proved to be a mistake. In any case, this meeting decided to accept the Potsdam Declaration based on my decision and arranged to send a telegram to that effect through Switzerland and Sweden. . . . The main motive behind my decision at that time was that if we . . . did not act, the Japanese race would perish and I would be unable to protect my loyal subjects [*sekishi*—literally, "children"]. Second, Kido agreed with me on the matter of defending the *kokutai*. If the enemy landed near Ise Bay, both Ise and Atsuta Shrines would immediately come under their control. There would be no time to transfer the sacred treasures [regalia] of the imperial family and no hope of protecting them. Under these circumstances, protection of the *kokutai* would be difficult. For these reasons, I thought at the time that I must make peace even at the sacrifice of myself.[87]

In this speech the emperor claims that his army minister told him that the capital could not be defended. Ever since June, however, he had known full well that continuation of the war was increasingly problematic. Why had he waited so long before making a policy decision to surrender immediately? And why, if Suzuki had wanted only one condition, and a real majority existed rather than a deadlock, didn't they end the war by majority decision, with Hirohito ratifying their decision after the fact?

The emperor already knew before Hiroshima was bombed that his cabinet was divided on accepting the Potsdam terms. He also knew that only he could unify government affairs and military command. Why, then, had he waited until the evening of the ninth—that is, until after yet another act of tremendous outside pressure had been applied—to call the Supreme War Leadership Council into session?[88]

In justifying his decision to surrender, Hirohito counterposes Hiranuma to the military hard-liners but then criticizes him for influencing the wording of the telegram that the Foreign Ministry sent to the Allies conditionally accepting the Potsdam Declaration. Yet Hiranuma joined the council, and the cabinet meeting that followed, precisely to *ensure* expression of the Shintoist, right-wing view of the *kokutai*. At the meetings on August 9–10, it was Hiranuma, not Tōgō, who voiced the sense of the majority on the fundamental need, which was to guarantee the theocratic view of the *kokutai* rather than Tōgō's secular, cultural view. At the time Hirohito supported Hiranuma and made no objection to that majority sentiment because he believed himself to be a monarch by divine right.

No discussion of Hirohito's speech should overlook his omission of the questioning of his responsibility for the defeat. Gen. Ikeda Sumihisa and Adm. Hoshina Zenshirō attended the August 9–10 meeting, and both later claimed that Privy Council President Hiranuma raised the matter. In Ikeda's account Hiranuma turned to Hirohito in the early morning hours of August 10 and said quietly, "Your majesty, you also bear responsibility [*sekinin*] for this defeat.

What apology [*mōshiwake*] are you going to make to the heroic spirits of the imperial founder of your house and your other imperial ancestors?" Hoshina, Chief of the Naval Affairs Department of the Navy Ministry, has Hiranuma saying virtually the same thing: "His majesty bears responsibility for reporting to the founder of his house and his other imperial ancestors. If he is not clear about this [matter], then his responsibility is grave."[89] Thus, at the August 9–10 Imperial Conference, Hiranuma may have raised with Hirohito the question of his atonement for the lost war. One wonders whether they did not also discuss the question of his abdication.

Once the emperor had made his "sacred decision," a cabinet conference deliberated on Tōgō's one condition. At Hiranuma's suggestion they agreed to reformulate their acceptance to read: "with the understanding that the said declaration does not comprise any demand that prejudices the prerogatives of his majesty as a sovereign ruler [*tennō no kokka tōji no taiken*]." Thus the *kokutai* concept of the right-wing ideologue Hiranuma emerged as the consensus, while Tōgō's more rational view that the imperial dynasty, not Hirohito, should be preserved, was ignored.

In effect this amounted to an affirmation that the emperor's rights of sovereignty, including his all-important right of supreme command, antedated the constitution and had been determined by the gods in antiquity, just as stated in the preamble to the Meiji constitution.[90] The Suzuki government was still fighting to maintain a view of the *kokutai* that included the emperor's political, military, and diplomatic prerogatives; and despite all that had happened, it was asking the Allies to guarantee the emperor's power to rule on the theocratic premises of state Shinto.[91] It was certainly not constitutional monarchy that the Suzuki cabinet sought to have the Allies assure, but rather a Japanese monarchy based on the principle of oracular sovereignty, with continued subjecthood or *shimmin* status for the Japanese people, and some postsurrender role for the military. In their extreme moment of crisis, the *kokutai* meant to them the orthodox Shinto-National Learning view of the state and the retention of real, substantial political power in the hands of the emperor, so that he and the "moderates" might go on using it to control his majesty's "subjects" after surrender.[92]

If the conservative Joseph C. Grew and the "Japan crowd" had gotten their way and the principle of unconditional surrender had been modified in advance, it is highly unlikely that Japan's postsurrender leaders, now the "moderates" around the throne, would ever have discarded the Meiji constitution and democratized their political institutions. Grew and those who took his position had very little understanding of the Japanese body politic, no faith in the capacity for democracy of ordinary Japanese people, and certainly no desire whatsoever to see the social foundations of the monarchy dismantled.

Secretary of State Byrnes's reply of August 11 to Japan's first surrender offer reiterated, but in no way compromised, America's basic unconditional surrender principle. Byrnes's note stated that "the authority of the Emperor and the Japanese Government to rule the state" had passed into the hands of the Supreme Commander of the Allied Powers; the emperor was to order all Japanese military authorities at home and abroad "to cease active operations and to surrender their arms;" it deliberately left unclarified the future status of both the emperor and the imperial institution. It was upon Japan's acceptance of an intact unconditional surrender principle, and of an uncertain status for the emperor, that the absolute authority of General MacArthur would be predicated and the institutional reforms of the early occupation period based.

To make the Byrnes note more palatable to Hirohito, the army leaders, and Hiranuma, Vice Foreign Minister Matsumoto Shinichi (after discussions with Tōgō), and Chief Cabinet Secretary Sakomizu resorted to mistranslation of several key words in the English text.[93] In the operative sentence, "From the moment of surrender, the authority of the Emperor and the Japanese Government to rule the state shall be subject to the Supreme Commander of the Allied powers," Matsumoto changed "shall be subject to" [*reizoku subeki*] to read "shall be circumscribed by" [*seigen no shita ni okareru*].

His change may have helped the still deeply divided Hirohito to accept peace. The next day, August 12, Hirohito informed the imperial family of his decision to surrender. When Prince Asaka asked whether the war would be continued if the *kokutai* could not be preserved, Hirohito replied "of course."[94]

At this point an attempt by a small group of middle-echelon officers in Tokyo to reject Byrnes's reply forced Hirohito to repeat his sacred decision on August 14. These last-minute coup attempts at the palace and at Atsugi air base did not amount to much and were aborted. Hirohito's decision of August 10 had totally demoralized the military bureaucrats at Imperial Headquarters and stripped them of the will to fight. Once Army Chief of Staff Umezu had explained to his subordinates that the emperor "had lost all confidence in the military," those in favor of fighting to the finish abruptly gave up.[95]

IV

At no time did the Japanese military ever exercise "complete dominance" over the political process or the conduct of the war, as Grew had maintained. As the war dragged on after the fall of the Tōjō cabinet, the senior leaders of the army and navy became increasingly beholden for their positions of power to the court group and the moderates around the throne. Not only were the latter closer to Hirohito; they also operated information exchanges, designed to obtain information for the emperor, which were more effective than the army's network of internal intelligence sources.[96]

At the end of the war as at its beginning, and through every stage of its unfolding, Emperor Hirohito played a highly active role in supporting the actions carried out in his name. When he is properly restored in the overall picture as supreme commander, the facts become abundantly clear: Neither (*a*) American unwillingness to make a firm, timely statement assuring continuation of the monarchy, as Grew had argued for, nor (*b*) the anti-Soviet strategy in the stance of Truman and Byrnes, who probably preferred use of the atomic bombs over diplomatic negotiation, were sufficient in and of themselves to account for use of the bomb, or for Japan's delay in surrendering. Rather, Emperor Hirohito's reluctance to face the fait accompli of defeat, and then to act decisively to end hostilities, plus certain official acts and policies of his government, were what mainly kept the war going, though they *also* were not sufficient causes for use of the bomb. In the final analysis, what counted on the one hand was not only the transcendent influence of the throne but the power, authority, and stubborn personality of its occupant, and on the other the power, determination, and truculence of Harry Truman.

From the very start of the Asia-Pacific war, the emperor was a major protagonist of the events going on around him. Before the Battle of Okinawa he had constantly pressed for a decisive victory. Afterward he accepted the need for an early but not an immediate peace. And then he vacillated, steering Japan toward continued warfare rather than toward direct negotiations with the Allies. When the final crisis was fully upon him, the only option left was surrender without negotiation. Even then he continued to procrastinate until the bomb was dropped and the Soviets attacked.

Generally speaking, it is true that any demand for surrender without prior negotiation has some retarding effect on the process of ending a war. But in this case it was not so much the Allied policy of unconditional surrender or "absolute victory" that prolonged the Asia-Pacific war, as it was the unrealistic and incompetent actions of Japan's highest leaders. The wartime emperor ideology that sustained their morale made it almost impossibly difficult for them to perform the act of surrender. Knowing they were objectively defeated, yet indifferent to the suffering that the war was imposing on their own people, let alone the peoples of Asia, the Pacific, and the West whose lives they had disrupted, the emperor and his war leaders searched for a way to lose without losing—a way to assuage domestic criticism after surrender and allow their power structure to survive.

Blinded by their preoccupation with the fate of the imperial house, and committed to an optimistic diplomacy vis-à-vis the Soviet Union, those leaders let pass several opportunities to end their lost war. Hirohito and his inner war cabinet—the Supreme War Leadership Council—could have looked reality in the face and acted decisively to sue for peace during February, when Prince Konoe made his report and both he and Foreign Minister Shigemitsu warned the emperor that the Neutrality Treaty offered no protection; the Soviet Union would not hesitate to intervene militarily in the Far East once the situation turned favorable in Europe. Military intelligence officers also alerted them to the likelihood of the Soviet Union entering the war against Japan by midsummer. By then the home islands had only been bombed on a small scale, but they knew for certain that the bombing of their cities would only intensify over time.

Their second missed opportunity came in early June, when the showdown Battle of Okinawa had been lost, when government analyses indicated that the war effort could soon continue no longer, and when General Umezu unveiled for the emperor the bleak results of his personal survey of the situation in China.[97] Considering that Foreign Minister Molotov had earlier notified Tokyo on April 5 that the Japan-Soviet Neutrality Pact would not be extended, and that the Germans had surrendered unconditionally on May 7–8, leaving Japan completely isolated, this certainly would have been a most opportune moment for them to have opened direct negotiations with the United States and Britain.

Instead, the Supreme War Leadership Council took two dangerous courses: preparations for a final battle on the homeland, and efforts to gain Soviet assistance in ending the war by offering Stalin limited territorial concessions. With Hirohito's approval the six constituent members of the council agreed to return to the situation that had existed prior to the Russo-Japanese War, while retaining Korea as Japanese territory and making south Manchuria a neutral zone. Before these negotiations could even begin, the council members adopted an infallible formula for wasting time. They authorized former foreign minister Hirota to confer with Ambassador Malik in order to discover the "intentions" of the Soviet leaders.[98]

Their third missed opportunity was July 27–28, when the Potsdam Declaration arrived and the Suzuki cabinet, after careful deliberation, twice publicly rejected it. At that time no member of the "peace faction" came forward with a proposal for accepting the Potsdam terms. Pinning their hopes on Konoe's not-yet-arranged mission to Moscow, the emperor and Kido delayed surrender and allowed the war to go on. During this interval between their receipt of the Potsdam Declaration on July 27 and the bombing of Hiroshima on August 6, the emperor and Kido waited and waited for a response from Moscow—a response that Ambassador Satō and others repeatedly stated would never come. Only *after* Hiroshima had been bombed did the emperor say, "We must bow to the inevitable;" now "is a good chance to end the war." More than ten thousand Japanese people died from conventional air raids during this eleven-day interval.[99]

The Japanese "peace" overtures to the Soviets, which had followed Germany's capitulation, were vague, feeble, and counterproductive. They certainly never constituted a serious attempt to negotiate an end to the war.[100] The thinking behind those maneuvers never progressed beyond decisions reached by the inner cabinet in mid-May 1945. As Konoe rightly suspected it would, the emperor's attempt to end the war via Moscow turned out to be a complete waste of time, and amounted to an imperial decision to postpone facing reality.

Would Japan's leaders have surrendered more promptly if the Truman administration had "clarified" the status of the emperor prior to the cataclysmic double shocks of the first atomic bomb and Soviet entry into the war? Probably not. On the other hand, they were likely to have surrendered in order to prevent the *kokutai* from being destroyed from within. The evidence suggests that the first atomic bomb and the Soviet declaration of war made Hirohito, Kido, and other members of the court group feel that continuation of the war would lead to precisely that destruction. They knew that the people were war-weary and despondent and that popular hostility toward the military and the government was increasing rapidly, along with popular criticism of the emperor himself. More particularly, Kido and Hirohito were privy to Home Ministry reports, based on information from governors and police chiefs all over the country, revealing that people were starting to speak of the emperor as an incompetent leader who was responsible for the worsening war situation.

At this critical moment the court group's very strong sense of internal threats had undoubtedly gone on hair-trigger alert. When the emperor back in February had said, "What worries me is whether the nation [could] endure" long enough to achieve victory, he was not so much expressing concern for the suffering of his subjects as fear that their suffering would result in social turmoil—in short, revolution. At that time he had been speaking of the ordinary, war-normal hardships of food shortages, air raids, burning cities, destroyed homes, and general discomfort as well as the ever-present death of loved ones. The atom bomb carried the infliction of death, pain, and suffering to unimaginably higher levels, and therefore also the threat from within. Of course there might have been only one bomb. But suddenly a second mushroom cloud rose; another city almost vanished. Yet the danger provided an opportunity: Hirohito now could save his suffering people from more suffering by surrendering, and at the same time shed responsibility for having led them into misery and assume an air of benevolence and the mantle of car-ing. Hirohito did indeed care. Not primarily for the Japanese people, however, but for his own imperial house and throne.

On July 16, the day of the successful American test of the first atomic bomb, Stalin, sensing what was about to happen, placed an urgent phone call to the commander of the Soviet Far Eastern forces, Marshal A. M. Vasilievsky, to ask how preparations for the campaign against Japan were progressing and whether he could move up the planned date by ten days. Vasilievsky replied that more time was needed to concentrate troops and needed supplies. Perhaps, if Stalin had been able to open war against Japan *before* the United States dropped the atomic bombs, the nuclear destruction of Hiroshima and Nagasaki might have been avoided. Or, if Japan had accepted the Potsdam Declaration on July 26, both the atomic bombs and Soviet entry into the war might have been avoided.[101]

Truman, at a White House meeting with the Joint Chiefs of Staff on June 18, had given the go-ahead for the invasion of Kyushu, with all that entailed in terms of high casualties and the logistics and manpower to sustain the operation into Spring 1946, when the invasion of Honshu was scheduled.[102] The recent Battle of Okinawa was on everyone's mind at that time, and Truman commented that "an Okinawa from one end of Japan to the other" was possible.[103] By the time he arrived at Potsdam, American battle casualties for the Kyushu invasion, scheduled to begin November 1, 1945, were projected as 22,576 killed, wounded, and missing during the first thirty days, increasing by nearly 11,000 during the next thirty days.[104]

It is not known if Truman was troubled by the massive American conventional bombing of Japanese noncombatants—actions that qualified as atrocities. But he was concerned with high American casualty projections. For him the alternative to dropping the atomic bombs would have been to wait for the effects of the Soviet ground attack in Manchuria and Korea, combined with the conventional bombing and shelling of the home islands, to become intolerable to Japan's leaders. Armed with a new doomsday weapon, however, Truman lacked the patience and foresight to wait. Japan's leaders, on the other hand, caught in the grip of a failed and endangered ideology, were willing to sacrifice huge numbers of their own people in order to maintain their and their monarch's power. It was partly to destroy that psychology—or, in the words of Army Chief of Staff Gen. George C. Marshall, spoken in 1957, "shock them [the leaders] into action"—that Truman and Marshall justified the dropping of the atomic bombs.[105]

V

Hirohito's staging of the *seidan* on the night of August 9–10, his repeat performance of it on the morning of the fourteenth, and finally, the dramatic radio reenactment of the *seidan* on a national scale, with the whole nation participating, at noon on the fifteenth—these events reinforced his charisma while preparing a new role for him in the drama called postwar that now would begin.

After the Hiroshima bombing, Hirohito procrastinated for a full day and a half before telling Kido, shortly before 10 A.M. on August 9, to "quickly control the situation" because "the Soviet Union has declared war and today began hostilities against us."[106] Kido immediately communicated with Prime Minister Suzuki, who began arrangements for the Imperial Conference held later that night. Following the *seidan* of August 10, chief cabinet secretary Sakomizu took charge of drafting the "Imperial Rescript Ending the War" on the basis of Hirohito's words. Assisted by two scholars of the Chinese classics, Kawada Mizuho and Yasuoka Masahiro, Sakomizu labored for over three days before submitting a version of the rescript to the Suzuki cabinet, which modified and approved it after six hours of contentious discussion on the night of August 14. Hirohito immediately signed it. Shimomura and Kido then persuaded him to record the suitably opaque final version for broadcast to the nation.

On the night of August 14 the Suzuki government notified the United States and other Allied governments that it had accepted both the Potsdam Declaration and the Byrnes letter of August 11. Hastening the emperor's actions in the climactic moment of the unconditional surrender drama was the American psychological warfare campaign. When a leaflet dropped from B-29s came into Kido's possession on the night of August 13 or the morning of the fourteenth, he met the emperor and explained the danger. The latest enemy leaflets were giving the Japanese people both the government's notification of surrender on one condition and the full text of Brynes's reply to it. If this continued, it would undermine the imperial government's reliance on secrecy to conceal from the nation the true nature of the lost war and the reasons for the long delayed surrender. Given Kido's and the emperor's worry about growing signs of defeatism, including criticism of the throne, they had to take immediate action to prevent people from acting on their own initiative. Hence the second *seidan*.[107]

At noon on August 15, the Japanese people gathered around their radio speakers and heard for the first time the high-pitched voice of their emperor telling them: "Our empire accepts the provisions of their Joint Declaration." There was no explanation of what those provisions were, but his next words went on to concede defeat, albeit indirectly, without ever using the word, and to seize the high moral ground from the Allies by declaring that he was acting to save "human civilization" from "total extinction" by "pav[ing] the way for a grand peace for all the generations to come." Hirohito also reiterated—just as his war rescript stated—that the aim of the war had been national "existence and self-defense," and he expressed regret only to the puppet and collaborationist regimes in Asia that had been Japan's allies.

In an emotionally powerful and astute last paragraph, the emperor revealed, but did not state, the real goals of his decision to end the war. He, who had made the war meaningful and valid for the people of Japan, wanted to obfuscate the issue of accountability, prevent expressions of strife and anger, and strengthen domestic unity centered on himself.

> Having been able to safeguard and maintain the structure of the imperial state, we are always with ye, Our good and loyal subjects, relying upon your sincerity and integrity. Beware most strictly of any outbursts of emotion that can engender needless complications, or any fraternal contention and strife that may create confusion, lead ye astray and cause ye to lose the confidence of the world. Let the entire nation continue as one family from generation to generation, ever firm in its faith of the imperishability of its divine land, ever mindful of its heavy burden of responsibilities, and of the long road before it.[108]

Hirohito's surrender rescript was the first text to redefine his new national image as a pacifist, antimilitarist, and completely passive onlooker in the war—none of which he had ever been. It cleverly underscored both his "benevolence" and his assertion of imperial sovereignty while obscuring his earlier reluctance to act concretely, on his own initiative, to end the war. But for those who heard the rescript, it was a shocking experience, a bolt from the blue that caught them totally unprepared. To ensure correct understanding of the message, which was written in obscure court style, radio announcer Wada Shinken reread the entire rescript in ordinary language. A cabinet announcement followed, condemning the United States for use of the atomic bombs in violation of international law, and the Soviet Union for declaring war against Japan. Thereupon Wada made these comments:

> We ourselves invited a situation in which we had no choice but to lay down our arms. We could not live up to the great benevolence of the emperor, but he did not even scold us. On the contrary, he said that whatever might happen to himself, "I can no longer bear to see my peo-

ple die in war." Before such great benevolence and love, who among us
can escape reflecting on his own disloyalty.[109]

Wada ended by reiterating the purpose of the imperial message:
"Since the situation has developed this way, the nation will unite
and, believing in the indestructibility of the divine land, put all of its
energies into rebuilding for the future." As the special surrender
broadcast drew to a close, a news commentary on the Potsdam Declaration again encouraged the audience to accept defeat, display the
proper moral attitude, and face reality "with a strong sense of self-
reproach. . . . Everyone must bear in mind that if we start blaming
one another, it will lead to economic, social, and moral confusion
that will destroy the imperial nation."[110]

The Japanese government, having accepted the Potsdam Declaration and the negative moral judgment it had rendered on all of
Japan's modern wars, was thereby obligated to pursue the issue of
war criminality. The imperial rescript and accompanying news
commentaries of August 14, however, were chiefly concerned with
maintaining order while preserving the monarchy and the official
ideology. The war in China was not mentioned; aggression was
ignored; troops were praised for their loyalty. Diffusing the
accountability of the decision makers, the notion was planted that
"the entire nation should share responsibility."

In the weeks and months that followed, vast amounts of secret
materials pertaining to Japanese war crimes and the war responsibility of the nation's highest leaders went up in smoke—in accordance with the August 14 decision of the Suzuki cabinet. Meanwhile
the media, and the cabinet of Prince Higashikuni Naruhiko, which
succeeded Suzuki's on August 17, represented the emperor to the
nation as the benevolent sage and apolitical ruler who had ended the
war. The surrender-broadcast "ritual" confirmed Hirohito's inherent power to create a radically new situation. Now the Japanese

people could return to peaceful economic pursuits, ever mindful that their emperor had saved them—and the rest of the world—from further destruction by atomic bombs.[111]

The very naming of this event was determined by the wartime needs of the ruling group, and ever since has impeded a deeper understanding of it. Hirohito's "sacred decision" both described and legitimized his act of ending the war by casting it in the most morally acceptable light. The device of the *seidan* shielded from criticism Hirohito's actions in the events of August 9–10, 14, and 15. At the same time those actions were tailored to fit the preexisting imperial narrative of his reign. The last *seidan* clearly served multiple political and memorializing functions.

The imperial rescripts announcing the *seidan* also abetted conflicting assessments of the atomic bombs' effect in hastening the conclusion of the war. The emperor's rescript of August 14 never used the word "surrender" and registered indirectly (with a single, vague phrase) Germany's defeat and the Soviet Union's entrance into the war, saying that "the general trends of the world have all turned against [Japan's] interest." It was unequivocally clear, however, in using the atomic bombs to portray Japan as victim and savior: "Moreover, the enemy has begun to employ a new and most cruel bomb, whose destructive power is quite incalculable; it has taken many innocent lives. Should we continue to fight, [that bomb] would result in the ultimate collapse and obliteration of the Japanese nation—even the total extinction of human civilization."

Obviously Hirohito sought to justify his decision to surrender by citing the dropping of the atomic bombs. The broadcast of his August 14 rescript became Japan's first official, public confirmation of the bombs' effectiveness. Whether the emperor and his advisers ever really believed that, however, is unlikely. For three days later, on August 17, Hirohito issued a second "Rescript to Soldiers and Sailors" in all war theaters of Asia and the Pacific, ordering them to cease fire and lay down their arms. This time, addressing only his military forces, he stressed the cause-and-effect relationship between Soviet entrance into the war and his decision to surrender, while conspicuously omitting any mention of the atomic bombs.

> Now that the Soviet Union has entered the war against us, to continue . . . under the present conditions at home and abroad would only recklessly incur even more damage to ourselves and result in endangering the very foundation of the empire's existence. Therefore, even though enormous fighting spirit still exists in the Imperial Navy and Army, I am going to make peace with the United States, Britain, and the Soviet Union, as well as with Chungking, in order to maintain our glorious national polity.[112]

The less-known August 17 rescript to the army and navy specified Soviet participation as the sole reason for surrender, and maintenance of the *kokutai* as the aim. Dissembling until the end—and beyond—the emperor stated two different justifications for his delayed surrender.[113] Both statements were probably true.

PART 4

THE UNEXAMINED LIFE, 1945–1989

14

A MONARCHY REINVENTED

Eleven-year-old Crown Prince Akihito had been evacuated to the safety of a hotel in the town of Nikkō, Tochigi prefecture, to escape the American bombing. Following the capitulation, Emperor Hirohito and Empress Nagako wrote to him, explaining why Japan had been beaten so badly. Their letters, filled with parental warmth, furnish glimpses of the tense situation in the beleaguered capital; more important, they reveal the mind-set of Japan's rulers in the immediate aftermath of defeat.

On August 30, 1945, Nagako reported: "Every day from morning to night B-29s, naval bombers, and fighters freely fly over the palace in all directions, making an enormous noise.... Unfortunately the B-29 is a splendid [plane]. As I sit at my desk writing and look up at the sky, countless numbers are passing over."[1] Hirohito too was impressed by the technological prowess of the Americans, embodied in their "superfortress." Many months earlier he had mentioned to Akihito how he and Nagako had been going around the garden of the Gobunko "picking up various articles related to B-29s."[2]

In a letter to his son dated September 9, the emperor skipped over the policy-making process in which he had been the central figure and laid out the large, general causes of the defeat:

Our people believed too much in the imperial country and were contemptuous of Britain and the United States. Our military men placed

too much weight on spirit and forgot about science. In the time of the
Meiji Emperor, there were great commanders like Yamagata, Ōyama,
and Yamamoto. But this time, as with Germany in World War I, military men predominated and gave no thought to the larger situation.
They knew how to advance but not how to retreat.

If we had continued the war, we would have been unable to protect the
three imperial regalia. Not only that, more of our countrymen would
have had to die. Repressing my emotions, I tried to save the seed of the
nation.[3]

Young Akihito's long diary entry, undated but written in
September 1945, and formally headed "Constructing the New
Japan," revealed other factors. Echoing what his parents and palace
tutors were teaching him about the nation's humiliating defeat, he
confessed that he felt "deeply mortified" by his father's having had
to take upon himself "the shame of the nation—unconditional surrender." Japan, however, had been defeated:

because of the overwhelming material superiority of Britain and the
United States . . . and the great skillfulness of the American way of
fighting. [The Anglo-Americans] were defeated at the start because
they were not then adequately prepared. But once they were prepared,
they came at us like wild boars. Their methods of attack were very
skillful and scientific. . . . Finally they used atomic bombs and killed
and wounded hundreds of thousands of Japanese, destroyed towns and
factories. . . . In the end we could fight no longer. The cause for this
was the inferiority of Japanese national power and scientific power.[4]

Akihito concluded by blaming the defeat on the Japanese people
rather than their leaders, and the political institutions under which
they lived. "It was impossible for the Japanese to win this total war
because from Taishō to early Shōwa, they thought only of their pri-

vate interests rather than the country, and behaved selfishly." Now the only course lay in following the emperor's words:

> ... maintain the spirit of protecting the *kokutai*, unite, and labor to climb out of this pit of darkness. No matter how one looks at it, individually, Japanese are superior to Americans in every respect. But as a group, we are inferior to them. So from now on we must have group training, foster science, and the entire nation must labor hard to construct a new, better Japan than today."[5]

The new Japan should foster science, tighten group commitment to national goals, and consider the past closed. From the outset, the elites dwelt on responsibility for the loss of the "War of Greater East Asia." Their autopsy ignored the pre–Pearl Harbor expansion into Manchuria, which Hirohito had abetted, the North China Incident of 1937 that, with his encouragement, the Konoe cabinet had escalated into an all-out war, and the role of Asian nationalism in contributing to defeat. Responsibility for having attacked China in 1931 and the United States and Britain in December 1941 shifted to responsibility for final defeat, which had cost the nation so much shame and misery. Naturally Hirohito did not in any way hold himself or the court group responsible for this consequence.

Crown Prince Akihito's sense that Japanese pursuit of self-interest was selfishness reflected another element in the official war autopsy. Hirohito's character and training disposed him to distrust individual self-assertion. Following the dictates of one's conscience posed, he believed, a threat to belief in the idealized collective self, and in the *kokutai*. From the start of Shōwa, Hirohito and the court entourage had actively encouraged the indoctrination of the nation in habits of self-effacement and obedience to officials. From 1937 onward they had supported policies designed to drastically lower living standards in order to rapidly build up war power. When it came time to consider how to construct the new nation, they initially imagined that they could continue this old emphasis. Hostile to liberalism, individualism, and democracy, they decried, on the one hand, the Japanese people's tendency to "follow blindly," and on the other, the blindness of putting self-interest ahead of state interest.

These widely held views on the nature of the war prevented Hirohito, his entourage, and the old-guard leaders from ever pursuing the connection between the causes of defeat and the construction of a new Japan. They also colored the tack that they now took toward their American occupiers.

I

Having ended his alliance with the military hardliners, thus reunifying the court group, Hirohito tried to reconcile himself to a period of temporary disarmament and foreign occupation. A new campaign of "spiritual mobilization" to protect the monarchy, based on his imperial rescript of August 15, and driving home its message, was now an obvious necessity. The next prime minister would need to explain to a dazed, demoralized, and battered nation what had happened, and why all loyal subjects must now change their thinking, courteously accept the enemy, and raise no questions as to who was responsible for the horrendous plight in which they found themselves. The immediate tasks of the next cabinet were to prepare a peaceful reception for the largely American army of occupation, and to hearten the nation by conveying an impression of continuity with the past. Only a member of the extended imperial family at the head of the next government could accomplish these tasks.

Acting on the recommendation of Kido, who dispensed with a conference of the senior statesmen and consulted only Hiranuma,

Hirohito, on August 17, appointed Prince Higashikuni as prime minister.[6] The prince had close ties to the imperial family. His wife was Emperor's Meiji's ninth daughter, and his son was married to Hirohito's daughter, Teru no miya. Having no reason at this time to think Higashikuni anything but trustworthy, even though he was a complete political novice, Hirohito charged him with overseeing a swift, peaceful, and preemptive demobilization of the army and navy. Higashikuni's "Imperial Family Cabinet," as the press immediately labeled it, was charged with demonstrating to the Allies that the monarchy alone had the power to demobilize Japan peacefully and control the situation. Higashikuni selected Konoe to be vice prime minister, and Ogata Taketora, vice president of the Asahi newspaper company, to be chief cabinet secretary. Both men were to play key roles in protecting the *kokutai*, legitimizing the emperor's actions, and shielding him from criticism. Ogata the propagandist directed the campaign to counter criticism of the war leaders; Konoe focused on preparations for the arrival of the American and British Commonwealth forces.

Although suicides occurred in different parts of the country immediately following surrender, the overwhelming majority of Japanese accepted the new situation. They also responded positively to Higashikuni's unprecedented radio speech to the nation, on August 17, informing them of his general principles for government. Act together "in accordance with the imperial will," he enjoined, and "we shall . . . construct the highest culture as advanced as any in the world. . . . Toward that end . . . I wish to encourage the development of constructive discussion and recognize the freedom to form healthy associations."[7] Peace would offer hope for the return of loved ones, and also allow some shedding of wartime constraints.

On the other hand few Japanese had any idea of what occupation would bring. Some, living in the vicinity of military bases, worried whether Allied troops would behave as their own soldiers had in China: pillaging, plundering, and raping, and voiced fear of a weakening of the race through miscegenation. The issue of rape and the fear of violence once the occupation troops landed was dealt with promptly. Konoe suggested, and Higashikuni approved, mobilizing prostitutes to deal with the sex-starved Allied troops who would, in only a few weeks, be descending upon the land.

On August 19 the Home Ministry ordered local government offices to establish "Recreation and Amusement Associations" (RAA), funded from the National Treasury. Almost overnight advertisements appeared in the national press and elsewhere informing women in need that food, clothing, and accommodation would be provided to all who volunteered to join. At the inaugural declaration of the RAA, crowds formed on the Imperial Plaza and an estimated fifteen hundred young women gathered on the street outside the temporary headquarters of RAA at Ginza 7 chōme (in the vicinity of today's Matsuzaka Department Store). There they listened as an RAA official read a declaration stating:

> [T]hrough the sacrifice of thousands of Okichis of the Shōwa era, we shall construct a dike to hold back the mad frenzy [of the occupation troops] and cultivate and preserve the purity of our race long into the future. . . . In this way we shall contribute to the peace of society. Stated differently, we are volunteering [our bodies] for the preservation of the *kokutai*.[8]

To deal with possible hostile reaction to such measures, the Home Ministry's Police Bureau, on August 23, issued secret "guidelines" for police officials throughout the country, warning them not to permit public criticism of the senior statesmen or of the emperor's decision to surrender. The imperial rescript had been issued, now the country must move forward, complying with the emperor's orders and "reflecting on one thing only: that, ultimately, we troubled the emperor's heart." The guidelines warned the police to "prevent disputes with the Allied forces by staying cool, calm, patient, and prudent under all circumstances. By doing these things we shall assuage the emperor's uneasiness and maintain the world's trust." Should any incident occur with the Allied armies, "it will be difficult to prevent the state and race from being destroyed."[9]

Opposition from the defeated armed forces, however, proved largely nonexistent. Morale among troops stationed on the home islands was low before August 15; over the next three weeks it disintegrated. Reports forwarded to the office of Privy Seal Kido from prefectural governors and police officials told of units demanding immediate discharge, of kamikaze pilots loading their planes with food and other supplies and flying off to their home villages, of army doctors and nurses in a hospital in Kagoshima competing with one another to flee their posts, leaving their patients behind. As scenes of military disorder, theft of military stocks, and general unruliness within the armed forces multiplied, civilian respect for the military collapsed. Men in uniform quickly found themselves objects of widespread civilian contempt.[10]

Higashikuni also had to contend with massive theft of government stockpiles of raw materials and goods by civil and military officials at the highest levels. Secret police reports in August indicated thousands of examples of government bureaucrats in the Munitions Ministry, the Ministry of Commerce and Industry, as well as the Army and Navy Ministries engaging in black market activities and covering up the sale of government stores by large corporations.[11] The one-sided way civil officials implemented wartime economic controls, arresting only small-scale black marketeers, exacerbated matters, and contributed to the nation's demoralization and its worsening economic plight.

Higashikuni was utterly unable to offer solutions to the problem of the burgeoning black market. In fact, at the start of his cabinet, he appointed as one of his cabinet councillors Kodama Yoshio, a black marketer and right-wing partisan. "Hereafter we're going to obey the commands of General MacArthur, so let's move smartly,"

Kodama told a Diet member from Tsu City who visited him in his Tokyo mansion in early September.[12] Kodama took charge of establishing sex and entertainment clubs for the occupation forces. So too did his friend Sasagawa Ryōichi, leader of the wartime National Essence League, who was not a cabinet councillor. Sasagawa's American Club in Minami Ward, Osaka, was one of the first to open in that city soon after American soldiers began arriving.[13]

Wittingly or not, the Higashikuni cabinet was laying a basis for the postwar reestablishment of ties between politicians, bureaucratic officials, and the underworld. The prime minister's main concern, however, was to win public support for the *kokutai* preservation movement. To that end, he appointed, as his second "cabinet counselor," Lt. Gen. Ishiwara Kanji, a man who had retired from active duty in 1941 and thereafter defined himself as an opponent of the Tōjō cabinet. Ishiwara was the leader of a new millenarian movement—the Tō'A renmei (East Asia League)—whose branches were spreading from northern Honshū to southern Kyushū.

Like Higashikuni, Ishiwara blamed the defeat on the degeneration of the Japanese people's morals. In his Tō'A renmei speeches he hammered home three themes: The gods had willed Japan's defeat in order to make the nation repent and renew its belief in the *kokutai*; the military, the police, and the bureaucracy, by oppressing the people, bore great responsibility for what had happened; and the nation should "surprise the enemy by carrying out reforms" before occupation rule even began. Abolish armaments for the duration of the occupation; get rid of the special higher police; end restrictions on speech and belief. And for the next several years, while in retreat from the world, Japan should learn as much as it could from the United States and imitate American ways.

To help Ishiwara spread this message, Higashikuni diverted railway trains to carry league members to conventions in different cities. In Morioka, Iwate prefecture, on September 14, 1945, Ishiwara (according to a police report) called on the entire nation to "repent" for having lost the war. He reminded his audience that by the end of the twentieth century, the "final global battle [between the United States and the Soviet Union] will be upon us," and that the principle of the *hakkō ichiu* (the "eight corners of the world under one roof") still lived.[14]

Hirohito kept close watch on Higashikuni's actions and appointments and received him in audiences at least once or twice a day from August 16 to September 2. During this crucial two weeks before their conquerors arrived en masse, Hirohito, the court group, and the Higashikuni cabinet focused on the issue that really mattered to them: controlling the people's reaction to defeat and keeping them obedient and unconcerned with questions of accountability. Nevertheless, no matter what they did, the feeling spread that once the foreign occupiers arrived, reform of the monarchy and punishment of those who had led the nation would ensue. The emperor himself, it was rumored, might even have to abdicate to assume responsibility for the war.

II

On August 30, 1945, General Douglas MacArthur, newly appointed supreme commander for the Allied Powers (SCAP), arrived in Japan to head the Allied military occupation. He set up his temporary headquarters in Yokohama. Three days later, on September 2, the emperor's representatives, led by Foreign Minister Shigemitsu, signed the formal surrender document aboard the U.S. battleship *Missouri*, moored in Tokyo Bay. Its concluding line was the operative sentence of Secretary of State Byrnes's reply to Japan's acceptance of the Potsdam Declaration: "The authority of the Emperor and the Japanese Government to rule the state shall be subject to the Supreme Commander for the Allied Powers who will take such steps as he deems proper to effectuate these terms of surrender."[15] That same day the Foreign Ministry established a "War Termination Liaison Committee," headed by diplomat Suzuki Kyūman, to obtain information from MacArthur and sound out his intentions. For many Japanese these were the first indications that "preservation of the *kokutai*" might prove harder than previously imagined, and would depend largely on General MacArthur.

On September 17 MacArthur finally established his General Headquarters (GHQ) in the Dai Ichi Life Insurance Building in central Tokyo, directly opposite the Imperial Palace. On the eighteenth, a secret directive arrived from the Pentagon, with the first part of the Truman administration's detailed blueprint for the reform of Japan.[16] On the twentieth MacArthur let it be known to Foreign Minister Yoshida Shigeru that an informal visit by Emperor Hirohito would not be inappropriate. That same day Grand Chamberlain Fujita Hisanori visited GHQ with a message from the palace: The emperor hoped that the general was enjoying good health; he wished to inform the general that Japan intended to carry out the terms of the Potsdam Declaration.[17]

Within this early occupation period, MacArthur's "military secretary" and former head of psychological warfare operations, Brig. Gen. Bonner F. Fellers, reestablished personal ties with two Japanese Quakers. One, Isshiki (Watanabe) Yuri, he had known from his days at Earlham College in Richmond, Indiana; the other, Kawai Michi, a former secretary-general of the YWCA and founder in 1929 of Keisen Girls School in Tokyo, he had met on his first visit to Japan in 1920. During their initial reunion meetings, Fellers spoke frankly of his urgent concern to prove that no grounds existed for holding the emperor responsible for the Pearl Harbor attack. With Kawai acting as his consultant and collaborator, Fellers was soon put into contact with her acquaintance, Sekiya Teizaburō, the high palace official who, since late Taishō, had played a leading role as a liaison between the court and government ministries. Sekiya too wanted to prove that the emperor was "a lover of peace."[18]

An entirely new, binational stage in the movement to protect Hirohito now began. Out of the interplay of efforts by GHQ, the emperor, Japanese government leaders, and Japanese Christians with prewar ties to influential Americans, came the shielding of Hirohito from war responsibility, his "humanization," and the reform of the imperial house. Henceforth, in the process of utilizing Hirohito's authority for their own respective purposes, MacArthur and the Japanese leadership would have to misrepresent a vital side of Hirohito's life and identity, just as they been misrepresented before the war.

In response to MacArthur's remark concerning an imperial visit, on the morning of September 27, 1945, the emperor donned formal morning dress complete with top hat, left his palace, and went to the American Embassy to pay a courtesy call on the general. The Japanese people were not informed beforehand of this visit. Neither were they aware of the serious personal crises both men were facing. MacArthur's conduct of the occupation had already come under criticism from the Russians and the British at the Council of Foreign Ministers meeting in London. Secretary of State James F. Byrnes was preparing to yield to Allied pressure for some form of group supervision of the freewheeling supreme commander. The prime minister of New Zealand had warned the American minister that "there should be no soft peace"; "the Emperor should be tried as a war criminal."[19]

Moreover, the Truman administration had been taken aback by certain statements issued (and later retracted) by MacArthur's GHQ concerning the duration of the occupation and the possibility of drastically downsizing Allied forces in Japan within a single year.[20] Acting Secretary of State Dean Acheson had openly rebuked MacArthur, saying "the occupation forces are the instruments of policy and not [its] determinants."[21] Truman was particularly displeased with MacArthur for ignoring State Department policy guidelines and for failing to return to the United States for consultations, despite having been urged to do so on two occasions by Army Chief of Staff Marshall.

Hirohito's position was also clouded and uncertain. His responsibility for beginning the war had become a controversial issue among the Allies. An unpublished Gallup opinion poll conducted in early June 1945 disclosed that 77 percent of the American public wanted the emperor severely punished.[22] On September 11, following the first round of arrests of suspected Japanese war criminals, the foreign press started to report rumors of the emperor's imminent abdication. On September 18 Joint Resolution 94 was introduced in the U.S. Senate (and referred to a committee), declaring that Emperor Hirohito of Japan should be tried as a war criminal.[23] And if these were not reasons enough for the emperor to worry, the Potsdam Declaration itself had deliberately left his future status uncertain: to be decided by "the freely expressed will of the Japanese people."

But the emperor's position was not all bleak. He and the Higashikuni cabinet, in keeping with their resolve to protect the *kokutai*, had begun disarming and demobilizing the seven-million-strong army and navy even before MacArthur's arrival in Tokyo. Their initiative made the demilitarization of Japan far easier than the Americans had expected or even imagined. President Truman had registered this important fact on September 6, 1945, when he announced the "U.S. Initial Post-Surrender Policy for Japan." This document instructed MacArthur to exercise his authority *through* Japan's existing governing structures and mechanisms, including the emperor, but only insofar as this promoted the achievement of U.S. objectives.[24]

Months earlier, between April and July 1945, MacArthur and Fellers had worked out their own approach to occupying and reforming Japan. In their view the principles of psychological warfare that Fellers had implemented in the Battle of the Philippines and elsewhere were solidly correct. They had played a key role in lowering Japanese morale, hastening surrender, and preparing the Japanese for occupation. Japanese military leaders alone bore responsibility for the war, and the emperor, the "moderates" around the throne, and the people had been totally deceived by them. All Japanese trusted the emperor. U.S. psychological warfare should build on their trust and turn it against them.[25] These ideas, the "common sense" of American psychological warfare experts in the Pacific, not to mention Chinese and Japanese Communist leaders in North China, had become MacArthur's fixed principles and were woven into his initial occupation plan.

Code-named Operation Blacklist, the plan turned on separating Hirohito from the militarists, retaining him as a constitutional monarch but only as a figurehead, and using him to bring about a great spiritual transformation of the Japanese people.[26] Because retaining the emperor was crucial to ensuring control over the population, the occupation forces aimed to immunize him from war responsibility, never debase him or demean his authority, and at the same time make maximum use of existing Japanese government organizations. MacArthur, in short, formulated no new policy toward the emperor; he merely continued the one in effect during the last year of the Pacific war, then drew out its implications as circumstances changed. More important, as MacArthur was under Potsdam Declaration orders to mete out stern punishment to war criminals, Hirohito's innocence should be established before the machinery for implementing that aspect of the declaration was set up.

Thus, at the very beginning of the occupation the Japanese defensive strategy for protecting the *kokutai* and MacArthur's occupation strategy coincided. The two sides did not yet know each other's thinking; nevertheless, where the emperor was concerned, they were proceeding on parallel tracks.

III

Frank L. Kluckhohn of the *New York Times* had earlier interviewed Prince Konoe, the vice prime minister in the Higashikuni cabinet. He had suggested to Konoe, quite probably at the request of GHQ, that the emperor send a four-point message to the American public via, naturally, Kluckhohn's own newspaper. So on September 25, two days before the emperor called on MacArthur, he granted brief, separate audiences to Kluckhohn and Hugh Baillie, president of the United Press and a former acquaintance of Konoe. The journalists submitted written questions. They received written replies, in English, drafted by Shidehara Kijurō. Two basic points were revealed: (*a*) democracy and pacifism (in the sense of Japan's temporary nonpossession of weapons) were the main ingredients in the postwar imperial image for overseas consumption; and (*b*) the emperor wished to avoid questions about Pearl Harbor.

Kluckhohn asked "whether [Hirohito] had intended for his war rescript [of December 1941] to be used as General Tōjō had used it—to launch the surprise attack on Pearl Harbor which brought the United States into the war." The emperor, answered "in effect, no, that had not been his intention."[27] So Tōjō, not the emperor, bore responsibility for the surprise attack on Pearl Harbor, which was precisely the message MacArthur wanted the American people to hear prior to his own meeting with Hirohito. It was also the line of defense for the emperor that Princes Konoe and Higashikuni and many of the other "moderates around the throne" had been advocating since 1944.[28]

Although Hirohito read and sanctioned Shidehara's reply, he could not possibly have believed it, because the attack on Pearl Harbor occurred eight hours before he had signed the imperial rescript declaring war, and he had personally taken great pains to ensure that the attack would be a surprise.[29] The Japanese government subsequently issued a statement, reported by the *New York Times* on September 29, that altered the emperor's words to avoid criticism of

Tōjō. Too much may not be made of this partial retraction, other than that it indicated poor communications between SCAP and the Higashikuni government, and that the latter had not yet fully worked out its *kokutai* preservation policy. The latter required that the emperor be protected by designating to stand in his place not only his chiefs of staff but Tōjō in particular.

Shortly after the audience granted to Kluckhohn and Baillie, the emperor visited MacArthur, hoping to learn what policies MacArthur would pursue toward the imperial house. Hirohito needed MacArthur's personal support if he was to preserve the *kokutai* and avoid taking legal and moral responsibility for his earlier actions as supreme commander and primary energizer of the political system. If MacArthur, for his part, was to use the emperor to legitimize occupation reforms, then he needed Hirohito to totally disown his "evil militarist" advisers.

Certain personal characteristics furnished additional bases for mutual support. MacArthur was older but dedicated to projecting himself as youthful and vigorous. Hirohito was just reaching middle age but accustomed to working with much older advisers. Both men had received prolonged and intense military educations, and had been set apart from their peers all their lives. MacArthur, the son of a Civil War hero who had won the Medal of Honor and later served as second-in-command during the American conquest of the Philippines, was a professional army officer. He had climbed to the highest command possible, becoming the youngest general and the youngest chief of staff in U.S. Army history.[30] During his rise, he had become a master at making efficient use of talented staff officers. MacArthur always felt he had been born to lead, but believed that all credit and acclaim for his accomplishments in command should accrue to himself alone. Similarly, when he failed the failure must never be his but the consequence of inadequate support or machination from above. Extremely egotistical, sometimes pompous and arrogant, MacArthur was driven by his family heritage to excel in everything he did. But nowhere is it recorded that any adult close to the supreme-commander-to-be ever sought to raise him to be unselfish and respectful of the views of others.

Both Hirohito and MacArthur valued loyalty and cultivated remoteness. They regarded themselves as their nation's leading asset and knew how to practice deception—MacArthur of his superiors at every single stage of his career; Hirohito of the entire Japanese nation. Both men combined in their persons multiple forms of authority and knew how to use it effectively. Despite these similarities, personalities more different than those of the emperor and the general could hardly be imagined. Hirohito did not share MacArthur's "dark side"—his eccentricity, extreme egoism, and pomposity. He was truly self-effacing, accustomed to ruling through others, by consensus rather than by dictate; and he was anything but physically imposing.

An American staff photographer was ready when the emperor arrived at the American embassy. He took three pictures of Hirohito standing with MacArthur in the embassy's main living room, and the two then retired to a specially prepared room. There they talked privately, through interpreter Okumura Katsuzō, for nearly forty minutes. MacArthur did most of the talking, and because they were both very concerned to protect the images they projected, they insisted that their conversation be kept off the record.

In the absence of a verbatim record, conflicting accounts of this private meeting were later put forward by MacArthur, by American journalists who based their reports on interviews with both the emperor and MacArthur, and by Japanese officials and historians.[31] Probably the most that can be said of their first meeting is that the two men encountered each other at a moment of uncertainty and realignment in their respective positions, and each came away feeling the meeting had been a success. Hirohito was pleased that

MacArthur was going to make use of him, and that he had not pursued the issue of war responsibility. MacArthur, in turn, was moved by the emperor's high evaluation of his conduct of the occupation and by his promise to cooperate. Presumably neither man said anything about the efforts already begun by their subordinates to save Hirohito from indictment as a war criminal.

Henceforth the Allied supreme commander would use the emperor, and the emperor would cooperate in being used. Their relationship became one of expediency and mutual protection, of more political benefit to Hirohito than to MacArthur because Hirohito had more to lose—the entire panoply of symbolic, legitimizing properties of the imperial throne.[32]

But for the American and Japanese leaders to interact amicably and cooperatively, the emperor would have to sever himself completely from militarism and militarists such as Tōjō, which he was very reluctant to do; MacArthur would have to ensure that the emperor was not held accountable for any of his actions during the war, especially the Pearl Harbor attack; and both GHQ and successive Japanese governments would have to carry out a struggle to reshape the historical consciousness of the Japanese people concerning the nature of the war and the role that the emperor had played in it.

For most Japanese living in the ruin of defeat, the importance of the first emperor-MacArthur meeting was not the spirit of mutual respect and cooperation the two leaders established. Nor was it the official announcements of what they had allegedly said to one another. The one good photograph taken by the American cameraman and run by all the leading Japanese newspapers on September 29, however, created a sensation. Shot from close in, it shows the bespectacled emperor, in formal morning coat and striped trousers, standing as if at attention, necktie straight and hands by his sides, while beside and towering over him is relaxed and casual MacArthur in an open-necked uniform, bereft of necktie or medals. The general's hands are on his hips and hidden from view. Both men are looking straight ahead at the camera.

What many Japanese saw in this picture led to renewed rumors that the emperor would soon abdicate. On August 15 his capitulation broadcast had forced his people to acknowledge the loss of the war. Now a single photograph forced them to confront the painful political implications of that loss.[33] The emperor they saw there was not a living god but a mortal human beside a much older human to whom he now was subservient. Hirohito perfectly exemplified the defeated nation; MacArthur stood completely relaxed and projected the confidence that comes from victory.

With that one photograph a small first step was taken in displacing the emperor from the center of Japanese collective identity and freeing the nation from the restrictions of the past.

No Japanese could possibly have taken such a photograph. Only photographers certified by the Imperial Household Ministry were permitted to record the emperor's image. And they had to use a telephoto lens from a distance of at least twenty meters, and usually (though not always) show only the upper half of the emperor's body, and never his back because it was slightly rounded.[34] He could not be shown smiling, for living gods were not supposed to smile. He could only be photographed standing motionless or at attention. Such photographers could be relied on not to use their photographic skills to undermine popular loyalty to the throne. Above all, they were expected to show their own personal feelings of reverence for their subject. But reverence for the emperor was an emotion few Americans at that time felt.

The Japanese government immediately banned reproduction of the picture. The reality of Hirohito's subordination to MacArthur was too disturbing. When no photograph accompanied the newspaper articles the day *after* the leaders' meeting, GHQ protested to the Japanese Foreign Ministry. The *next* day, September 29, the *Asahi*,

Mainichi, and *Yomiuri-Hōchi* newspapers did publish the censored photograph together with a "corrected" account of the emperor's reply to Kluckhohn's questions and Baillie's "interview." Home Minister Yamazaki Iwao immediately intervened, and all copies of those papers were seized on the grounds that the emperor never criticized his subjects and that the picture was sacrilegious to the imperial house and would thus have a detrimental effect on the nation.

Conflict between the Higashikuni government and GHQ now ensued, and ended when General Headquarters not only ordered the printing of the photograph but also the repeal of all restrictions on publishing.[35] On October 4 MacArthur issued the "Civil Liberties" directive that abolished some of the major obstacles to democratization: the Peace Preservation Law, the National Defense Security Law, and the "special higher police." Overnight thought control loosened, the legal taboo on criticism of the emperor broke, and the whole apparatus of laws and ordinances established in order to "protect the *kokutai*" came crashing down. The personnel of the "special higher police" remained at their work, however, still thinking of themselves as "the emperor's police."

The Higashikuni cabinet resigned immediately. Four days later (October 8), MacArthur tightened SCAP censorship of the Tokyo newspapers, while endorsing the emperor's choice of Shidehara Kijūrō, a seventy-four-year-old former diplomat and prewar moderate, to replace Higashikuni. Shidehara, the leading candidate of the "moderates" ever since the wartime cabinets of Koiso Kuniaki and Suzuki Kantarō, would follow the same policy of protecting the *kokutai* but rely on a less confrontational, more flexible approach.

Over the next few weeks GHQ began to attack "feudal remnants" and the emperor system. On October 10, it banned the display of the sun flag (*hinomaru*), a symbol that antedated the Meiji restoration, but left undisturbed the more important singing in unison of the official national anthem ("Kimigayo"), a paean to the glories of the monarchy that had been made part of daily school education in 1931.[36]

On October 11 GHQ freed nearly five hundred Communist political prisoners and announced "five great reforms": emancipation of women; promotion of labor unions; and democratization of the educational, legal, and economic systems. With the announcement of these goals, the occupation passed to a new phase. The people gained freedom to criticize their government, their emperor, and the institution of the throne. Political parties soon restarted. Communists began to criticize the emperor publicly and to pursue the issue of his legal and moral responsibility for more than a decade of futile warfare.

On October 22 GHQ issued a directive ordering education reform and the dismissal of all teachers who had advocated militarism or were hostile to occupation policies. Henceforth wartime leaders in all fields were at risk. On October 30, 1945, GHQ made public the total assets of the imperial house, based on grossly understated figures provided by the Imperial Household Ministry. Emperor Hirohito's subjects learned that he owned assets of more than 16 billion yen. Drawing income from enormous holdings of productive forests; livestock farms; corporate stocks; and national, prefectural, and municipal bonds, and with large holdings of bullion specie and currency, Hirohito was far and away the nation's biggest landowner and wealthiest individual.[37] With the public seizing on the issue of the emperor's vast wealth, and with criticism of the most prominent war leaders appearing daily in print, and the Communists calling for abolition of the "emperor system," both the Shidehara cabinet and politicians in the Diet soon became uncertain about preserving not only the *kokutai* but their own jobs.[38]

Also in October, the problem of abdication resurfaced in the Japanese press. On October 12 Prince Konoe informed a reporter that the emperor was aware of the problem; on the twenty-first, Konoe told Russell Brines of the Associated Press that the Imperial

Household Law did not provide for abdication; four days later the *Mainichi shinbun* reported that the emperor could not possibly abdicate because he had accepted the Potsdam Declaration and had a duty to carry it out. The abdication rumors of October aroused the trepidations of Hirohito's court defenders and kept alive the problem of his moral, political, and legal responsibility for the war. Court officials responded by making minor reforms, while signaling to the nation the emperor's intention to remain on the throne.[39] In addition, from this time onward arguments for the emperor's abdication began to intersect with the search by conservative intellectuals for an "indigenous" democratization based on the reconstruction of the national morality—something that could not occur while Hirohito was monarch.[40]

Meanwhile military agencies were steadily being lopped off. On September 13 the Imperial Headquarters that had existed for seven years and ten months was abolished. On October 10 the Combined Fleet and the Navy General Headquarters were formally dissolved. Five days later the general headquarters of both the army and navy closed, and on December 1, the two service ministries themselves were abolished.[41] By the end of 1945 the armed forces Hirohito had commanded no longer existed. Still, despite the demystifying effect of the emperor-MacArthur photograph, the image of him as uniformed supreme commander of the nation persisted.

IV

The emperor's advisers now focused on extinguishing his military image. Availing themselves of MacArthur's personal generosity, they sought, and were quickly granted, permission for him to worship "privately" at Ise Shrine in Mie prefecture.

Accompanied by high court officials, as well as curious Allied journalists, Hirohito departed Tokyo on November 12 for a three-day trip to the national Shinto shrines of his imperial ancestors.

Outwardly the trip seemed a simple undertaking for purely religious purposes. He visited the inner and outer shrines of Ise and the mausoleum of the legendary first emperor, Jimmu (in Nara), and the Meiji emperor (in Kyoto), staying overnight at the Kyoto Palace on both occasions. The hidden purpose of the trip was to affirm, in the new context of defeat, the viability of imperial history, based on religion and myth. Hirohito used the occasion to test public opinion and shed his military image. The trip was his first opportunity to display a new, postwar royal uniform. It closely resembled the duty garb of a railroad conductor, the collar closed and stiffly stand-up. Understandably he never wore this outfit again, but went completely civilian in a plain, poorly fitting business suit. The manufacture of the imperial railwaymanlike uniform may have signaled an intention to impress the public, at home and abroad, with his determination to remain on the throne rather than to abdicate.[42]

The signal Hirohito received from his subjects, however, was clear. When the imperial train stopped for six minutes at Numazu Station on October 12, Lord Keeper of the Privy Seal Kido was anxious, wondering whether people living in the burnt-out area around the station "might throw stones or something."[43] Wherever the emperor appeared in Ise and Kyoto, however, he was warmly welcomed, thus putting to rest Kido's fear. Even though the mystique of the throne had been punctured by defeat, his subjects remained loyal, and many still regarded him as "sacred and inviolable." The Ise-Kyoto tour thus contributed to the emperor's later decision to go out among the people, something he disliked doing and had always kept to a necessary minimum. A month after returning to Tokyo, Hirohito visited the tomb of his father, the Taishō emperor. His October train trip and this visit were his first announced postwar tours.

On November 29, 1945, the emperor told Vice Grand Chamberlain Kinoshita Michio that seven of the imperial princes were going to visit the imperial mausoleums on his behalf, and that he intended to tell them that "his last tour to the Kansai region [that is, his Ise-Kyoto trip] had a great effect in promoting intimacy between the high and the low. The imperial family, which is a presence between him and the people, should make great efforts [to nurture that intimacy]."[44]

Concurrently, following Hirohito's return from Kyoto, the Japanese people learned that the imperial portrait would be removed from display in all schools, government offices, and overseas embassies and consulates. The Imperial Household Ministry planned a new portrait as replacement, which the emperor would eventually "bestow" on the nation, as he had before. Unlike his military uniform, however, the imperial likeness could not be carelessly discarded. If it were, the emperor's bond with his people might be weakened.[45]

Three weeks after the emperor's train trip for ostensibly private religious purposes, GHQ's Civil Information and Education Section (CIE) launched a carefully prepared campaign to remold Japanese opinion on the lost war and the evils of militarism. Bradley Smith, chief of CIE's Planning Division, wrote a series of ten articles that were translated into Japanese by the official news agency, Kyōdō Tsūshinsha. "A History of the Pacific War: The Destruction of Deceit and Militarism in Japan," was described as having been "Contributed by Allied General Headquarters." The prologue for the first installment started in all national newspapers on December 8, 1945, the anniversary of Pearl Harbor. It listed Japan's main war crimes and declared that "the concealment of the truth" by successive wartime governments had produced the "gravest consequences."

> [For] even after Japan retreated on many fronts and its navy ceased to exist, the true situation was never publicized. Recently, the emperor himself said that it had not been his wish to attack Pearl Harbor without warning, but the military police [*kempeitai*] exerted every effort to prevent [his statement] from reaching the people. . . . It is absolutely

essential for the people to know the full history of this war so they may understand why Japan was defeated and . . . why they now suffer such a miserable plight. Only in this way will they gain the knowledge and strength to oppose militaristic actions and reconstruct the state as a member of international peaceful society. . . . [46]

The "History of the Pacific War" emphasized "the crimes resulting from Japanese militarism," including the rapes and other outrages in Nanking, but also highlighted the efforts for peace of the "moderate faction," centering on Emperor Hirohito. Reaching back, the initial article described Prime Minister Shidehara (the main defender of the Kwantung Army during its 1931 Manchurian aggression) as a man who had respected "the principles of peace and international cooperation" during his tenure as foreign minister. But by placing the most blame on a handful of "military cliques," thus depicting the people one-sidedly as deceived victims—as even the emperor had been deceived—this GHQ effort to reshape historical consciousness ultimately confused the Japanese acceptance of war responsibility.

CIE reinforced its press campaign with a radio news program designed to remold Japanese opinion. From December 9 to February 10, 1946, NHK radio broadcast a thirty-minute, thrice-weekly evening program called "Shinsō wa kō da" [Now it can be told]. Based on the "History of the Pacific War" and produced by Americans, it was designed as the Japanese version of America's best-known news program of the 1930s: "The March of Time."[47] The opening scene began with an announcer's authoritative voice declaring melodramatically,

We, the people of Japan, already know the war criminal suspects. Those who betrayed us are now being exposed to the light of day.

Who? Who are they?

Be patient and I'll tell you. Above all, I'll give you the facts so you can draw your own conclusions.

[Music rises, dies out.]

Announcer: This is the first in a series of radio broadcasts entitled "Now It Can Be Told." Through these broadcasts you will come to understand the true facts about the great war and the circumstances that brought it about.[48]

"Now It Can Be Told" spread the message that Japan had fought a war of aggression rather than of self-defense; its leaders had deceived the nation. Directly contradicting familiar wartime propaganda about the "War of Greater East Asia," the program hit its Japanese listeners hard, infuriating many. Hundreds of letters poured into NHK protesting the punitive spirit of the program and the dogmatic style of presentation by its unidentified Japanese performers.[49]

Japan's political elites could not recognize the lost war as one of aggression, for then they would have had to discuss where responsibility for starting and losing it lay. They would have been unable to push the entire blame onto the military. Yet they had to prevent GHQ from driving too deep a wedge between the military and the people, or it would affect the emperor. Ever since the emperor's surrender broadcast, they had tried to counteract the Allied information on the war by sedulously avoiding issues of accountability while emphasizing "the emperor's gracious consideration and benevolence for the people." Prime Minister Higashikuni set the tone at his first press conference, on August 28:

We have come to this ending because the government's policies were flawed. But another cause [of the defeat] was a decline in the moral behavior of the people. So at this time I feel the entire nation—the military, the government officials, and the people—must thoroughly reflect and repent. Repentance of the whole nation is the first step in reconstruction, and the first step toward national unity.[50]

Later, at a press conference on September 4, Higashikuni repeated the message: Imperial initiative had ended the war, national repentance was now in order, and "protection of the national polity" was called for. The war had ended thanks to "the gracious benevolence of His Majesty, who paved the way to an eternal peace in order to save the people from suffering. Never before had we been so profoundly moved by the deep sympathy of His Majesty. We deeply regret having caused Him so much concern." [51]

Higashikuni's plea for general repentance and national unity had mixed consequences. Some Japanese were immediately persuaded, but the reaction of most was bafflement or anger. Hard economic times, combined with the recent experience of vast inequalities in the sacrifices that had been demanded of the people during the war, undercut Higashikuni's message and contributed to growing distrust of the national leadership. His admission that a major cause of Japan's defeat had been the enormous discrepancy between its war power and the national strength of its enemies made many feel that their leaders had acted recklessly in waging war against the United States and Britain.[52]

After Higashikuni resigned, Prime Minister Shidehara went further in rewriting history. On November 5, 1945, the Shidehara cabinet adopted a document on war responsibility that eventually became a major prop in the postwar conservative politicians' view of the war. Entitled "Matters Concerning War Responsibility and Other Issues," the document showed that the conservatives believed that "the empire was compelled to embark on the Greater East Asian War in view of the surrounding circumstances." This was tantamount to saying that the Tōjō cabinet's surprise attack on the United States and Britain had been in self-defense. The document also laid down the egregiously false, official line that the emperor had always been a peace-minded constitutionalist, kept in the dark about the actual details of the attack on Pearl Harbor.[53]

If CIE's "History of the Pacific War" slighted Japan's war against the peoples of Asia, Shidehara's dishonest policy document simply ignored Japanese aggression in China since 1931, and in Southeast Asia starting in 1940. Inverting cause and effect, the November 5 policy decision on war responsibility began the lost war from the commencement of "ABCD encirclement," a term that denoted the military and economic pressure the United States, Britain, China, and the Netherlands had placed on Japan during the very last stage of its pre–Pearl Harbor aggression.[54]

At the end of 1945, men in the emperor's entourage, and former members of the wartime cabinets, were acting independently to protect Hirohito and the *kokutai*. The *Asahi shinbun*, for example, published a serialized account of Hirohito's heroic role in the surrender process. Authored by Sakomizu Hisatsune and titled, in Japanese, "In the Time of Surrender," it ran concurrently with the publication of CIE's "History of the Pacific War" series, reflecting the basic consensual agreement between GHQ and Japan's "moderate" leaders on the matter of protecting the emperor.

Thus, in defending the emperor, GHQ and the conservative ruling elites were also promoting their respective versions of Japan's lost war. GHQ succeeded in establishing only the militarists as aggressors, not the emperor who had commanded them. The Japanese conservatives were unable to negate openly the American version of the "Pacific War." Nevertheless they wished at least to keep alive the position that the war had been fought for self-defense, just as the imperial rescript said, and that Japan had been forced into it. Eventually, both sides were successful in implanting their views. Japan never pursued war crimes on its own with a view to seeking punishment of those who had committed them, and its government paid reparations only to other governments, never to individuals.

V

While the battle to shape historical consciousness unfolded, GHQ resumed arrests of suspected war criminals, extended its investigations to include the imperial family, and continued to await the Japanese government's plans for revision of the constitution that would inaugurate the new era of democracy. Japanese public opinion surveys showed a strong desire to have the imperial system reformed. According to one such survey, 15.9 percent "wanted the prewar system to remain"; 45.3 percent wanted "the center of morality placed outside of politics; and 28.4 percent wanted a British-style emperor system."[55] But the Shidehara cabinet was deliberately procrastinating while crafting a plan for only token revision of the Meiji constitution that would leave the *kokutai* virtually unchanged. Watching these developments, and desiring to encourage "spontaneous" popular organizational efforts, the reformers in GHQ turned their attention to the "emperor system."

On December 15 a GHQ directive ended state support of Shinto shrines and eliminated Shinto from the education system by banning militaristic and ultranationalistic teachings connected with Shinto. The "Shinto Directive" introduced the principle of the separation of state and religion, thereby effectively ending the "unity of rites and politics" (*saisei itchi*) that all governments had professed to uphold since early Meiji. It also banned the use in official documents of terms such as "War of Greater East Asia" and "eight corners of the world under one roof."

On January 1, 1946, the Japanese press printed the entire text of Emperor Hirohito's first-ever New Year's rescript to the nation, formally titled "Rescript to Promote the National Destiny" but popularly known as the "Declaration of Humanity" (*ningen sengen*).[56] Couched in obscure, classical language, it quoted in its entirety Emperor Meiji's egalitarian-sounding imperial oath of five articles, starting with: "We shall determine all matters of state by public discussion, after assemblies have been convoked far and wide;" and ending: "We shall seek knowledge throughout the world and thus invigorate the foundations of this imperial nation."[57] Buried in the text was a denial that the emperor's ties with his people was based on "the false conception" of him as "a living deity" (*akitsumikami*).

Drafted earlier at GHQ, the rescript had undergone translation and revision by the Shidehara cabinet and the court. The draft-translation-revision process had imaged the interplay between the court, intent on defending the *kokutai*, and American policy makers, who were ambivalent about the monarchy but believed that its reform was best approached indirectly. Both sides intended to use the rescript to open a new phase in their campaigns to rehabilitate Hirohito's image.

Hirohito's failure to deny his reputed descent from the sun goddess, Amaterasu Ōmikami, stands out. To emphasize the union of monarchy and democracy since the Meiji period, he inserted the oath Meiji had sworn not to the Japanese people but to Amaterasu Ōmikami. In so doing, he pushed into the background the message that his relationship with the people was not based on his supposed divinity. Certainly the thinking of the Japanese leadership, including the emperor, was changing at this time. By putting forth the view that "mutual trust and reverent affection" (*shin'ai to keiai*) between the emperor and the people were the basis of the imperial system, they could downplay, without ever explicitly repudiating, the Shinto foundation myths that, in any event, few Japanese still believed.[58]

GHQ and Western journalists chose to deemphasize the New Year's rescript's primary focus on political continuity and instead gave importance to its repudiation of false doctrine. Western press coverage of the rescript also ignored the emperor's failure to refer to the doctrine that his sovereign powers of state derived from the sun goddess, thereby leaving undenied the myth that was the basis of his renounced divinity in the first place. Hirohito's omissions did not stop the *New York Times* from saying, in its lead editorial, that by issuing the rescript, the emperor had become "one of the great reformers in Japanese history."[59] Nor did they prevent MacArthur from promptly declaring that: "The emperor's New Year's statement pleases me very much. By it he undertakes a leading part in democratization of his people. He squarely takes his stand for the future along liberal lines. His action reflects the irresistible influence of a sound idea. A sound idea cannot be stopped."[60]

What MacArthur did not report to the American public, and what the American press also slighted, was Emperor Hirohito's false linkage of the Meiji past with the current postwar democracy. In effect Emperor Meiji, dead since 1912, was made the founding father of the political system about to be born in 1946. Far from the progressive and liberating statement MacArthur called it, the Declaration of Humanity was one more attempt by Hirohito and his advisers to limit, not to lead, the "democratization of his people," something he had been doing all his adult life.

Hirohito's attempt to integrate the concept of democracy with Japanese history, thus avoiding a break with the past that the Japanese enemies of democracy could seize on and later use to argue that democracy was a foreign importation, was not the problem. Rather the issue was *which past* should prevail in the context of the Declaration of Humanity and the political situation at the time. The articulate Left wanted to ground democracy in the post-World War I era of "Taishō democracy." Some were even seeking to link the notion of democracy to the thirteenth-century Buddhist saint Shinran. Hirohito deliberately sought to undercut these more radical notions of democracy. And three decades later he revealed in a press interview that he had "adopted democracy" not because the people were sovereign but "because [democracy] was the will of the Meiji emperor."[61]

The leading Japanese dailies gave front-page coverage to the rescript and ran special sections on the imperial family. Banner headlines across the front page of the *Mainichi* declared, WE

BESTOW AN IMPERIAL RESCRIPT FOR THE NEW YEAR, TIES OF TRUST AND AFFECTION, WE ARE WITH THE NATION."[62] The *Asahi shinbun* carried Prime Minister Shidehara's "Respectful Remarks," written in simple language:

> We are deeply moved with awe before his majesty's kind considera-
> tion. At the beginning of this rescript his majesty cited the Charter
> Oath of Five Articles that was promulgated in March 1868, and on
> which the development of democracy in our country was founded.
> The intention of the Charter Oath became manifest only gradually:
> First came the Imperial Instruction of 1881 to open a Diet; next, the
> promulgation of the Meiji constitution in 1889; then the development
> of parliamentary politics. Our parliamentary politics from the begin-
> ning has been based on these fundamental principles. The promise
> had been made and our parliamentary politics should have developed
> vigorously. Unfortunately, in recent years the process was held back
> by reactionary forces. . . . The benevolent intention of the great Meiji
> emperor was lost sight of. Now, however, we have a new opportunity
> to start afresh. . . . We shall construct a new state that is thoroughly
> democratic, pacifistic, and rational. Thereby we shall set his majesty's
> heart at ease.[63]

The prime minister chose his words carefully. "Development of democracy in our country" contrasted, implicitly but effectively, Japanese imperial democracy with American-style democracy. It also made the adoption of democracy a matter of respecting "the imperial will" instead of the will of the people. In this way, Hirohito and Shidehara had indirectly checked MacArthur, who had hoped to make 1945 represent the decisive break in Japanese political culture.[64]

Nevertheless, a way now opened for the Japanese people to see their relationship with their sovereign in a different light. The New Year's rescript made a deep impact and contributed to reshaping the emperor's image. By emphasizing his qualities as a human being and asserting that the basis of his relationship with the people had always been one of trust and affection, the emperor, in effect, had inaugurated his own "adoration." Interestingly, the issue of the *Asahi* that carried the New Year's rescript and the prime minister's comments also featured an interview with Hirohito's brother Prince Takamatsu that related concrete episodes illustrative of the emperor's character and contained themes that would figure in his re-presentation over the next few years.[65]

Popular books and news articles followed during 1946–47, giving the Japanese public what had been denied them by the "military" and other evil types around the throne: a full view of the private life of the "human emperor" and his family. These writings, and the photographic image-manipulations that accompanied them, typically described the emperor as an extraordinary natural scientist, a "sage," a "personality of great stature," and, above all, a "peace-loving, highly cultured intellectual" who was "always with the people."[66]

Scholarly writers also joined the campaign for the new "symbol" emperor. Right after Hirohito had disavowed his divinity, an article by the historian Tsuda Sōkichi appeared in the April 1946 issue of the new postwar intellectual journal *Sekai* and quickly came to be recognized as the earliest full-blown defense of the new monarchy. Tsuda argued that emperors are compatible with democracy, and that throughout most of Japanese recorded history, power and authority had always been divided between emperor and ruling class. In his view, state and people had been fused from the very onset of Japanese history, or, as he put it, "The Japanese imperial house was generated from within the Japanese people and unified them." Tsuda's conflation of imperial house–state–nation was an expression of romantic nationalism that captured nicely the sensibility of the political class in the aftermath of defeat. Yoshida Shigeru echoed Tsuda's outlook when he asserted in his autobiography: "According to our historical concepts and traditional spirit ever since antiquity, the imperial house is the progenitor of our race."[67]

Tsuda went on to argue that "the great majority of the people" were mainly to blame for having led Japan astray. While the imperial house "always accommodated itself to change and adapted to the politics of every period," the people did not; they "trusted statesmen who ultimately led the country into its present predicament" and they should "accept responsibility for this" rather than blame the Shōwa emperor. He ended his article with a ringing exhortation to "love" and "embrace" the imperial house and to make it "beautiful, secure, and permanent" by their love. For "love is the most thoroughgoing form of democracy."[68]

Tsuda's widely read and discussed article awakened memories of Prime Minister Higashikuni's argument for the "repentance of the one hundred million" for Japan's defeat. His polemic on unilateral emperor love also reminded his readers that the lexicon of Japanese monarchy is rich with concepts and phrases that can easily accommodate a peaceful, demilitarized "nation of culture." Many of Tsuda's arguments became pillars of postwar orthodoxy concerning the throne. Defenders of the imperial house generally agreed with him that vertical "love," directed upward to the emperor, was the key to saving "our emperor." But for critics of the emperor system the real problem was the degree to which the imperial house could be "humanized," given the Japanese people's difficulty in loving the emperor "within the limits of [mere] human propriety."[69]

To grasp the conflict between the postwar defenders of the monarchy and its critics—those who sympathized with the emperor and those who found him repugnant—Tsuda's response to the Declaration of Humanity should be balanced against the response of *Shinsō*, a highly popular, left-wing muckraking magazine that first appeared on March 1, 1946. Its "Statement of Purpose" captured nicely the new spirit of irreverence toward the throne:

> "Influence the people but do not inform them" was the political injunction of the great feudal politician Tokugawa Ieyasu. Ever since Meiji, from its Charter Oath of Five Articles, the emperor's government has pretended to be carrying out democracy. But we all know that for nearly eighty years, until the moment of unconditional surrender last summer, the emperor's government followed Ieyasu's injunction, and has kept the people in ignorance.

Stressing the need to "liberate the people from this feudal political idea," the essay expressed a desire to "expose every lie from ancient times to the present" and to examine "the true nature of government under the emperor system" so as to determine whether Japan had really fought a "holy war." "From such a viewpoint, basing ourselves on facts not excuses, we shall thoroughly examine the emperor system [*tennōsei*] and the structure of capitalism with a view to making some contribution to the democratic education of our fellow Japanese." [70]

One of *Shinsō*'s contributions to undermining emperor worship was its cartoon strips treating the transmogrified Shōwa emperor as a butt for humor—a comic victim of his palace guardians, the politicians in the Diet, and even ordinary people. *Shinsō*'s running gags on the "human" and "great" emperor highlighted many controversies of the occupation years: the calls for his abdication, the phenomenon of pretenders to the throne (such as the fifty-six-year-old shopkeeper Kumazawa Hiromichi, whom the press referred to as the "Kumazawa emperor"), the imperial portrait, and the imperial visitations, which *Shinsō* ridiculed by depicting the emperor in a drawing as a "broom." [71] Ironically, despite their debunking aim, these irreverent, leftist depictions of the emperor "humanized," whether in a frock coat or a business suit, unintentionally reinforced the official government position that he had always been only a normal constitutional monarch, never one who made important decisions on his own.

VI

Shortly after the Declaration of Humanity, a directive from Washington on the drafting of a Japanese constitution had requested that MacArthur encourage that "the Emperor institution" be abolished or reformed "along more democratic lines." MacArthur was now forced to clarify Hirohito's responsibility for ordering the attack on Pearl Harbor and, at the same time, end his ambiguous new status. On January 25, 1946, he sent a "Secret" telegram to Gen. Dwight D. Eisenhower, then U.S. Army Chief of Staff, stating his belief in the emperor's total innocence. The MacArthur telegram, based on a memorandum sent to him three months earlier by his Japan "expert" General Fellers, asserted that:

> No specific and tangible evidence has been uncovered with regard to [the emperor's] exact activities which might connect him in varying degree with the political decisions of the Japanese Empire during the last decade. I have gained the definite impression from as complete a research as was possible to me that his connection with affairs of state up to the time of the end of the war was largely ministerial and automatically responsive to the advice of his councillors. . . .

No official U.S. document unearthed so far has indicated that MacArthur or his staff investigated the emperor for war crimes. What they investigated were ways to protect Hirohito from the war crimes trial. As early as October 1945, in a brief memorandum intended for MacArthur, Maj. John E. Anderton had laid out the key elements of a defense: "in the interest of peaceful occupation and rehabilitation of Japan, prevention of revolution and communism, all facts surrounding the execution of the declaration of war and subsequent position of the Emperor which tend to show fraud, menace or duress be marshalled." And "if such facts are sufficient to establish an affirmative defense beyond a reasonable doubt, positive action [should] be taken to prevent indictment and prosecution of the Emperor as a war criminal."[72]

Seeking to shock the Truman administration, MacArthur concluded his telegram to Eisenhower by predicting dire consequences should the emperor face trial as a war criminal:

> His indictment will unquestionably cause a tremendous convulsion among the Japanese people, the repercussions of which cannot be overestimated. He is a symbol which unites all Japanese. Destroy him and the nation will disintegrate. . . . It is quite possible that a million troops would be required which would have to be maintained for an indefinite number of years.[73]

On January 29 MacArthur met with part of the newly established Far Eastern Commission in his Tokyo office to answer questions concerning the position of the emperor. Then on February 1, the *Mainichi shinbun* published the Japanese government's draft constitution, produced, under pressure from GHQ, by Minister of State Matsumoto Jōji and his committee.[74] An English translation of the Matsumoto draft reached MacArthur that same day. Noting that it left the status of the emperor unchanged, he concluded, correctly, that the Shidehara cabinet was incapable of writing a democratic constitution. Unless he himself acted quickly, before the first formal meeting of the Far Eastern Commission (scheduled for February 26), the initiative in constitutional revision could pass from his hands, and the preservation of the monarchy might be endangered by nations hostile to the Japanese throne.

The general met his dilemma by giving the Government Section of GHQ, headed by Gen. Courtney Whitney, one full week, February 3–10, to write a new draft of a model Japanese constitution. The drafters set to work, intent on realizing the goal of preventing Japan from ever again becoming a military threat to the United States. They concentrated first on reforming the monarchy.

The emperor, severed from real political power, became (and was defined as) only a "symbol" of unity. He was made so "symbolic" that neither the man nor the institution could ever again become an instrument for a revival of militarism. But the draft did permit the emperor to perform a few specified imperial "acts in matters of state" "on the advice and approval of the cabinet."

Next, the imperial armed forces were eliminated by inserting into the constitution an article—the famous Article 9—renouncing war:

> Aspiring sincerely to an international peace based on justice and order, the Japanese people forever renounce war as a sovereign right of the nation and the threat or use of force as a means of settling international disputes.
>
> In order to accomplish the aim of the preceding paragraph, land, sea, and air forces, as well as other war potential, will never be maintained. The right of belligerency of the state will not be recognized.[75]

Thanks to the American drafters, guarantees of civil liberties went right into the text of the constitution; women were enfranchised. The modus operandi of the Japanese state was partially reshaped. The draft weakened in theory the power of bureaucrats, strengthened that of the Diet, and enhanced the power of the judiciary. The final product permitted Japan its monarchy, and shifted political power to the Diet and the cabinet, should such a need arise.[76]

The model constitution was drafted and deliberated by both houses of the Diet at a very strange moment of crisis in postwar history. The power of ordinary people to act from below to realize their aspirations was still weak. There had been no domestic antiwar movement during all of 1945, let alone a viable Communist movement.[77] Yet the mystique of the monarchy had been deflated. Many people no longer held the emperor in exaltation. The antiemperor sentiment of the left was no longer being restrained. Even the communists defined the Americans as an "army of liberation." Most important, public opinion was shifting rapidly, with former diehard militarists switching overnight into fervent "democrats."[78]

Most Japanese *politicians*, with the notable exception of the Communists and a few iconoclasts, however, still held the monarchy in reverential awe. Their old guard attitude was in fundamental conflict with the democratic spirit of the American draft constitution. The primary concern of nearly all politicians, conservative, socialist, and liberal, was to preserve the *kokutai*. In their view that required a politically empowered monarch available for use in an *internal* crisis. Minor revision might be necessary to prevent public opinion from swinging in favor of abolition of the monarchy. Some of the emperor's powers might be taken away, but not all; least of all should he be turned into a "mere decoration."

At this crucial moment Hirohito was unable to fathom the aspirations of his subjects for fundamental reform of society. On February 12, he told Kinoshita, "Matsumoto seems to want to conclude the constitutional revision while he is still in office. I think I shall mention this to Shidehara. There is no need to hurry. Simply to indicate willingness to revise is enough."[79]

When Foreign Minister Yoshida and State Minister Matsumoto received the American model constitution at the Foreign Ministry on February 13, they were shocked. Committed to preserving the *kokutai* under the Meiji constitution, they believed that they would be unable to use an emperor unless he was allowed to reign and rule, combining power with authority. Over the next few weeks most members of the Shidehara cabinet changed on this crucial point. The progressive American draft at least retained the hereditary principle and guaranteed the continuance of the throne. In this moment of crisis for the monarchy, only Hirohito himself procrastinated.

The diary of Ashida Hitoshi, a moderate conservative who served as Shidehara's welfare minister and chaired an important lower-house subcommittee on constitutional revision, discloses that on the second day of the cabinet's deliberations on the American draft, February 22, Shidehara reported on his visit to GHQ the previous day: "MacArthur, as usual, started on an oration. 'I am working from the bottom of my heart for the good of Japan. Ever since my audience with the emperor, I have been telling myself I must insure his safety at all costs.'" The supreme commander went on, however, to warn of "unpleasant" discussions for Japan at the Far Eastern Commission in Washington and the uncertainty of his own tenure. As the American draft kept the emperor on the throne, he saw "no unbridgeable gap" between the Japanese and GHQ drafts. Under the latter, he felt the emperor was protected and his authority enhanced because it derived from his people's trust in him rather than from his ancestry.[80]

Shidehara's cabinet members were unhappy with the "symbol monarchy" and the renunciation of war as a sovereign right of the state. Ashida, however, pointed out that, "the idea that international disputes should be resolved by mediation and conciliation without recourse to armed force was a policy already accepted by our government in the Kellogg[-Briand] Pact and the Covenant [of the League of Nations]. It's certainly not something new."[81] Clearly Ashida did not think the renunciation of war would prejudice Japan's inherent right of self-defense, nor did he envision that its codification in Article 9 of the constitution would become a tremendous point of controversy in the postoccupation period. What Ashida and other members of the cabinet worried about was the emperor's loss of political power.

Wanting to avoid a hopeless dispute with MacArthur, Shidehara and his cabinet probably would have accepted the American model more quickly had the emperor permitted it. The evidence suggests that Hirohito did not assent. While he delayed, pressure for his abdication increased. On February 27 Hirohito's youngest brother, thirty-one-year-old Prince Mikasa, stood up in the privy council and indirectly urged him to step down and accept responsibility for Japan's defeat. Ashida attended that meeting together with the emperor and members of the imperial family, and recorded Mikasa as saying:

> "Various debates are going on concerning the present emperor and also the imperial family. I fear we shall regret it later on if the government fails to take bold action immediately." His implication was that it would be extremely unfortunate if [the government], dominated by old thinking, took inadequate measures. Everyone seemed to ponder [Mikasa's] words. Never have I seen his majesty's face so pale.[82]

Moreover, that same day, the *Yomiuri-Hōchi* ran a front-page story on the emperor's "abdication," based on AP correspondent Russell Brines's interview with Prince Higashikuni. The article claimed that many members of the imperial family approved of the emperor's stepping down in order to be free to acknowledge his moral responsibility for the war. It suggested that the emperor was isolated. Only the imperial household minister and prime minister opposed abdication.[83] A similar article, based on another interview with former prime minister Prince Higashikuni, appeared in the *New York Times* on March 4, and indicated that Prince Takamatsu, the second in line to the throne, would probably serve as regent until Crown Prince Akihito came of age.[84] The fact that pressure to abdicate came not only from Prince Higashikuni, but from his own younger brothers must have helped Hirohito overcome his reluctance to accept the MacArthur draft. Sibling rivalry in the imperial family, exploited by the militarists during the 1930s, now benefited MacArthur's constitutional reform.

On March 5 Shidehara came to the emperor bearing the MacArthur draft text and a draft of an imperial message declaring the emperor desired that the constitution be drastically revised. If Hirohito wished to maintain the unequal partnership with MacArthur that guaranteed him protection, it was time to move decisively. As reported by Kinoshita in his diary, "the reason for the big rush" on constitutional revision "was the article in yesterday's *Yomiuri* in which Prince Higashikuni discussed the problem of the emperor's abdication with a foreign journalist. . . . . Initially, M [MacArthur] agreed that the Matsumoto draft could be presented to him by [March] 11. [Now] they cannot wait [that long]."[85]

The next day the Japanese people read in their newspapers an outline of the Japanese government's draft constitution. They learned that sovereignty would be placed in them rather than in the will of the emperor, and that Japan would henceforth renounce war. On March 9 the *Mainichi shinbun* published the view of liberal international law scholar Yokota Kisaburō. Shown an advance draft of the constitution by GHQ officials, Yokota now opined that the clause renouncing war was equivalent to the idealistic Kellogg-Briand Pact, and that it did not make impossible the use of military force for self-defense, or "in cases involving international cooperation."[86]

Diet debate and revision of the constitution took place between April and August 1946. There is no evidence that members of the all-important lower-house subcommittee on the constitution, chaired by Ashida, accepted the interpretation of Yokota that the possibility of using armed force for self-defense and for international security was inherent in the wording of Article 9. The prevailing consensus was total, absolute denial of military force in keeping with public opinion at the time.

The new Constitution of Japan was promulgated eight months after Hirohito accepted the MacArthur draft, and went into effect the next year, on May 3, 1947. By then, the Imperial Household Ministry had become the Imperial Household Office (*Kunaifu*), and the number of its employees had been greatly reduced. The peerage had been abolished. The National Treasury had taken over the budget of the Imperial Household Office, and the state had taken title to the imperial museums, which now became national museums.[87]

So the end came swiftly for most of the supporting institutions, practices, and powers of monarchy created during Meiji. Pressured by MacArthur and Shidehara, threatened by talk of abdication from his siblings and his uncles, and fearing the Tokyo war crimes trials, Hirohito resisted for two weeks, then gave in. Bleakly he told Shidehara, "As the matter has gone this far, it can't be helped."[88] It was exactly the sort of remark he had made at every other critical juncture of his reign: from his assent to the bombing of Chinchow in south Manchuria in October 1931 and the military alliance with Hitler and Mussolini of September 1940, to his approval of the attack on Pearl Harbor in December 1941.

Yoshida Shigeru would later claim in his memoirs that it was the emperor himself who made the "sacred decision" to accept the MacArthur draft. Thereupon the divided Shidehara cabinet saw the light, and agreed to accept it.[89] The American author of the chapter on "The New Constitution of Japan" in GHQ's official history of the occupation also left the impression that the emperor was an enthusiastic supporter of MacArthur's draft constitution and that he conveyed his enthusiasm to Shidehara, Yoshida, and chief cabinet secretary Narahashi Wataru during an audience on February 22, 1946.[90]

Historian Watanabe Osamu, however, has revealed how the American version of events was based on Narahashi's account of his alleged imperial audience. In fact, there was no audience culminating in a decisive imperial assent on February 22. Ashida did not record one in his diary, and Yoshida himself denied having had an audience with the emperor that day. Years later Yoshida created his own version of the emperor's role in order to strengthen Japanese acceptance of the new constitution at a time when it was under attack from former Class A war criminal suspects and once-purged, subsequently pardoned, politicians. By the mid–1950s the latter (associated with Hatoyama Ichirō of the Democratic Party) had become the mainstream conservatives in the Diet and were leading a drive to amend the constitution totally. In an informal tape-recorded interview in 1955 with Kanamori Tokujirō, a former minister of state during his first cabinet, Yoshida indicated that the emperor was not an enthusiastic supporter of a constitution that barred him from *any* political role. Referring to Shidehara's audience of March 5, 1946, Yoshida told Kanamori that Emperor Hirohito merely said (referring to his loss of all political functions) "something to the effect of 'Let it go.'"[91]

Thus, when the constitutional moment arrived, Hirohito did sanction the most progressive reform ever presented to him. By his assent he himself became a symbol of the nation that claimed descent from the "homogeneous" Yamato race, and also a symbol— no longer a wielder—of sovereignty. After clinging tenaciously to the *kokutai* longer than anyone else, he finally acted from fear, at the moment when he felt the whole world was against him: fear he would be pressured into abdication, and, most of all, fear that with prolonged public discussion of his hesitancy would come an uncontrollable debate on republicanism, which would end in the monarchy itself being eliminated. Thereafter, for the rest of his life, he continued at odds with his symbolic status, psychologically unable to adjust to it.[92]

Chapter 1, Article 1, of the final Japanese version of the new constitution, redefined the emperor as "the symbol of the state and of the unity of the nation, deriving his position from the will of the nation with whom resides sovereign power." During subsequent deliberations on the constitution by the Ninetieth (and last) Imperial Diet, the members declared themselves loyal subjects of the emperor and downplayed this new basis of political legitimacy. But they did not try to restore the emperor's powers. The Shōwa emperor had failed in his most important duty—coordinating the army, the navy, and the government and making the system work. Failure would not be rewarded. More important, the unpurged politicians did not want to return to the authoritarian prewar system in which even conservative political parties had been unable to exercise the full powers of the state. As for Article 9, until the Korean War changed the circumstances, no politician dared to challenge public opinion by arguing that Japan had retained the right to maintain war power for self-defense.

Up to 1947 the real constitutional quarrel in occupied Japan had pitted supporters of the *kokutai*, centered on the court group and old guard politicians, against a small number of Japanese reformers who wanted a ceremonial monarchy and a genuine civil society but lacked the political power to achieve those goals on their own.[93] Thanks to GHQ, the reformers won, leaving the extremes in the debate isolated: Communists on the left and die-hard protectors of the *kokutai* on the right, plus a few prewar constitutional scholars who were so committed to the Meiji constitution as to be unable to conceptualize a democratic state.

Hirohito's teacher of constitutional law, Shimizu Tōru, and Professor Minobe Tatsukichi represented the latter. Shimizu was so depressed by the new constitution, and by newspaper reports of crowds jostling the emperor in his walkabouts, that he committed suicide.[94] Minobe, once the foremost liberal influence on prewar parliamentary politics, argued against the new constitution in newspaper and journal articles during 1946. Still fixated on German theories of constitutional law, Minobe emerged from the war as a staunch opponent of popular sovereignty and majority rule. He insisted that the only way to integrate the nation and realize "true democracy"—as opposed to the "American-style" practice, which easily led to "tyranny"—was for Japan to have a monarch in whom political power was concentrated.[95]

Nevertheless Emperor Hirohito remained on the throne—unindicted, unrepentant, and protected as well as crippled by the new constitution. And so the monarchy too remained a political issue, and the old constitution continued to exert influence through the debate on Hirohito's war responsibility. For the Meiji constitution now furnished the theoretical basis for putting all blame for the war on the military. Hereafter both apologists and critics of Hirohito's wartime behavior would repeatedly make use of different interpretations of its articles. The apologists (including of course Hirohito) would use the old constitution to exonerate him of responsibility on the general ground that constitutional monarchs are, by definition, politically passive and nonaccountable for their actions. They would also invoke the specific ground that Articles 3 and 55 immunized him and placed responsibility in the hands of his advisers.

Critics of the emperor would deny the very premise of constitutional monarchy. Arguing that Hirohito had been more akin to an absolute monarch, they would stress the responsibility that accrued to him as supreme commander and sole issuer of military orders, responsible for determining the organization and peacetime standing of the armed forces. The critics would also point to the prewar system of "independence of the right of supreme command," and to the emperor's unique power to proclaim military orders. Ultimately they claimed that the whole issue had been left unresolved precisely because he had never been indicted.[96]

The Constitution of Japan stripped the emperor of all political authority, removed him from the system of power, and linked him to the notion of the "peace state." It thereby foreclosed public discussion on the monarchy before it had really begun. At the same time the new constitution changed the emperor from an absolute value into a relative one, from a "sacred and inviolable" divinity into a mere human being under the law. Henceforth it was the constitution, not the emperor, that articulated the highest ideals, aspirations, and purposes of the Japanese people. And instead of Hirohito having enacted the constitution, the Diet had enacted Hirohito. On paper at least, he possessed none of the prerogatives of power of a British monarch and could be criticized like any other official organ of state. Constitutionally speaking Japan had indeed created a new variant of the genus "constitutional monarchy"—one that was in step with modernity, quite unlike the archaic institution still perpetuating itself in Great Britain.

Constitutions, however, are living things, put into practice in accordance with existing conventions, precedents, and beliefs. At the deepest levels of national identity, emperorism retained its hold over the minds of many Japanese. Because of what many influential people believed him and the imperial house to be and to stand for, Hirohito still could influence Japanese political evolution. Powerful emotional barriers to questioning his conduct or criticizing his status continued throughout the occupation and for the rest of his life.

Moreover, although the Diet had enacted an Imperial House Law in 1947, the new law resembled the old even in name, and was drafted simply by deleting from the original those articles that could be construed as contradicting the 1947 constitution, such as the system of "era names" and the "great food-offering ceremony." An attempt to insert a clause on the emperor's abdication was rejected in the Diet. The new Imperial House Law was no longer on a par with the constitution as the old had been. Yet its existence allowed some scholars to argue that precisely because of its system of hereditary succession to the throne, Japan had an unwritten constitution in addition and prior to the Constitution of Japan.[97]

The new constitution also generated problems that were to beset Japan for the remainder of the twentieth century. One such problem was the great divide between the concept of the state held by Japan's political rulers in 1946–47, and the modern secular, demilitarized, civil state concept enshrined in the new constitution, in conformity with the wishes and aspirations of most Japanese.[98]

The political elites had not been the original drafters of the constitution they were duty bound to implement. Like Hirohito, they too did not believe in many of its ideals, including especially the notion of the demilitarized state and the principle of the separation of politics and religion.

The Constitution of Japan also left unresolved the problem of the symbol monarchy's place in Japanese national identity. How were the inherently incompatible principles of monarchy and democracy to be reconciled? How were Japanese citizens supposed to regard their formerly divine emperor who remained on his throne, though now only a "symbol," and had never accepted responsibility for his earlier behavior? Were they to pretend that no conflict existed?

The answers to these questions changed as historical circumstances changed. But at the rebirth of the monarchy in February-March 1946, around the time the lists of the war crimes indictees were being settled and the emperor and his aides were preparing his defense, Vice Grand Chamberlain Kinoshita gave an interview to the editor of the magazine *Chōryū*. When asked what Hirohito thought about the democratization of Japan, Kinoshita answered,

His majesty thinks that to democratize Japan is to carry out thoroughly the spirit of the imperial house ever since antiquity. That is to say, for the emperor the heart of the imperial house is the heart of the people, and the way to democratize Japan is to make this spirit thoroughgoing.

Question: In order for us to ask the heart of the imperial house to become the people's heart, I think, first, that the political form has to be one that allows the heart of the people to develop.

Kinoshita: Indeed, yes. The imperial house has to become the spiritual center of the people rather than the center of politics. His majesty the emperor will ensure that politics by the people for the people is not wiped out from this country.

Question: From the form, it seems as though the emperor's powers of state might be narrowed. But in reality they will actually be more fully expanded.

Kinoshita: Yes, indeed.[99]

15

THE TOKYO TRIAL

Emperor Hirohito had known as early as 1942 that the trial of major war criminals was an official Allied war aim.[1] In November 1943 the Moscow Declaration had confirmed the point. The Potsdam Declaration of July 1945 had reiterated it; and the Charter of the International Military Tribunal (IMT), signed in London on August 8, 1945, definitively stated Allied policy toward war criminals.[2] Thus on August 9–10, when the time came for him and the leaders of the government to consider capitulation, the issue of war crimes was of serious concern. That concern deepened on September 11, 1945, when MacArthur ordered the arrest and imprisonment of the first batch of suspected war criminals, including the emperor's favorite prime minister—so hated by the Japanese people not only for brutal repression by the military police under his control but for the unfair way in which food rationing was carried out—General Tōjō.

Quite alarmed at this risk to the ruling elites, the Higashikuni cabinet immediately voted to seize the initiative from the Allies by convening an independent Japanese war crimes tribunal. Hirohito was not pleased. If war criminals were punished under national law, in his name, he would be placed in a contradictory position and deeply embarrassed. Up to this time Higashikuni had been seeing the emperor daily; abruptly his audiences were reduced. Nevertheless, the next day Foreign Minister Shigemitsu requested GHQ's permission to hold independent trials. GHQ refused.[3] There would be no official Japanese war crimes trial, no participation by Japanese judges on the bench in the Tokyo trial, and no trial of crimes committed by Japanese troops against other Japanese. The dirty work would be left to foreigners.

MacArthur personally found the prosecution of war criminals distasteful. Get-the-trials-over-with-quickly was his principle, and he was careless about and indifferent to abuses arising from GHQ's loosely defined and sparse rules of evidence and procedure. When he tried the surrendered Japanese generals who had commanded against him in the Philippines—Homma Masaharu and Yamashita Tomoyuki—justice was swift. After the trial, conviction, and sentencing to death of both men for failing to take all measures to prevent troops under their command from committing atrocities, two U.S. Supreme Court justices sharply criticized the procedures followed by the military commissions in the Philippines and the spirit of revenge that informed them. MacArthur, obviously angered, fired back: "Those who would oppose such an honest method can only be a minority . . . no sophistry can confine justice to any [particular] form. It is a quality. Its purity lies in its purpose, not in its detail. The rules of war, and military law . . . have always proved sufficiently flexible to accomplish justice within the strict limits of morality."[4]

MacArthur confirmed both death sentences and later wrote that "the remaining United States cases of this kind were tried by the International tribunal in Tokyo." For him there appeared to be little difference between an American military commission and an international war crimes tribunal.[5]

I

Brigadier General Fellers had joined MacArthur's Southwest Pacific Command in Australia in late 1943, after having worked for a year in the Office of Strategic Services (OSS), predecessor of the CIA. Immediately on landing in Japan (in the same plane that carried MacArthur), Fellers went to work to protect Hirohito from the role he had played during and at the end of the war. Fellers's overriding goals were to confirm the effectiveness of his own wartime propaganda program, and, at the same time, to shield Hirohito from standing trial.

Fellers conducted private interrogations of about forty Japanese war leaders, including many who would later be charged as the most important Class A war criminals. His interrogations were carried out mainly in visits to Sugamo Prison in Tokyo over a five-month period—September 22, 1945, to March 6, 1946—through two interpreters. Fellers's activities placed all the major war criminal suspects on alert as to GHQ's specific concerns, and allowed them to coordinate their stories so that the emperor would be spared from indictment.[6] Thus, at the same time the prosecuting attorneys were developing evidence to be used in trying these people, Fellers was inadvertently helping them. Soon the prosecuting attorneys found the war leaders all saying virtually the same thing. The emperor had acted heroically and single-handedly to end the war. This theme (unknown to them) coincided with Fellers's goal of demonstrating the effectiveness of his own propaganda campaign against Japan.

Equally helpful to Japan's wartime leaders in protecting Hirohito were the interviews conducted by civilian and military members of the U.S. Strategic Bombing Survey (USSBS) between late September and December 1945. The purposes of the Survey were to assess the effectiveness of aerial bombardment on Japan's decision to surrender, and the impact of the atomic bombs in particular. USSBS members also sought to fathom the workings of Japan's wartime political system. Needless to say top Japanese political and military leaders, such as Privy Seal Kido; former prime ministers Konoe, Yonai, and Suzuki Kantarō; as well as Suzuki's secretary Sakomizu, Kido's secretary Matsudaira Yasumasa, and Adm. Takagi Sōkichi, viewed their interactions with the survey as a way of protecting the *kokutai*. Extremely cooperative in answering questions, they became the main source of evidence on the surrender process and were able to use their interrogations to shape official American perceptions of Hirohito's role in ending the war.[7]

On the same day Fellers concluded his private interrogations of the indicted, he summoned Admiral Yonai Mitsumasa to his office in the Dai Ichi Life Insurance Building. Yonai had recently served as navy minister in the Higashikuni cabinet and had met MacArthur.[8] On March 6, 1946, Yonai and his interpreter, Mizota Shūichi, went to Fellers's office and were told that some Allied countries, particularly the Soviet Union, wanted to punish the emperor as a war criminal:

> To counter this situation, it would be most convenient if the Japanese side could prove to us that the emperor is completely blameless. I think the forthcoming trials offer the best opportunity to do that. Tōjō, in particular, should be made to bear all responsibility at his trial. In other words, I want you to have Tōjō say as follows:
>
> "At the imperial conference prior to the start of the war, I had already decided to push for war even if his majesty the emperor was against going to war with the United States."[9]

Admiral Yonai responded that he certainly agreed. The best way to establish his majesty's innocence would be to have Tōjō and Shimada take all responsibility. "However, as far as Shimada is concerned, I am already convinced he is prepared to take full responsibility."[10]

There was a reason for Yonai's confidence in Admiral Shimada. The Shidehara government had been implementing its own policy of immunizing the emperor from war responsibility and, through Suzuki Tadakatsu, head of the War Termination Liaison Bureau in Yokohama, had already secured Shimada's consent to take responsibility for the opening of the war. A similar assurance from Tōjō had apparently not been forthcoming.

Two weeks later Mizota penned a memorandum concerning a second conversation with Fellers on March 22 in which Fellers said:

> The most influential advocate of un-American thought in the United States is COHEN [*sic*] (a Jew and a Communist), the top adviser to Secretary of State Byrnes. As I told Yonai . . . it is extremely disadvantageous to MacArthur's standing in the United States to put on trial the very emperor who is cooperating with him and facilitating the smooth administration of the occupation. This is the reason for my request. . . . "I wonder whether what I said to Admiral Yonai the other day has already been conveyed to Tōjō?"[11]

The explicit anti-Semitism of Fellers (like his and MacArthur's hatred of President Franklin D. Roosevelt, the New Deal, and all liberals), and how he and MacArthur transmitted their bigotry to Japan's leaders, had not been reflected in the draft version of the new constituion and had no influence on the conversion of the monarchy to "symbol."[12] But MacArthur's truly extraordinary measures to save Hirohito from trial as a war criminal had a lasting and profoundly distorting impact on Japanese understanding of the lost war.

Months before the Tokyo tribunal commenced, MacArthur's highest subordinates were working to attribute ultimate responsibility for Pearl Harbor to Gen. Tōjō Hideki. So too were Tōjō's own army colleagues. Back in September, Tōjō, on receiving word that his arrest was imminent, had attempted suicide. While he was recovering, his former subordinates had again gotten word to him that he had to live in order to protect the emperor. Tōjō understood, and wanted to own up to his disgrace by shouldering all responsibility for the defeat. Since his testimony would be vital, either absolving or implicating Hirohito, it could not be left to chance.

Apparently it was Maj. Gen. Courtney Whitney who first confronted the problem of Tōjō's testimony about the emperor's war responsibility. According to Shiobara Tokisaburō, Tōjō's defense lawyer, sometime before Tōjō began giving his pretrial depositions (and probably before Yonai and his interpreter had met Fellers), Whitney had told Yonai that MacArthur and President Truman "wanted to protect the *kokutai* by making the emperor bear no responsibility." But there was "considerable opposition" in the United States to doing that. Tōjō could either answer his American interrogators in a way that encouraged the emperor's opponents or he could help to control the situation.[13] Whitney's remarks reflected MacArthur's hypersensitivity to any interference from the United States in the conduct of the occupation, as well as the supreme commander's determination to use the Tokyo trials as his instrument for waging peace.

Yonai reported this conversation to lawyer Shiobara, and the latter promised to help Tōjō plan his defense with American public opinion in mind. Subsequently, both in his depositions and in his court testimony, Tōjō followed the Japanese government's official line on the emperor's role in 1941: namely, that only the advisers to whom the emperor delegated authority bore responsibility for the decisions made then, and "since the highest organs of the state had decided there was no alternative, the emperor had to give his sanction" to war.

Years afterward, Tōjō's defense counselor revealed that at the time Whitney, Yonai, and even the chief prosecutor had been pressuring Tōjō to testify the way MacArthur wanted, Hirohito had checked up on their progress in a phone call to Prince Higashikuni.[14]

II

A difficult situation had met American chief prosecutor Joseph B. Keenan and his staff when they gathered in Tokyo on December 6 and 7, 1945, to organize the International Military Tribunal for the

Far East (IMTFE) and the International Prosecution Section (IPS), two groups that would soon be staffed by judges and prosecutors from eleven nations. GHQ had just gotten around to ordering the Japanese government to preserve official top-secret documents that could have a bearing on war crimes. Since the Occupation was operating indirectly through the Japanese government, IPS officials were unable to check pertinent ministry records until January 3, 1946.[15]

More important, Keenan found that MacArthur had been directed by a policy paper sent to him from Washington on September 12, and a Joint Chiefs order based on it of October 6, to draft a charter for an international court and to establish a unified prosecution organ (the IPS). The policy document (SWNCC 57/3) restricted what the IPS could do and reserved to MacArthur alone "the power to reduce, approve, or . . . alter" any punishments meted out. Its last paragraph, no. 17, instructed him to "take no action against the Emperor as a war criminal" without an explicit directive from Washington, thereby leaving open the possibility of his indictment. The supreme commander was to operate under orders from Washington and at the same time be an international civil servant, the representative of those Allied Powers who had signed the instrument of surrender and would now be asked to send judges and prosecutors. MacArthur's dual role and the way he played it added to the complexity of the ensuing trial. It blurred the nature of the tribunal's authority, and made it inevitable that the defense would claim that the Tokyo trial was, de facto, an American proceeding.[16]

At the beginning of 1946, the financial resources of the Imperial Household Ministry had been frozen, its staff downsized, and its sources of information curtailed. In order for Hirohito and his advisers to plan effectively for the forthcoming war crimes trials, new information sources had to be tapped. Consequently Matsudaira Yasamasa drew on the expertise of a secret Army Ministry research group that since the surrender was continuing its work but within the legal section of the Demobilization Bureau. Col. Matsu-tani Makoto, leader of the group, had participated in wartime plan-ning and had served as secretary to Army Ministers Sugiyama and Anami, as well as Prime Minister Suzuki. The colonel had tried unsuccessfully to reach Hirohito, via Kido's secretary, with the plea that as the war was obviously lost, it had to be ended. Now Matsu-tani and his group were examining damage-control measures for the forthcoming war crimes ordeal.

Their work began with a series of secret conferences held on January 3, 4, and 5, 1946, that were attended by elites from the pri-vate and imperial universities, the Bank of Tokyo, the Foreign Min-istry, Finance Ministry, and Ministry of Commerce and Industry, as well as by Matsudaira, representing Hirohito. Also present and con-tributing significantly to the conference's objectivity were Marxist historian Hirano Yoshitarō and political scientist Yabe Teiji—the former, Marxist or not, had stoutly supported the War of Greater East Asia, while Yabe was a longtime advocate of Japanese-style fas-cism. The conferees concluded that during the American occupa-tion, Japan's politics, economy, and thought would develop steadily and positively for about two years. Debate on the monarchy would gradually intensify in step with Soviet exploitation of ideological confusion.

Their final report emphasized the need to spread but also con-trol "cooperative democracy" in every area. The moderating assumption was that any real revolution in popular consciousness could be avoided if the emperor were retained as a "centripetal force" and "symbol"—in other words, as a concession to the irra-tional and traditional aspects of Japanese society. The war crimes trial would be a "political" spectacle, best dealt with from behind the scenes. Friendships with the judges and the lawyers for both the prosecution and the defense should be cultivated. The line for the defense should emphasize the army's sole responsibility for the war, and no hint of responsibility should be allowed to touch Hirohito.

The trial should be used to preserve and defend the state, and to this end individual defendants should be given minor priority.[17]

Nevertheless, Hirohito and his aides could not be sure he would escape interrogation either as witness or defendant, so in March 1946, five of his aides helped him to prepare his defense. The Japanese press was then filled with speculation that the war trial indictments would focus mainly on responsibility for spreading the war to the United States and Britain. Thus Hirohito and his aides felt the need to defend mainly on this issue rather than his role in the China war. Questions that MacArthur's headquarters wanted answered were conveyed to them by the newly appointed liaison officer between the palace and GHQ, Terasaki Hidenari, whose American wife had spent the war years in Japan and was a relative of General Fellers. The emperor's aides posed these questions to him and took down his responses.

There were five dictation sessions extending over eight hours. Terasaki then wrote out, in pencil, certain portions of this longer stenographic transcript on the basis of notes compiled and selected largely by Inada Shūichi, the director of the Imperial Palace Records Bureau. Terasaki's account is dated June 1, when the Tokyo trial had been in session for nearly one month. Work on the larger dictated text—originally entitled "The Emperor's Account of the Secret History of Shōwa"—from which Inada made his notes, continued into late July. After that time the text, which Terasaki had no hand in making and may never even have seen, was retitled "Record of the Emperor's Conversations" [*Seidan haichōroku*].

The political intention behind the initial "monologue" was first to defend Hirohito from the Tokyo tribunal and second to generate information the Americans could use against those who would actually stand trial for Japan's war crimes. Hirohito approved of these purposes. He wanted his views clearly conveyed to General Headquarters, but he also wanted to defend General Tōjō Hideki, whom he knew was being set up to take the fall for him.

During the first dictation session on March 18, Hirohito called attention to racial tensions in the background to the Pacific War. He began by noting that the Great Powers had rejected "Japan's call for racial equality, advocated by our representatives at the peace conference following World War I. Everywhere in the world discrimination between yellow and white remained, as in the rejection of immigration to California and the whites-only policy in Australia. These were sufficient grounds for the indignation of the Japanese people." Hirohito seemed to be criticizing the principle of white supremacy that he believed underlay U.S. Asian policy. He ignored, of course, what Japan's delegates had really advocated at Versailles: racial equality for Japanese only, not people of color all over the world.

He then expounded on seven questions that his aides knew were going to be dealt with by the tribunal. He started with an incident about which he and his government had, before the defeat, deliberately misinformed the Japanese people: Chang Tso-lin's assassination by staff officers of the Kwantung Army in Manchuria and the resignation of the Tanaka Giichi cabinet (1927–29). He spoke next about the London Naval Conference of 1930, the Manchurian Incident of 1931, and the Shanghai Incident of 1932. He continued with the February 26, 1936, incident, the decision to "limit the army and navy ministers to active-duty officers," and "Peace Negotiations with China and the Tripartite Pact."[18]

At the second session Terasaki informed everyone in the room that General MacArthur had sent a secret telegram to Washington in January exonerating the emperor of war crimes. He probably would not be indicted but could still be called as a witness. The work of preparing to counteract the Tokyo tribunal must continue. That day, March 20, Hirohito answered seven questions addressed to him by his aides concerning the causes of the collapse of the cabinets of Abe and Yonai, the Tripartite Pact, the Imperial Conferences of July 16 and September 6, questions about Tōjō, and the Pearl Harbor attack plan.[19]

During his third session two days later, Hirohito continued expounding on the Tōjō cabinet, Tōjō's efforts to prevent war, the imperial rescript declaring war, and disunity between the army and navy.[20] He heaped lavish praise on Tōjō, calling him "a man of understanding" who "became notorious as a sort of despot because he held too many posts, was too busy to communicate his feelings to subordinates, and made excessive use of the military police." Hirohito also admitted that he had resisted removing Tōjō because Tōjō "had been in contact with people all over Greater East Asia and without him [we] would have lost our ability to control their hearts."[21] The next two dictation sessions were held on April 8, at which time the five aides again listened to Hirohito's recollections from afternoon to evening. There was also a sixth dictation session, on April 9, that was not included in the "Monologue."

By this time, Hirohito was also preparing for his second meeting with General MacArthur, which he wanted to have before the Tokyo trial opened. A tentative date had been set for the meeting, April 23. Terasaki was to serve as the interpreter. But on the twenty-second, Terasaki had to ask Fellers for a postponement due to the unexpected resignation of the Shidehara cabinet. The cancellation deprived Hirohito of the chance to see MacArthur prior to the trial and to explain in person his purposes during the first twenty years of his reign. In this situation (as NHK documentary writer Higashino Shin hypothesized), Terasaki made available to Fellers his own brief (undated and untitled) summary, in English, of key points from the emperor's previous dictation sessions. Terasaki had intended to use this material as reference in interpreting for the cancelled meeting. As Fellers was personally duty bound to keep MacArthur informed of precisely such matters, "there is a very strong possibility that MacArthur read the English version."[22] He may also have read Terasaki's longer version of the "Monologue," though that document has not, so far, turned up in the papers of MacArthur or other American participants.

In the longer Japanese version, the emperor addressed thirty topics; the shorter English version contains only ten and puts emphasis on the emperor's powerlessness, omitting completely his role during the China war. The aim of both documents is clearly to present the argument that Hirohito had not been able to prevent the opening of war, and to explain why he could act independently only when the cabinet was not functioning.

III

During February and March 1946, while the Japanese public was learning about the new constitution, the work of the IPS continued. The executive committee of the IPS was composed mainly of "associate counsels" from each of the countries comprising the tribunal. Chaired by Chief Prosecutor Keenan and assisted by the most experienced lawyers on his staff, the IPS focused on interrogating and selecting those suspects who would be charged with "crimes against peace." Thirty names appeared on the Class A suspects list compiled by American prosecutors, but only eleven on the British list; neither mentioned the emperor. The Australians, however, presented a "provisional list of 100" possible indictees, including Hirohito for "crimes against peace and crimes against humanity." The Australians also furnished a detailed memorandum supporting the charges against the emperor. Never "at any time," it stressed, was Hirohito "forced by duress to give his written approval" to any aggressive military action. The memorandum asked rhetorically, "[I]s his crime not greater because he approved of something in which he did not believe?"[23]

The executive committee whittled the number of indictees down to twenty-eight. Excluded, among others, was Ishiwara Kanji, the mastermind of the Manchurian Incident. Ishiwara had not been interviewed during the preparatory stage. His removal from the indictees list was probably owed to Keenan's positive image of Ishiwara as one who had opposed Tōjō and tried to over-throw his regime. But it may also have reflected the American pros-ecutors' mistaken belief that middle-echelon staff officers, like their American counterparts, were never prime movers in initiating aggression.[24]

In the end only twenty-six defendants were indicted. There were no businessmen, no university intellectuals, no Buddhist priests, no judges, and no journalists who had preached militarism and racial fanaticism. When the Soviet delegates tardily arrived on April 13, they tried to include three businessmen who had played leading roles in organizing the economy for war, but succeeded in adding only Gen. Umezu Yoshijirō and diplomat Shigemitsu Mamoru. Former foreign minister Matsuoka Yōsuke and former naval chief of staff Nagano Osumi died before the trial was con-cluded. One defendant—Ōkawa Shūmei—was declared mentally incompetent.

A serious distorting effect on the selection of the Tokyo defen-dants, and later on the trial itself, arose from the overwhelming U.S. military and economic domination of the Asia-Pacific region, and from MacArthur's excessive power. But above all, distortions stemmed from the subordination of international law to *realpolitik* by *all* the Allied governments. Those governments tended to rank their national interests first, law and morality second. So did Hiro-hito and his advisers, working covertly behind the unfolding legal drama.

Thus the Soviet delegation, on instructions from Stalin, chose to follow the leader and call for Hirohito's indictment only if the Americans did. The representatives of the only three Asian coun-tries that participated in the tribunal—China, the Philippines, and India—also sought to avoid conflict with American policy as much as possible and to pursue their own lines of inquiry.

No country had suffered more from Japan's aggression than China; and no Allied war leader understood the close connection

between the Japanese monarchy and militarism better than did Chiang Kai-shek. But Chiang also believed Hirohito to be a check on
the spread of Communism, and so opted not to indict. Although his
own military courts indicted and tried 883 Japanese for war crimes
in ten different cities, he did not accord high priority to the Tokyo
trial. Chiang's war with the Communists was about to resume. He
needed American financial aid and military assistance, and hoped to
persuade Japanese military personnel to stay on after surrender so
that he could use them in his war against the Communists.

The small legal team Chiang dispatched to Tokyo reflected
these priorities: one judge (Mei Ju-ao), one prosecutor (Hsiang
Che-chun), and only two secretaries. Later Chiang sent more personnel and had materials collected pertaining to war crimes, but
never enough to allow the Chinese to take the initiative. During the
China stage of the prosecution's case, in the summer of 1946, American prosecutors did the main work of investigating accusations of
Japanese criminal behavior, Prosecutor Hsiang merely assisting. On
the other hand Hsiang energetically probed the Nanking atrocities
and the killing of civilians and disarmed soldiers in many other Chinese cities. He also presented evidence on the crime of rape, though
without treating it as a crime against humanity.

Nationalist China chose not to hand over to IPS investigators
the vast amount of data on Chinese war casualties that Chiang's
"Commission on Reparations" had been accumulating ever since
1938. Nor did it pursue Japan's forced recruitment of civilian laborers, the "kill all, burn all, steal all" (sankō sakusen) campaigns in
North China, and the use of poison gas. These "crimes against
humanity" (with the exception of the last) had taken place mostly in
the Communist base areas, so Chiang Kai-shek was not interested
in them.[25] This may explain why Chiang's chief of staff, Gen. Ho
Ying-ch'in, treated Gen. Okamura Yasuji, architect of the liquida-
tion campaigns, and Okamura's subordinate officers "in and around
Nanking . . . like honored guests instead of defeated enemies."[26]

When a Chinese military court in Nanking convicted Okamura of war crimes in July 1948, Chiang protected the general, first ordering Okamura released so he could recover from tuberculosis in a Shanghai hospital, then allowing him to return safely to Japan. A year later, while GHQ turned a blind eye, the Nationalist high command, operating through their Tokyo mission, secretly enlisted Okamura's services in recruiting high-ranking Japanese officers as military advisers to go to Taiwan and aid in the reconstruction of Taiwan's armed forces.[27]

The Philippines had lost more than one million noncombatants and suffered enormous damage during the war. Most Filipinos held Hirohito responsible. The Philippine government nominated judge Delfin Jaranilla, a participant in the Bataan "death march," as its representative on the bench, and later appointed Pedro Lopez as associate prosecutor. During the Philippines stage of the trial, Lopez introduced 144 cases of atrocities committed by Japanese forces against Filipino non-combatants and American and Filipino POWs, thereby laying a basis for later reparations claims. On the payroll of the American government, Lopez, like Jaranilla, never made an issue of Hirohito's absence from the list of indictees.[28]

The Indian appointee to the court was sixty-year-old Radhabinod Pal of the High Court of Calcutta. Pal had been a supporter of the pro-Axis Indian nationalist, Chandra Bose, and a longtime Japanophile. Unlike most Indian elites, who condemned both British and Japanese imperialism and never embraced the ideology of the Greater East Asia Coprosperity Sphere, Pal was an outright apologist for Japanese imperialism. Arriving in Tokyo in May, he accepted his appointment under the charter in bad faith, not believing in the right of the Allies to try Japan, let alone judicially sanction it any way. Determined to see the tribunal fail from the outset, Pal intended to write a separate dissenting opinion no matter what the other judges ruled. Not surprisingly he refused to sign a "joint affirmation to administer justice fairly."[29]

Thereafter, according to the estimate of defense lawyer Owen Cunningham, Pal absented himself for 109 of 466 "judge-days," or more than twice the number of the next highest absentee, the president of the tribunal, Sir William Webb himself (53 "judge-days").[30] Whenever Pal appeared in court, he unfailingly bowed to the defendants, whom he regarded as men who had initiated the liberation of Asia. Pal, the most politically independent of the judges, refused to let Allied political concerns and purposes, let alone the charter, influence his judgment in any way. He would produce the tribunal's most emotionally charged, political judgment. Many who repudiated the Tokyo trial while clinging to the wartime propaganda view of the "War of Greater East Asia," believed that the main cause of Asian suffering was Western white men—that is, Pal's "victors." They would cite Pal's arguments approvingly. So too would others who saw the war primarily in terms of the "white" exploitation of Asia.

Throughout the process of selecting among those accused, the prosecutors worked feverishly, their eyes peeled to the clock and to Nuremberg, fearing that world interest would vanish once the German trial of twenty-two major war criminals ended.[31] Nuremberg was both their legal model and a source of psychological pressure. MacArthur, through Keenan, exerted pressure to wind up the preparatory stage and begin the proceedings. He denied the prosecution the right to interrogate Hirohito; he also determined that Hirohito would neither give testimony as a witness nor be asked to provide his diary or other private papers.

Diaries and prison depositions, both formal and informal, played a crucial role in the decisions to indict because so many of the incriminating Japanese documents had been burned or otherwise disposed of by cabinet decisions transmitted orally to avoid a written trail.[32] Secret records of the Japanese armed forces were also hidden away. Most though not all of the depositions were completed by April 9—one week after Keenan had ordered them stopped. All deponents sought to protect Hirohito and to lay blame for the war on a very small number of army officers, singled out by name. Participating in the trial behind the scenes, through their depositions, the pro-Anglo-American "moderates" now took their revenge on the army elite for having lost the war. The senior statesmen, Adms. Yonai Mitsumasa and Okada Keisuke, who like others in the court milieu had served as informants for the prosecution, defended the navy, exaggerated the army's influence, and minimized that of the emperor and his entourage.[33]

IV

On May 3, 1946, the trial opened in the large, newly renovated auditorium of the War Ministry Building in Ichigaya, near the center of Tokyo. Keenan had had this nerve center of Japanese militarism converted into a courtroom, refitted with dark wood paneling and a long, highly elevated mahogany bench for the judges. One microphone was provided solely for the use of the tribunal president. A witness box was set near the center of the room with tables and benches nearby for the lawyers and court stenographers. Carpenters built high lecterns for the chief prosecutor and chief defense counsel, and platforms for the Allied movie cameramen and still photographers who filmed the entire proceeding. Special galley areas were set aside for the domestic and foreign press, radio broadcasters, and some thirty translators who worked in the two official languages of the trial, English and Japanese.[34] Seats in the rear upper balcony accommodated 660 spectators, while first-floor seats increased the total to nearly 1,000. Clerks moved around the courtroom with traveling microphones, and large klieg lights, hung from the ceiling, brightly illuminated the whole scene.[35]

Three days later, at the third open session, defendants, judges, lawyers, white-helmeted military policemen, and hundreds of diplomats and journalists from all over the world packed the courtroom at 9:15 A.M. to hear the pleas of the defendants. First the defense lawyers were introduced, then a dispute arose over a mistranslation in the indictment. Once that was cleared up, the indictees, starting with Araki Sadao, stood up as their names were called in alphabetical order. All pleaded not guilty to each and every charge. A show trial in the best pedagogical sense—that is, a major criminal trial intended to teach not lies, as in Stalin's show trials, but positive lessons about the criminality of war—was now off to a slow start, with the courtroom packed and the Japanese nation looking on, still in the middle of a food crisis.

The prosecution team presented its case in phases over a period of nearly eight months, starting with Keenan's dramatic opening statement on June 4. The Tokyo tribunal was trying men who had "declared war upon civilization" itself, and should therefore be viewed as part of a just "battle of civilization to preserve the entire world from destruction." He then proceeded to outline the theory of the prosecution.[36] Thereafter the prosecutors daily introduced treaties, agreements, and other documents in order to establish what American and Japanese foreign policies had been. The prosecution called 109 witnesses who testified orally, and entered written testimony (in the form of statements, affidavits, and interrogations) from 561 others. Step-by-step the evidence against the accused accumulated. The first story to emerge was of Japan's preparations for war through propaganda, censorship, and centralized educational indoctrination; next the narrative of its conduct of aggressive wars was constructed, with the spotlight on the war crimes of the imperial forces in different countries.

As early as the second week, American defense attorney Maj. Ben Bruce Blakeney challenged the participation of the Soviet judge on the bench because the Soviet government had earlier been expelled from the League of Nations for its limited war of aggression against Finland. The defense had raised the issue of Allied behavior in the just-concluded era of global repartition (1938–45);

thereafter it began raising *tu quoque* ("you did it too") arguments, intended to weaken the accusations of the prosecution without actually refuting them. On each occasion the bench rejected them—in effect telling the defense which acts of violence were "aggression" and war crimes and which were not.

On June 13 the Australian associate prosecutor, Alan Mansfield, introduced documents that clarified both the various Hague treaties to which Japan had been a party, and the Japanese political and bureaucratic systems. The life history of each defendant was read out, and the prosecutors summarized how the war was prepared. Japanese witnesses Shidehara Kijūrō and Wakatsuki Reijirō, among others, described a virtually autonomous army, a "police state," and the ethos that informed its politics during the 1930s. The impression deepened that the "militarists" had staged "incidents," challenged the authority of successive cabinets, and gradually consolidated power. But whenever the question arose of who was constitutionally and morally responsible for the army high command, no answer could be given, for Hirohito was being kept "hidden behind a *shōji* screen."[37]

After a short summer recess, during which air-conditioning was installed in the courtroom, the tribunal reconvened and began hearing testimony on Japanese aggression in China, starting around the time of the Manchurian Incident. On June 27, Inukai Takeru, the son of assassinated prime minister Inukai Tsuyoshi, took the witness stand for the prosecution. In giving evidence, he made a direct and unexpected reference to Hirohito, claiming that his father, for whom he had worked as secretary, had been granted an audience at which he had asked the emperor directly to order the army to withdraw from Manchuria. Rather than state outright that the emperor refused, Inukai declared that the prime minister "failed to achieve his aim." In later cross-examination of Inukai, Hozumi Shigetaka, lawyer for defendants Kido and Tōgō, asked why the emperor had not granted Prime Minister Inukai's request for an imperial rescript ordering the army out; furthermore, whether read in English or Japanese, the witness's "statement can be taken to mean that the emperor had responsibility for the expansion of the Manchurian Incident."[38] Inukai tried to correct his statement, but the bench had been stirred by the dramatic, unexpected way in which responsibility had been attributed to the emperor.

The next day Webb informed the court that some of the judges "would like to hear the witness make a fuller statement on the emperor's position to clear up a contradiction, if there be one, in his own evidence." Inukai partially retracted his previous day's statement by saying that when he and his father spoke of "withdrawal from Manchuria" they meant the ordering of the Korean Army back to Korea, and the Railway Garrison troops back to the railway zone. Ultimately Inukai failed to clear up the contradiction, however.[39] Seven months later, when the prosecution completed its narrative of the conspiracy and closed its case, the question of Hirohito's role in events hung like a cloud over the proceedings. Not a single defendant had dared to discuss his war responsibility.

V

The defense took eleven months trying to establish the nonculpability of each accused—most of 1947, longer than the entire first Nuremberg trial. It presented, in addition to the defendants, 310 witnesses and written testimony by 214 others. The defense generally followed Japanese wartime propaganda in explaining why Japan had gone to war against the United States and Britain, and made use of numerous postwar writings critical of Roosevelt's foreign policy.[40] When the defense concentrated on justifying Japan's actions in China and the Pacific, the prosecution pointed to the many gross errors of fact that riddled the defense presentation. The tribunal ruled again and again that the bulk of the defense material was irrelevant or immaterial. Rejected documents included details of Japan's efforts to counter Soviet communism in Asia and the U.S. congressional investigations of the Pearl Harbor attack. When attorney Blakeney attempted to submit a summary of former secretary of war Stimson's account of the decision to drop atomic bombs on Japan, the tribunal, by majority, rejected that as well. Rebuttals and summations by both sides went on through the winter and spring of 1948.[41]

The American and Japanese defense lawyers performed badly from the outset. In the words of leading defense lawyer and former member of the Diet Kiyose Ichirō, they tried "to disprove each and every charge of criminality lodged against" their clients but were unable to agree on a common strategy.[42] Kiyose's long opening statement made the point that war atrocities "alleged to have been committed against the Jews in Germany [were] never present in Japan, [and] we are prepared to produce evidence to explain the difference between the war crimes of Germany and the alleged acts of the accused."[43] Next, defense lawyer Takayanagi Kenzō rose and attacked the legitimacy of the charter. A succession of Japanese senior army officers, some under investigation as possible war criminals themselves, were called as witnesses for the defense. Many defense attorneys claimed their clients had acted under superior orders and/or had fought to stop the spread of Communism in Asia. Many referred to the "Hull note," a term introduced into the Japanese lexicon during the trial and charged with malevolent connotations ever since. The real villain, they insisted, had been the United States, which had forced Japan into a war of "self-defense." The defense lawyers also pursued delaying tactics, hoping that the worsening ideological conflict between the United States and the Soviet Union would help Japan's militarists to make their case.

The highlights of the defense phase were the testimonies of ex–Privy Seal Kido, ex–Foreign Minister Tōgō, and General Tōjō. In cross-examination by Chief Prosecutor Keenan, all three inadvertently drew in the absent emperor.

During Kido's first two days on the witness stand, October

14–16, 1947, his defense lawyer, William Logan, read out the entire 297-page English text of his lengthy deposition, omitting nothing despite Keenan's complaint that it duplicated court documents. When Logan finished, ten lawyers questioned Kido in turn for nearly five days. Then Keenan began several days of cross-examination, designed to establish that "from the beginning of [Kido's] political career until the surrender of Japan," he had (in Keenan's words) "constantly opposed any movement upon the part of the Emperor . . . in a practical way to bring about law and order . . . and stop the rule of lawlessness and violence . . . ."[44] Using the diary of Harada Kumao to question assertions in Kido's diary, Keenan showed that Kido had gone along with, rather than fought against, the militarists during the China war; despite his claims of having had nothing to do with politics, Kido had exercised enormous political power behind the scenes.

The chief prosecutor also charged Kido with constantly shifting blame onto his friends: Harada and Konoe—both conveniently deceased—and the elderly Makino Nobuaki. On the twenty-third several tense exchanges ensued between Keenan and Kido: focusing on what had been Hirohito's authority in military and diplomatic affairs on the eve of the Pearl Harbor attack, and on Kido's advice to the emperor, including his role in the making of the Tripartite Pact; his recommendation of Tōjō as prime minister, and his handling of President Roosevelt's last-minute letter to the emperor.[45] By the time Kido left the stand, the emperor's war responsibility was again at issue.

In late December 1947 former foreign minister Tōgō took the witness stand and drew national attention by declaring that Tōjō, Shimada Shigetarō, and Suzuki Teiichi had been the main advocates of declaring war in 1941. More important, Tōgō also claimed, on December 26, that Secretary of State Hull had demanded an immediate and complete withdrawal of all Japanese military and police forces from China and French Indochina.

Not only that, the Hull note . . . demanded that we withdraw from the Manchurian area as well, which would have immediately affected Korea, causing us to withdraw from there also. Stated differently, I can boldly state our external situation would have been the same as we face right now. . . . In sum, the Hull note demanded that Japan return to [its] pre-Russo-Japanese War situation. This would have been suicidal for Japan in East Asia. If we had done so, then economically we would have been unable to exist.[46]

Tōgō implied that the government was forced to opt for war after it had carefully studied the "Hull note." In fact there was (and is) no record of such an examination. What Tōgō sought to obscure in addition to the professional incompetence of his Washington diplomats, was that Hull had never challenged Japan's continued control of Manchukuo; and that he, Tōgō, might have, but did not, insist on postponing war with the United States at that time by making Hull's document a focus for negotiations.

When General Tōjō took the stand on December 27, 1947, both GHQ's and the Japanese government's lobbying campaign to protect Hirohito shifted into high gear. The *Asahi shinbun* gave most of its front page to Tōjō's testimony. Its headline that day read, "The Emperor Bears No Responsibility. [Tōjō] Insists Adamantly That It Was a War of Self Defense."[47] Three days later, on December 30, after his American lawyer had read into the record excerpts from his earlier depositions, Tōjō defended not only the emperor but the entire Japanese political process leading to the decision for war in December 1941. Japanese politics had not undergone any reactionary transformation, he insisted, but had remained government-as-usual-under-the-Meiji-Constitution. All Japanese war atrocities were accidental; neither ideological indoctrination nor the ethos that informed the armed forces had anything to do with them. Addressing the Japanese public at large, rather than the courtroom audience, Tōjō depicted himself as an aggrieved victim.

He denied that aggressive war was a crime and declared:

> I insist that right up to the very end this was a war of self-defense and
> did not violate international law as understood at that time. I have
> never imagined, not even to this day, that as an official and an individ-
> ual of a defeated nation I would be indicted by the victors and accused
> of being a violator of treaties and a criminal under international law
> because my country fought this war.

Tōjō then cleverly displaced his and the emperor's responsibility
for starting the war behind the very different responsibility for losing
it. The defeat had occurred during the last year and a half of the war,
when Tōjō was out of power. On the stand he was magnanimous:
"The second problem is my responsibility for the defeat as the prime
minister at that time. In this sense, I not only accept my responsibility, but from the bottom of my heart I am happy to bear it."[48]

Tōjō's performance evoked strong emotions and helped to
restore his standing among those who were hostile to the tribunal
and wanted to see at least one of the accused stand up as a model of
loyalist behavior. Keenan's response was ineffective. The next day,
however, under questioning by Kido's American defense attorney,
William Logan, Tōjō created a stir by inadvertently and indirectly
implicating the emperor.

> *Logan*: Do you remember even one example where Kido proposed
> something or acted against the emperor's wish for peace?
> *Tojo*: So far as I know, such an instance never arose. Not only that, no
> Japanese subject, let alone a high official of Japan, would ever go
> against the will of the emperor.[49]

Tōjō's slip, undermining the argument that Hirohito bore no
responsibility for the decision to start the war, was immediately
pointed out to the prosecution by tribunal president Webb. It could

not be ignored. One of Hirohito's close aides immediately sent word to Kido in Sugamo prison to get Tōjō to correct his error. With the help of Chief Counsel Keenan, Tōjō did so the next time he took the stand, January 6, 1948. Nevertheless, more damage had been done: the prosecution's evidence and Tōjō's testimony had once again implicated the emperor who was not on trial.[50]

VI

The threat of forced abdication had hung heavily over Hirohito before, during, and long after the war crimes trial. The danger came from his immediate family members who wanted to have a voice in political affairs, and from all who believed that there are moral standards applicable *only* to leaders of nations.

Prince Takamatsu was one of several family members who wanted Hirohito out. Soon after Japan's formal surrender, on September 20, 1945, he confided to his diary that it was unwise for the emperor to remain on the throne simply because he had accumulated years of experience as monarch or because his abdication would disturb MacArthur.[51] Anticipating a regency but unable to openly promote his own candidacy, he endorsed the idea of Chichibu as regent. Ten days later he wrote that Prince Chichibu's return to the capital after a long convalescence "means he will meet people and when the time comes he could become regent."[52] Takamatsu, clearly believing Hirohito was not licensed to stay on the throne permanently, maintained a steady stream of criticism of him. Other family members, such as Princes Mikasa and Higashikuni, also supported early abdication.

Soon several prominent intellectuals, such as the liberal philosopher Tanabe Hajime, publicly called on Hirohito to "muster the courage to express a more sincere sense of responsibility" by abdicating.[53] The president of Tokyo Imperial University, Nambara Shigeru, also asked him to step down. Among the first to state the moral case against the emperor from the standpoint of soldiers who had laid down their lives for him in battle was the famous poet Miyoshi Tatsuji. There will "be no morality in the world" unless the emperor abdicates "as quickly as circumstances permit," Miyoshi declared in a series of influential articles during the spring and into early summer of 1946:

> As the head of state, his majesty must take primary responsibility for this defeat. . . . . The emperor bears responsibility for being extremely negligent in the performance of his duties. He permitted the violent behavior of the military cliques and for many years did not do what he should have done. His loyal subjects trusted him as a benevolent father, as in the phrase "the children of the emperor." They believed that as emperor he was the supreme commander of the emperor's military; they obeyed military regulations posted in his name; and they died in battle shouting, "His Majesty the Emperor, Banzai!" Yet the emperor lamented, "The army is a nuisance . . . ." It is the emperor who is guilty for betraying the loyal soldiers.[54]

Vice Grand Chamberlain Kinoshita Michio rightly perceived the long-term nature of this threat. In an unsigned, undated memorandum in his diary, probably written in early spring 1946, on Imperial Household Ministry stationery, Kinoshita (or someone who shared his ideas) wrote that even though the United States and MacArthur had decided to maintain the monarchy,

> as the war crimes trials go forward, the problem will arise of whether to retain the present emperor or install a successor. I am sure [the United States and General MacArthur] anticipate all-out resistance from the Japanese people if they call for the abolition of the emperor system. But they probably don't anticipate similar resistance to a call for abdication of the current emperor and enthronement of a new one. Depending on the circumstances, they may begin to advocate this. We will have to be prepared.

It is vital of importance not to allow them to talk about the abdication
of the emperor. The way to do that is to plant the impression that, for
the United States, the present emperor is the most desirable, trustworthy person to be in control of Japan and also [the most reliable
person] in international relations, particularly in the Orient.[55]

By July 1946 even Hirohito's most enthusiastic defender in
GHQ, General Fellers, was urging him to repent to the nation in
the interest of preventing long-lasting harm to the monarchy.[56]
Meanwhile, Kido, in detention at Sugamo Prison, mulled over the
question of Hirohito's war responsibility but put off recommending
abdication until his own ordeal and the occupation itself had ended.

On November 4, 1948, around the time the Communist armies of
Mao Tse-tung captured Mukden and Stalin was challenging the
"Truman Doctrine" by blockading Berlin, the Tokyo trial drew to a
close after a six-month recess.

Judge Webb read out in open session the majority judgment,
but first reviewed the law of the Charter—issued and later amended
by MacArthur—which defined three broad categories of crime.[57]
The initial category was "the planning, preparation, initiation or
waging of a . . . war of aggression, or a war in violation of international law, treaties, agreements . . . or participation in a common
plan or conspiracy for the accomplishment of any of the foregoing."
Following Nuremberg precedent, the waging of such a war was
termed "crimes against peace." During the trial it had denoted
mainly violations of the Covenant of the League of Nations, the
Nine-Power Treaty concerning the sovereignty, independence, and
territorial integrity of China, and the Kellogg-Briand Pact
renouncing war of aggression as an instrument of national policy.
Unlike conventional war crimes, "crimes against peace" could be
committed only by policy makers.[58] The prosecution had argued not
that aggressive war per se was illegal but only that every act of
aggressive war with which Japan was charged was covered by

treaties to which Japan was a party. Because pursuit of this charge had forced the prosecutors to investigate the causes of the Asia-Pacific War, a hornet's nest of unresolved historical debate had opened, particularly after the defense was not allowed to introduce in evidence documents having to do with communism in Asia. On the other hand, neither at Nuremberg nor Tokyo were death sentences handed down solely on the basis of "crimes against peace."

The second, less controversial category of offense was "violation of the laws or customs of war." This offense was based upon the Hague and Geneva Conventions on the laws of land warfare and the treatment of prisoners of war, respectively. Both had come to be recognized as customary law embodying minimum standards of humane conduct, applicable to all states engaged in international armed conflict. Defense attempts to rebut charges of "violations of the laws and customs of war" invariably fell flat in the face of the enormous evidence the prosecution marshaled to prove Japanese criminality in the prosecution of war.[59]

"Crimes against humanity" was the third category. The term (which had first emerged in World War I in connection with Turkish atrocities against Armenians) was defined exactly as in the four-nation London Charter on which the IMT at Nuremberg was based. It denoted "murder, extermination, enslavement, deportation, and other inhumane acts committed before or during the war, or persecutions on political or racial grounds . . . ." These crimes, mainly against the civilian population, "were punishable under international law only insofar" as they were committed in connection with war crimes. At Tokyo the prosecutors, following the fifty-five count indictment, highlighted the catchall crime of murder taken broadly "as resulting from illegal warfare confined to aggressive attacks or in violation of treaties when the nations attacked were at peace with Japan."[60] "Murder" so taken was an enormous umbrella that could and did cover both the Japanese attack on Pearl Harbor and the "rape of Nanking."

Judge Webb went on to discuss the conduct of the trial and the facts of the individual cases. Though the tribunal found the Japanese army guilty of usurping power by intimidation and assassination, it exonerated the Japanese people for the behavior of their armed forces. It also greatly reduced the number of counts in the original indictment that were considered to have been proved. Webb concluded by summarizing the majority view "that the charge of conspiracy to wage [a succession of] aggressive wars has been made out . . . these acts are . . . criminal in the highest degree."[61]

He then handed down guilty verdicts on all twenty-five principal defendants. Tōjō received the death sentence, along with five other generals: Itagaki Seishirō, Kimura Heitarō, Doihara Kenji, Matsui Iwane, and Mutō Akira. One civil official, former diplomat and prime minister Hirota Kōki, was also sentenced to die. After MacArthur had dismissed all appeals for a stay of execution, seven of the defense lawyers appealed to the U.S. Supreme Court. Their ground was constitutional: The Tokyo tribunal was really an American court established without the consent of Congress; it had derived, from and been conducted entirely on the basis of, President Truman's executive powers. Shortly before the Justices heard their "appeal," an angry MacArthur told British representative Alvary Gascoigne, that even if the Supreme Court issued a writ of habeas corpus, he would "ignore it" and "entrust the matter to the Far Eastern Commission."[62] On December 15, the day before the case was argued at the Supreme Court, the Far Eastern Commission hastily announced that the tribunal "is an international court appointed and acting under international authority."[63] Five days later the Court ruled that it had no power or authority to set aside the sentences.

The defense lawyers had sought to highlight the political nature of the Tokyo tribunal. They succeeded only in revealing its complexity, and emphasizing the dual, ambiguous nature of MacArthur's authority. The Supreme Commander now went ahead and ordered the seven executed by hanging. Their bodies were then cremated and most of their ashes scattered at sea in the mistaken belief that this would prevent them from someday being enshrined as martyrs.[64] A chamberlain alleges that on hearing the news of Tōjō's death, Hirohito went into his office and wept.

Sixteen defendants, including former privy seal Kido and former prime minister Hiranuma, received life imprisonment. Ex–Foreign Minister Tōgō received twenty-five years' confinement while diplomat Shigemitsu Mamoru, not regarded as one of the main persons responsible for starting the war, received seven years for having participated as foreign minister in the Kōiso cabinet and for having made no effort to stop the mistreatment of prisoners of war.

In his own separate, concurring opinion, Webb agreed in general with the verdict of the majority but felt that the Japanese accused should be treated with more consideration than their German counterparts, whose "crimes were far more heinous, varied and extensive." Webb saved his sharpest criticism for the total immunity given to the emperor. Firmly rejecting the defense of duress, he declared: "No ruler can commit the crime of launching aggressive war and then validly claim to be excused for so doing because his life would otherwise have been in danger."[65]

Judge Henri Bernard of France wrote a dissenting opinion which also brought in the emperor. Japan's declaration of war, he concluded, "had a principal author who escaped all prosecution and of whom in any case the present Defendants could only be considered as accomplices."[66]

Judge B. V. A. Röling of the Netherlands found nothing objectionable in Hirohito's immunity, for he believed him to have been a complete figurehead. Röling based his dissent instead on the imperfections of the charter, whose validity he had questioned from the outset. He rejected the notion of "aggression" as a crime under international law, and felt that four of the defendants—Kido, Hata,

Hirota, Shigemitsu, and Tōgō—should have been acquitted.

Judge Pal completed his dissenting opinion in early August, and asked Webb to have the entire text read in open court, according to Indian practice. The majority voted to have only its existence announced, which Webb did on the day of sentencing, November 12.

Pal's judgment, declaring all the defendants innocent on all charges, was unique, in no way representative of the Indian or any other Asian government.[67] From the standpoint of legal theory, he denied (as did Röling, whose views were close to his) the criminality of launching and waging war as a sovereign right of the state. The international legal order as it had existed in the nineteenth century could not be developed and expanded; the concept of "aggression" remained legally undefined. The Nuremberg and Tokyo tribunals, having exceeded the framework of international law as it existed before World War I, were illegal. Ergo the defendants were not in violation of law.

Serious errors of fact marred Pal's historical analysis of Japan's actions—the second element of his dissent. He asserted, for example, that Chang Tso-lin had not been assassinated by the Japanese military, and that the "Hull note" was an American ultimatum. "Even the contemporary historians," he wrote, "could think that '[a]s for the present war, the Principality of Monaco [and] the Grand Duchy of Luxembourg would have taken up arms against the United States on receipt of such a note as the State Department sent the Japanese Government on the eve of Pearl Harbor.'"[68] Pal contravened the political purpose of the trial and one of the occupation's main educational goals: namely, to make the Japanese people understand the criminality of war. Despite his professed intention, he ended up arguing the innocence of Japan and strongly endorsing the official Japanese view of wartime history.

Although CIE's "war guilt program" prohibited the publication in full of the dissenting opinions in the Tokyo trial, Judge Webb noted in open court the dissents by nearly half the judges on the tribunal.[69] The independence of the foreign judges and the existence of minority verdicts impressed the Japanese public and contributed to acceptance of the trial results.

VII

The Tokyo trial, despite its defective procedures and complex political nature, had a deep, many-sided impact on the Japanese people and their view of the lost war.[70] Some right-wing opinion was highly critical, resentful, and angry, and never reflected on Japan's aggression. Kishi Nobusuke, in his Sugamo Prison diary described the war crimes trial as a "farce" and devoted the rest of his political life to trying to undo its effects.[71] Other rightists, feeling that Japan, stripped naked, had been shamed before the world, tried to ignore the trial, put it out of mind, block the transmission of any positive political and cultural lessons. Former conservative prime minister Ashida predicted that the trial would not cause great domestic repercussions.[72]

The Communists had been virtually the only ones vigorously to demand pursuit of war responsibility and harsh punishment for convicted criminals. But in academia, intellectuals of Marxist persuasion tended to dismiss the trial as a lost opportunity for deepening Japan's democratization, and as historically insignificant. The charter for the tribunal had been revised to allow heads of state to escape responsibility, they noted, and the judicial process had been corrupted by MacArthur's grants of total immunity to the emperor and the nation's business and financial leaders. Some Marxist historians also pointed out, correctly, that the Tokyo tribunal had promoted an elitist view of history insofar as it made the course toward war "pivot on the conflict between extreme militarists and moderate political leaders."[73] Outside the universities, however, according to an American military intelligence report prepared in August 1948, the majority of Japanese took a "passive" attitude toward the accused national leaders, but also felt they had received a fair trial under the circumstances.[74] After the verdicts were handed down, popular reaction to the trial was expressed positively in continued efforts to reconstruct, improve, and make Japan a genuine "peace state."

To this one may add: It is doubtful the defendants would have been treated as fairly if they had been judged in a Japanese court for defying the emperor's "spirit of peace" as envisioned in an undated document—a draft emergency imperial decree that provided for trials and the death sentence—found in the Makino Nobuaki papers and believed to have been written during the Shidehara cabinet.[75]

More important, the Tokyo trial was never a straightforward adversarial proceeding, pitting victors against vanquished. The charge of "victors' justice," leveled most vehemently by Pal, was and remains extremely simplistic, and has impeded understanding of what really happened. The proceedings at Tokyo amounted, in fact, to a joint—American-Japanese—political trial.[76] During its preparatory stage Hirohito and those closest to him participated behind the scenes, helping to select and influence the persons charged with war crimes. Imperial aides Terasaki and Matsudaira served as informants for members of the executive committee of the IPS, which drew up the list of indictees. So too did other members of the entourage, who sought to protect both the emperor and the senior statesmen. Palace aides and Foreign Ministry officials instructed the Class A suspects in Sugamo Prison on what to say; at the same time they cultivated relations with Keenan and many of the lawyers for both defense and prosecution.

Members of the imperial family, particularly Prince Takamatsu, and palace aides such as Matsudaira invited the American attorneys to cocktail parties, receptions, and imperial "duck hunts" with the aim of winning favor, nurturing collaborators, and gaining information. Hirohito personally sanctioned increases in palace spending precisely for such entertainments. His officials cooperated in the interrogations and gave depositions because they wanted to pin responsibility for aggression on a handful of military cliques—while leaving the impression that the emperor and his people had been completely deceived. Members of the reorganized and expanded court group of the early postsurrender period succeeded in inserting into the official American version of the ending of World War II a false account that obscured Hirohito's role in delaying the surrender. These conservative elites, whom Keenan called "peace lovers," influenced to some extent the indictment process, the court proceedings, and even the final verdicts.

The Tokyo tribunal succeeded in revealing both the deceit of the war leaders and their unwillingness to admit criminal liability for their actions while in office. It disclosed, for the first time in Japan, the facts about the assassination of Chang Tso-lin and the Kwantung Army conspiracy that led to the Manchurian Incident. It documented the mistreatment and murder of Allied prisoners of war and civilians at scores of places in Asia and the Pacific, including most famously Bataan and the Thai-Burma railway over the river Kwai.[77] Evidence of mass atrocities at Nanking was admitted, and during the trial of General Matsui Iwane was reinforced for the Japanese people by press reports of the war crimes trial in Nanking, which sentenced to death Gens. Tani Hisao and Isogai Rensuke, among others, for their role in the mass atrocities of 1937–38. The Japanese killing of civilians in Manila, where indiscriminate American artillery bombardment also contributed to the high death toll, were described in detail. The introduction of evidence on the rape of female prisoners and females in occupied territories, and the prosecution of rape in an international war crimes trial, set positive precedents for the future.[78]

The Tokyo trial affected Japanese political attitudes in the long run. Influenced by what they had learned about war as a national enterprise, many people resolved that Japan should never go to war again, and dedicated themselves to making democratic ideals and international norms work. Because the trial strengthened popular hatred of militarism and war, it contributed to acceptance of the new constitution. The Japanese peace movement drew on the trial's evidence to condemn the old value structure of imperial Japan. The Japanese press, at CIE's insistence, reported daily on the proceedings, and though subject to occupation censorship, presented an account of the road to war much more accurate than the story the average Japanese had been led to believe. In addition an enormous amount of documentation amassed by the prosecution and defense was preserved, and still serves today as an invaluable historical archive.

Nevertheless, in the eyes of some Japanese and foreign critics then and since, the Tokyo trial was irrevocably flawed. The tribunal had not adequately protected the rights of defendants under international criminal law. In its indictment, the prosecution laid great emphasis on the charge of conspiracy—a legal concept grounded in the European natural-law tradition and in Anglo-Saxon common law but regarded as vague, unfamiliar, and historically anachronistic by Continental lawyers.[79] Keenan and MacArthur, following Truman policy, obfuscated the Japanese decision-making process by omitting the one person in power during the entire seventeen-year period of the alleged conspiracy (January 1, 1928 to September 2, 1945). That person was the emperor: He alone could have validated a conspiratorial union of wills to wage an illegal "war of aggression and a war in violation of international law, treaties, agreements and assurances."

Moreover the Allies had also committed war crimes but refused to apply the Nuremberg principles to their own conduct. Over the thirty-one months that the trial unfolded, the U.S.–Soviet Cold War steadily worsened, and that influenced the proceedings. Western colonialism in Asia remained alive and well, which meant that the Tokyo trial highlighted, in a way that Nuremberg did not, the problematic relationship between imperialism and international law. The fact that no judges from either the "Dutch East Indies" or former colonial Korea sat on the bench was telling. Even more telling were the actions of the French and Dutch governments in seeking to restore their colonial rule in Southeast Asia, and the Americans their influence everywhere in Asia and the Pacific. The Truman administration gave economic aid to France while it was fighting against the Viet Minh. In China it permitted surrendered Japanese troops to fight on the side of Chiang Kai-shek, and provided Chiang's military forces with equipment and advisers to aid in his renewed civil war against the Communists.[80] In the underdeveloped parts of Asia and the Pacific, American leaders seemed to be following Japan's example of keeping whole nations in their "proper place."

The final indictment, together with five "Appendices" containing the particulars for all of the counts alleged against the accused, had been lodged with the tribunal on May 4, 1946. The indictment specified Japan's production and distribution of drugs; Appendix D, Section Nine, of the indictment specified Japan's poison gas operations in China, also in violation of international laws. The prosecution pursued the drug issue but dropped the toxic gas charge.[81]

Col. Thomas H. Morrow, the lawyer whom Keenan had placed in charge of "All China Military Aggression 1937–45," had traveled to China in March 1946 and investigated this issue. His April 26 report to Keenan triggered a secret counterattack from the U.S. Chemical Warfare Service (CWS), which insisted, on the basis of specious legal reasoning, that Japan had not been acting illegally in waging chemical warfare. Having developed the world's most advanced poison gas arsenal and been denied the chance to use its new weapons during World War II, CWS wanted the tribunal to take no action that might lead to the criminalization of poison gas, especially when it believed war with the Soviet Union to be imminent. To this day it is unclear whether MacArthur or someone else high up in the army chain of command made the actual decision not to pursue the indictment of the Japanese army for its use of chemical weapons. But sometime during the first two months of the trial the issue was dropped. President Truman, who lacked the imagination to see the implications of what was at stake, in effect allowed Roosevelt's wartime policy condemning poison gas as an illegal, inhumane method of warfare to be reversed. Japanese officers involved in chemical warfare and American army leaders who did not want their hands tied by international law were the main beneficiaries. Concurrently the world lost the opportunity to prevent the spread of chemical weapons. On August 12, 1946, a disappointed Colonel Morrow resigned, probably over this issue, and returned to the United States.[82]

Among the numerous personal immunities from prosecution that MacArthur and the Allies granted for reasons of national interest were those to General Ishii Shirō and the officers and men of Unit 731 who had been responsible for Japan's biological warfare in China. The estimates that three to ten thousand mostly Chinese prisoners of war had been killed in Ishi's biological experiments were ignored. Access to the experimental data on the killings was considered by the Joint Chiefs of Staff and MacArthur more vital than justice.[83]

Lingering consciousness of the "holy war" and continuation of the old sense of values among many Japanese undoubtedly shortened the period of introspection that followed the war crimes revelations. The widespread Japanese belief that war is a natural social phenomenon, something that just happens among nations through no fault of their own, blocked self-reflection on war atrocities in China; and in the view of some Japanese writers, so too did a weak sense of individual autonomy and an ethical life overly dependent on the opinion of others.[84] But the main reason why Japanese war crimes were so quickly forgotten had to do with Hirohito himself. The legitimacy of Japan's wars of aggression—the belief that it had invaded various Asian and Pacific countries in order to liberate them—could not be fully discredited unless he was subjected to trial and interrogation in some forum for his role in the wars, especially his inability or disinclination to hold Japan's armed forces to any standard of behavior morally higher than loyalty and success. Many Japanese, after all, had been complicit with him in waging war, and the nation as a whole came to feel that because the emperor had not been held responsible, neither should they.

The Japanese people began a very serious confrontation with war guilt—but the early decision of MacArthur and Truman not to distribute accountability justly, letting Kido and Tōjō bear the emperor's share, cut short that confrontation; so did Truman's drastic policy changes in 1947–48. The same thing happened in divided Germany, where Truman's policy, implemented by the U.S. high commissioner, John McCloy, limited the reach of the denazification program by redefining it to apply to only a small number of German perpetrators. The Tokyo trial, and the purges that accompanied it, failed to solve Japan's many-sided problem of war responsibility; in some ways they made the problem more intractable.

Protecting the emperor and remaking his image were complex political undertakings that could be achieved only by grossly exaggerating the threat of social upheaval in Japan, rigging testimony, destroying evidence, and distorting history.[85] It is not known if Hirohito was offended by this tampering with justice, or if he included it in his reports to the spirits of his imperial ancestors. We can be certain that throughout the trial, down through the execution of Tōjō, Hirohito never lost sight of his larger aims, which were to stave off domestic and foreign pressure for his abdication, to preserve the monarchy, and thus to maintain a realm of stability and a principle of legitimacy in Japanese political life.

16

SALVAGING THE IMPERIAL MYSTIQUE

As the fifth month of occupation came in with the new year, 1946, the Japanese nation seemed to be torn in half. On the one hand demobilized veterans and displaced civilians continued to be repatriated from the Asian continent; millions remained homeless; food rationing had broken down; and black markets were flourishing everywhere. Farmers had begun political struggles for the democratization of local village government. Land reform had not yet begun, but tenants and small owner-cultivators were demonstrating their grievances against the landlord class—a social pillar of the prewar monarchy ever since Meiji. On the other hand the confusion and demoralization so noticeable earlier were starting to give way to intellectual ferment and excitement. It appeared to many, not all of whom were leftists, that defeat and occupation might soon result in radical, thoroughgoing reform. Major institutional change was in the air and could be imminent.

On January 13, 1946, one Reginald Blyth, a teacher at the Peers' School who was also, informally, an adviser to GHQ's Civil Information and Education Section, sent Hirohito's Grand Chamberlain a letter. Taking cognizance of the near collapse of the food rationing system, Blyth proposed that the emperor counter this serious problem:

> The Emperor alone has the chance to . . . provide the emotional motive power for the proper distribution of food without a black mar-

ket. He should make a trip round Japan, visit the coal mines and farming districts. He should listen to them, talk to them, ask them questions. On his return he should issue a statement concerning e. g. the hoarding of food, the necessity of sacrifices now, just as in war time. He should uncork some feeling, pull out the vox humana stop, and appeal to the Japanese to share their stocks.[1]

Hirohito began his travels to shore up the endangered status quo by means of "blessed visitations" (gyōkō), actively supported by MacArthur and his public relations advisers in GHQ, who wanted him to show that he was "really interested in the people."[2] On his part extreme awkwardness marked the initial encounters, and on the people's part, shock and uncertainty.

On March 26, 1946, journalist Mark Gayn met the touring emperor at a hospital for the war wounded in Takasaki City, Gumma prefecture. Hirohito was then in an early phase of being "humanized," and wanting to help the process along, Gayn left this unforgettable description:

I had had a good look at the emperor, or "Charlie," as we called him. He is a little man, about five feet two inches in height, in a badly cut gray striped suit, with trousers a couple of inches too short. He has a pronounced facial tic and his right shoulder twitches constantly. When he walks, he throws his right leg a little sideways, as if he has no control over it. He was obviously excited and ill at ease, and uncertain of what to do with his arms and hands.

At first, he shuffled past the men, stopping occasionally to read the charts. Then he apparently decided the moment called for a few words. He tried several questions, but they all seemed out of place. At last he settled on the simple "Where are you from?" He now walked from man to man, asked his question, and when the patient answered, the emperor said, "Ah, so!" He sounded as if he was surprised to learn that the man had come from Akita or Wakayama or the

Hokkaido. His voice was high-pitched, and as time passed it grew thinner and higher.

The irreverent Americans were now all waiting for the inhuman sound of "Ah, so," and when it came they nudged each other, and laughed, and mimicked the sound. But the joke wore out. We could now see the emperor for what he was: a tired, pathetic little man, compelled to do a job distasteful to him, and trying desperately to control his disobedient voice and face and body. It was hot and hushed, and there were no sounds other than the emperor's shrill voice and the heavy breathing of his escorts.[3]

Soon, however, the people became accustomed to seeing the emperor traveling about in his "democratic," ill-fitting business suit, giving mechanical responses, sometimes even smiling—body movements that living gods were not supposed to make. Gradually popular enthusiasm grew, aided by loyalist officials acting as shills, and by GHQ and the censored Japanese press, which repeatedly magnified the significance of his travels. At one level the Imperial Household Ministry sought to reach out to the people during 1946 by distributing (with MacArthur's permission) money, land, buildings, and lumber for public purposes. At an entirely different level a new monarchy was in the process of being born in a country that had also changed its name from the very masculine "Great Imperial Japan" (*Dai Nippon teikoku*) to the more feminine "Japan" (*Nihon koku*).[4]

The court officials who planned the tour—Ōgane Masujirō and Katō Susumu—stressed that it was "his majesty's idea," and cited the precedent of Meiji's grand progresses of the period from 1872 to 1885. This analogy was misleading. Emperor Meiji had toured in a time of crisis marked by violent disturbances and political agitation that posed a danger to the emerging monarchy. His tours were part of the larger process of making his presence known among the people and establishing his authority as a wielder of real power—setting up, in short, the hard and impersonal relationship between emperor and subject that marked his reign.

In contrast Hirohito himself described his intention as therapeutic. He wanted to "comfort the people in their suffering" and to "encourage their efforts at reconstruction." He believed (as Kinoshita's diary entry of March 31, 1946, reveals) that he could go around the entire country quickly and complete his task in a single year. He wanted to forestall possible republican sentiment by reversing and softening the harshness of the earlier emperor-people relationship, and thus make the monarchy more popular and "democratic." Of course, in comparing Hirohito's travels with Meiji's, it should not be forgotten that there would not have been any tours without MacArthur's strong support.

The early tours took place when GHQ had ended national rituals in honor of the war dead by ordering the emperor, on April 30, 1946, to stop visiting or sending envoys to Yasukuni Shrine. As the tours gradually caught the public imagination, Hirohito and his staff grasped the possibilities they offered not only for demonstrating his popularity, and thus his usefulness to General Headquarters and the Far Eastern Commission, but also for regaining some of his lost authority. Indifference to the emperor had become common in urban areas where people were caught up in the everyday struggle for food and shelter. But among many segments of the public the old sense of awe and trust in the emperor remained, complicated by feelings of pity and sympathy for him as a person who, having lost the war, now needed the protection of MacArthur.[5] Also, having disavowed myths about his divinity and exposed himself to the glare of democracy under conditions of relative freedom of expression, neither he nor his entourage could easily control his growing audiences.

In early October 1946 Hirohito had his third, carefully rehearsed meeting with MacArthur. He began by thanking the general for his generous food assistance during May, after which he brought up the "bad feeling" toward Japan in the United States compared to the friendly feelings that existed within GHQ. MacArthur answered that, with "reeducation," American public opinion would improve. Smiling, he added, "I always tell American visitors that the emperor is the most democratic person [here], but none of them believe me." MacArthur mentioned the new peace constitution; Hirohito cited the troubled international situation and expressed fear that Japan might be endanged. MacArthur predicted that someday the world would praise the new constitution and in a century Japan would be "the moral leader of the world." Hirohito then expressed his worries about labor unrest. The Japanese as a people, he claimed, had a low level of education and "lack a sense of religion." MacArthur told him not to worry: "[T]he healthy nature of the Japanese is manifested in their love and respect for you, [now] just as in the past." At the end of the meeting MacArthur encouraged him to continue his tours.[6]

On this and other occasions during 1946, Hirohito confided to MacArthur that the Japanese people were like children. They "lacked calmness" and were "blind followers," always ready to imitate examples from abroad. He said the same thing to Inada and Kinoshita, who took down his secret account of the war. Privately he added that because of the revised constitution, "defeat was better for the nation than if we had become extremely militaristic as a result of victory."[7] Eager to cast defeat in a hopeful light, Hirohito repeatedly told the nation's highest leaders what they already knew: defeat in war could have a positive outcome provided they cooperate with the enemy and facilitate moderate reform. Remember, he cautioned them at his summer residence in Hayama on the first anniversary of the surrender, "This is not the first time Japan has lost a war. Long ago [in the seventh century A.D.] we dispatched troops to Korea and withdrew them after having been defeated in the battle at Hakusukinoe. Thereafter we made many reforms and they became a turning point for developing Japanese culture."[8]

I

The year 1947 constituted a crucial second stage in the development of Hirohito's new image as a "human," "democratic" emperor who had suffered together with his people. At this time, the Ministry of Education edited and published an immensely influential textbook, *Atarashii kenpō no hanashi* (The Story of the new constitution), that emphasized the ideals of democracy, internationalism, popular sovereignty, and the abandonment of war, while using the highest honorifics in referring to the emperor.[9] The Japanese mass media also reached agreement with the government on the rules for use of the highest honorifics in news stories concerning him, while the imperial court renewed the prewar practice of bestowing imperial accolades. The emperor wrote to President Truman, sending the letter via Chief Prosecutor Joseph B. Keenan. He inaugurated the practice of receiving New Year's felicitations on January 2 at the Nijū Bridge of the imperial palace.

When Hirohito resumed his tours in 1947, they turned overnight into wildly emotional mass events that far surpassed the expectations of their planners. The tours moved from prefecture to prefecture and city to city against a news background of daily reports on the war crimes trial and on steadily worsening relations between the Soviet Union and the United States. The Truman Doctrine of March 12, 1947, marked the formal start of the Cold War in Europe. As the Cold War intensified, U.S.–Japan policy became increasingly conservative, shifting emphasis from reformation and top down democratization to reconstruction and economic development—and the restoration of management's prerogatives in the work place.[10]

Signs of a softening appeared in American reparations policy: By March 17, MacArthur told foreign journalists that the United States had no intention of destroying Japan's industrial capability. His letter to Prime Minister Yoshida ordered a comprehensive plan prepared to restart the economy. By the second postwar general

election on April 25, 1947, GHQ had given the Japanese government a new priority: Japan must become economically self-sufficient, able to take its place in a reconstructed world order under
United States leadership.

From Hirohito's viewpoint these developments seemed to indicate that GHQ was relaxing its control, and suggested possibilities
for him to maneuver independently that had not existed before. On
May 6, 1947, three days after the promulgation of the new constitution, Hirohito again met with MacArthur. He was more concerned
about security matters than of deepening democracy. According to
former diplomat Matsui Akira, the emperor asked the supreme
commander, "After the United States leaves, who is going to protect
Japan?" With magnanimous disregard for Japan's national independence, MacArthur answered, "Just as we protect California, so shall
we protect Japan," and went on to underscore the ideal of the
United Nations.[11] Hirohito was hardly reassured. But the next
month in a meeting with a group of American journalists,
MacArthur declared that "[t]he Japanese will not be opposed to
America keeping Okinawa because the Okinawans are not
Japanese."[12] Already the general was thinking that a Japan that had
constitutionally "forever renounce[d] war as a sovereign right of the
nation" could be protected by the transformation of Okinawa into a
vast and permanent American military base.

In the summer of 1947 Hirohito resumed touring. The imperial
trains and motorcades grew larger; each trip was more elaborate,
more costly, and more popular. Conservative Diet members and
local politicians, judging that their standing with the public would
benefit from close association with the emperor, rushed to get
aboard the imperial tour wagon. When the emperor reached Osaka
in early June, the tours, which had started as inspections of damaged
areas, had become vast victory parades. The banned sun flag flew
from rooftops and was waved by thousands of cheering welcomers.
A disinterested observer would have had the impression that the

whole nation was celebrating its emperor, who now appeared to be a victor after all.

On June 1, 1947, after the Diet had chosen him under the new constitution, Katayama Tetsu formed a coalition cabinet. Hirohito, displeased that now he was shut out of the process of choosing the next prime minister, could only express his dissatisfaction by saying "Katayama is not strong enough."[13] Afterward he insisted that the new prime minister make a formal report to him at his Kyoto Palace. On July 24 he asked Katayama's foreign minister, Ashida Hitoshi, to continue giving him informal reports on matters of foreign policy.[14] Even Ashida, a very loyal subject, felt that the emperor's requests violated the letter as well as the spirit of the new constitution. Reluctantly he complied, and thereafter briefed Hirohito regularly, particularly on preparations for an eventual peace treaty and the problem of Japan's future security.

Hirohito now made a second return to an activist role in state affairs, in violation of the new constitution. On June 5, 1947, Foreign Minister Ashida remarked to the foreign press corps that the Japanese people wished to have Okinawa returned to Japan. General MacArthur's response came some three weeks later, on the twenty-seventh, when in widely noted remarks to a group of American editors and publishers, he declared that "The Ryukyus are our natural frontier;" there was no Japanese opposition to the United States retaining Okinawa, for "the Okinawans are not Japanese." And moreover, American air bases on Okinawa were important for Japan's own security. At this point—after both Ashida and MacArthur had spoken publicly on Okinawa, but before the State Department and the Pentagon had come together and firmed up American policy concerning the strategic island—Hirohito intervened with an unconstitutional political statement asserting Japanese sovereignty while endorsing the views of MacArthur, protector of the Japanese monarchy.[15]

On September 20, 1947, Hirohito conveyed to MacArthur's

political adviser, William J. Sebald, his position on the future of Okinawa. Acting through Terasaki, his interpreter and frequent liaison with high GHQ officials, the emperor requested that, in view of the worsening confrontation between the Soviet Union and the United States, the American military occupation of Okinawa and other islands in the Ryukyu chain continue for ninety-nine years. Hirohito knew MacArthur's latest views on the status of Okinawa when he made this offer. The emperor's thinking on Okinawa was also fully in tune with the colonial mentality of Japan's mainstream conservative political elites, who, like the nation in general, had never undergone decolonization. Back in December 1945, the Eighty-ninth Imperial Diet had abolished the voting rights of the people of Okinawa along with those of the former Japanese colonies of Taiwan and Korea. Thus, when the Ninetieth Imperial Diet had met in 1946 to accept the new "peace" constitution, not a single representative from Okinawa was present.

Hirohito's "Okinawa message" proved that he was continuing to play a secret role in both foreign and domestic policy affairs that had nothing to do with the ceremonial role to which the constitution confined him.[16] But it also suggested the great weight he placed on "the growth of [Japanese] rightist and leftist groups" who could provoke an incident which the Soviet Union might exploit.[17] Hirohito, like the Foreign Ministry, wanted to retain an American military presence in and around Japan after the signing of a peace treaty. At the same time, he may also have felt the need to draw closer to the United States for protection while the Tokyo Trials continued. But above all, his message shows the connection between the new symbol monarchy, Article 9 of the new postwar constitution, and the American militarization of Okinawa.

On October 10, 1947, while Hirohito was touring Nagaoka City, Niigata prefecture, Chief Prosecutor Joseph B. Keenan announced that neither the emperor nor the business community bore responsibility for the war.[18] In the United States the previous year, Keenan had disclosed that "high political circles" had decided against trying the emperor for war crimes.[19] Keenan's public reiteration of this decision in Japan was welcome news for Hirohito, who months earlier, in March 1946, had already learned informally that he would not be indicted. For the leaders of the Japanese business world, who would soon become the main financial supporters of the new monarchy, Keenan's announcement was welcome, but partially offset by MacArthur's continued enthusiasm for the dissolution of Japan's great industrial conglomerates and for limited economic democratization.[20]

Meanwhile, pressure continued for the emperor's abdication and for further court reform. On October 14, 1947, GHQ again reduced the number of royal family members who could possess imperial status. More unwelcome news for Hirohito and his supporters followed. Foreign Minister Ashida recorded in his diary a meeting with former general Tanaka Ryūkichi, a man on "close terms" with Chief Prosecutor Keenan. Tanaka told Ashida that Keenan refused to entrust the cross-examinations of Kido, Tōjō, and Tōgō to anyone but himself, but feared that his and others' efforts might be wasted if the empress and crown prince acted "too conspicuously" in traveling about the country. Keenan (according to General Tanaka, via Ashida) intended to visit the emperor after the trials to discuss the "problem of abdication and other matters." Tanaka also said that "MacArthur is convinced that monarchical rule is needed in order to stabilize Japan and suppress the Communist Party."[21] One month later, on November 14, 1947, Hirohito met General MacArthur for the fifth time. Nothing they discussed in their ninety-minute meeting is known, though it is likely that as in previous meetings concrete political matters were aired. On the twenty-sixth he departed for the Chūgoku region of southwestern Honshu on his final trip of the year.

On December 7, 1947—six years after the Pearl Harbor attack and twenty-six months after the end of the war—Hirohito and his party arrived at atom-bombed Hiroshima. The streets had been specially cleaned and dusted for the occasion. Wearing a dark gray Homburg and clothes that in the opinion of an Australian observer might "have been deliberately chosen so as not to be too much on the smart side," he seemed to "symbolize the down at the heels but determined look characteristic of present-day Japan." Thousands of adults and children lined the long, meticulously planned route of his motorcade into the city. At the first stop, war orphans in black robes were on their knees waiting for him:

> and standing beside them were a few mothers, their faces scarred with keloids, who held children in more or less serious stages of disfigurement. While the cameras clicked and turned and the crowd pushed in more and more excitedly, the emperor listened, hat in hand, to a short explanation of what had happened to this group. He murmured a few "Is that so's" and made as though to speak into a microphone that was being held out toward him. Then his lip trembled and with a short bow, he turned back to his car. At this point, the crowd went berserk. Shouting banzais at the top of their voices, the people rushed forward, their eyes shining and all their mask of unemotionalism wiped off their faces. [Imperial] Household officials and police were jostled and trampled on before he got back to his car. None of the crowd touched the emperor, but many of them seemed happy just to touch the body of his car.
>
> Our party went ahead at the next stop, on to the improvised plaza where the mayor, the city officials and a crowd of 50,000—a quarter of the city's present population, were waiting to welcome him. . . . Here again you could see people weeping with emotion. . . . The Emperor mounted a rostrum . . . and once again was photographed from every angle. [Pulling a slip of paper from his pocket] he read a short simple speech. . . . At the city hall he climbed up to the roof where the mayor was waiting with a map showing the city as it was, as it is, and as it is planned that it will be. . . . A pair of field glasses rested on a purple

handkerchief for the Emperor's use, but he did not touch them. For the first time that day he was obviously overcome with nervousness and seemed anxious to get away.[22]

By this time GHQ had begun to reevaluate the imperial tours in response to growing foreign and domestic criticism as well as criticism within headquarters itself. Paul J. Kent of the Political Affairs Division was assigned to accompany the emperor to the Chūgoku region. Kent's initial report, dated December 16, 1947, noted the huge size of the imperial party: almost a hundred officials and attendants, plus countless Japanese newspaper and magazine reporters and photographers who "followed the Imperial Party at every stage of the journey . . . [and] were provided with space on the train, and with buses, or automobiles, for local travel." Kent blamed "this multitude of votaries, satellites, dog robbers, and seneschals" for "the monstrous expenditure of funds by Local governments and private corporations." He went on to note that:

> virtually every street over which the Imperial party travelled had been newly repaired . . . [and] spots of ground on which he stood to see rice fields and farms were covered with floorings and canopies. Pillars, columns, and arches, usually covered with flowers and branches, were erected at the entrances to squares and street corners and on the approaches to bridges. Railings upon which he laid his hand were covered with cloth, paths upon which he walked were not infrequently covered with matting. If one considers the total effort . . . one is forced to conclude that a staggering sum was devoted to enterprises which serve no useful purpose and which are . . . completely unjustified in a nation standing upon the verge of financial collapse.

The emperor, he insisted, "does not see actual conditions" and his inspection tours, which were more like "campaign tours," served mainly to keep him in the public eye for days and weeks in advance of each visit. Worst of all, rather than democratizing the monarchy, the tours were increasing "the power and influence of the Imperial tradition."

Kent did not dare criticize Hirohito himself for this sorry state of affairs, but instead described him as:

> nervous to the point of looking physically handicapped; his gestures and movements are jerky and uncoordinated. He hesitates before speaking or acting. If not thoroughly self-conscious, he is certainly ill-at-ease. . . . On almost all occasions his face was devoid of any expression. He did smile a few times, when speaking to children, and when the *Banzai*'s assumed great proportions. He is even poorly dressed.

Ultimately Kent attributed the emperor's uneasiness to the attitude of the imperial house officials, whom he also blamed for two incidents he found particularly disturbing. One was the emperor's tour of Hiroshima, on the sixth anniversary of Pearl Harbor.[23] The other incident that aroused Kent's anger was the "organized widespread display of the [sun] flag" that occurred on December 11, the last day of the Chūgoku tour.[24]

GHQ took quick action. On January 12, 1948, GHQ's Government Section ordered the emperor's "campaign tours" discontinued on the ground that officials of the Imperial Household Office had contravened the spirit of numerous GHQ orders. They had conducted themselves arrogantly and undemocratically, and the Japanese bureaucracy, flagrantly misusing public funds, had levied unjust taxes to finance the emperor's touring.[25] GHQ also took note of rumors of plots against the emperor's life, involving alleged Korean Communists who were upset about the newly enacted Alien Registration Law. Unstated was deeper concern that, rather than removing all traces of the emperor's renounced divinity and freeing the Japanese citizenry from their feeling of subjecthood, the tours were actually promoting the old idolatry.

II

On New Year's Day 1948, Hirohito welcomed tens of thousands who gathered on the palace plaza to greet him. In mid-January he staged the popular "Imperial New Year's Poetry Reading" (*utakai hajime*) at the palace. This ceremony had been introduced in the second year of the Meiji restoration, 1869, and with each stirring of democracy had been progressively opened up to more and more Japanese subjects, then to citizens. Contestants submitted *waka* on assigned themes, and the best *waka* were selected for the reading. To court officials and ideologues, such ceremonial readings served to dissolve social and political differences among the Japanese. In reality, the effect was quite contrary. As the emperor deigned to hear the merely ordinary people's poems and the lowly people humbly listened to his, emperor and people became one. Conservative ideological and political values were thereby reproduced by the *utakai hajime*, and the make-believe of the nation as a classless monolith resymbolized.[26]

Later in 1948 Hirohito made highly publicized charitable donations and experimented with three new, truncated types of imperial visitations: short trips to attend tree-planting ceremonies, appearances at athletic events, and appearances at cultural and social projects sponsored by private organizations that worked closely with the palace.

When the emperor convoked the Diet in January 1948, the continued practice of the "crab walk" by Diet members provoked an incident. Whenever the emperor entered the Diet building through the special door reserved for his use, he would first receive the leaders of the two houses in a special audience room. Traditionally Diet members who entered that room to be received by the emperor walked to a point directly in front of him, bowed deeply, then exited walking sideways or backward to the nearest door, in this manner avoiding the disrespectful exposure of their profiles or the backs of their heads. But in January 1948, when the emperor entered that special audience room expecting to receive bows from the president and vice president of the upper and lower houses of the Diet, Matsumoto Jiichirō, vice president of the House of Councillors and Socialist Party member, failed to appear. He later explained, addressing his colleagues, "Why must I imitate the sideways walk of a crab? . . . Hasn't he become [only] a human being?"

Matsumoto had revealed how prewar customs inappropriate to the new constitutional order were still being observed. Instead of being honored for his courage, however, he was sanctioned. His behavior and speech (as journalist Matsuura Sōzō noted) totally alienated Yoshida Shigeru and other staunch conservatives who had been fighting since the "placard incident" of 1946 to restore the crime of lèse-majesté in the new criminal code. Within a short time, Matsumoto was purged by GHQ, with assistance from Yoshida, and his political career temporarily came to an end, while crab-walking in the presence of the emperor continued.[27]

The "crab walk" incident clearly highlighted the need for additional reform of the rules of behavior pertaining to the new monarchy. Despite the ban on imperial campaigns, and the absence of articles about the tours in the major daily newspapers, the emperor's efforts to court the people continued; so too did the process of circumscribing the monarchy.

On February 10, 1948, the Socialist-led Katayama cabinet resigned en masse as a result of conflict between its left and right factions. Katayama thereupon reported his resignation to the throne, although the new constitution in no way required him to.[28] Four weeks later, on March 10, Ashida Hitoshi formed a second unstable coalition cabinet. Hirohito told him in good traditional imperial fashion, "[D]o something about the Communist Party." Ashida explained that the party was quite legal and the government could not prosecute Communists unless they acted illegally. He went on to warn the emperor that his tours had been generating "mountains of letters" to GHQ and endangering the new monarchy.[29] In this way, Ashida revealed his intention to continue Katayama's unsuccessful effort to democratize the court. For two months Hirohito resisted, calling on his favorite "pendulum theory" of gradual reform.[30] But, eventually, Ashida persuaded him to dismiss his top advisers. During the summer the principal stage managers of the campaign tours, Ōgane, Katō, and Matsudaira, exited from the scene.

Meanwhile the prestige of the emperor remained under assault. In April the war crimes tribunal adjourned for the preparation of its final verdicts. Intellectuals concerned with the future of the new monarchy once again addressed Hirohito's continued avoidance of all moral and political responsibility for his actions during the war, and for the suffering he had caused the nation. Some even expected he would use the conclusion of the Trial to declare his abdication.

The year 1948 was a time of transition in the shaping of Japanese domestic politics by the U.S.–Soviet confrontation. On October 7 the Ashida cabinet collapsed after seven months in office; a few days later the more conservative Yoshida Shigeru formed his second cabinet. One month later the Tokyo war crimes trials drew to an end. Sentences were pronounced on the afternoon of November 12. On December 23, 1948, the seven condemned to die were hanged in Sugamo Prison.

The next day MacArthur released from prison or house arrest nineteen Class A war crimes suspects, none yet indicted and tried. Included were former ministers of state such as Kishi Nobusuke, who had signed the declaration of war against the United States in 1941; Abe Genki, the police bureaucrat in charge of repressing political dissent under the Tōjō and Suzuki cabinets; and right-wing gang bosses Kodama Yoshio and Sasagawa Ryōichi.[31]

Over the next few years Japanese politicians and the emperor himself would call for the release of all convicted A, B, and C class criminals, and in most instances MacArthur and his successor, Gen. Matthew B. Ridgway, would comply. By the time the San Francisco

Peace Treaty with Japan went into effect in April 1952, SCAP had freed, with Washington's approval, a total of 892 war criminals, including B and C class detainees who had never been brought to trial.[32] The release of these men, followed by the swift rise of a few of them to the very highest positions of power in the postwar state, had a profoundly polarizing influence on Japanese politics throughout the 1950s.

On December 1, 1948, National Security Council document 13/2 was transmitted to MacArthur. It formally approved the shift in U.S. occupation policy from political democratization to economic reconstruction and remilitarization. Henceforth the United States would be concerned to strengthen Japan not only economically and politically but militarily—a violation of the peace constitution. Some two weeks after receiving the document and a follow-up directive from Truman, on December 18, MacArthur ordered the second Yoshida cabinet to carry out "nine principles" designed to ensure wage and price control and maximize production for export. Early the next year Detroit banker Joseph M. Dodge arrived in Japan to implement a drastic deflationary fiscal policy projected to revive Japanese capitalism by generating massive unemployment.[33] With these policy shifts mandated from Washington, MacArthur suffered a loss of power and the "reverse course" in Japanese politics suddenly accelerated.

III

Hirohito's imperial tours resumed under new stage management in 1949 and continued until the end of 1951. At the start of that period, GHQ relaxed its tight restrictions on public discussion of the effects of the atomic bombs on Hiroshima and Nagasaki, thereby stimulating the peace movement; by its end the occupation had a new military leader and was rapidly moving to a close.

During these years the international situation in East Asia

changed drastically. In 1949 the Russians developed and tested atomic weapons, and Chinese Communist armies under Mao Tse-tung defeated Chiang Kai-shek's Nationalists on the mainland of China. The Nationalists fled to Taiwan. In late February 1950, the chairman of the Joint Chiefs of Staff, Gen. Omar Bradley, flew to Tokyo to confer with MacArthur on defense plans in the event of an emergency in the Far East. The Truman administration at that point permitted MacArthur to expand his sphere of authority in an emergency, and gave him control of a vast oceanic area surrounding Japan, including the Ryukyu Islands. Concurrently Truman adopted a provocative risk-taking strategy, as seen first in National Security Council document 48/2 of December 1949 and later NSC–68 of March 1950. Three months later, on June 25, the Korean War broke out. Largely in response to these developments, Japan rearmed, strengthened its police forces, and began to receive large infusions of economic assistance from the United States. Soon Japan experienced not only its first postwar economic boom, but also its first renewal of nationalism. Largely as a reaction to these developments, the Japanese peace movement was born, a branch of the international movement for peace.

On May 17, 1949, in response to calls for imperial visits from prefectural assemblies, Hirohito departed for a twenty-four-day tour of Kyushu.[34] Two years had passed since the promulgation of the constitution that converted the monarch from ruler to symbol, and the mood of the country had altered. Yoshida Shigeru had returned to power in October 1948. In February 1949 he formed his third cabinet, the first based on a solid conservative majority. Occupied Japan, on its way to becoming the "workshop" for Asia, no longer paid token reparations to the victims of its aggression. The American occupiers no longer made efforts to democratize its economy. GHQ still dictated policies, however, and still maintained post-publication censorship of the Japanese media. But more administrative authority was gradually passing to the Japanese government, which, in May 1949, assumed full responsibility for guarding the imperial palace and the emperor. In June the Imperial Household Office became an agency (*kunaichō*) under the Prime Minister's Office.[35]

Hirohito's Kyushu tours were less lavish in scale than his earlier travels. They were welcomed, however. Renewed media appeals for support of the monarchy, and continuous efforts by government at all levels insured that the tours elicited the greatest possible degree of very uniform, yet "spontaneous" enthusiasm from the people. Wearing worker's clothing, the emperor inspected a Mitsui coal mine. He held meetings with journalists, academics, and famous literary figures. At Nagasaki he momentarily put the focus on the A-bomb survivors by having himself photographed at the Nagasaki Hospital standing by the bedside of dying Professor Nagai Takashi, a medical professor and victim of radiation poisoning. In early 1949 Nagai's testimonial, *The Bells of Nagasaki* [*Nagasaki no kane*], had captured the imagination of the nation, arguing that Nagasaki had been chosen by God as a pure sacrificial offering in order to end the war. The "Nagai boom," into which the emperor skillfully tapped, was part of a belated national discovery of Japan's suppressed nuclear experience.

Under conditions of deepening Cold War, the citizens of the new Japan had begun learning, belatedly, about the experience of the A-bomb victims. Works such as Ōta Yōko's *City of Corpses* [*Shikabane no machi*], Hara Tamiki's *Summer Flowers* [*Natsu no hana*], and Imamura Tokuyuki and Ōmori Minoru's *The Green Buds of Hiroshima* [*Hiroshima no midori no me*] became 1949–50 national bestsellers.[36] The conjunction of increasing nuclear consciousness and deepening cold war brought a more relevant appreciation of the peace principle in the new constitution. But the gap between the conception of the state held by conservative politicians who were ruling under the new constitution, and that held by the great majority of Japanese, remained wide. As if reflecting this discrepancy between constitutional ideal and reality, the public, despite all the careful planning and organization by court officials, continued to disagree over the appropriate behavior for the emperor. Some wanted him to deepen his humanization. Others felt that if he became too "human," the monarchy itself would be discredited.

In the summer of 1949 national athletic events such as the All-Japan Swimming Champion Tournament helped to heighten nationalism for the first time under the occupation. The emperor and empress attended, and Hirohito afterwards gave words of encouragement to the athletes. When the Japanese swimming champion Furuhashi Hironoshin won a gold medal at the Los Angeles Olympics, he and his teammates were later granted an audience at the palace and a tea in their honor.[37] National pride was also enriched that year by the award of the Nobel Prize in physics to Professor Yukawa Hideki. Once again Hirohito made a widely reported appearance in the presence of these "symbolic leaders" of the new Japan.[38]

Early in 1950 Hirohito published poems about his Kyushu visit and his joy at Professor Yukawa's Nobel award, then embarked on another series of tours.[39] His nineteen-day journey through Shikoku and Awajishima began on March 13.[40] He visited prefectural government offices, public schools and universities, agricultural experimental stations, homes for orphans, paper mills, chemical plants, and textile and machine tool factories. As always, people responded variously. Most often the touring emperor was warmly received as an embodiment of the spirit of love, a person of benevolence, and a celebrity. A minority, however, still believed him to be a sacred presence, a living deity, and a force so powerful as to animate their very gestures and reflexes. Upon seeing him approach, they would shout *banzais* and be moved to tears. Their facial muscles would tighten, their bodies vibrate, and their legs tremble as if struck by a strong electric current. Emotional paralysis would follow, and they might momentarily lose consciousness of where they were. This phenomemon, the physical expression of an intact sense of subject-hood, has been repeatedly described in the reminiscences of those who experienced it.[41] The common theme is the affirmative sense of having worked hard and suffered harshly together with the emperor.

On the other hand no amount of image manipulation could wipe away his war responsibility. Feelings of indifference toward the emperor were also widespread. And for a small minority on the left he remained the butt of jokes and an object of derision elicited by his inarticulateness.

American and Japanese diplomatic preparations were moving ahead swiftly toward a peace treaty that would incorporate Japan in an American-led bloc against the Soviet Union and the new Communist dictatorship in China. Hirohito now secretly interjected himself into this process, making it easier than it might have been for the United States to negotiate a one-sided military alliance with Japan that gave the Truman administration virtually everything it wanted.

As reconstructed by historian Toyoshita Narahiko, Hirohito's diplomatic interventions began right after his tenth meeting with MacArthur, on April 18, 1950. The issue between the two leaders (ever since their fourth meeting on May 6, 1947) was still the war-renouncing constitution and the weight that each man attached to it. According to the emperor's interpreter for their ninth and tenth meetings, Matsui Akira, they had discussed the "peace problem" on November 26, 1949, when debate over the peace treaty was heating up, and at the April 18 meeting the subject was the threat to Japan from the Communist camp. On both occasions MacArthur reportedly preached the "spirit of Article 9." Hirohito, who had never been pacifistically inclined except for public relations purposes, held that only military power could protect Japan. Perhaps feeling that his differences with the supreme commander on the future security of Japan were unbridgeable, the emperor finally decided to bypass him.

Two background factors may have influenced him. In February 1950 the Soviet Union had reopened the issue of Hirohito's war criminality by demanding that he be brought to trial for having sanctioned biological and chemical warfare during World War II.[42]

And on April 6 the Republican lawyer John Foster Dulles was appointed a special adviser to Secretary of State Dean Acheson, fueling speculation in Tokyo and Washington that the peace treaty negotiations, stalled ever since Fall 1949 by disagreements between the Pentagon and the State Department, would start moving forward again. Toyoshita conjectures that right after Hirohito's tenth meeting with MacArthur, when Finance Minister Ikeda Hayato went to Washington, he delivered a secret personal message from the emperor to Joseph M. Dodge, MacArthur's financial adviser. The emperor's message to Dodge was "to the effect that the [Yoshida] Government desires the earliest possible treaty. As such a treaty probably would require the maintenance of U.S. forces [on Japanese soil] . . . if the U.S. Government hesitates to make these conditions, the Japanese Government [itself] will try to find a way to offer them."[43] In short Hirohito, not Yoshida, made the first effort to hurry the peace treaty that would end the occupation, leave American military forces and bases in Japan, and return Japanese independence.

Dulles went to Tokyo in late June to open full-scale negotiations on a peace and security treaty to end the occupation. At his first meeting with Yoshida, he found the prime minister disappointing. Unlike Hirohito, Yoshida appeared unrushed and reluctant to commit on security matters. Three days later, on June 25, the North Korean dictator Kim Il-sung, having secured prior, tacit support from Stalin and Mao Tse-tung, sent his army across the 38th parallel deep into South Korea. The endemic fighting in the divided Korean peninsula had turned into full-scale civil war. The Truman administration, always quick on the trigger, immediately ordered U.S. military intervention, overnight internationalizing the conflict. MacArthur's command in Tokyo, though caught psychologically unprepared, responded with air, ground, and sea operations against North Korea.

Hirohito, meanwhile, had learned of Yoshida's disastrous meeting with Dulles. The next evening, he dispatched an "oral message" to Dulles through Matsudaira Yasumasa of the Imperial Household Agency, registering his loss of confidence in Yoshida. By Dulles's account the "main point" was that when officials from the United States "came to investigate conditions in Japan, they only saw Japanese in the Government of Japan who had been officially approved by SCAP. . . . SCAP apparently feared contacts with some of the older Japanese because of their alleged former militaristic outlook." Yet it was precisely these veteran officials, most of whom were purgees, who could "give most valuable advice and assistance to Americans interested in future relations between our two countries." Hirohito "suggested that before any final action with regard to the . . . provisions of a peace treaty be taken there should be set up some form of advisory council of Japanese who would be truly representative of the people."[44]

Two *Newsweek* journalists, Harry Kern and Compton Packenham, had arranged the dinner at which Matsudaira conveyed this "oral message" to Dulles. Critical of MacArthur's economic reforms and his purge of war criminals, they had organized, two years earlier, an "American Council on Japan," dedicated to fostering trade between the United States and Japan. Hirohito may have believed that, where the peace treaty and rearmament were concerned, "loyal Shigeru" was no longer "truly representative of the people of Japan." To him Kern and Packenham represented a new, independent channel by which, circumventing his prime minister, as he had earlier circumvented MacArthur, he could communicate with Washington. It was constitutionally reprehensible; it was characteristically Hirohito. In effect, he was reviving the prewar tradition of "dual diplomacy."[45]

On January 25, 1951, Dulles returned to Tokyo to work out

remaining problems. At his first staff meeting, Dulles stated that the crux was "Do we get the right to station as many troops as we want [,] where we want and for as long as we want [,] or do we not?"[46] Wanting unlimited military access to all areas of Japan, Dulles worried that the Japanese might try to extract concessions. But Yoshida, rather than make an effort, even a pro forma one, to limit America's special privileges in postoccupation Japan, simply yielded. The United States would have its bases and its extraterritorial privileges; Japan would even establish a fifty-thousand-man "token" national defense force. Yoshida was obviously inept. But his failure in these negotiations—to gain leverage from granting bases, and to counter Dulles's argument that the United States was performing an act of benevolence by leaving its military in Japan—may have had more to do with the influence of Hirohito than with his own blundering.

How often Hirohito and his entourage communicated with key members of the American Council on Japan to facilitate discussions and negotiations cannot be determined. One must not overemphasize their influence. But neither should his role be ignored. On February 10, 1951, Hirohito hosted a banquet for Dulles at the Imperial Palace. He also met him on at least two other occasions that year. The American secretary of state certainly regarded the Shōwa emperor as more than a merely ceremonial figure.

The Korean War contributed to a sharp change in the Japanese national mood. The earlier passion to develop democracy cooled. Left-led labor unions came under attack. A climate of political repression of the left ensued and the Yoshida government and the Japanese public showed a growing intolerance of the nascent peace movement and of criticism of the emperor. That summer the satirical magazine *Shinsō* reported that a young man from Sasebo city in Nagasaki prefecture claimed to be Hirohito's "hidden child."[47] Prime Minister Yoshida, acting on behalf of Hirohito, sued. *Shinsō*'s publisher, Sawa Keitarō, soon found himself locked up for libel.[48] Even Hirohito's youngest brother, Prince Mikasa, came in for criticism after publicly opposing the revival of "National Foundation Day" (Kigensetsu) and warning of the danger of militarism.[49]

In late November 1950, two months after receiving authorization from Truman to cross the thirty-eighth parallel and occupy the north, and many weeks after having been warned by China that such an offensive by American (but not Korean) troops would threaten its security and bring a direct Chinese response, MacArthur learned that the threatened response had happened. The Chinese had crossed into Korea with an army of three hundred thousand. Recklessly overextended, the Americans were forced to beat a swift, long retreat and suffered heavy losses. By January 1951 the now panicky, depressed supreme commander who had ordered them to march to the Yalu River had become, in the eyes of the Truman administration, dangerously political and nothing more than "a prima donna figurehead who had to be tolerated."[50]

After a new Eighth Army field commander, Lieutenant General Ridgway, had halted the Chinese advance at roughly the thirty-eighth parallel, MacArthur again exceeded his authority by issuing unauthorized public statements threatening China and declaring, "There is no substitute for victory."[51] On April 11 an angry, disgusted Truman finally fired MacArthur for repeated insubordination and for his intention to spread the fighting beyond Korea. Four days later Hirohito paid a final, farewell visit to his friend, the prestigious general who had defeated him in war and defended him in peace. On April 16, 1951, MacArthur headed home without ever having visited the palace despite all the efforts of Hirohito's entourage to get him to do so. Huge, subdued crowds lined the way as he was driven to Haneda Airport. Prime Minister Yoshida and a representative of the Imperial Household Agency were on hand to wave good-bye.

Douglas MacArthur had been the most important person in Hirohito's life for more than six years. He had admired the general's constancy of purpose and imagined him to be a successful role player, capable of adapting to new situations. His dismissal shocked Hirohito. Did it portend a delay in the peace treaty? A shift perhaps in basic U.S. policy? A new escalation of the fighting in Korea? On April 22 Hirohito tried to find out by twice questioning Dulles directly. Dulles was irked. He replied that he "had no desire to discuss the merits of the matter, but . . . at least there had been a demonstration of the supremacy of civil over military authority under our system, and . . . that phase of the matter might usefully be pondered in Japan."[52] End of discussion.

In October 1951 Hirohito prepared to visit Kyoto and three other prefectures. More than a thousand Kyoto University students convened a peace assembly to protest the San Francisco Peace Treaty and the U.S.–Japan Security Treaty the Yoshida government had signed on September 8. They issued an "open letter" appealing to the "human emperor" and focusing on rearmament: "We have been forced to recognize that you, through the unilateral peace [treaty] and the rearmament of Japan, have again, just as in the past, attempted to act as an ideological pillar of war."[53] When Hirohito appeared at Kyoto University, on November 12, a huge placard saluted him: "Because you once were a god, those who studied here before us died on your battlefield. Please, never again be a god; never again have us cry out 'Listen! The voices of the sea! [*kike wadatsumi no koe*].'"[54]

More than two thousand students welcomed the emperor to the campus, singing peace songs instead of the traditional national anthem, "Kimigayo." Shocked by their symbolic action and breach of etiquette, about five hundred armed riot and regular police stormed on to the campus and started skirmishing with the students. The next day's newspapers announced that an "unprecedentedly disgraceful incident" had occurred at the university, and sided with the police against the students. Eight students were expelled for peacefully protesting. The student association was dissolved.

For weeks, the reined-in and self-censored Japanese press sensationalized the incident, treating it as an act of lèse-majesté. Nationally and locally, many condemned the students as "heartless Reds" or as juveniles lacking in moral etiquette. Their equally numerous defenders, however, either expressed antipathy toward the emperor or declared total disinterest in him.[55]

The Kyoto University protest incident marked the relicensing of de facto lèse majesté and the resumption of more traditional ways of protecting the emperor. It brought an abrupt end to the "human emperor" campaign. It warned Japan's leaders that times had changed, bringing real danger to the restoration of any part of monarchical authority. In this tense encounter, one can see already the problems Hirohito would have in adapting to Japan's emerging anti-militarism and one-nation pacifism.

IV

Hirohito's first meeting with MacArthur confirmed the general's belief that the emperor could be used as the American government desired. Hirohito came away convinced that he could benefit by collaborating. So began the great historical trade-off of the occupation period: MacArthur's use of the emperor and the emperor's utilization of GHQ to remake his role without sacrificing everything. Hirohito's tours were for a time part of that trade-off. He both gained and lost from them. With the war still so overwhelmingly present in people's memories, many sided with the defeated emperor partly out of mortification and shame at having lost. In effect, they used Hirohito to say to the world "we have been defeated, but we haven't lost everything; we still have the emperor, and our pride." At the height of their popularity in 1947, the "blessed visitations" were a powerful counter to the war crimes trials, displacing public attention to the happier spectacle of the smiling, hat-doffing emperor in motion. The media helped by glorifying him as the "emperor of love and peace," and by interpreting his performances as supportive of democracy.

By 1948 the Cold War in Europe had become more confrontational and a U.S.–Soviet showdown over Berlin seemed likely. Hirohito's preoccupation with national security problems deepened. Hampered by his lack of constitutional authority, he worked behind the scenes to encourage the United States to retain Okinawa as a military base and later to consolidate Japan's military alliance with Washington. For him anti-Sovietism and cooperation with the United States and Britain were a return to the policy from which his earlier deviation had brought disaster to Japan. He could not allow that to happen again.

17

THE QUIET YEARS AND THE
LEGACIES OF SHŌWA

He said the Emperor had remarked to him several times that the name given his reign—Shōwa [meaning] Enlightened Peace—now seemed to be a cynical one but he wished to retain that designation and hoped that he would live long enough to insure that it would indeed be a reign of "Splendid Peace."

from the papers of Gen. Courtney Whitney

On April 28, 1952, the San Francisco Peace Treaty, the Japan–U.S. Security Treaty, and the Administrative Agreement granting American military forces in Japan special privileges all went into effect simultaneously. GHQ was abolished; the occupation ended. Thousands of American armed forces began to go home.

Japan now, at last, regained formal independence. At last also the long era of combined military-civilian rule, which had begun in the mid–1880s under Meiji and endured through MacArthur and Ridgway, came to an end. Hirohito finally realized his often stated wish that the occupation be long and followed by an alliance with the United States that would protect Japan militarily into the future. Probably the emperor had even foreseen that the alliance (as opposed to the presence of large numbers of American troops) would be relatively popular with about half the nation, as indeed it proved to be.[1] That the peace treaty had been signed with forty-eight nations but not with the Soviet Union, the People's Republic of China, the Philippines, and India did not bother Hirohito as it did most leftist and some conservative politicians. They opposed both the one-sided peace and the defensive military alliance that had as its main object the containment of China and the Soviet Union.

Japan's return to independence brought home to Hirohito once again the personal losses he had suffered from the defeat and MacArthur's democratizing reforms. His tours of the country, originally undertaken to strengthen domestic integration and save the throne, had largely ended. He could no longer intervene in foreign and domestic affairs by secretly communicating his views to American officials. How was he to convey to the leadership of a new Japan his vision of peace and security through military alliance and economic development? He wanted still to be considered an important political figure, and a large constituency of emperor-enthusiasts continued to believe that he ought to be a driving force in politics. How could he adjust to the role the new constitution required, that of a merely ceremonial monarch?

It was clear that these questions preoccupied him at a time when his only chance to play an active political role in rebuilding the nation depended on the continued loyalty of conservative politicians. When, at the formation of the Progressive Reform Party in February 1952, some of those politicians began to advocate constitutional revision, Hirohito's hopes brightened. A few years later politicians in Yoshida's Liberal Party and members of the Progressive Reform Party launched a movement to partially amend the new constitution in order to eliminate Article 9, entitle him "the head of state," and revive some of the authority he had held under the Meiji constitution. Hirohito backed it. Popular opposition proved too strong, however, and by the end of the 1950s the movement was defeated.[2]

At the return of independence, Japan was absorbed with physical reconstruction, restoration of foreign trade, and economic development. Territorial issues with the Soviet Union over the Kuriles and the United States over the Ryukyu and Ogasawara Islands remained to be negotiated. Memories of the lost war were still vivid; fear of militarism was strong and hatred of the upper echelons of the old officer corps widespread. People remembered that the emperor had sent their sons, brothers, husbands, and fathers off to war. Yet few still argued about his direct responsibility for launching the war, or for the many violations of domestic and international law that had occurred during its course. Where the "symbol" of the nation's unity was concerned, most Japanese were reluctant to exercise their new freedoms. Hirohito's continuation on the throne after independence clearly inhibited popular exercise of the constitution's guarantee of freedom of thought and expression.

Shortly before the treaties became effective, in January 1952, a thirty-four-year-old conservative politician, Nakasone Yasuhiro, declared during questioning in the Budgetary Committee of the House of Representatives that "responsibility for having degraded the glory of modern Japan lies with the Shōwa emperor." Nakasone wanted Hirohito, whom he called "a pacifist," to acknowledge "his responsibility for having driven Japan into a reckless war" by abdicating so that "the crown prince [could] become emperor" and "the moral foundation of the monarchy firmed up and made eternal." Prime Minister Yoshida angrily labeled Nakasone "un-Japanese"; the rest of the nation just ignored him.

So too did Hirohito. He had no sense of moral accountability to any but his ancestors, and when under pressure to abdicate, he sometimes intimated to aides that he continued to think of himself as a monarch by divine right. In early 1952, in private remarks to Grand Chamberlain Inada Shūichi, Hirohito observed that regardless of what others had said of him during the occupation, he himself had never said he intended to abdicate. He believed he had a divine mission to remain on the throne and rebuild Japan. "The Meiji emperor said that unlike ministers who can resign, emperors can't abdicate because they must carry out the divine order as written in the dynastic histories. . . . My duty is to bequeath this country, which I received from my ancestors, to my descendants."[3] Hirohito's self-image could not have been more unsuitable and unrealistic for a "symbol" monarch under a democratic constitution. Postwar standards of morality were changing; Hirohito's were not.

While Hirohito clung to his old self-image, speculation that he might abdicate ended around 1952, and Japanese media attention shifted to his nineteen-year-old son, Crown Prince Akihito. With no dark shadow of war guilt hanging over him, Akihito had been hailed in the press as the "future hope of Japan." He had received a Western-style education, was at ease with social conversation and spoke Japanese in a normal voice, with a normal intonation (neither of which his father did). Moreover, Akihito had been tutored in the virtues of Britain's George V rather than Meiji, and in English by a Philadelphia Quaker, Mrs. Elizabeth Vining. He was now being prepared for his ceremonial investiture, a "state ceremony" scheduled for November 1952, and the press reported that he would soon be sent abroad to attend the coronation of Queen Elizabeth. At the start of the postoccupation period, Hirohito, the Imperial Household Agency, and the Yoshida cabinet strove to convey, through the crown prince, a message of close friendship with the island nation of Britain, praised as the model of apolitical constitutional monarchy.[4]

I

Compared to military occupations of other countries by other armies, the occupation of Japan had been mild and correct; now the peace treaty was extremely generous and nonpunitive. Virtually the only reparations that Japan would ever have to pay—a mere 1.02 billion dollars worth of goods and "services" spread out over many years—were to the Philippines, Indonesia, Burma, and (later) South Vietnam.[5] Nevertheless, at the end of 1952, some 260,000 American military personnel remained posted at bases throughout the country, while strategically important Okinawa and the Ogasawara Islands continued to be occupied.[6] Emperor Hirohito had personally given his consent for these arrangements to the State Department's special consultant on the treaty, John Foster Dulles. For Hirohito understood, better than most Japanese at the time, the unbreakable connection between Japan's renunciation of war and armaments in Article 9 of the constitution, and Okinawa's ongoing status as a giant military base under direct American military rule.

The entire experience of war, defeat, foreign occupation, and reform left Japan deeply divided about its recent past and uneasy about the future. For the Yoshida cabinet two tasks held priority: controlling the deep divisions of national opinion on the issue of the new Security Treaty, and correcting the "excesses" in the occupation-era reforms by pursuing a Japanese-initiated "reverse course." Favorable international conditions and a clever strategy for remembering the war dead facilitated the achievement of both tasks. Generally the U.S.–Soviet Cold War permitted Japan's ruling conservatives to be tricky in their treatment of war criminals, and it freed them from foreign criticism as they went about reimposing censorship in education where the war and the role of the emperor were concerned. In signing the peace treaty, Prime Minister Yoshida acknowledged only minimal Japanese war responsibility. He assented (in Article 11) to the charges against the convicted felons and accepted the judgments rendered by the Tokyo tribunal and other Allied war crimes trials. Yet at home Yoshida was able to deny or leave unquestioned the war leaders' and the state's responsibility to the nation and the world.[7]

This denial could be seen in the way Japanese government officials, as well as an influential minority of private citizens, dismissed
the Tokyo trial as one-sided "victor's justice," denied launching and
escalating the China war, and avoided all discussion of war responsibility. Between 1951 and 1960, various movements arose seeking
the release of "detained comrades" still held in prison. In the Diet
conservatives and socialists passed resolutions demanding the
release of the convicted criminals. Concurrently the government
paid their back salaries and restored their pensions—on the grounds
that they had not been tried under Japanese domestic law and therefore should not be treated as ordinary, standard, home-style criminals. A very small number of those who had been imprisoned as war
criminals or suspects, such as Shigemitsu Mamoru, Kaya Okinori,
and Kishi Nobusuke, actually rose to high positions at the very center of Japanese politics.[8] External acceptance of war responsibility
but internal denial—or as historian Yoshida Yutaka termed it, the
"double standard"—both in the actual treatment of those convicted
of war crimes, and as a framework for thinking about the lost war,
first formed as the occupation ended, then spread through Japanese
society during and after the Korean War.[9]

Hirohito was the ultimate symbol of this "double standard," just
as he was an integral part of the conservative approach to containing dissent and keeping everyone aimed toward steady economic
development. He played a key role in demonstrating to the nation
that the leaders of the state understood the importance of according
proper treatment to the war dead and their families. On the first
May Day after restoration of independence, May 1, 1952, demonstrators protesting both the peace treaty and pending Diet legislation to "prevent destructive activities," clashed with police in front
of the Imperial Palace. Two people died and approximately 2,300
were injured. The next day, against this background of a deeply
divided populace, the government staged the first national war

memorial service at the Shinjuku Imperial Gardens in Tokyo. To the strains of the former national anthem, "Kimigayo" (May the imperial reign endure), Hirohito, wearing morning clothes and top hat, mounted the memorial platform together with Empress Nagako and read aloud these lines:

> Due to the recent succession of wars, countless numbers died on the battlefields, sacrificed their lives in the course of work or met untimely deaths. I mourn for all of them from the bottom of my heart and am always pained when I think of their bereaved families. On this occasion, my thoughts are with them and I renew my condolences to them.[10]

Seven years earlier Hirohito had pronounced similar words in his rescript announcing surrender. Then his intention had been to protect the *kokutai*. Now it was to move closer to the bereaved families and bind the nation together while also indicating, subtly and indirectly, that the question of his own war responsibility should not be reopened.[11]

Significantly Prime Minister Yoshida's eulogy stressed that the war dead had laid the foundation for Japan's peace and future prosperity. Their "sacrifice" for the nation, said Yoshida, bound the dead to their living heirs. For the next quarter century, all conservative governments would make repeated and powerful use of the word "sacrifice."

In June 1952, Hirohito visited Ise Shrine, and in July the shrine of the Meiji emperor. In August he had honored the war dead. Now, on October 16, he resumed worshiping at Yasukuni Shrine. Thereafter, down to 1975, Hirohito visited the shrine on eight occasions. It was as if there had been no occupation, or at least no reforms. He was completely indifferent to Yasukuni's disestablishment from the state for its role in channeling religious energy into war.[12]

II

Conservatives and progressives divided in the early 1950s not only over their characterization of the Asia-Pacific war, but also about the highly subordinate military relationship that the United States had forced upon Japan. The Security Treaty, which was presented to the Yoshida cabinet as a precondition for ending the occupation, brought Japan under the U.S. "nuclear umbrella" and ceded to American military forces many special rights and prerogatives. Militarily, diplomatically, and psychologically, Japan remained dominated by its former conqueror—a kingpin state in America's Asian-Pacific network of alliances and military bases.

Many Japanese perceived their military entanglement with the United States as both highly dangerous and a flagrant negation of the peace ideals inscribed in their new constitution; others, including Hirohito, saw things differently. They took a "realist" view and recognized only the favorable international conditions for economic growth created by subordination to the strongest Western power. The security alliance with the United States relieved Japan of the costs of providing for its own defense, freed its industries to profit enormously from the war in Korea, and insured access to U.S.–controlled markets, technology, and raw materials. The other side was that the American-Soviet rivalry was turning into a world-endangering arms race, and Japan was being drawn into it just as it was developing a culture of pacifism and anti-militarism.

Lacking confidence in their ability to govern in a democracy torn by fierce social conflicts between unions and business firms, Japan's political elites felt a deep uncertainty. Conservatives (including the very small but significant minority who had spent the occupation years behind bars), drafted plans to revise the "peace constitution" and strengthen the emperor's powers by changing his status from a vague "symbol" to a "head of state" who once again could have the power to declare national emergencies and promulgate emergency decrees. Their aim was not to revive the prewar or wartime "emperor system." Neither was it to educate future generations in the old imperial-nation view of history rooted in mythology. Rather, conservatives sought to bolster the emperor's authority so they could use it for their own purposes. They hoped to restrict the human rights provisions of the constitution for the sake of "public welfare." They also wanted to insert new clauses to protect rights of inheritance, thereby strengthening the family system, while containing most of the women's rights so dramatically expanded under the occupation.[13]

Extremely concerned about his people's preoccupation with their rights rather than their obligations, Hirohito welcomed these restorationist efforts. He was happy to once again sanction official documents and to have the credentials of foreign diplomats presented to him. His years of active participation in politics and decision making had been personally fulfilling and he longed to resume meaningful political activity. But his constitutional status was now merely that of a "symbol." Intervention in military, diplomatic, and political affairs was denied him. When established in June 1954, the "Self-Defense Forces" and "Self-Defense Force Agency" were placed under the command of the prime minister with the principle of civilian control written into their enabling legislation. Being severed from the new Japan's military was painful for Hirohito. His growing irrelevance to Japanese politics and policy making was even more painful.

What remained to him? Only the secret briefings he received from cabinet ministers, and the year-end reports on law and order from the head of the Metropolitan Police and the governor of Tokyo. Neither briefings nor reports were provided for by constitutional law, however, and either could be ended at any time.[14] As the political battles of the mid- and late 1950s unfolded, Hirohito could only hope that influential politicians would seek out his political counsel, continue the briefings he received, and refrain from insisting he be hobbled by his constitutional "symbol" status.

The political turmoil began during the government of Yoshida's successor, seventy-two-year-old Hatoyama Ichirō, who was committed (prematurely as it turned out) to a policy of economic *and* political independence for Japan. On the day Hatoyama formed his first cabinet, December 10, 1954, Foreign Minister and ex-convicted-felon Shigemitsu Mamoru came to the Palace to brief Hirohito. An innately conservative, yet also intellectually innovative and ambitious person, Shigemitsu during the late 1930s had been an advocate of the "new order" and direct imperial rule. Five years in prison had not changed his fondness for abstract plans to devise new orders. Neither had prison dulled his lively sense of himself as the emperor's loyal servant, or his belief that the emperor lay at the interstices of power and could still be used to serve the purposes of his ministers just as under the old constitution.

Throughout 1955 Shigemitsu and Hirohito discussed important diplomatic issues about twice a month. After the Socialists had gained strength in the Diet and achieved party unity, the conservatives joined to form the Liberal Democratic Party (LDP), with Hatoyama as its first president. In 1955, also, the Japanese economy finally surpassed its prewar and even wartime peak output in virtually all areas except one—trade.[15] While Hatoyama sought revision of the constitution to eliminate Article 9, and to elevate the status of the emperor, Shigemitsu moved to normalize relations with the Soviet Union and widen trade with China. The latter especially would be difficult to accomplish given that the United States was still under the influence of McCarthyism and refused even to recognize China while that country was pursuing a Stalinist model of autarchic development.

At his meetings with Shigemitsu, Hirohito worried aloud about Communist infiltration of Japan should relations with Moscow be restored. He cautioned the foreign minister to avoid a situation where Japan could again become a strategic rival of the United States. In late August 1955, with Nikita Khrushchev in power and seeking a peace treaty with Japan, Hirohito spoke with Shigemitsu at his mansion in Nasu, Tochigi prefecture, and, according to Shigemitsu, stressed "the need to be friendly with the United States and hostile to communism. He said that [American] troops stationed in Japan must not withdraw."[16] Hatoyama and Shigemitsu soon tired of Hirohito's uninvited anti-Communist admonitions and stopped consulting. Their effort to negotiate with Moscow over the normalization of relations failed when they insisted that the Soviets return the southern Kurile Islands, seized at the end of World War II. Hirohito, unhappy with their diplomatic line, was probably pleased to see both of them depart.

By 1956 more and more Japanese were throwing off old authoritarian political attitudes under the influence of the new constitution and improved economic conditions. Nevertheless, the public was not yet ready to accept Japanese veterans who put down myths of wartime innocence and victimization. That year, determined to fill the void of knowledge about Japan's campaigns in China, veterans of those campaigns who had been imprisoned for war crimes in China returned home and began making public confessions to acts of genocide. In 1957 their book entitled, in Japanese, *Sankō (Burn All, Kill All, Steal All)*, became a national bestseller and introduced to the general public the term "*sankō* operations." Reaction was swift. The veterans were accused of "disgracing all Japanese." They were branded as communist dupes, "brainwashed by the Chinese Communist Party." Under threat from right-wing thugs, the publisher soon discontinued it. *Kill All, Burn All, Steal All* had no place in Japanese collective memory at a time when the government was supporting the U.S. policy of containing China and commemorating the nation's losses in war.[17]

Moreover, many still remained attached to the older forms of nationalist belonging centered on the emperor. Hirohito and his brother Prince Takamatsu took a close interest in the restorationist organizations that formed during the first wave of postoccupation nationalism. Occasionally, the emperor's former military aide, one Hayata Noboru, came to the palace to report on veterans groups such as the Japan Veterans Friendship League, of which he was the vice president, as well as on the Japan War-Bereaved Families Association—an early-occupation-era group that had grown increasingly conservative since its reorganization in 1953.

On August 15, 1958, these two national associations joined with the Association of Shinto Shrines and various right-wing organizations, to carry out a memorial service at the large Kudan Hall, near Yasukuni Shrine. The purpose of the service was to "enshrine the heroic spirits [*eirei*] of all those who died for the country in the War of Greater East Asia." The term "heroic spirit," connoting an outstanding person who had made a great achievement in war, had once been associated with the notion of "holy war." It had come to imply also a positive attitude toward the imperial state and a negative evaluation of the postwar values inscribed in the constitution. Hirohito and Empress Nagako sent flowers and an imperial message for these unofficial August 15 memorial services.[18] They did not personally attend the annual ceremony, however, until 1963, when the name of the event was changed to the less ideologically charged "National War Dead Memorial Service."

Even among veterans and bereaved families, who in remembering the war dead at the same time reaffirmed the moral justness of the "War of Greater East Asia," there were many who also remembered that Hirohito represented all those leaders who had never admitted responsibility for the war. Such sentiment was usually expressed indirectly, as when the *Shizuoka shinbun* in October 1957 launched a campaign to induce the emperor to visit the "Nation-Protecting Shrine" [*gokoku jinja*], Shizuoka's local branch of Yasukuni Shrine. "Because the emperor is the representative of the nation and the symbol of the state, he expresses the nation's sentiment and so should bow down to the spirits of the war dead by visiting *gokoku jinja*. . . . They died for the Japanese state, for the nation, and for this emperor. Why should he not bow before them, show them his gratitude, and ask for their forgiveness?" And every request for Hirohito to show his "gratitude" and ask "forgiveness" of the war dead, contained the possibility of rekindling discussion of his war responsibility.[19]

Partly in response to this renewed nationalist activity by veterans and other conservative groups, a political backlash from the Left developed during the mid- and late 1950s. A small number of historical studies espousing critical views of the lost war gained national attention. On the university campuses, criticism rekindled in certain famous intellectuals who had supported expanding war during the 1930s and early 1940s. Communists, left-wing socialists, and liberals, but also some student groups and many white- and blue-collar workers increasingly condemned the LDP's efforts to revise the constitution. Fueling their opposition were fears of Japan being drawn into war between the United States and the Soviet Union, and fear of rearmament.

The LDP government's reinstitution of state control of education, and its heavy-handed attempt to resuscitate patriotic enthusiasm, also kindled distrust. During the mid-1950s the Ministry of Education checked the influence of the progressive Japan Teachers Union and abolished publicly elected school boards. In place of the latter, it installed the mechanism of school textbook examinations—an ideal device for perpetuating the "double standard." The system of textbook control implemented between 1956 and 1958 played down Japan's aggressive Asian colonialism and wars. The ministry also attempted to require schools to display the "Rising Sun" flag and to teach the singing of "Kimigayo," even though neither of them enjoyed legal sanction, both closely associated with the prewar empire. (This was finally achieved in 1999.)

During the first decade of independence, Hirohito gradually ceased to be an object of frequent media attention. He continued to make public appearances at sports events and tree planting ceremonies, to travel to different parts of the country for very short visits, and to perform the limited duties prescribed for him in the constitution. Soon two antagonistic imperial images began to emerge. One was the postwar "human" emperor, a "scientist," a "scholar," and a "family man," popular with his people and in tune with the democratic and liberal values codified in the constitution and practiced in the emerging consumer society. The other was the remote, hard, awe-inspiring, high-voiced emperor, stiffly bound into Shinto and the old value structure, and supportive of the unreformed imperial system. Many middle-aged and elderly supporters of the LDP embraced the latter image and clung to the traditional political values.

III

In February 1957 Kishi Nobusuke, who had served as minister of commerce and industry, and later vice minister of munitions under Tōjō, formed a cabinet bent on revising the Japan-U.S. Security Treaty, and developing a more independent foreign policy. Kishi's goals included reestablishing close economic ties with the nations of Southeast Asia and securing the release of Class B and C war criminals who still were imprisoned for such crimes as torture, rape, and murder. Some were in Sugamo Prison; others remained in the custody of former Allied nations. Their early parole and pardon, Kishi argued, would make it easier for Japan to forget the past and move closer to the United States. The Eisenhower administration agreed and helped to expedite the release of the remaining war criminals.

Kishi, like Hatoyama before him, hoped to revise Articles 1 and 9 of the constitution (on the emperor and the abandonment of war), and to expand the small Self-Defense Forces. Anticipating public demonstrations protesting renewal of the Security Treaty, Kishi introduced a bill to strengthen the powers of the police. In late October 1958 the mass media and most of the nation's labor unions turned against the proposed police law and a national coalition soon emerged calling for Kishi's removal.

In early November the four-million-strong Sōhyō labor federation went on strike against the police bill. As opposition to Kishi escalated, his government, on November 27, happily announced the engagement of Crown Prince Akihito and Shōda Michiko, daughter of the president of a large flour-milling company and the product of a Catholic upbringing. Public attention immediately turned from nasty politics to romantic love as palace officials and the media carefully orchestrated all the details. An astonishing "Mitchii" craze swept Japan, and Kishi safely escaped the headlines for awhile.

The engagement and marriage of the crown prince marked an important shift in the evolution of the monarchy. To hear the words "commoner" and "love" joined to the imperial family was distinctively new and very popular. Emperor Hirohito and Empress Nagako opposed the marriage because they believed Michiko might not be able to handle the intricacies of palace customs.[20] What most concerned Hirohito was neither Michiko's Christianity nor even the maintenance of the imperial house's ties to state Shinto, but rather the break with tradition that the marriage connoted. Hirohito was uncomfortable with the very notion of an "open, popular monarchy." But like everyone, he and Nagako could also appreciate how an alliance with one of the nation's prominent business families could serve to strengthen a legally and politically weakened monarchy.

In February 1959 a Japanese opinion poll showed 87 percent support for Akihito's choice of a commoner.[21] But in addition to general approval, there was also public uneasiness about the marriage. Some worried that a perfectly normal woman marrying into the imperial family would suffer from the loss of her accustomed freedom and become unhappy. A small number of critics and writers of fiction, including the well-known novelist Fukazawa Shichirō, urged that imperial males never marry outside the royal pale so that continued inbreeding would eventually lead to the extinction of the whole imperial lot. Die-hard traditionalists and Shintoists were also opposed.[22] To them there was only threat in the new society of mass consumption and hedonistic aspiration: prewar values were fast eroding, and the marriage suggested that if the throne were brought down to earth, it would eventually be debased also—by popular acclaim and approval.

Crown Prince Akihito and Michiko were united on April 10, 1959, before a huge television audience estimated at fifteen million viewers; another half million lined the route of their marriage parade.[23] The newlyweds then disappeared on their honeymoon, and from public attention, which now reverted to the great political issues. On January 19, 1960, Kishi signed in Washington, D.C., a renegotiated and more equitable Japan–U.S. Security Treaty. The United States promised to consult before committing its forces in Japan to military action. American bases remained on Japanese soil, however, and the Japanese Self-Defense Forces were obligated to aid U.S. forces should Washington find itself at war with some other Far Eastern nation (such as China), and should that other nation attack American bases in Japan.

Ratification was fiercely resisted by the opposition parties within the Diet and by organized labor and student groups outside the Diet. On May 19 five hundred uniformed policemen were brought into the House of Representatives; the vote on ratification was literally a forced vote. This proceeding triggered a month of the largest demonstrations in Japanese history, culminating on June 15 with the death of a student protester in a clash with police in front of the Diet building, followed by calls for a general strike by a coalition of union federations and groups of private citizens. Kishi immediately canceled the scheduled visit of President Eisenhower to Japan. Four days later the Security Treaty went into effect, and the next month Kishi and his entire cabinet resigned, having accomplished their primary mission.

For Hirohito the whole ratification experience was an emotional ordeal. He had wanted relations with the United States improved and the alliance strengthened at all costs. Until the very last minute he had hoped to travel to Haneda airport to greet visiting President Eisenhower, and be seen riding back to the Palace with him in a limousine past crowds of cheering well-wishers. Kishi would then have gotten his treaty renewed while Eisenhower's visit would have helped the emperor raise his status as de facto "head of state," with no need for constitutional revision. The cancellation had denied him that while the struggle over the treaty had temporarily turned the majority of the nation against any tampering with the constitution.[24]

Thus the results of the whole effort were mixed. Hirohito's and the LDP's wish for an American military alliance that would insure continuation of Japan's diplomatic course for the remainder of his reign had been realized. But the struggle over the Security Treaty, anti-Kishi and prodemocracy in its aims, had been a learning process for the ruling elites. They had weathered the biggest national crisis of the postoccupation period without ever calling on help from the emperor. The rising generation of LDP leaders drew the lesson that the monarchy was not needed as a crisis-control mechanism. Hirohito's dream of someday regaining political relevance was only a dream.

While the treaty struggle was unfolding in Japan, in South Korea student demonstrators were overthrowing American-sponsored dictator Syngman Rhee. In this heated atmosphere of revolutionary hope on the Left and counterrevolutionary fear on the Right, Fukazawa Shichirō wrote a political parody entitled "Fūryū mutan" (A Dream of courtly elegance).[25] In December 1960, in the immediate wake of the treaty struggle, *Chūō kōron* (Central review), a popular journal of opinion and the arts, published the story. It begins when the first-person narrator purchases a strange wristwatch that keeps correct time only while he sleeps. As his dream unfolds he witnesses an uprising in central Tokyo resulting in the takeover of the palace by left-wing revolutionaries. At the plaza in front of the palace, crowds enjoy watching as their "superiors" are laid low. The dreamer sees Crown Prince Akihito (in a tuxedo) and Princess Michiko (in a kimono) lying on the ground bellies-up, awaiting execution. The narrator realizes that it is his own ax being wielded by the executioner. The royal heads come off with a *swoosh*, roll across the plaza, and disappear from sight with a clinking metallic sound of tin cans.[26]

Presently the narrator meets an elderly court chamberlain who tells him nonchalantly: "Now, if you go over there, their majesties the emperor and empress are being killed." He proceeds as instructed, and as he looks at the deceased royal couple, he notices the foreign labels "Made in England" on Hirohito's business suit and Nagako's skirt. The high point of the dream is an exchange with Emperor Meiji's wife—that is, Hirohito's grandmother, who had died in 1914, and whom he confuses with Teimei kōgō, Hirohito's mother.

> "You scum wouldn't even be alive if it weren't for us! You owe us everything."
>
> "How can you say that, you shitty old hag? Owe what? To you? Why, you sucked our blood and lived high on our money."
>
> "What! So you've forgotten August 15? When *our* Hirohito saved all of you by surrendering? Unconditionally! And *he* did it!"
>
> "Damn you! Our lives were saved because people around your grandson persuaded him to! Unconditionally!"[27]

Later the dowager empress mutters defiantly, "All the people are grateful to us. They do this and they do that for us. Then in the end they say we were bloodsuckers who squeezed money out of them. But who wanted war? You, you idiots! What insolence!"

A satirical attack on the institution of the "symbol" monarchy, and on the fabricated myth that Hirohito had heroically saved the nation from destruction, the "Dream" can be seen as revealing a miscellany of thrusts and cuts that say much about the emperor problem when the era of rapid economic growth began. At a time when most Japanese opted to avoid confronting the emperor's responsibility for the war of aggression, the actors in Fukazawa's story, including the narrator, all have a bald spot on the crown of their heads. That common scar, baldness, is Fukazawa's metaphor for the emperor problem buried deep inside the Japanese conscience. The "Dream," in effect, asserts a mutual relationship of culpability shared by emperor and people, nearly all of whom had enthusiastically identified with him and cooperated in the unjust war of aggression. Fukazawa implies that having made the monarchy a unifying "symbol" for their own purposes, the people have not yet liberated themselves from their emperor. By failing to pursue *his* war responsibility, they avoid pursuing their own.

Fukazawa's fictionalized murder of the nation's "symbolic family" provoked expressions of delight and approval from some readers, but these quickly gave way to cries of outrage from others, and finally to a real homicide. The Imperial Household Agency sought to bring suit against both author and publisher but the Ikeda cabinet refused to take up the issue. Right-wing groups saw the struggle against the Security Treaty and Fukazawa's "Dream" as springing from the same source—a desire for revolution. They were more successful than the government in enforcing sanctions against such an act of "lèse majesté." The rightists gathered outside the Chūō Kōron Company's Tokyo headquarters to berate and threaten its employees. The furor built until, on February 1, 1960, a seventeen-year-old member of a radical right-wing party invaded the residence of the company president, Shimanaka Hōji. Finding him not at home, the youth killed the family maid with a short sword and severely wounded Shimanaka's wife.

After the murder Fukazawa went into hiding for five years. Apparently he never published again. According to literary historian John W. Treat, he devoted "himself to making bean paste" and later "ran a muffin stall—grandly dubbed the Yumeya or 'Dream Shop' in a working-class district of Tokyo."[28] Shimanaka disavowed any association with the writer. Rather than criticize the rightists for the bloodbath at his home, or defend freedom of speech and artistic expression, he repeatedly issued public apologies in the newspapers for having troubled the throne.[29] Then, to further mollify right-wing and respectable opinion alike, *Chūō Kōron* changed its editorial direction and became an outlet for articles that made the behavior of the wartime state appear less condemnable. Other large commercial publishers followed suit, censoring themselves more strictly on subjects concerning the throne. No one (except for a few small, underground presses) thereafter dared publish parodies mocking the authority of emperors.

The "Fūryū mutan" and "Shimanaka incidents" highlighted the limits of free expression in the new, more tolerant Japan. In their wake, the mass media stopped publishing articles that could be construed as critical or demeaning of Hirohito and the imperial house. The scope of this "chrysanthemum taboo" widened in 1963 when the publisher Heibonsha ended its magazine serialization of Koyama Itoko's novel, *Lady Michiko (Michikosama)* following its criticism in the Diet as "entertainment" unsuitable for the nation.[30] Such actions did not silence intellectual argument about the monarchy, however, and their overall impact on the mass media was ephemeral. In the middle-class consumer society that had emerged from war and occupation, the constitution had gained a high level of legitimacy. A postwar generation had become the main bearer of democratic, antiauthoritarian values, in conflict with the values of the older generations, educated under the prewar and wartime regimes, for whom unthinking loyalty and reverence for the throne remained strong. In this conflict Hirohito stood with the older generation but was always very careful never openly to defend their view of the "War of Greater East Asia."

Some 233 organized crime and rightist groups were disbanded during the early occupation years. Between 1958 and 1961 right-wing terrorism returned briefly to the Japanese political scene. There is no clear evidence that Kishi and his "mainstream" faction of the LDP directly ordered terrorism against political opponents. Nevertheless, their hard-line policies probably did foster a climate in which such incidents could occur while the police, passive if not complicit, looked the other way. Right-wing hit men struck at leftist Diet members and intimidated opponents of the Security Treaty. Asanuma Inejirō, chairman of the Socialist Party, was assassinated while giving a speech on live television. Radical rightists also ventured into the cultural arena. For the first time in the postwar era, they targeted for intimidation and death writers like Fukuzawa who were effective in expressing the need for continued reform of the monarchy.

IV

Drawing a lesson from Kishi's downfall, his successor, Prime Minister Ikeda Hayato, abandoned constitutional revision and hoisted the slogan "Tolerance and Patience." Ikeda is mainly remembered for his plan to "double" the nation's income within a decade by increasing its GNP by 9 percent annually. During his years in power—June 1960 to November 1964—Japan entered a period of extraordinary economic growth that continued until the first "oil shock" in 1973. Though it slowed at that time, the rate of growth still remained well above that of all Western nations. The decline in the Japanese farm population also accelerated, going from almost a third of the total employed in 1960 to under a fifth in 1970 and less than a tenth in

1980. When Hirohito turned sixty-seven in 1968, Japan had achieved the second largest GNP in the capitalist world; by the time he reached eighty in 1981, few of the agricultural communities that years earlier had been important mainstays of the monarchy still even existed.[31]

In 1963 Ikeda succeeded in making surrender day, August 15, the anniversary for memorializing the nation's war dead in a purely secular, non-Shinto ceremony of condolence. Avoiding all historical evaluation of the war itself, Ikeda, like Yoshida before him, declared the war dead to be "the foundation of the remarkable development of our economy and culture." Henceforth War Memorial Day would be an occasion for other prime ministers to evoke that Yoshida-Ikeda memorial mantra: From the sacrifices of the war dead had come, in time, postwar economic prosperity.[32] In such ways were small steps taken in the direction of legitimizing the war and reconstituting an inclusive national community. Also in 1963, the Ikeda government passed a new law on textbooks designed to "normalize education." The new law quickly led to the production of history texts and teaching guides that completely skirted the issue of Japan's culpability for aggression and Hirohito's role in the war.

Ikeda also revived the practice, originally stipulated in the Meiji constitution and abandoned during the occupation, of having the emperor bestow imperial awards on distinguished citizens who had made important contributions to the nation in the arts and sciences. The award ceremonies, held at the palace, affirmed a cultural hierarchy based on excellence and political conformity, and at the same time strengthened the societal hierarchy atop which was Hirohito on the imperial throne. From 1963, awards for battlefield survivors were included, and from April 1964, posthumous awards to servicemen killed in combat. The leader of the LDP drew up the awards lists twice annually from 1963 onward and transmitted them to the emperor. Conferring these imperial accolades always just before election days served not only to honor deserving artists, intellectuals, and war veterans, but also gave popular support to the LDP, which was precisely their purpose.[33] Spreading imperial accolades in order to strengthen a ruling party's electoral support base was certainly "a new use of the imperial institution," though it had well established counterparts overseas.[34]

By middle and later Shōwa, the 1960s into the 1970s, Japan was transforming rapidly into an intensely urbanized society, oriented to meet the infrastructural, financial, technical, and social requirements of huge capitalist enterprises. Above all, postwar Japan was politically dedicated to supporting big business, big manufacturing, and big trade, no matter what the human and environmental costs. And as big business expanded and consolidated, the Japanese middle class also expanded. During the occupation, large enterprises joined together in business federations. Representing corporate and financial interests with their ever changing requirements, these federations essentially mediated between corporate interests and key ministries of the state, such as Finance, Post and Telecommunications, and International Trade and Industry and the Bank of Japan, and the ruling party establishment.[35] Prosperity and affluence unified this new Japanese society, and the role constitutionally assigned to the "symbol" was now merely supplementary.

Unlike most of the wartime generation who had identified with the emperor or paid lip service to (if they did not actually believe in) the ideological principles of the state, the "younger generation" of the 1970s, for example, had been brought up in the emerging enterprise society. They identified with the company, tended to be distrustful of the state, and affirmed the values of economic growth and democracy. Stated differently: The series of ideological changes that had gone from pre-Meiji samurai loyalty to feudal lords and post-Meiji loyalty of all "subjects" to the emperor had shifted to employee loyalty to the firm in a company-centered society. With Japan fast becoming a major economic power, but not yet having regained its status as a great political power, the monarchy was no longer needed to actively mold the nation as in Meiji, or to prevent and constrain democratic change as in Taishō and early Shōwa. Nevertheless, because the constitution preserved the monarchy, and the monarchy contravened the principle of equality and nondiscrimination under the law, it remained a constraint on the freedom of the individual. This was not because the conservative political establishment of the 1960s and 1970s ordered it to perform as such: the enterprise society itself generated hierarchy and discrimination, and the monarchy, situated at its apex, served to validate those principles.[36]

After Kishi no LDP government could ignore the division in values between liberals and progressives on one side, and conservatives on the other, especially when the division was expressed at the polls. Accordingly, divisive issues of constitutional revision and remilitarization remained off the agenda of Ikeda's successor, Satō Eisaku (Kishi's half brother). Prime Minister Satō's goal was one of economic growth and national unity based on material affluence. By pursuing "consensus politics," and encouraging forgetfulness of Japan's militarist and colonialist past, he was able to stay in office for eight years, 1964 to 1972, longer than any other prime minister. Like his predecessor Ikeda, Satō idolized Yoshida Shigeru, and from the start of his tenure he sought to please the old emperor, as Yoshida had, by his pro-American policy and also by keeping Hirohito fully abreast of political developments.

On December 26, approximately six weeks after forming his cabinet, Satō visited the palace to brief the emperor for the first time.[37] They soon developed a warm personal relationship. Thereafter (except when campaigning or traveling abroad) Satō went out of his way to report to Hirohito on international affairs, national politics, education and defense issues, the economy, and agricultural policy. He reported frequently and at length, sometimes even while visiting the palace for investiture ceremonies and imperial awards. Eager to follow, and be part of, state affairs, Hirohito plied Satō with questions.

In the mid- and late 1960s President Lyndon Johnson was beginning to escalate the war in Vietnam, and protesting Japanese students were focusing on the American bases in Okinawa from which B-52s were taking off to bomb North Vietnam. Satō fully supported the American aggression against North Vietnam. As the war intensified, the importance of both Japan and Okinawa to the United States increased. In October 1964 China tested its first atomic bomb. Exactly two years later China, which was descending into the chaos of the Cultural Revolution, test-fired a missile capable of carrying a nuclear warhead to any target in East Asia. It soon became clear to some in Washington that in due time continental-size China would acquire a nuclear arsenal. This meant Okinawa would be more important to the United States. A rethinking of U.S.–China relations was clearly necessary.

Hirohito's personal thoughts about the first Chinese bomb and the later missile launch are not known. It is likely, however, that neither he nor Satō questioned the usefulness of the American "nuclear umbrella" even though China was now embarked on nuclear missile development. Hirohito's questions, according to Satō, focused on the increasingly troubled economic relationship with the United States. At such times Satō would try to keep him abreast of the progress he was making in the textile dispute. They also talked about the course of the Vietnam War, how the prime minister was dealing with student protests, and the policies of President Johnson and those of the even more inscrutable Nixon. While Hirohito appreciated Satō's handling of foreign and domestic affairs, he would occasionally express anger at the corruption of LDP Diet members and cabinet officials.[38]

During Satō's tenure in office, Hirohito moved into a new, scaled-down palace (1964), participated in the hosting of the Olympic Games in Tokyo (also in 1964), the staging of the "Meiji Centennial" ceremonies (1968), which celebrated a century of "successful modernization," and the World Exposition in Osaka, where he and the empress twice made appearances (1970). These events strengthened pride in Japan's economic achievements and asserted the dignity of the nation. National pride and dignity were further enhanced when Satō negotiated the retrocession of Okinawa to Japan's control (1972). A large continuing American military presence was allowed, however, because both sides wanted the island to remain America's "Gibraltar of the Pacific." On the occasion of the final return ceremony in Tokyo, Hirohito met visiting foreign dignitaries and gave a short speech expressing his condolences for the sacrifices made by the people of Okinawa both during and following the war.[39]

While Satō and the LDP conservatives governed, the elderly Hirohito once again could dream of becoming more active, even again the head of state. He did continue meeting foreign dignitaries and royals. As during the early, youthful years of his reign, he hosted palace receptions and elegant garden parties—though they were of course quite different gatherings. He attended national sports events and helped the LDP convey to the world the Japanese idea of peace and prosperity. In 1970 Satō suggested Hirohito travel to Europe again. Hirohito agreed and the next year, after he had turned seventy, he and Empress Nagako departed. Fifty-five years earlier, rightists had protested his grand tour. This time the protests came from the Left, and made his journey literally a rude awakening, both for him and the Japanese nation. In the seven countries he visited, but especially in the Netherlands, West Germany, and Britain, angry demonstrators hurled objects and insults at his motorcade. They clearly did not see him as a symbol of peace or regard the Japanese people as only or primarily victims of war—at that time, a view still widely held in Japan. Hirohito and Nagako returned home but the protests in Europe reminded many that "war responsibility" was not just an issue of the past.

After Hirohito's European tour Japan turned to normalization of relations with the People's Republic of China, which was achieved by Satō's successor, Tanaka Kakuei (1972–74). Under

Tanaka, Japanese politicians continued the "double standard" in public comments on the lost war. When, on February 2, 1973, Prime Minister Tanaka was asked by a Communist Diet member whether he thought the Japan-China war had been a war of aggression, he replied blandly and blankly: "It is true that Japan once sent troops to the Chinese continent; this is a historical fact. But when you ask me straightforwardly whether that constituted, as you say, a war of aggression, it is very hard for me to answer. This is a question for future historians to evaluate." Few Japanese found Tanaka's evasion objectionable.[40] Fewer still saw any connection between his nonreply and a need to protect Hirohito.

Hirohito had continued to receive—as a courtesy, though one in violation of the constitution—secret informal briefings on international and military affairs. These opportunities for him to convey his views to the leaders of government did not become known to the Japanese public until May 1973, when Masuhara Keikichi, the head of the Self-Defense Agency under the Tanaka cabinet, disclosed to a journalist that the emperor had counseled him to "firmly incorporate [into the expansion plan for the Self-Defense Forces] the good points of the old army and avoid the bad ones."[41] Public criticism resulted: Why had the seventy-two-year-old "symbol" emperor been secretly briefed? Hirohito's reference to "the good points of the old army," forced Tanaka to dismiss Masuhara and led the emperor to lament, "If something like this can become an issue, then I am nothing more than a papier-mâché doll."[42]

Following this incident Tanaka and his immediate successors (Miki Takeo, Fukuda Takeo, and Ōhira Masayoshi) ended the emperor's military briefings by the head of the Self-Defense Forces, which had been going on since the early 1960s. Yet Hirohito's passionate interest in all matters military, political, and diplomatic never waned. During the late 1970s, when Japanese companies were expanding their activities throughout Southeast Asia and China, helping to make Japan an economic "superpower," high government officials continued reporting to their elderly monarch on military and diplomatic matters, and professors from different universities continued lecturing to him on foreign affairs.

By mid-1975 approximately one half the Japanese population had been born after World War II.[43] The "heroic war dead" view of the lost war, which had reaffirmed the values of imperial Japan, was no longer so popular as it had been during the first two decades after independence. Whether as sightseeing tourists, or as serious pilgrims traveling to old World War II battlefields, as if to religious shrines, to collect bones, Japanese were going abroad in ever-growing numbers. In China, Southeast Asia, and the islands of the Pacific, they gradually discovered how foreigners had suffered at the hands of the Japanese military, and how many in Asia still viewed Japan as inherently militaristic and aggressive. They were starting to overcome a narrow concentration on their own war sacrifices.

In September 1975 Emperor Hirohito and Empress Nagako paid their only state visit to the United States. Five years earlier Prime Minister Satō Eisaku and the emperor had discussed the idea of a trip to assuage economic frictions. The actual planning for the trip did not begin until 1973. On the eve of his departure, seventy-four-year-old Hirohito gave an exclusive interview to *Newsweek* journalist Bernard Krisher. As reported in the evening *Asahi* of September 22, 1975, one of Krisher's eleven questions was: "It is well known that at the time of the ending of the war you took an important role. How then do you answer those who claim that you participated also in the policy process leading to the decision to open hostilities?" Hirohito replied:

> Yes, I myself made the decision to end the war. The prime minister sought my opinion because he couldn't unify the views of the cabinet. . . . But at the time of opening hostilities, the cabinet made the decision, and I was unable to overturn it. I believe my action was in agreement with the articles of the constitution of Japan.[44]

Nearly seven years after the Japanese publication of the Kido diaries, which showed that the emperor had never blindly followed the will of anyone, either cabinet or military, and the *Sugiyama memo*, which had revealed how highly active and interventionist a monarch he had been, Hirohito still mechanically reiterated the false litany that had helped to sustain him and conservative politics through three postwar decades: He had been a faithful constitutional monarch, who bore no responsibility for having started the war but deserved all the credit for having ended it; the Meiji constitution had required him to accept the advice of the cabinet when exercising his power of supreme command and his right to declare war and make peace. And so on.

On September 22 foreign journalists who resided in Tokyo asked Hirohito more questions. "[M]any Americans expect your majesty to say something about the Japan-U.S. war of the 1940s. How do you intend to answer this question?" Hirohito replied, "I am examining this question. Right now I prefer not to express my views." In short, no comment. Further into the interview, he was asked: "Your Majesty, do you think the values of the Japanese people have changed over the past thirty years?" Hirohito replied, "I know various people have stated many different views since the end of the war, but seen broadly I don't think there has been any change [of values] from prewar to postwar."[45] Hirohito's strong emphasis on continuity could be taken as a denial that foreign occupation and reform had changed the essentials in the Japanese value-structure. Yet it could also be heard as an expression of his resolve to assert the old nonsense of the monarchy's unchanged nature.

At the end of this interview, Hirohito was asked again about his role in starting and ending the war. "You said that you had acted in accord with the stipulations of the [Meiji] constitution. That statement seems to imply that you did not oppose the military at that time. Consequently I would like to ask your majesty whether you, personally, ever felt that Japan's military leaders led it into a fruitless and wrong adventure?" Hirohito replied: "The facts may have been as you have stated, but as the people involved are still living, if I comment now I will be criticizing persons who were leaders of that time. I do not care to do so."[46] It was unclear as to which leaders he was referring, though clearly not to himself, for throughout the occupation Hirohito had criticized everyone around him, except for Tōjō and Kido, for having lost the war.

A few weeks after this series of interviews, while on his first formal state visit to Washington, Hirohito expressed his "profound sadness" over World War II to President Gerald Ford, who had visited Japan the previous year. There followed a whirlwind tour of the United States. The climax was at Disneyland, in California, where the smiling emperor made a walkabout with Mickey Mouse. Later he petted a koala bear at the San Diego Zoo.[47] Photographs of the elderly emperor delighted many Americans, and seemed to confirm the false stereotype of him as a monarch who had always been peaceminded but helpless.

On returning to Tokyo, Hirohito was interviewed on television (October 31). Alerted to the war responsibility issue by the emperor's interviews with the foreign press corps and his remark to President Ford, a Japanese newsman pounced, asking the "improper" and embarrassing question: "Your majesty, at your White House banquet you said, 'I deeply deplore that unfortunate war.' Does your majesty feel responsibility for the war itself, including the opening of hostilities [that is, not just for the defeat]? Also, what does your majesty think about so-called war responsibility?"

Hirohito's face stiffened: "I can't answer that kind of question because I haven't thoroughly studied the literature in this field, and so don't really appreciate the nuances of your words." When asked about the atomic bombing of Hiroshima, he said, "It's very regrettable that nuclear bombs were dropped, and I feel sorry for the citizens of Hiroshima. But it couldn't be helped because that happened in wartime."[48] Hirohito's pretense of ignorance, as if he had been an innocent bystander to the events of his reign, was too much for many Japanese viewers. His "it couldn't be helped" remark, denying any role in the events that had led to the tragedy of Hiroshima, especially angered professional historians. That year Inoue Kiyoshi published the first carefully documented account of Hirohito's contributions at each stage of the China and Pacific wars. Nezu Masashi followed with the first critical biography. The work of unmasking the emperor had begun.

Three months after this interview, the Kyōdō News Agency surveyed three thousand men and women on the state of the monarchy. More than 80 percent responded. Nearly 57 percent of these respondents either believed that the emperor bore war responsibility or were unsure if he did. By his answers to the various interview questions, Hirohito showed, once again, that he was out of step with the feelings of the majority of the Japanese people.[49]

V

Hirohito's European and American visits, together with his various press interviews, helped the Japanese people to reengage with the long-buried question of his war responsibility. But for Hirohito the foreign tours and the interviews had no such effect. For him, the event that triggered a confrontation with the past was more personal. Certain reminiscences on the war by his brother, Prince Takamatsu, had appeared in the February 1975 issue of the popular journal *Bungei shunjū*. Hirohito seems not to have learned about the article until January 1976.[50] Interviewed on the war by journalist Kase Hideaki, Prince Takamatsu implied that he had been a dove and Hirohito a reckless hawk. He told of the incident on November 30, 1941, when he had spoken to his brother for five minutes, warning him that the navy high command could feel confident only if the war lasted no longer than two years. Takamatsu also recalled warning his brother to end the war right after the Battle of Midway. And he told how, in June 1944, he had shocked a meeting of staff officers at Navy General Headquarters by telling them that "Since the absolute defense perimeter has already been destroyed ... our goal should be to focus on the best way to lose the war." Finally, Takamatsu revealed that he and Prince Konoe had considered asking the emperor to abdicate prior to surrender.[51]

Learning of these disclosures, Hirohito grew very upset. He felt his brother had gone too far. What could he do to save his reputation as emperor? For the first time since he dictated his "Monologue" and, with Inada Shūichi and Kinoshita Michio, made the first "Record of the Emperor's Conversations" (*Haichōroku*), Hirohito returned to the task of setting the historical record straight. The project to record the events of his reign and define the place that he would occupy in history focused on his role during the years of war and occupation. It quickly turned into a consuming interest that haunted him for the rest of his life. By nature the least self-reflective of men, Hirohito became obsessed with his past.

In February 1976, assisted by his last grand chamberlain, Irie Sukemasa, Hirohito began to make the second *Haichōroku*. Irie worked on the revisions until his death in 1983. It is tempting to imagine Hirohito continuing, helped by some other aide, almost until his own death six years later. The process involved Hirohito dictating to Irie, ordering him to put in new "facts" as he, the emperor, remembered them. Hirohito would then reread Irie's revised version of some event, correct it, and return it for polishing and copying out in ink on high-quality paper. Sometimes Hirohito would summon Irie daily or twice daily to make a change in the text. But hardly a week went by when the two old men were not at work together.

On November 10, 1976, Hirohito, now seventy-five years old, took time off from his secret history project to celebrate his fiftieth year on the throne. The state ceremony at the heavily guarded Martial Arts Hall (Budōkan) in Tokyo was attended by some 7,500 dignitaries. Noticeably absent were representatives of the Socialist and Communist Parties and several prefectural governors who were opposed in principle to honoring the first twenty years of his "Shōwa" reign, when he was at the height of his power. When it was over, Hirohito went back to his dictation, and to relying on Irie's literary skills. By the end of 1976, Irie had filled more than "nine notebooks plus a conclusion" with the emperor's revised account of events.[52]

Hirohito worked on the revised memoir of his reign all through 1977, 1978, and 1979. He insisted on continuing with it into his eighties, just as he insisted on performing some of the more physically exhausting court ceremonies and on not letting his son take over as regent while he lived. He never seemed to tire of the project. Irie, in his diary entries for 1980, notes how the emperor worried about Honjō Shigeru's account of the February 26, 1936, military uprising. The names of some of the prime movers in saving him from indictment during the occupation period are mentioned: Fellers, Terasaki, Keenan, and so on.[53] Voices from the past kept recurring, as did the events of 1941. His concern with what his brother Takamatsu had said about him in print had become obsessive.

While Hirohito was tirelessly reconstructing the version of the war years he had narrated many decades earlier in 1946, others had begun thinking of Japan after Shōwa. The Association of Shinto Shrines, organizations of veterans and bereaved families, conservative Diet members, and many local prefectural assemblymen were campaigning to strengthen the authority of the monarchy. One of their objectives was to mandate by law the use of era-names (such as Meiji, Taishō, Shōwa) in counting time in official documents. In 1979, after years of debate in which opposition to the measure always prevailed, the Diet finally passed the "Era-Name Law"—a regressive measure that prescribed the use of each emperor's reign title to indicate contemporary time.

Some three decades earlier, GHQ had ordered this institution of "imperial time" deleted from the revised Imperial Household Law. When the conservatives tried to legislate the practice into law, GHQ had declared the era-name system to be incompatible with the spirit of the new constitution because the emperor no longer ruled. Now, in 1979, the bill had become law, ensuring that people would go on thinking in terms of imperial eras which ended with the physical death of each emperor. The notion of the uniqueness of the Japanese people was once again reaffirmed. Hirohito's reaction to this outcome is unknown but he could hardly have been displeased. The passage of the Era Name Law set the stage for a new attempt, during the next decade, to strengthen the authority of the throne.

During the early and mid–1980s, Asian nations once invaded and colonized by Japan were achieving rapid economic growth, making productivity gains, and, in the process, finding that their voices were heard in international affairs. As Japan came under scathing criticism in the United States for its protectionist economic practices, its domestic policies were also subjected to closer scrutiny by nations in East Asia. Starting in fall 1981, the South Korean press criticized the wording of Japanese textbooks. The textbooks whitewashed Japan's invasion of China (calling it an "advance" rather than an "invasion") and misdescribed its harsh colonial role in Korea (labeling the March 1 Independence Movement a "riot"). These practices of the Ministry of Education only attracted worldwide attention, however, the following summer when China, for a combination of historic and diplomatic reasons, joined in pushing into the limelight Japan's responsibility for the Asia-Pacific war.

Behind the protests lay concern over Japan's economic power, but also unease at the way top Japanese officials persisted in trying to enhance the authority of the emperor, while contending that Japan needed a new national identity grounded in glory rather than shame. Prime Minister Suzuki Zenkō (1980–82) quickly defused the international uproar over Japan's slanted textbook practices, and some improvements were registered in Japan-China relations. But during the tenure of Suzuki's successor, Nakasone Yasuhiro (1982–87), Japan continued to remain under a cloud of mistrust in the eyes of many Asian and Western peoples. Having resolved to achieve greater participation in international society for Japan, Nakasone promised to rectify the textbook problem, and over the next decade, as Japanese perceptions of the lost war continued to change, substantial progress was made under different LDP prime ministers.

Hirohito, like many other Japanese, worried less about China than about Japan's worsening relations with the United States. The United States was buffeted by rising inflation, and the American public had come to feel that their country was stagnating under President Jimmy Carter. In 1980 they elected Republican Ronald Reagan as president. Reagan and his advisers immediately rekindled the nuclear arms race with the Soviet Union and inaugurated an aggressive policy of imperial interventions. Japan's elites responded by increasing defense spending on the premise that the United States' global economic and military hegemony was declining and it was time for Japan to prepare to stand on its own. Nakasone immediately sought to improve relations with the Reagan administration, strengthening defense, and raising the annual military budget above the ceiling of one percent of gross national product, formally fixed by a cabinet decision six years earlier.

For Hirohito, Reagan's policies carried the danger of war, and the Nakasone initiatives had both positive and negative sides. As he told Irie on October 17, 1982, after learning that the Reagan administration had requested that Japan not only share the burden of air defense over its sea-lanes but also blockade the Sōya Strait, "If we do this, isn't there a danger of war with the Soviet Union? Go tell the director [of the Defense Agency] that I think so."[54] On the twenty-sixth he confided to Irie his concern that "If Japan increases the size of its armed forces, the Soviet Union might be provoked."[55] Three days later, riding by car with Irie to view field birds and ducks, "All he talked about on the way was defense issues. 'We have no politicians who can view these matters from a broad perspective. How foolish to provoke the Soviets by strengthening defense, to become so preoccupied with the percentage of GNP we spend on defense!'"[56]

Grand Chamberlain Irie Sukemasa died in 1983. The last two years of his diary record Hirohito's continuing uneasiness with problems in Japan–U.S. relations.

Another political issue that roiled the Japanese political scene during the early and mid–1980s was state protection for Yasukuni Shrine. Although Hirohito had stopped visiting Yasukuni after 1975, he did not object to public officials worshiping at the shrine where the souls of those who had died for him and Japan reposed. On the other hand he did not want to deepen domestic divisions over the issue of state support for Yasukuni. The same was true of most LDP politicians in the Diet. Anxious to retain the support of the Bereaved Families Association and the Association of Shinto Shrines, while also not alienating the opposition, they had tabled a "Yasukuni Shrine Protection Bill" five times between 1969 and 1974. On each occasion the bill was defeated after discussions with the opposition Socialist Party; and all involved breathed a sigh of relief. After 1978, when the Class A war criminals, executed for "crimes against humanity," were secretly enshrined at Yasukuni, the issue of furnishing state support for the Shinto institution became more controversial than ever. Moreover, this action made it virtually impossible for the image-conscious Hirohito ever again to visit the shrine which extols Japanese militarism and the "War of Greater East Asia."

Nakasone, like his precedessor Suzuki, hoped to effect a symbolic strengthening of ties with the past. Legalizing state support for Yasukuni Shrine and perpetuating the practice of cabinet ministers worshiping there were ways of accomplishing that goal. On August 15, 1985, Nakasone became the first postwar prime minister to worship at Yasukuni in his official capacity. His attempt to curry favor with conservative and right-wing constituencies by legitimizing official worship at Yasukuni provoked strong criticism within Japan. To minimize the significance of his action Nakasone declared that he had bowed only once instead of twice and clapped his hands only once instead of twice, thereby indicating that to visit a Shinto shrine was not necessarily to perform a religious act. But once the governments of South Korea and China added their voices to the criticism, Nakasone stopped worshiping there. Soon the issue waned, along with national support for a law authorizing state protection of Yasukuni.[57]

Given Hirohito's political concern to maintain amicable relations with China and Korea, he was probably relieved to see the Yasukuni Shrine bill shelved. It is doubtful, however, that Hirohito gave much thought to the ethical or constitutional dimensions of the problem. By this time, the Yasukuni War Museum had transformed the Asia-Pacific war symbolically by removing the emperor from nearly all Shōwa-era exhibits. Virtually all connection between him, emperor ideology, and the wars of the 1930s and early 1940s was effaced. Visitors could come and depart the museum without ever suspecting that Hirohito had once been the vital energizing leader of the war.

In Prime Minister Nakasone the elderly Hirohito found a leader with a clear position on the uses of the monarchy in an era when Japan had regained its status as a great power. Nakasone argued that power and authority had been separated in Japan since antiquity; hence the true form of the emperor was that of a "symbol" as specified in the constitution. However, Nakasone wanted to raise the emperor's status and enhance his authority, so that he could become the symbol of the "state" rather than of high economic growth, which he had been since the early 1960s. This he was unable to bring about. All Nakasone succeeded in doing, in the course of many speeches on the theme of state and emperor, was to revive the long-smoldering resentment of right-wing nationalists against the judgments of the Tokyo war crimes trial. Echoing earlier attacks on the trials by proponents of constitutional revision, Nakasone charged that the left-wing had been trying to impose a "Tokyo trials view of history" on the nation's youth. During his last month in office—while the United States and the Soviet Union reached agreement on intermediate range nuclear missiles—he reiterated his ideological position, calling for a "general settlement of accounts with the past" and a strengthening of the prime minister's powers.

When Nakasone stepped down, in late October 1987, Hirohito's life was drawing to its end. The Cold War, which had long been winding down, was almost over. Soon Japanese politicians would find it harder to practice their political double standard about the lost war. On September 18, 1987, the eighty-six-year-old emperor was reported to have an undisclosed intestinal disease. He was soon hospitalized for surgery, the first emperor to undergo such a procedure. The operation was successful but a year later, on September 19, 1988, he was gravely ill. Crown Prince Akihito was informed that his father had cancer; the press was left to speculate. The nation plunged into a mood of prolonged grieving. For one hundred and eleven days Japan raptly followed an old and dying emperor's temperature, blood pressure, and other vital signs. Long lines of Japanese citizens queued to pray for him and to sign official "get well" registers provided by government agencies. The condolence-wishers represented a small minority, and many signed because their company superiors did first. Yet it seemed as if the entire nation was in vigil.

While Hirohito lay dying in the inner recesses of the Fukiage Palace, the Japanese media censored itself on discussion of his and the monarchy's role in Japanese military aggression. Elsewhere, in Asia and Europe, media coverage concentrated almost exclusively on his war role, and the way Japanese officials avoided confronting that past. The stance of the Japanese toward Hirohito in his dying days, and the feelings of the rest of the world toward him could not have been more different.[58]

In early December 1988 a mood of calmness and detachment returned, moderating the excessive "self-restraint" that had descended on the entire nation when the news of Hirohito's illness was first disclosed. On the seventh, Nagasaki's Catholic mayor and LDP member, Motoshima Hitoshi, addressing the Nagasaki City Assembly, spoke matter-of-factly about the "war responsibility" of the dying emperor. His words, reported in the media, touched off a fury of rightist reaction. His own LDP turned against him. A year later a right-wing thug shot Motoshima, but the mayor survived.

Death came to Hirohito at 6:33 in the morning on January 7, 1989, with family members around him. The attending physicians, astonished at his tenacious will to live, attributed his stamina to the chaste, disciplined life he had led since youth. In the view of chief physician Tamaki Akira, the emperor was sustained by his belief in the power of spirit. At the end he simply refused to surrender.

Prime Minister Takeshita delivered the official eulogy. He reiterated two of the unrealities on which Japanese politics during the second half of the twentieth century had been based. "The great emperor," declared Takeshita, had always been a pacifist and constitutional monarch. For sixty-two turbulent years he "had prayed for world peace and the happiness of the Japanese nation," and every day he practiced what he preached. "Regarding the great war, which had broken out contrary to his wishes, when he could no longer bear to watch the nation suffering its evils, he made the heroic decision and, disregarding his own welfare, ended it."

Fifty-six-year-old Crown Prince Akihito took on his imperial duties the next day. A father with three grown children, Princes

Hiro and Aya and Princess Nori, he faced no such succession problem as Hirohito had. During a brief ceremony he declared his loyalty to the Constitution of Japan.

The new era of "Heisei" (achieved peace) began as East and West Germany finally united, the Cold War ended, and the Union of Soviet Socialist Republics—the world's largest empire—started to break up. Politics everywhere became more fluid. In Japan, a minor political crisis, triggered by the usual recurring corruption scandal, once again shook the political establishment. This time, for the first time in an upper house election (July 1989), the LDP went down to temporary defeat. In the course of a single year, three prime ministers came and three prime ministers went. Hirohito's funeral and the accession ceremonies for Akihito were held up by serious disputes among the ruling elites. Many months passed beyond the customary one year of national mourning before Emperor Akihito could begin his various enthronement ceremonies. Like that of the Shōwa emperor before him, the pageantry was all government-financed, but less elaborate this time and less hyped. The public looked on with pleasure, but few seemed moved by it.

The enthronement culminated in a ceremony staged in the palace on November 12, 1990. Some 2,500 dignitaries attended, fifteen hundred of them from 158 countries around the world. This was followed two weeks later by a "Great Food-Offering Ceremony" in the imperial palace garden, November 23, with 733 guests in attendance. Neither event was a gain or a favorable portent for Japanese democracy. At the enthronement the symbolism was medieval—sacred regalia, emperor seated on high, and servile prime minister standing below and looking humbly up. Even the thought of popular sovereignty was mocked.[59] The six-hour-long food offering was based on an imperial ordinance of 1909 that had nothing at all to do with the constitution of 1947. Nevertheless, Akihito's oath was to uphold that constitution.

The *daijōsai* religious ceremony revived state Shinto rituals based on the political culture of Meiji-era absolutism. In that sense it flouted the constitutional separation of politics and religion.[60] When criticism arose, spokesmen for the cabinet pointed out that the first religious act of the new reign did not require constitutional justfication. Akihito's installation ceremony had merely given him an opportunity to pray on behalf of his people; it had in no way transformed him into a living deity.[61] And in fact, the enthronement had been an incomplete Shinto ritual as compared with that of Shōwa. Nor had officials and journalists used this occasion to enhance his popularity.

In December 1990, when the imperial transition was over, and quickly forgotten, Emperor Akihito granted a press interview. Responding to questions about the lost war, he replied: "My generation has lived for a long time without war, and so I have had no occasion to reflect on the war."[62] His reply could have been voiced by Shōwa. Thereafter, although an annual birthday press conference became traditional, no more serious war questions would be asked.

Emperor Akihito and Empress Michiko soon resumed visits abroad. In October 1992, their visit to China, at the insistence of the Peking government, divided opinion at home about the value of "imperial house diplomacy." In August 1995, on the fiftieth anniversary of the surrender, they embarked on a less controversial "journey of condolence" to the cities of Hiroshima and Nagasaki, and the island of Okinawa. Thus apologizing only for the suffering caused by Japan's wartime past, Akihito avoided any acknowledgment of his father's war guilt.

As the twentieth century ended, although developments in Japan hinted that constitutional change might take place, it seemed unlikely that Akihito would ever be brought forward to lead the nation as dramatically as Meiji or as disastrously as Shōwa. His personality, abilities, education, and interests all seemed to rule out such a role. So too did the many problems still unresolved from World War II—problems inherent in the institution of the Japanese monarchy itself rather than in the particular occupant of the throne. Nonetheless, like Itō and the *genrō* with Meiji; and Kido, the militarists, and MacArthur with Shōwa, some future national leadership may rise and find effective ways to make use of the new monarch or his successors. Whether they will move the institution as their predecessors did—to prevent the deepening of democracy and growth in the popular sense of political empowerment—is a crucial issue for Japan in the new millennium.

NOTES

ABBREVIATIONS USED IN THE NOTES

FRUS   *Foreign Relations of the United States.* U.S. State Department documents pertaining to peace and war, from 1928 to 1941, and the Far East for 1944–54 (Washington, D.C.: USGPO).

Harada nikki Harada Kumao, *Saionji kō to seikyoku*, vols. 1–9 (Iwanami Shoten, 1950–56).

HSN   *Zoku gendaishi shiryō 4: rikugun, Hata Shunroku nisshi* (Misuzu Shobō, 1983). The diary of Hata Shunroku.

ISN   Irie Sukemasa, *Irie Sukemasa nikki*, vols. 1–6 (Asahi Shimbunsha, 1990–91). The diary of Irie Sukemasa.

Jō nikki Jō Eiichirō, *Jijūbukan, Jō Eiichirō nikki, Kindai Nihon shiryō sensho 4*, Nomura Minoru, ed. (Yamakawa Shuppansha, 1982). The diary of Jō Eiichirō.

KYN   *Shōwa shoki no tennō to kyūchū: jijūjichō Kawai Yahachi nikki*, vols. 1–6, Takahashi Hiroshi et al., eds. (Iwanami Shoten, 1993–94). The diary of Kawai Yahachi.

MNN   *Makino Nobuaki nikki.* Itō Takashi, Hirose Junkou, eds. (Chūō Kōronsha, 1990). The diary of Makino Nobuaki.

NH   Nakazono Hiroshi, "Seitō naikaku-ki ni okeru Shōwa tennō oyobi sokkin no sei-jiteki Kōdō to yakuwari: Tanaka naikaku o chūshin ni," master's thesis, Aoyama Gakuin Daigaku, Daigakuin, 1992.

Senshi sōsho Japan's official war history in 102 vols., ed. by Bōeichō Bōei Kenshūjo, Senshishitsu (Asagumo Shinbunsha, 1966–80); many documents on which it is based remain closed to the public.

TN   Takamatsu no miya Nobuhito Shinnō, *Takamatsu no miya nikki*, Vols. 1–8 (Chūō Kōronsha, 1997). The diary of Prince Takamatsu.

TWCT *The Tokyo War Crimes Trial: The Complete Transcripts of the Proceedings of the International Military Tribunal for the Far East*, edited by R. John Pritchard and Sonia Maganua Zaide (N. Y. & London: Garland, 1981). Vols. 8, 12, 13, 20, and 21 are cited in the notes.

STD   *Shōwa tennō dokuhakuroku, Terasaki Hidenari, goyōgakari nikki*, Terasaki Hidenari and Mariko Terasaki Miller, eds. (Bungei Shunjūsha, 1991).

INTRODUCTION

1. Adding to Hirohito's stress, by reminding him of the insecurity of monarchs in the wake of lost wars, were press reports on the forthcoming general election in Italy, which would determine not only the fate of his former Axis ally, the fascist King Victor Emmanuel III, but decide whether Italy itself would become a republic. See *Asahi shinbun*, Mar. 15, *Mainichi shinbun*, Mar. 21, and news reports thereafter until the abolition of the Italian monarchy and establishment of a republic following the general election on June 2, 1946.

2. See Higashino Shin, *Shōwa tennō futatsu no 'dokuhakuroku'* (NHK Shuppansha, 1998), p. 158, citing historian Yoshida Yutaka.

3. "Inada Shūichi 'Bibōroku' yori bassui," March 18, 1946, in Higashino Shin, pp. 224–25. Inada, the director of the Imperial Palace Records Bureau, probably made the original stenographic record from which all versions of the "Monologue" derive. The other participants were Hirohito's liaison and interpreter with GHQ, Terasaki Hidenari, Imperial Household Minister Matsudaira Yasumasa, Vice–Grand Chamberlain Kinoshita Michio, and Matsudaira Yoshitami.

4. Terasaki Hidenari and Mariko Terasaki Miller, eds., *Shōwa tennō dokuhakuroku—Terasaki Hidenari goyōgakari nikki* (Bungei Shunjūsha, 1991), p. 136. Cited hereafter as *STD*.

5. "Eigoban, 'Shōwa tennō dokuhakuroku' genbun," in Higashino Shin, p. 212. The original is untitled and undated. Internal evidence, analyzed by Higashino, suggests that it was drafted by Terasaki Hidenari about a week after the completion of the Japanese version of the "Monologue" and presented to Gen. Bonner F. Fellers, MacArthur's secretary, on or around April 23, 1946, the day Hirohito was scheduled to have (but at the last minute was forced to cancel) his second meeting with MacArthur.

6. No one knows the true dimensions of the human losses from World War II in Asia and the Pacific because accurate figures on war deaths were never really collected. It can be said with some certainty that China sustained the most casualties at the hand of Japan, including more than 10 million killed. The Philippines (according to official Filipino sources) suffered 1.1 million wartime deaths. Approximately 1.5 to 2 million Vietnamese died from war-related starvation. Official casualty estimates for Indonesia seem to have been buried (probably deliberately) within the figure of 4 million "forced laborers" put forward by Indonesian officials during reparations talks with Japan; famine was the main cause of their deaths. An estimated 150,000 Burmese, more than 100,000 Malaysians and residents of Singapore, 200,000 Koreans, and more than 30,000 residents of Taiwan died during or immediately after the war, including many from noncombat situations. There appear to be no official casualty figures for Pacific islanders, especially those who suffered in the jungle fighting in the Solomons and New Guinea. Australia suffered nearly 18,000 dead. More than 60,000 Allied soldiers, civilians, and prisoners of war were killed by the Japanese. Japan, the aggressor in Asia and the Pacific, suffered 3.1 million deaths, of which nearly one-third were noncombatant fatalities. Like Nazi Germany, Japan incurred gross human losses smaller than those it inflicted on some of the nations that were the objects of its aggression. Finally, huge as these Asian losses were, the European losses from the war were greater, especially in the Soviet Union, which did most of the fighting against Nazi Germany. See Otabe Yuji, Hayashi Hiroshi, and Yamada Akira, *Kiiwaado Nihon no sensō banzai* (Yuzankaku Shuppan, 1997), p. 54; for Soviet casualties, see John Erickson, "Soviet War Losses: Calculations and Controversies," in John Erickson and David Dilks, eds., *Barbarossa, the Axis and the Allies* (Edinburgh University Press, 1994), pp. 255–77.

7. Tadokoro Izumi, *Shōwa tennō no waka* (Sōjusha, 1997), p. 11.
8. On the tenth anniversary of Hirohito's death, the *Yomiuri shinbun* reported that the Imperial Household Agency had already spent over 97 million yen on the Shōwa annals project and "a further 12.74 million yen was budgeted for fiscal 1999." *Daily Yomiuri* (Jan. 8, 1999), p. 3.
9. Higashino Shin, p. 142. He identifies this as Record Group 331, Box 763.
10. Yasuda Hiroshi, *Tennō no seijishi: Mutsuhito, Yoshihito, Hirohito no jidai* (Aoki Shoten, 1998), p. 277.
11. An imperial household law, promulgated at the same time, blurred the distinction between the ancient customs and institutional practices of the imperial house and the many newly constructed ones of the Meiji era. Together with imperial ordinances, it formed a legal tradition entirely separate from parliamentary law based on the constitution. Yokota Kōichi, "'Kōshitsu tempan' shichū" in Yokota Kōichi et al., ed. *Shōchō tennōsei no kōzō: kenpō gakusha ni yoru kaidoku* (Nihon Hyōronsha, 1990), pp. 105–106.
12. Both the oligarchs and Emperor Meiji believed that the emperor's "right of supreme military command" did not require for its exercise the advice of any minister of state. From their viewpoint the essence of the Restoration was precisely the revival of the emperor's position as a military monarch.
13. Kimijima Kazuhiko, "Shokuminchi 'teikoku' e no michi," in Asada Kyōji, ed., *Kindai Nihon no kiseki 10, 'Teikoku' Nihon to Ajia* (Yoshikawa Kōbunkan, 1994), pp. 60–61. The fighting on Taiwan lasted for more than a decade and cost 9,592 Japanese combatant deaths.

CHAPTER 1 THE BOY, THE FAMILY, AND THE MEIJI LEGACIES

1. Kojima Noboru, *Tennō 1: wakaki shinnō* (Bungei Shunjūsha, 1980, 1989), p. 12.
2. Kawahara Toshiaki, *Tennō Hirohito no Shōwashi* (Bungei Shunjū, 1983), pp. 10–11; Hosaka Masayasu, *Chichibu no miyato Shōwa tennō* (Bungei Shunjū, 1989), p. 21; Nezu Masashi, *Tennō to Shōwashi, jō* (San Ichi Shinsha, 1988), p. 11.
3. Asukai Masamichi, *Meiji taitei* (Chikuma Raiburarii, 1989), p. 211.
4. In 1895 Emperor Mutsuhito allowed the German physician Erwin Baelz to begin treating Yoshihito for his various illnesses on a regular basis. See *Awakening Japan: The Diary of a German Doctor: Edwin Baelz* (Indiana University Press, 1974), pp. 105–6, 116, 167, 359–60, 376; Iwai Tadakuma, *Meiji tennō "taitei" densetsu* (Sanseidō, 1997), p. 139.
5. Tanaka Sōgorō, *Tennō no kenkyū* (San Ichi Shobō, 1974), p. 218.
6. Nezu, *Tennō to Shōwashi, jō*, p. 14.
7. Kawahara, *Tennō Hirohito no Shōwashi*, p. 14.
8. Hosaka, *Chichibu no miya to Shōwa tennō*, pp. 30–31.
9. Cited in Kawahara, *Tennō Hirohito no Shōwashi*, p. 30.
10. Hosaka, *Chichibu no miya to Shōwa tennō*, p. 26.
11. Suzuki Taka, "Kinjō Tennō, unmei no tanjō," in *Bungei Shunjū tokushūgō: tennō hakusho* (Oct. 1956), p. 74.
12. Takamatsu no miya Nobuhito Denki Kankō Iinkai, eds., *Takamatsu no miya Nobuhito shinnō* (Asahi Shinbunsha, 1991), p. 81.
13. Ibid., p. 72.
14. Togashi Junji, "Tennō hakusho: shirarezaru heika," in *Tennō no Shōwashi, Sandē Mainichi fukkokuban, kinkyū zōkan* (Feb.–April 1989), p. 88, citing Chichibu no miya, "Omoide no ki."
15. Zaidan Hōjin Chichibu no miya Kinenkai, ed., *Yasuhito shinnō jikki* (Yoshikawa Kōbunkan, 1972), p. 44.

16. *Twenty-Third Annual Statistics of the City of Tokyo* (Tokyo, 1927), p. 150; *Historical Statistics of Japan*, vol. 1 (Japan Statistical Association, 1987), p. 168.

17. Takashi Fujitani, *Splendid Monarchy: Power and Pagentry in Modern Japan* (University of California Press, 1996), pp. 128, 131; Iwai Tadakuma, *Meiji tennō "taitei" densetsu*, p. 156.

18. Watanabe Osamu, "Sengo seiji no nagare ni miru tennō to Nihon nashionarizumu no henyō," in Nihon Jyânarisuto Kaigi, ed., *Yameru masu komi to Nihon* (Kōbunkyū, 1995), pp. 98–99, 100.

19. Masuda Tomoko, "Tennō: kindai," in *Nihonshi daijiten, yonkan* (Heibonsha, 1994).

20. Itō removed the top of the military chain of command from the prime minister's jurisdiction and deliberately weakened the prime minister's powers in order to enhance the emperor's. He also strengthened the independent advisory authority of ministers of state and made cabinet decisions depend on unanimous consent rather than on simple majority vote. In the final stage of his constitution making, Itō established a privy council to deliberate on the constitution. Although Emperor Meiji actively participated in virtually all of its meetings, it is doubtful if he really understood the enormous political and military obligations he was foisting on himself—obligations that would fall with even greater weight on the shoulders of Hirohito. For details see Minobe Tatsukichi, *Chikujō kenpō seigi, zen* (Yūhikaku, 1931), p. 523; Sakano Junji, "Naikaku," in *Nihonshi daijiten, dai gokan* (Heibonsha, 1993), pp. 289–90; Masuda Tomoko, "Meiji rikken kunshusei ni okeru Sūmitsuin," in *Rekishi to chiri* 355 (March 1985), pp. 1–14; and Tanaka, *Tennō no kenkyū*, p. 168.

21. Mitani Taichirō, "The Establishment of Party Cabinets, 1898–1932," in Peter Duus, ed., *The Cambridge History of Japan*, vol. 6, *The Twentieth Century* (Cambridge University Press, 1988), pp. 55–86.

22. Iwai, *Meiji tennō "taitei" densetsu*, pp. 85–86.

23. Masuda, "Tennō: kindai," p. 1243.

24. Itō Hirobumi, *Commentary on the Constitution of the Empire of Japan* (1906; reprint, Greenwood Press, 1978), p. 7.

25. First used in an official document in 1881, *shinmin* became a legal term only in 1889. Until 1946, an unusually strong sense of "subjecthood" distinguished Japan from other nation-states. See Asukai, "Meiji tennō, 'kōtei' to 'tenshi' no aida: sekai rekkyō e no chōsen," in Nishikawa Nagao and Matsuya Hideharu, eds., *Bakumatsu, Meiji-ki no kokumin kokka keisei to bunka henyō* (Shinshōsha, 1995), p. 46.

26. For the text of the Education Rescript, see David J. Lu, *Sources of Japanese History*, vol. 2 (McGraw-Hill, 1974), pp. 70–71.

27. Asukai Masamichi, "Kindai tennōzō no tenkai," in Asao Naohiro et al., eds., *Iwanami kōza, Nihon tsūshi, kindai 2, dai 17 kan* (Iwanami Shoten, 1994), p. 246.

28. Ienaga Saburō, "Nihon no minshushugi," in Ienaga, ed., *Gendai Nihon shisō taikei 3, minshushugi* (Chikuma Shobō, 1965), pp. 24–25.

29. Yasuda Hiroshi, "The Modern Emperor System Before and After the Sino-Japanese War of 1894–95," in *Acta Asiatica: Bulletin of the Institute of Eastern Culture* 59 (Tōhō Gakkai, 1990), p. 57.

30. Wakamori Tarō, *Tennōsei no rekishi shinri* (Kōbundō, 1973), pp. 199–200.

31. Ishida Takeshi, *Meiji seiji shisōshi kenkyū* (Miraisha, 1954), chaps. 1, 2.

32. Quoted in Brian Victoria, *Zen at War* (Weatherhill, 1997), p. 44, citing Kashiwagi Ryūho, *Taigyaku jiken to Uchiyama Gudō* (JCA Shuppan, 1979), pp. 198–201. I have altered the translation slightly.

33. Masuda, "Meiji rikkensei to tennō," pp. 120–21.

34. Yasuda, *Tennō nō seijishi*, pp. 150–51.

35. Yoshida, "Nihon no guntai," in Asao Naohiro et al., eds., *Iwanami kōza, Nihon tsūshi, kindai 2, dai 17 kan*, p. 153.
36. Ōe Shinobu, p. 84; Yoshida, "Nihon no guntai," p. 154.
37. Yoshida, "Nihon no guntai," pp. 156–57.
38. Yi O Un Den Kankōkai, *Ei shinnō Yi Un denki* (Kyōei Shobō, 1978), pp. 78, 83, 89; Yoshida Kōichi, "Nihon no Kankoku tōji ni okeru Kankoku kōshitsu no sonzai." 1992 nendo Hitotsubashi daigaku, shakai gakubu, gakushi ronbun (January 1993, unpublished), pp. 28–31; and Chichibu no miya Kinenkai, *Yoshihito shinnō jiseki shiryō* (n.p., 1952), pp. 14–15. After Itō's assassination, Meiji's frequent audiences with Yi Un seem to have ended.
39. H. D. Harootunian, "Introduction," in B. S. Silberman and H. D. Harootunian, eds., *Japan in Crisis: Essays in Taisho Democracy* (Princeton University Press, 1974), pp. 6–7.
40. *Takamatsu no miya Nobuhito shinnō*, p. 68.
41. Fujiwara Akira, *Shōwa tennō no jūgonen sensō* (Aoki Shoten, 1991), p. 11.
42. Nezu, *Tennō to Shōwashi, jō*, p. 14.
43. Watanabe Osamu, *Sengo seiji shi no naka no tennōsei* (Aoki Shoten, 1990), p. 395.
44. Nagazumi Torahiko, *Shōwa tennō to watakushi* (Gakushū Kenkyūsha, 1992), p. 41. Starting in 1927 and continuing for the rest of his working life, Nagazumi served Hirohito as chamberlain, vice grand chamberlain, and chief ritualist.
45. Iwai, *Meiji tennō—"taitei" densetsu*, pp. 138–39.
46. Nezu, p.14; Kanroji Osanaga, *Sebiro no tennō* (Tōzai Bunmeisha, 1957), p. 57; Ōtake Shūichi, *Tennō no gakkō: Shōwa no teiōgaku to Takanawa ogakumonjo* (Bungei Shunjū, 1986), pp. 248–49.
47. Yoshida Yutaka, *Shōwa tennō no shūsenshi* (Iwanami Shinsho, 1992), p. 224.
48. Nagazumi, pp. 39–40; the prayer room was also used for purposes of admonishment.
49. Ogasawara notes Hirohito's visit in 1916 to the crematorium of Emperor Juntoku, who had been sent into exile on Sado for participating in the Shōkyū Disturbance of the early thirteenth century. See Ogasawara Naganari, "Sesshō no miya denka no gokōtoku," in *Taiyō* (Jan. 1, 1922), p. 5.
50. Suzuki Masayuki, *Kindai no tennō: Iwanami bukkuretto shiriizu, Nihon kindaishi 13* (Iwanami Shoten, 1992), p. 44.
51. Yoshida, pp. 223–24.
52. Ibid., p. 224.
53. That year Hirohito received Japan's highest award, the Grand Order of the Chrysanthemum, in the form of a little button. When Chichibu saw Hirohito in his special uniform with the button on it, he was jealous and said to him, "You're not that important. You don't even have the Order of the Golden Kite or a medal from a foreign country." The gentle rivalry and tension between the brothers would continue into their adulthood. See Togashi Junji, "Tennō hakusho: shirarezaru heika," p. 88.
54. Yasuda Hiroshi, "Kindai tennōsei ni okeru kenryoku to ken'i: Taishō demokurashii-ki no kōsatsu," in *Bunka hyōron*, No. 357 (Oct. 1990), p. 179.
55. Yasuda, *Tennō no seijishi*, p. 159.
56. Ibid., pp. 164–65.
57. Suzuki Masayuki, *Kōshitsu seido: Meiji kara sengo made* (Iwanami Shinsho, No. 289, 1993), p. 138; Mitani Taichirō, *Kindai Nihon no sensō to seiji* (Iwanami Shoten, 1997), p. 43.
58. Mitani Taichirō, "Taishō demokurashii to Washinton taisei, 1915–1930," in Hosoya Chihiro, ed., *Nichi-Bei kankei tsūshi* (Tokyo Daigaku Shuppankai, 1995), p. 78.
59. Hosaka, *Chichibu no miya to Shōwa tennō*, p. 46.
60. Yamaga Sokō's *Chūkō jijitsu* [True facts of the central realm], printed in 1669, extolled

Shinto teachings, asserted the innate superiority of the Japanese people, and claimed that Japan's early emperors had realized an ideal government. The other book was Miyake Kanran's *Chūkō kangen*. Notions of reverence for the Imperial House permeated both works. See *Takamatsu no miya Nobuhito*, p. 84.

61. Uchikawa Yoshimi et al., *Taishō nyūsu jiten, dai ikkan* (Mainichi Komyunikēshion Shuppan Jigyōbu, 1986), p. 621.

62. *Asahi shinbun*, Sept. 20, 1912, cited in *Taishō nyūsu jiten*, p. 629.

63. *Taishō nyūsu jiten, dai ikkan*, p. 620; Carol Gluck, *Japan's Modern Myths: Ideology in the Late Meiji Period* (Princeton University Press, 1985), p. 221.

64. Okada Kyūji, *Senjinkun to Nihon seishin* (Gunji Kyōiku Kenkyūkai, 1942), p. 320.

65. *Asahi shinbun*, Sept. 14, 1912.

66. *Shinano Mainichi shinbun*, Sept. 19 and 20, 1912, cited in *Taishō nyūsu jiten*, pp. 627–29.

67. *Asahi shinbun*, Sept. 15, 1912.

68. Tsurumi Shunsuke, Nakagawa Roppei, eds., *Tennō hyakuwa, jō* (Chikuma Shobō, 1989), pp. 58–59.

69. Tokoro Isao, "Shōwa tennō ga mananda 'kokushi' kyōkasho," *Bungei shunjū* (Feb. 1990), p. 131; Tanaka Hiromi, "Shōwa tennō no teiōgaku," *This Is Yomiuri* (Apr. 1992), pp. 87–106. Prince Chichibu embarked on an army career after graduating from the Peers' School; Prince Takamatsu pursued a naval career; Prince Mikasa graduated from the Army College in 1941.

70. The Ogakumonjo was located on the site of the Edo mansion of the Hosokawa daimyō, where in 1703 Ōishi Yoshio and sixteen others of the famous forty-seven *rōnin* of the Akō fiefdom were interred and committed suicide after they had avenged the death of their lord Asano. The incidents took place from 1701 to 1703 and were later dramatized for the puppet and Kabuki theaters.

71. On Capt. Alfred T. Mahan and Japan, see Walter LaFeber, *The Clash: A History of U.S.-Japan Relations* (W. W. Norton, 1997), p. 56; Anders Stephanson, *Manifest Destiny: American Expansionism and the Empire of Right* (Hill & Wang, 1995), pp. 84–87.

72. On Prince Fushimi, see Hata Ikuhiko, ed., *Nihon rikukaigun sōgō jiten* (Tokyo Daigaku Shuppankai, 1991), p. 228; Nomura Minoru, *Tennō, Fushimi no miya to Nihon kaigun* (Bungei Shunjū, 1988), p. 55.

73. On Ugaki see Hata, ed., *Nihon rikukaigun sōgō jiten*, p. 22; Inoue Kiyoshi, *Ugaki Kazushige* (Asahi Shinbunsha, 1975).

74. Nara Takeji, "Nara Takeji kaikoroku (sōan)," manuscript, pp. 298–99.

75. Anatol Rappaport, "Introduction" to Carl von Clausewitz, *On War* (Penguin Books, 1968), p. 28; C. L. Glaser and C. Kaufmann, "What Is the Offense-Defense Balance and Can We Measure It?" in *International Security* 22, no. 4 (Spring 1998), p. 54, n. 35, citing Edward N. Luttwak, *Strategy: The Logic of War and Peace* (Harvard University Press, 1987).

76. Yamada Akira, *Gunbi kakuchō no kindaishi: Nihongun no kakuchō to hōkai* (Yoshikawa Kōbunkan, 1997), pp. 37–40.

77. Nagazumi, p. 74.

78. Ibid., pp. 57–67.

79. Tanaka Hiromi, "Shōwa tennō no teiōgaku," in *This Is Yomiuri* (April 1992), pp. 97–100. Kojima, *Tennō, dai ikkan*, p. 85.

80. Both as regent and emperor, Hirohito bestowed gifts and accolades on the *kōzoku*, hosted them at his annual birthday dinner, and at New Year's celebrations received them in audience, allowing certain *kōzoku* to attend imperial lectures. Author's interview with Professor Yamashina (Asano) Yoshimasa, Tokyo, July 10, 1993; Tanaka

Nobumasa, *Dokyumento Shōwa tennō: dai ikkan shinryaku* (Ryokufū Shuppan, 1984), pp. 122–24. Tanaka has termed the *kōzoku* and *kazoku* "the imperial guard without weapons." For insight into the vanished world of the *kōzoku*, see Otabe Yūji, *Nashimoto no miya Itsuko-hi-no nikki: kōzokuhi no mita Meiji, Taishō, Shōwa* (Shōgakukan, 1991); on the *kazoku*, see Sakai Miiko, *Aru kazoku no Shōwashi* (Kōdansha, 1986).

81. Ihara Yoriaki, *Zōho kōshitsu jiten* (Toyamabō, 1938), p. 45.

82. During the 1930s "imperial family members accounted for 9 out of 134 army generals and 3 out of 77 navy admirals. Of this number, 5 of 17 field marshals and 3 of 11 fleet admirals were members of the imperial family. Ten military councillors were appointed from the imperial family, including one from the Korean Imperial House." See Sakamoto Yūichi, "Kōzoku gunjin no tanjō: kindai tennōsei no kakuritsu to kōzoku no gunjika," in Iwai Tadakuma, ed., *Kindai Nihon shakai to tennōsei* (Kashiwa Shobō, 1988), pp. 230–31.

83. Fujiwara Akira, "'Tennō no guntai' no rekishi to honshitsu," in *Kikan sensō sekinin kenkyū*, No. 11 (Spring 1996), p. 65.

84. *Yamato* was an ancient name for a clan (one of many) that by dint of martial prowess established the first state in ancient Japan.

85. Asano Kazuo, "Taishō-ki ni okeru rikugun shōkō no shakai ninshiki to rikugun no seishin kyōiku: *Kaikōsha kiji* no ronsetsu kiji no bunseki," in Nakamura Katsunori, ed., *Kindai Nihon seiji no shosō: jidai ni yoru tenkai to kōsatsu* (Keiō Tsūshin, 1989), p. 447.

86. Kōketsu Atsushi, "Tennō no guntai no tokushitsu: zangyaku kōi no rekishiteki haikei," in *Kikan sensō sekinin kenkyū* 8 (Summer 1995), p. 11.

87. Shibuno Junichi, "Taishō jūnen Kawasaki, Mitsubishi dai sōgi no bunken to kenkyū," *Rekishi to Kobe* (August 1967), p. 11.

88. Kurozawa Fumitaka, "Gunbu no 'Taishō demokurashii' ninshiki no ichidanmen," in Kindai Gaikōshi Kenkyūkai, ed., *Hendōki no Nihon gaikō to gunji: shiryō to kentō* (Hara Shobō, 1987), esp. pp. 55–56; Kataoka, "Shōwa shoki, Nihon rikugun e no shakaigakuteki apurōchi," pp. 19–21.

89. Kurozawa, p. 32.

90. Ibid., pp. 49–53. *Kaikōsha kiji* was published by Kaikōsha, the army officers' friendship and aid society. For discussion of its contents from a viewpoint contrary to Kurozawa's, see Asano Kazuo, "Taishōki ni okeru rikugun shōkō no shakai ninshiki to rikugun no seishin kyōiku," p. 443, n. 5.

91. Aizawa Seishisai, of the nationalist Mito school of neo-Confucian thinkers, published *Shinron* (The new theses) in 1825. It contains the line: "Sacred integration between gods and men characterized this form of military organization." Similar arguments could be found in the popular *Nihon gaishi* (Unofficial history of Japan), completed in 1827 by the Kyoto historian Rai San'yō, and in the thought of "men of spirit" who, in the 1860s, powered the movement to "revere the emperor and expel the barbarian." See Bob T. Wakabayashi, *Anti-Foreignism and Western Learning in Early Modern Japan: The New Theses of 1825* (Harvard University Press, 1986), p. 174; Fujiwara, *Shōwa tennō no jūgonen sensō*, pp. 11, 18.

92. The idea that the emperor directly commanded the military and supervised its affairs was related to the dominant belief behind the Meiji restoration—the restoration of direct imperial rule—and therefore integral to the very notion of a *tennō* whom the Ogakumonjo sought to inculcate. See Fujiwara, "Tōsuiken to tennō," pp. 197–98.

93. Kōketsu, "Tennō no guntai no tokushitsu," pp. 9–10.

94. Kazuko Tsurumi, *Social Change and the Individual: Japan Before and After Defeat in World War II* (Princeton University Press, 1970), pp. 92–93.

95. Kataoka Tetsuya, "Shōwa shoki, Nihon rikugun e no shakaigakuteki apurōchi," in *Gunji shigaku* 22, no. 4 (1987): p. 16.

CHAPTER 2
CULTIVATING AN EMPEROR

1. Fujiwara Akira, "Tōsuiken to tennō," in Tōyama Shigeki, ed., *Kindai tennōsei no tenkai: kindai tennōsei no kenkyū II* (Iwanami Shoten, 1987), p. 199.
2. Yasumaru Yoshio, *Kindai tennōzō no keisei* (Iwanami Shoten, 1991), pp. 12–13.
3. Togashi Junji, "Tennō hakusho: shirarezaru heika," in *Tennō no Shōwashi, Sandē Mainichi fukkokuban, kinkyū zōkan* (Feb.-Apr. 1989), p. 89.
4. Ōtake Shūichi, *Tennō no gakkō: Shōwa no teiōgaku to Takanawa Ogakumonjo*, p. 29.
5. Saeki Shinkō, "Seibutsugaku to arahitogami no hazama," in *Bungei shunjū, tokushūgō: ōinaru Shōwa* (Mar. 1989), p. 490.
6. Kawahara, *Tennō Hirohito no Shōwashi*, p. 41.
7. Between 1953 and 1989 the Imperial Household Biological Laboratory published many other works bearing the inscription, "Collected by His Majesty the Emperor of Japan" and "described by" or "annotated by" others. Occasionally Hirohito "wrote" prefaces to his biological works that were transcribed by chamberlains and given to publishers. Typically they began with the words, "I, availing myself of the leisure time spared from my duties . . . " Itō Kenji. "The Shōwa Emperor Hirohito's Marine Biological Research," p. 8. Seminar paper, Harvard University, May 15, 1997.
8. Collective authorship—a normal scientific practice—may have signified, in Hirohito's case, continuity with the prewar mindset of protecting the emperor from the buffeting criticism of fellow scientists in case any errors had inadvertently crept into his work. This is suggested by Itō, "The Shōwa Emperor Hirohito's Marine Biological Research."
9. *Sandē Mainichi*, Oct. 1949, p. 5; "Kagakusha tennō [Hirohito] no seitai," in *Shinsō*, No. 36 (Dec. 1, 1949), p. 9; Komae Hisashi, "Heika to seibutsugaku," in *Tennō no inshō* (Sōgensha, 1949), pp. 150–64.
10. Kenneth B. Pyle, "Meiji Conservatism," in Marius B. Jansen, ed., *The Cambridge History of Japan*, vol. 5, *The Nineteenth Century* (Cambridge University Press, 1989), p. 692.
11. In 1935, at the height of the dispute over Minobe's "emperor organ theory," members of the court entourage openly discussed, in Hirohito's presence, the whole issue of the legitimate line of succession. At that time the emperor reportedly said to his chief aide, Gen. Honjō Shigeru: "I think the decision as to the legitimate line of succession requires further study. Actually, I too am from the northern bloodline of descent. Of course, generally speaking, it doesn't make any difference, though it is odd." Cited in Yoshida, *Shōwa tennō no shūsenshi*, p. 222.
12. Nezu, *Tennō to Shōwashi, jō*, p. 15.
13. Igari Shizan, "Teiō rinri shinkō no Sugiura Jūgō sensei," in *Kingu* (Dec. 1928), pp. 124–25.
14. Sugiura Shigetake, *Rinri goshinkō sōan*, ed. Igari Matazō (Tokyo, privately printed, 1936), p. 1103.
15. Ibid., p. 1105.
16. Ibid., p. 1106.
17. Nezu, *Tennō to Shōwashi, jō*, p. 15. Nezu did not allow for the possibility that Sugiura's single lecture on the Meiji constitution may also have indicated that other tutors had more responsibility for lecturing on the constitution. The Boshin Edict, issued after the Russo-Japanese War, called on the Japanese people to be frugal, upright, and

attentive to duty, while the Imperial Rescript to Soldiers and Sailors taught them to offer their lives for the emperor and blindly obey the orders of superior officers as though they were the orders of the emperor.

18. Nezu, *Tennō to Shōwashi, jō*, p. 16.

19. A speech by Professor Miura Shūkō, published in the Osaka *Mainichi shinbun* on July 31, 1912, is believed to contain the earliest expression of the term "Meiji the Great." Miura cited Meiji's abolition of military house politics, his establishment of direct imperial rule, and his transformation of a small island nation into a great empire as his main achievements. A key text that helped spread the myth of "Meiji the great" was the special, book-length supplement to the popular magazine *Kingu*, which appeared in late 1927. The "foreword," by Education Minister Mizuno Rentarō, boasted that "no other country in the world . . . has a national polity in which the imperial line has been unbroken for ages eternal and the emperor becomes one with the gods at the time of his enthronement." Inumaru, "Kindai tennōsei, jō," *Bunka hyōron* 385 (Feb. 1993), p. 129.

20. Sugiura Shigetake, *Rinri goshinkō sōan*.

21. Ibid., pp. 1055–61. Wilhelm II, an emotionally unstable monarch who had recently aspired to be the dictator of Europe, resided in exile in the Netherlands. As a political and symbolic leader, he personified not only the forces of his times but the historic weaknesses of the German people: their glorified, megalomaniacal image of themselves as a people who deserved to rule all of Europe, their deep insecurities, and their radical anti-Semitism. (See Thomas A. Kohut, *Wilhelm II and the Germans: A Study in Leadership* [Oxford University Press, 1991], p. 178.)

22. Ibid., pp. 958–64.

23. Ibid., p. 122.

24. Ibid., p. 581.

25. Ibid., p. 881. Anti-Japanese racial discrimination was particularly strong in the United States and its Territory of Hawaii, where Japanese were denied the right to be naturalized or to own land.

26. Ibid., p. 884.

27. Herbert P. Bix, *Peasant Protest in Japan, 1590–1884* (Yale University Press, 1986), pp. 81, 112, 175.

28. Ibid., p. 887.

29. Nezu, *Tennō to Shōwashi, jō*, p. 16. Nezu writes: "It would have been a miracle if, after having received in his young mind for seven years this sort of education, [Hirohito] had not become a militarist. Only a person like Sugiura would have had the courage to give this sort of conservative education in an age of rising democracy."

30. Shiratori Kurakichi, "Shina kodensetsu no kenkyū," in *Tōyō jihō* 131 (Aug. 1909), pp. 38–44.

31. Tokoro Isao, "Shōwa tennō ga mananda 'kokushi' kyōkasho," in *Bungei shunjū* (Feb. 1990), p. 133. My next few paragraphs mainly summarize Tokoro's very useful account.

32. Shiratori Kurakichi, *Kokushi, dai ikkan* (n.p., 1914), pp. 6–7. I am indebted to Professor Tokoro for a copy of volume 1.

33. Iwai Tadakuma, *Meiji tennō "taitei" densetsu* (Sanseidō, 1997), p. 47.

34. Shiratori, *Kokushi, dai ikkan*, p. 26; cited in Tokoro, p. 134.

35. Shiratori, *Kokushi, dai ikkan*, p. 28.

36. In 1928–29, Shiratori acknowledged indirectly that the power of myth to legitimate the political order had weakened, and the national ideology had to be reformulated to place it on a more rational basis. See his lectures published in the organ of the Navy Officers Association: "Nihon minzoku no keitō," *Yūshū* 15, no. 178 (Sept. 1928), and "Kōdō ni tsuite," *Yūshū* 16, no. 190 (Sept. 1929).

37. Tokoro, "Shōwa tennō ga mananda 'kokushi' kyōkasho," p. 140.
38. Ibid., p. 136.
39. H. Paul Varley, "Nanbokucho seijun ron," in *Kodansha Encyclopedia of Japan*, vol. 5 (Kodansha Ltd., 1983), pp. 323–24.
40. Tokoro, "Shōwa tennō ga mananda 'kokushi' kyōkasho."
41. Shiratori Kurakichi, *Kinsen "Kokushi"* (Benseisha, 1997), pp. 711–713.
42. Tokoro, "Shōwa tennō ga mananda 'kokushi' kyōkasho," p. 136.
43. Tokoro has argued that Sugiura used historical materials and interpreted them "deductively," whereas Shiratori's aim in the *Kokushi* was to explain the process of development of Japanese history "inductively." Shiratori's textbook simply recorded the circumstances of the succession to the throne and how many emperors worked hard and tried to promote the happiness of the people. Tokoro believes it is historically "precise and fair," sometimes pointing out defects and shortcomings in the rule of different emperors. He compares the *Kokushi* to Kitabatake Chikafusa's *Jinnō shōtōki* of 1339, but does not use Kitabatake to explicate Shiratori. His comparison is essentially rhetorical, designed to drive home his point that Shiratori's *Kokushi* still has "persuasive power" and "may be called a modern version of the *Jinnō shōtōki*." See Tokoro, "Shōwa tennō ga mananda 'kokushi' kyōkasho," p. 140.
44. Iwai, *Meiji tennō "taitei" densetsu*, p. 5.
45. Nagazumi, *Shōwa tennō to watakushi*, p. 76.
46. Suzuki Yasuzō, *Nihon no kenpōgakushi kenkyū* (Keisō Shobō, 1975), p. 260.
47. Ibid., pp. 261–62.
48. Quoted in ibid., p. 263.
49. A typical example is Konoe Atsumaro, "Kunshu musekinin no riyū," in *Kokka gakkai zasshi* 5, no. 55 (1892), pp. 1224–31.
50. Minobe Tatsukichi, *Chikujō kenpō seigi* (Yūhikaku, 1927), p. 512, cited in Yamauchi Toshihiro, "Tennō no sensō sekinin," in Yokota Kōichirō, Ebashi Takashi, eds., *Shōchō tennōsei no kozō: kenpō gakusha ni yoru kaidoku* (Nihon Hyōronsha, 1990), p. 247.
51. Shimizu expressed the relationship between the emperor and the state in terms of an organic—brain/body—metaphor, but also added that "there is no contradiction between saying that the state is an entity which possesses the right of sovereignty and, at the same time, the emperor is the subject of sovereignty. Unless one reasons this way, one cannot explain the Japanese national polity." Quoted by Suzuki (*Nihon no kenpōgakushi kenkyū*, p. 266) from Shimizu Tōru, *Kokuhōgaku dai ippen kenpōhen*, p. 21.
52. From 1885, when the cabinet system was established, until 1945, no Japanese prime minister ever ran for the Diet, and only three—Hara Kei, Hamaguchi Osachi, and Inukai Tsuyoshi—had been elected to the House of Representatives. Prime ministers did not lead the majority of the House, though they were tacitly accepted by it. The *genrō* chose the prime minister; later, at the start of his reign, Hirohito and his court group became the appointers, taking into account, when it served their purposes, the preferences of the majority conservative party in the lower house, but just as often ignoring them. Thus imperial Japan had a "party cabinet" system of government rather than a parliamentary cabinet government. This is not to imply either that the Westminster model of parliamentary cabinet government worked democratically in the interwar decades. Neither Lloyd George nor Ramsay MacDonald were leaders of the majority party of their governments, but the distinction between the Japanese party setup and the British model of parliamentary government is useful and worth making.

CHAPTER 3
CONFRONTING THE REAL WORLD

1. On May 28, 1919, Foreign Minister Uchida Kōsai cabled the Japanese ambassador in Paris that the kaiser's trial would have a negative influence "on popular beliefs concerning our *kokutai*." Afterward Makino joined Wilson and Lansing in opposing the trial of Wilhelm II. See Uchida to Matsui, May 28, 1919, in *Nihon gaikō bunsho, dai san satsu, gekan, 1919* (Gaimushō, 1971), p. 1078.

2. *Tokyo nichi nichi shinbun*, May 8, 1919.

3. Quoted from Tanaka Hiromi, "Shōwa tennō no teiōgaku," in *This Is Yomiuri* (Apr. 1992), pp. 101–2. Tanaka termed these congratulatory accounts a "report card."

4. Ibid., p. 102; Hatano Masaru, "Taishō jūnen Kōtaishi hō-Ō: sono kettei e no purosesu to seika," in *Keiō Gijuku Daigaku Hōgaku kenkyū* 66, no. 7 (July 1993). Miura Gorō had won notoriety as the head of the Japanese legation in Seoul. He was implicated in the murder of Korea's Queen Min in 1895.

5. Nara Takeji, diary, pp. 292–94; Tanaka Hiromi, p. 102. I am indebted to Professor Tanaka for a copy of this portion of the Nara diary.

6. Quoted from the Nara diary, p. 294.

7. The talking habit increased over time and is discussed in many memoir sources, including Okabe Nagaakira, one of twelve chamberlains who served Hirohito from March 1936 to April 1946. See Okabe Nagaakira, *Gekidō jidai no Shōwa tennō: aru jijū no kaisōki* (Asahi Sonorama, 1990), pp. 97–99.

8. Makino's diary entry of Oct. 28, 1926, furnishes a good example of Hirohito's taciturnity:

> I visited Prince Saionji as promised, and he told me that he had an audience the other day with the prince. He told him that he was getting old and worried about the future. Hereafter you question the privy seal if there is political strife or change. Even after I am gone, question him chiefly. If the privy seal needs to seek other opinions or consult with others, he will ask you for permission to do so; you should grant it so that he can question them. . . . Saionji added that . . . the prince didn't reply, but of course he expected that.

MNN, pp. 261–62.

9. The novelist Ōe Kenzaburō remembered the strange dread that came over him when, as a little boy, he laughed on hearing Hirohito's voice for the first time on the day Japan capitulated:

> We didn't understand what he was talking about, but we certainly heard his voice. One of my playmates, wearing dirty short pants, was able to skillfully mimic it. We all laughed loudly as he spoke in the "emperor's voice."
> Our laughter rang through the quiet mountain village at high noon on a summer day and vanished with an echo into the blue sky. Suddenly a feeling of anxiety, of having committed a sin, gripped us disrespectful children. Falling silent, we stared at one another. Even for mere grammar school students, the emperor was an august and overwhelming presence.

Ōe Kenzaburō, "Tennō," *Shūkan Asahi* (Jan. 4, 1959), p. 30. For a fuller account of the different ways the Japanese people received Hirohito's voice on the day of the famous broadcast, see Takeyama Akiko, *Gyokuon hōsō* (Banseisha, 1989), pp. 53–54.

10. After 1927 the Photography Department of the Imperial Household Ministry banned the taking of pictures that showed the upper half of Hirohito's body or his

back (he had a slight curvature). Thereafter he was typically photographed with an unsmiling expression, standing motionless or at ramrod attention, his arms straight down at his sides. Nakayama Toshiaki, *Noriko hi no migite: "okaminaoshi" shashin jiken* (K. K. Jōhō Sentaa Shuppan Kyoku, 1992), p. 104.

11. Watanabe Ikujirō, *Meiji tennō no goseitoku to gunji* as cited in Fujiwara Akira, *Shōwa tennō no jūgonen sensō* (Aoki Shoten, 1991), p. 46.

12. Nezu, *Tennō to Shōwashi*, p. 20.

13. Tanaka Hiromi, "Shōwa tennō no teiōgaku," pp. 101–2; and Tanaka Hiromi, "Nisshin, Nichi-Ro kaisenshi no hensan to Ogasawara Naganari (2)," in *Gunji shigaku* 18, no. 4 (1983), pp. 43–44. Ogasawara was a prodigious literary creator of paragons of military virtue such as "Commander Hirose" of Japanese textbook fame and "Tōgō Heihachirō the Great."

14. According to Ogasawara, "All his essays on politics are particularly deeply moving. His brightness is almost unbelievable.... Once, when Sugiura was giving a lecture on apothegems, he asked the crown prince which saying most impressed him and [Hirohito] answered: 'Ten ni shifuku nashi' [Heaven has no self-interest]." Ogasawara Naganari, "Sesshō no miya denka no gokōtoku," *Taiyō* (Jan. 1, 1922).

15. *MNN*, pp. 21–23. Makino was shown the composition by Sugiura, and reproduced it in his diary entry of August 17, 1921. This is a rare example of an early piece by Hirohito, and also one of the relatively few instances in which he makes a reference to his own father. Another reference to his father can be found in the Honjō diary.

16. Yasuda Hiroshi, "Kindai tennōsei ni okeru kenryoku to ken'i—Taishō demokurashii-ki no kōsatsu," in *Bunka hyōron* 357 (Oct. 1990), p. 183.

17. Nearly 20 percent of all lèse majesté incidents in the early 1920s involved loose talk and symbolic desecrations of the imperial photograph. Common offenses included the cutting up of newspaper pictures of the emperor; the use, for unspecified, improper purposes, of the special sections on the imperial house; destruction of material objects, artifacts, and facilities that symbolized the emperor. Regardless of the motivation behind criticism of the throne, the government treated all acts of disrespect as crimes of lèse-majesté. See Watanabe Osamu, "Tennōsei kokka chitsujo no rekishiteki kenkyū josetsu," pp. 252, 258–61.

18. Ibid., p. 253.

19. Yasuda, "Kindai tennōsei ni okeru kenryoku to ken'i—Taishō demokurashii-ki no kōsatsu," p. 183.

20. Hara Kei, *Hara Kei nikki, dai hakkan* (Kangensha, 1950), pp. 46–47; cited in Suzuki Masayuki, "Taishō demokurashii to kokutai mondai," in *Nihonshi kenkyū* 281 (Jan. 1986), p. 56, from a different edition of the same diary (*dai gokan*).

21. Kuroda Hisata, *Tennōke no zaisan* (San Ichi Shobō, 1966), p. 133.

22. Gotō Yasushi, "Tennōsei kenkyū to teishitsu tōkeisho," in *Teishitsu tōkeisho 1, Meiji 32 nendohan* (Kashiwa Shobō, 1993), p. 3.

23. Watanabe Katsuo, "Kyūchū bōjūdai jiken no zenbō," in *This Is Yomiuri* (Apr. 1993), p. 70. My own interpretation departs from Watanabe's in significant ways. For an older version of the incident, see George M. Wilson, *Radical Nationalist in Japan: Kita Ikki 1883–1937* (Harvard University Press, 1969), pp. 100–101.

24. Watanabe, "Kyūchū bōjūdai jiken no zenbō," p. 81.

25. On pan-Asianism, see John Welfield, *An Empire in Eclipse: Japan in the Postwar American Alliance System* (Athlone Press, 1988), pp. 8–10.

26. Ibid., pp. 108–9.

27. Takahashi Hidenari, "Hara Kei naikakuka no gikai," in Uchida Kenzō et al., eds., *Nihon gikaishi roku 2* (Dai Ichi Hōki Shuppan K. K., 1990), p. 251.

28. Takahashi, "Hara Kei naikakuka no gikai," p. 250.

29. Fujiwara Akira, "Dai Nihon teikoku kenpō to tennō," in Fujiwara et al., *Tennō no Shōwa-shi* (Shin Nihon Shinsho, 1984, 1990), p. 32. The connection between the imperial court and right-wing extremists and gangsters antedates the Meiji period and can be traced back to the influence of the Shinto revivalists on the court nobility at Kyoto.

30. "Every four or five days Kita visited Ogasawara and furnished him with various kinds of information. Sometimes Kita cried in front of Ogasawara and Ogasawara comforted him." Tanaka Hiromi, "Shōwa shichinen zengo ni okeru Tōgō guruupu no katsudō: Ogasawara Naganari nikki o tōshite (1)," manuscript, p. 15, n. 4.

31. Ibid., pp. 1–10.

32. Hatano Masaru, "Taishō jūnen kōtaishi hō-Ō: sono kettei e no purosesu to seika," in *Keiō Gijuku Daigaku, Hōgaku Kenkyūkai, hen, Hōgaku kenkyū* 66, no. 7 (July 1989), p. 48.

33. Hata Nagami, "Makino Nobuaki kankei bunsho: kyūchū gurūpu o chūshin toshite," in *Shien* 43, no. 1 (May 1983), pp. 69–70.

34. *MNN*, p. 751. During the Feb. 1936 army uprising, Makino held the post of "economic consultant" to the Imperial Household Ministry.

35. *ISN.*

36. Suzuki, "Taishō demokurashii to kokutai mondai," pp. 57–58; Hatano, "Taishō jūnen kōtaishi hō-Ō: sono kettei e no purosesu to seika," p. 57.

37. *Hara Kei nikki, dai hakkan*, pp. 555–56; *dai kyūkan*, pp. 95–96, 111; cited in Suzuki, "Taishō demokurashii to kokutai mondai," p. 58.

38. *Hara nikki, dai kyūkan*, entry of Oct. 28, 1920, p. 118; Suzuki, "Taishō demokurashii to kokutai mondai," p. 59.

39. Quoted in Sasaki Ryūji, *Gendai tennōsei no kigen to kinō* (Shōwa Shuppan, 1990), p. 88.

40. *Hara Kei nikki, dai kyūkan*, p. 149, entry of Dec. 8, 1920; Suzuki, "Taishō demokurashii to kokutai mondai," p. 59.

41. On Dec. 11, 1920, while pleading with Yamagata not to resign his presidency of the privy council, Hara observed that the regency was of vital importance because "[t]he third generation is crucial for both the imperial family and the families of subjects. The Tokugawa family established itself through Iemitsu, the third shogun. Although Germany failed, the third emperor brought it to the height of its prosperity." The notion that dynastic lineages ossify quickly after a certain length of time is of ancient origin and can be found in many civilizations.

42. Suzuki, "Taishō demokurashii to kokutai mondai," pp. 59–60.

43. *Hara nikki, dai kyūkan*, p. 118; cited in ibid., p. 59.

44. Telegram from Shidehara to Foreign Minister Uchida, as cited in Hatano Masaru, "Taishō jūnen kōtaishi hō-Ō: sono kettei e no purosesu to seika," in *Keiō Gijuku Daigaku Hōgaku kenkyū* (July 1993), p. 47; see also Kisaka Junichirō, "Minshū ishiki no henka to shihai taisei no dōyō," in Fujiwara Akira, ed., *Minshū no rekishi 8, Dan'atsu no arashi no naka de* (Sanseidō, 1975), p. 76.

45. Hatano Masaru, *Hirohito kōtaishi Yōroppa gaiyūki* (Sōshisha, 1998), p. 59.

46. On Hara's accompanying the party to Yokohama, then leading the farewell cheers aboard the *Katori*, see Itō Yukio, "Hara Kei naikaku to rikken kunshusei (3)," in *Hōgaku ronsō* 143, no. 6 (Sept. 1998), pp. 8–9.

47. *Osaka Mainichi* (*yūkan*), Mar. 13, 1921, in *Taishō nyūsu jiten, dai gokan* (Mainichi Komunikēsionzu, 1988), pp. 229–30.

48. The description of the Western tour in this and the next three paragraphs is based largely on "Nara Takeji kaisōroku (sōan)," draft.

49. Hatano, *Hirohito kōtaishi Yōroppa gaiyūki*, p. 119.

50. Itō, "Hara Kei naikaku to rikken kunshusei (3)," p. 9.

51. Kisaka Junichirō, "Minshū ishiki no henka to shihai taisei no dōyō," in Fujiwara Akira, ed., *Minshū no rekishi 8, Dan'atsu no arashi no naka de* (Sanseidō, 1975), p. 76.

52. Ibid., p. 77.

53. Ibid.

54. Itō, "Hara Kei naikaku to rikken kunshusei (3)," p. 10.

55. Nagura Bunichi, "Eikoku inshō danpen," in *Shin shōsetsu* (Apr. 1922), pp. 63, 64–65.

56. Mitearai Tatsuo, "Denka oyobi Nihon no eta tokoro: kōshitsu to kokumin no kankei ni isshin kigen," in *Shin shōsetsu* (Apr. 1922), p. 65.

57. Mitearai, pp. 65–67. He went on to say that "the day after our arrival in Windsor . . . the whole city turned out in force and shouted, 'Hurrah! Hirohito.'"

58. *Hara Kei nikki, dai kyūkan*, p. 357; Suzuki, "Taishō demokurashii to kokutai mondai," p. 60.

59. The *Katori* returned on Sept. 2, one day ahead of schedule, forcing Hirohito to stay aboard ship because the official welcome had been prepared for the third. See ibid.

60. *Hara Kei nikki, dai kyūkan*, Sept. 19, 1921, p. 445.

61. Ibid., p. 452, entry of Sept. 21; cited in Suzuki, *Kōshitsu seido*, pp. 150–51.

62. "Nara Takeji kaisōroku (sōan)," p. 319.

63. *MNN*, p. 26.

64. Ibid., p. 65. *Kannamesai*, held annually on Oct. 17, was the ritual exercise of offering the new grain crops to Amaterasu Ōmikami.

65. On Chinda's indebtedness to the Meiji emperor and his keen sense of responsibility for nurturing the virtues of Hirohito, see Kusazawa Gakutō, "Chinda Sutemi," *Gendai* (June 1, 1927), p. 291.

66. Kojima Noboru cites the alleged deathbed comment of Empress Nagako's father, Prince Kuni no miya Kuniyoshi, uttered on Jan. 27, 1929. "The present emperor has in him a weakness of the will; he needs the empress's assistance. Do your best; do your best." One can only wonder how many other court officials during the 1920s thought Hirohito had a weak will. See Kojima, *Tennō, dai nikan* (Bungei Shunjū, 1974), p. 56.

67. Sasaki, *Gendai tennōsei no kigen to kinō*, p. 86.

68. Harold Nicolson, *King George V: His Life and Reign* (London: Constable & Co. Ltd., 1952), pp. 141–42.

69. Ibid., p. 252.

70. Sasaki, *Gendai tennōsei no kigen to kinō*, p. 87.

71. James F. Willis, *Prologue to Nuremberg: The Politics and Diplomacy of Punishing War Criminals of the First World War* (Greenwood Press, 1982), p. 103.

72. Sasaki, *Gendai tennōsei no kigen to kinō*, p. 87.

73. Ibid., p. 88.

74. The tour could not compensate for Hirohito's isolated upbringing, or teach him to conceive freedom as also meaning relief from toil and scarcity of goods. Nor did his sudden encounter with Western living in Europe lead him to espouse the modern ideal of freedom as being true to oneself.

75. Sasaki, *Gendai tennōsei no kigen to kinō*, p. 86.

76. Ibid., p. 89.

77. Ilse Hayden, *Symbol and Privilege: The Ritual Context of British Royalty* (University of Arizona Press, 1987), p. 45.

78. "Nara Takeji kaisōroku (sōan)," pp. 318–19.

79. Ibid., pp. 319–20.

80. On Hara's assassination, see Gotō Takeo, "Kōtaishi no gaiyū o habamu mono," in

Bungei shunjū tokushūgō, tennō hakusho (Oct. 1956), pp. 96–97; *Tokyo nichi nichi shinbun*, Nov. 5, 1921, in *Taishō nyūsu jiten, dai gokan*, p. 567.
81. *MNN*, p. 34, entry of Nov. 5, 1921.

CHAPTER 4
THE REGENCY AND THE CRISIS OF TAISHŌ DEMOCRACY

1. Yasuda, *Tennō no seijishi*, p. 196.
2. "Nara Takeji kaisōroku (sōan)," p. 329.
3. Makino's entry of Aug. 23, 1921, notes: "Yesterday the chief military aide-de-camp visited me and said, 'I think it's necessary to devise a method for him to learn political affairs following his return.' I agreed emphatically . . . and told him to study the matter." *MNN*, p. 25.
4. Regular lectures are mentioned in Nagazumi, *Shōwa tennō to watakushi*, pp. 109–11.
5. Other lecturers during the 1920s included Hirohito's teacher of Japanese literature, Professor Haga Yaichi; a Professor Toribe, who taught Chinese literature; Professor Katō Shigeru, who lectured on Chinese history and philosophy; Yamamoto Shinjirō, Hirohito's translator and teacher of French; and the right-wing constitutional scholar Kakei Katsuhiko.
6. Shimizu Tōru, "Kenpō to kōshitsu tenpan o goshinkō mōshiagete," in *Jitsugyō no Nihon zōkan: gotaiten kinen shashingō* (Nov. 1928), pp. 20–21.
7. *MNN*, pp. 109–10.
8. *KYN, dai ikkan* (Iwanami Shoten, 1993), p. 49; *MNN*, p. 263.
9. *KYN, dai ikkan*, pp. 115, 142, 152, 219, 252, 260; *dai nikan*, p. 32.
10. *KYN, dai ikkan*, p. 55.
11. Ibid., pp. 79–80, 85, 87.
12. Shinohara Hatsue, "An Intellectual Foundation for the Road to Pearl Harbor: Quincy Wright and Tachi Sakutarō." Paper presented at the Conference on the United States and Japan in World War II, Hofstra University, Dec. 1991, p. 3. The material in this and the next paragraph comes from Ms. Shinohara's helpful paper.
13. Tachi's massive study of international law was published in two parts—peacetime law and wartime law—in 1930–31. Kawai Yahachi's earliest diary entries on Tachi occur on Sept. 30 and Oct. 14, 1926. See *KYN, dai ikkan*, pp. 31, 36.
14. *KYN, dai gokan*, p. 16, entry of Jan. 29, 1931.
15. Makino believed that Hirohito's participation in military exercises was useful for instructing both himself and the emperor in the politics of war expenditures. Hirohito's partiality for navy leaders such as Adms. Suzuki Kantarō and Okada Keisuke may have reflected Makino's influence. See *MNN*, pp. 289–91, where he discusses Hirohito's and his own participation in naval exercises staged outside Tokyo Bay between Oct. 20–25, 1927.
16. Watanabe Osamu, "Tennōsei kokka chitsujo no rekishiteki kenkyū josetsu," in *Shakai Kagaku Kenkyū* 30, no. 5 (Mar. 1977), p. 259.
17. The Imperial Household Ministry announced on Nov. 21, 1921, that soon after the Taishō emperor's birth he had contracted an illness similar to cerebral meningitis and from around 1914–15 "he not only lost a decent posture and walked unsteadily, but his speech also faltered." Shikama Kōsuke, *Jijūbukan nikki*, Nov. 25, 1921, as cited in Yasuda Hiroshi, "Kindai tennōsei ni okeru kenryoku to ken'i—Taishō demokurashiiki no kōsatsu" in *Bunka hyōron* 357 (Oct. 1990), p. 186.
18. Asukai Masamichi, *Meiji taitei* (Chikuma Shobō, 1989), p. 287; Watanabe Ikujirō, *Kōshitsu shinron* (Waseda Daigaku Shuppanbu, 1929), p. 320.
19. *MNN*, pp. 68–69.

20. Ibid.
21. Wakabayashi Masahiro, "1923-nen tōgū Taiwan gyōkei to 'naichi enchōshugi'" in *Iwanami kōza, 2 teikoku tōchi no kōzō, kindai Nihon to shokuminchi* (Iwanami Shoten, 1992), p. 108.
22. Ibid., p. 113.
23. Ibid., pp. 99–100.
24. Ibid., pp. 103–4, quoting the *Taiwan jippō* (May–June 1923), pp. 7–8.
25. Tasaki Kimitsukasa, "Kantō daishinsai 70 shūnen kinen shū sankaki" in *Rekishigaku kenkyū* 653 (Dec. 1993), pp. 32–34.
26. Chōsenshi Kenkyūkai, ed., *Nyūmon Chōsen no rekishi* (Sanseidō, 1998), pp. 166–70; also see the discussion of the Kantō earthquake in Roman Cybriwsky, *Tokyo: The Shogun's City at the Twenty-First Century* (John Wiley & Sons, 1998), pp. 82–85.
27. "Nara Takeji kaisōroku (sōan)," pp. 344, 348; Fujiwara Akira, *Shōwa tennō no jūgonen sensō* (Aoki Shoten, 1991), p. 42.
28. Ōe Shinobu, "Hajimete kōkai sareta kizokuin himitsukai giji sokkirokushū," in *Tokyo Daigaku Shuppankai UP 276* (Oct. 1995), pp. 30–31.
29. Watanabe, "Tennōsei kokka chitsujo no rekishiteki kenkyū josetsu," p. 187.
30. Ōe, "Hajimete kōkai sareta kizokuin himitsukai giji sokkirokushū," p. 30.
31. *Asahi shinbun*, June 5, 1995.
32. Kojima, *Tennō, dai ikkan*, pp. 320, 328.
33. Watanabe, "Tennōsei kokka chitsujo no rekishiteki kenkyū josetsu," p. 256.
34. Ibid., p. 257. Watanabe calls this "the second great treason trial in modern Japanese history"—the first having been the trial in 1911–12 of Kōtoku Shūsui and ten others, including the Sōtō Zen sect priest Uchiyama Gudō, over their alleged involvement in a plot to assassinate the Meiji emperor.
35. *MNN*, pp. 107–8.
36. Kojima, *Tennō, dai ikkan*, p. 304, paperback edition, p. 298.
37. Ibid., p. 299, paperback edition.
38. Watanabe, "Tennōsei kokka chitsujo no rekishiteki kenkyū josetsu," p. 257.
39. Nezu, *Tennō to Shōwashi, jō*, p. 37. In 1928 alone the number of lèse-majesté incidents jumped to twenty-eight.
40. Watanabe, "Tennōsei kokka chitsujo no rekishiteki kenkyū josetsu," p. 257.
41. "Zōshō no gōgi okonawareru," in *Tokyo nichi nichi shinbun (yūkan)*, Jan. 26, 1924, in *Taishō nyūsu jiten, rokkan* (Mainichi Komunikēshionzu, 1988), pp. 344–45.
42. Koyama Itoko, *Kōgōsama* (Suzakusha, 1959), pp. 43–44.
43. *Osaka Mainichi*, Jan. 27, 1924, in *Taishō nyūsu jiten, rokkan*, p. 347.
44. Ōsawa Satoru, "Kōshitsu zaisei to 'Teishitsu tōkeisho,'" in *Teishitsu tōkeisho 1, Meiji 32 nendo hen* (Kashiwa Shobō, 1993), pp. 12–14.
45. Kawahara, *Tennō Hirohito no Shōwa-shi*, p. 75.
46. *MNN*, entry of Jan. 28, 1922, pp. 44–45.
47. Takahashi Hiroshi, "Kaisetsu," in Kinoshita Michio, *Sokkin nisshi* (Bungei Shunjūsha, 1990), p. 289.
48. *MNN*, p. 44.
49. The term "peace code" comes from Dorothy V. Jones, *Code of Peace: Ethics and Security in the World of the Warlord States* (University of Chicago Press, 1991).
50. Kobayashi Michiko, "Sekai taisen to tairiku seisaku no henyō," in *Rekishigaku kenkyū* 656 (Mar. 1994), pp. 1–16.
51. Saitō Seiji, "Nichi-Doku sensō no kaisen gaikō," in Nihon Kokusai Seiji Gakkai, ed., *Kokusai seiji* 4 (Oct. 1998), pp. 192–208.
52. Fujiwara, *Shōwa tennō no jūgonen sensō*, pp. 40–48.
53. Jones, *Code of Peace*, p. 44, observes that the Japanese "symbolic statement on racial

equality . . . was left out of the covenant (along with a statement on religious tolera-
tion that Wilson very much wanted) [but] the principle of the equality of nations was
resoundingly affirmed . . . in the very structure of the League."

54. Shibata Shinichi, "Hakken! Shōwa tennō ga mananda teiōgaku kyōkasho," in *Bungei shinjū* (Feb. 1998, special issue), p. 131.

55. Nagai Kazu, *Kindai Nihon no gunbu to seiji* (Shibunkaku Shuppan, 1993), p. 256.

56. Kurono Taeru, "Shōwa shoki kaigun ni okeru kokubō shisō no tairitsu to konmei: kokubō hōshin no dainiji kaitei to daisanji kaitei no aida," in *Gunji shigaku* 34, no. 1 (June 1998), pp. 10–11.

57. Fujiwara, *Shōwa tennō no jūgonen sensō*, p. 42.

58. Military spending fell from a high of 60.14 percent in 1920 to 28.52 percent in 1930. Expressed in terms of GNP, the decline was from 5.86 percent to 3.03 percent. See Yamada Akira, *Gunbi kakuchō no kindaishi: Nihongun no bōchō to hōkai* (Yoshikawa Kōbunkan, 1997), p. 10.

59. Russians who surrendered during the four-year long Siberian war were not treated as POWs, suggesting that Japanese soldiers either killed them on the spot or, less prob-able, released them after they had pledged not to fight again. Yui Daizaburō, Kosuge Nobuko, *Rengō koku horyo gyakutai to sengo sekinin* (Iwanami Bukkuretto no. 321, 1993), p.16.

60. Yoshida Yutaka, *Tennō no guntai to Nankin jiken* (Aoki Shoten, 1985), p. 191.

61. Ibid.

62. Ibid., pp. 193–94.

63. Ibid., p. 191.

64. Kataoka Tetsuya, "Shōwa shoki: Nihon rikugun e no shakaigakuteki apuroochi" in *Gunji shigaku* 22, no. 4 (1987), pp. 20–21.

65. Ibid., pp. 23–24.

66. Kataoka, p. 25, notes that in 1928 Gens. Araki Sadao, Obata Toshishirō, and Suzuki Osamichi revised *Tōsui kōryō*, making the principle of the offensive and the primacy of spirit over material force the dominant ideas of the Japanese army.

67. Maehara Tōru, "'Tōsuiken dokuritsu' riron no gunnai de no hatten keika" in *Gunji shigaku* 23, no. 3 (Jan. 1998), pp. 18–19.

68. Nagai, *Kindai Nihon no gunbu to seiji*, p. 255.

69. Maehara, "'Tōsuiken dokuritsu' riron no gunnai de hatten keika," pp. 27–28.

70. In February 1922 the General Staff Office produced a top-secret study titled "Concerning the Independence of the Right of Supreme Command," which may have been the first official document whose title included the term "independence of the right of supreme command." See Maehara, p. 30.

71. Quoted in Maehara, p. 34; also, p. 40, n. 50.

72. Tanaka Hiromi, "Kyozō no gunshin Tōgō Heihachirō," in *This Is Yomiuri* (Sept. 1993), p. 240.

73. "Nara Takeji kaisōroku (sōan)," pp. 357–58.

74. Ibid., p. 355; *Jiji shinbun* (Aug. 10, 1925).

75. "Nara Takeji kaisōroku (sōan)," p. 355.

76. Asano Kazuo, "Taishōki ni okeru rikugun shōkō no shakai ninshiki to rikugun no seishin kyōiku: *Kaikōsha kiji* no ronsetsu kiji no bunseki," in Nakamura Katsunori, ed., *Kindai Nihon seiji no shosō: jidai ni yoru tenkai to kōsatsu* (Keiō Tsūshin, 1989), p. 455.

77. Fujiwara, *Shōwa tennō no jūgonen sensō*, p. 43.

78. Ibid., p. 44.

79. Miyaji Masato, "Seiji shi ni okeru tennō no kinō" in Rekishigaku kenkyūkai, ed., *Tennō to tennōsei o kangaeru* (Aoki Shoten 1988), p. 97.

80. Yasuda Hiroshi, "Kindai tennōsei ni okeru kenryoku to ken'i—Taishō demokurashii-ki no kōsatsu," in *Bunka hyōron* 357 (Oct. 1990), p. 188.

81. Ibid., p. 157. Article 1 of the new thought-control law stated:

> Anyone who has formed an association with the object of altering the national polity [*kokutai*] or the form of government [*seitai*], or disavowing the system of private ownership, or anyone who has joined such an association with the full knowledge of its objects, shall be liable to imprisonment with or without hard labor for a term not exceeding ten years.

82. Suzuki, "Taishō demokurashii to kokutai mondai," p. 63.

83. Kojima, *Tennō, dai ikkan*, pp. 342–43. Kaneko Fumiko eventually committed suicide while in prison.

84. Kanazawa Fumio, "Gyōzaisei seiri, fusen, chian ijihō: dai 49 kai teikoku gikai–dai 52 kai teikoku gikai," in Uchida Kenzō et al., eds., *Nihon gikai shi roku 2* (Dai Ichihōki Shuppan K. K., 1990), pp. 400–401.

85. Suzuki, *Kōshitsu seido*, p. 167.

86. Ibid., p. 167.

87. Suzuki, *Kindai no tennō*, p. 52.

88. Tokoro Shigemoto, *Kindai shakai to Nichirenshugi* (Hyōronsha, 1972), pp. 130–32.

89. Ibid., p. 133.

90. Ibid., p. 135.

91. Maruyama Teruo, "Tennōsei to shūkyō," in Inoue Kiyoshi et al., *Shōwa no shūen to tennōsei no genzai* (Shinsensha, 1988), p. 183.

92. Right-wing organizations increased from 23 in 1926 to 196 in 1932. After 1929 many of them added anticapitalist rhetoric to their usual anti-Westernism. The more important ones were the new study associations in which young bureaucrats played leading roles. See Suzuki, *Kōshitsu seido*, p. 170.

93. In the early 1930s, Yasuoka reaffirmed the separation of the *kokutai* from the form of government (*seitai*), and preached that any form of government, whether parliamentarism or military dictatorship, should be tolerated as long as it served to protect the *kokutai*. Otabe Yūji, "Tennōsei ideorogii to shin Ei-Bei ha no keifu: Yasuoka Masahiro o chūshin ni" in *Shien* vol. 43, no. 1 (May 1983), pp. 27, 29, and n. 3.

94. Suzuki, *Kindai no tennō*, pp. 51–52.

95. Ibid., p. 53, citing Nagata, p. 85.

96. Ibid., p. 54.

97. Kurozawa Fumitaka, "Gunbu no 'Taishō demokurashii' ninshiki no ichidanmen," in Kindai Gaikōshi Kenkyūkai, ed., *Hendōki no Nihon gaikō to gunji: shiryō to kentō* (Hara Shobō, 1987), p. 49.

98. Ibid., p. 48.

99. Ibid., p. 49, citing Inspector General of Military Education Mutō Nobuyoshi in Mar. 1932.

100. Kawano Hitoshi, "Taishō, Shōwa-ki gunji eriito no keisei katei: rikugun shōkō no gun kyaria sentaku to gun gakkō tekiō ni kansuru jisshū bunseki," in Tsutsui Kiyotada, ed., *'Kindai Nihon' no rekishi shakai gaku: shinsei to kōzō* (Bokutakusha, 1990), pp. 95–140.

101. Hata Ikuhiko, ed., *Nihon riku-kaigun sōgō jiten* (Tokyo Daigaku Shuppankai, 1991), p. 735.

102. Kawano, "Taishō-Shōwa-ki gunji eriito no keisei katei," pp. 105–6.

103. Ibid., p. 120.

104. *KYN, dai ikkan*, pp. 33–35, 37, 41–42.

105. Watanabe, "Tennōsei kokka chitsujo no rekishiteki kenkyū josetsu," p. 264.

106. Ibid., p. 265.

107. Ibid., p. 262.

108. Takahashi Yōichi, "Inoue Tetsujirō fukei jiken saikō" in Terasaki Masao et al., eds., *Kindai Nihon ni okeru chi no bunpai to kokumin tōgō* (Dai Ichihōki K. K., 1993), p. 347. The pamphlet carried the names Tōyama Mitsuru, Tanaka Hiroyuki, Iogi Ryōzō, and Ashizu Kōjirō.

109. Ibid., pp. 349, 358.

110. Tokoro, *Kindai shakai to Nichirenshugi*, p. 119.

111. Tanaka Hinosuke, *Shishiō dan sōhen, 6* (Shishiō Zenshū Kankōkai, 1937), pp. 343 ff.

112. Tamura Yoshirō, "Kindai Nihon no ayumi to Nichirenshugi," in Tamura Yoshirō and Miyazaki Eishū, eds., *Kōza Nichiren 4, Nihon kindai to Nichirenshugi* (Shunjūsha, 1972), p. 3.

CHAPTER 5
THE NEW MONARCHY AND THE NEW NATIONALISM

1. *KYN, dai ikkan*, p. 66. The number 124 was concocted centuries earlier by not counting empresses, deleting the emperors of the southern court, and lopping off names that did not accord with certain sources. No one knows exactly how many emperors Japan has had because the dynastic records do not correlate and are contradictory, and the way of naming them has changed over time.

2. The four rescripts are reproduced and discussed in Senda Kako, *Tennō to chokugo to Shōwashi* (Sekibunsha, 1983), pp. 21–25.

3. Hatano Sumio, "Manshū jihen to 'kyūchū' seiryoku," in *Tochigi shigaku* 5 (1991), p. 108. Nara did not always "act in unison" with the court group but frequently gave priority in his actions to the army organization to which he belonged.

4. Problems connected with defining the court group are addressed in *NH*.

5. When Kichizaemon died in June 1926, Saionji expressed his concern to Makino over how to secure the Sumitomo family after the death of its head. "The new head of the Sumitomo family is very young, but that family's influence is great and is not limited to them. Since Sumitomo is a state organ it is desirable for the public interest and security to have its foundation strengthened. I agree completely with the prince." See *MNN*, p. 259.

6. Hatano, "Manshū jihen to 'kyūchū' seiryoku," p. 107.

7. Hirohito summoned Saionji to Tokyo after Prime Minister Inukai was assassinated in May 1932, and again following the army mutiny of February 26, 1936, at which time Saionji participated in the selection of Hirota Kōki as prime minister. See Harada Kumao, *Saionji kō to seikyoku, dai gokan* (Iwanami Shoten, 1951), pp. 6, 8. Cited hereafter as *Harada nikki*.

8. Masuda Tomoko, "Tennō: kindai," in *Nihonshi, 4 kan*, p. 1244.

9. *NH*, p. 28.

10. On Harada's career, see Thomas F. Mayer-Oakes, *Fragile Victory: Prince Saionji and the 1930 London Treaty Issue, from the Memoirs of Baron Harada Kumao, Translated with an Introduction and Annotations* (Wayne State University Press, 1968), pp. 41–42.

11. Although Konoe and Hirohito differed profoundly on certain foreign policy issues, Konoe remained personally close to Hirohito until mid–1941.

12. Shōji Junichirō, "Konoe Fumimaro-zō no saikentō: taigai ishiki o chūshin ni," in Kindai Gaikōshi Kenkyūkai, hen, *Hendōki no Nihon gaikō to gunji* (Hara Shobō, 1987), esp. pp. 101–5.

13. Gōtō Muneto, "Taishō demokurashii to kazoku shakai no saihen," in *Rekishigaku kenkyū* 694 (Feb. 1997), pp. 19–34, 63.

14. Mizutani Taichirō, "Kyūtei seijika no ronri to kōdō: Kido Kōichi nikki ni tsuite," in

Mizutani Taichirō, *Taishō demokurashiiron: Yoshino Sakuzō jidai to sonogo* (Chūō Kōronsha, 1974), pp. 176–287.

15. Masuda, "Tennō: Kindai," p. 1243.

16. Watanabe Osamu, "Tennō," in *Nihonshi, yonkan* (Heibonsha, 1994), p. 1246.

17. Itō Takashi, "Kaisetsu," in *MNN*, p. 715; also pp. 321, 323; Suzuki, *Kōshitsu seido*, p. 169.

18. *KYN, dai ikkan*, pp. 79–80. After conveying Konoe's views to high Imperial Household Ministry officials, Kawai went back to Konoe at the House of Peers. When Kawai returned to the palace, he mailed a copy of his proposal to Konoe. Kawai also sought the advice of constitutional law scholar Uesugi Shinkichi.

19. "Nara Takeji kaisōroku (sōan)," p. 327. Meiji was not enshrined and worshiped as a god until 1920, eight years after his death.

20. Nakajima Michio, *Tennō no daigawari to kokumin* (Aoki Shoten, 1990) p. 116; *KYN, dai ikkan*, pp. 73–80.

21. *KYN, dai ikkan*, p. 219, entry of Oct. 8, 1927; *Japan Times and Mail*, Nov. 5, 1928.

22. See Kawai's diary entry of May 1, 1929; Takahashi Hiroshi, "Kaisetsu: tsukurareta kyūchū saishi," in *KYN, dai rokkan* (Iwanami Shoten, 1994), pp. 256–57. Takahashi notes that both rice cultivation and the practice of sericulture were deeply related to the Harvest Festival, the most important ceremony of the imperial house. The new, unhulled harvest was offered by the emperor to the gods, while silk drapery was employed in the requiem for dead emperors, held on the eve of the Harvest Festival.

23. For details see *NH*; Kanazawa Shio, "Gyōsei seiri, fusen, chian ijihō: dai 49 kai teikoku gikai- dai 52 kai teikoku gikai," in Uchida Kenzō et al., eds., *Nihon Gikai shiroku 2* (Dai Ichi Hōki Shuppan K. K., 1990), pp. 401–6.

24. See the long entry of June 15, 1927, in *MNN*, pp. 268–69.

25. *NH*, p. 5.

26. On Oct. 30, 1928, General Ugaki criticized the money lavished on the enthronement ceremonies at a time when "the masses are suffering for lack of adequate food and clothing." He later noted: "Police control throughout the period of the succession ... was extraordinarily severe and many critical voices are saying that it exceeded the bounds of common sense." Cited in Ogino Fujio, "'Shōwa tairei' to tennōsei keisatsu: Shōwa tairei keibi kiroku o chūshin ni," in Nishi Hidenari et al., *Shōwa tairei kiroku shiryō: kaisetsu* (Fuji Shuppan, 1990), pp. 30, 55.

27. In 1927 the Tokyo Broadcasting System (today's NHK) produced the first live broadcast of the National Middle School Baseball Tournament from Kōshien Stadium in Nishinomiya City, Hyōgo prefecture. The following year saw its first broadcast of a sumō wrestling tournament. Sasaki Ryūji, *Gendai tennōsei no kigen to kinō*, p. 90.

28. In contrast to state Shinto, a complete creature of the Japanese government, sectarian Shinto had more leeway in interpreting Shinto, except where its teachings clashed with *kokutai* ideology.

29. See Takahashi Hiroshi, "Shinkakuka no kizashi: Shōwa no tairei," in *KYN, dai ikkan*, pp. 307–8.

30. Nakajima, *Tennō no daigawari to kokumin*, p. 109.

31. Takashi Fujitani, *Splendid Monarchy: Power and Pageantry in Modern Japan* (University of California Press, 1996), p. 236.

32. Sasaki, *Gendai tennōsei no kigen to kinō*, pp. 90–91.

33. Cited from *Mochizuki Keisuke den*, p. 361, in Nakajima, *Tennō no daigawari to kokumin*, p. 119.

34. Nakajima (*Tennō no daigawari to kokumin*, p. 110) furnishes a good example of such

counterpoint in the following instruction given by Education Minister Shōda Kazuo to a conference of local officials on July 13, 1928:

> Nowadays many people harbor thoughts that run counter to national sentiment based on the *kokutai*. Influenced by these ideas, some students have been violating their duties; others have even been implicated in the recent Communist Party incident. This is a matter of grave concern for the state. . . . In order to save this situation, we first should have them understand the founding principles of our country and thereby nurture in them a firm, unshakable national spirit. . . . I believe the forthcoming grand enthronement ceremonies provide the greatest opportunity for us to heighten the spirit of students and get them to master the concept of the *kokutai*.

35. Fujiwara Akira, ed., *Nihon minshū no rekishi 8, dan'atsu no arashi no naka de* (Sanseidō, 1975), p. 180.
36. Nakajima, *Tennō no daigawari to kokumin*, pp. 60–61.
37. Nishi Hidenari, "'Shōwa tairei' to kokumin: 'Shōwa tairei yoroku' o chūshin toshite," in Nishi Hidenari et al., *Shōwa tairei kiroku shiryō: kaisetsu*, p. 25.
38. Ibid.
39. For the material in this and the next paragraph, I am indebted to Christine Kim, "Imperial Pageantry in the Colonies: An Examination of the Korean Response to Hirohito's Enthronement" (paper, Harvard University, Apr. 1997).
40. Senda, *Tennō to chokugo to Shōwa-shi*, p. 77; Nezu, *Tennō to Shōwa-shi, jō* (San Ichi Shobō, 1976), pp. 46–47; *Tokushū Bungei shunjū: tennō hakusho* (Oct. 1956), p. 77; Okada Seiji and Hikuma Takenori, "Sokui no rei, daijōsai no rekishiteki kentō," in *Bunka hyōron* 357 (Oct. 1990), pp. 62–87.
41. The historian Yasumaru Yoshio notes that the *daijōsai* rite was discontinued from 1466 to 1687, replaced by a ritual of purification by water, and it was no longer needed. The *daijōsai* was resumed in 1687, under the influence of Suika Shinto, which emphasized the emperor's *bansei ikkei*. Henceforth the emperor was a god not only for reasons of bloodline descent but also because Amaterasu Ōmikami had directly invested him with divinity as a result of his sharing of sacred grain with her. This was the concept of the *daijōsai* adopted by the Meiji elite in an official instruction on the *daijōsai* in 1871. See Yasumaru Yoshio, *Kindai tennōzō no keisei* (Iwanami Shoten, 1992), p. 23. The adherents of the heretical Shinto sects of Ōmotokyō and Tenrikyō rejected this official view.
42. Nakajima, *Tennō no daigawari to kokumin*, p. 58; Okada, Hikuma, "Sokui no rei, daijōsai no rekishiteki kentō," p. 79.
43. Tomura Masahiro, *Shinwa to saigi: Yasukuni kara daijōsai e* (Nihon Kitoku Kyōdan Shuppankyoku, 1988), p. 68; Yuge Tōru, "Roma kōtei reihai to tennō shinka," in *Rekishi hyōron* 406 (Feb. 1984), where he notes that in contrast to the ancient Romans who deified their emperors in broad daylight, usually after death, the Japanese deified their emperors while they were still living, at night. Also see Okada, Hikuma, "Sokui no rei, daijōsai no rekishiteki kentō," p. 77; Ihara Yoriaki, *Kōshitsu jiten* (Toyamabō, 1943), p. 75. *Gyoza* or *goza* is defined as the seat or seats in front of a deity, where the emperor, empress, or grand dowager sits.
44. The *Tokyo nichi nichi shimbun* reported on Nov. 15, 1928: "There is no way to view the *shinza* within the innermost chambers since it has always been the most sacred, awe-inspiring mystery," and, "One should not make indiscriminate inferences about the mysteries within the innermost chambers." Cited in Yuge, "Roma kōtei reihai to tennō shinka," p. 9.

45. Nishi, "'Shōwa tairei' to kokumin: 'Shōwa tairei yoroku' o chūshin toshite," p. 26.
46. *Japan Times and Mail*, Dec. 3 and 4, 1928.
47. Nakajima, *Tennō no daigawari to kokumin*, pp. 79–80.
48. *Japan Times and Mail*, Nov. 23, 1928.
49. Yasumaru, *Kindai tennōzō no keisei*, pp. 23–24. The theory of Hirohito's deification was strengthened by the publication in 1928 of *Daijōsai no hongi* (*Cardinal principles of the great food offering ceremony*) by the ethnologist Origuchi Nobuo, who argued that the emperor has a divine nature because of his sacred marriage during the *daijōsai*.
50. Sasaki, *Gendai tennōsei no kigen to kinō*, p. 91.
51. Nakamura Masanori, *Nihon no rekishi 29, rōdōsha to nōmin* (Shōgakukan, 1976), p. 325; Hōsei Daigaku Ōhara Shakai Mondai Kenkyūjo, ed., *Shakai, rōdō undō dai nenpyō, dai ikkan, 1858–1945* (Rōdō Junpōsha, 1986), p. 278.
52. One procession (May 28 to June 9, 1929) was to the Kansai region (Osaka-Kobe-Kyoto); another to Shizuoka prefecture from May 18 to June 3, 1930: a third to Gumma, Tochigi, and Saitama prefectures in Nov. 1934, and a fourth to Hokkaido from Sept. 24 to Oct. 12, 1936.
53. Sakamoto Kōjirō, *Shōchō tennōsei e no pafuoomansu: Shōwa-ki no tennō gyōkō no hensen* (Kamakawa Shuppansha, 1989), pp. 4–5; Dai Kasumi Kai, ed., *Naimushōshi, dai sankan* (Chihō Zaimu Kyōkai, 1971), p. 770. Nara linked the 1928 revision of the Peace Preservation Law to the government's fear of direct appeals to the emperor while on tour. See "Nara Takeji kaisōroku (sōan)," p. 367.
54. *Naimushō-shi, dai sankan*, pp. 761–62.
55. Ibid., pp. 761–63.
56. Yasumaru, *Kindai tennōzō no keisei*, pp. 289–90.
57. *Jitsugyō no Nihon zōkan: gotaiten kinen shashingō* (Nov. 1928), p. 57.
58. Hoshino Teruoki, "Tairei no shogi oyobi sono igi," in *Jitsugyō no Nihon* (Nov. 1928), p. 69.
59. During 1927–28, the initiative in promoting the divine and militaristic image of the emperor came directly from the palace, and from key figures in the court milieu and civil bureaucracy. They began the proselytization of the Japanese spirit and gave new life to extremism originating from within orthodoxy.
60. Nakajima, *Tennō no daigawari to kōkumin*, pp. 123–24.
61. From "The Great Enthronement Ceremony and National Morality: Strive to Promote the Way of the Father and the Mother," an editorial in "Yokohama bōeki shimpō," July 14, 1928, cited in Nakajima, *Tennō no daigawari to kokumin*, p. 125.
62. Ibid., p. 128.
63. Ibid.
64. Ibid., pp. 129–30.
65. Ibid., p. 129, from "Young Japan and Its Wordly Mission," Dec. 1, 1928.
66. Ibid., p. 130.
67. D. C. Holtom, *Modern Japan and Shinto Nationalism: A Study of Present-Day Trends in Japanese Religions* (Universty of Chicago Press, 1943), pp. 23–24.
68. Yasumaru, *Kindai tennōzō no keisei*, pp. 12–13.
69. Nakajima, *Tennō no daigawari to kokumin*, p. 131.
70. Fujiwara Akira, ed., *Nihon minshū no rekishi 8, danatsu no arashi no naka de*, pp. 178–79.

CHAPTER 6
A POLITICAL MONARCH EMERGES

1. Suzuki Masayuki, *Kindai tennōsei no shihai chitsujo* (Azekura Shobō, 1986), part 2.
2. *Senshi sōsho 31, kaigun gunsenbi 1* (1969), pp. 375–76; Kurono Taeru, "Shōwa shoki

kaigun ni okeru kokubō shisō no tairitsu to konmei: kokubō hōshin no dainiji kaitei to daisanji kaitei no aida," in *Gunji shigaku* 34, no. 1 (June 1998), pp. 12–13.

3. For chronology see Nakamura Masanori, ed., *Nenpyō Shōwa shi* (Iwanami Shoten, 1989), p. 5.

4. Hirohito attended the privy council deliberations on the edict, was aware of the crackdown being mounted against the Left, and sought to have certain unspecified conditions or reservations added to the rescript before approving it. What they were, and what he found objectionable in Prime Minister Tanaka's reporting of the matter to him, is not known. *KYN, dai nikan*, pp. 110–11; *MNN*, pp. 321, 322.

5. Kanda Fuhito, "Kindai Nihon no sensō: horyo seisaku o chūshin toshite," in *Kikan sensō sekinin kenkyū* 9 (Autumn 1995), p. 15.

6. Yui Daizaburō, Kosuge Nobuko, *Rengō koku horyo gyakutai to sengo sekinin* (Iwanami Bukkuretto no. 321, 1993), p. 19. In opposing the ratification of the Geneva Treaty of July 27, 1927, Concerning the Treatment of Prisoners of War, naval leaders, on Nov. 15, 1934, argued that "Japanese military personnel are forbidden to become prisoners;" and "[i]f we adopt the treaty as it stands . . . we would have to revise the regulations governing punishment in the military, which would make discipline very difficult to maintain."

7. Gordon M. Berger, "Politics and Mobilization in Japan, 1931–1945" in Peter Duus, ed., *The Cambridge History of Japan*, vol. 6, *The Twentieth Century* (Cambridge University Press, 1988), pp. 105–6.

8. Cited in Tanaka Hiromi, "Kyozō no gunshin Tōgō Heihachirō," in *This is Yomiuri* (Sept. 1993), p. 220.

9. Katō Kanji, "Kokka minjinron no seishinka," in *Kokuhon* (Jan. 26, 1926).

10. Ogasawara's *Tōgō gensui shōden* first appeared in a limited edition in the spring of 1921; it was reissued in an inexpensive popular edition in 1925. See Tanaka Hiromi, "Kyozō no gunshin Tōgō Heihachirō," pp. 234–35.

11. Tanaka, "Kyozō no gunshin Tōgō Heihachirō," pp. 225, 236, 239.

12. Answer to Japan, Southwest Pacific Area, July 1, 1944, p. 9. From the Bonner F. Fellers collection at the Hoover Institution.

13. Kiyozawa Retsu, *Gendai Nihon bunmeishi, dai sankan, gaikōshi* (Tōyō Keizai Shinpōsha, 1941), p. 437; Stephen Pelz, *Race to Pearl Harbor: The Failure of the Second London Naval Conference and the Onset of World War II* (Harvard University Press, 1974), pp. 2–3.

14. *MNN*, p. 417.

15. *NH*, pp. 59–60, cited with the permission of the author.

16. Masuda Tomoko, "Tennō, kindai," in *Nihonshi, yonkan* (Heibonsha, 1994), p. 1243–44.

17. On the first floor of Hirohito's redesigned palace were waiting rooms and a large (twenty-mat-size), chastely furnished audience chamber, partitioned into two sections. A telephone manned by a chamberlain was mounted on a wall in the carpeted corridor leading from the reception rooms to the outer audience chamber. When Hirohito was ready to receive someone, he or an aide would phone, signaling the guest to advance into the "outer room." The guest would bow slightly on entering, bow again after stepping into the "inner room," and execute a very deep bow before the imperial table. Exiting in the emperor's presence required doing the "crab walk," making sure, that is, to retreat by walking sideways to the door so as never to turn one's back to him.

Hirohito's audience chamber, which doubled as his lecture room, contained a mantelpiece screening a recessed electric heater. In front of the mantelpiece were his chair and desk. A long oval table abutted the desk. Display shelves lined one wall, painted in a traditional pattern of royal purple waves with golden plovers and mist above. The same design adorned the wall behind his seat.

Above this audience room on the second floor were his study, library, and office, where the imperial seals were stored and only high court officials and chamberlain were allowed. There he would read and countersign documents that required his sanction. See Nihon Gendaishi Shiryō Kenkyūkai, "Okabe Nagaakira shi danwa kiroku," n.d., pp. 11–12. I am indebted to historian Okabe Makio for a copy of this record.

18. *NH*, pp. 5–6.
19. *KYN, dai ikkan*, p. 81.
20. Suzuki, *Kōshitsu seido: Meiji kara sengo made*, p. 168. According to Makino (p. 317) Prime Minister Tanaka had asked Chinda to ask the emperor to say a kind word to Mizuno.
21. Ibid.
22. Kojima, *Tennō, dai nikan*, p. 33; Akira Iriye, *After Imperialism: The Search for a New Order in the Far East, 1921–1931* (Harvard University Press, 1965), pp. 197–205.
23. *MNN*, p. 322.
24. *NH*, pp. 22–24.
25. Ibid., p. 23.
26. *KYN, dai sankan*, p. 23; *MNN*, pp. 336–37; and *NH*, p. 23.
27. Okabe Nagakage, *Okabe Nagakage nikki: Shōwa shoki kazoku kanryō no kiroku*. Shōyū Kurabu, ed. (Kashiwa Shobō, 1993), pp. 60–61.
28. *NH*, p. 24 and n. 261; also *MNN*, p. 350.
29. Ibid., p. 19.
30. Bix, "The Shōwa Emperor's 'Monologue' and the Problem of War Responsibility," *Journal of Japanese Studies* 18, no. 2 (Summer 1992), p. 338–42.
31. Ibid., pp. 341–42; and the discussion in Fujiwara, Awaya et al., *Tettei kenshō: 'Shōwa tennō dokuhakuroku'* (Ōtsuki Shoten 1991), pp. 33–34.
32. Railroad Minister Ogawa Heikichi, nettled by the anachronism of the emperor's action, remarked, "It is most irrational in the present era for the prime minister to be forced into confinement due to the emperor's anger." Cited in Masuda, "Tennō: kindai," p. 1244.
33. Ikō Toshiya, "Shōwa tennō, kyūchū gurūpu no Tanaka naikaku tōkaku undō," in *Rekishi hyōron* 496 (Aug. 1991), pp. 16–17, as cited in Bix, p. 342.
34. Watanabe Osamu, *Sengo seiji shi no naka no tennōsei* (Aoki Shoten, 1990), p. 86.
35. Uchida's instruction stated that "Manchuria is Japan's outer rampart. . . . We have not the least intention of making Manchuria into a protectorate or committing territorial aggression against it." However, because the "Kuomintang government . . . has levied taxes, stirred up strikes against foreigners . . . and taken many extreme actions similar to those of the communists, the imperial government cannot ignore the intrusion into the Three Eastern Provinces of the southern forces who have such tendencies." Gaimushō hen, *Nihon gaikō nenpyō narabi shuyō monjo II* (Hara Shobō, 1969), pp. 117–19.
36. Whitney R. Harris, *Tyranny on Trial: The Evidence at Nuremberg* (Southern Methodist University Press, 1954), writes (p. 523) that, "The International Military Tribunal construed the Briand-Kellogg Pact as making aggressive war criminal, as well as illegal, and as affording the juridical basis for the punishment of individuals who initiated and waged wars of aggression in violation of its terms." The Tokyo tribunal took the same position. See "Trial of Japanese War Criminals: Documents" (Washington, D.C.: GPO, 1946), pp. 14–15.
37. For the text of the treaty see *FRUS, 1928*, vol. 1 , pp. 153–56.

38. Kiyozawa, *Gendai Nihon bunmeishi, dai sankan, gaikōshi*, pp. 435–37.
39. Hatsue Shinohara, "An Intellectual Foundation for the Road to Pearl Harbor: Quincy Wright and Tachi Sakutarō." Paper presented at the Conference on The United States and Japan in World War II, Hofstra University, Dec. 1991.
40. The treaty was signed in Paris (August 27, 1928) and ratified in Japan (June 27, 1929) with the government declaring that it understood the offending phrase did not apply to Japan. It went into force on July 24, 1929.
41. Suzuki, *Kōshitsu seido*, pp. 168–70.
42. In "A View of International Law in the Kellogg-Briand Pact" and "Britain's New Monroe Doctrine and the Effect of the No-War Treaty," both published in 1928, Tachi belabored the obvious point that the signatories to the pact had renounced war "as an instrument of national policy," but not the right of self-defense. Focusing on the interpretive notes that France, Great Britain, and the United States exchanged prior to signing the Pact on August 27, 1928, he observed that:

> Britain does not recognize the application of the No-War Pact in regions where it claims to have a vital interest. . . . If other countries recognize this claim of Britain, it will lead to a situation where the United States too will claim that war based on the principle of the Monroe Doctrine is not prohibited by the No War Pact. I have to acknowledge, therefore, that, in addition to cases of the activation of the right of self-defense, wars exist that cannot be prohibited by the Pact in connection with the Monroe Doctrine of the United States and the New Monroe-ism of Britain.

Tachi Sakutarō, "Eikoku no shin-Monrōshugi sengen," in *Gaikō jihō* 577 (Dec. 15, 1928), p. 3. See also Quincy Wright, "The Interpretation of Multilateral Treaties," in *American Journal of International Law* 23 (1929), p. 105.
43. *KYN, dai sankan*, pp. 41, 53, 55, 79, 83, 89, and 228.
44. Shinohara, pp. 6–7.
45. Ibid., p. 11.
46. Sasaki, *Gendai tennōsei no kigen to kinō*, p. 91.
47. Ikō Toshiya, "Kokusai renmei ni okeru anzen hoshō rongi to Nihon, 1927–1931," in *Tokyo Bunka Tanki Daigaku Kiyō, dai 16 gō* (1999), pp. 31–31.
48. "Nara Takeji kaisōroku (sōan)," p. 385.
49. Masuda Tomoko, "Seitō naikakusei no hōkai," in Tokyo Daigaku Shakai Kagaku Kenkyūjo, ed., *Gendai Nihon shakai, 4 rekishiteki zentei* (Tokyo Daigaku Shuppankai, 1991), p. 188.
50. Masuda Tomoko, "Saitō Makoto kyokoku itchi naikakuron: rikken kunshusei no saihen to Nihon fuashizumu," in *Shiriizu Nihon gendaishi 3, kōzō to hendō, gendai shakai e no tenkai* (Iwanami Shoten, 1993), pp. 245–46.
51. Sentenced to death in late 1933, Sagoya, along with fellow murderer and Shinto lay priest Inoue Nisshō, was pardoned in Hirohito's great amnesty of 1940. Sagoya served only six years in prison; Inoue served eight. See *NH*, p. 59, and *Konsaisu Nihon jinmei jiten, kaiteiban* (Sanseidō, 1991), p. 565.
52. Yamada Akira, *Gunbi kakuchō no kindaishi: Nihongun no bochō to hōkai* (Yoshikawa Kōbunkan, 1997), p. 10.
53. Masuda, "Saitō Makoto kyokoku itchi naikakuron," p. 247.
54. Ibid., pp. 247–248.
55. Otabe Yūji, "Kaisetsu: Manshū jihen to tennō, kyūchū," p. 256, citing *KYN, dai gokan*, p. 103.
56. Cited in Seki Hiroharu, "The Manchurian Incident, 1931," in James W. Morley, ed., *Japan Erupts: The London Naval Conference and the Manchurian Incident, 1928–1932*.

Selected translations from Taiheiyō sensō e no michi: kaisen gaikō shi (Columbia University Press, 1984), p. 177.

57. Parks M. Coble, *Facing Japan: Chinese Politics and Japanese Imperialism, 1931–1937* (Harvard University Press, 1991), pp. 24–25.

58. Otabe, "Kaisetsu: Manshū jihen to tennō, kyūchū," p. 257; Seki Hiroharu, "The Manchurian Incident, 1931," pp. 189–92.

59. Ibid., p. 179, citing from *Harada nikki, bekkan*, p. 356.

60. Ibid., pp. 185–86.

61. James B. Crowley, *Japan's Quest for Autonomy: National Security and Foreign Policy, 1930–1938* (Princeton University Press, 1966), p. 109.

62. Three days later, at Hirohito's insistence, Makino again discussed the problem of military discipline with Chief Aide-de-Camp Nara and Grand Chamberlain Suzuki, but took no further action. See Hatano Sumio, "Manshū jihen to 'kyūchū' seiryoku," p. 109; *MNN*, entries of August 19 and 21, 1931; and *Harada nikki, dai nikan*, pp. 39–40.

63. By practicing austerity in a time of acute depression, while insisting that his bureaucratic servants do likewise, Hirohito probably imagined that he was setting a good example, when he was really contributing to the demoralization of the bureaucracy. On the salary reduction issue, see Otabe, "Kaisetsu: Manshū jihen to tennō, kyūchū," in *KYN, dai gokan*, p. 255, citing Kawai's entries of May 27 and 30.

64. *KYN, dai gokan*, p. 152.

65. The Army General Staff officers who hosted the meeting were Gens. Kanaya Hanzō, Ninomiya Harushige, Hata Shunroku, and Tatekawa Yoshitsugu. Their guests from the Navy General Staff were Adms. Oikawa Koshirō, Taniguchi Naomi, Nagano Osami, and Kondō Nobutake. The navy's "special organ" in Manchuria was not established until Jan. 27, 1932. See Shinmyō Takeo, ed., *Kaigun sensō kentō kaigi kiroku: Taiheiyō sensō kaisen no keii* (Mainichi Shinbunsha, 1976), pp. 118–19; Kōketsu, *Nihon kaigun no shūsen kōsaku—Ajia taiheiyō sensō no saikentō*, pp. 10–11; Hata Ikuhiko, ed., *Nihon rikukaigun sōgō jiten*, p. 452.

66. *KYN, dai gokan*, p. 153.

67. Hatano, "Manshū jihen to 'kyūchū' seiryoku," pp. 109, 136 n. 4, citing "Nara Takeji nikki," entries of Sept. 8, 10, 11, 1931. Around this time Assistant Imperial Household Minister Sekiya also warned Minami not to let the situation get out of control. Hatano, "Manshū jihen to 'kyūchū' seiryoku," pp. 110, 136 n. 7, citing *MNN*, entry of Sept. 15, 1931.

68. Kunegi Toshihirō, "Shidehara Kijūrō—'heiwa gaikō' no honne to tatemae," in Yoshida Yutaka et al., *Haisen zengo: Shōwa tennō to gonin no shidōsha* (Aoki Shoten, 1995), pp. 89–90.

69. Seki, "The Manchurian Incident, 1931," p. 205; Hatano, "Manshū jihen to 'kyūchū' seiryoku," p. 110.

70. Arai Naoyuki, "Tennō hōdō no nani ga kawari, nani ga kawaranakatta no ka," in Nihon Jyānarisuto Kaigi, ed., *Yameru masu komi to Nihon* (Kōbunkyū, 1995), pp. 181, 182, 189.

71. Fujiwara, *Shōwa tennō no jūgonen sensō*, pp. 63–74.

Chapter 7
The Manchurian Transformation

1. Eguchi Keiichi, *Jūgonen sensō shōshi, shinpan* (Aoki Shoten, 1991), pp. 36–37.

2. Hatano Sumio, "Manshū jihen to 'kyūchū' seiryoku," *Tochigi shigaku* 5 (1991), p. 110, citing "Nara nikki," Sept. 19, 1931.

3. On Sept. 19, 1931, General Nara told Army Minister Minami that, "Although the

Kwantung Army can independently determine the sphere of action of its duties as specified in its regulations, it must await the decision of the cabinet if its actions go beyond that sphere. If large-scale troop movements are necessary, we may need to convene an imperial conference." *KYN, dai gokan*, p. 156; Yamada, *Dai gensui Shōwa tennō*, pp. 49, 83.

4. *Harada nikki, dai nikan*, p. 64; Fujiwara, *Shōwa Tennō no jūgonen sensō*, p. 68. Chang Hsueh-liang's forces probably numbered closer to 130,000.

5. All present were core members of the Jūichikai (Association of the eleventh), a group of titled peers, of whom Kido was the most active. Formed in 1922 and representing the reform faction of the titled nobility, they shared Konoe's view that Nationalist China denoted merely a region of raw territory to be used to secure Japan's survival.

6. Kido Kōichi nikki, jō, p. 101.

7. Fujiwara, *Shōwa tennō no jūgonen sensō*, p. 72.

8. Eguchi, *Jūgonen sensō shōshi, shinpan*, p. 40.

9. Hatano, "Manshū jihen to 'kyūchū' seiryoku," p. 114, citing "Nara nikki," Sept. 21, 1931.

10. "Nara Takeji jijūbukanchō nikki (shō)," in *Chūō kōron* (Sept. 1990), pp. 340–41.

11. Eguchi, *Jūgonen sensō shōshi, shinpan*, p. 41.

12. "Nara Takeji jijūbukanchō nikki (shō)," p. 342.

13. Gary B. Ostrower, *Collective Insecurity: The United States and the League of Nations During the Early Thirties* (London: Associated University Presses, 1993), pp. 94–96.

14. "Nara Takeji jijūbukanchō nikki (sho)," p. 344.

15. Hatano, "Manshū jihen to 'kyūchū' seiryoku," p. 122.

16. Ibid., citing Nara, Oct. 8, 1931.

17. "Nara Takeji jijūbukanchō nikki (sho)," p. 345.

18. Hatano, "Manshū jihen to 'kyūchū' seiryoku," p. 129, citing *MNN*, Nov. 8, 1931. Hsi Hsia (Ko-min) graduated from a Japanese army cadet school in 1911 and later served with Chang Tso-lin. After Sept. 18, he declared the independence of Kirin Province and soon joined the Manchukuo puppet regime.

19. Ibid., pp. 129–30.

20. Masuda Tomoko, "Seitō naikakusei no hōkai," in Tokyo Daigaku Shakai Kagaku Kenkyūjo, ed., *Gendai Nihon shakai, 4 rekishiteki zentei* (Tokyo Daigaku Shuppankai, 1991), pp. 193–94.

21. Ostrower, *Collective Insecurity*, pp. 94–96.

22. Shimada Toshihiko, "The Extension of Hostilities, 1931–1932," in *Japan Erupts: The London Naval Conference and the Manchurian Incident, 1928–1932* (Columbia University Press, 1984), p. 287; Hatano, "Manshū jihen to 'kyūchū' seiryoku," pp. 121–22, 123, n. 64.

23. After World War II the *New York Times*, on June 24, 1946, accused Shidehara of being an "accomplice of the militarists," who had "helped to confuse the world about an event which the Japanese later extolled as the beginning of the Second World War."

24. Seki Hiroharu, "The Manchurian Incident, 1931," p. 164. After the failure of the March coup incident, many middle-echelon officers became convinced that military action in Manchuria was the essential precondition to political reform at home.

25. *Harada nikki, dai nikan,* p. 81, cited in Hatano, "Manshū jihen to 'kyūchū' seiryoku," p. 126.

26. *KYN, dai gokan,* p. 265.

27. Otabe Yūji, "Nii ten niiroku jiken, shubōsha wa dare ka," in Fujiwara Akira et al., eds, *Nihon kindaishi no kyozō to jitsuzō 3, Manshū jihen—haisen* (Ōsuki Shoten, 1989), p. 81; and, in the same volume, Abe Hirozumi, "Nihon ni fuashizumu wa nakatta no ka," p. 206.

28. Ikō Toshiya, "Seitō seiji wa naze owatta no ka," in Fujiwara et al., eds., *Nihon kindaishi no kyozō to jitsuzō 3,* pp. 68–70. Ikō discusses Inukai's speech of Nov. 3, 1931, to a general meeting of Seiyūkai members.

29. *KYN, dai gokan,* pp. 219–20.

30. Ibid., p. 225.

31. Ibid., entry of Dec. 27, 1931, p. 227.

32. Aoyama Teruaki, "Ima, naze Tōgō Heihachirō ka?" in *Bunka hyōron* 436 (Dec. 1989), p. 68.

33. *ISN, dai ikkan,* p. 47. Hirohito regarded their ennoblement as "no big deal." See *Kido Kōichi nikki, jō,* p. 445.

34. Masuda, "Seitō naikaku no hōkai," in Tokyo Daigaku Shakai Kagaku Kenkyūjo, ed., *Gendai Nihon Shakai, 4 rekishiteki zentei,* pp. 204–205.

35. Miyaji Masato, "Seijishi ni okeru tennō no kinō," in Rekishigaku Kenkyūkai, ed., *Tennō to tennōsei o kangaeru* (Aoki Shoten, 1986), p. 98; Masuda, "Seitō naikakusei no hōkai," p. 214.

36. *Japan Times,* Jan. 12, 1932, reported that the emperor also notified the Sun Goddess of his safe deliverance from the assassin by performing rites at the Kashikodokoro (Place of Awe) within the palace, and by dispatching messengers to the Grand Shrine at Ise and to the Mausoleum of Emperor Jimmu in Nara prefecture.

37. *Kido Kōichi nikki, jō,* p. 127, entry of Jan. 8, 1932; Otabe Yūji, "Kaisetsu: gō ten ichigō jiken zengo no tennō, kyūchū," in *KYN, dai rokkan,* p. 273.

38. Jonathan Haslam, *The Soviet Union and the Threat from the East, 1933–41* (University of Pittsburgh Press, 1992), p. 8.

39. Katsuno Shun, *Shōwa tennō no sensō* (Tosho Shuppansha, 1990), p. 60.

40. Walter Lafeber, *The Clash: A History of U.S.-Japan Relations* (W. W. Norton & Co., 1997), p. 172.

41. Shimada, "The Extension of Hostilities, 1931–1932," pp. 306–7.

42. Fujiwara Akira, "Nitchū sensō ni okeru horyo gyakusatsu," in *Kikan sensō sekinin kenkyū* 9 (Autumn 1995), p. 18.

43. Ibid., p. 19.

44. Ibid.

45. In his "Monologue," Hirohito noted that he had brought an end to the fighting in Shanghai. "When the suspension of hostilities occurred on March 3," it was "because I had expressly ordered Shirakawa beforehand not to expand the conflict." His decisive action in an area where Britain and the United States had substantial interests should be contrasted with his silence and lack of reflection about having sanctioned the aggression in Manchuria. See *STD,* p. 28; Fujiwara Akira et al., *Tettei kenshō: Shōwa tennō 'dokuhakuroku'* (Ōtsuki Shoten, 1991), p. 82.

46. Fujiwara Akira, "'Tennō no guntai' no rekishi to honshitsu," in *Kikan sensō sekinin kenkyū* 11 (Spring 1996), p. 67. During the China war, Japanese pilots shot down

over enemy territory and taken prisoner often committed suicide on their return. Around the time of the Nomonhan Incident in 1939, repatriated noncommissioned officers were frequently court-martialed, and some felt compelled to commit suicide. The reverse side of this battlefield psychology was the organized murder of Chinese prisoners of war.

47. On the glorification of militarism during this period, see Louise Young, *Japan's Total Empire: Manchuria and The Culture of Wartime Imperialism* (University of California Press, 1997); Kinbara Samon, Takemae Eiji., eds., *Shōwashi, zōhoban* (Yūhikaku Sensho, 1989), pp. 93–97.

48. *Kido Kōichi nikki, jō*, p. 167. The naval officers had been influenced by Ōkawa Shūmei and Lt. Comm. Fujii Hitoshi, an ultranationalist killed at Shanghai in February 1932. See *TN, dai nikan* (Chūō Kōronsha, 1995), May 20, 1933, p. 78.

49. Five days after Inukai's murder, Army Minister Araki warned divisional commanders that "movements of the emperor's army are made on irreversible orders from him. The entire imperial army must be held monolithic and never allowed to form free, vertical commands and act like private armies. In short, it . . . can take action only on the basis of the emperor's orders." Cited in Masuda, "Saitō Makoto kyokoku itchi naikakuron," in *Shiriizu Nihon kingendaishi, kōzō to hendō, 3 gendai shakai e no tenkai* (Iwanami Shoten, 1993), p. 234.

50. *Harada nikki, dai nikan*, pp. 287–88, Masuda, "Saitō Makoto kyokoku itchi naikakuron," p. 235; Kojima, *Tennō, dai nikan*, pp. 220–27.

51. Otabe Yūji, "Tennōsei ideorogii to shin Ei-Bei-ha no keifu: Yasuoka Masahiro o chūshin ni," in *Shien* 43, no. 1 (May 1983), pp. 26–28. By 1932 Yasuoka had acquired a reputation as the "ideologue of the new bureaucrats."

52. Masuda, "Saitō Makoto kyokoku itchi naikakuron," p. 238.

53. Otabe, "Kaisetsu: gō ten ichigō jiken zengo no tennō, kyūchū," in *KYN, dai rokkan*, p. 276.

54. *NH*, p. 60.

55. Masuda, "Saitō Makoto kyokoku itchi naikakuron," pp. 237–38.

56. Miyaji, "Seijishi ni okeru tennō no kinō," p. 99. The army's famous pamphlet, *Kokubō no hongi to sono kyōka no teishō*, issued in Oct. 1934, expounded the idea of a national defense state.

57. On the Meiji political order, see Nagai Kazu, *Kindai Nihon no gunbu to seiji* (Shibunkaku Shuppan, 1993), p. 260.

58. Masuda, "Saitō Makoto kyokoku itchi naikakuron," p. 256.

59. Yu Shinjun, *Manshū jihenki no Chū-Nichi gaikōshi kenkyū* (Tōhō Shoten, 1986), p. 380. Concerned to counter charges of violating the Nine-Power Pact, the Foreign Ministry commissioned Hirohito's teacher of international law, Tachi Sakutarō, to devise legal justifications for the recognition of Manchukuo.

60. Yu Shinjun, *Manshū jihenki no Chū-Nichi gaikōshi kenkyū*, p. 381.

61. Ibid.

62. Ibid.

63. James B. Crowley, *Japan's Quest for Autonomy: National Security and Foreign Policy, 1930–1938* (Princeton University Press, 1966), p. xv.

64. Masuda, "Saitō Makoto kyokoku itchi naikakuron," p. 255.

65. Nakamura Kikuo, *Shōwa rikugun hishi* (Banchō Shobō, 1968), pp. 41–43.

66. "Nara Takeji jijūbukanchō nikki (sho)," Nov. 22, 1932, p. 346.

67. Ibid.; *MNN*, pp. 534–35.

68. "Nara Takeji jijūbukanchō nikki (sho)," pp. 346–349; Yamada, *Dai gensui Shōwa tennō*, p. 53.

69. *MNN*, p. 538, *Kido Kōichi nikki, jō*, p. 215.

70. Yamada, *Dai gensui Shōwa tennō* pp. 50–51.

71. For the Soviet military buildup in the Far East, its costs and consequences, see Haslam, *The Soviet Union and the Threat From the East, 1933–41*, pp. 24–39.

72. "Nara Takeji jijūbukanchō nikki (sho)," p. 348.

73. Joseph C. Grew, Diary No. 17, Feb. 11, 1933, p. 453. In Joseph Grew Papers, Houghton Library, Harvard University.

74. "Nara Takeji jijūbukanchō nikki (sho)," p. 348.

75. Ibid., pp. 348–49; Yamada, *Dai gensui Shōwa tennō*, p. 52.

76. "Nara Takeji jijūbukanchō nikki (sho)," p. 349.

77. Ibid.; Yamada, *Dai gensui Shōwa tennō*, pp. 51–53.

78. Parks M. Coble, *Facing Japan: Chinese Politics and Japanese Imperialism, 1931–1937* (Harvard University Press, 1991), pp. 94–95.

79. "Nara Takeji jijūbukanchō nikki (sho)," p. 351, entries of Feb. 21–22, 1933.

80. *Kido Kōichi nikki, jō*, p. 216. On the League's mandate system, see Sharon Korman, *The Right of Conquest* (Oxford, Clarendon Press, 1996), pp. 142–43.

81. Otabe Yūji, "Han Ei-Bei datta Konoe shushō, 'dokudansha' Matsuoka zō no shūsei mo," in *Shinano Mainichi* (June 5, 1995).

82. Although Japan contributed financially to the League on a reduced basis until 1938, Matsuoka's walkout ended its thirteen-year political relationship with the international body.

83. *Harada nikki, dai sankan*, p. 46. Honjō Shigeru, in his diary entry of Feb. 8, 1934 (pp. 185–86) claims that the emperor told him that "[a]t the time of our withdrawal from the League, groups such as the Imperial Military Reservists Association sent telegrams directly to the League of Nations, or forcefully conveyed their opinions to the chief aide-de-camp and the grand chamberlain. Worried that they were exceeding their spheres of authority, I cautioned that everyone should fulfill their own duties."

84. Inoue, *Tennō no sensō sekinin*, p. 58; *Harada nikki, dai sankan*, p. 46.

85. *MNN*, p. 546.

86. On Sept. 19, 1931, Sasagawa Ryōichi, leader of the right-wing Kokusui Taishūtō [National Essence Mass Party] visited the Osaka *Asahi shinbun* to complain about the *Asahi's* "lukewarm" editorials about the army in Manchuria. A few days later Uchida Ryōhei, president of the Kokuryūkai, threatened the *Asahi* for not doing a properly patriotic job. Such pressure, applied early, easily turned the major dailies into avid supporters of militarism. See Arai Naoyuki, "Tennō hōdō no naniga kawari, nani ga kawaranakatta no ka," in Nihon Jyânarisuto Kaigi, ed., *Yameru masu komi to Nihon* (Kōbunkyō, 1995), pp. 181–82.

87. The forced conversion to emperor ideology of many imprisoned communist intellectuals—the most dynamic opponents of Japanese militarism—occurred around the same time, paving the way for the destruction of the Left. However, the most privileged group in Japanese society set the precedent of apostasy.

88. During the secret session of the House of Peers, Akaike Atsushi, former superintendent of the Metropolitan Police, raved about a conspiracy against Japan by "the

secret society called the Freemasons, or the Jews behind the scene." Professor Yamamuro Shinichi of Kyoto University criticized the reasoning of his fellow peers who "self-righteously" insisted on believing that Japan alone was correct and the League was "one-sidedly oppressing" it. See *Asahi shinbun*, June 5, 1995; Shūgiin Jimukyoku, ed., *Teikoku gikai shūgiin himitsukai giji sokkirokushū 1* (Shūeikai, 1996), pp. 247–55.

89. For a helpful overview, see Waldo H. Heinrichs, Jr., "1931–1937," in Ernest R. May and James C. Thomson, Jr., ed., *American-East Asian Relations: A Survey* (Harvard Univ. Press, 1972).

90. Haslam, *The Soviet Union and the Threat from the East, 1933–41*, p. 28. Citing a British military intelligence estimate, Haslam notes that "[by] June [1932] . . . east of Irkutsk in Siberia Soviet forces had grown to just over 200,000 men, excluding border troops." The Soviet war preparations to counter the threat from Japan's Kwantung Army exacerbated food shortages in European Russia.

91. Katsuno, *Shōwa tennō no sensō*, p. 59; *KYN, dai rokkan*, p. 18. Minami's views on Manchuria were quickly challenged by Prime Minister Inukai, who opposed the creation of Manchukuo. The population of Japan in 1940 had risen to 71.4 million. See *Historical Statistics of Japan*, vol. 1 (Japan Statistical Association, 1987), p. 168.

92. *KYN, dai rokkan*, p. 25; Katsuno, *Shōwa tennō no sensō*, pp. 59–60. Matsuoka's court sponser was Privy Seal Makino.

93. Quoted in Shōji Junichirō, "Konoe Fumimaro zō no saikentō: taigai ishiki o chūshin ni," in Kindai Gaikōshi Kenkyūkai, ed., *Hendōki no Nihon gaikō to gunji* (Hara Shobō, 1987), pp. 101–2.

94. Yabe Teiji, ed., *Konoe Fumimaro, jō* (Kōbundō, 1952), pp. 239–40.

95. Kido Kōichi acknowledged these motivating factors in his Sugamo prison interrogations. See the Kido-Sackett exchanges of Jan. 28 and Feb. 7, 1946. For concise accounts of the Manchurian Incident and the Asia-Pacific war, see Eguchi, *Jūgonen sensō shōshi*, pp. 11–75, and Okabe Makio, "Ajia-Taiheiyō sensō," in Nakamura Masanori et al., eds., *Sengō Nihon, senryō to sengo kaikakū, dai ikkan. Sekaishi no naka no 1945* (Iwanami Shoten, 1995), pp. 30–40.

96. Kobayashi Michiko, "Sekai taisen to tairiku seisaku no henyō," in *Rekishigaku kenkyū* 656 (Mar. 1994), p. 15.

97. Shōji, "Konoe Fumimaro zō no saikentō: taigai ishiki o chūshin ni," p. 14.

98. Quoted in Yoshida, "Konoe Fumimaro: 'kakushin-ha kyūtei seijika no gosan," in Yoshida Yutaka, Ara Kei, et al., *Haisen zengo Shōwa tennō to gonin no shidōsha*, p. 15.

99. Masuda, "Saitō Makoto kyokoku itchi naikakuron," p. 258; Yoshida Yutaka, "Tennō to sensō sekinin," in Fujiwara et al., *Tennō no Shōwa shi* (Shin Nihon Shinsho, 1990), p. 61.

100. "Jokan no nichijō no aramashi," in *KYN, dai rokkan*, pp. 218–20; Koyama Itoko, *Kōgōsama: Nagako Empress of Japan* (Suzakusha, 1959), p. 368.

101. Fujiwara, *Shōwa tennō no jūgonen sensō*, pp. 76–77.

102. From Sept. 1931 through July 1936, Japan's combatant dead and wounded numbered 3,928, while Chinese (anti-Japan, anti-Manchukuo) forces, fighting mainly a guerrilla war, suffered 41,688 deaths. Kisaka Junichirō, "Ajia-Taiheiyō sensō no rekishiteki seikaku o megutte," in *Nenpō: Nihon gendaishi, sōkan, sengo gojūnen no rekishiteki kenshō* (Azuma Shuppan, 1995), pp. 29–30.

103. Youli Sun, *China and the Origins of the Pacific War, 1931–1945* (St. Martin's Press,

1993), pp. 41–62, discusses the "gradualist" rationale behind Chiang's policy and the dilemmas it engendered.

104. *TN, dai nikan*, pp. 89–91; also see pp. 116–17.

105. Uryū Tadao, "Kōsaku eiga, Nihon nyūsu shōshi," in *Bessatsu ichiokunin no Shōwashi: Nihon nyūsu eiga shi* (Mainichi Shinbunsha, 1977), p. 520.

106. The analysis in this and the next few paragraphs is based on the incomplete script of *Hijōji Nihon* and the open-court testimony of Mizuno Yoshiyuki, who in 1933 headed the movie department of the Osaka Mainichi. Both documents are reproduced in *GS40*.

107. Mizuno in *GS40*, pp. 253–54.

108. *GS40*, pp. 242–43.

109. Ibid., p. 248, reel/segment 9.

110. Ibid., pp. 251–52. Meiji's three poems were: "The bravery of the Yamato spirit always manifests itself in an emergency"; "A man pierces iron with an arrow. Our Yamato spirit carries it through"; "If we gather together the strength of hundreds of thousands of loyal subjects, we can accomplish anything."

111. Material in this and the following paragraphs, unless otherwise noted, is drawn from Suzaki Shinichi, "Sōryokusen rikai o megutte: rikugun chūjiku to 2.26 jiken no seinen shōkō no aida," in *Nenpō Nihon gendaishi, No. 3 1997* (Gendai Shiryō] Shuppan, 1997).

112. Ibid., p. 35.

113. Ibid., p. 56.

114. Tōjō Hideki, "Shōhai no bunkiten wa shisōsen: senji heiji tomo sunkokumo yudan wa naranu," in Rikugun, ed., *Hijōji kokumin zenshū* (Chūō Kōronsha, 1934), pp. 54, 65.

115. Suzaki, "Sōryokusen rikai o megutte," p. 63.

CHAPTER 8
RESTORATION AND REPRESSION

1. Emilio Gentile, *The Sacralization of Politics in Fascist Italy*, trans. Keith Botsford (Harvard University Press, 1996), p. 14.

2. Miwa Yasushi, "Sensō to fuashizumu o soshi suru kanōsei wa nakatta no ka," in Fujiwara et al., eds., *Nihon kindaishi no kyozō to jitsuzō 3, Manshū jihen—haisen* (Ōtsuki Shoten, 1989), p. 49. Most of those seized by police were Marxists who had dwelt on class exploitation and redefined the emperor as an oppressor.

3. David G. Goodman, Masanori Miyazawa, *Jews in the Japanese Mind: The History and Uses of a Cultural Stereotype* (Free Press, 1995), pp. 104–5; 106–34.

4. Yasumaru, *Kindai tennōzō no keisei*, p. 267.

5. "Senjinkun," in Bushidō Gakukai, ed., *Bushidō no seizui* (Teikoku Shoseki Kyōkai, 1941), p. 15.

6. Robert J. Smith and Ella Lury Wiswell, *The Women of Suye Mura* (University of Chicago Press, 1982), pp. 112–13.

7. Grand Chamberlain Suzuki may have urged Hirohito to change his foreign policy mainly to avoid such criticism. See Otabe, "Kaisetsu: Manshū jihen to tennō, kyūchū," in *KYN, dai goken*, p. 26.

8. Okabe Nagakage, *Okabe Nagakage nikki: Shōwa shoki kazoku kanryō no kiroku*. Shōyū Kurabu, ed. (Kashiwa Shobō, 1993), pp. 77, 356; *Harada nikki, dai nikan*, p. 47; *KYN, dai goken*, p. 198, entry of Nov. 14, 1931; Otabe, "Kaisetsu: Manshū jihen to tennō, kyūchū," p. 26.

9. *TN, dai nikan,* p. 124, entry of Aug. 6, 1933.

10. "Nara Takeji kaisōroku," May 28, 1932, p. 415. Nara notes (p. 416) that the reassignment of Prince Chichibu to the Army General Staff occurred on August 24, 1932, "in response to the emperor's wish."

11. Ibid., p. 426.

12. In interrogation documents compiled by the International Prosecution Section but not used at the Tokyo war crimes trial, Kido Kōichi identified General Araki as a person who had given approval for assassinations. See Awaya Kentarō et al., eds., *Tokyo saiban shiryō: Kido Kōichi jinmonchōsho* (Ōtsuki Shoten, 1987), p. 547.

13. Kinbara Samon, Takemae Eiji, eds., *Shōwa shi (zōhoban): kokumin no naka no haran to gekidō no hanseiki,* p. 101.

14. *TN, dai nikan,* Sept. 26, 1933, pp. 147–48.

15. *MNN,* p. 636, cited in Matsuzaki Shōichi, "Saikō 'Umezu-Ho Ying-ch'in kyōtei'," in Gunjishi Gakkai, ed., *Nitchū sensō no shosō* (Menshōsha, 1997), p. 45.

16. Foreign Ministry official Amou Eiji had declared Japan responsible for the maintenance of peace and order in East Asia, and opposed in principle to any offers of significant financial or technical assistance to China. For discussion, see Kobayashi Motohiro, "Hirota Kōki ni sensō sekinin wa nakatta ka," in Fujiwara et al., eds., *Nihon kindaishi no kyozō to jitsuzō 3, Manshū jihen—haisen,* p. 100.

17. Katsuno, *Shōwa tennō no sensō,* p. 76.

18. Masuda Tomoko, "Tennō kikansetsu haigeki jiken to kokutai meichō undō," in *Nagoya daigaku, Hōsei ronshū* 173 (Mar 1998). My page citations are to the galley proofs of this article, kindly made available to me by the author.

19. On Mazaki's intervention see Wakatsuki Yasuo, *Nihon no sensō sekinin: saigo no sensō sedai kara, jō* (Hara Shobō, 1995), p. 181; *Mazaki Jinzaburō nikki, dai nikan* (Yamakawa Shuppansha, 1981), p. 64.

20. Katsuno, *Shōwa tennō no sensō,* p. 75.

21. The first Okada statement had been drafted entirely by civil officials: namely, his private secretary Sakomizu Hisatsune, the director general of the Cabinet Legislation Bureau Kanamori Tokujirō, chief of the Cabinet Research Bureau Yoshida Shigeru, and Cabinet Secretary Shirane. See Masuda Tomoko, "Tennō kikansetsu haigeki jiken to kokutai meichō undō," p. 20.

22. Cited in ibid., p. 21. The Okada cabinet's second statement on Minobe's organ theory was issued on Oct. 15.

23. Minobe, *Kenpō satsuyō,* cited in Suzuki Masayuki, *Kōshitsu seido,* p. 183.

24. Masuda, "Tennō kikansetsu haigeki jiken to kokutai meichō undō," p. 23.

25. Suzuki, *Kōshitsu seido,* p. 185.

26. Miyaji Masato, "Seijishi ni okeru tennō no kinō," in Rekishigaku Kenkyūkai, ed., *Tennō to tennōsei o kangaeru,* p. 101.

27. Honjō Shigeru, *Honjō nikki* (Hara Shobō, 1989), Mar. 29, 1935, p. 204.

28. "Shōwa tennō no dokuhakuroku hachi jikan" in *Bungei shunjū* (Dec. 1990), p. 104.

29. Masuda, "Tennō kikansetsu haigeki jiken to kokutai meichō undō," p. 22. Although Masuda argues that the emperor defended Minobe indirectly, there seems to be no concrete evidence to support that view.

30. *Honjō nikki,* p. 204; also cited in Katsuno, *Shōwa tennō no sensō,* p. 77. Honjō kept arguing with the emperor about the organ theory right through April and May.

31. *TN, dai nikan,* p. 375.

32. On the connection between the Aizawa trial and the February 26 mutiny, see Crowley, pp. 267–73; Ben-Ami Shillony, *Revolt in Japan: The Young Officers and the February 26, 1936, Incident* (Princeton University Press, 1973), pp. 113–14. On other

triggering causes see, Otabe, "Nii ten niiroku jiken, shubōsha wa dare ka," p. 82.

33. Suzuki Kenji, *Sensō to shinbun* (Mainichi Shinbun, 1995), p. 117–18. Intimidation worked. The major urban dailies avoided editorial criticism of the military, leaving discussion of the incident mainly to smaller, local papers.

34. Hata Ikuhiko, *Shōwa-shi o juso suru* (Gurafusha, 1984), p. 70.

35. Otabe, "Nii ten niiroku jiken, shubōsha wa dare ka," pp. 76–77, 93. My analysis of the uprising is based largely on Otabe's essay. Hata Ikuhiko, *Hirohito tennō itsutsu no ketsudan* (Kōdansha, 1984), Yamada Akira, *Daigensui Shōwa tennō* (Shin Nihon Shuppansha, 1994), Kido Kōichi's dairy, the interrogation of Kido by Henry R. Sackett, plus other sources cited below. One of the few studies in English on the mutiny is Shillony's *Revolt in Japan*.

36. Yasumaru, *Kindai tennōzō no keisei*, pp. 281–82.

37. Hata, *Hirohito tennō itsutsu no ketsudan*, p. 25, citing *Kido Kōichi kankei bunsho*, p. 106.

38. Ibid., p. 26.

39. Otabe, "Ni ten niroku jiken, shubōsha wa dare ka," p. 77.

40. *Kido Kōichi nikki, jō*, p. 464. "If I cannot ask your majesty's opinion directly, can I query the lord keeper of the privy seal?" To this question too Hirohito replied no.

41. Cited in Otabe, "Nii ten niiroku jiken, shubōsha wa dare ka," p. 77; also see the discussion of the "army minister's instruction" in Shillony, *Revolt in Japan*, pp. 153–54.

42. Hata, *Hirohito tennō itsutsu no ketsudan*, p. 26.

43. Yamada, *Daigensui Shōwa tennō*, p. 58.

44. Hata, *Hirohito tennō itsutsu no ketsudan*, pp. 29, 39.

45. Ibid., p. 37.

46. On March 27, 1938, Saionji told Harada, "with a pained expression" that:

> Awfully dark facts exist in Japanese history. Emperor Suizei, who followed Emperor Jimmu was enthroned as emperor only after his brothers were murdered. . . . Of course, I'm sure no such thing will ever happen of the prince's own will. But if those who surround him should ever create such a situation, then I don't know. I cannot believe any member of the imperial family would ever do such a thing today. But we have to bear this possibility in mind and be very careful hereafter.

Saionji returned to the problem of sibling rivalry exactly one month later, on April 27, when he instructed Harada to warn Kido and Konoe to be alert to any tensions in the emperor's relations with his brothers:

> . . . there are many instances in Japanese history in which young brothers murdered their elder brothers and enthroned themselves. . . . I am sure there are no problems with Princes Chichibu and Takamatsu. [But] tell them to always pay attention to situations where dangerous elements might emerge from among the imperial household . . .

Harada nikki, dai rokkan (Iwanami Shoten, 1956), pp. 265, 297.

47. Koyama Itoko, *Kōgōsama* (Suzakusha, 1959), p. 211.

48. Yamada Akira, *Gunbi kakuchō no kindaishi: Nihongun no bōchō to hōkai* (Yoshikawa Kōbunkan, 1997), pp. 9–10.

49. Otabe, "Nii ten niiroku jiken, shubōsha wa dare ka," pp. 83–84.

50. Cited in Suzaki Shinichi, "Sōryokusen rikai o megutte: rikugun chūjiku to ni ten niroku jiken no seinen shōkō no aida," in *Nenpō Nihon gendaishi* 3 (1997), p. 73.

51. Ibid., p. 77.

52. Imaoka Yutaka, "Shina jihen mae no sanbō no ugoki," in Dōdai Kurabu Kōenshū, *Shōwa gunji hiwa, ge* (Dōdai Keizai Konwakai kan, 1989), p. 116.

53. *STD*, pp. 32–33. Hirohito forced the resignation of Generals Araki, Hayashi, Mazaki, Nishi, Abe, Ueda, and Terauchi and sanctioned the placing of four of them on the reserve list. See Hillis Lory, *Japan's Military Masters: The Army in Japanese Life* (Greenwood Press, 1943, 1973), p. 115.

54. Yamada, *Dai gensui Shōwa tennō*, pp. 56, 59.

55. "When I made cabinet reports to the throne," Admiral Okada later recollected, "His majesty would clearly reply 'yes' when he agreed but say nothing when he disagreed. On occasions when he took issue with documents that were offered him, he frequently kept them in his hand." Cited in Yoshida Yutaka, "Tennō no sensō sekinin," in Fujiwara et al., *Tennō no Shōwashi* (Shin Nihon Shuppansha, 1984), p. 43.

56. Shibata Shinichi, *Shōwa-ki no kōshitsu to seiji gaikō* (Hara Shobō, 1995), p. 32. On March 4, 1936, the emperor told Honjō:

> . . . to pay careful attention to the words I use because if they are too strong, then once again it will cause resentment against the Lord Keeper of the Privy Seal. As for myself, I deeply regret that they murdered my most loyal and trusted ministers and general. This is like strangling me with raw silk. What they did violated both the constitution and the rescripts of the Meiji emperor.

Shibata, pp. 34–35.

57. "Case 212, Hirota Kōki," in Awaya Kentarō, Yoshida Yutaka, eds., *Kokusai kensatsu kyoku (IPS) jinmon chōsho, dai 28 kan* (Nihon Tosho Sentā, 1993), pp. 414, 417, 506. Hirota later denied having restricted the candidates for ministerial position to the active duty list, since prime ministers were still permitted to search the inactive list and to have reserve officers appointed to the ministerial position.

58. Figuring in Hirota's indictment as a war criminal was the charge of restricting ministerial posts to active-duty officers, made by Admiral Yonai among others. American occupation officials uncritically accepted the charge because it dramatized the enfeeblement of civilian politicians. Since the army already had the power to topple cabinets by withholding a service minister, this event has as much to do with postwar as with prewar history.

59. Eguchi Keiichi, "Chūgoku sensen no Nihongun," in Fujiwara Akira, Imai Seiichi, eds., *Jūgonen sensōshi 2: Nitchū sensō* (Aoki Shoten, 1988), p. 51, citing the *Tokyo nichi nichi shinbun*, Dec. 12 and 13, 1935.

60. Eguchi, *Jūgonen sensō shōshi, shinpan*, p. 108.

61. Fujiwara Akira, "Tennō to kyūchū," in Igarashi Takeshi, Kitaoka Shinichi, eds., *"Sōron," Tokyo saiban to wa nan datta no ka* (Tsukiji Shokan, 1997), p. 174.

62. Antony Best, *Britain, Japan and Pearl Harbor: Avoiding War in East Asia, 1936–41* (Routledge, 1995), p. 17.

63. Best, *Britain, Japan and Pearl Harbor*, pp. 27–28.

64. Kobayashi Motohiro, "Hirota Kōki ni sensō sekinin wa nakatta ka," in Fujiwara et al., eds., *Nihon kindaishi no kyozō to jitsuzō 3*, pp. 105–7.

65. The Criteria of National Policy stated that Japan would advance by gradual, peaceful means "toward the southern Seas." The Foreign Policy of the Empire declared "the South Seas region" to be "essential for the empire's industry and national defense," and "a natural region for our future racial development. We must refrain, however, from provoking countries that have relations there, strive to dispel their fears of the Empire, and advance peacefully and gradually." Gaimushō, ed., *Nihon*

gaikō nenpyō narabi ni shuyō bunsho, ge (Hara Shobō, 1969), pp. 344–45, 347.

66. Yoshizawa Minami, *Sensō kakudai no kōzu: Nihongun no "Futsuin shinchū"* (Aoki Shoten, 1986). This is a pioneering study of how conflicts and splits developed among the groups formulating national policy during 1940. His thesis of "parallel arguments" in policy documents is as applicable to the period following the February 1936 uprising as it is to the situation in 1940. A useful study of policy making that applies Yoshizawa's insights is Moriyama Atsushi, *NichiBei kaisen no seiji katei* (Yoshikawa Kōbunkan, 1998).

67. "Kokusaku no kijun," Aug. 7, 1936, in Yamada Akira, ed., *Gaikō shiryō: kindai Nihon no bōchō to shinryaku* (Shin Nihon Shuppansha, 1997), p. 250.

68. Yamada, *Gunbi kakuchō no kindaishi*, p. 10. For a contemporary discussion of Hirota's policies, see T. A. Bisson, *Japan in China* (Macmillan Company, 1938), pp. 222–35.

69. Kōketsu, *Nihon kaigun no shūsen kōsaku*, pp. 19–20. The material in this and the next four paragraphs draws on this incisive analysis.

70. Ibid., p. 21.

71. Ibid., p. 22.

72. Ibid., pp. 21–22.

73. Ibid.,, p. 22.

74. Ibid., p. 23.

75. Aizawa Kiyoshi, "Nitchū sensō no zenmenka to Yonai Mitsumasa," in Gunji Shigakkai, ed., *Nitchū sensō no shosō* (Kinseisha, 1997), pp. 128–30.

76. Cited in Suzuki Kenji, *Sensō to shinbun*, p. 116.

77. Cited in Suzuki Masayuki, *Kōshitsu seido*, pp. 186–87.

78. Eguchi Keiichi, *Taikei Nihon no rekishi: futatsu no taisen* (Shōgakukan, 1989), pp. 299–300.

79. Otto D. Tolischus, *Tokyo Record* (London: Hamish Hamilton, 1943), p. 415.

80. Eguchi, *Taikei Nihon no rekishi*, p. 300.

CHAPTER 9
HOLY WAR

1. Kobayashi Hideo, "Ryūjōkō jiken o megutte: Ryūjōkō jiken rokujussūnen ni yosete," in *Rekishigaku kenkyū* 699 (July 1997), pp. 30–35.

2. Yamada Akira, *Daigensui Shōwa tennō*, p. 65; for slightly different, less detailed versions, Jonathan Haslam, *The Soviet Union and the Threat From the East, 1933–41: Moscow, Tokyo and the Prelude to the Pacific War* (University of Pittsburgh Press, 1992), pp. 89–90; and Clark W. Tinch, "Quasi-War Between Japan and the U.S.S.R., 1937–1939," in *World Politics* 3, no. 2 (July 1951), pp. 177–78.

3. *Harada nikki, dai rokkan*, p. 30.

4. Matsudaira Yasumasa, secretary to Privy Seal Yuasa, informed Saionji's secretary, Harada, of the emperor's linking of the Manchurian and Marco Polo Bridge Incidents during his scolding of Army Minister Itagaki Seishirō. Harada dutifully recorded the story a week later on July 28, 1938. According to Matsudaira, the emperor said, "Both at . . . the time of the Manchurian Incident and at the Marco Polo Bridge, the first episode of this incident, the field [officers] completely ignored their orders from the center and acted arbitrarily." Hirohito could only have been referring to the regimental and the batallion commanders in the vicinity of Marco Polo Bridge who were directly responsible for expanding the incident, Mutaguchi Renya and Ichiki Kiyonao; but Harada's diary entry fails to name them. Hirohito's view of the war's outbreak directly challenged the Konoe cabinet's official version. See *Harada nikki, dai nanakan*, p. 51; Eguchi Keiichi, "Rokōkyō jiken to Tsūshū jiken no hyōka o megutte," in *Kikan sensō sekinin kenkyū* 25 (Fall 1999), p. 4.

5. *Kido Kōichi nikki, ge*, p. 802.

6. Gaimushō hensan, *Nihon gaikō nenpyō narabi shuyō bunsho, ge* (Hara Shobō, 1969), p. 366.

7. In a political intelligence report of 1941, naval analysts concluded that the first Konoe cabinet had "lacked passion and implementing power to forge ahead strongly in a particular direction with all the ministers united. " Cited in Kōketsu, *Nihon kaigun no shūsen kōsaku: Ajia-Taiheiyō sensō no saikenshō*, p. 47.

8. The imperial order (*Rinsanmei* No. 64) is cited, along with detailed chronology, in *Senshi sōsho: rikukaigun nenpyō, fuki heigo, yōgo no kaisetsu* (1980), p. 11, and reproduced in full in *Senshi sōsho: Shina jihen rikugun sakusen (1): Shōwa jūsannen ichigatsu made* (1975); see also Fujiwara Akira, "Tennō to kyūchū," in Igarashi Takeshi, Kitaoka Shinichi, eds., *"Sōron" Tokyo saiban to wa nan datta no ka* (Tsukiji Shokan, 1997), p. 147.

9. Fujiwara, *Shōwa tennō no jūgonen sensō*, p. 92.

10. Eguchi, "Rokōkyō jiken to Tsūshū jiken no hyōka o megutte," pp. 2–4; T. A. Bisson, *Japan in China* (The MacMillan Co., 1938; reprinted by Greenwood Press, 1973), p. 31.

11. *Kido Kōichi nikki, jō*, p. 581; *TN, dai nikan*, pp. 510, 512, 514. Right after the Tungchow massacre, Ishiwara Kanji, leader of the nonexpansionists, delivered a lecture to Hirohito on operations against the Soviet Union in which he warned about the disadvantages of spreading the fighting in North China.

12. Fujiwara, "Tennō to kyūchū," p. 147.

13. Edgar Snow, *The Battle for Asia* (Random House, 1941), p. 46; Dick Wilson, *When Tigers Fight: The Story of the Sino-Japanese War, 1937–1945* (Viking Press, 1982), p. 33.

14. On Yonai, his sudden reversal of attitude toward the Kuomintang, and the start of the war, see Aizawa Kiyoshi, "Nitchū sensō no zenmenka to Yonai Mitsumasa," in Gunji Shigakkai, ed., *Nitchū sensō shosō* (Kinseisha, 1997), pp. 137–38

15. Kasahara Tokushi, *Nankin jiken* (Iwanami Shinsho, 1997), p. 221.

16. Fujiwara, *Shōwa tennō no jūgonen sensō*, pp. 93–94.

17. Kōketsu, *Nihon kaigun no shūsen kōsaku: Ajia-Taiheiyō sensō no saikenshō*, p. 18.

18. Kasahara, *Nankin jiken*, p. 27.

19. Usui Katsumi, *Nitchū sensō: wahei ka sensen kakudai ka* (Chūkō Shinsho, 1967), p. 46.

20. *Senshi sōsho: Shina jihen rikugun sakusen (1): Shōwa jūsannen ichigatsu made* (1975), p. 283.

21. Ibid., p. 283.

22. Ibid., p. 284. The report of the chiefs of staff explicitly noted that the capture of Nanking could be accomplished only by a large force over a long period of time.

23. Ibid., p. 285.

24. Ibid., pp. 290–91.

25. Ibid., pp. 297–99. The 13th and 101st Divisions were composed mainly of reservists who, on average, were over thirty years old. Fujiwara Akira, *Nankin no Nihongun: Nankin daigyakusatsu to sono haikei* (Ōtsuki Shoten, 1997), p. 13.

26. Fujiwara, "Nitchū sensō ni okeru horyo gyakusatsu," in *Kikan sensō sekinin kenkyū* 9 (Autumn 1995), p. 23, citing from *RikuShi himitsu dai nikki*, Bōei Kenkyūjo, Toshokan, secret telegram number 1,679 sent to China in 1937, bearing the title "Rikugun daijin kunji sōfu no ken."

27. Senda Kakō, *Tennō to chokugo to Shōwa shi* (Sekibunsha, 1990), pp. 257–58.

28. For a discussion of "compassionate killing," see Brian A. Victoria, *Zen at War* (Weatherhill, Inc., 1997), pp. 86–91.

29. Hara Takeshi, Yasuoka Akio, ed., *Nihon rikukaigun jiten* (Shinjinbutsu Ōraisha, 1997), p. 152; Mori Shigeki, "Kokusaku kettei katei no henyō: dai niji, dai sanji Konoe naikaku no kokusaku kettei o meguru 'kokumu' to 'tōsui,'" in *Nihonshi kenkyū* 395 (July 1995), pp. 36 ff.

30. Mori, "Kokusaku kettei katei no henyō," p. 41.
31. Ōe Shinobu, *Gozen kaigi*, p. 101. Official minutes were not kept, but the two volumes of documents and notes dictated by General Sugiyama, largely written by Sanada Jōichirō, and known as the Sugiyama memo, are an invaluable source. For the conferences of 1940–41, see Sanbōhonbu, ed., *Sugiyama memo, jō* (Hara Shobō, 1994).
32. *Tokyo nichi nichi shinbun* and *Tokyo Asahi shinbun* for Jan. 12, 1938; July 28, 1940; Sept. 20, 1940; Nov. 14, 1940; and July 2 and 3, 1941. The all-important imperial conferences of Sept. 6 and Nov. 5, 1941, were not, so far as I can tell, reported in the press.
33. The constituent members of the imperial conferences were the prime minister, privy council president, ministers of the army, navy, finance, and foreign affairs, the president of the cabinet Planning Board, the two chiefs of the general staffs, and the two chiefs of the army and navy Military Affairs Sections. Participants stated their views; the president of the privy council raised questions, often on the emperor's behalf; and the emperor usually (though not always) sat silently through the proceedings. Decisions were invariably reached by consensus.
34. Yasuda Hiroshi, *Tennō no seijishi: Mutsuhito, Yoshihito, and Hirohito no jidai*, pp. 272–73. The notion of the monarchy itself as a "system of irresponsibility" was first enunciated by the political scientist Maruyama Masao.
35. Hirohito's Imperial Headquarters departed from Meiji's practice in excluding civil officials on the ground that they had no right to know military secrets. His Imperial Headquarters also allowed the military to participate in shaping national policy and global strategy from a more privileged position than in the past. Conversely, it strengthened the emperor's (and thus his advisers') voice in military and political decision making. Power that Hirohito had lost to the military earlier in the decade was recovered as the war expanded and the defective nature of Japan's total war machine became increasingly apparent.
36. Sejima Ryūzō, "Taiken kara mita Dai Tō'A sensō," in Gunjishi Gakkai, ed., *Dai niji sekai taisen (3): shūsen* (Kinseisha, Sept. 1995), pp. 398–99. Final decisions of the Imperial Headquarters on matters of grave strategic import, like important decisions of the liaison conference, required meetings in the emperor's presence. However, as Yamada Akira pointed out, sometimes the two chiefs of staff made decisions of the Imperial Headquarters without ever convening a formal conference. When such a decision was formally submitted to the emperor, and approved by him, it went into effect automatically. Yamada, *Dai gensui Shōwa tennō*, p. 70.
37. Minoru Genda, a staff officer at Imperial Headquarters from November 1942 until January 1945, would later state that only the emperor could make the system work because "[t]he whole organization was split into three—that is, the Navy, the Army, and what is known as the government— and the only one [who] could coordinate the three was the emperor." Leon V. Sigal, *Fighting to a Finish: The Politics of War Termination in the United States and Japan, 1945* (Cornell University Press, 1988), p. 74.
38. Mori, "Kokusaku kettei katei no henyō," pp. 37–38.
39. Yamada Akira, "Shōwa tennō no sensō shidō: jōhō shōka to sakusen kanyo," in *Kikan sensō sekinin kenkyū* 8 (Summer 1995), p. 18. He goes on to note (p. 19) that the first Imperial Headquarters Army Order was issued on November 27, 1937, and the last, bearing the number 1,392, on August 28, 1945. The navy, following a similar procedure, issued a total of 304 Imperial Headquarters Navy Orders between July 28, 1937, and September 6, 1941. After Hirohito sanctioned the Pearl Harbor attack, the navy restarted the series, issuing Imperial Headquarters Naval Number 1 on November 5, 1941, and Number 57, its last, on September 1, 1945.
40. In his short "Introduction" to his translation of the 1941 policy conferences,

Nobutaka Ike seriously misdescribes Hirohito's relationship to the high command. See Nobutaka Ike, *Japan's Decision for War: Records of the 1941 Policy Conferences* (Stanford University Press, 1967), p. xviii.

41. Yamada, *Daigensui Shōwa tennō*, p. 185.

42. Suzaki Shinichi, "Tennō to sensō" in *Seiji taisei to sensō shidō* (n.d., n.p.), p. 218. Kido alluded to this reality in discussing the emperor's war responsibility on July 21, 1964. "When the emperor was not persuaded," he explained, "the question would be suspended and the decision postponed or the cabinet would reconsider the matter. That was the custom." *Kido Kōichi nikki—Tokyo saibanki* (Tokyo Daigaku Shuppankai, 1980), p. 454.

43. Fujiwara Akira, Imai Seiichi, Ōe Shinobu, eds., *Kindai Nihonshi no kiso chishiki* (Yūhikaku, 1972), p. 418; Yoshida, *Tennō no guntai to Nankin jiken*, p. 41; Fujiwara, *Nankin no Nihon gun: Nankin daigyakusatsu to sono haikei*, p. 18.

44. Fujiwara, *Nankin no Nihon gun*, p. 16.

45. Ibid., p. 20.

46. Kasahara, *Nankin jiken*, p. 225; Eguchi, *Jūgonen sensō shōshi, shinpan*, p. 129.

47. Kasahara, *Nankin jiken*, pp. 181–87.

48. Ibid., p. 190.

49. *TWCT*, vol. 20: *Judgment and Annexes*, transcript p. 49,608.

50. Yoshida Yutaka, *Tennō no guntai to Nankin jiken* (Aoki Shoten, 1988), p. 160; Fujiwara Akira, "Nankin daigyakusatsu no giseishasū ni tsuite—'Tokyo saiban shikan' hihan ga imi suru mono," in *Rekishi chiri kyōiku* 530 (Mar. 1995), p. 72; Daqing Yang, "Convergence or Divergence? Recent Historical Writing on the Rape of Nanjing," in *American Historical Review* 104, no. 3 (June 1999), p. 850.

The ill-preparedness of Japanese recruits for the sacrifices they were forced to make during and after the Battle of Shanghai often figures in explanations of their mass murder of Chinese POWs at Nanking. Competing with one another to reach and completely encircle the city, the soldiers craved revenge for the heavy losses they had suffered up to its fall. The vagueness of Japan's proclaimed war aims contributed to their frustration and confusion. Above all they held Chinese in contempt as an inferior race. Deeper reasons for the Nanking atrocity had to do with the characteristics of the Imperial Army itself. For recent discussions see Kōketsu Atsushi, "Tennō no guntai no tokushitsu: zangyaku kōi no rekishiteki haikei," p. 12; Fujiwara Akira, "Nitchū sensō ni okeru horyo gyakusatsu," in *Kikan sensō sekinin dai kyūgō* (Autumn 1995), pp. 22–23.

51. Eguchi Keiichi, *Taikei Nihon no rekishi 14: futatsu no taisen* (Shōgakukan, 1989), p. 259, citing the *Chicago Daily News*, Dec. 15, 1937. Using estimates made years earlier by members of the Nanking International Relief Committee, journalist Edgar Snow claimed that "the Japanese murdered no less than 42,000 people in Nanking alone" and another "300,000 civilians . . . in their march between Shanghai and Nanking." See Snow, *The Battle for Asia*, p. 57.

52. Yoshimi Yoshiaki, ed., *Jūgun ianfu shiryōshū* (Ōtsuki Shoten, 1992), see the chart on p. 191; Kōketsu, "Tennō no guntai no tokushitsu: zangyaku kōi no rekishiteki haikei," p. 14.

53. Hora Tomio, *Nankin jihen* (Shinjinbutsu Ōraisha, 1972), pp. 84–85; Kasahara Tokushi, *Nitchū zenmen sensō to kaigun: Panai gō jiken no shinsō* (Aoki Shoten, 1997), p. 283; Suzuki Kenji, *Sensō to shinbun* (Mainichi Shinbunsha, 1995), pp. 123–24.

54. Hora Tomio, *Nankin daigyakusatsu: "maboroshi" ka kōsaku hihan* (Gendaishi Shuppankai, 1975), pp. 22–26.

55. Yanaihara Tadao, "Seijiteki kaihōsha to reiteki kaihōsha," in *Kashin*, dai sankan, dai ichigō (Jan. 1940).

56. In his postwar deposition to the International Prosecution Section of the Tokyo Tribunal (May 1, 1946), Prince Asaka denied any massacre of Chinese prisoners and claimed never to have received complaints about the conduct of his troops. General Matsui also denied atrocities and went out of his way to protect Prince Asaka by shifting blame for incidents to lower ranking division commanders. Both generals may be counted among the first of the Nanking massacre deniers. For their depositions see Awaya Kentarō, Yoshida Yutaka, ed., *Kokusai kensatsukyoku (IPS) jinmonchōsho, dai 8 kan* (Nihon Tosho Centâ, 1993), Case No. 44, esp. pp. 358–66; and *Kokusai kensatsukyoku (IPS) jinmonchōsho, dai 12 kan*, p. 306.

57. Etō Genkurō then informed fellow reserve general Mazaki Jinzaburō, who wrote in his diary on Jan. 28, 1938: "Military order and discipline have collapsed. Unless they are reestablished, we will be unable to fight a serious war. It is almost unbearable to hear the stories of robbery, rape, and pillaging." Cited in Kasahara, *Nankin jiken*, p. 212.

58. Yoshida Yutaka, "Nankin jihen to kokusai hō," in Yoshida Yutaka, *Gendai shigaku to sensō sekinin* (Aoki Shoten, 1997), p. 120.

59. Shigemitsu Mamoru, *Zoku Shigemitsu Mamoru shuki* (Chūō Kōronsha, 1988), p. 295.

60. "Records of the U.S. Dept. of State Relating to Political Relations between the U.S. and Japan, 1930–1939," reel no. 3, file no. 711.94/1184, Grew's review of developments up to March 18, 1938.

61. "Hidaka Shinrokurō," in Awaya Kentarō, Yoshida Yutaka, eds., *Kokusai kensatsukyoku (IPS) jinmon chōsho, dai 42 kan* (Nihon Tosho Sentā, 1993), pp. 79–98. Hallett Abend, the *New York Times* correspondent in China at the time of the "rape," wrote in 1943 that an unnamed "high civilian Japanese official who had made a personal investigation of the atrocities" told him that he had had a "private conversation with the Emperor" in which he informed Hirohito of the details. Abend's informant may have been Hidaka Shinrokuro. Abend has him saying:

> I was accorded the very rare honor of a summons to the palace and of more than two hours of private conversation with the Emperor. . . . When I entered the great hall of audience, he ordered all attendants to retire to the doors, beyond hearing. Then he had a pillow placed for me, and I spent two hours on my knees at his feet, while he bent over and had me whisper into his ear all that I knew about the events following the capture of Nanking. I kept back nothing, and he asked many searching questions.

Abend's overdramatization of this audience, with Hirohito bending over while the kneeling informant whispers in his ear, appears false, more Chinese than Japanese. In other respects his account seems credible. In his deposition to the IPS, given on May 1, 1946, Hidaka admitted knowing Abend from his days in Shanghai. At the Tokyo trial, he testified for the defense on behalf of Gen. Matsui Iwane but was not questioned about his earlier deposition implicating the emperor. See Abend, *Pacific Charter: Our Destiny in Asia* (Doubleday, Doran & Co., 1943), pp. 38–39; *Kyokutō kokusai gunji saiban sokkiroku, dai rokkan* (Yūshōdō Shoten, 1968), dai 210 go, pp. 270–73.

62. Lt. Col. Chō Isamu, serving on the general staff of the Shanghai Expeditionary Force and as chief of the Intelligence Section of the Central China Area Army, is known to have issued orders that controlled the massacres. Fujiwara, *Nankin no Nihongun*, p. 80.

63. Kasahara, *Nitchū zenmen sensō to kaigun*, p. 168, citing Kaigunshō kaigun gunji fukyūbu, *Shina jihen ni okeru teikoku kaigun no kōdō*, p. 37.

64. *Ibid.*, pp. 161–62, citing *Shina jihen rikugun sakusen*, pp. 406–416.

65. The "Imperial Message of His Majesty the Supreme Commander" read: "We are deeply gratified that various units of the Army and Navy in the Central China Area, following up their operations in Shanghai and its environs, have pursued [the enemy] and captured Nanking. Transmit our feelings to your officers and men." Kasahara, *Nankin jiken*, p. 164, citing the *Nankin senshi shiryōshū II*.

66. Ibid., p. 213.

67. Awaya, Yoshida, ed., *Kokusai kensatsukyoku (IPS) jinmonchōsho, dai 8 kan*, p. 356.

68. The USS *Panay*, built in Shanghai in 1928 and named after the island of Panay in the American colony of the Philippines, was one of three gun boats of the American Asiatic Fleet's "Yangtze Patrol." Its "right" to navigate the river and protect American lives and property derived from the 1860 Treaty of Peking, which ended the second Opium War. For details, see Kasahara, *Nitchū zenmen sensō to kaigun*, p. 22.

69. See *Washington Post*, Dec. 14, 1937; *Los Angeles Times*, Dec. 15, 1937; *New York Times*, Dec. 1937; *Manchester Guardian*, Dec. 14 and 20, 1937; and *The Times* of London, Dec. 14 and 16, 1937.

70. Kasahara, *Nitchū zenmen sensō to kaigun*, p. 302.

71. The American press in the late 1930s generally "tended to slight events in the Pacific" and seldom gave Asian news stories front-page attention. See James C. Schneider, *Should America Go to War? The Debate over Foreign Policy in Chicago, 1939–1941* (University of North Carolina Press, 1989), p. 150.

72. Kasahara, *Nitchū zenmen sensō to kaigun*, pp. 304–5.

73. *Chicago Daily News*, Dec. 14, 1937; Kasahara, *Nitchū zenmen sensō to kaigun*, pp. 247, 303.

74. *Los Angeles Times*, Dec. 14, 1937.

75. See Allan Robert Brown, "The Figurehead Role of the Japanese Emperor: Perception and Reality." Ph.D. dissertation, Stanford University (Ann Arbor, Michigan: Univ. Microfilms, 1971), pp. 197–98.

76. Ishijima Noriyuki, "Chūgoku no kōsen taisei to taigai kankei," in Rekishigaku Kenkyūkai, ed., *Kōza sekaishi 8, Sensō to minshū: dai niji sekai taisen* (Tokyo Daigaku Shuppankai, 1996), pp. 53–54; Youli Sun, *China and the Origins of the Pacific War, 1931–1941* (St. Martin's Press, 1993), pp. 92–95.

77. Fujiwara, *Shōwa tennō no jūgonen sensō*, p. 96.

78. Kasahara, *Nitchū zenmen sensō to kaigun*, pp. 214–15.

79. Sun, *China and the Origins of the Pacific War, 1931–1941*, p. 97.

80. Fujiwara, *Shōwa tennō no jūgonen sensō*, p. 96.

81. Yamada, *Daigensui Shōwa tennō*, p. 81, citing *Gendaishi shiryō, dai kyūkan, Nitchū sensō I*, p. 50.

82. *Harada nikki, dai rokkan*, p. 204.

83. Yamada, *Daigensui Shōwa tennō*, p. 84, citing *Harada nikki, dai rokkan*, p. 207. The *Tokyo Nichi Nichi shinbun* (evening edition), Jan. 12, 1938, carried the banner head-lines: HISTORICAL IMPERIAL CONFERENCE HELD, EMPIRE'S UNSHAKEABLE POLICY DECIDED, HOPE TO ERADICATE ANTI-JAPANESE REGIME AND STRIVE TO ESTAB-LISH PEACE IN THE ORIENT. The *Tokyo Asahi shinbun*'s announcement described the seating arrangements and the layout of the conference room.

84. James B. Crowley, *Japan's Quest for Autonomy: National Security and Foreign Policy, 1930–1938* (Princeton University Press, 1966), p. 372.

85. Fujiwara, *Shōwa tennō no jūgonen sensō*, p. 97.

86. Yamada, *Daigensui Shōwa tennō*, pp. 83–84.

87. Fujiwara, *Shōwa tennō no jūgonen sensō*, p. 98.

88. Eguchi, *Taikei Nihon no rekishi 14: futatsu no taisen*, p. 263; Kōketsu, *Nihon kaigun no shūsen kōsaku*, p. 192; Kasahara, *Nitchū zenmen sensō to kaigun*, pp. 294–95.

89. Fujiwara, *Shōwa tennō no jūgonen sensō*, p. 98.

90. Yamada, *Daigensui Shōwa tennō*, p. 85.

91. Rikusen Gakkai Senshi Bukai, ed., *Kindai sensōshi gaisetsu: shiryōshū* (Rikusen Gakkai, Kudansha, 1984), n.p. These casualty figures, compiled by Demobilization Bureau No. 1 in Dec. 1945, may be the best currently available.

92. *Senshi sōsho, Chūgoku hōmen rikugun kōkū sakusen* (1974), pp. 163–64, 223–24; see also pp. 150 and 180–201.

93. Eguchi, "Chūgoku sensen no Nihongun," p. 60.

94. *Harada nikki, dai nanakan*, p. 51, entry of July 28, 1938. Harada also drew attention, several weeks later, to Kido's growing criticism of Privy Seal Yuasa Kurahei. On Sept. 16, Harada wrote that he had seen Kido on the eleventh and heard him say that "the privy seal goes by the law on everything. Whenever something happens, he says deal with the matter in accordance with the law. He urges the chief of the Metropolitan Police to apply the law. He doesn't understand the times. . . . [Yuasa] can't get along with the prime minister. The right wing, for instance, is more advanced." *Harada nikki, dai nanakan*, p. 108.

95. Tanaka, *Dokyumento Shōwa tennō, I, shinryaku* (Ryokufū Shuppan, 1989), p. 84.

96. Hsi-Sheng Ch'i, "The Military Dimension, 1942–1945," in James C. Hsiung and Steven I. Levine, *China's Bitter Victory: The War with Japan 1937–1945* (M. E. Sharpe, Inc., 1992), p. 179.

97. Inoue Kiyoshi, *Tennō no sensō sekinin* (Iwanami Shoten, 1991), p. 121.

98. Yoshimi Yoshiaki, *Kusa no ne fuashizumu: Nihon minshū no sensō taiken* (Tokyo Daigaku Shuppankai, 1991), p. 27. Tacked on to the three principles was a statement that Japan would not insist on territory or reparations, would respect China's sovereignty, abolish extraterritoriality, and give positive consideration to returning its concessions in China.

99. Okabe Makio, "Ajia-Taiheiyō sensō," in Nakamura Masanori, et al., eds, *Sengo Nihon, senryō to sengo kaikaku, dai ikkan, Sekaishi no naka no 1945* (Iwanami Shoten, 1995), p. 35.

100. *Harada nikki, dai nanakan*, pp. 249, 258. Hiranuma's designated foreign minister, Arita Hachirō, also made opposition to a tripartite pact a condition for his entering the cabinet. On Hiranuma's dissolution of the Kokuhonsha, see Christopher A. Szpilman, "The Politics of Cultural Conservatism: The National Foundation Society in the Struggle Against Foreign Ideas in Prewar Japan, 1918–1936," Ph.D. dissertation, Yale University, 1993.

101. Watanabe Toshihiko, "Nanajū ichi butai to Nagata Tetsuzan," in Chūō Daigaku Jinbun Kagaku Kenkyūjo, ed., *Nitchū sensō: Nihon, Chūgoku, Amerika* (Chūō Daigaku Shuppanbu, 1993), pp. 275–76, 296, citing (among other sources) Alvin D. Coox, *Nomonhan: Japan Against Russia, 1939*, vol. 2, p. 919; Tsuneishi Keiichi, *Kieta saikin butai*, and Eda Kenji et al., eds., *Shōgen jintai jikken*. Watanabe notes (p. 302, n. 68) that biological warfare weapons were transported to Nomonhan and that Japanese war crimes defendants at the Khaborovsk Soviet military tribunal (Dec. 1950) testified to having used them.

102. Kojima, *Tennō, dai yonkan*, p. 73; Eguchi, *Taikei Nihon no rekishi 14, futatsu no taisen*, p. 274. A higher casualty figure of 19, 714 killed is given in Watanabe Toshihiko, "Nanasan ichi butai to Nagata Tetsuzan," in Chūō Daigaku Jinbun Kagaku Kenkyūjo, ed., *Nitchū sensō: Nihon, Chūgoku, Amerika* (Chūō Daigaku Shuppanbu, 1993), p. 296.

103. By 1943 Hattori had risen to become chief of the Operations Section of the Army General Staff. In his postwar comment on the Nomonhan incident, Hirohito takes credit for the imperial command that led to the fighting:

Because the Soviet-Manchukuo border in the Nomonhan area is not clearly demarcated, both sides made false accusations of illegal encroachment. Since an imperial command had been issued to Yamada Otsuzō [this is an error; Hirohito means Gen. Ueda Kenkichi], the Kwantung Army commander, to strictly defend the Manchukuo border, there was a reason why the Kwantung Army engaged the invading Soviet troops in battle. . . . Later . . . the orders were changed so that they did not have to rigorously defend the border in undefined or remote areas.

STD, pp. 44–45, Eguchi, *Taikei Nihon no rekishi 14, futatsu no taisen*, pp. 273–74.

104. Fujiwara Akira, Awaya Kentarō et al., *Tettei kenshō: Shōwa tennō 'dokuhakuroku'* (Ōtsuki Shoten, 1991), p. 49.

105. See Donald Cameron Watt, *How War Came: The Immediate Origins of the Second World War, 1938–1939* (William Heinemann Ltd., 1989), pp. 349–60.

106. Tanaka, *Dokyumento Shōwa tennō, I: shinryaku* (Ryukufū Shuppan, 1984), pp. 98–99.

107. *Harada nikki, dai nanakan*, pp. 334, 335–36; Inoue, *Tennō no sensō sekinin*, pp. 127–29.

108. On U.S., British, and Japanese "monetary warfare" in China between 1935 and 1941, see Jonathan Kirshner, *Currency and Coercion: The Political Economy of International Monetary Power* (Princeton University Press, 1995), pp. 51–61.

109. Quoted in Tanaka, *Dokyumento Shōwa tennō, I: shinryaku*, p. 89, citing "Jijū bukanchō nikki," in *Bungei shunjū rinji zōkan* (May 1971).

110. Geoffrey Roberts, *The Soviet Union and the Origins of the Second World War: Russo-German Relations and the Road to War, 1933–1941* (London: MacMillan Press Ltd., 1995), pp. 92–93.

111. *HSN*, p. 231.

112. *Kido Kōichi nikki, ge*, p. 742–743, entry of Aug. 28, 1939.

113. *HSN*, pp. 218, 231.

114. For the circumstances surrounding Yonai's appointment, see *Kido Kōichi nikki, ge*, p. 766; *Harada nikki, dai hakkan*, pp. 166, 176; Iwabuchi Tatsuo, *Jūshinron* (Takayama Shoin, 1941), pp. 190–91; *STD*, p. 49.

115. Hosaka Masayasu, "Shōwa rikugun no kōbō, dai 6 kai Shōwa tennō to Tōjō Hideki," in *Gekkan Asahi* 3, no. 2 (Feb. 1991), p. 161.

116. Iwai Tadakuma, "Tennōsei no gojūnen," in Ritsumeikan Daigaku Jinbun Kagaku Kenkyūjo, ed., *Sengo gojūnen o dō miru ka, ge, nijū isseiki e no tenbō no tame ni* (Jinbun Shoin, 1998), p. 247.

117. Jonathan Haslam, *The Soviet Union and the Threat from the East, 1933–41*, pp. 92–94. Since mid-1937 China had benefited from having signed a secret nonaggression pact with the Soviet Union, which was delighted to have Japanese power embroiled in China. Soviet aid took the form of military advisers, pilots, planes, equipment and munitions shipped overland from Siberia and Central Asia, and by sea to Haiphong, then to Rangoon for movement over the Burma Road. Though substantial, it could never compensate for Chiang's repeated defeats on the battlefield.

CHAPTER 10
STALEMATE AND ESCALATION

1. *Senshi sōsho: Shina jihen rikugun sakusen (1): Shōwa jūsannen ichigatsu made* (1975), p. 239; Awaya and Fujiwara, "Kaisetsu," in Ki Gakujin, *Nihongun no kagakusen: Chūgoku senjō ni okeru dokugasu sakusen* (Ōtsuki Shoten, 1996), p. 374; Fujiwara Akira, "Nitchū sensō ni okeru horyo gyakusatsu," in *Kikan sensō sekinin kenkyū* 9 (Autumn 1995), p. 22.

2. Awaya Kentarō, "Ima, miketsu no sensō sekinin to wa—shazai, hoshō yōkyū to saikin, dokugasusen mondai o chūshin ni," in *Sekai* 558 (Sept. 1991).

3. Yoshimi Yoshiaki, Matsuno Seiya, "Dokugasusen kankei shiryō II, Kaisetsu," in *Jūgonen sensō gokuhi shiryōshū, hokan 2, Dokugasusen kankei shiryō II* (Funi Shuppankan, 1997), p. 27.

4. *Gendai shishiryō (9), Nitchū sensō (2).* Elucidated by Usui Katsumi (Misuzu Shobō, 1964), pp. 211–212; Tanaka Nobumasa, *Dokyumento Shōwa tennō 2, Kaisen* (Ryokufū Shuppan, 1985), p. 96. Prior to the establishment of the Imperial Headquarters, the emperor's direct orders to his commanders in chief in the field were called *rinsanmei*.

5. Yoshimi, Matsuno, "Dokugasusen kankei shiryō II, Kaisetsu," pp. 25, 29. Because eventual retaliation was feared, great care was also taken to prevent the use of gas against Westerners in China, though not against Chinese noncombatants.

6. Ibid., p. 28.

7. Ibid.

8. Awaya and Fujiwara, "Kaisetsu," p. 376. On May 14, 1938, the League of Nations adopted a resolution condemning the Japanese use of poison gas.

9. Ibid., p. 377.

10. Yoshimi, Matsuno, "Dokugasusen kankei shiryō II, Kaisetsu," p. 28.

11. Ibid., p. 29.

12. Ibid. For a discussion of the emperor and biological warfare, see Yoshimi Yoshiaki, Ikō Toshiya, *Nana san ichi butai to tennō, rikugun chūō* (Iwanami Bukkuretto No. 389, 1995), pp. 8–9.

13. Yoshimi, Ikō, *Nana san ichi butai to tennō, rikugun chūō,* pp. 8–9; Stephen Endicott, Edward Hagerman, *The United States and Biological Warfare: Secrets from the Early Cold War and Korea* (Indiana University Press, 1998).

14. Maeda Toshio, *Senryaku bakugeki no shisō: Gerunika, Jūkei, Hiroshima e no kiseki* (Asahi Shinbunsha, 1988), pp. 156, 157, 167, 420.

15. The warning of what could happen did little to check the growth of Japanese purchases of American products. By 1940 the United States still accounted for 36 percent of Japan's total imports. Oil constituted 75 percent of that total. Seventy percent of Japan's iron, 35 percent of its cotton, 32 percent of its machinery, and 90 percent of its copper all came from the United States. Ōe Shinobu, *Tōsuiken* (Nihon Hyoronsha, 1990), p. 195.

16. Eguchi, "Chugoku sensen no Nihongun," p. 61, citing the document drafted by Tanaka Ryūkichi.

17. Himeta Mitsuyoshi, "Nihongun ni yoru 'sankō seisaku, sankō sakusen' o megutte," in Chūō Daigaku Jinbun Kagaku Kenkyūjo, ed., *Nitchū sensō: Nihon, Chūgoku, Amerika* (Chūō Daigaku Shuppanbu, 1993), p. 120.

18. Fujiwara Akira, "'Sankō sakusen' to kita Shina hōmengun (1)," in *Kikan sensō sekinin kenkyū* 20 (Summer 1998), p. 23.

19. Eguchi, "Chūgoku sensen no Nihongun," p. 61.

20. Fujiwara, "'Sankō sakusen' to kita Shina hōmengun (1)," p. 27.

21. Ibid., p. 28.

22. Ibid., p. 73, citing Himeta Mitsuyoshi, *"Sankō sakusen towa nan dattaka—Chūgokujin no mita Nihon no sensō"* (Iwanami Bukkuretto, 1996), p. 43.

23. Moriyama Atsushi, *Nichi-Bei kaisen no seiji katei,* p. 53.

24. For the full text, see Yamada Akira, ed., *Gaikō shiryō: kindai Nihon no bōchō to shinryaku* (Shin Nihon Shuppansha, 1997), pp. 317–18.

25. Takagi's views were laid out in his report of July 27, 1940, entitled "The Recent Situation of the Empire and the Position of the Navy" [Teikoku no kinjō to kaigun no tachiba]. See Kōketsu, *Nihon kaigun no shūsen kōsaku,* pp. 51–54.

26. Ibid., pp. 51–52.

27. *Harada nikki, dai hakkan,* p. 32.

28. *Harada nikki, dai nanakan*, p. 339.

29. Ibid., p. 108.

30. Tanaka, *Dokyumento Shōwa tennō, I, shinryaku*, pp. 109–12.

31. *HSN*, p. 258; Yasuda Hiroshi, *Tennō no seijishi*, p. 268.

32. *Kido Kōichi niki, ge*, p. 794.

33. *HSN*, p. 268.

34. *Senshi sōsho: Rikukaigun nenpyō: fu heigo, yōgo no kaisetsu* (1980), p. 336; Gerald Bunker, *The Peace Conspiracy: Wang Ching-wei and the China War, 1937–1941* (Harvard University Press, 1972), pp. 58, 238–41.

35. *Kido Kōichi nikki, ge*, p. 802.

36. Tanaka, *Dokyumento Shōwa tennō I, shinryaku*, pp. 113–16.

37. Confidential telegram from Grew to Hull, July 21, 1940, in *Records of the U.S. Department of State Relating to the Internal Affairs of Japan, Political Affairs: July 1940 to July 1941.*

38. Yasuda, *Tennō no seijishi: Mutsuhito, Yoshihito, Hirohito no jidai*, pp. 4, 8.

39. For details of the procedures for enacting the policy document "Main Principles for Dealing with the Situation Accompanying Changes in the World Situation," see Mori Shigeki, "Kokusaku kettei katei no henyō: dainiji, daisanji Konoe naikaku no kokusaku kettei o meguru 'kokumu' to 'tōsui,'" in *Nihonshi kenkyū* 395 (July 1995), pp. 39ff.

40. Jonathan Marshall, *To Have and Have Not: Southeast Asian Raw Materials and the Origins of the Pacific War* (University of California Press, 1995), pp. 7–32, 36–53.

41. Mori Shigeki, "Kokusaku kettei katei no henyō," p. 34.

42. "Interrogation of (Marquis) Kido Kōichi, Feb. 27, 1946," in Awaya Kentarō, Yoshida Yutaka, ed., *Kokusai kensatsu kyoku (IPS) jinmonchōsho, dai sankan*, p. 533; Mori Shigeki, "Sūjiku gaikō oyobi nanshin seisaku to kaigun," in *Rekishigaku kenkyū* 727 (Sept. 1999), p. 17.

43. Moriyama, *Nichi-Bei kaisen no seiji katei*, p. 54, citing *Senshi sōsho* 65, pp. 73, 115–19.

44. Sawada Shigeru, *Sanbō jichō Sawada Shigeru kaisōroku* (Fuyō Shobō, 1982), pp. 72–73.

45. Ibid., pp. 73–74.

46. Ibid., p. 74.

47. *Kido Kōichi nikki, ge*, p. 812.

48. Yoshizawa Minami, *Sensō kakudai no kōzu: Nihongun no "Futsuin shinchū"* (Aoki Shoten, 1986), pp. 68, 70, 72.

49. Marshall, *To Have and Have Not: Southeast Asian Raw Materials and the Origins of the Pacific War*, argues that by 1940, if not earlier, both sides had come to define their national interests in mercantilist terms of control over raw materials.

50. *Kido Kōichi nikki, ge*, p. 821.

51. Ibid., p. 825.

52. For the text of the treaty, see James W. Morley, ed., *Deterrent Diplomacy: Japan, Germany, and the USSR, 1935–1940* (Columbia University Press, 1976), pp. 298–99.

53. Inoue, *Tennō no sensō sekinin*, p. 125.

54. *Harada nikki, dai nanakan*, p. 280.

55. *Kido Kōichi nikki, ge*, p. 822.

56. *Harada nikki, dai hakkan*, p. 347.

57. Yasuda, *Tennō no seijishi*, p. 270.

58. In the "Monologue" Hirohito twice noted that "Prince Chichibu advocated the Tripartite Pact." He added that "since [Chichibu] later became ill, I did not know his views [at the time]. Prince Takamatsu usually disagreed with the opinions of those in authority. . . . After the Tripartite Pact he glorified war, but with the coming of the Tōjō cabinet he changed to an antiwar view." *STD*, p. 129.

59. On Oct. 19, 1940, Kido wrote that the emperor had informed Admiral Oikawa that "Prince Chichibu is recuperating from tuberculosis and we might have to ask Prince Takamatsu to become regent should an emergency arise. Do not send him to the front line." *Kido Kōichi nikki, ge,* p. 830; Chichibu no miya Kinenkai, *Yasuhito Shinnō jikki* (Yoshikawa Kōbunkan, 1972), p. 639.

60. *Kido nikki—Tokyo saibanki* (Tokyo Daigaku Shuppankai, 1980), p. 460. Although the professed intention of the act's architects was to prevent a Japan–U.S. war, their true feelings were quite different. See Tanaka, vol. 1, pp. 117–18; Inoue, *Tennō no sensō sekinin,* p. 139.

61. Senda, *Tennō to chokugo to Shōwashi,* pp. 311–13.

62. Mori Shigeki, "Matsuoka gaikō ni okeru tai-Bei oyobi tai-Ei saku: Nichi-Doku-I sangoku dōmei teiketsu zengo no kōsō to tenkai," in *Nihonshi kenkyū,* 421 (Sept. 1997), p. 50, citing *Asahi shinbun,* morning edition, Oct. 5, 1940.

63. *Kido Kōichi nikki, ge,* p. 830, entry of Oct. 17, 1940.

64. Furukawa Takahisa, "Kigensetsu nisen roppyaku nen hōshuku kinen jigyō o meguru seiji katei," in *Shigaku zasshi* 103, no. 9 (Sept. 1994), p. 1 (1573).

65. Matsuo Shōichi, *Kindai tennōsei kokka to minshū, Ajia, ge* (Hōsei Daigaku Shuppan Kyoku, 1998), p. 183.

66. *Tokyo nichi nichi shinbun, yūkan rinji* (Nov. 11, 1940). For English translations of Hirohito's messages see *The Oriental Economist* 7, no. 11 (Nov. 1940), p. 640.

67. Antony Best, *Britain, Japan and Pearl Harbor: Avoiding War in East Asia, 1936–41* (Routledge, 1995), p. 130.

68. Edward S. Miller, *War Plan Orange: the U.S. Strategy to Defeat Japan, 1897–1945* (U.S. Naval Institute Press, 1991), 269–70. Roosevelt approved the plan's premise in November 1940, and also "assented to secret talks with the British to cast it into a combined plan for use when the nations became combat allies [p. 270]." Joint Anglo-American war planning began in early 1941.

CHAPTER 11
PROLOGUE TO PEARL HARBOR

1. Moriyama Atsushi, *Nichi-Bei kaisen no seiji katei* (Yoshikawa Kōbunkan, 1998), p. 164.

2. Mori Shigeki, "Kokusaku kettei katei no henyō: dainiji, daisanji Konoe naikaku no kokusaku kettei o meguru 'kokumu' to 'tōsui.'" *Nihonshi kenkyū* 395 (July 1995), pp. 58, 59, 60.

3. Fujiwara, *Shōwa tennō no jūgonen sensō,* p. 97.

4. Hata Ikuhiko, ed., *Rikukaigun sōgō jiten* (Tokyo Daigaku Shuppankai, 1991), p. 497.

5. Mori Shigeki, "Yamada Akira, *Daigensui Shōwa tennō,*" in Tokyo Rekishi Kagaku Kenkyūkai, *Jinmin no rekishigaku* 124 (July 1995), p. 27.

6. Sejima Ryūzō, "Taiken kara mita Dai Tō'A sensō," in Gunjishi gakkai, ed., *Dai niji sekai taisen (3): shūsen* (Kinseisha, 1995), p. 400.

7. Yamada Akira, "Shōwa tennō no sensō shidō: jōhō shūka to sakusen kanyo," in *Kikan: sensō sekinin kenkyū* 8 (Summer 1995), pp. 17–18.

8. Sejima, "Taiken kara mita Dai Tō'A sensō," pp. 389–400.

9. See Yamada's report in Fujiwara Akira, Awaya Kentarō et al., *Tettei kenshō: Shōwa tennō 'dokuhakuroku'* (Ōtsuki Shoten, 1991), p. 101.

10. Yamada, "Shōwa tennō no sensō shidō: jōhō shūka to sakusen kanyo," p. 18.

11. Morimatsu Toshio, "Shōwa tennō o oshinobi tatematsuru: Ogata jijūbukan nikki kara," in Dōdai Kurabu Kōenshū, *Shōwa gunji hiwa chūkan* (Dōdai Keizai Konwakai kan, 1989), pp. 7–8.

12. Yamada, "Shōwa tennō no sensō shidō: jōhō shūka to sakusen kanyo," p. 19.

13. Imoto Tokuma, *Sakusen nisshi de tsuzuru Dai Tō'A sensō* (Fuyō Shobō, 1979), pp. 37–38.
14. Haslam, *The Soviet Union and the Threat from the East, 1933–41*, p. 136.
15. At the railway station just before his departure, Hitler is alleged to have forewarned Matsuoka: "When you get back to Japan, you cannot report to your emperor that a conflict between Germany and the Soviet Union is out of the question." Paul Schmidt, *Hitler's Interpreter* (New York: Macmillan, 1951), p. 231.
16. Cited in Borisu Suravinsukii, *Kōshō Nisso chūritsu jōyaku: kōkaisareta Roshia gaimushō kimitsu bunsho* (Iwanami Shoten, 1996), pp. 114–16.
17. Ibid., p. 117.
18. Joseph Gordon, "The Russo-Japanese Neutrality Pact of April 1941," in S. H. Jones, Jr., and John E. Lane, eds., Columbia University East Asian Institute Studies 6: *Researches in the Social Sciences on Japan* 2 (June 1959); Suravinsukii, *Kōshō Nisso chūritsu jōyaku: kōkai sareta Roshia gaimushō kimitsu bunsho.*
19. Suravinsukii, *Kōshō Nisso chūritsu jōyaku*, pp. 129–30, 134–35.
20. Ibid., p. 134.
21. Ibid., pp. 134–42.
22. Ibid., p. 143, citing the unpublished diary of Fujii Shigeru.
23. Abe Hikota, "Dai Tō'A sensō no keisuteki bunseki," in Kondō Shinji, ed., *Kindai Nihon sensōshi, Dai Tō'A sensō* (Tokyodō Shuppan, 1997), p. 824.
24. Yoshida Yutaka, who makes this argument, also identifies the "emergency war funds special account" as the mechanism that allowed the army and navy to accumulate tremendous war power. Both services diverted emergency military appropriations, earmarked for the China war, to build up their basic war power. Both services fought the war in China on the cheap and saved the greater part of their emergency military funds for purposes of stockpiling and arms expansion. Citing the official history of the Finance Ministry (*Shōwa zaiseishi, dai yonkan* [Tōyō Keizai Shinpōsha, 1955], he estimates that the direct cost of the China war down to 1945 was only one-third of the entire emergency military allocation.

    See Yoshida Yutaka, *Nihonjin no sensōkan* (Iwanami Shoten, 1995), pp. 17–19; and Captain John Weckerling, "Military Attaché Report No. 9221," Feb. 3, 1938, p. 4, National Archives, Reel no. 13.
25. Nobutake Ike, ed. and trans., *Japan's Decision for War: Records of the 1941 Policy Conferences* (Stanford University Press, 1967), pp. 78–79. I have altered Ike's translation in part. See also Sanbōhonbu, ed., *Sugiyama memo, jō* (Hara Shobō, 1967), p. 251.
26. Awaya Kentarō et al., eds., *Tokyo saiban shiryō: Kido Kōichi jinmonchōsho* (Ōtsuki Shoten, 1987), p. 557.
27. Tanaka Nobumasa, *Dokyumento Shōwa tennō, dai ikkan, shinryaku* (Ryokufū Shuppan, 1984), p. 129; Shimada Toshihiko, *Kantōgun* (Chūkō Shinsho, 1965), pp. 168, 175.
28. In his "Monologue" Hirohito and his aides tried to pass lightly over the July 2 imperial conference and its decision to move into southern Indochina. For its main effect—the hardening of American policy toward Japan—he blamed the military. "An imperial conference on July 2," Hirohito says, "put a stop to those advocating war with the Soviet Union and, at the same time, as compensation, I sanctioned an advance into the southern part of French Indochina." Hirohito (or one of his aides) then added the preposterous statement: "Just around August, when our troops were in the process of gathering at Hainan Island and we still had time to recall them, I had military aide-de-camp Hasunuma [Ban] tell Tōjō that because of the extremely bad domestic rice crop, the nation would surely starve if rice imports from the south were

stopped, and that he should therefore discontinue the advance. But Tōjō did not obey; thus the Japanese army's advance into southern Indochina, announced on July 26, resulted finally in dreadful economic sanctions against Japan." See *STD*, p. 59.

29. Sanbōhonbu, ed., *Sugiyama memo, jō*, p. 284.

30. Moriyama, *NichiBei kaisen no seiji katei*, p. 171.

31. Ibid., pp. 164–65.

32. Yoshizawa, *Sensō kakudai no kōzu: Nihongun no Futsuin shinchū*, p. 232.

33. Michael Schaller, "The Debacle in the Philippines," in Robert Love, Jr., ed., *Pearl Harbor Revisited* (Macmillan Press Ltd., 1995), pp. 111–29; John E. Costello, "Remember Pearl Harbor," in *U.S. Naval Academy, Proceedings* (Sept. 1983), p. 55. According to Brian McAlister Linn, *Guardians of Empire: The U.S. Army and the Pacific, 1902–1940* (University of North Carolina Press, 1997), MacArthur commanded 10,569 American troops and 11,963 Filipino "scouts," for a total of 22,532. This force was considerably augmented in December. By the time Japan attacked, the "American contingent had increased to almost 19,000 with another 19,000 en route" (pp. 254, 245). In Washington many politicians and military officials familiar with MacArthur's weak defense setup understood that the Philippines were indefensible.

34. *FRUS, Japan 1931–1941, Vol. II* (Washington, D.C.: USGPO, 1943), pp. 266–67.

35. Moriyama, *Nichi-Bei kaisen no seiji katei*, pp. 166–67, citing unpublished navy records, including the diaries of Vice Navy Minister Sawamoto Yorio and Fujii Shigeru of the Military Affairs Bureau of the Navy Ministry.

36. *Sugiyama memo, jō*, p. 286.

37. Moriyama, *Nichi-Bei kaisen no seiji katei*, p. 169, citing *Sawamoto nikki*, n.p., and *Kido Kōichi nikki, ge*, p. 895.

38. Moriyama, *Nichi-Bei kaisen no seiji katei*, pp. 171–76.

39. Robert J. C. Butow, "The Hull-Nomura Conversations: A Fundamental Misconception," in *American Historical Review* 64, no. 4 (July 1960), pp. 822–36; Butow, "Backdoor Diplomacy in the Pacific: The Proposal for a Konoye-Roosevelt Meeting, 1941," in *Journal of American History* 59, no. 1 (June 1972), pp. 48–72.

40. Sudō Shinji, *Nichi-Bei kaisen gaikō no kenkyū: Nichi-Bei kōshō no hattan kara Haru nōto made* (Keiō Tsūshin, 1986), p. 184; *Kido Kōichi nikki, ge*, p. 897.

41. Moriyama, *Nichi-Bei kaisen no seiji katei*, p. 177; Sudō, *Nichi-Bei kaisen gaikō no kenkyū*, p. 184.

42. A recent example of such polemic is Seishiro Sugihara, *Between Incompetence and Culpability: Assessing the Diplomacy of Japan's Foreign Ministry from Pearl Harbor to Potsdam*, trans. Norman Hu (University Press of America, 1997).

43. Sudō, *Nichi-Bei kaisen gaikō no kenkyū*, p. 186.

44. Kōketsu Atsushi, *Nihon kaigun no shūsen kōsaku: Ajia-Taiheiyō sensō no saikentō* (Chūkō Shinsho, 1996), pp. 57–58.

45. Cited in ibid., pp. 58–59.

46. Kido's reply to Henry R. Sackett, Mar. 4, 1946, Sugamo Prison, p. 603, in case 5, vol. 5, series 81180, National Archives Record Group 331, Records of Allied Operational and Occupation Headquarters, World War II.

47. *TN, dai sankan*, pp. 283–84.

48. Yamada Akira, *Gunbi kakuchō no kindaishi: Nihongun no kakuchō to hōkai*, p. 223, citing *Senshi sōsho 65, Dai hon'ei rikugunbu, Dai Tō'A sensō kaisen keii (1)* p. 368–69.

49. Koketsu, *Nihon kaigun no shūsen kōsaku: Ajia-Taiheiyō sensō nō saikenshō*, p. 66.

50. Sanbōhonbu, ed., *Sugiyama memo, jō*, pp. 303–5, 312.

51. Ibid., p. 310.

52. *Kido Kōichi nikki, ge*, especially entries of August 11 and 28, pp. 900–901, 904. See

also *Senshi Sōsho, Daihon'ei rikugunbu, Dai Tō'A sensō kaisen keii (4)* (1974), pp. 543–44, which draws on the diaries of Konoe and Kido.

53. Shigemitsu Mamoru, *Zoku Shigemitsu Mamoru shuki* (Chūō Kōronsha, 1988), pp. 104–6.

54. According to Kido's postwar prison diary, Konoe first spoke with Kido, telling him that "the military had forced the document upon him." Kido then conferred with Hirohito and recommended that he summon General Sugiyama and Admiral Nagano.

> In connection with their replies to the emperor's questions, the emperor scolded Sugiyama but ... Nagano came to his defense, saying ... "Sometimes an operation is needed." His Majesty's biggest doubt concerned the fact that the first item in the draft document was the decision to decide whether to initiate hostilities while diplomatic negotiations came second.

Kido's account supports the image of an emperor who exhibited ambiguity because he was reluctant to initiate war with the United States and Britain. General Sugiyama's notes on the Sept. 5 briefing seem to validate this antiwar image. The notes have Hirohito saying, in a loud voice (and Konoe's later recollection of the meeting confirms this): "Do you think you can carry out the southern operations as planned?" ... "When you were a minister of state, you told me that Chiang Kai-shek would give up right away, but you still can't beat him even today!" ... "You say the interior of China is huge; isn't the Pacific Ocean even bigger than China?" Konoe's question to the emperor, however, is not in the *Sugiyama memo*. See *Kido Kōichi nikki—Tōkyo saibanki* (Tōkyo Daigaku Shuppankai, 1980), part 3, "Kyokutō kokusai gunji saiban ni kansuru danwa," pp. 461–62; Sanbōhonbu, hen, *Sugiyama memo, jō*, pp. 310–11; Yabe Teiji, *Konoe Fumimaro* (Kōbundō, 1952), p. 361.

55. Takagi Sōkichi historical documents: "Seikai shojōhō—Shōwa jūninen kara," pp. 589, 591, 592–95. The first ellipsis after "you were army minister" and the second ellipsis after "big difficulties" are in Takagi's original text; this document, in the Takagi papers at the War History Archives in Tokyo, is also cited in Kōketsu, *Nihon kaigun no shūsen kōsaku: Ajia-Taiheiyō sensō no saikenshō*, pp. 71–72.

56. Shiina Takeo, ed., *Kaigun sensō kentō kaigi kiroku: Taiheiyō sensō kaisen no keii* (Mainichi Shinbunsha, 1976), p. 28.

57. Domon Shūhei, *Tatakau tennō* (Kōdansha, 1989), p. 22.

58. *Kido Kōichi nikki, ge*, p. 905.

59. *Sugiyama memo, jō*, p. 322.

60. Domon, *Tatakau tennō*, p. 22

61. James W. Morley, ed., David A. Titus, trans., *Taiheiyo senso e no michi. English Selections: The Final Confrontation: Japan's Negotiations with the United States, 1941* (Columbia University Press, 1994), p. 176.

62. Iwai Tadakuma, *Meiji tennō "taitei" densetsu* (Sanseidō, 1997), pp. 150–51.

63. *Sugiyama memo, jō* (Hara Shobō, 1967 edition), p. 331, also cited in Domon, *Tatakau tennō*, p. 20.

64. Ibid.

65. Kōketsu, *Nihon kaigun no shūsen kōsaku*, pp. 74–75.

66. *Kido Kōichi nikki, ge*, p. 909. Writing in prison after Konoe's suicide, Kido gave this account of his Sept. 26, 1941, meeting with Konoe: "If the army insists on opening hostilities on October 15, then I have no confidence and must think about resigning." I [Kido] told him, "Since you are the one who made the decision at the impe-

rial conference of September 6, it is irresponsible for you to quit now leaving that decision as it stands." Kido, "Sensō kaihi e no doryoku," in *Kido Kōichi kankei bunsho* (Iwanami Shoten, 1966), p. 30.

67. *Kido Kōichi nikki, ge*, p. 914; also cited in Tanaka, *Dokyumento Shōwa tennō, dai ikkan*, pp. 141–42.

68. *Sugiyama memo, jō*, pp. 348–349. The day before Konoe's last cabinet meeting, the emperor had told Kido: "There seems little hope in the present situation for the Japan–U.S. negotiations. This time if hostilities erupt, I might have to issue a declaration of war." See *Kido Kōichi nikki, ge*, p. 914.

69. Otabe Yūji, "Han Ei-Bei datta Konoe Shusō, 'dokudansha' Matsuoka zō no shūsei mo" in *Shinano Mainichi* (June 5, 1995).

70. *STD*, p. 69.

71. For Konoe's letter of resignation see Yabe, *Konoe Fumimaro, ge*, pp. 395–96.

72. Hosaka Masayasu, "Shōwa rikugun no kōbō, dai roku kai, Shōwa tennō to Tōjō Hideki," *Gekkan Asahi* 3, no. 2 (Feb. 1991), p. 164, citing Tōjō's diary.

73. *Kido Kōichi nikki, ge*, p. 918.

74. *TN, dai sankan*, p. 307.

75. Fujiwara, *Shōwa tennō no jūgonen sensō*, p. 126, citing Tomita Kenji, *Haisen Nihon no uchigawa* (Kōdansha, 1962).

76. *STD*, p, 67.

77. Kaigun chūjō Hoshina Zenshirō Kaisōki, *Dai Tō'A sensō hishi: ushinawareta wahei kōsaku* (Hara Shobō, 1975), p. 43. Vice Admiral Hoshina, chief of the Navy Ministry's Weapons Bureau and a planner of the Pearl Harbor attack, attended the seventeen-hour-long liaison conference on Nov. 1 and took notes.

78. Ibid., p. 43.

79. Tanaka, *Dokyumento Shōwa tennō, dai ikkan*, pp. 270–71.

80. *Sugiyama memo, jō*, p. 387.

81. Ibid. Hirohito was referring to "Hitler's pope," the anti-Semitic Pius XII.

82. The "Plan for Ending the War with the U.S., Britain, the Netherlands, and Chiang Kai-shek" contained the following lines—the last two inserted at Hirohito's request:

> Wait for a good opportunity in the European war situation, particularly collapse of mainland England, ending of the German-Soviet war, and success of our policies toward India.
> ... [S]trengthen diplomatic and propaganda measures vis-a-vis various countries in South America, Sweden, Portugal, and the Vatican. Conclude separate agreements with Germany and Italy not to make unilateral peace.... [F]ind ways to avoid immediately concluding peace with Britain at the time of its surrender, and immediately take measures that will force Britain to induce the United States [to make peace].

The document is reproduced in full in Yamada Akira, ed., *Gaikō shiryō: kindai Nihon no bōchō to shinryaku* (Shin Nihon Shuppansha, 1997), p. 355.

83. Yamada Akira, *Daigensui Shōwa tennō* (Shin Nihon Shuppansha, 1994), p. 156.

84. Ibid., p. 156, citing *Shōwa jūroku nen jōsō kankei shorui tsuzuri, dai ikkan*. At Okehazama in Central Honshū in 1560 the first of the great unifiers of Japan, Oda Nobunaga, defeated a much larger opponent and opened the path to a new national hegemony. The penchant for discussing their modern "total war" with analogies from feudal and prefeudal history was widely shared among Japanese officers.

85. *Kido Kōichi nikki, ge*, p. 921.

86. *Kimitsu sensō nisshi*, entry of Nov. 4, 1941, p. 194. For their questions and answers, see *Sugiyama memo, jō*, pp. 388–406.

87. *Senshi sōsho: Daihon'ei rikugunbu: Dai Tō'A sensō kaisen keii (5)* (1974), pp. 338–39.

88. Fujiwara, *Shōwa tennō no jūgonen sensō*, p. 129.

89. Tanaka, *Dokyumento Shōwa tennō, dai nikan, kaisen* (Ryokufū Shuppan, 1988), p. 265.

90. Nobutake Ike, trans. and ed., *Japan's Decision for War: Records of the 1941 Policy Conferences* (Stanford University Press, 1967), p. 204; James MacGregor Burns, *Roosevelt: The Soldier of Freedom* (Harcourt Brace Jovanovich, Inc., 1970), p. 155.

91. *Kido Kōichi nikki, ge*, p. 921. Having registered in his diary the imperial conference of Nov. 5, Kido could only play down its significance when later questioned about it by American investigators after the war. Tōjō repeatedly denied the very existence of the Nov. 5 conference. When finally cornered, he lied again about its contents. Hirohito simply omitted all mention of it in his "Monologue." The prosecutors at the Tokyo tribunal had great difficulty grasping the full import of this key meeting. See: "Case File No. 20, Tōjō Hideki." in Awaya, Yoshida, eds., *Kokusai kensatsu kyoku (IPS) jinmon chōsho, dai gokan* (Nihon Tosho Centā, 1993), pp. 108, 134; and the Tōjō interrogations of March 12 and 15, 1946, in *Kokusai kensatsu kyoku (IPS) jinmon-chōsho, dai gokan.*

92. Yoshida, *Nihonjin no sensōkan*, pp. 178–79; *Senshi sōsho: Rikukaigun nenpyō, fu-heigo, yōgo no kaisetsu* (1980), p. 85.

93. *Sugiyama memo, jō*, p. 431.

94. Sudō Shinji, *Haru nōto o kaita otoko: Nichi-Bei kaisen gaikō to "yuki" sakusen* (Bungei Shunjū, 1999), p. 176.

95. Moriyama, *Nichi-Bei kaisen no seiji katei*, pp. 222–25.

96. Tanaka, *Dokyumento Shōwa tennō, dai nikan*, p. 256, citing *Sugiyama memo, jō*, p. 536.

97. Ibid., pp. 259–260, citing *Sugiyama memo, jō*, p. 535 and *Kido Kōichi nikki, ge*, pp. 926–27.

98. *Kido Kōichi nikki, ge*, p. 928. Vol. 3 of Prince Takamatsu's diary contains no entries for the crucial seventeen days from Nov. 14 to 30, 1941. Calling attention to this fact, editor Akagawa Hiroyuki asks whether Takamatsu or someone else destroyed this portion of the diary. "We investigated, and it didn't seem as though it was deliberately removed, but still the true reason for these missing entries remains unknown." *TN, dai sankan* (Chūō Kōronsha, 1995), pp. 422–23.

99. Ike, *Japan's Decision for War*, p. 279; Sudō, *Haru nōto o kaita otoko*, p. 180.

100. Ike, *Japan's Decision for War*, p. 279.

101. Sudō, *Haru nōto o kaita otoko*, pp. 188–189. Japan's actions in Manchuria were an established fact neither Hull nor Roosevelt wanted to question for fear of immediately precipitating war.

102. *Sugiyama memo, jō*, p. 542; Ike, *Japan's Decision for War*, p. 282. Here I have generally followed Ike's translation.

103. Ike, *Japan's Decision for War*, p. 283. I have made slight alterations to Ike's translation; Tanaka, *Dokyumento Shōwa tennō dai nikan*, p. 287.

104. *Sugiyama memo, jō*, p. 543; Ike, *Japan's Decision for War*, p. 283. Kido, in his diary entry, simply stated that, "At 2:00 P.M. the imperial conference convened and war against the United States was finally decided upon by the emperor. At 4:30 the prime minister visited me and we conferred about the imperial rescript declaring war." *Kido Kōichi nikki, ge*, p. 931.

105. Tanaka, *Dokyumento Shōwa tennō dai nikan*, p. 291, citing *Rikugunbu kaisen keii 5*, p. 517.

106. Inoue, *Tennō no sensō sekinin*, p. 181.

107. Cited in Okabe Makio, "Ajia taiheiyō sensō no kaisen tetsuzuki," in *Kikan sensō sekinin kenkyū* 8 (Summer 1995), p. 29.

108. *Kido Kōichi nikki, ge,* entries of Dec. 5, 6, 1941, p. 932; Tanaka, *Dokyumento Shōwa tennō dai nikan,* pp. 361–63.
109. Okabe, "Ajia taiheiyō sensō no kaisen tetsuzuki," pp. 29–30.
110. The opening line of the *Senjinkun,* adopted in Jan. 1941, read: "The battlefield is where the Imperial Army, acting under the imperial command, displays its true character, conquering whenever it attacks, winning whenever it engages in combat, in order to spread KŌDŌ [the Imperial Way] far and wide so that the enemy may look up in awe to the august virtues of his majesty."
111. *Jō nikki,* p. 119. The most credible version of Hirohito's reaction to the Roosevelt letter is in Prince Takamatsu's diary. On Dec. 10, 1941, Takamatsu recorded Hirohito telling him that the letter from Roosevelt came through Grew and that "We answered [Grew] just as we have been saying in government-to-government talks. What a meaningless thing to come and tell us." Takamatsu then added that "because the media was distracted by the president's letter on the night of the seventh, it helped conceal our military operation." The least trustworthy version is Hirohito's "Monologue" account, which blames Tōgō for his nonreply:

> I knew beforehand . . . that a telegram would probably be coming to me by short-wave from Roosevelt; but it didn't come. I was wondering what had happened . . . when, finally, at 3 A.M. on December 8, Tōgō [Shigenori] brought it to me. I understand that Ambassador Grew sought an audience so that he could hand it to me personally. I wanted to answer this presidential telegram but Tōgō said that already on the 6th "Two of our submarines were sunk off the coast of Hawaii; it is better not to answer now." At his suggestion, I decided not to reply.

TN, dai sankan, p. 333; and *STD,* pp. 77–78.
112. *Jō nikki,* pp. 119–20.

CHAPTER 12
THE ORDEAL OF SUPREME COMMAND

1. The United States annually produced twelve times the steel, five times the amount of ships, one hundred and five times the number of automobiles, and five and a half times the amount of electricity that Japan did at the time it attacked Pearl Harbor. Yamada Akira, *Gunbi kakuchō no kindaishi: Nihongun no kakuchō to hōkai* (Yoshikawa Kōbunkan, 1997), pp. 219–20; Abe Hikota, "Dai Tō'A sensō no keisuteki bunseki," in Kondo Shinji, ed., *Kindai Nihon sensōshi, Dai Tō'A sensō* (Tokyōdō Shuppan, 1997), p. 824.
2. *Kido Kōichi nikki, ge,* pp. 999–1000.
3. *Jō nikki,* p. 139.
4. Ibid., p. 218.
5. Ibid., p. 235. This entry, for Jan. 28, 1943, refers to a secular, not a religious, ceremony that dates from Jan. 24, 1869, the second year of the Meiji restoration, when the "tradition" was first introduced of using the ancient lyric poetry to tie the modern monarchy firmly to the past, and to the emperor's subjects. It also serves as a reminder that the commander in chief was expected to be a poet.
6. Ibid., p. 293. June 30 and Dec. 31 were "Grand Purification" days, when Hirohito donned special garments made of white silk and flax in order to perform rites that wiped away the crimes "committed unintentionally by the nation." See Ihara Yoriaki, *Hozō, kōshitsu jiten* (Toyamabō, 1938), p. 194.
7. Abe, "Dai Tō'A sensō no keisuteki bunseki," p. 839.
8. As of late Sept. 1943, the Imperial Army had only five of its seventy divisions in the

Pacific—almost all of them in the south and southwest, where it had deployed about two hundred thousand light infantry troops. Until the last year of the war, despite the overwhelming firepower that Allied forces concentrated against them, the army failed to abandon the doctrine of hand-to-hand combat. It neither drew new lessons from defeat nor restructured itself to cope with the kind of war it was actually fighting. Instead, as the war dragged on, the army reduced the size of its divisions while failing to increase either their fire-power or mobility; and it continued to underestimate American and British fighting capability. Thus everywhere the Japanese army fought, it dispersed rather than concentrated its forces, and threw in troops only as they were needed. See Abe, "Dai Tō'A sensō no keisuteki bunseki," pp. 830, 845, and chart 41 on p. 850; Yamada, *Gunbi kakuchō no kindaishi: Nihongun no kakuchō to hōkai*, pp. 209, 221.

9. Nakao Yūji, "Dai Tō'A sensō ni okeru bōsei teni chien no yōin," in Gunjishi Gakkai, ed., *Dainiji sekai taisen (3), Gunji shigaku* 31, nos. 1 & 2 (Sept. 1995), p. 110.

10. *Senshi sōsho: rikukaigun nenpyō, fu heigo yōgo no kaisetsu* (1980), p. 104; Shiryō Chōsakai, ed., *Daikairei: kaisetsu* (Mainichi Shinbunsha, 1978), p. 122; see also the interpretation of these moves in Nakao, "Dai Tō'A sensō ni okeru bōsei teni chien no yōin," p. 110.

11. Shiryō, *Daikairei, kaisetsu*, p. 97.

12. *Sugiyama memo, ge*, pp. 81–82, cited in Nakao, pp. 110–11. The policy document was entitled "Kongo torubeki sensō shidō no taikō" (Outline for conducting future war guidance). Its third item stated: "We will decided on concrete measures for more positive war guidance after giving consideration to our national power, changes in operations, the war situation between Germany and the Soviet Union, U.S.–Soviet relations, and trends in Chungking."

13. Yamada, *Daigensui Shōwa tennō*, p. 180.

14. Ibid., p. 181.

15. Kita Hiroaki, *Gunritsu hōtei: senjika no shirarezaru "saiban"* (Asahi Sensho, 1997), pp. 53–54.

16. HSN, p. 376; Kita, *Gunritsu hōtei: senjika no shirarezaru "saiban*," pp. 54–55.

17. Yamada, *Daigensui Shōwa tennō*, p. 185; Fujiwara, *Shōwa tennō no jūgonen sensō*, pp. 135–38.

18. Fujiwara, *Shōwa tennō no jūgonen sensō*, p. 136, citing *Senshi sōsho: Shōwa 17, 18 nen no Shina hakengun*, n.p. On the Gogō operation see also *Senshi sōsho: Dai hon'ei rikugunbu, 5, Shōwa jū shichi nen jūnigatsu made*, pp. 76–81.

19. Yamada Akira, "Nihon fuashizumu ni okeru dagekiteki gunjiryoku kensetsu no zasetsu: Nihon kaigun kōkūheiryoku no tokuchō oyobi sono hōkai no gunjiteki yōin," *Jinbun gakuhō*, Tokyo Toritsu Daigaku Jinbun Gakubu 199 (Mar. 1988), p. 104, citing *Senshi sōsho: Nantō hōmen kaigun sakusen (1)* (1971), pp. 272, 284, 288, 294, 319.

20. Tanaka Nobumasa, *Dokyumento Shōwa tennō, dai sankan: hōkai* (Ryokufū Shuppan, 1986), pp. 203–4. Citing only Japanese sources, Tanaka estimates U.S. losses in the Battle of Midway at 354 dead, of whom 210 were pilots.

21. *Sugiyama memo, ge*, pp. 130–31. At the liaison conference of June 10, the navy reported only one aircraft carrier sunk, one missing, and one heavily damaged.

22. *Kido Kōichi nikki, ge*, pp. 966–67.

23. Nakao, "Dai Tō'A sensō ni okeru bōsei teni chien no yōin," p. 111.

24. "Commentary" by Nomura Minoru in *Jō nikki*, p. 8. Jō served as a naval aide to Hirohito from Nov. 15, 1940, to Jan. 19, 1944.

25. Ibid., pp. 288–92.

26. Ibid., pp. 6–7.

27. Uryū Tadao, "Kokusaku eiga, Nihon nyūsu shōshi," in *Bessatsu Ichiokunin no Shōwashi: Nihon nyūsu eiga shi* (Mainichi Shinbunsha, 1977), p. 522.

28. *Jō nikki*, pp. 142–43.

29. Ibid., p. 159.

30. Ibid., pp. 142–44.

31. Ibid., p. 144.

32. *Kido Kōichi nikki, ge*, p. 949.

33. Nakao, "Dai Tō'A senso ni ōkeru bōsei teni chien no yōin," p. 8.

34. *Jō nikki*, pp. 149, 151–53.

35. Yamada, *Daigensui Shōwa tennō*, p. 196. Just as Japanese war planners in late 1941 and again in late 1942 underestimated American industrial and military capacity, so they erred in seriously overestimating Germany's industrial capacity. According to historian Abe Hikota, the Army General Staff estimated that Germany in Oct. 1942 was producing monthly 2,000 tanks and and 3,000 airplanes, when its actual production in Dec. 1942 was only 760 tanks and 1,548 planes. The general staff was off by factors of 2.6 on tanks and about 1.9 on airplanes. See Abe, "Dai Tō'A senso no keisuteki bunseki," p. 853.

36. *Kido Kōichi nikki, ge*, p. 970.

37. Yamada, *Daigensui Shōwa tennō*, p. 196, citing "Yōhei jikō ni kanshi sōjō," July 11, 1942 (unpublished).

38. *Senshi sōsho: Dai hon'ei rikugunbu* 5 (1973), p. 350.

39. Yamada, *Daigensui Shōwa tennō*, pp. 198–99.

40. Domon Shūhei, *Tatakau tennō* (Kōdansha, 1989), p. 61.

41. Ibid., p. 63.

42. Nakao, "Dai Tō'A senso ni okeru bōsei teni chien no yōin," p. 118, citing Itō Shōtoku, *Teikoku rikugun no saigo—kessen ed.* (Kadokawa Bunko, 1973), p. 25.

43. Tōgō Shigenori, *Jidai no ichimen: taisen gaikō no shuki* (Kaizōsha, 1952), pp. 294, 298.

44. Ibid., pp. 296–97; *Kido Kōichi nikki, ge*, pp. 980–81, entry of Sept. 1, 1942. Tōjō did not relinquish the foreign ministership until Hirohito appointed Shigemitsu Mamoru to that post on Apr. 20, 1943. After leaving office, Tōgō turned against Tōjō and advised the senior statesmen and the court entourage during 1943 to force Tōjō to step down. Tōgō Shigenori, *Gaikō shuki* (Hara Shobō, 1967), p. 314.

45. Yamada, *Daigensui Shōwa tennō*, p. 203; Grace P. Hayes, *The History of the Joint Chiefs of Staff in World War II: The War Against Japan* (Naval Institute Press, 1982), p. 190.

46. Ugaki Matome, *Senmoroku* (Hara Shobō, 1968), p. 224.

47. Ibid., p. 224.

48. Yamada, *Daigensui Shōwa tennō*, p. 205.

49. Domon, *Tatakau tennō*, p. 65.

50. Yamada, *Daigensui Shōwa tennō*, pp. 199, 201.

51. Ibid., p. 201.

52. Ibid., p. 202.

53. Nakao, "Dai Tō'A senso ni okeru bōsei teni chien no yōin," p. 119, citing *Senshi sōsho: Minami Taiheiyō rikugun sakusen (2)* (1969), p. 444.

54. Yamada, *Daigensui Shōwa tennō*, p. 207.

55. Ibid., p. 218.

56. *Kido Kōichi nikki, ge*, p. 999; *Jō nikki*, p. 218; Domon, *Tatakau tennō*, p. 68.

57. *Senshi sōsho 63, daihon'ei rikugunbu (5)* (1973), p. 561.

58. Nakao, "Dai Tō'A senso ni okeru bōsei teni chien no yōin," p. 119, citing Imoto Kumao, *Sakusen nisshi de tsuzuru Dai Tō'A senso* (Fuyō Shobō, 1979), p. 275.

59. Right after the imperial headquarters conference ended, Hirohito reportedly told Sugiyama, "I was thinking of bestowing an imperial rescript if they could recapture

Guadalcanal. What do you think? The officers and men fought hard and suffered. So why not grant them an imperial rescript. If I do grant one, when would be the best time?" The rescript was granted on January 5, 1943, but not publicized. See Bōei Kenshūjo Senshishitsu, "Senshi shiryō riku dainigō (Nantō hōmen sakusen shiryō): *Sanada Jōichirō shōshō shuki*, June 25, 1956," p. 19.

60. Ibid., pp. 18–19. These are Sanada's handwritten notes, based on his diary, of the circumstances leading up to the imperial decision to withdraw from Guadalcanal.

61. Yamada, *Daigensui Shōwa tennō*, pp. 213–14.

62. Charles W. Koburger, Jr., *Pacific Turning Point: The Solomons Campaign, 1942–1943* (Praeger, 1995), p. 75.

63. *Jō nikki*, p. 235; Koburger, *Pacific Turning Point*, p. 78.

64. *Senshi sōsho: Nantō hōmen kaigun sakusen (3): Ga tō tesshūgō* (1976), p. 106.

65. Koburger, *Pacific Turning Point*, p. 90. U.S. losses on New Georgia were about one thousand killed and four thousand wounded.

66. Fujiwara, *Shōwa tennō no jūgonen sensō*, p. 140, citing Satō Kenryō, "Dai Tō'A sensō kaikoroku."

67. *Kido Kōichi nikki, ge*, p. 1020.

68. *Kido Kōichi kankei bunsho*, pp. 128–29.

69. *Sugiyama memo, ge*, "Kaisetsu," pp. 20–21. The briefings were held on June 6 and 7.

70. Ibid., p. 21.

71. Yamada, "Shōwa tennō no sensō shidō: jōhō shūka to sakusen kanyo," in *Kikan: sensō sekinin kenkyū* 8 (Summer 1995), p. 20.

72. For the full exchange at the Aug. 5, 1943, audience, see *Sugiyama memo, ge*, "Kaisetsu," pp. 24–25.

73. Nakao, "Dai Tō'A sensō ni okeru bōsei teni chien no yōin," p. 120, citing "Sanada Jōichirō shōshō nikki" (unpublished).

74. Yamada, *Daigensui Shōwa tennō*, pp. 240–42, citing *Daihon'ei kaigunbu, rengō kantai (4)*, pp. 493–94.

75. *Senshi sōsho: Daihon'ei rikugunbu 7: Shōwa jūhachinen jūnigatsu made* (1973), p. 148.

76. Ibid., pp. 158–59.

77. *Sugiyama memo, ge*, p. 471.

78. Ibid., pp. 471–472.

79. Yamada, *Daigensui Shōwa tennō, p*, 239.

80. For the draft made at the Imperial Headquarters Government Liaison Conference on September 25, 1943, and adopted five days later at the imperial conference, see *Senshi sōsho: Daihon'ei rikugunbu (7), Shōwa jūhachi nen jūni gatsu made* (1973) , p. 185, Yamada, *Daigensui Shōwa tennō*, p. 242; and for the full text of the Sept. 30, 1943, policy document ("Kongo torubeki sensō shidō no taikō") see Yamada, ed., *Gaikō shiryō kindai Nihon no bōcho to shinryaku* (Shin Nihon Shuppansha, 1997), pp. 373–74.

81. Yamada, *Daigensui Shōwa tennō*, p. 242.

82. *Jō nikki*, p. 324.

83. Harry A. Gailey, *Bougainville 1943–1945: The Forgotten Campaign* (University Press of Kentucky, 1991), p. 3.

84. *Jō nikki*, p. 341.

85. *Jō nikki*, "Kaidai," pp. 19–20.

86. Stephen Taaffe, *MacArthur's Jungle War: the 1944 New Guinea Campaign* (University Press of Kansas, 1998), pp. 3, 53.

87. Inaba Masao, "Shiryō kaisetsu" and "Tōjō rikusō no sanbō sōchō kennin keii" in *Sugiyama memo, ge*, p. 31.

88. Ibid., pp. 26–34.

89. Domon, *Tatakau tennō*, p. 99.

90. Hatano Sumio, *Taiheiyō sensō to Ajia gaikō* (Tokyo Daigaku Shuppankai, 1996), pp. 77–78.

91. In his Jan. 5, 1944, talk to young staff officers in Nanking, Prince Mikasa boldly criticized the venality, corruption, and lack of humility of Japanese army officers. He urged that they change their ways and give full support to "the national government so that it can implement . . . policies for the sake of 400 million Chinese people." His prepared text, in a question-and-answer form, allowed him to register also the facile, anti-Semitic bigotry of his fellow staff officers, and to call attention to Japanese racism and Anglo-American policies toward East Asia. See Mikasa no miya Nobuhito [Wakasugi sanbō], "Shina jihen ni taisuru Nihonjin toshite no naisei [bakuryōyō]," in *This is Yomiuri* (Aug. 1994), pp. 63, 65, 67, 69, 71.

92. Akashi Yōji, "Taiheiyō sensō makki ni okeru Nihon gunbu no Yenan seiken to no heiwa mosaku: sono haikei," in Gunji Shigakkai, ed., *Dai niji sekai taisen (3): shūsen* (Kinseisha, 1995), pp. 177–78. Field commanders fiercely resisted implementation of the policy change.

93. *Senshi sōsho: Inpaaru sakusen, Biruma no bōei* (1968), pp. 151–59.

94. Hara Takeshi, Yasuoka Akio, eds., *Nihon rikukaigun jiten* (Shin Jimbutsu Ōraisha, 1997), pp. 101–2, and comments by Yamada Akira in Fujiwara et al., *Tettei kenshō: Shōwa tennō 'dokuhakuroku'* (Tokyo: Ōtsuki Shoten, 1991), p. 96. The Allies suffered approximately eighteen thousand casualties in the Imphal campaign.

95. Rekishi Kyōikusha Kyōgikai, ed., *Maboroshi dewa nakatta hondo kessen* (Kōbunken, 1995), pp. 16–17.

96. Ibid., p. 17.

97. American losses on Saipan were 3,426 marines killed and 13,099 wounded. The stubborn Japanese defense gave rise to the belief among strategic planners in Washington that it would "cost approximately one American killed and several wounded to exterminate seven Japanese soldiers." Many American planners thereafter used this "Saipan ratio" for making "strategic-level casualty projections in the Pacific." On this point, see D. M. Giangreco, "Casualty Projections for the U.S. Invasions of Japan, 1945–1946: Planning and Policy Implications," in *Journal of Military History* 61, no. 3 (July 1997), p. 535. I am indebted to the author for bringing his important article to my attention.

98. *Senshi sōsho: Daihon'ei kaigunbu, rengō kantai (6): dai sandankai sakusen kōki* (1970), p. 21, citing "Gunreibu dai ichi buchō Nakazawa Tasuku shōshō gyōmu nisshi" (unpublished).

99. Ibid.

100. *Senshi sōsho: Daihon'ei kaigunbu, rengō kantai (6): dai sandankai sakusen kōki*, p. 22, citing the unpublished recollections of Comm. Fujimori Yasuo, a staff officer in the operations section of the First Department who had worked on the Saipan recapture plan.

101. Ibid., p. 33.

102. Ibid., p. 37.

103. Nihon Heiki Kōgyōkai, ed., *Rikusen heiki sōran* (Tosho Shuppansha, 1977). pp. 540.

104. *TN, dai nanakan*, pp. 514–15, 517.

105. Hosokawa Morisada, *Jōhō tennō ni tassezu, jō: Hosokawa nikki* (Isobe Shobo, 1953), pp. 117–20.

106. For the text see *Mainichi Shinbun*, Mar. 19, 1995. Tōjō had this rescript in his possession on the day of his botched suicide attempt, Sept. 11, 1945.

107. Yamada Akira, Kōketsu Atsushi, *Ososugita seidan: Shōwa tennō no sensō shidō to sensō sekinin* (Shōwa Shuppan, 1991), pp. 132–33; Leon V. Sigal, *Fighting to a Finish: The*

Politics of War Termination in the United States and Japan, 1945 (Cornell University Press, 1988), p. 31.

108. Yamada, Kōketsu, *Ososugita seidan*, p. 148.
109. Yoshida Yutaka, *Shōwa tennō no shūsenshi* (Iwanami Shinsho, 1992), p. 14.
110. *Kido Kōichi nikki, ge*, p. 1131, entry of July 26, 1944.
111. *Maboroshi dewa nakatta hondo kessen*, pp. 20–21.
112. Yamada, Kōketsu, *Ososugita seidan*, pp. 167–68.
113. For the full text, see Senda Kakō, *Tennō to chokugo to Shōwashi* (Sekibunsha, 1983), p. 373.
114. *Nihon rikukaigun jiten*, pp. 109–12. American casualties in the Leyte and Philippine Sea battles numbered approximately fifteen thousand.
115. *STD*, p. 100; *Senshi sōsho 45: Dai hon'ei kaigunbu, rengō kantai (6)* (1970), p. 472.
116. For the text of the balloon-bomb orders, see Morimatsu Toshio, ed., *"Dai hon'ei rikugunbu" tairikurei, tairikushi sōshūsei, dai 9 kan, Shōwa jūkyūnen* (Emutee Shuppan, 1994), pp. 270–71, 513, 532–33.
117. *Maboroshi dewa nakatta hondo kessen*, pp. 23–24; *"Dai hon'ei rikugunbu" tairikurei, tairikushi sōshūsei, dai 9 kan, Shōwa jūkyūnen*, pp. 532–33.
118. According to a recent Japanese assessment of damage inflicted by "body-smashing" attacks on all Allied ships during the last phase of the Pacific war, 57 aircraft carriers were sunk, 108 warships and escort carriers were so heavily damaged as to be out of action for the remainder of the war; 84 other naval ships sustained light damage with heavy personnel casualties; and 221 ships were lightly damaged, for a total of 470 ships. See Kamikaze Kankō Iinkai, eds., *Shashinshū—Kamikaze: riku, kaigun tokubetsu kōgekitai, jō* (KK Besutoseraazu, 1996), p. 19; for a recent American study, see D. M. Giangreco, "The Truth About Kamikazes," in *Naval History* (May–June 1997), pp. 25–30.
119. Yoshihashi Kaizō, "Jijū bukan toshite mita shūsen no toshi no kiroku" in *Gunji shigaku 2* (Aug. 1965), pp. 96–97; Katsuno Shun, *Shōwa tennō no sensō*, p. 200; Uryū, "Kokusaku eiga, Nihon nyūsu shōshi," p. 522.
120. Yoshihashi, "Jijū bukan toshite mita shūsen no toshi no kiroku," p. 97.
121. Domon, *Tatakau tennō*, p. 192.
122. *Nihon rikukaigun jiten*, p. 112; Craig M. Cameron, *American Samurai: Myth, Imagination, and the Conduct of Battle in the First Marine Division, 1941–1951* (Cambridge University Press, 1994), pp. 251–54, addresses the American symbolism of the flag-raising. Cameron (pp. 252–53) notes that there were actually two flag raisings, the famous second one designed to "replace the smaller initial flag with a larger, more visible one. The men who fought their way to the top of the volcano and whose actions were preserved in a photographic record . . . were quickly lost in obscurity that Marine Corps publicists actively fostered so as not to confuse the desired symbolism of the second raising."
123. *Senshi sōsho: Daihon'ei rikugunbu (10) Shōwa nijūnen hachigatsu made* (1975), p. 113.
124. Fujiwara Akira et al., *Okinawasen to tennōsei* (Rippū Shobō, 1987), p. 28, citing Ōta Yoshihiro, *Okinawa sakusen no tōsui* (Sagami Shobō, 1984), pp. 401–2;
125. *Senshi sōsho: Daihon'ei rikugunbu (10) Shōwa nijūnen hachigatsu made* (1975), p. 113.
126. Domon, *Tatakau tennō*, p. 192.
127. Ibid., p. 193.
128. Ibid.
129. *Senshi sōsho: Daihon'ei rikugunbu (10) Shōwa nijūnen hachigatsu made*, p. 128.
130. Ibid., pp. 211–12. On May 9 Hirohito shocked the Army Operations Section by refusing General Umezu's request to place the Seventeenth Area Army in Korea under the command of the Kwantung Army. Such a move, he believed, would

destroy the distinction between Manchuria, a foreign country, and Korea, "the national territory." Ibid., pp. 224–25.

CHAPTER 13
DELAYED SURRENDER

1. Dick Wilson, *When Tigers Fight: The Story of the Sino-Japanese War, 1937–1945* (Viking Press, 1982), pp. 234–45.

2. Yoshida Yutaka, *Nihonjin no sensōkan* (Iwanami Shoten, 1995), p. 102, chart 13, citing Ōkurashō Shōwa Zaisei-shi Henshūshitsu, ed., *Shōwa zaisei-shi 4* (Tōyō Keizai Shinbunsha, 1955).

3. Ibid., p. 102, chart 12, citing Ōe Shinobu, ed., *Shina jihen Dai Tō'A sensōkan dōin gaishi* (Fuji Shuppan, 1988).

4. Reduced to 250 warships of all types by the end of December 1944, the navy had only 53.8 percent of the tonnage with which it had started the war in December 1941. Yamada Akira, *Gunbi kakuchō no kindaishi: Nihongun no kakuchō to hōkai* (Yoshikawa Kōbunkan, 1997), p. 205.

5. Rekishi Kyōikusha Kyōgikai, ed., *Maboroshi dewa nakatta hondo kessen* (Kōbunken, 1995), pp. 19–20; Yamada, *Gunbi kakuchō no kindaishi*, p. 210.

6. Katsuno Shun, *Shōwa tennō no sensō* (Tosho Shuppansha, 1990), pp. 205–6.

7. Yabe Teiji, a Tokyo Imperial University scholar and ideologue who served as Konoe's political adviser, observed after the war that Konoe's private audience with the emperor in February was the first he had been allowed to have in nearly three years. Yabe also noted: "Until around the time of the fall of Saipan, Kido had absolute faith in Tōjō, and what anyone told Kido was immediately passed on to Tōjō." See Yabe Teiji, "Kōshitsu no chi nagareru Konoe Fumimaro," in *Bungei shunjū, tokushūgō: tennō hakusho* (Oct. 1956), p. 190.

8. The words are those of the U.S. Strategic Bombing Survey, *Japan's Struggle to End the War* (Washington, D.C., July 1946), p. 2.

9. *TN, dai rokkan* (Chūō Kōronsha, 1997), pp. 466–67.

10. Sometime in January or early February 1945, Konoe drafted an analysis of the situation facing Japan and used it as his reference in writing the "memorial." In this unsigned handwritten document, Konoe explicitly rejected the view of the Soviet Union held by Hirohito and the high command; he also identified the Japan-Soviet Neutrality Treaty as an instrument designed to "worsen the conflict between Japan and the United States and Britain." For Konoe's text see Shōji Junichirō, "Konoe Fumimaro shuki 'Soren no Tō'A ni taisuru ito,'" in *Gunji shigaku* 34, no. 2 (Sept. 1998), pp. 45–48. For Finance Ministry bureaucrat Ueda Shunkichi's input see Ueda Shunkichi, "Shōwa demokurashii no zasetsu" and "Gunbu, kakushin kanryō no Nihon kyōsanka keikakuan," in *Jiyū* (Oct. and Nov. 1960).

11. For translation and analysis of the Konoe memorial see John W. Dower, *Empire and Aftermath: Yoshida Shigeru and the Japanese Experience, 1874–1954* (Harvard University Press, 1979), pp. 260–64.

12. Kōketsu Atsushi, "'Potsdamu sengen' to hachigatsu jūgonichi—judaku chien no haikei niwa nani ga atta no ka," in *Rekishi chiri kyōiku* 536 (Aug. 1995), pp. 13–14, citing Harada Kumao's version of the emperor-Konoe exchange from "Harada danshaku naiwa oboe, March 21, 1945," in "Takagi Sōkichi shiryō."

13. Fujita Hisanori, *Jijūchō no kaisō* (Chūō Kōronsha, 1987), pp. 66–67; Yamada Akira, Kōketsu Atsushi, *Ososugita seidan: Shōwa tennō no sensō shidō to sensō sekinin* (Shōwa Shuppan, 1991), p. 180, citing the 1978 Chūō Kōronsha version of *Hosokawa nikki*.

14. Domon, *Tatakau tennō*, p. 192.

15. *Haisen no kiroku: sanbōhonbu shozō, Meiji hyakunen-shi sōsho, dai 38 kan* (Hara Shobō, 1967), pp. 230–31.

16. "Renritsu kyōryoku naikaku, Koiso, Yonai," January to February 1945, notebook 6, folder 1B–74, in the Shigemitsu papers held at the Kensei Kinenkan in Tokyo; also see Takeda Tomoki, "Shigemitsu Mamoru no senji gaikō ninshiki to seiji senryaku: kyuchū, tennō to no kakawari ni oite," in *Nenpō kindai Nihon kenkyū 20: kyūchū kōshitsu to seiji* (Yamakawa Shuppansha, 1998), p. 197.Shigemitsu's handwritten notations, scrawled right after the audience, make clear that the thought of the two men also went back to the kaiser and the collapse of the German Empire.

17. Kinbara Samon, Takemae Eiji, eds., *Shōwa-shi—zōhoban* (Yūhikaku Sensho, 1989), p. 218; Walter LaFeber, *The Clash: A History of U.S.-Japan Relations* (W. W. Norton, 1997), p. 236.

18. Yoshihashi Kaizō, "Jijū bukan toshite mita shūsen no toshi no kiroku," in *Gunji shigaku* 2 (Aug. 1965), pp. 97–98.

19. Cited in Kunegi Toshihiro, "Shidehara Kijūrō—'heiwa gaikō' no honne to tatemae" in Yoshida Yutaka, Ara Kei et al., *Haisen zengo: Shōwa tennō to gonin no shidōsha* (Aoki Shoten, 1995), p. 96.

20. The letter was addressed to Ōdaira Komatsuchi, Shidehara's friend from university days. Cited in ibid., p. 97.

21. Prince Konoe Fumimaro, Mar. 30, 1945, cited in *Hosokawa nikki* (Chūō Kōronsha, 1978), pp. 373–74.

22. In his "Monologue" Hirohito claimed that General Koiso "lacked common sense" for trying to negotiate peace through a person who was acting behind the back of the Nanking government. The incident revealed Hirohito's rigid adherence to rules of procedure as well as confusion over how to conduct negotiations with China. See *STD*, pp. 106–7; Shi Yuan-hua, "Nitchū sensō kōki ni okeru Nihon to Ō Chō Mei seifu no 'bōwa' kōsaku," translated by Itō Nobuyuki in Gunji Shigakkai, ed., *Nitchū sensō no shosō* (Kinseisha, 1997), pp. 294–95; Saitō Haruko, "Nihon no tai-So shūsen gaikō," in *Shiron* (Tokyo Joshi Daigaku) 41 (Mar. 1988), p. 54.

23. *Kido Kōichi nikki, ge*, pp. 1208–9; Ōe Shinobu, *Gozen kaigi: Shōwa tennō jūgokai no seidan* (Chūō Kōronsha 1991), p. 235. June 8 was also the day on which Hirohito told his chief aide-de-camp that he would not leave Tokyo, thereby setting at naught army plans to build a rock fortress for him in Matsushiro, Nagano prefecture.

24. *Kido Kōichi nikki, ge*, p. 1210; Hata Ikuhiko, *Hirohito tennō itsutsu no ketsudan* (Kōdansha, 1984), p. 46, citing the diary of army aide-de-camp Ogata Kenichi.

25. *Kido Kōichi nikki, ge*, pp. 1212–13.

26. Yamada, Kōketsu, *Ososugita seidan*, pp. 204–6.

27. John Ray Skates, *The Invasion of Japan: Alternative to the Bomb* (University of South Carolina Press, 1994), p. 102. An English translation of the Ketsu-Gō plan can be found in *Reports of General MacArthur: Japanese Operations in the Southwest Pacific Area*, vol. 2, part 2 (Washington, D.C.: USGPO, 1966), pp. 601–7.

28. Matsuura Sōzō, *Tennō to masu komi* (Aoki Shoten, 1975), pp. 3–14.

29. Heiwa Hakubutsukan o tsukurukai, ed., *Kami no sensō, dentan: bōryaku senden bira wa kataru* (Japan Peace Museum, Emiiru K. K., 1990), p. 125.

30. "Report on Psychological Warfare Against Japan, Southwest Pacific Area, 1944–1945," Mar. 15, 1946, p. 13. Bonner F. Fellers Collection, Hoover Institution Archives, Stanford, Calif.

31. Reproduced and cited in Higashino Shin, *Shōwa tennō futatsu no "dokuhakuroku"* (NHK Shuppan, 1998), p. 79.

32. Awaya Kentarō, Kawashima Takamine, "Gyokuon hōsō wa teki no bōryaku da," in

This Is Yomiuri (Nov. 1994), p. 47. The *Chian jōhō* material, published in seven volumes by Nihon Tosho Sentā in Tokyo in late 1994, is an invaluable source for understanding Japanese opinion at the time of the ending of the war.

33. Twice in the late thirteenth century, the "winds of the gods" decimated invading Mongol armadas off the shores of Kyushu. By taking the name *kamikaze*, the pilots who attacked Allied ships evoked one of the most powerful memories in Japanese history.

34. Yui Daizaburō, "Beikoku no sengo sekai kōsō to Ajia" in *Senryō kaikaku no kokusai hikaku: Nihon, Ajia, Yōroppa*, Yui Daizaburō et al., eds. (Sanseidō, 1994), pp. 12–13.

35. Awaya Kentarō, "Nihon haisen wa jōkentsuki kōfuku ka" in *Nihon kindaishi no kyozō to jitsuzō 4: kōfuku- 'Shōwa' no shūen*, edited by Fujiwara Akira et al. (Ōtsuki Shoten, 1989), pp. 14–20.

36. The key State Department document clarifying the unconditional surrender principle for Japan is PWC–284a of Nov. 13, 1944. For the text see *FRUS, Diplomatic Papers 1944, Vol. V: The Near East, South Asia, and Africa, The Far East* (USGPO, 1965), pp. 1275–85; for essential background see Robert E. Sherwood, *The White House Papers of Harry L. Hopkins: An Intimate History*, vol. 2, *January 1942-July 1945* (London: Eyre & Spottiswoode, 1949), pp. 690, 693–94.

37. William L. Shirer, *The Rise and Fall of the Third Reich* (New York, 1990), p. 1139. Italian partisans summarily executed Mussolini on April 28, and the war in Italy ended on May 2. Hitler committed suicide on April 30. Germany's total surrender was realized by the unconditional surrender of its armed forces. After having arrested all the members of Grand Admiral Dönitz's new Nazi government on May 23, the United States, the Soviet Union, Great Britain, and France signed the Berlin Declaration on June 5, 1945, making the nature of Germany's surrender crystal clear. See Arai Shinichi, "Kyōkasho kentei to mujōken kōfuku ronsō," in *Rekishigaku kenkyū* 531 (Aug. 1984), p. 15.

38. Within a few hours of Truman's statement, naval Capt. Ellis M. Zacharias began a series of weekly broadcasts to Japan reiterating Truman's message but without mentioning the emperor. See Allan M. Winkler, *The Politics of Propaganda: The Office of War Information, 1942–1945* (Yale University Press, 1978), p. 145.

39. The "queen bee" analogy comes from Grew's speech to a U.S. Senate committee hearing on December 12, 1944. See Nakamura Masanori, *The Japanese Monarchy: Ambassador Joseph Grew and the Making of the 'Symbol Emperor System,' 1931–1991* (M. E. Sharpe, Inc., 1992), p. 66.

40. Joseph C. Grew, *Turbulent Era: A Diplomatic Record of Forty Years, 1904–1945*, vol. 2 (Boston: Houghton Mifflin, Co., 1952), p. 1435. Grew endorsed the Truman administration's decision to retain the emperor for postwar purposes, but even he never imagined that Hirohito would be able to absolve himself of war guilt and not step down.

41. Ibid., pp. 1425–26.

42. Nakamura, *The Japanese Monarchy*, pp. 70–77.

43. The declaration was largely the work of Secretary of War Henry L. Stimson and his aides, but Secretary of State James Byrnes polished it, eliminated the clarification of the emperor's status, and influenced the timing of its release.

44. The direct repatriation home of Japanese military forces was a major difference between Japan's unconditional surrender and Germany's. The official American policy at the time of the declaration was that unconditional surrender applied "to Japan" and "thus cover[ed] not only the armed forces, but also the emperor, the government and the people. All are to acquiesce in any acts which the allies consider appropriate in carrying out their policy." See the undated State Department memorandum,

"Comparison of the Proclamation of July 26, 1945, with the Policy of the Department of State," prepared on July 30, in *FRUS, Diplomatic Papers: The Conference of Berlin (The Potsdam Conference) 1945*, vol. 2 (Washington, D.C.: USGPO, 1960), p. 1285.

45. The deleted lines included the following: "(1) We . . . agree that Japan shall be given an opportunity to end this war. . . . (4) The time has come for Japan to decide whether she will continue to be controlled by those self-willed militaristic advisers whose unintelligent calculations have brought the Empire of Japan to the threshold of annihilation, or whether she will follow the path of reason."

46. Minomatsu Jō, ed., Takagi Sōkichi copy, *Kaigun taishō Yonai Mitsumasa oboegaki* (Kojinsha, 1978), pp. 143–44, as cited in Tanaka Nobumasa, p. 434. Churchill did indeed lose the British general election of July 5, 1945. A Labour Party cabinet headed by Clement Attlee replaced Churchill's Conservative-dominated coalition government on the twenty-seventh.

47. Truman notes in his memoirs, "On July 28 Radio Tokyo announced that the Japanese government would continue to fight. There was no formal reply to the joint ultimatum of the United States, the United Kingdom, and China. There was no alternative now. The bomb was scheduled to be dropped after August 3 unless Japan surrendered before that day." *Memoirs by Harry S. Truman*, vol. 1, *Year of Decisions* (Garden City, N.Y.: 1955), p. 421.

48. Tanaka, *Dokyumento Shōwa tennō, dai gokan*, p. 449. Needless to say Stalin did not need Suzuki's *mokusatsu* statement or the Yalta agreement to enter the war against defeated Japan. He would have done so in any case.

49. LaFeber, *The Clash*, p. 247.

50. The Soviet declaration of war stated: "Japan remains the only great power after the defeat and surrender of Hitlerian Germany which still insists on continuing the war, and has rejected the demand for the unconditional surrender of its armed forces, put forth on July 26 by the three nations: the United States of America, Britain, and China." Nihon Jyānarizumu Kenkyūkai, ed., *Shōwa "hatsugen" no kiroku* (Tokyū Ejenshi Shuppan Jigyōbu, 1989), p. 94.

51. Tanaka, *Dokyumento Shōwa tennō, dai gokan*, p. 475. See also Committee for the Compilation of Materials on Damage Caused by the Atomic Bombs, *Hiroshima and Nagasaki: The Physical, Medical, and Social Effects of the Atomic Bombings* (New York, 1981), p. 114. Even today the entire picture of the human damage wrought by the atomic bombs is difficult to grasp.

52. Cyril Clemens, ed., *Truman Speaks* (Columbia University Press, 1960), p. 69.

53. *Kido Kōichi nikki, ge*, pp. 1220–21.

54. Ishiguro Tadaatsu, *Nōsei rakuyōrō* (Oka Shoin, 1956), pp. 421–22; Suzuki Kantarō Denki Hensan Iinkai, ed., *Suzuki Kantarō den* (1960), p. 372. Minister of State Shimomura conveyed the concerns of the Advisory Council to the cabinet. Agricultural Minister Ishiguro in his memoirs commented on Suzuki's motivations (p. 422):

> I still don't know his true intention in making this statement. . . . At cabinet meetings [Suzuki] only stressed fighting through to the end. He maintained the same attitude in his press conferences and toward the Potsdam Declaration. So I couldn't understand whether this cabinet was going to continue the war or end it. Judging solely from appearances, I could only understand that the cabinet intended to continue fighting. There was not a single sign of their wanting to quit. Yet I imagined that precisely because the prime minister did not give expression to quitting the war meant that, at heart, he wanted to.

This was Ishiguro's invocation of the *haragei* defense on Suzuki's behalf. *Haragei* is the Japanese cultural practice whereby two parties in a negotiation advance their respective positions by subtle, nonverbal mutual deception.

55. *STD*, p. 120.

56. Wada Haruki, "Nisso sensō," in Hara Teruyuki, Sotogawa Tsugio, eds., *Kōza Suravu no sekai 8, Suravu to Nihon* (Kōbundō, 1995), p. 110.

57. Saitō Haruko, "Nihon no tai-So shūsen gaikō," in *Shiron* (Tokyo Joshi Daigaku) 41 (Mar. 1988), p. 49; see Wada Haruki, "Nisso sensō," p. 110.

58. Saitō, pp. 49, 52. In May 1943 Stalin had declared: "Only when it is facing grave danger does the fascist camp talk about peace." On Nov. 6, 1944, he called Japan an "aggressor state."

59. *STD*, p. 121.

60. Arita concluded his memorial with the words: "Your majesty confronts this crisis with his inherent wisdom. I humbly ask your majesty to view the trend of the war and resolutely act to save the imperial nation at its critical moment. I am respectfully reporting this with utter trepidation and awe." See Gaimushō, ed., *Shūsen shiroku 3*, p. 208.

61. Satō to Tōgō, June 8, 1945, in ibid., p. 191.

62. Satō to Tōgō, Moscow, July 13, 1945, in *FRUS, Diplomatic Papers: The Conference of Berlin (The Potsdam Conference), 1945*, vol. 1 (Washington, D.C.: USGPO, 1960), p. 881.

63. Satō to Tōgō, no. 1227, Moscow, July 19, and no. 1228, Moscow, July 20, 1945, in *FRUS, Diplomatic Papers: The Conference of Berlin (The Potsdam Conference), 1945*, vol. 2 (Washington, D.C.: USGPO, 1960), pp. 1251 and 1256. For the Japanese original see Gaimushō, ed., *Shūsen shiroku 3* (Hokuyōsha, 1977), p. 199.

64. Tanaka Nobumasa, *Dokyumento Shōwa tennō, dai gokan*, p. 439, citing Gaimushō ed., *Shūsen shiroku* (Shinbun Gekkansha, 1952), pp. 524–25.

65. Ibid., p. 440.

66. Ibid., p. 444.

67. Cited in David Holloway, *Stalin and the Bomb: The Soviet Union and Atomic Energy, 1939–1956* (Yale University Press, 1994), p. 128.

68. Tanaka, pp. 461–62. In his memoirs Truman claims not to have been surprised by the Soviet decision. On the initial Soviet reaction to Hiroshima, see Holloway, *Stalin and the Bomb*, pp. 127–29, and the review of Holloway by Vladislav Zubok in *Science* 266 (Oct. 21, 1994), pp. 466–68.

69. Historians of the A-bomb decision generally conclude that Truman knew of the contents of the intercepted and decoded Japanese "peace feelers," and that Secretary of the Navy James Forrestal and Army Chief of Staff Marshall were also informed of the cables. But these cables were evidence only of the Japanese government's desire to make peace, not of its commitment to surrender unconditionally, because there was no such commitment prior to Hiroshima and the Soviet entry into the war. What the emperor and Kido were asking for up to that time was not "peace" but the preservation of the emperor's power and the entire monarchical system. On U.S. knowledge, see Walter Millis, ed., *The Forrestal Diaries* (Viking Press, 1951), pp. 74–77; Robert H. Ferrell, ed., *Off the Record: The Private Papers of Harry S. Truman* (Harper & Row, 1980), pp. 53–54; and *Memoirs by Harry S. Truman*, vol. 1, p. 396.

70. Yamada, Kōketsu, *Ososugita seidan*, pp. 212–13. The "emperor's letter" that Konoe was to have carried to Moscow was apparently quite short. A précis of the text can be found in Gaimushō, ed., *Shūsen kiroku 3*, pp. 160–61.

71. On Yonai and Takagi, see Yoshida, *Shōwa tennō no shūsenshi*, p. 27; and, for the full

statement quoted here, *Takagi kaigun shōshō oboegaki* (Mainichi Shinbunsha, 1979), p. 351, cited in Tanaka, *Dokyumento Shōwa tennō, dai gokan*, p. 475.

72. Kido always tried to leave the impression that he and Hirohito were consistent opponents of the militarists. Interviewed on April 6, 1966, he declared: "On the whole, our minds were already prepared [for surrender] earlier. That's why we weren't shocked by the atomic bombs. . . . There was also a plus aspect to the atomic bombs and the Soviet entry into the war. I assumed at the time that if there had been no atomic bombs and the Soviet Union hadn't joined in, we might not have succeeded." The following year he opined boastfully: "Because the Soviets and the atomic bombs did the job for us, one could say that Japan was able to revive to this extent." "Kido Kōichi-shi to no taiwa," in Kanazawa Makoto et al., eds., *Kazoku: Meiji hyakunen sokumenshi* (Hakuyō Sensho, 1978), p. 185; Wada Haruki, "Nisso sensō" in Hara Teruyuki et al., eds., *Kōza Suravu no sekai 8, Suravu to Nihon* (Kōbundō, 1995), p. 119.

73. For the text of "Wahei kōsho no yōkō," see Yabe Teiji, *Konoe Fumimaro, ge* (Kōbunkan, 1952), pp. 559–62.

74. Yoshida, *Shōwa tennō no shūsenshi*, pp. 23–24.

75. Yoshida Yutaka, "Konoe Fumiraro: 'kakushin' ha kyūtei seijika no gosan" in Yoshida et al., *Haisen zengo: Shōwa tennō to gonin no shidōsha*, p. 40. In Aug. 1945 Soviet troops captured 639,676 Kwantung Army soldiers, "including 26,583 officers and 191 generals." Except for the generals, most (about 570,000) were forced to work at hard labor in the camps. See S. I. Kuznetsov, "Kwantung Army Generals in Soviet Prisons (1945–1956)," in *Journal of Slavic Military Studies* 11, no. 3 (Sept. 1998), p. 187.

76. Around the time of capitulation, Kido met frequently with civil and military police officials, and collected the latest information about the worsening domestic situation. Rear Admiral Takagi recalled after the war that on July 12, 1945, when Prince Konoe told the emperor, "The situation today has reached the point where people hold a grudge against the Imperial House," Hirohito "agreed completely." See Yoshida, *Shōwa tennō no shūsenshi*, pp. 29–30, citing Takagi Sōkichi, *Takagi kaigun shōshō oboegaki* (Mainichi Shinbunsha, 1979); Hayashi Shigeru, Andō Yoshio et al., eds., *Nihon shūsenshi jōkan, hachi gatsu jūgonichi no kūdetā hoka* (Mainichi Shinbunsha, 1962), pp. 196–210; Tanaka, *Dokyumento Shōwa tennō, dai gokan*, p. 460; and John W. Dower, "Sensational Rumors, Seditious Graffiti, and the Nightmares of the Thought Police," in Dower, *Japan in War and Peace: Selected Essays* (New Press, 1993), pp. 101–54.

77. Kimishima Kazuhiko, "'Shūsen kōsaku' to 'kokutai' ni kansuru ichi shiron," in *Tokyo Gakugei Daigaku Kiyō*, Dai Sanbumon, Shakai Kagaku 34 (Dec. 1982), p. 157, citing Toyoda Soemu, *Saigo no teikoku kaigun* (Sekai no Nihonsha, 1950), pp. 206–7.

78. In his dictated statement to interviewer Ōi Atsushi of GHQ's Historical Section on November 28, 1949, Tōgō said, "I cannot recall that Minister of the Navy Yonai introduced all the four conditions," and went on to accuse Anami, Umezu, and Toyoda of adding three conditions to the single one that he, Tōgō, had proposed. But other officials interrogated in the follow-up interviews stated otherwise.

79. According to Tanaka Nobumasa's reconstruction, based on the memoirs of Toyoda Soemu and Tōgō Shigenori, General Umezu stated the case for self-disarmament as follows:

> The word "surrender" is not in the Japanese military lexicon. In our military education, if you lose your weapons, you fight with your bare hands. When your hands will no longer help, you fight with your feet. When you can no longer use your hands and feet, you bite with your teeth. Finally, when you can no longer fight, you bite off your tongue and commit suicide.

That's what we teach. I do not think that it will go smoothly to order such an army to abandon its weapons and surrender. We should request that our army and the allied army designate the place and time in each theater of operations and the units will gather there to hand over their weapons. We ourselves will collect them . . .

Tanaka, *Dokyumento Shōwa tennō, dai gokan*, pp. 479–80.

80. Awaya Kentarō, "Tokyo saiban ni miru sengo shori" in Awaya Kentarō, et al., *Sensō sekinin, sengo sekinin: Nihon to Doitsu wa dō chigau ka*, pp. 79–80.

81. Tanaka, *Dokyumento Shōwa tennō, dai gokan*, pp. 493–94; Tōgō's dictated statements to investigators from the Historical Section of GHQ in the follow-up interviews of May 17, 1949 and August 17, 1950, in *U.S. Army Statements of Japanese Officials on World War II* (n.p. 1949–50), vol. 4, Microfilm Shelf No. 51256.

82. Gaimushō, ed., *Nihon gaikō nenpyō narabi shuyō bunsho, ge*, (Nihon Kokusai Rengō Kyōkai, 1955), p. 630; Kimishima Kazuhiko, "'Shūsen kōsaku' to 'kokutai' ni kansuru ichi shiron," p. 161.

83. Prince Takamatsu, maneuvering behind the scenes for the overthrow of the Tōjō cabinet, reportedly said at a meeting of the Naval General Staff Headquarters, on June 29, 1944, that, "Since the absolute defense perimeter has been broken from New Guinea and Saipan to Ogasawara, we should now abandon the former ideal of establishing the Greater East Asia Co-Prosperity Sphere and focus our war goal on—to put it bluntly—how cleverly we should be defeated." Hosokawa Morisada, *Jōhō tennō ni tassezu, ge* (Dōkōsha Isobe Shobō, 1953), p. 252.

84. Yoshida, *Shōwa tennō no shūsenshi*, p. 31.

85. Matsudaira's essay, "The Japanese Emperor and the War," appears as the "Appendix" to volume 2, part 2" of the *Reports*, which MacArthur's staff group printed in Tokyo in 1950, under the general editorship of Maj. Gen. Charles A. Willoughby. See *Reports of General MacArthur: Japanese Operations in the Southwest Pacific Area*, vol. 2, part 2 (Washington, D.C.: GPO, 1966), pp. 763–71.

86. *Kido Kōichi nikki, ge*, p. 1223.

87. *STD*, pp. 125–26.

88. Tanaka, *Dokyumento Shōwa tennō, dai gokan*, p. 472.

89. Hoshina's notes of the imperial conference can be found in Gaimushō, ed., *Nihon gaikō nenpyō narabi shuyō bunsho, ge*, p. 630. See also Yoshida, *Nihonjin no sensōkan*, pp. 42–43, citing Ikeda Sumihisa, *Nihon no magarikado* (Senjō Shuppan, 1986) and Hoshina Zenshirō, *Dai Tō'A sensō hishi* (Hara Shobō, 1975).

90. Tanaka, *Dokyumento Shōwa tennō, dai gokan*, p. 506.

91. Ibid., p. 507.

92. Yokota Kisaburō, *Tennōsei* (Rōdō Bunkasha, 1949), pp. 183–84.

93. Ōmori Minoru, *Sengo hishi 2: tennō to genshi bakudan* (Kōdansha, 1975), p. 267, and Tanaka, *Dokyumento Shōwa tennō dai gokan: haisen, ge* (Ryokufū Shuppan, 1989), p. 531.

94. *STD*, p. 129.

95. Yamada, *Daigensui Shōwa tennō*, p. 304.

96. Yoshida, *Shōwa tennō no shūsenshi*, p. 226.

97. In his "Monologue" Hirohito says, "Umezu returned from Manchuria the day after the [imperial] conference [of June 8]. According to his report, even with all our forces in China we could only resist eight American divisions. If the United States landed ten divisions in China, there was absolutely no chance of winning. It was the first time that Umezu ever complained like this." *STD*, pp. 116–17.

98. At the mid-May meetings of the inner cabinet, Prime Minister Suzuki opined:

"Stalin's character resembles Saigō Nanshū [Takamori], so don't you think we should put all of our efforts into peace mediation through the Soviet Union." Army Minister Anami declared: "We have considerable room for negotiation because after the war the Soviet Union will confront America and not want Japan to become too weakened." Navy Minister Yonai said: "Why not transfer warships to them and ask for oil and airplanes in return." Saitō Haruko, "Nihon no tai-So shūsen gaikō," in *Shiron* 41 (Tokyo Joshi Daigaku), (Mar. 1988), p. 55, citing *Nihon gaikō nenpyō narabi shuyō bunsho, ge*, p. 612.

99. Tanaka, *Dokyumento Shōwa tennō, dai gokan*, pp. 459–460, citing Kido's response to written questions concerning the ending of the war, given in Sugamo prison on May 17, 1949.

100. Tōgō himself conceded as much when he said, on August 17, 1950, that "although I asked the Soviet Union to act as peace mediator, I was unable to advise her of our peace conditions in any concrete form." See Tōgō statement of Aug. 17, 1950, p. 4, in *U.S. Army Statements of Japanese Officials on World War II*, vol. 4, microfilm shelf no. 51256.

101. Saitō, "Nihon no tai-So shūsen gaikō," p. 58.

102. D. M. Giangreco, "Casualty Projections for the U.S. Invasions of Japan, 1945–1946: Planning and Policy Implications," *Journal of Military History* 61, no. 3 (July 1997), pp. 521–81. Giangreco has reproduced and annotated the minutes of the June 18 White House meeting. For the full text, together with the military estimates, see "Appendix" to Martin J. Sherwin, *A World Destroyed: Hiroshima and the Origins of the Arms Race* (Vintage Books, 1987), pp. 355–63.

103. Giangreco, "Casualty Projections," p. 560.

104. Ibid., pp. 574–77. His analysis should be compared with Barton Bernstein's discussion of casualty forecasting in "The Struggle Over History: Defining the Hiroshima Narrative," in Philip Nobile, ed., *Judgment at the Smithsonian* (Marlowe & Co., 1995), pp. 127–256.

105. Forrest C. Pogue, *George C. Marshall: Statesman*, vol. 4 (Viking, 1987, p. 19, from Pogue's February 1957 interview with Marshall.

106. *Kido Kōichi nikki, ge*, p. 1223.

107. Matsuura Sōzō, *Tennō Hirohito to chihō toshi kūshū* (Ōtsuki Shoten, 1995), pp. 175–78.

108. For the official English translation, see Butow, *Japan's Decision to Surrender*, appendix 1, p. 248; for discussion see Bix, "The Shōwa Emperor's 'Monologue' . . . ," pp. 300–302; Fujita Shōzō, *Tenkō no shisōshi teki kenkyū* (Iwanami Shoten, 1975), pp. 227–30.

109. Takeyama Akiko, *Gyokuon hōsō* (Banseisha, 1989), p. 128.

110. Ibid., p. 103.

111. The idea of the surrender as a broadcast "ritual" comes from ibid., p. 71.

112. Senda Kakō, *Tennō to chokugo to Shōwa shi* (Sekibunsha, 1983), p. 394.

113. Ōe Shinobu, "Hiroshima-Nagasaki o menzai shita Shōwa tennō no sekinin," in *Shūkan kinyōbi* (Apr. 28, 1995), p. 40. For an English language translation of the August 17 rescript see U.S. Pacific Fleet and Pacific Ocean Areas, *Psychological Warfare Part Two, Supplement No. 3* (n.p., CINCPAC-CINCPOA Bulletin No. 164–45, 15 Aug. 1945).

CHAPTER 14
A MONARCHY REINVENTED

1. Reprinted in *Bungei shunjū, tokubetsugō: Ōinaru Shōwa* (Mar. 1989), p. 364.

2. Hirohito's letter to Akihito, dated Mar. 6, 1945, in ibid., p. 362.

3. Kinoshita Michio, *Sokkin nisshi* (Bungei shunju, 1990, p. 48.

4. Tsurumi Shunsuke, Nakagawa Roppei, eds., *Tennō hyakuwa, ge* (Chikuma Bunko, 1989), pp. 39–41. This letter was released to the nation's press by the Kyōdō News Agency on Apr. 15, 1986. The cabinet of Nakasone Yasuhiro was then preparing for the sixtieth anniversary of Hirohito's reign while conducting a campaign celebrating the centennial of the Meiji Restoration. See Sakamoto Kōjirō, *Shōchō tennōsei e no pafōmansu: Shōwa-ki no tennō gyōkō no hensen* (Yamakawa Shuppansha, 1989), p. 65; *Asahi Evening News*, Apr. 15, 1986.

5. Kinoshita, *Sokkin nisshi*, pp. 48–49.

6. Chimoto Hideki, *Tennōsei no shinryaku sekinin to sengo sekinin* (Aoki Shoten, 1990), p. 141.

7. Cited in Chimoto, p. 144; and Iokibe Makoto, *Senryōki: shushōtachi no shin Nihon* (Yomiuri Shinbunsha, 1997), p. 39.

8. Cited in Kinbara Samon, Takemae Eiji, *Shōwashi: kokumin no naka no haran to gekidō no hanseiki—zōhoban* (Yūhikaku Sensho, 1989), p. 244.
   Okichi was the name of a young woman assigned by the *bakufu* (the government of the Tokugawa shogun) magistrate of Shimoda around 1856 to be the mistress of Townsend Harris, the first American consul to Japan

9. Cited in Awaya Kentarō, ed., *Shiryō Nihon gendaishi 2: Haisen chokugo no seiji to shakai 1* (Ōtsuki Shoten, 1980), p. 24.

10. Awaya Kentarō, Kawashima Takamine, eds., *Haisenji zenkoku chian jōhō, dai rokkan: kokusai kensatsu kyoku ōshū jūyō bunsho* 1 (Nihon Tosho Centā, 1994), pp. 8–10, 242–245; Awaya, Kawashima, "Gyokuon hōsō wa teki no bōryaku da," in *This Is Yomiuri* (Nov. 1994), pp. 50–52.

11. See the *chian jōhō* material cited in Awaya, Kawashima, "Gyokuon hōsō wa teki no bōryaku da," p. 44.

12. Ibid., p. 56.

13. Report of the Osaka Municipal Special Higher Police, First Section, Sept. 19, 1945, as cited in ibid., pp. 55–56.

14. The material in this and the preceeding paragraph on Ishiwara's Tō'A renmei is drawn from *Kokusai kensatsu kyoku ōshū jūyō bunsho 1: Haisenji zenkoku chian jōhō, dai nikan*, pp. 84–85, 90; also cited in Awaya, Kawashima, "Gyokuon hōsō wa teki no bōryaku da," pp. 58–60.

15. "Text of the Instrument of Surrender" in Ramond Dennett and Robert K. Turner, eds., *Documents on American Foreign Relations*, vol. 3, *July 1, 1945—December 31, 1946* (Princeton University Press, Kraus Reprint Co., 1976), pp. 109–10.

16. Theodore Cohen, *Remaking Japan: The American Occupation as New Deal* (Free Press, 1987), p. 4. MacArthur did not receive the second half of his reform directive until October 22.

17. For nearly a year MacArthur had been hoping to get the emperor to call on him. In Manila, he had conveyed his wish to Col. Sidney Mashbir, the head of the Allied Translation and Interpreter Service (ATIS). "I'll start proceedings along that line as soon as we arrive in Japan," Mashbir replied. See Sidney F. Mashbir, *I Was an American Spy* (Vantage Press, Inc., 1953), pp. 308–9. On Fujita's visit to GHQ, see *TN, dai hakkan*, p. 152.

18. Takahashi Hiroshi, "Shōchō tennō no sekkeishatachi," *Shokun* (January 1995), pp. 66–68. Several excerpts from Sekiya's unpublished diary, cited by Takahashi, show how Sekiya, Kawai, and Fellers conferred on making sure that the emperor was not held responsible for the war.

19. *FRUS, Diplomatic Papers 1945: The Far East*, vol. 6, p. 720.

20. *New York Times*, Sept. 26, 1945.

21. Ibid., Sept. 23, 1946.

22. Cited in Awaya Kentarō, NHK Shuzaihan, *Tokyo saiban e no michi* (Nihon Hōsō Shuppan Kyōkai, 1994), pp. 13–14.

23. Frederick B. Wiener, "Comment: *The Years of MacArthur*, Vol. III: MacArthur Unjustifiably Accused of Meting Out 'Victors' Justice" in War Crimes Cases," in *Military Law Review* 113 (Summer 1986), p. 217.

24. Report of Government Section Supreme Commander for the Allied Powers, *Political Reorientation of Japan, Sept. 1945 to Sept. 1948* (Washington, D.C.: USGPO, 1949), vol. 2, p. 423.

25. Higashino Shin, *Shōwa tennō futatsu no "dokuhakuroku"* (NHK Shuppan, 1998), pp. 62–68. In his psychological warfare report entitled "Answer to Japan," drafted in mid-1944, Fellers had written, "It is a profanity for Japanese to doubt the Emperor's correctness just as it is for Catholics to doubt the chastity of the Virgin Mary."

26. The final "Blacklist" plan, dated August 8, 1945, assumed an occupation by acquiescence; what developed was an occupation in which Japan's leaders actively participated in influencing American policy from the very start. See *Reports of General MacArthur, MacArthur in Japan: The Occupation: Military Phase*, Vol. 1 Supplement. Prepared by His General Staff (Washington, D.C.: USGPO, 1966), pp. 2–12.

27. Toyoshita Narahiko, "Tennō/Makkāsā kaiken no shoken" in Iwanami Shinsho Henshūbu, ed., *Shōwa no shūen* (Iwanami Shoten 1990), p. 81; Matsuo Takayoshi, "Kōshō Shōwa tennō, Makkāsā gensui dai ikkai kaiken," in *Kyoto daigaku bungakubu kenkyū kiyō*, dai 29 go (Mar. 1990), pp. 46–48. The corrected answer, given afterward by a spokesman, was: "As to the strategic details of the war, such as the disposition of military and naval forces and the time, place, and manner of the attack, the emperor was not generally consulted, these being decided almost exclusively by the high command. At any rate, it was his majesty's intention to issue a formal declaration of war before the commencement of hostilities."

28. Hosokawa Morisada, *Jōhō tennō ni tassezu: Hosokawa nikki* (Isobe Shobō, 1953), p. 173; Kinoshita, *Sokkin nisshi*, pp. 34–35; *Sugiyama memo, jō*, pp. 387–88.

29. Tanaka Nobumasa, *Dokyumento Shōwa tennō 6, senryō* (Ryokufū Shuppan 1990), p. 237; *ISN, dai nikan*, p. 11.

30. Theodore Cohen, *Remaking Japan*, p. 64.

31. Douglas MacArthur, *Reminiscences: General of the Army Douglas MacArthur* (McGraw-Hill Book Co., 1964), p. 288; Richard E. Lauterbach, "Secret Japan War Plans: Official Reports Reveal Pearl Harbor Strategy," *Life*, Mar. 4, 1946, p. 22; John Gunther, *The Riddle of MacArthur: Japan, Korea and the Far East* (Harper & Brothers, 1957), p. 116; *Kido Kōichi nikki, ge*, pp. 1237–38; and Toyoshita, "Tennō/Makkāsā kaiken no shoken," p. 78.

32. Toyoshita, "Tennō/Makkāsā kaiken no shoken," pp. 83–84.

33. D. Clayton James, The Years of MacArthur, vol. 3, *Triumph and Disaster 1945–1964* (Boston: Houghton Mifflin Co., 1985), pp. 322–23.

34. Kaneko Shōichirō, *Shinbun Kameraman no shōgen* (Nihon Shinbun Kyōkai, 1986) pp. 28–33.

35. *New York Times*, Sept. 29, 1945; Yui Daizaburō, "Democracy From the Ruins: The First Seven Weeks of the Occupation in Japan" (Apr. 30, 1986; unpublished paper).

36. "Kimigayo" (His majesty's reign) first became the official national anthem during the decade between the Sino- and Russo-Japanese Wars (1895 to 1905).

37. The figures GHQ disclosed on Oct. 30, 1945, were based on early postsurrender monetary standards. Subsequent reevaluation, raised the total value of the imperial property sharply. Nezu, *Tennō to Shōwashi, ge* (San Ichi Shōbō, 1976, 1983), pp. 265–66.

38. Herbert P. Bix, "The Shōwa Emperor's 'Monologue' and the Problem of War Responsibility," in *Journal of Japanese Studies* 18, no. 2 (Summer 1992), p. 307.

39. Abdication was a live issue throughout the entire occupation period. For discussion, see ibid., pp. 312–18.

40. Yasuda Tsuneo, "Shōchō tennōsei to minshū ishiki: sono shisōteki kanren o chūshin ni," in *Rekishigaku kenkyū* 621 (July 1991), p. 36.

41. Yamada, *Dai gensui Shōwa tennō*, p. 306. The last remnants of the army and navy ministries—the First and Second Demobilization Bureaus—were closed down in Oct. 1947.

42. Tanaka, *Dokyumento Shōwa tennō 6, senryō*, pp. 167–68. He cites the reaction to the Nov. 8 press report of antiwar activist and writer Watanabe Kiyoshi, who had survived the sinking of the battleship *Musashi*.

43. *Kido Kōichi kankei bunsho* (Tokyo Daigaku Shuppankai, 1966), pp. 139–40. Kido adds, "However, when the train arrived at Numazu Station, the station [had been] burned down and a temporary hut stood in its place. A crowd was standing by the fence looking at us. Overall the mood was peaceful. Some bowed their heads; others smiled. It was a very natural scene and before I knew it, the six minutes . . . had passed."

44. Kinoshita, *Sokkin nisshi*, p. 64.

45. Tanaka, *Dokyumento Shōwa tennō*, p. 169, referring to the *Asahi shinbun* of Nov. 24.

46. Takeyama Akiko, "Senryōka no hōsō: 'Shinsō wa kō dā,'" in Minami Hiroshi, Shakai Shinri Kenkyūjo, eds., *Zoku, Shōwa bunka 1945–1989* (Keisō Shōbō 1990), p. 121; *Asahi shinbun (yūkan)*, Dec. 8, 1945.

47. John Dunning, *Tune in Yesterday: The Ultimate Encyclopedia of Old-Time Radio, 1925–1976* (Prentice-Hall, Inc., 1976), pp. 393–96.

48. Takeyama, "Senryōka no hōsō: 'Shinso wa ko da,'" pp. 105–6; see also Mark Gayn, *Japan Diary* (William Sloane Associates, 1948), p. 6. After watching a rehearsal of the show, Gayn wrote (p. 7):

    > The only thing that disturbed me in the broadcasts, as well as in the series of twenty [*sic*] newspaper articles starting tomorrow, was their politics. They described the timid Premier Kijuro Shidehara as a courageous foe of militarism; they concentrated their fire mainly on men of the sword, to the exclusion of such obvious war criminals as the emperor or heads of the super-trusts; they naively interpreted, or even distorted, some of the recent Japanese history.

49. Takeyama, pp. 131–34. CIE-GHQ responded by altering the format and changing the style to accommodate Japanese listeners. The pilot for a new, toned-down version went on the air in late January 1946. Called "Now It Can Be Told—Question Box," it was later renamed "Truth Box," and ran from Feb. 17 to Nov. 29, 1946. After further modifications this show too was renamed "Question Box," a program of questions and answers concerning the Pacific war, labor unions, the new constitution, and school integration. In Jan. 1948 "Question Box" became NHK's daily "Information Hour." See Takeyama, p. 140.

50. *Asahi shinbun*, Aug. 30, 1945, cited in Yoshida, *Nihonjin no sensōkan*, pp. 26–27.

51. *Mainichi Shimbun*, Sept. 5, 1945, quoted in Ōkubo Genji, *The Problems of the Emperor System in Postwar Japan* (Nihon Taiheiyō Mondai Chōsakai, 1948), p. 9. Higashikuni's speech is reproduced in Kokkai Hyakunen-shi Kankōkai, ed., *Nihon kokkai hyakunen shi, chūkan* (Kokkai Shiryō Hensankai, 1987), pp. 583–93.

52. Yoshida, *Nihonjin no sensōkan*, p. 27.

53. For discussion of the Nov. 5, 1945, policy document, see Bix, "The Shōwa Emperor's 'Monologue' . . . ," pp. 306–7.

54. Kisaka Junichirō, "Ajia-taiheiyō sensō no rekishiteki seikaku o megutte," *Nenpō: Nihon gendaishi, sōkan, sengo gojūnen no rekishiteki kenshō* (Azuma Shuppan, 1995), p. 9.
55. Akazawa Shirō, "Shōchō tennōsei no keisei to sensō sekininron," in *Rekishi hyōron* 313 (July 1976), p. 47.
56. For the text of the rescript see Senda, *Tennō to chokugo to Shōwashi*, pp. 401–4.
57. For detailed analysis of Meiji's imperial oath, see John Breen, "The Imperial Oath of April 1868: Ritual, Politics, and Power in the Restoration," in *Monumenta Nipponica: Studies in Japanese Culture* 51, no. 4 (Winter 1996), p. 410; for analysis of the "Declaration of Humanity" see Bix, "The Shōwa Emperor's 'Monologue'. . . ," pp. 318–21.
58. Akazawa, "Shōchō tennōsei no keisei to sensō sekininron," p. 46.
59. *New York Times*, Jan. 1, 1946.
60. *Chicago Daily Tribune*, Jan. 1, 1946.
61. For the full text of Hirohito's press interview of Aug. 23, 1977, see Takahashi Hiroshi, *Heika otazune mōshiagemasu* (Bungei Shunjū, 1989), p. 253.
62. Tanaka Nobumasa, *Dokyumento Shōwa tennō, dai hakkan: shōchō* (Ryokufū Shuppan, 1993), p. 115.
63. Cited in Sakamoto, *Shōchō tennōsei e no pafōmansu*, p. 96.
64. For contrasting commentary on the New Year's rescript, see Hata Ikuhiko, *Hirohito tennō itsutsu no ketsudan* (Kōdansha, 1984), p. 221; Tanaka Nobumasa, *Dokyumento Shōwa tennō: dai hakkan: shōchō*, pp. 115–19.
65. Yoshida, *Shōwa tennō no shūsenshi*, p. 78.
66. A typical example of such writing is Ono Noboru, *Ningen tennō* (Ichiyōsha, 1947), which went through four editions in its first year.
67. Cited from *Yoshida Shigeru, IV*, in Ito Satoru, "Yoshida Shigeru: senzen sengo o tsū-jita shin-Bei-ha" in Yoshida Yutaka, Ara Kei, et al., *Haisen zengo: Shōwa tennō to gonin no shidōsha* (Aoki Shoten, 1995), p. 260.
68. Tsuda Sōkichi, "Kenkoku no jijō to bansei ikkei no shisō," in *Sekai* (Apr. 1946), pp. 53–54.
69. Sakaguchi Ango, "Tennō heika ni sasaguru kotoba," in *Teihon Sakaguchi Ango zenshū, dai nana kan* (Sanyōdō Insatsu K. K., 1967), p. 404.
70. "Sōkan no kotoba," in *Shinsō* (Mar. 1, 1946), p. 3.
71. "Tennō wa hōki de aru," in *Shinsō*, Sept. 1, 1947, inside front cover. The reason offered was because "everywhere the emperor goes, even in deep mine shafts or the corners of the towns through which his entourage passes, the walls of the buildings are cleaned with brooms and instantaneously the towns and villages are beautified."
72. The Anderton memorandum to "The Commander in Chief" through "Military Secretary" is in the Fellers papers.
73. *FRUS, Diplomatic Papers 1946: The Far East*, vol. 8, p. 396.
74. The Matsumoto draft merely altered some of the phraseology of the Meiji constitution while retaining the authority and powers of the emperor and the system of separate Imperial House Law. Worse still, it reduced the rights and increased the duties of "subjects," and, except for subjecting the war- and treaty-making authority of the emperor to the consent of a permanent Diet committee, failed to strengthen substantially the power of the Diet. See *Political Reorientation of Japan: September 1945 to September 1948. Report of Government Section, Supreme Commander for the Allied Powers* (Washington, D.C.: USGPO, 1949), pp. 98–101.
75. The phrase "In order to accomplish the aim of the preceding paragraph" was added by Ashida Hitoshi in Diet deliberations.
76. Watanabe Osamu, "Sengo kaikaku to hō: tennōsei kokka wa datōsareta ka," in

Hasegawa Masayasu et al., eds., *Kōza, kakumei to hō, dai sankan, shimin kakumei to Nihon-hō* (Nihon Hyōronsha, 1994), pp. 126–29.

77. Watanabe, "Sengo kaikaku to hō: tennōsei kokka wa datōsareta ka," p. 227.
78. Ibid., p. 226.
79. Kinoshita, *Sokkin nisshi*, p. 145.
80. Ashida Hitoshi, *Ashida Hitoshi nikki, dai ikkan* (Iwanami Shoten, 1986), pp. 78–79.
81. Ibid., p. 80.
82. Ibid., p. 82.
83. Watanabe, "Sengo kaikaku to hō: tennōsei kokka wa datōsareta ka," p. 123.
84. *New York Times* (Mar. 4, 1946), p. 6.
85. Kinoshita, *Sokkin nisshi*, pp. 163–64.
86. Tanaka Akihito, *Nijusseiki no Nihon, dai nikan, Anzen hoshō: sengo gojūnen no mosaku* (Yomiuri Shinbunsha, 1997), p. 33. Yokota later abandoned his initial interpretation of Article 9 and distanced himself from earlier criticism of Hirohito. After the outbreak of the Korean War, both he and Ashida became strong supporters of rearmament. By 1960 Yokota had moved sufficiently to the right to qualify as a justice of the Supreme Court.
87. Takahashi Hiroshi, "Kaisetsu—Shōwa tennō to 'Sokkin nisshi' no jidai" in Kinoshita, *Sokkin nisshi*, p. 268.
88. *Ashida nikki, dai ikkan*, p. 90. The emperor's resistance has been argued persuasively by Watanabe Osamu in *Sengo seiji shi no naka no tennōsei* (Aoki Shoten, 1990) and "Tennō," in *Nihonshi daijiten, yonkan* (Heibonsha, 1994), p. 1246.
89. See Yoshida Shigeru, *Kaisō jūnen* (Shinchōsha, 1957–58).
90. The GHQ account, written by Alfred R. Hussey, states: "On the 22nd, as a last recourse, the Prime Minister, accompanied by Yoshida and Narahashi, consulted the Emperor. Hirohito did not hesitate. He advised Shidehara that he fully supported the most thorough-going revision, even to the point of depriving the Emperor himself of all political authority." *Political Reorientation of Japan*, p. 106.
91. Watanabe, *Sengo seijishi no naka no tennōsei* , pp–119–120, citing *Asahi shinbun*, Apr. 18, 1977.
92. The following day, Mar. 6, 1946, Kinoshita (p. 165) tried to comfort Hirohito regarding the loss of his sovereign powers by telling him it was better to discard the old constitution:

> . . . and obtain freedom to guide the spirit of politicians and the people. The emperor seems to have the same idea.
>
> Concerning abdication, the emperor said that it would probably be easier for him if he abdicated, for then he wouldn't have to experience today's difficulties. But Prince Chichibu is sick; Prince Takamatsu had been pro-war and at the hub of the military at that time, so he was unsuitable to be regent. Prince Mikasa was young and inexperienced. He felt especially disappointed at the rash act of Prince Higashikuni and said that Higashikuni probably never considered these sort of circumstances.

93. Watanabe, "Sengo kaikaku to hō: tennōsei kokka wa datōsareta ka," pp. 235–38. Watanabe emphasizes (p. 239) the highly limited nature of the constitutional revision process, rebutting the argument that the 1946 revision continued the tradition of constitution making of the 1870s-early 1880s. "The heightening of the movement for postwar reform had barely begun," he writes, "when the basic framework of the constitution was determined from above."
94. Shimizu Tōru, at seventy-nine, committed suicide in Sept. 1947, leaving behind a last testament expressing anger at the new constitution for having turned Hirohito

into a puppet, and sadness at newspaper pictures that showed him being jostled by crowds. See Shimizu Terao, "Meiji kenpō ni junshishita kenpō gakusha," in *Bungei shunjū* 42 (Nov. 1964), pp. 274–81.

95. Minobe Tatsukichi, "Minshushugi to waga gikai seido," *Sekai* (Jan. 1946) and "Minshushugi seiji to kenpō," *Seikatsu bunka* (Feb. 1946).

96. Yamada Akira, "Gendai ni okeru 'sensō sekinin' mondai: tennō no 'sensō sekinin' o chūshin ni," in *Rekishi hyōron* 545 (Sept. 1995), pp. 24–25; Yamauchi Toshihiro, "Tennō no sensō sekinin," in Yokota Kōichi, Ebashi Takashi, eds., *Shōchō tennōsei no kōzō: kenpō gakusha ni yoru kaidoku*, (Nihon Hyōronsha, 1990), pp. 241–58.

97. See Yokota Koichi, "'Koshitsu tempan' shichū" in Yokota, Ebashi, *Shōchō tennōsei no kōzō: kenpō gakusha ni yoru kaidoku*, pp. 106–8; for the English text, *Political Reorientation of Japan*, pp. 846–48.

98. Watanabe Osamu, "Nihon koku kenpō unyōshi josetsu," in Higuchi Yōichi, ed., *Kōza, kenpōgaku* 1, 116–32.

99. Kinoshita Michio, "Seijō no goshinkyō," in *Chōryū* (Mar. 1946), p. 86; Kinoshita, *Sokkin nisshi*, p. 169; cited in Tanaka, *Dokyumento Shōwa tennō, dai hakkan*, pp. 424–25. This interview appeared after the emperor had read and approved it. Hirohito obviously believed he could remain the moral and spiritual center of the nation.

Chapter 15
The Tokyo Trial

1. Under-Secretary of State Sumner Welles made the earliest declaration of this war aim. Kurusu Saburo, ex–ambassador to the United States, cited Welles on Nov. 26, 1942, in an address before the Imperial Rule Assistance Association, in which he noted that punishment of war criminals was a principal U.S. war aim.

2. Timothy L. H. McCormack, "From Sun Tzu to the Sixth Committee: The Evolution of an International Criminal Law Regime," in Timothy McCormack and Gerry J. Simpson, *The Law of War Crimes: National and International Approaches* (Boston: Kluwer Law International, 1997), p. 57.

3. While waiting for GHQ's reply, the Japanese army prosecuted seven people, in fake trials designed to protect the army by destroying, manipulating, and fabricating evidence. GHQ ordered the Japanese government to stop its prosecution of war criminals on March 9, 1946. See Nagai Hitoshi, "War Crimes Trials by the Japanese Army," in *Kantō Gakuin Daigaku Keizai Gakubu Sōgō Gakujutsu Ronsō* (Jan. 99).

4. Evan J. Wallach, "The Procedural and Evidentiary Rules of the Post–World War II War Crimes Trials: Did They Provide An Outline for International Legal Procedure?" in *Columbia Journal of Transnational Law* 37, no. 3 (1999), pp. 873–74. Justice Murphy in the *Homma* case objected to the absence of safeguards concerning the use of coerced evidence; Justice Rutledge in the *Yamashita* case condemned MacArthur's charter, which made the Military Commission in Manila "a law unto itself." For details of the trials in the Philippines and elsewhere in Asia, see Philip R. Piccigallo, *The Japanese on Trial: Allied War Crimes Operations in the East, 1945–1951* (University of Texas Press, 1979), esp. pp. 49–68.

5. Piccigallo, *The Japanese on Trial*, p. 66; citing Douglas MacArthur: *Reminiscences: General of the Army Douglas MacArthur* (McGraw-Hill, 1964), p. 298.

6. Higashino Shin, *Shōwa tennō futatsu no "dokuhakuroku"* (Nihon Hōsō Kyoku Shuppankai, 1998), pp. 102–3.

7. Gordon Daniels, ed., "A Guide to the Reports of the United States Strategic Bombing Survey: Europe, The Pacific" (London: Offices of the Royal Historical Society, 1981), pp. xxiii-xxiv; Yoshida Yutaka, *Shōwa tennō no shūsenshi* (Iwanami Shinsho, 1992), pp. 179–80.

8. Toyoda Kumao, *Sensō saiban yoroku* (Taiseisha Kabushiki Kaisha, 1986), p. 170.

9. Takada Makiko, "Shinshutsu Shiryō kara mita 'Shōwa tenno dokuhakuroku,'" in *Seiji keizai shigaku* 299 (Mar. 1991), p. 41. The Mizota documents were first published in Toyoda, *Sensō saiban yoroku*, pp. 171–72.

10. Ibid.

11. Takada, "Shinshutsu Shiryō kara mita 'Shōwa tennō dokuhakuroku,'" p. 42. Fellers is referring here to Benjamin V. Cohen, a New Deal lawyer who later served as assistant to Secretary of State Byrnes.

12. The espousal, by people like Fellers, of anti-Semitic views to Japanese officials, as evidenced in the Mizota notes, was not innocuous. Such behavior allowed the wartime anti-Semitism that Japanese governments had fostered in order to ensure ideological conformity against the West to persist. To this day anti-Semitism without Jews remains a visible element of continuity between late imperial and present-day Japan.

13. "Moto kyokutō kokusai gunji saiban bengonin Shiobara Tokisaburō kara no chōshusho (dai ikkai)," July 4, 1961, in *Kyokutō kokusai gunji saiban kankei chōshu shiryō* (Yasukuni Kaikō Bunko Shozō, Inoue Tadao Shiryō, n.p., n.d.). This is the stenographic record of Shiobara's questioning by officials of the Research Department of the Ministry of Justice.

14. Ibid.

15. "Investigative Division Progress Report," Memorandum of Lt. Colonel B. E. Sackett to Joseph B. Keenan, Jan. 22, 1946, in *Tokyo saiban e no michi—kokusai kensatsu kyoku, seiji kettei kankei bunsho, dai nikan*, p. 149.

16. *FRUS, Diplomatic Papers 1945: The Far East*, vol. 6, pp. 926–36; Higurashi Yoshinobu, "Rengōkoku no kyokutō shuyō sensō hanzai saiban ni kansuru kihon seisaku," in *Nihon rekishi* 495 (Aug. 1989), pp. 55–60; Arnold Brackman, *The Other Nuremberg: The Untold Story of the Tokyo War Crimes Trials* (William Morrow & Co., 1987), p. 47. SWNCC 57/3, which was sent to all the nations that signed the document of surrender, and JCS directive No. 1512 formed the legal framework for the IPS.

17. Matsutani Makoto, *Nihon saiken hiwa: Tokyo saiban ya saigunbi, nado: doran no hanseiki o ikita moto shushō hishokan no kaisō* (Asagumo Shinbunsha, 1983), pp. 94–105. The research group, which in October 1947 became part of the Ministry of Health and Welfare, continued its work until the end of the trials.

18. Kinoshita, *Sokkin nisshi*, pp. 170–72.

19. Ibid., p. 175.

20. Ibid., p. 176.

21. *STD*, pp. 88, 96.

22. Higashino, *Shōwa tennō futatsu no "dokuhakuroku,"* pp. 65–66. The English "Monologue" appears on pp. 209–219.

23. See Australian "List No. 1" of the major Japanese war criminals, dated January 16, 1946, in *Tokyo saiban e no michi—kokusai kensatsu kyoku, seiji kettei kankei bunsho, dai nikan*, pp. 402–35.

24. Katō Yōko, "Tōjō Hideki to Ishiwara Kanji," in Igarashi Takeshi, Kitaoka Shinichi, eds., *"Sōron" Tokyo saiban to wa nan datta no ka* (Tsukiji Shokan, 1997), pp. 118–28.

25. Yoshida Yutaka, "Sensō sekinin to Kyokutō kokusai gunji saiban," in Nakamura Masanori et al., *Sengo Nihon: senryō to sengo kaikaku, dai gokan* (Iwanami Shoten, 1995), pp. 75–76.

26. Donald G. Gillin with Charles Etter, "Staying On: Japanese Soldiers and Civilians in China, 1945–1949," in *Journal of Asian Studies* 42, no. 3 (May 1983), p. 499.

27. Awaya Kentarō, "Senryō, hisenryō: Tokyo saiban o jirei ni," in *Iwanami kōza: Nihon*

tsūshi, dai 19 kan (Iwanami Shoten, 1995), p. 198; Yoshida Yutaka, "Sensō sekinin to Kyokutō kokusai gunji saiban," in *Sengo Nihon: senryō to sengo kaikaku, dai gokan*, pp. 74–75; Nakamura Yūetsu, *Paidan: Taiwangun o tsukutta Nihongun shōkōtachi* (Fuyō Shobō, 1995), pp. 74–83.

28. Nagai Hitoshi, "Fuirippin to Tokyo saiban: daihyō kenji no kensatsu katsudō o chūshin toshite," in *Shien* 57, no. 2 (Mar. 1997), p. 58.

29. Brackman, *The Other Nuremberg*, pp. 92, 344.

30. Meirion and Susie Harries, *Sheathing the Sword: The Demilitarisation of Japan* (London: Hamish Hamilton, 1987), p. 149; Higurashi Yoshinobu, "Pāru hanketsu saikō: Tokyo saiban ni okeru bekkō iken no kokusai kankyō," in Itō Takashi, ed., *Nihon kindaishi no saikōchiku* (Yamakawa Shuppansha, 1993), p. 396.

31. International Prosecution Section 315, Microfilm Reel 28, R 2/163, p. 667; and R2/147, p. 661. The first, precedent-setting Nuremberg Trial taught the lesson that crimes "against peace" and "against humanity" (or, more accurately, "the human status") were of international concern, and that individuals, not just states, were culpable for violating them. See McCormack, Simpson, *The Law of War Crimes: National and International Approaches*, p. xxii; Simon Chesterman, "Never Again . . . And Again: Law, Order, and the Gender of War Crimes in Bosnia and Beyond," in *Yale Journal of International Law* 22, no. 299 (1997), p. 318.

32. "Burning of Confidential Documents by Japanese Government," case no. 43, serial 2, in *International Prosecution Section*, vol. 8; Tanaka, *Dokyumento Shōwa tennō, dai hakkan, shochō*, p. 421. In a letter to the *Far Eastern Economic Review* (July 6, 1989), Aristides George Lazarus, former defense lawyer for Gen. Hata Shunroku, claimed that, at the urging of an emissary of President Truman, who was most likely Keenan, he had participated in saving Hirohito from the trials. "With Hata, I arranged that the military defendants, and their witnesses, would go out of their way during their testimony to include the fact that Hirohito was only a benign presence when military actions or programmes were discussed at meetings that, by protocol, he had to attend."

33. Yoshida, *Shōwa tennō no shūsenshi*, pp. 183–85.

34. John L. Ginn, *Sugamo Prison, Tokyo: An Account of the Trial and Sentencing of Japanese War Criminals in 1948, by a U.S. Participant* (MacFarland & Co., Pub., 1992), p. 39. The IPS Language Division established Chinese and Russian sections but was never able to keep up with the demands on its services.

35. Figures on total seating vary considerably: see Brackman, *The Other Nuremberg*, p. 89; Tokyo Saiban Handobukku Henshū Iinkai, ed., *Tokyo saiban handobukku* (Aoki Shoten, 1989), p. 31.

36. "Opening Statement" by Keenan, in *Trial of Japanese War Criminals: Documents* (Washington, D.C.: USGPO, 1946), p. 1.

37. Brackman, *The Other Nuremberg*, p. 133; Asahi Shinbun Hōtei Kishadan, *Tokyo saiban, jō* (Tokyo Saiban Kankōkai, 1963), pp. 258–60.

38. *Kyokutō kokusai gunji saiban sokkiroku*, No. 20, (June 27, 1946), p. 12; Brackman, *The Other Nuremberg*, p. 134. During the defense phase of the trial, in September 1947, General Araki also rebutted Inukai Takeru's testimony. See *TWCT, Vol. 12: Transcript of the Proceedings in Open Session Pages 27,839 to 30,420*, pp. 28, 131–32.

39. Brackman, *The Other Nuremberg*, p. 135; *Kyokutō kokusai gunji saiban sokkiroku* 21, June 28, 1946, p. 3.

40. Harries and Harries, *Sheathing the Sword*, p. 157.

41. *TWCT, Vol. 8: Proceedings of the Tribunal/Pages 17542–20,105*, p. 17,662. Fifty years after the end of World War II, eight volumes of these rejected defense documents were published in Japanese. Tokyo Saiban Shiryō Kankōkai, ed., *Tokyo saiban kyakka*

miteishutsu bengogawa Shiryō, vols. 1–8 (Kokusho Kankōkai, 1995). Vol. 1 contains the *Nippon Times* summary of Stimson's famous *Harper's* article.

42. Brackman, *The Other Nuremberg*, p. 284.

43. Ibid.

44. *TWCT, Vol. 13: Transcript of the Proceedings in Open Session Pages 30,421 to 32,971*, p. 31,310.

45. Asahi Shinbun Hōtei Kishadan, *Tokyo saiban, chū* (Tokyo Saiban Kankōkai, 1963), p. 8; "False Answers and Criticism of the Senior Statesmen," *Asahi shinbun* (Oct. 23, 1947).

46. *Kyokutō kokusai gunji saiban sokkiroku, dai hakkan*, No. 342, December 26, 1947 (Matsudo Shoten, 1968), p. 8.

47. *Asahi shinbun*, Dec. 27, 1947.

48. *Kyokutō kokusai gunji saiban sokkiroku, dai hakkan*, No 344 (Matsudo Shoten, 1968), pp. 216–17; Kainō Michitaka, "Nitchū sensō to Taiheiyō sensō: Nihon fuasshizumuron no josetsu toshite," pp. 2, 6. Although scheduled for publication in *Chūgoku kenkyū*, No. 6 (Nihon Hyōronsha, 1949), the article was censored by SCAP.

49. *Kyokutō kokusai gunji saiban sokkiroku, dai hakkan*, No. 345, pp. 221–22.

50. When *Life* magazine, on Jan. 26, 1948, criticized the trial, Webb wrote to MacArthur (Feb. 11) denying he had ever "questioned any witness to show the Emperor . . . was guilty of crime of any kind or in any way responsible for the war. . . . I also pointed to [Keenan] that the Prosecution's evidence implicated the Emperor."

51. *TN, dai hakkan*, p. 159.

52. Ibid., p. 41.

53. Akazawa Shirō, "Shōchō tennōsei no keisei to sensō sekininron," in *Rekishi hyōron*. 313 (July 1976), pp. 48, 50. He cites Tanabe's essay, "Seiji tetsugaku no kyūmu" in *Tenbō* (Mar. 1946).

54. Miyoshi Tatsuji, "Heika wa sumiyaka ni gotaii ni naru ga yoroshii," serialized in the Jan., Mar., Apr., and June 1946 issues of *Shinchō* under the title "Natsukashii Nihon." Reprinted in Tsurumi Shunsuke, Nakagawa Roppei, eds., *Tennō hyakuwa, ge* (Chikuma Shobō, 1989), pp. 326–27; the essay is discussed in Bix, "The Shōwa Emperor's 'Monologue'. . . ," pp. 314–15.

55. "Kokutai goji no hōryaku (Kinoshita no memo)" in Kinoshita, *Sokkin nisshi*, p. 225.

56. Just before returning to the United States to work in Republican and extreme right-wing organizations, Fellers wrote Hirohito a letter on "matters of spiritual importance." Delivered to Ōgane Shūjirō at the Palace by diplomat Kasai Jūji, it was apparently read by Hirohito. Seventeen years later, in April 1963, Kasai wrote Fellers to say:

> Today is the emperor's birthday. Thanks to MacArthur and you the emperor's position was saved. I am truly grateful to you. . . . Do you remember that you had tried to appeal to the emperor to express his imperial repentance? If he had done that, he would have obtained the love and respect not only of the Japanese people but of the whole world.

Cited in Higashino Shin, pp. 192–93.

57. MacArthur, partly following SWNCC 57/3, amended the Nuremberg Charter in significant ways. His Charter for the IMTFE deleted the article in the Nuremberg Charter denying immunity to "heads of state" in wartime (Article 74). It failed to provide for the appointment of alternate judges as at Nuremberg; and it stipulated that a majority vote of the judges present at any particular time determined decisions and judgments. An absent judge could take part in subsequent proceedings unless he declared in open court that he was unfamiliar "with the proceedings which took

place in his absence." See Wallach, "The Procedural and Evidentiary Rules of the Post–World War II War Crimes Trials: Did They Provide An Outline For International Legal Procedure?" pp. 864–65; Yoram Dinstein and Mala Tabory, eds., *War Crimes in International Law* (The Hague, Boston: Martinus Nijhoff Publishers, 1996), p. 270.

58. Dinstein and Tabory, eds., *War Crimes in International Law*, p. 5.

59. International lawyer Theodor Meron has pointed out that the Tokyo tribunal, "in contrast to the the IMT, did not view the entirety of the Hague Regulations as necessarily an accurate mirror of customary law." See Theodor Meron, *Human Rights and Humanitarian Norms as Customary Law* (Oxford: Clarendon Press, 1989), p. 39.

60. "Opening Statement" by Joseph B. Keenan in *Trial of Japanese War Criminals: Documents*, p. 19.

61. Cited in Brackman, *The Other Nuremberg*, p. 374; Tokyo Saiban Handobukku Henshū Iinkai, ed., *Tokyo saiban handobukku*, p. 63. The final judgment stated that Japan waged wars of aggression against France, the United States, Britain, and the Netherlands, but failed to include a similar statement labeling as aggression its campaigns in China.

62. Higurashi Yoshinobu, "Tokyo saiban no sogan mondai," in *Gunji kenkyū* 35, no. 2 (Sept. 1999), p. 52.

63. Brackman, *The Other Nuremberg*, p. 399.

64. *Asahi shinbun* journalists claim that some of their bones, buried at the cremation site in Yokohama, were excavated after the occupation and offered to family members by Health Ministry officials in a formal ceremony at Ichigaya. See Asahi Shinbun Hōtei Kishadan, *Tokyo saiban, ge*, pp. 970–72.

65. "Separate Opinion of the President," in B. V. A. Röling and C. F. Ruter, eds., *The Tokyo Judgment: The International Military Tribunal for the Far East (I.M.T.F.E.) 29 April 1946–12 November 1948*, vol. 1 (APA–University Press, 1977), p. 478.

66. "Dissenting Judgment of the Member from France," in Röling, Ruter, *The Tokyo Judgment*, vol. 1, p. 496.

67. It seems more accurate to say that Pal viewed World War II as an antiwhite Asian nationalist, rather than "from an interpretive perspective located in the South," as Richard Falk claims in "Telford Taylor and The Legacy of Nuremberg," in *Columbia Journal of International Law* 37, no. 3 (1999), p. 697, n. 12.

68. "Judgment of Mr. Justice Pal, Member from India," in Röling and Ruter, *The Tokyo Judgment*, vol. 1, p. 929; *TWCT*, vol. 21, *Separate Opinions*, p. 963. On Pal's dissent and his role at Tokyo, see Nagao Ryūichi, "Pāru hanji no ronri," in Igarashi Takeshi, Kitaoka Shinichi, eds., *"Sōron" Tokyo saiban to wa nan datta no ka* (Tsukiji Shoten, 1997); Higurashi Yoshinobu, "Pāru hanketsu saikō: Tokyo saiban ni okeru bekko iken no kokusai kankyō," in Itō Takashi, ed., *Nihon kindaishi no saikōchiku* (Yamakawa Shuppansha, 1993).

69. CIE officials considered the Tokyo trial a part of the demilitarization and democratization process. Their "war guilt program" centered on the publication in the Japanese press of daily news reports on the court proceedings.

70. Yoshimi Yoshiaki, "Senryōki Nihon no minshū ishiki—sensō sekininron o megutte," in *Shisō* 811 (Jan. 1992); Yoshida Yutaka, "Senryōki ni okeru sensō sekininron," in *Hitotsubashi ronsō* 5, no. 2 (Feb. 1991); Ara Kei, "Tokyo saiban, sensō sekininron no genryū—Tokyo saiban to senryōka no seron," in *Rekishi hyōron* 408 (Apr. 1984).

71. Nakamura Masanori, "Tokyo saiban to Nihon gendaishi," in Nakamura Masanori, *Gendaishi o manabu: sengo kaikaku to gendai Nihon* (Yoshikawa Kōbunkan, 1997), pp. 98–99.

72. *Ashida Hitoshi nikki, dai nikan* (Iwanami Shoten, 1986), p. 247.

73. Nakamura, "Tokyo saiban to Nihon gendaishi," p. 97.

74. Awaya Kentarō, "Tokyo saiban ni miru sengo shori," in Awaya et al., *Sensō sekinin, sengo sekinin: Nihon to Doitsu wa dō chigau ka* (Asahi Sensho, 1998), p. 117; U.S. State Dept., "Japanese Reactions to Class A War Crimes Trial," Aug. 27, 1948, in *O.S.S./State Dept. Intelligence and Research Reports*, part 2, *Postwar Japan, Korea, and Southeast Asia*, reel 5 (University Publications of America, Inc.).

75. The decree was discovered and introduced in English by Awaya Kentarō. See "In the Shadows of the Tokyo Tribunal," "Appendix" in Hosoya C. et al., eds., *The Tokyo War Crimes Trial: An International Symposium* (Kōdansha International Ltd., 1986), pp. 79–88.

76. Yoshida Yutaka, "'Shōwa tennō dokuhakuroku' no rekishiteki ichizuke," in Higashino, *Shōwa tennō futatsu no "dokuhakuroku,"* p. 266.

77. Nakamura Masanori, *Gendaishi o manabu: sengo kaikaku to gendai Nihon* (Yoshikawa Kōbunkan, 1997), pp. 93–120.

78. In section 12 of appendix D, rape was defined traditionally as "failure to respect family honour and rights" rather than as violence against women per se. *Tokyo saiban e no michi: kokusai kensatsu kyoku, seisaku kettei kankei bunsho, dai yonkan*, p. 416.

79. "The Crime of Conspiracy," memorandum for Joseph B. Keenan, Washington, D.C., May 23, 1946; Arieh J. Kochavi, *Prelude to Nuremberg: Allied War Crimes Policy and the Question of Punishment* (University of North Carolina Press, 1998), p. 225. The prosecution of "conspiracy" had also divided the British and Americans from the French and Soviets during the London negotiations over the IMT Charter.

80. Kainō Michitaka, "Tokyo saiban, sonogo," in *Shisō* 348 (1953), p. 28.

81. Awaya, "Tokyo saiban ni miru sengo shori," in *Sensō sekinin, sengo sekinin*, p. 97; Awaya et al., eds., *Tokyo saiban e no michi: kokusai kensatsu kyoku, seisaku kettei kankei bunsho, dai yonkan* (Gendai Shiryō Shuppan, 1999), p. 416.

82. Yoshimi Yoshiaki, "Sensō hanzai to meneki," in *Kikan sensō sekinin kenkyū* 26 (Winter 1999), pp. 1–6; Awaya, "Tokyo sabian ni miru sengo shori," p. 97.

83. Stephen Endicott, Edward Hagerman, *The United States and Biological Warfare: Secrets from the Early Cold War and Korea* (Indiana University Press, 1998), pp. 37–41.

84. Sakuta Keiichi, "Nihonjin no renzokukan," in Sakuta Keiichi, *Kachi no shakaigaku* (Iwanami Shoten, 1972), p. 413.

85. Awaya, "Tokyo saiban ni miru sengo shori," in *Sensō sekinin, sengo sekinin*, pp. 112–15.

CHAPTER 16
SALVAGING THE IMPERIAL MYSTIQUE

1. Kinoshita Michio, *Sokkin nisshi*, p. 112.

2. Reginald Blyth, as reproduced (in English) in Kinoshita, p. 112.

3. Mark Gayn, *Japan Diary* (Sloane Associates, Inc., 1948), pp. 137–138.

4. On the gender shift, see Takashi Fujitani, *Splendid Monarchy: Power and Pagentry in Modern Japan* (University of California Press, 1996).

5. Shimizu Ikutarō, "Senryōka no tennōsei," *Shisō*, No. 358 (June 1953), p. 638.

6. Yamagiwa Akira, et al., *Shiryō Nihon senryō 1: tennōsei* (Ōtsuki Shoten, 1990), pp. 570–74.

7. Kinoshita, *Sokkin nisshi*, p. 215.

8. "Inada Shūichi 'Bibōroku' yori bassui," entry of August 14, 1946. *Hakusukinoe* (in A.D. 663) was a naval battle between Japanese warriors coming to the aid of the Kudara Kingdom in the southern part of Korea, around Pusan, against Chinese and Korean forces. Defeat forced the Japanese to flee the peninsula and led to domestic reform.

9. Yamazumi Makimi, "Sengo kyōiku wa seikō shita ka," in *Nihon kindaishi no kyozō to jitsuzō 4, kōfuku— Shōwa no shūen* (Ōtsuki Shoten, 1989), pp. 272–76.

10. Earlier MacArthur had slowed the momentum of the democratization movement from below and given encouragement to the defendants in the Tokyo Trial by banning a national general strike planned for February 1, 1947.

11. Matsui was Hirohito's interpreter for his 8th through 11th meetings with MacArthur, and for his two meetings with Dulles on Feb. 10 and April 22, 1951. See *Sankei shinbun*, Jan. 6, l994; Shindō Eiichi, "Bunkatsu sareta ryōdo," *Sekai* (April 1979); *Pacific Stars & Stripes* (May 7, 1947).

12. Cited in Arasaki Moriteru, *Okinawa dōjidaishi, dai gokan: "datsuhoku nyūnan" no shisō 1991–1992* (Tokyo: 1993); also see Nakamura Masanori, "Kenpō dai kyūjō to tennō-sei," in *Gekkan, Gunshuku mondai shiryō* (May 1998).

13. Watanabe Osamu, "Sengo kaikaku to hō," pp. 245–246.

14. *Ashida Hitoshi nikki, dai nikan* , pp. 13–14.

15. Arasaki Moriteru, *Okinawa dōjidaishi, dai gokan*, pp. 219–20, 230; *Nippon Times*, June 29, 1947; *Pacific Stars & Stripes*, June 29, 1947.

16. Shindo Eiichi, "Bunkatsu sareta ryōdo."

17. Aketagawa Tōru, "Gyōsei kyōtei no teiketsu 'senryō no ronri,'" in Toyoshita Narahiko, ed., *Ampo jōyaku no ronri: sono seisei to tenkai* (Kashiwa Shobō, 1999), p. 68, emphasizes Hirohito's fear of revolution.

18. Suzuki Shizuko, p. 65; on the Niigata tour in general, see Suzuki Masao, pp. 166–69.

19. *New York Times*, June 18, 1946. At his Washington news conference, Keenan declared that the emperor was not a war criminal so much as "a figurehead and a fraud perpetrated on the Japanese people." The idea of the imperial institution itself as a "fraud" designed to control an unenlightend people dates back to Basil Hall Chamberlain's essay of 1912, *The Invention of a New Religion*.

20. A year earlier, on April 13, 1946, MacArthur had released from prison Gokō Kiyoshi, chairman of Mitsubishi Heavy Industries, imperial Japan's main arms-maker, and also Prince Nashimoto. Shortly afterwards, he released four other top business leaders, including Ikeda Seihin, managing director of the Mitsui zaibatsu. See Awaya, "Tokyo saiban ni miru sengo shori," in Awaya, et al., *Sensō sekinin, sengo sekinin: Nihon to Doitsu wa dō chigau ka*, p. 98.

21. *Ashida nikki, dai nikan*, p. 27.

22. "The Emperor's Visit to Hiroshima," Dec. 9, 1947, Departmental Despatch No. 45/1947: From Australian Mission in Japan, Australian Archives, ACT CRS A 1838, Item 477/511.

23. Suzuki Masao, *Shōwa tennō no gojunkō* (Tentensha, 1992), pp. 210–11.

24. "The Emperor's Tour of the Chūgoku Region," Dec. 16, 1947, in National Diet Library, GHQ/SCAP Records Box No. 2195, Microfiche Sheet No. GS (B)–01787.

25. "Memorandum for the Record," Jan. 12, 1948, by Guy Swopes, Chief of GHQ's Political Affairs Division. After citing the huge amount of yen spent on Hirohito's four-day visit to Hiroshima prefecture, he noted that prefectural assemblies, local governments, and private corporations had also appropriated "staggering" amounts of money for large-scale street repair and road improvements in connection with Hirohito's travels. "The Japanese Emperor has been humanized," but he still "occupies today essentially the same position he has held for decades."

26. John W. Treat, "Beheaded Emperors and the Absent Figure in Contemporary Japanese Literature," in *PMLA* (Jan. 1994), p. 106.

27. Matsuura Sōzō, *Tennō to masu komi*, p. 29; Ito Satoru, "Nihon koku kenpō to tennō," in Fujiwara Akira, et al., *Tennō no Shōwa shi*, pp. 129–30.

28. *Nippon Times*, Feb. 25, 1948.

29. *Ashida nikki, dai nikan*, March 10, 1947, pp. 72–73.

30. According to this view of political history, Japanese development alternated between periods of radical (usually rightist) reform and periods of moderation.
31. On the release of war crimes suspects, see Sebald to Sec. of State, Dec. 24, 1948, in *FRUS 1948*, vol. 6, *The Far East and Australasia*, pp. 936–37; and Far Eastern Commission policy decisions of Feb. 24 and March 31, 1949.
32. In the San Francisco Peace Treaty, the U.S. abandoned reparations claims against Japan and obliged the Japanese government to acknowledge only minimal war responsibility in the form of accepting, in Article 11, the verdict of the Tokyo tribunal.
33. On NSC 13/2 and what followed, see Michael Schaller, *The American Occupation of Japan: The Origins of the Cold War in Asia* (Oxford University Press, 1985), pp. 136–39; Nakamura Masanori, "Nihon senryō no shodankai: sono kenkyū shiteki seiri," in Yui Daizaburō, et al., eds., *Senryō kaikaku no kokusai hikaku: Nihon, Asia, Yōroppa* (Sanseidō, 1994), pp. 94–96.
34. Takahashi Hiroshi, "Shōchō tennō no sekkeishatachi," pp. 95–96.
35. Sakamoto, *Shōchō tennōsei e no pafōmansu*, p. 244.
36. Ubuki Satoru, "Hibaku taiken to heiwa undō," in Nakamura Masanori, et al., eds, *Sengo Nihon, senryō to sengo kaikaku 4, sengo minshushugi* (Iwanami Shoten, 1995), p. 117. For discussion, see John W. Treat, *Writing Ground Zero: Japanese Literature and the Atomic Bomb* (University of Chicago Press, 1995).
37. *Shōchō tennōsei e no pafōmansu,*, pp. 250–52.
38. Ibid., p. 253.
39. Ibid., p. 244.
40. On the Shikoku tour, see Suzuki Masao, pp. 295–324.
41. Yasuda Tsuneo, "Shōchō tennōsei to minshū ishiki: sono shisōteki kanren o chūshin ni," pp. 32–33; Yoshimi, "Senryōki Nihon no minshū ishiki: sensō sekininron o megutte," pp. 94–99.
42. The Soviet indictment grew out of the findings of the military trial of Kwantung Army commander Gen. Yamada Otozō and eleven other Japanese at Khabarovsk in Dec. 1949. The Soviet report alluded to eighteen volumes of evidence accumulated by the court, including "secret newsreels depicting operations" of the bacteriological warfare Units 731 and 100.
43. *FRUS 1950*, vol. 6, *East Asia and the Pacific*, pp. 1195–96.
44. Ibid., pp. 1236–37.
45. Toyoshita, *Ampo jōyaku no ronri: sono seisei to tenkai*, p. 116; John G. Roberts, "The 'Japan Crowd' and the Zaibatsu Restoration," in *Japan Interpreter* 12, no. 3–4 (Summer 1979), pp. 402–3; Howard B. Schonberger, *Aftermath of War: Americans and the Remaking of Japan, 1945–1952* (Kent State University Press, 1989), pp. 151–56. In mid-August 1950, at the request of Commerce Secretary W. Averell Harriman, Packenham and members of Hirohito's entourage committed Hirohito's "oral message" to writing. Toyoshita, *Ampo jōyaku no ronri: sono seisei to tenkai*, p. 116, Schonberger, *Aftermath of War*, p. 156.
46. Toyoshita, *Ampo jōyaku no ronri: sono seisei to tenkai*, pp. 110–11; Ronald W. Pruessen, *John Foster Dulles: The Road to Power* (Free Press, 1982), p. 473.
47. See the unsigned article, "Hirohito o chichi ni motsu otoko," in *Shinsō* 43 (July 1950), pp. 7–17.
48. Matsuura, *Tennō to masu komi*, p. 29.
49. Mikasa no miya Takahito and M. Lester, "Heiwa wa tabū ka," in *Bungei shunjū* (Dec. 1951), pp. 129–30.
50. David McCullough, *Truman* (Simon & Schuster, 1992), p. 834. For a more realistic assessment, see Arnold A. Offner, "'Another Victory': President Truman, American

Foreign Policy, and the Cold War," in *Diplomatic History* 23, no. 2 (Spring 1999), pp. 127–55.

51. Cited in James Chace, *Acheson: The Secretary of State Who Created the American World* (Simon & Schuster, 1998), p. 313.

52. "Memorandum of Conversation," in John Foster Dulles Papers, "Japan Peace Treaty Files," reel 7, box 4, p. 604.

53. Itō Satoru, "Nihon koku kenpō to tennō," p. 141.

54. Kyoto Daigaku Sākuru, "'Kimigayo' o kakikeshita: Kyōdai tennō gyōkō jiken," in *Jinmin bungaku* (Jan. 1952), p. 41. *Wadatsumi no koe* is a collection of posthumously published letters of Japanese students who died in the Asia-Pacific War.

55. Minami Hiroshi, "Tennōsei no shinriteki jiban," in Kuno Osamu, Kamishima Jiro, eds., *"Tennōsei" ronshū* (San Ichi Shobō, 1974), pp. 194–95; Sakamoto, *shōchō tennōsei e no pafōmansu*, p. 359.

CHAPTER 17
THE QUIET YEARS AND THE LEGACIES OF SHŌWA

1. James J. Orr, "The Victim as Hero in Postwar Japan: The Rise of a Mythology of War Victimhood." Ph.D. dissertation, Department of East Asian Studies, Bucknell University, Lewisberg, Pennsylvania, p. 230–31. Japanese opinion polls show that the majority of the public turned against the Security Treaty only during the 1960 crisis over its renewal. By the early 1970s, a national consensus in support of the treaty had nearly been restored. The percentage favoring the treaty rose from about 41 percent in 1969 to 69 percent in 1984. On the eve of Hirohito's death, 67 percent supported it.

2. Watanabe Osamu, "Tennō," *Nihonshi daijiten, yonkan*, p. 1248; Watanabe Osamu, *Nihonkoku kenpō "kaisei" shi* (Nihon Hyōronsha, 1987), pp. 236–37, 245. Early pressure for constitutional revision also came from Vice President Richard Nixon, who visited Japan on Nov. 19, 1953, and declared that the war-renouncing constitition was "a mistake."

3. *Asahi shinbun*, Jan. 6, 1999. The document ("Gist of What I Heard From Grand Chamberlain Inada on April 24, 1968, Concerning the Problem of Abdication") was discovered in papers attached to the unpublished diary of former Grand Chamberlain Tokugawa Yoshihiro. Twenty-three years after the surrender, Hirohito had conveniently blocked out three occasions—mid-August 1945, right after the Tokyo trial in 1948, and at the end of the occupation in 1951—when he had indeed contemplated stepping down. In Dec. 1945, Tokugawa himself communicated Hirohito's intention to abdicate to George Atcheson, Jr., the State Department's political adviser to MacArthur [POLAD]. See Itō Satoru, ed., *Kan, sei, shikisha kataru sengo kōsō* (Azuma Shuppan Kabushiki Kaisha, 1995), p. 157.

4. Shimizu Ikutarō, "Senryōka no tennōsei," in *Shisō* 348 (June l953), pp. 640–41.

5. Takushi Ohno, *War Reparations and Peace Settlement: Philippines-Japan Relations 1945–1956* (Manila: Solidaridad Publishing House, 1986), p. ix. Although mainland China sustained the greatest loss of life and property from Japanese aggression, the Kuomintang received only trifling reparations down to mid–1949; the CCP received nothing. At the San Francisco Peace Conference, Taiwan was forced to accept the U.S. position waiving claims against Japan. Seven hours before signing the peace treaty, Chiang Kai-shek also approved a "Normalization Treaty" with Japan that, at Tokyo's insistence, omitted reference to any Japanese obligation to pay war reparations, even though it was the wish of nearly all Kuomintang officials, not to mention the Taiwanese people, that Japan pay for the damage it had caused. To this day the complicated issue of reparations payments to China remains unsettled. See In En-

gun, "Nihon no sengo shori: Nitchū, Nittai kankei o chūshin ni," *Nenpō Nihon gendaishi*, No. 5 (1999), pp. 85–116; Nishikawa Hiroshi, "Sengo Ajia keizai to Nihon no baishō mondai," in ibid., pp. 11–15.

6. By 1959 their number had declined to 58,000; in 1990 there were still 47,770 American troops on Japanese soil. See Muroyama Yoshimasa, *Nichi-Bei anpo taisei, jō* (Yūhikaku, 1992), p. 243; Ara Takashi, "Saigunbi to zai-Nichi Beigun," in *Iwanami kōza: Nihon tsūshi, dai nijukkan: gendai 1* (Iwanami Shoten, 1995), p. 169.

7. Yoshida, *Nihonjin no sensōkan*, p. 82.

8. Yoshioka Yoshinori, "Sengo Nihon seijō to A-kyū senpan," in *Bunka hyōron* 372 (Jan. l992), p. 114. Shigemitsu, released on parole in late l950, went on to become president of the Progressive Party, vice president of the LDP, vice prime minister and foreign minister in the Hatoyama Ichirō cabinet (Dec. l954 to Dec. l956). Kaya, paroled in 1955, won election to the Diet five times, starting in 1958, and entered the Ikeda Hayato cabinet in 1960, rising to the post of justice minister in 1963.

9. Yoshida, *Nihonjin no sensōkan*, p. 17; Yoshida, "Sensō no kioku," in *Iwanami koza, sekaishi 25: sensō to heiwa, mirai e no messeeji* (Iwanami Shoten, 1997), p. 99.

10. Tanaka Nobumasa, *Sensō no kioku: sono inpei no kōzō, kokuritsu sensō memoriaru o tōshite* (Ryokufū Shuppan, 1997), p. 60.

11. Ibid., p. 61.

12. Yoshida Yutaka, lecture, Waseda University, Tokyo, Dec. 20, 1997.

13. Watanabe Osamu, "Nihon koku kenpō unyōshi josetsu," in Higuchi Yoichi, ed., *Kōza: kenpōgaku 1* (Nihon Hyōronsha, 1995), pp. 136–37.

14. Watanabe Osamu, *Sengo seijishi no naka no tennōsei* (Aoki Shoten, 1990), p. 199.

15. Banno Junji, "Introduction: The Historical Origins of Companyism: From Westernization to Indigenization," in Banno Junji, ed., *The Political Economy of Japanese Society*, vol. 1, *The State or the Market?* (Oxford University Press, 1997), p. 1.

16. Shigemitsu Mamoru, *Zoku Shigemitsu Mamoru shuki* (Chūō Kōronsha, 1988), p. 732; Watanabe, *Sengo seijishi no naka no tennōsei*, p. 239.

17. Kasahara Tokushi, *Nankin jiken to sankō sakusen: mirai ni ikasu sensō no kioku* (Ōtsuki Shoten, 1999), pp. 81–82.

18. Yoshida, "Sensō no kioku," in *Iwanami kōza, sekai rekishi 25*, p. 105; Nihon Gōyū Renmei, *Nihon gōyū renmei jūnenshi* (privately published, 1967), pp. 157–58; Nakajima Michio, "Sensō to Nihonjin," in *Iwanami kōza: Nihon tsūshi dai nijukkan, gendai 1* (Iwanami Shoten, 1995), p. 234.

19. Yoshida, "Sensō no kioku," p. 108.

20. Nakamura Masanori, *The Japanese Monarchy: Ambassador Joseph Grew and the Making of the 'Symbol Emperor System,' 1931–1991* (M. E. Sharpe, Inc., 1992), p. 124.

21. Yasuda Tsuneo, "Shōchō tennōsei to minshū ishiki: sono shisōteki kanren o chūshin ni," in *Rekishigaku kenkyū* 621 (July 1991), p. 36.

22. Ashizu Uzuhiko, a right-wing spokesman for the forces of Shintoism, wrote sarcastically at the time of the marriage that it "was conducted before the Place of Awe because Shōda Michiko was a good student of a Catholic school. If the Shōda family had not been Catholic, the government would not have taken such a bold step to recover the traditions of the imperial house." Ashizu Uzuhiko, "Kōtaishi denka goseikon no hamon," in *Miyabe to haken* (Jinja Shinpōsha kan, 1980), p. 165, cited in Watanabe Osamu, "Sengo seiji ni okeru tennō riyō no rekishi to gendaikai" (unpublished).

23. Tsurumi, Nakagawa, *Tennō no hyakuwa, ge*, p. 477.

24. Watanabe, "Sengo seiji ni okeru tennō riyō no rekishi to gendankai," p. 30.

25. Kawahara Toshiaki, *Tennōke no gojūnen*, pp. 172–75; Takeda Taijun, "Yume to gen-

jitsu," in *Gunzō* (Feb. 1961), pp. 192–94; John W. Treat, "Beheaded Emperors and the Absent Figure in Contemporary Japanese Literature," in *PMLA* (Jan. 1994).

26. Fukazawa Shichirō, "Fūryū mutan," *Chūō kōron* (Dec. 1960), p. 333.
27. Ibid., p. 336.
28. Treat, "Beheaded Emperors and the Absent Figure in Contemporary Japanese Fiction," p. 111.
29. Matsuura, *Tennō to masu komi*, pp. 110–11.
30. Kunegi Toshihiro, "Gunkokushugi no fukkatsu to tennō," in Fujiwara Akira, et al., *Tennō no Shōwashi* (Shin Nihon Shinsho, 1984), p. 161.
31. Nakamura, *The Japanese Monarchy*, pp. 132–33.
32. Yoshida, *Nihonjin no sensōkan*, p. 110.
33. Kunegi, "Gunkokushugi no fukkatsu to tennō," p. 183.
34. Watanabe, *Nihon to wa dō iu kuni ka, doko e mukatte iku no ka: 'kaikaku' no jidai, Nihon no kōzō bunseki*, p. 287.
35. Watanabe, "The Weakness of the Contemporary Japanese state," in Banno, ed., *The Political Economy of Japanese Society, Vol. 1*, pp. 120–24.
36. Yasumaru, *Kindai tennōzō no keisei*, pp. 291–92.
37. Satō Eisaku, *Satō Eisaku nikki, dai nikan* (Asahi Shinbunsha, 1998), p. 211.
38. On August 6, 1966, Satō wrote that Hirohito had "scolded" him "for letting the press write so much about the appointments to the Supreme Court. I am truly struck with awe. I also apologised to him for the Tanaka Shōji incident." Tanaka, a LDP Diet member, had used his position on the Lower House Audit Committee to extort millions of yen in a land deal. Two months later Satō again apologized to Hirohito for the misconduct of two other ministers of state. See *Satō Eisaku nikki, dai nikan*, pp. 469, 502.
39. *ISN, dai yonkan* (Asahi Shinbunsha, 1991), pp. 359, 407.
40. Yoshida, *Nihonjin no sensōkan*, p. 138.
41. Iwami Takao, "Shinpen: sengo seiji 15, 'Haribote ni naraneba'—'Masuhara jiken' de gokansō morasu," in *Mainichi shinbun*, July 14, 1991; cited in Bix, "The Shōwa Emperor's 'Monologue' . . . " in *Journal of Japanese Studies*, Vol. 18, No. 2 (Summer 1992), pp. 362–363.
42. Iwami Takao, *Heika no goshitsumon: Shōwa tennō to sengo seiji* (Mainichi Shinbunsha, 1992), pp. 85–88; Iwai Tadakuma, "Tennōsei no gojūnen," in Ritsumeikan Daigaku Jinbun Kagaku Kenkyūjō, ed., *Sengo gojūnen o dō miru ka, ge: nijū isseiki e no tenbō no tame ni* (Jinbun Shoin, 1998), p. 254; Nakamura, *The Japanese Monarchy*, p. 139.
43. Yoshida, *Nihonjin no sensōkan*, p. 140.
44. *Asahi shinbun*, Sept. 22, 1973.
45. Ibid., Sept. 23, 1975; Matsuura, *Tennō to masukomi*, p. 242 ff.
46. *Asahi shinbun*, Sept. 23, 1975.
47. *Time* [intl. ed.], Oct. 20, 1975, pp. 14–15; *Newsweek*, Oct. 20, 1975, p. 25.
48. Nakamura, *The Japanese Monarchy*, p. 140.
49. Yoshida, *Nihonjin no sensōkan*, p. 163.
50. *ISN, dai gokan*, pp. 208, 210–213.
51. Kase Hideaki, "Takamatsu no miya kaku katariki: sensō makki, Miya wa wahei e no ugoki o sasaeru shuchū no ippon datta," in *Bungei shunjū* (Feb. 1975), pp. 193, 198, 200.
52. *ISN, dai gokan*, p. 273.
53. Ibid., pp. 56, 57, 111, 114, 132. The 1980 entries on the "Haichōroku" are terse and occur on a daily, weekly, monthly basis.
54. Ibid., p. 214.

55. Ibid., p. 217.

56. Ibid.

57. Watanabe Osamu, "Kyūjū nendai Nihon kokka to tennōsei," in *Bunka hyōron* 357 (Oct. l990), p. 45.

58. Yun Koncha, "Kozetsu no rekishi ishiki: 'Shōwa' no shūen to Ajia," in *Shisō*, No. 786 (Dec. l989), p. 12.

59. "Sokui no rei no shoten," *Asahi shinbun*, Oct. 19–21, 1990.

60. Sasagawa Norikatsu, "Sokui no rei to daijōsai," in Yokota Kōichi et al., eds., *Shōchō tennōsei no kōzō: kenpōgakusha ni yoru kaidoku* (Nihon Hyōronsha, 1990), pp. 1193–212; *Japan Times*, Nov. 13,1990.

61. *Japan Times*, Nov. 23, l990.

62. *Mainichi shinbun*, Dec. 23, 1990.

INDEX